Reader's Digest

WRITE BETTER, SPEAK BETTER

The Reader's Digest Association, Inc.
Pleasantville, New York · Montreal

The acknowledgments that appear on pages 728-730
are hereby made a part of this copyright page.

Library of Congress Catalog Card Number 75-183859

ISBN 0-89577-006-7

Printed in the United States of America

Eighth Printing, February 1985

Introduction

Your verbal ability is among the most important skills you possess. Throughout your life, in all kinds of situations from the classroom to the board room, people form their opinions of you on the basis of how you speak and how you write. Understanding how to use words effectively can bring you increased confidence and pave your way to success in school, in business, in your social life—in every area where communication is important.

WRITE BETTER, SPEAK BETTER is designed to help you achieve this goal. It brings together in one place the most practical advice available from experts in the field of communications. Its fifty-nine chapters have been carefully selected and organized by the editors of the Reader's Digest to give you a complete course in the writing and speaking skills that are essential in your everyday life, whether you are a housewife, a businessman, a student, or simply a person who wants to say what you mean and get results.

The book is divided into four parts. The first, "How to Write Better," covers in detail the many writing situations you encounter, from sending an invitation to preparing a business report or writing your congressman. Sample letters and lists of tips make the material clear and easy to understand. Part Two reviews the basic elements of word power: vocabulary, grammar, punctuation, and spelling. Part Three, "How to Speak Better," gives helpful, concrete advice on speaking situations that include everyday conversation, what to say on the telephone, job interviews, running a meeting, how to use anecdotes in a speech, and organizing a formal talk complete with visual aids. The final section tells you how to detect and correct flaws in your voice or pronunciation. The special fifty-page feature, "A Dictionary of Usage," provides ready reference to common problems in writing and speaking.

Study the chapters, review the tips, take the progress tests, and you'll soon find that words really can work wonders for you.

Contents

Part one

■ HOW TO WRITE BETTER

Part two
■ THE TOOLS OF THE TRADE

Part three
■ HOW TO SPEAK BETTER

Part four
■ LEARN TO USE YOUR VOICE

How to write better

1

Good writing — a skill you can learn

The ability to communicate clearly in writing is one of the most important skills you will ever master. It will help you to get your ideas across effectively and to get the results you want in your business and personal life. There is no mystery to good writing—it is a skill you can learn.

Like fine food, good writing is something we approach with relish and enjoy from the first taste to the last. And good writers, like good chefs, do not suddenly appear full-blown, as Athena sprang from the head of her father, Zeus. Quite the contrary, just as the chef serves an intensive apprenticeship mastering the skills of his trade, the writer sits at his table and devotes long hours to achieving a style, a precision, a clarity in his writing, whatever its purpose—schoolwork, matters of business, or purely social communication. You may be sure that the more painstaking the effort, the more effective the writing, and the more rewarding.

There are still some remote places in the world where you might find a public scribe to do your business or social writing for you, for a fee. There are a few executives who are blessed with that rare kind of secretary who can take care of all sorts of correspondence with no more than a quick memorandum to work from. But for most of us, if there is any writing to be done, we have to do it ourselves.

We have to write school papers (book reports, term papers, college applications), business papers (memos, reports, letters of inquiry, letters of adjustment), home papers (everything from notes to the milkman to invitations to a church supper). We are constantly called on to put words to paper. It would be difficult to count the number of such words, messages, letters, and reports put into the mails or delivered by hand, but the daily figure must be enormous. What is more, everyone who writes expects, or at least hopes, that his writing will be read.

Yet we know very well, from our own experience, that much that is handwritten and more that is typed is only skimmed, and sometimes not read at all. Every day too much reading matter (newspapers, magazines, leaflets, as well as letters) comes into our hands. With all the duties and responsibilities we have in our business and personal lives, there simply isn't the time to go through all those pages which clutter our desks or cram our mail boxes. And our own correspondence, whatever its form and shape and size, must compete with the letters and correspondence of everyone else who is doing exactly what we are doing: writing.

Under these circumstances we must turn out a more attractive, more interesting, more tasteful product. We want to arouse and hold the interest of the reader of our correspondence or communication. We want whatever we write to be read, from first word to last, not just tossed into some "letters-to-be-read" file or into a wastepaper basket. This is the reason we bend our efforts toward learning and practicing the skills of interesting, effective writing.

Keep it brief

"That writer does the most, who gives the reader the *most* information, and takes from him the *least* time," wrote Charles C. Colton, churchman, gambler, and author, some two hundred years ago. This is an observation which everyone who writes should commit to heart, an observation to post above the desk of every businessman who dictates a memo, of every housewife who pens a letter, and of every student who taps out a term study on his typewriter.

The purpose of writing is to communicate: a thought, an idea, a sentiment, a fact. The more concrete and concise these elements in a communication, the more precise, the more rewarding they are to the reader. The manner in which you communicate information is enormously important. It must come to us in palatable form to command our attention, and to hold it.

"Brevity is the soul of wit," said Shakespeare's Polonius in *Hamlet*. This was a nice touch of irony since, as we all know, Polonius was a

rather long-winded gentleman. Nevertheless, his maxim warrants remembering, along with Mr. Colton's admonition that we demand the
least time from our readers. But brevity, too, requires a skillful hand.
We can do very well without the reams of unnecessary detail (especially
of that "he said, she said" variety) which we so frequently encounter.

Make it clear and complete

On the other hand, nothing can be more irritating and sometimes frus-
trating than the omission of essential detail. Suppose, for example, the
shirts you manufacture come in several styles, colors, and sizes, but the
order you have received in the mail gives no specifications. Or you are
driving to visit a friend in the country and you come to a fork in a country lane; you consult the map he has sent you and he has omitted both
the fork and the road you are to take. Or someone writes down a telephone message from your out-of-town friends, telling you they're going
to be in the city and will drop in to see you; but the message contains
no date, no time, and nothing to indicate whether they are coming alone
or with their children. And there are the instructions for setting up your
hi-fi phonograph and tape recorder which take for granted that you
know what a "patch cord" is.

Unquestionably there is virtue in brevity, but as these examples show,
you must never assume that your reader is as expert or as knowledgeable as you are about whatever it is you are writing. Brevity is not an
excuse for lack of clarity. And clarity, above all, is essential to what you
have to say on paper.

Clarity, precision, conciseness—each is of utmost importance to effective writing. But what of style, the way in which you pen your correspondence, business or social? Certainly you want to avoid stiffness and
rigidity in any kind of writing you do (even when you send off an angry letter to the manager of your local department store to complain
that the bed you ordered arrived with just three legs and no head-
board). At the same time, you wouldn't write a report on the market
conditions in Hong Kong in the "chummy" manner of a letter to a
cousin in Duluth or to that college roommate who has just become
president of some giant, and competitive, organization.

The simplest and best approach toward developing your own particular style in writing is to write as you speak. This would seem to be just
about as easy a task as you could set yourself—but in reality it isn't.

That old mystique which hovers over the written word seems to get into the way; even when we use a dictaphone to bridge the gap between what we wish to say and what we put to paper, the subliminal discomfort still lingers.

"It is not easy to write with a familiar style," wrote William Hazlitt, the sagacious English essayist, more than 150 years ago, "to write as anyone would speak in common conversation. . . ." But, given a modicum of time and a soupçon of effort, it can be done.

KEEP YOUR LANGUAGE LIVELY

As you write, concentrate on keeping your language active, spare and precise. Habitual use of the passive voice, unnecessary words and vague generalities makes your prose flabby, thus:

WEAK: The demand for the prisoners' release was not accepted by the chief executive.
BETTER: The president refused to free the prisoners.
WEAK: It was decided by the group that the matter would be considered at the next meeting.
BETTER: The school board decided to consider nominations next week.
WEAK: And illumination was called for by the supreme being.
BETTER: And God said, Let there be light . . .

The more you speak, the more freely you speak. The more you write, the more fluent your writing will become. Studying models and drills designed to develop your skills will help. And the keener your studies and more ardent your practice, the sooner will that antique, constricting dread of words lose its hold on you; and the sooner will that problem of getting off a memo to your secretary, that school application, that letter you owe your aunt in Toronto, be dissipated.

Effective, interesting writing is a skill you can master. In this first section of *Write Better, Speak Better* we shall analyze in detail the techniques involved in writing everything from business and personal letters to the productive college application, from mannerisms in writing that should be avoided to the art of intelligent editing. There will be numerous examples of model letters to guide you in your efforts, and a number of drills which should help you sharpen the essential skills. In later chapters, we will deal with the other kinds of writing, and with the bricks and mortar of the craft—grammar, spelling, sentence structure, and the rules governing good form and usage—which often make the difference between effectiveness and flatness in your writing.

2

Secrets of
good letter writing

Most of the writing you do is probably for business or personal letters. Here are some surprisingly simple tips on how to give your letters the impact you want them to have—how to say what you want to say in the way you want to say it—plus a list of troublesome words and phrases.

If you're a typical American, you're in trouble. At least you're in trouble when it comes to writing a large percentage of your letters. For the chances are that a good share of them are going to people who know nothing—and care less—about you.

Consider how it was in our parents' and grandparents' time. Most of their letters were written to their families and to friends. Occasionally, the head of the household might sit down and dash off a stern letter to the local newspaper stating in no uncertain terms that the condition of the streets, or the nation, was disgraceful. But for the most part, personal correspondence consisted of letters to people whom our forebears knew reasonably well.

Think about your own correspondence. Undoubtedly, some of it is still personal. But the chances are that a great deal is written to strangers. Here are a few typical situations; you'll probably find several of them reflected in your own life.

The Smiths have a sixteen-year-old son with a fine scholastic record. They write to a college inquiring about scholarship possibilities. If they know the right things to say, they may receive a letter and a number of forms, one of which will request them to have friends send in character references. This vitally important letter must be just right.

Question: What should the Smiths say in their original letter in order to make a favorable impression on the school officials? How should they fill in the forms? Which of their friends should they ask to write references, if they expect to impress the school? And what should the references say?

A year ago, Mr. Smith bought a power mower from a local retailer. Two days after his warranty expired, the engine housing broke. The retailer says he can't do anything about it.

Question: Can Mr. Smith get a free repair by writing a letter to the manufacturer? He may be able to if he knows the right things to say.

The Smiths' daughter is graduating from college, and would like to work in Washington for the government.

Question: Should she write to her congressman or her senator or to some federal office? What should she say?

Mrs. Smith's brother recently died and left his small business to her. She'd like to find someone to manage it or buy it.

Question: If she puts a classified ad in the newspaper, what's the best thing to say?

Mr. Smith has just received a letter from the Internal Revenue Service, saying that he owes $153 in back taxes. Mr. Smith is sure they're wrong, but he doesn't want to waste a day arguing with an agent at the local IRS office.

Question: How can he straighten it out by mail?

In each of these cases, the Smiths are writing not to an individual, but to an institution. Today, much of our life is influenced by, and depends upon, impersonal institutions. What this section will do is suggest how to influence those institutions by mail—how to get them to answer your questions, or persuade them to do whatever it is you want done.

The ABC's of good letter writing

Writing successfully to virtually any institution, or any public figure, requires an understanding of one fact: The person you're writing to is harried. He doesn't have time to do his job as well as he'd like; his boss is on his back; his peers are wondering if he really knows his business; and his subordinates, he is sure, are either incompetent or angling for his desk.

As a result, anything you can say in your letter that will make his job easier will be of enormous help in getting a satisfactory answer.

What *can* you do to make things easier for him? There are three things, and they can be called the ABC's of good letter writing. ABC stands for Accuracy, Brevity, and Clarity. Let's take a close look at each.

A IS FOR ACCURACY

Accuracy is very important because the person you're writing to does not, in all probability, know you, nor is he likely to be familiar with the circumstances which caused you to write. Therefore, be as specific as possible, giving all the pertinent information as accurately as you can in your letter to him.

For example, if you're complaining about a product you've bought that has become defective, include all the pertinent facts—where you bought it, the date you bought it, the model number of the product, if it has one. (For a more detailed discussion, see Chapter 7.)

Remember, much of today's institutional business is run by the number. Computers shape the activities of a surprisingly large number of institutions, from setting up college classroom schedules to renewing your magazine subscription.

For instance, here's an excellent example of just how firmly we are all locked into this situation. A neighbor's wife received a renewal form for her driver's license. A clerk in the license bureau had apparently made an error, and the computer-produced form listed her middle name as her last name.

When she notified the bureau of the mistake and asked them to correct it, they sent her a computer-produced change-of-name form, along with a computer-produced form letter saying that since she had changed her name, she should now send them her correct name, along with proof that she *had* changed her name legally. She had not, of course, changed her name since her marriage some twenty years before. But, as far as the license bureau was concerned, she must have changed it, since the computer said so.

She finally managed to straighten out the matter by sending them an old library card with her correct name on it, as proof that she did exist. Her license still shows the incorrect name, but she is fairly certain that in three years, when she's due for another renewal, they may admit that she has a right to her own name.

Once we're in a nightmare like this, we can do little but slog on to the end. But, forewarned, we can take steps to avoid it.

Accuracy is a major rock of salvation here. Give the important facts

WRITE BETTER, SPEAK BETTER

and the pertinent figures correctly, and you may be able to save considerable time and annoyance.

B IS FOR BREVITY

You can take it for granted that the person you're writing to hasn't time to wade through a long letter. If he receives a piece of correspondence that runs more than a page, or at most, two, he'll probably slip it at the bottom of his pile of incoming mail, with the thought that he'll look at it when he has more time.

Don't blame him. You'd probably do the same. So, pare your letter down to essentials, eliminating every sentence that will not help the letter's recipient to help you.

As a general rule, you can organize your letter into three parts:
1. Tell why you're writing.
2. Give the important facts.
3. Describe what you'd like the recipient to do.

1. Telling the recipient why you're writing immediately lets him know what's on your mind. It gives him, so to speak, a framework in which to read your letter, or a signpost telling him where he's to focus his attention.

For example, suppose you were writing to a television station to complain about the contents of a certain show. A good way to begin would be a simple declaration of that fact; for example, "I object strongly to the slurring remarks you made about civil service workers on the program 'Last Man' which was shown last night on Channel 4."

Or, suppose you're writing to urge a congressman to vote Yes on a certain measure. You might start: "Your support of HR 347, the immigration bill, will help strengthen the traditions on which this country was founded."

Contrast this with less direct methods. The recipient will wonder what it's all about if you write, in the case of the television station: "I feel there is too much joking about the civil service in your programs," or, in the case of the congressman, "We need to strengthen our constitutional heritage."

2. Giving the important facts to support your first sentence will show that you're businesslike and thoughtful. Limit the facts to the one or two or three which are most important. If you give a long string of reasons why, the letter becomes boring and irritating. *Remember: You*

don't want to irritate the reader, you want to get him on your side. One excellent, subtle way of doing it is to keep the letter clear and simple.

One useful practice is to put each of your reasons or arguments in a separate paragraph, preceded by a number. Thus, a letter to the editor of a newspaper might read:

> I believe we should install street lights at the corner of 16th Avenue and A Street.
> There are several reasons why this is desirable:
> First: It is the only block in the area without overhead illumination.
> Second: There were three nighttime accidents there in the past year.
> Third: The city has promised in the past that this would be done, but so far, there has been no action.

3. Finally, describing what you'd like the recipient to do gives him something to act upon. If you're complaining to a company, tell them what you want of them: "I believe you should refund my purchase price," or, "I want to exchange this for an undamaged model."

If you're writing to a government agency: "Please send me the correct forms," or "Can you tell me where I can find this information?"

■The guidelines are worth repeating:

Why are you writing?

What facts support your reasons for writing?

What should the reader do?

C IS FOR CLARITY

It is difficult to tell somebody, "Go out and be clear." It is like saying, "Be funny." But if you follow the suggestions given above for accuracy and brevity, you'll have gone a long way toward achieving clarity.

Here are a few additional suggestions which will make your letters— and any other writing you do—more easily understood.

Keep your paragraphs short. Frequent paragraphing breaks up the solid look of a letter, and even if it isn't easy to understand, the indentations make it *look* easier, and give the reader courage to go on. As a general rule, try to keep typewritten paragraphs under ten lines. Handwritten letters might well be paragraphed every five or six lines.

Keep your sentences short. Your harried reader simply does not have great powers of concentration, and even if he does, he'll probably be too busy to exercise them. If any sentence runs more than four lines, try to break it up into two shorter sentences.

11

Keep your words short. Don't try to impress the reader with long or unusual words or phrases. You may not be using them correctly, in the first place. In the second place, the reader will tend to be put off by them or consider them pompous and phony.

AVOID ROUNDABOUT VERBIAGE

The General Services Administration of the federal government has published a booklet called "Plain Letters," to help government employes improve their correspondence. It includes a list of common, roundabout phrases and suggests shorter alternatives. We reprint it here because the disease is not limited to government correspondents. The words in parentheses are the ones to use.

in regard to (about, concerning)
with regard to (about, concerning, on)
in relation to (toward, to)
in connection with (about, of, in, on)
on the part of (for, among)
with reference to (on, about, concerning)
in view of (because, since)
in the event of (if)
in order to (to)

on behalf of (for)
in accordance with (with, by)
by means of (with, by)
in the case of (if, in)
in the matter of (in)
in the amount of (for)
for the purpose of (for)
in the majority of instances (usually)
in a number of cases (some)
on a few occasions (occasionally)
in the time of (during)

On the next pages is a list of hackneyed, overlong, and misused words. Familiarize yourself with them and you'll have taken another step on your journey to clarity.

A young prep-school lad we know is still trying to decipher the following letter from his current girl friend:

"Dear John, I hope you are not still angry. I want to explain that I was really joking when I told you I didn't mean what I said about reconsidering my decision not to change my mind. Please believe I really mean this. Love, Grace."

—*E. E. Kenyon in The American Weekly*

Troublesome words and phrases

By avoiding overworked and exhausted words and phrases, you can add considerable liveliness to your letters. And there are a number of other words that don't mean exactly what you think they mean. Read this list (which is based on a similar list in "Plain Letters," published by the General Services Administration) and improve your writing.

about "He will arrive at about nine o'clock" is incorrect. Use "at" or "about," but not both.

accompanied by The preposition *with* is usually better. "I am enclosing a form with this letter," rather than "This letter is accompanied by a form."

acquaint Use "tell" or "inform"; "acquaint" is terribly stiff and a bit dated. "Advise" is another word that you can eliminate; use "tell" or "inform" here, too.

affect, effect "Affect" is always a verb meaning to modify or influence. "Effect" may be noun or verb. As verb, it means "to accomplish" or "bring about"; as a noun, it means "outcome" or "result." Thus, correct examples would be: *affect:* "The accident affected my health"; *effect as noun:* "The program has a bad effect on my children"; *effect as verb:* "I cannot effect a solution to this problem."

all-around is incorrect. Use "all-round."

all, all of Say "all the people," not "all of the people."

all ready, already The first is an adjectival phrase, and is correctly used in the following example: "When the hour came, they were all ready." The second is an adverb that oftener than not should be omitted: "We have (already) written."

alternative Don't say, "the only other alternative"; say instead, "the alternative."

anxious is proper only when anxiety exists. Do you really mean "eager"? If so, use it.

appreciate your informing me is a clumsy phrase. Use something simple, such as "Please write me" or "Please tell me."

apt Don't use this word when you mean "likely." "Apt" suggests a predisposition, as in, "A tactless person is apt to write a blunt letter." "Likely" suggests the idea of possibility, as in "Delayed replies are likely (not apt) to damage your chances."

at all times Say "always."
    this time Say "now."
    the present time Say "now."
    an early date Say "soon."
    your earliest convenience Do you mean this? A convenient time may never come.
    the earliest possible moment Say "soon" or "immediately."

13

WRITE BETTER, SPEAK BETTER

attached please find
    herewith
    hereto
    These are all unnecessary. "Attached" is enough.

between, among "Between" refers to two only. "Among" refers to more than two.

biannual is the same as semiannual. Both mean "twice a year."

biennial means "every two years."

bimonthly means "every two months"; it may also mean "twice a month" but *semimonthly* is better.

commence "Begin" and "start" are less pompous; why not use them?

communicate, communication
Avoid these long words by being specific. Instead of "communicate," use "write," "wire," or "telephone." Instead of "communication," use "letter," "telegram," "memorandum."

conclude It is better to close a letter than to conclude it.

continuously, continually The first word means "without interruption"; the second, "intermittently," "at frequent intervals."

demonstrates "Shows" is a good simple word to use instead of this long one.

desire "If you wish" or "if you want" is usually better than "if you desire."

determine is overworked. "Decide" or "find out" are better.

different is often unnecessary, as in this typical sentence: "Six different plans were discussed at the meeting."

due to the fact that is a roundabout way of saying "because."

earliest practicable date what is a "practicable" date?

effectuate A word mothered by bureaucrats, nourished by journalists, and beloved by all who cherish hollow pomposity. "Effect" means exactly the same thing and is shorter.

enclosed herewith
    please find
    with this letter
    "Enclosed" is sufficient.

equivalent is seldom better than "equal."

farther, further "Farther" indicates distance; "further" denotes quantity or degree. You go farther away; you hear nothing further.

few, less "Few" is for numbers; "less" for quantities or amounts. Write fewer letters and say less.

finalize, finalization These are manufactured words. Why not use such natural words as "end," "conclude," "complete"?

for your information Superfluous.
    the month of July Say "for July."
    the reason that Use "since," "because," "as."

fullest possible extent Meaningless padding. Say "full extent," or just "fully."

14

furnish Use "give" as a preferable, shorter, and more direct substitute.

further See FARTHER.

implement Say "carry out."

in compliance with your request Say "as you requested."
    addition to Say "besides."
    a satisfactory manner Say "satisfactorily."
    the near future Say "soon."
    the event that Say "if."
    the amount of Say "for."
    the meantime Say "meantime" or "meanwhile."
    order to Say "to."
    regard to Say "about."
    view of the fact that Say "as."

inasmuch as "As," "since," and "because" are a lot shorter.

indicate "Show" is a better word, not nearly so overworked.

kindly should not be used for "please." "Please reply," not "kindly reply."

liquidate Say "pay off" if that is what you mean.

none as a subject is usually plural unless a single subject is clearly indicated. "None of the jobs are open." "None of the work is done."

notwithstanding the fact that is a long-winded way of saying "although" or "even though."

on is superfluous in stating days and dates. "He arrived Tuesday," not "He arrived on Tuesday."

previous to, prior to Why not say "before"?

principal, principle The noun "principal" means "head" or "chief," as well as capital sum. The adjective "principal" means "highest" or "best in rank or importance." "Principle" means "truth," "belief," "policy," "conviction," or "general theory."

quite means "really," "truly," "wholly," "positively." Avoid its use in phrases like "quite a few" and "quite some."

rarely ever, seldom ever "Ever" is superfluous in these two cases.

reside The conversational word "live" is preferable.

submitted "Sent" is shorter, more direct.

subsequent to "After" is shorter, more direct.

this is to inform you You can generally omit this phrase.
    is to thank you Why not simply "Thank you"?

utilization An inflated word for "use."

wish to apologize, wish to advise Instead of the first phrase, simply say, "We apologize." Instead of the second phrase, start off with what you want to say.

15

test your skills

SECRETS OF GOOD LETTER WRITING

1. *Rewrite the following letter, substituting simpler words:*

Dear Sir:

On January 6 I purchased a kit from your establishment: Model #316–B. Subsequently it came to my attention that several of the components were in absentia: the wing-nut bolts, the six brass screws and the lockwedge. The components are insignificant in monetary value, but without them I cannot implement the directions and conclude the project. I trust that you will cooperate to the fullest extent possible by sending these components at the earliest practicable date.

Yours sincerely,
Mr. George Widgen

2. *Rewrite the following letter, taking out every unnecessary word:*

Dear Sir:

This is the occasion of the third time I have written to you about a kit I ordered and subsequently received with three missing parts. My first two letters, which outlined the problem in minute detail, were not answered, although I sincerely requested prompt service. The missing parts, as noted previously, are two wing-nut bolts, six brass screws, and a lockwedge, which the man at the local hardware had never heard of. Notwithstanding the fact that I have already lost three precious weeks because of your policy of refusing to acknowledge customer complaints and your failure to answer my previous letters, I would appreciate having the missing parts without even further delay so I don't suffer the loss of even more wasted time.

If this letter is also ignored like the last two, I shall feel forced to make formal complaint to the Post Office Department in order to get the restitution I deserve.

I hope to hear from you soon so I don't have to take this dire step, and I trust that you will demonstrate your good faith by communicating with me at once.

Sincerely yours,
George Widgen

3. *Evaluate each of the following letter openings:*

a. I need a replacement head gasket for the model 7-B whammle I bought from you last August 10.

b. As far as I'm concerned, your recent vote was criminal!

c. This is the third time I've written you about my problem.

d. Things are pretty slow here, so I thought I'd drop you a line.

Answers to this quiz appear on page 699.

16

3

Handling your
personal correspondence

You can write the kind of personal letter we all love to receive. In this chapter, columnist Elizabeth Post tells how to phrase gracious notes of congratulation or apology, how to acknowledge hospitality or write letters of introduction, and how to communicate the human touch.

The practice of personal letter writing is diminishing to such an extent today that the letter threatens to become a telegram, a telephone message, or just a postcard. Since daily events are communicated by newspapers, radio, and television with far greater accuracy and dispatch than they could have been by the efforts of a Voltaire himself, the circulation of general news—which formed the chief reason for letters in the stagecoach and sailing-vessel days—has no part in the hurried correspondence of the twentieth century. Still, people *do* write letters, and there are some who possess a gift for a fresh turn of phrase with which to charm the reader.

The letter we all love to receive is the one that carries so much of the writer's personality that he or she seems to be sitting beside us and talking as if we were together, instead of by proxy in ink-made characters on paper. To achieve this happy feeling of *talking* through a letter, you must use certain devices to diminish the stilted quality of the written word. Here are a few specific suggestions that may help to make your letters reflect your personality.

It is quite correct to type a personal letter, but only if the writer is a proficient enough typist so that the number of errors does not distract the reader. Leave ample margins to make the letter attractive.

Punctuation can add interest and variety to your letters, much as the change in tone of a speaker's voice adds zest and color to his story. Underlining a word or using an exclamation point after a phrase or sentence gives emphasis where you want it. A dash is effective instead of a longer, possibly more grammatical phrase. "We went to a dance last night—what a party!" is more colorful than "We went to a dance last night and it was a great party."

In a personal letter use phrases typical of your speech rather than more formal language. A young person who commonly uses the expression "a real doll" would sound unnatural and self-conscious if she wrote "she is a lovely girl."

Occasionally insert the name of the person to whom you are writing to give your letter an added touch of familiarity and affection. "And, Helen, guess what we are going to do this summer!" makes Helen feel as though it will be of special interest to *her*.

Use contractions to make your writing sound more natural. Since you would probably never say "I do not know" for "I don't know" or "I am so glad" for "I'm so glad," why write it that way?

And, finally, don't stop too long to think of *how* to say it. Decide what you want to say, and then write it as quickly as possible; that way, it will seem as if you are truly talking to your friend.

The difficulty in beginning

Most people who wonder how they will ever fill a blank sheet of paper find that the difficult part of a letter is the beginning. The instruction of an English professor—"Begin at the beginning of what you have to say, go on until you have finished, and then stop"—is just about as useful as the explanation of the celebrated artist who proclaimed, "You simply take a little of the right color of paint and put it on the right spot." Perhaps the following suggestions will be more helpful.

Even someone who loves the very sight of your handwriting could hardly be expected to enjoy a letter beginning "I know I ought to have written sooner, but I haven't had anything to write about." Or one saying "I suppose you think I've been very neglectful, but you know how I hate to write letters."

Suppose you merely change the wording of the above sentences, so that instead of slamming the door in your friend's face, you hold it open. "Do you think I have forgotten you entirely? You don't know, Ann, how

LETTERS THAT SHOULDN'T BE WRITTEN

No USEFUL PURPOSE is ever served by writing needlessly of misfortune or unhappiness—even to members of your family. Our distress at hearing about illness or unhappiness among those we love is intensified by the number of miles that separate us from them.

The chronic calamity writers seem to wait until the skies are darkest and then, rushing to their desks, luxuriate in pouring out all their troubles to their friends.

Every day the mails carry letters of another kind whose fallout would be spectacular if they fell into the wrong hands. Silly girls and foolish men, for example, often write things that sound quite different from their original intent.

Remember this above all: Never write a letter to anyone that you would be embarrassed to see in a newspaper above your signature. Thousands upon thousands of people, inspired by every known emotion, have poured words on paper, and few of the many made public have had charm or beauty.

If you are determined to write an emotional letter to someone, put it away overnight in order to reread it and make sure that you have said nothing that may sound different from what you intended.

The point to remember is that written words have permanency, and thoughts carelessly put on paper can come back to haunt you.

The light, jesting tone that saves a quip from being offensive cannot be expressed in writing, and remarks that are amusing when spoken can become sharp and insulting when written. Moreover, words expressing a fleeting mood can take on a frightening permanence when written down.

Anger in a letter carries with it the effect of solidified fury. Bitter spoken words fade away once the cause is forgiven; written words are fixed on the page forever. Admonitions from parents to their children may very properly be put on paper—provided they are meant to endure and to be remembered—but momentary annoyance should be expressed briefly.

One point cannot be overstressed: Letters written under strong emotion should be held for twenty-four hours and reread before being sent—or probably torn into small pieces and not sent at all.

many letters I planned to write you." Or "Time and time again I've wanted to write you but each moment that I saved for myself was always interrupted by—*something.*"

It is easy enough to begin a letter in answer to one you have just received. You have fresh news to comment on, and the impulse to reply needs no prodding. Nothing can be simpler than to say, "We were all so pleased to hear from you this morning," or "Your letter was the most welcome thing the postman has brought for ages." Then you take up the various subjects in Ann's letter, which should certainly lead into topics of your own.

Remember to answer all of her specific questions. It is not only unflattering to give the impression that you read them hurriedly, but often very upsetting if you omit long-awaited information.

On ending a letter

Just as the beginning of a letter should give the reader an impression of greeting, its ending should express friendly or affectionate leave-taking. Nothing can be worse than to flounder for an idea that will effect your escape. "Well, I guess you've read enough of this," and "You're probably bored by now so I'd better close" are obvious phrases of desperation. Certainly they are ungraceful.

When you leave a good friend's house, you don't have to invent a special sentence in order to say good-by. Leave-taking in a letter is the same. In personal letters to friends or family, it is not necessary to use the standard forms of closing.

Will write again in a day or two.

Martin

Lunch was announced half a page ago! So good-by for now.

Nancy

Counting the hours till next weekend!

Betsy

The note of apology

If you find that you can't keep a dinner date or other social engagement you should always telephone or send a wire before the appointed time to warn your host or hostess that you will not be there. But you should also follow up with a written explanation. The note of apology should offer a valid excuse for your absence and express sincere regret at the inconvenience you may have caused.

Dear Mrs. Town,

I do apologize for having had to send you the telegram about Monday night.

When I accepted your invitation, I stupidly forgot entirely that Monday was a holiday and that my own guests, naturally, were not leaving until Tuesday morning; Arthur and I could not very well go out by ourselves and leave them!

We were disappointed and hope that you know how sorry we were not to be with you.

Very sincerely,
Ethel Norman

Tuesday morning

The note of apology for an unfortunate mishap should explain the circumstances and offer a sincere apology.

Dear Mrs. Johnson,

My little boy has just told me that our dog got into your flower beds and did a great deal of damage.

The fence around his pen is being built higher at this moment, and he will not be able to escape again. I shall send you some plants to replace those that were ruined, although I know that new ones cannot compensate for those you have lost. I can only ask you to accept my apologies.

Sincerely yours,
Katherine Pennybacker

Thank-you letters

The most important qualification of a thank-you letter is that it sound sincere. Therefore, use the expressions most natural to you, and write as enthusiastically as if you were talking.

LETTERS OF THANKS FOR WEDDING PRESENTS

Insofar as possible, thank-you notes for wedding presents should be written as soon as the gift is received. This is not always possible, but if they are not sent before the wedding, they must be written as soon as the bride returns from her honeymoon. Even for a very large wedding, all thank-you notes should be mailed within two months.

All wedding presents are sent to the bride, and she writes all the thank-you notes. But she generally words her letters to include the bridegroom, especially if the gifts have been sent by friends of his. Some girls prefer to sign the notes with both their names. This is a matter of choice. She might write something like this:

Saturday

Dear Mrs. Beck,

To think of your sending us all those wonderful glasses! They are perfect, and Jim and I want to thank you a thousand times!

The presents will be shown on the day of the wedding, but do come over this Tuesday morning for a cup of coffee and an earlier view.

Thanking you again, and with love from us both,

Joan

More formally, the bride-to-be might write:

Dear Mrs. King,

It was more than thoughtful of you and Mr. King to send us such a lovely clock. I have never been noted for my punctuality, and your gift will surely help me to improve. Thank you very, very much.

Looking forward to seeing you on the tenth,

Very sincerely,
Joan McCord

The salutation is addressed to Mrs. King only, but sometimes, as in the examples above, thanks to the husband is definitely expressed.

For a present received after the wedding, the bride might write:

Dear Mrs. Chatterton,

The mirror you sent us is going over our living-room mantel just as soon as we can hang it up! It is exactly what we most needed, and we both thank you ever so much.

Please come in soon to see how beautiful it looks in the room.

Affectionately,
Mary Smartlington

THANKS FOR CHRISTMAS AND OTHER PRESENTS

Thank-you notes for Christmas—and all other—presents should be written within two or three days of the time the gift is received. In the case of Christmas gifts a slightly longer period is permissible, but the notes should be sent before New Year's Day.

Dearest Aunt Lucy,

We just love our armchair! Jack says I'll never get a chance to sit in it if he gets there first. We both thank you so much, and are looking forward to seeing you at Easter.

With much love,
Sally

For his high school graduation, I sent my nephew a check. Several weeks went by without a thank-you note. But when my next bank statement arrived, I found on the back of his canceled check, scrawled above his endorsement: "Dear Aunt Virginia—You know how I hate to write, but thanks a lot!"   —*Virginia S. Pendarvis*

Dear Kate,

I am fascinated with my jewel box—it is so unusual. You are really clever at finding what no one else can, and what everyone wants. I don't know how you do it!

Again, thanks so much.

With love,
Edie

THANKS FOR A BABY PRESENT

Dear Mrs. Foster,

No one else in the world can knit like you! The sweater you made for the baby is perfectly adorable on her. Thank you, so much, from both of us.

Affectionately,
Robin

Dear Mrs. Cooper,

Thank you ever so much for the blanket you sent the baby. It is by far the prettiest one he has, and so soft and warm that I am really envious of him.

Do come in and see him, won't you? We love visitors, any day between 4 and 5:30.

Affectionately,
Helen

Bread-and-butter letters

When you have stayed overnight or longer at someone's house, it is absolutely necessary to write a letter of thanks to your hostess within a few days after the visit.

Why bread-and-butter letters, as they are called, are so difficult for nearly everyone is hard to say unless it is because they are often written to persons with whom you are on formal terms, and you want your letter to be informal in tone. Possibly you have been visiting a friend

WRITE BETTER, SPEAK BETTER

and must write to her mother, whom you scarcely know, or perhaps you are a bride and have been on a first visit to relatives or old friends of your husband who were strangers to you until now.

In the first case, when you have been visiting a girl friend and must write a letter to her mother, you write "Dear Mrs. Town" at the top of a page, and nothing in the memory of Mrs. Town encourages you to go further. It would be easy enough to write to Pauline, your friend. Very well, write to Pauline then—on a different piece of paper—about what a good time you had, how nice it was to be with her. Then copy the note you composed to Pauline on the page beginning "Dear Mrs. Town." You have only to add "Love to Pauline, and thank you again for asking me," end it "Very sincerely," or better, "Affectionately"—and there you are!

Don't be afraid that your note is too informal. Never think, because you cannot write a letter easily, that it is better not to write at all. The most awkward note imaginable is better than none.

AFTER A HOUSE-PARTY WEEKEND

Dear Franny,

You and Jim are such wonderful hosts! Once again I can only tell you that there is no other house to which I go with so much pleasure, and leave with so much regret.

Your party over this last weekend was the best yet, and thank you very, very much for having included me.

With much love to you all,
Betty

Dear Mrs. Farthingham,

Last weekend was the high spot of the summer. Everything you planned was wonderful, but the best of all was the trip to the country fair on Sunday.

I truly enjoyed every minute with your family, and thank you more than I can say for including me.

Very sincerely,
Elliot Sandstrom

AFTER VISITING A CLOSE FRIEND

Dear Ellen,

It was hideously stuffy in town this morning after the coolness of Strandholm, and a back alleyway is not an alluring outlook after the beauty of your place.

It was so good being with you and I enjoyed every moment.

With love,
Caroline

24

Dearest Bett,

We both had a wonderful time! Bob's sunburn has turned to a beautiful tan, and the rest did him a world of good.

You were good to ask us so soon again, and we thank you very, very much. Call us as soon as you get home.

Yours,
Mary

TO A STRANGER WHO HAS ENTERTAINED YOU

When someone has shown you special hospitality in a city where you are a stranger:

Dear Mrs. Duluth,

It was so good of you to give my husband and me so much of your time. We enjoyed and appreciated all your kindness to us more than we can say.

We hope that you and Mr. Duluth may be coming East before long and that we may have the pleasure of seeing you then in our home.

In the meanwhile, thank you for your generous hospitality, and my husband joins me in sending kindest regards to you both.

Very sincerely yours,
Katherine Starkweather

FROM A BRIDE TO HER NEW RELATIVES-IN-LAW

The following letter, written by a bride after paying a first visit to her husband's aunt and uncle, won her at a stroke the love of the whole family:

Dear Aunt Anne,

Now that we are home again I have a confession to make! Do you know that when Dick drove me up to your front door and I saw you and Uncle Bob standing on the top step—I was simply paralyzed with fright!

"Suppose they don't like me," was all that I could think. Of course, I know you love Dick, but that only made it worse. How awful, if you didn't like—me! The reason I stumbled coming up the steps was that

---

As Prince of Wales, Edward VII was known by his friends for his sense of humor. One intimate, relying on the prince's joviality, declined a dinner invitation with the following telegram: "Sorry cannot come. Lie follows." Edward was immensely amused.

---

my knees were actually knocking together! And then you were both so perfectly adorable to me and made me feel as though I had always been your niece—and not just the wife of your nephew.

I loved every minute of our being with you, just as much as Dick did, and we hope you are going to let us come again soon.

With best love from us both,

Your affectionate niece,
Nancy

Letters of congratulation

ON AN ENGAGEMENT

Dear Stella,

While we are not altogether surprised, we are both delighted to hear the good news of your engagement. Ted's family and ours are very close, as you know, and we have always been especially devoted to him. He is one of the finest—and now luckiest—of young men, and we send you both every good wish for all possible happiness.

Affectionately,
Nancy Jackson

Dear Ted,

Just a line to tell you how glad we all are to hear of your wonderful news. Stella is lovely, and, of course, from our point of view, we don't think she's exactly unfortunate either! This brings our very best wishes to you from

Arthur and Nancy Jackson

LETTER FROM A MOTHER TO A SON'S FIANCÉE

When it is impossible for a mother to go to meet her son's new fiancée, a letter should be written to her. The general outline is:

Dear Mary,

John has just told us of his great happiness, which, of course, makes us very happy, too. Our one distress is that we are so far away [or whatever else] that we cannot immediately meet you in person.

We do, however, send you our love and hope that we shall see you very soon.

Sincerely and affectionately,
Martha Jones

ON THE BIRTH OF A BABY

Dear Sue,

We were so delighted to hear the news of Jonathan Junior's birth. Congratulations to all three of you!

May I come to see you and the baby the first time that I'm in town?
I'll call and let you know when that will be.

> Much love,
> Helen

OTHER LETTERS OF CONGRATULATION

Dear Mrs. Steele,

We are so glad to hear the good news of David's success; it was a
very splendid accomplishment, and we are all so proud of him and
happy for you. When you see him or write to him, please give him our
love and congratulations.

> Sincerely,
> Mildred Bowen

Dear Michael,

We were all so happy to hear of the confirmation of your appointment. The state needs men like you—if we had more of your sort, the
ordinary citizen would have less to worry about. Our warmest congratulations!

> Jim

Letters of introduction

A business letter of introduction is somewhat different from a social one,
although it carries your implicit approval of the person you wish to introduce. It also implies the writer's request that the receiver pay due attention to the person being introduced. Since these letters are often
written to important people with little time to spare, they must not be
written casually.

A business letter of introduction does not necessarily oblige the receiver to entertain the subject socially. If he wishes to, he certainly may,
but generally his attention to the bearer's business is sufficient.

The social introduction is, in a way, more of a responsibility, because
the writer must decide on the compatibility of the people he is introducing. Therefore, there is one firm rule: Never *ask* for such letters of
introduction, and be very sparing in your offers to write them.

Few people realize that a letter of social introduction carries an immediate obligation. The form might as well be "The bearer of this note
has the right to demand your interest, your time, your hospitality—liberally and at once, no matter what you think of him." Therefore, it is far
better to refuse to write a note of introduction in the beginning than to
inconvenience a friend or acquaintance.

PUT IN YOUR FEW CENTS' WORTH!

ONE OF THE BEST THINGS in life costs just a few cents—sometimes only six. Plus the gracious impulse to write a letter, an unlooked-for letter, the kind of letter that brings to the lucky recipient a lift for the whole day.

Too often it goes unwritten. Too often we fool ourselves that we haven't the time.

Was anyone ever busier than Abraham Lincoln, or was there anyone who should have grown more sick of the onerous weight of correspondence? When thousands were dying daily on the battle-field, and his heart was bowed with all the griefs of the nation, he could still find a minute to write that famous letter to Mrs. Bixby:

> Dear Madam:
>   I have been shown in the files of the War Department a statement of the Adjutant General of Massachusetts that you are the mother of five sons who have died gloriously on the field of battle. I feel how weak and fruitless must be any word of mine which should attempt to beguile you from the grief of a loss so overwhelming. But I cannot refrain from tendering you the consolation that may be found in the thanks of the republic they died to save. I pray that our Heavenly Father may assuage the anguish of your bereavement, and leave you only the cherished memory of the loved and lost, and the solemn pride that must be yours to have laid so costly a sacrifice upon the altar of freedom.
>   Yours very sincerely and respectfully,
>
>   A. Lincoln

We all intend to write letters, of condolence, of congratulation, of appreciation, and friendship—tomorrow, or next week. For years I intended to write my fifth grade teacher, who had started me, as I realized looking back much later, on my career as a scientist and writer on nature.

Finally I wrote that letter. It came back, enclosed in a note from the school principal, saying that my old teacher had died two years before.

So I tried once more, this time to the professor of one of the stiffest science courses in college. He was regarded as an unapproachable old bear, but finding that his teaching had stuck as almost none other had, I wrote him how much his course had meant to me. Here is the answer I received:

> I found your letter last night just at a time when I was feeling particularly low. It seemed to make my whole lifework worthwhile. I may say that in thirty-five years of giving the best I know how to give, I have never before received one word of appreciation from a student. Thanks.

I was riding in a bus one day when there was an accident. Women and children, bruised and cut with flying glass, became panicky. The driver took charge of everybody and everything at once, helping the injured, marshaling witnesses, sending someone to telephone for the ambulance, and keeping calm under the unjust abuse of the truck driver who had run into him. After the ambulance had come, the driver got into his seat, wiped some blood off his eyebrow, and started to finish his run with his battered bus. Said a man next to him, "I'm going to report you!" Indignantly, I began to intervene, but he hastened on: "For efficiency and courtesy. If you'll tell me where to write, and give me your name, I'll tell your company you're the best man in a pinch I ever saw."

"Gee, mister," said the driver, letting out a long breath, "I wish there was more in the world like you." How often someone performs unusual services for us that we allow to pass unpraised, taking courtesy and helpfulness for granted!

The mails are available to everyone, and correspondence is not an intrusion comparable to a personal call on a stranger. There is no reason why, if you have something friendly to say, you shouldn't say it in a letter, even to an exalted personage whom you have never met. And its results can be momentous for you.

Why anyone should deprive himself of a friend that he might have, even at long range, is hard to understand, with the postal department delivering once a day in most communities.

True, we are not all of us as fluent as men of letters are. But no flowery style is required. Your friends want to hear from *you* in your own characteristic style. No rhetoric takes the place of sincerity.

—*Donald Culross Peattie*

When you know someone who is going to a city where you have other friends and when you believe that it will be a mutual pleasure for them to meet, a letter of introduction is proper and very easy to write. But sent to a casual acquaintance—no matter how attractive or distinguished the person to be introduced—it is a gross presumption.

THE MORE FORMAL NOTE OF INTRODUCTION

Dear Mrs. Miller:

Julian Gibbs is going to Buffalo on January tenth to deliver a lecture on his Polar expedition, and I am giving him this note of introduction to you. He is a very great friend of ours, and I think that perhaps you and Mr. Miller will enjoy meeting him as much as I know he would enjoy knowing you.

With kindest regards, in which Arthur joins,

Very sincerely,
Ethel Norman

If Mr. Norman were introducing one man to another, he would give his card to the visitor, inscribed as follows:

Introducing Julian Gibbs

Mr. Arthur Lees Norman

Mr. Norman would also send a private letter by mail, telling his friend that Mr. Gibbs is coming.

Dear Jack,

I am giving Julian Gibbs a card of introduction to you when he goes to Buffalo on the tenth to lecture. He is delightfully entertaining and a great friend of ours. I feel sure that Betty would enjoy meeting him. If you can conveniently ask him to your house, I know he would appreciate it; if not, perhaps you could put him up for a day or two at a club or arrange for a reservation in a good hotel.

Faithfully,
Arthur Norman

INFORMAL LETTER OF INTRODUCTION

My dear Ruth,

I am giving this letter to George Perrin, a good friend of ours, who is going to be in Chicago the week of January 7.

I want very much to have him meet you and hope that this will find you in town.

Affectionately,
Louise Hill

At the same time a second and private letter of information is written and sent by mail.

Dear Ruth,

I have sent you a letter introducing George Perrin. He is young, about thirty-five or so, very good company, and altogether likable. We have known him for some years.

He is very interested in modern art, and knowing that you count a number of artists among your friends, we thought you might be able to arrange some introductions for him.

I know it would be a pleasure for everyone concerned, and hope you will be able to get together.

Affectionately,
Louise

PROCEDURE ON ARRIVAL

A letter of introduction is always handed to you unsealed. It is correct for you to seal it at once in the presence of its author.

If you are a man and your introduction is to a lady, you go to her house soon after you arrive, introduce yourself, and give her your letter of introduction. If you feel presumptuous in going directly to her home, you may telephone and explain who you are and by whom you are introduced. She should, and undoubtedly will, set a time for you to meet, and when you arrive, you give her your letter of introduction.

A letter to a man is mailed to his house, unless the letter is a business one. In the latter case, if there has not been time to mail the introduction ahead, you go to his office and send in your business card and the letter. You wait in the reception room until he has read the letter and calls you into his office. If at all possible, it is much better to write or call him first, letting him know your business and when you will arrive. This will ensure his having time to see you, as well as preparing him to discuss whatever your business may be.

A woman mails her letter of introduction and does nothing further until she receives an acknowledgment. But the obligation of a written

FOUR TIPS FOR WRITING THE SICK

FOR THE BEDRIDDEN, either in a hospital setting or at home, few pleasures are greater than those of receiving a letter from a friend, unless it be a visit. Even if you send a letter to an invalid whom you visit occasionally, it can help lift his spirits enormously. If you cannot always send a letter, a tastefully selected greeting card is better than nothing. Here are four general principles that may be useful.

First, this is one of the rare occasions when I cannot counsel you to be brief. The longer the letter, the better. An invalid or convalescent has a great deal of time on his hands. He may feel up to reading only part of a long letter at a time; then he will look forward to taking it up again later.

Second, make sure your letter is easy to read. The energy level of an invalid is likely to be low; don't make him work any harder than necessary. If you can type, by all means do so—and be sure to double-space your lines. If your handwriting isn't easily legible, print the letter in large, easy-to-read characters.

Third, keep the letter reasonably cheerful, but not so much so that you run over into the trivial. Be careful to make comments on the person's own situation and to ask questions as you would in a conversation, even if the invalid is not able to write you a reply. Essentially, the letter should act as a proxy for you.

Fourth, if the invalid is going to be confined for quite some time, and you're worried because the routines of your life make poor material for an interesting series of letters, consider sending along clippings from newspapers and magazines that you think will interest the patient. Jokes, humorous columns, even serious articles that will help make him feel a part of the world will be morale building.

Several years ago, I was confined to bed for nearly a year, and I remember that my greatest source of gloom was the feeling that the world was passing me by, that my acquaintances were all making their way in the world, while I was vegetating. Letters which cheered me most were those which generally followed the suggestions I've offered in the preceding paragraphs.

—Lassor Blumenthal

introduction is so strong that only illness or absence can excuse the recipient from asking you to her house—either formally or informally.

When a man receives a letter introducing another man, he calls the
person introduced on the telephone and asks how he may be of service.
If he does not invite the newcomer to his house, he may arrange a hotel
reservation or ask him to lunch or dinner at a restaurant, as the circumstances seem to warrant. But it is absolutely necessary that he show the
stranger what courtesy he can.

THE INDIRECT LETTER OF INTRODUCTION

When the Franklins move to Strangetown, an indirect letter of introduction is better than a direct one. An indirect letter is one written by
Mrs. O'Connor to a friend of hers in Strangetown. As already explained,
a letter of introduction *presented* by Mrs. Franklin puts its recipient in a
position where she must do something for the Franklins, no matter how
inconvenient or distasteful it may be.

If, on the other hand, Mrs. O'Connor merely writes to Mrs. Hartwell,
"My friends, the Franklins, are going to live in your neighborhood," the
latter is free to make advances only insofar as she feels inclined.

Mrs. Franklin, knowing nothing about this letter and expecting nothing in the way of hospitality, is far more likely to be pleased when Mrs.
Hartwell calls on her than when she is invited to Mrs. Hartwell's house
because the invitation is obligatory. A letter of introduction, as you can
see, is often an inconvenience and can be a very real burden.

The letter of condolence

The two most important things about letters of condolence are that they
be written immediately, and that they be sincere.

Intimate letters of condolence are like love letters in that they are too
personal to follow a set form. Say what you truly feel. Say that and
nothing else. Sit down at your desk; let your thoughts be with the person you are writing to.

Don't dwell on the details of illness or the manner of death; don't
quote endlessly from the poets and Scripture. Remember that a person
with an aching heart will not wish to wade through interminably sor-
rowful thoughts. The more nearly a note can express a thought of sympathy, and a genuine love or appreciation for the one who has gone, the
greater comfort it brings.

Write as simply as possible and let your heart speak truly but briefly. Forget, if you can, that you are using written words. Think merely how you feel—then put your feelings on paper.

Suppose it is the death of a man who has left a place in the whole community that will be difficult, if not impossible, to fill. You remember all he stood for that was fine and helpful to others and how much he will be missed. All you can think of is "Steve—what a wonderful man he was! I don't think anything will ever be the same again without him." Say just that! Ask if there is anything you can do at any time to be of service. There is nothing more to be said. A line into which you have put a little of the genuine feeling that you had for Steve is worth pages of eloquence. A letter of condolence may be abrupt, badly constructed, ungrammatical—never mind. Grace of expression counts for nothing; sincerity alone is of value.

Occasionally a letter from one who has suffered an undeniably equal loss, who in sincerity writes words of encouragement and assurance that in time the pain will grow less instead of greater, is of genuine help.

The few examples below are intended merely as suggested guides for those at a loss to construct a short but appropriate message.

My dear Mrs. Sutphen,
    We are so very shocked to hear of the sorrow that has come to you.
    If there is anything that either my husband or I can do, I earnestly hope that you will call upon us.

                  Alice Blake

My dear Mrs. Conrad,
    I know how little words written on a page can possibly mean to you at such a time. But I must at least tell you that you are in our thoughts and in our hearts, and if there is anything that we can do for you, please send us a message—whatever it may be.

             With deepest sympathy,
             Mary Newling

The letter to someone whose loss is for the best is difficult in that you want to express sympathy but cannot feel sad that one who has suffered so long has found release. The expression of sympathy in this case should not be for the present death, but for the illness or whatever it was that occurred long ago. The grief for a paralyzed mother is for the stroke that cut her down many years before, and your sympathy, though you may not have realized it, is for that. You might write: "Your sorrow during all these years—and now—is in my heart; and all my thoughts and sympathy are with you."

4

Give your letters
the right look

Part of the impression your letters make depends on their appearance. When is a typewritten letter improper? Where should you put your return address, and in what form? Are there different styles for formal and informal letters? Here are the answers you need to know.

The letter you write, whether you realize it or not, is a mirror that reflects your appearance, taste, and character. A sloppy letter—the writing running up and down, badly worded, badly spelled, paper and envelope unmatched, smeared—proclaims the sort of person who probably has uncombed hair, run-down heels, a run in her stockings, or a stain on his tie. Conversely, a neat, precise, evenly written note portrays a person who has those happy characteristics. Therefore, while it cannot be said that a person's future can be read in his handwriting, his character may well be revealed. Furthermore, a messy letter is discourteous, clearly implying a lack of interest and care on the part of the writer which invites a similar reaction by the reader.

The executive picks a secretary not only because his or her neat and efficient letters are good advertising, but because they indicate that the secretary is well organized and tidy.

Excellent secretaries have an advantage over most of us in that they have had training in the preparation of business correspondence. And, of course, the mechanical nature of the typewriter itself simplifies such matters as the evenness of margins and the regular spacing of lines and words. Writing letters by hand is more difficult, but it is possible to make graceful letters, to space words evenly, and to put them on a page so that their appearance is pleasing. No matter how badly formed each individual letter may be, the page as a whole will look fairly neat if the writing is consistent and the lines level. Avoid such exaggerated styles of writing as dotting "i" with a circle, for no amount of attention to other matters can compensate for such childish habits.

You can make yourself write neatly and legibly. You can—with the help of a dictionary if need be—spell correctly. You can be sure that you understand the meaning of every word you use. If it is difficult for you to write in a straight line, use the lined guide that comes with some stationery, or make one yourself. If you find it impossible to keep an even margin, draw a light perpendicular line at the left of the page so that you can start each new line of writing on it. A guide line one inch from the right edge of your paper to tell you where to stop will also help. Far better to use these guides than to send envelopes and pages of writing that slide uphill and down in uncontrolled disorder, so that the recipient must all but stand on his head to read them.

These calligraphic complications may be avoided by using a typewriter. All business letters—from home as well as office—should be typed if you have access to a machine, and letters to friends certainly may be if you wish. However, some forms of correspondence must always be written by hand, and the following rules are unbreakable except for handicapped people who otherwise could not write at all.

Never type an invitation, an acceptance, or a regret.

Never type letters of congratulations or thanks.

Never type letters or notes of condolence.

Choose the right stationery

Suitability should be considered in choosing your stationery, just as it is in choosing your wardrobe. For a handwriting that is habitually large, pick a paper of a larger size than you would choose for writing that is small. The shape of paper should also depend somewhat upon the writer's usual spacing of the lines and on whether a wide or narrow margin is used. Low, spread-out writing looks better on a square sheet of paper; tall, pointed writing looks better on paper that is high and narrow.

Whether the paper is rough or smooth is entirely a matter of personal choice—but its quality should be good and its shape and color conservative. Paper should never be ruled or highly scented or oddly shaped, nor should it have elaborate or striking ornamentation.

When the paper is thin, envelopes with colored linings should be used so that the writing cannot be read through the envelope, or you may fold a blank sheet outside the pages. The monogram or address may be stamped on the paper in a color to match the lining. Young girls may use gay envelope linings and paper, and the device on the paper may correspond, but it must not be so large or loud as to be ostentatious. Oblong envelopes are excellent for business, but those more nearly square are smartest for personal use.

Linings for Christmas-card envelopes may be as bright as the ornaments that decorate a Christmas tree. This is the time one may go overboard. But unrestrained masses of red and gold, swirls of purple and green, or other striking colors are in poor taste at any other time.

PAPER FOR A MAN A man's writing paper should always be conservative. White or cream, gray, or granite-colored paper, medium size or larger, is the best choice. The color of the engraving (or printing) should be black, gray, or dark blue. Writing ink should be black or blue-black.

A very practical man's paper is a single sheet 7 or 7¼ inches by 10 or 10½ inches marked in plain block letters in dark blue at the top. His name (without title), his address including zip code, and his telephone number all appear. This paper can be used for typewriting or handwriting and for all types of correspondence. It is folded in thirds to fit into a 7¼-inch or 7½-inch-by-4-inch envelope. For purely social correspondence, he may use paper of the same color and size, with initials in block letters or a crest if he has one. A man who has occasion to write short notes frequently may also have single sheets in a slightly smaller size, so that the message will not look as lost as it would on the larger paper. (See sample letterheads on next page.)

PAPER FOR A WOMAN White, cream, light blues, grays, and light greens are in best taste. Paper should be of small or medium size, single or double sheets, plain or with colored border, stamped with a monogram, initials, or name and address in color to match the border. Writing ink should be black or blue, and green may be used if that is the color of the paper.

A married woman's paper is engraved "Mrs. William Frost," not "Mrs. Mary Frost" or "Mary Frost." An unmarried woman uses "Miss" only in

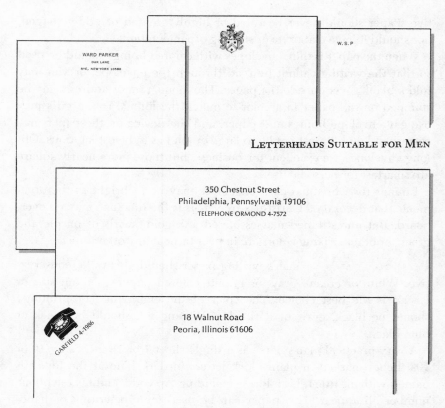

WARD PARKER
OAK LANE
RYE, NEW YORK 10580

W. S. P

LETTERHEADS SUITABLE FOR MEN

350 Chestnut Street
Philadelphia, Pennsylvania 19106
TELEPHONE ORMOND 4-7572

GARFIELD 4-1986

18 Walnut Road
Peoria, Illinois 61606

PAPER FOR THE WHOLE FAMILY

the return address on the envelope. A professional woman often uses her professional name without title—"Jane Author" rather than "Mrs. Robert Author"—on paper used for business correspondence.

PAPER FOR EVERYONE IN THE FAMILY   Paper suitable for use by all the members of a family has the address engraved or printed in plain letters at the top of the first page. Frequently the telephone number is put in small letters under the address or in the upper left-hand corner with the address in the center. This paper is especially practical if you have a country or vacation home, as it can also be used by your guests.

FOR THE YOUNG CORRESPONDENT   A girl's first name—either Elizabeth in full or Betty—is popular for all of a young girl's personal correspondence, but it should not be used by an older woman. If her first name is not distinctive, the young girl may wish to use her surname also. Available for very young ladies are attractive papers with designs in the upper left-hand corners or along the left or top borders, usually flowers, birds, or perhaps a kitten or puppy. A name or monogram is not used. and the style of the picture varies with the age of the girl.

Many stationers also sell paper for very young girls or boys. It is ruled, usually has an illustration of animals, toys, or something from a familiar story or nursery rhyme, and may come in a variety of shapes. It is designed to amuse the young child and make him consider letter writing a pleasure rather than a chore.

NOTEPAPER   For short notes, for acceptances or regrets, and for invitations, a supply of fold-over notepaper, half the size of a single sheet of lady's writing paper, is invaluable. It may be of any color properly used for letter paper and engraved or printed with initials or with the owner's name and address, and possibly telephone number. If not marked with initials or a name, it is useful for every female member of the family.

OFFICIAL WRITING PAPER   An ambassador or minister has his country's coat of arms—usually in gold—stamped at the top of writing paper and on cards of invitation for official or formal use. For his personal use and for the use of all who live at the embassy or the legation, notepaper is engraved merely

AMERICAN EMBASSY
LONDON

A governor's letter paper is stamped

EXECUTIVE MANSION
COLUMBUS
OHIO

and is usually surmounted by the state coat of arms. EXECUTIVE OFFICE is also correct as the heading for official letters. Paper engraved with EXECUTIVE MANSION, but without the coat of arms, may be used by the governor's family if the address is also that of their home. Otherwise their paper is engraved with their personal address.

A senator's wife has no right to use stationery headed THE SENATE, nor may the wife of a representative write on paper engraved HOUSE OF REPRESENTATIVES.

MOURNING PAPER   Few people use mourning paper at all, and plain white paper has almost replaced that with a black border. A ¼-inch bor-

39

der is considered deepest mourning; borders of $\frac{3}{16}$, $\frac{1}{16}$, or $\frac{1}{32}$ inch are also appropriate. Colored paper or stationery with gay floral or other designs is never appropriate for those in mourning.

PRINTING AS WELL AS ENGRAVING

Years ago the paper used by a woman was either engraved, die-stamped, or left plain. Today paper upon which one's full name and address are printed has become indispensable to everyone who must write many letters. Therefore, a small supply of engraved paper at un-avoidably higher cost is used only for formal correspondence and is augmented by a larger supply of printed paper for informal social cor-respondence and for business letters.

The mechanics of the letter

SEQUENCE OF PAGES Folded stationery may cause problems about the proper order in which to use the pages. If a letter is two pages long, it is customary to use the first and third pages, as this leaves the fourth page blank and prevents the writing from showing through the enve-lope. For longer letters, one may write first, second, third, fourth, in reg-ular order; or first and fourth, then, opening the sheet and turning it sideways, write across the two inside pages as one. The sequence is not important, and there is no fixed rule. If any possibility of confusion exists, it is best to number all pages but the first.

One may write on both sides of single-sheet stationery, but not if it is airmail weight, since this thin paper allows the writing to show through, making the letter difficult to read.

On fold-over or informal notepaper, when the address is at the top and there is nothing in the center, the letter or note begins on the first page and follows into the center pages. The paper is opened flat and written on vertically as if it were a single page. If there is an initial or name in the center of the front page, the note begins at the top of the opened center pages if it is long enough to cover more than half, and on the lower half if it is to be only a few words.

YOUR HOME ADDRESS AND THE DATE If your stationery is not marked with your address, it is only courteous to provide it for your correspond-ent's convenience in replying. The upper right-hand corner of the first page of your letter is the usual place for an address, but sometimes, es-pecially on a short note, it may be included in the lower left-hand part

of the page, just below the level of your signature. In either case the
date goes below the address.

> Sincerely,
> Mary Swenson
> (Mrs. John Swenson)

45 Barton Street
Racine, Wisconsin
May 5, 1971

When your address is already engraved or printed on the stationery,
the date is placed in the same place—in the upper right-hand corner of
the first page of a letter or at the end and to the far left of the signature
of a note. May 9, 1971, is preferable to 5–9–71.

At the end of a note "Thursday" is sufficient unless the note is an invitation for more than a week ahead, in which case you write, as in a
letter, "January 9." The year is not essential.

RECIPIENT'S ADDRESS The correct form for business letters demands
that the receiver's address be put at the left, five lines below the level
of the date and two lines above the salutation, exactly as it appears on
the envelope.

Mr. James Johnson
Smith, Johnson & Co.
20 Broadway
New York, New York 10027

Dear Mr. Johnson:

Smith, Johnson & Co.
20 Broadway
New York, New York 10027

Dear Sirs:

Personal letters and notes, however, never have the address of the receiver anywhere except on the envelope itself.

THE SALUTATION When writing business correspondence without the
name of a person to whom the letter should be directed, the salutation
may be "Dear Sir," "Dear Sirs," or "Gentlemen." When addressing
women, "Dear Madams" is acceptable. If you are writing to a specific
person whose name is known, use the salutation "Dear Mr. Brown,"
"Dear Mrs. Smith," "Dear Miss Jones," or "Dear Ms. White." (The
term "Ms." has gained wide acceptance and is now used interchangeably with "Mrs." and "Miss" in business and personal correspondence.)

If the writer of a business letter personally knows the man or woman
to whom the letter is being sent, the salutation "Dear Jim" or "Dear
Anne" may be used. A good rule to follow is to address the person as

you ordinarily do when speaking with him or her. Discretion should always be used when using first names, however, as there are some people who, despite their friendly nature, prefer being addressed with their titles, such as Mr., Mrs., Miss, or Ms. where business matters are concerned.

When writing a social letter, a formal beginning is "My dear Mr. Johnson" or "My dear Mrs. Johnson." Less formal and often more appropriate when writing to close friends are the salutations "Dear Sally" and "Dearest Sally." In this area, too, discretion should be used. Bear in mind that it is usually better to err on the side of formality when you are not absolutely certain of how the recipient of your correspondence would view your intimacy.

In a business letter it is proper to follow the salutation with a colon, while in a social or friendly letter the salutation is followed by a comma.

THE CLOSING   It is too bad that, for personal letters and notes, the English language does not permit the charming closing of letters in the French manner, those little flowers of compliment that leave such a pleasant glow. But ever since the eighteenth century, English-speaking people have been busy pruning away all ornament of expression; even the last remaining graces—"kindest regards," "with kindest remembrances"—are fast disappearing, leaving us little but an abrupt "Sincerely yours."

The best ending to a formal social note is "Sincerely," "Sincerely yours," "Very sincerely," or "Very sincerely yours."

"I have the honor to remain . . ." is used only in correspondence to very prominent people in the government, diplomatic corps, or church.

The close of a business letter should be "Yours truly" or "Very truly yours." "Sincerely" is also correct. "Respectfully" is used only by a tradesman to a customer or by an employe to an employer. No woman should ever sign a letter "Respectfully," except as part of the long, formal "I have the honor to remain" close of a letter to the President of the United States or to a bishop or a mother superior.

"Faithfully" and "Faithfully yours" are appropriate for a man when he is writing to a woman or for any formal social correspondence, such as a letter to the President of the United States, a member of the Cabinet, an ambassador, a clergyman, etc.

"As always" is useful to someone with whom you may not be on intimate terms, especially when you have not seen or been in communication with the person for some time.

"Sincerely" in formal notes and "Affectionately" or "Love" in friendly notes are the most frequently used closings at present. Between the first and last two there is a blank; in English we have no adequate expression to fit sentiment more friendly than the first and less intimate than the others. "Cordially" was brought into use no doubt to fill this need, but it sounds a bit condescending.

"Yours in haste" and "Hastily yours," while not bad form, are rather carelessly rude unless for some reason your communication indicates real and necessary haste.

"Gratefully" is used only when a benefit has been received, as to a lawyer who has skillfully handled a case or to a friend who has gone to unusual trouble to do you a favor.

In an ordinary letter of thanks, the signature is "Sincerely," "Affectionately," "Devotedly"—whatever your usual close may be.

THE SIGNATURE   John Hunter Titherington Smith, finding his name too much of a penful for letters and documents, may choose J.H.T. Smith instead, or perhaps at the end of personal letters, John H.T. Smith. Of course, if he is writing a business associate with whom he is on terms of close personal acquaintance, he signs simply "John" or "Jack" over the typed "J.H.T. Smith." Mail is addressed to him in the typed form (or the printed form, if the letterhead carries his full name).

A married woman always signs a letter to a stranger, a bank, a business firm, etc., with her legal name. If her stationery is marked with her full married name and address, her signature—Mary Jones Mathews or Mary J. Mathews—needs no further explanation. But if it is not, she should give her married name (to which the reply will be sent) in one of several ways. When she writes by hand, she adds her married name beneath her signature, or to the left of it, in parentheses, thus:

> *Very truly yours,*
> *Mary Jones Mathews*
> *(Mrs. John Mathews)*

When the letter is typed, her married name is typed beneath the space left for her signature, where it need not be enclosed in parentheses.

> Very truly yours,
> *Mary Jones Mathews*
> Mrs. John Mathews

The only times when a woman actually uses "Mrs." in her signature are in a hotel register, on a business telegram, on a charge account, or in a letter ordering a purchase from a store. And then it must be Mrs. John Smith. To a servant who works for her, it is Mrs. Smith.

An unmarried woman uses much the same form in a typed letter:

> Sincerely,
> *Mary Mathews*
> Miss Mary Mathews

When she writes by hand, she may use this style:

> *Sincerely,*
> *(Miss) Mary Mathews*

And a final warning about the signature: Avoid a flourishing, unrecognizable one. While the reader may be able to decipher a word in a sentence because of its context, he cannot possibly make sense of an illegible signature if he does not already know who wrote the letter.

A PROFESSIONAL WOMAN'S SIGNATURE When an unmarried woman starts a professional career using her maiden name, she may continue to use it throughout her business life. She uses "Miss" in combination with that name even after she marries.

Many women start their careers after their marriage and wish to use their married names. Professionally called Mary T. Forsyth or Helen Horton Hughes, they should use business stationery with their names

---

A professor at an eastern university driving to the West Coast one summer had been invited to stop en route at the homes of half a dozen of his former students. A methodically efficient man, he wrote all his thank-you notes beforehand. He sealed, addressed, and stamped the letters, bundled them up with a rubber band, and put them in his suitcase.

His first stop was in Buffalo. Next night, unpacking in a hotel room about 300 miles farther west, he discovered the thank-you notes were missing. Telephoning his Buffalo host, he asked with studied casualness, "Did you by any chance find a bundle of letters in the guest room?"

"Why, yes," said his friend. "I mailed them for you this very morning." —*Regina Schirmer*

printed that way. This can be most confusing to a correspondent. In order to make it clear what title he should use in addressing a reply, Mary or Helen may precede her typewritten signature with (Mrs.). This should *never* be done except on business correspondence—in all other cases their husbands' names are used below the handwritten signature when clarification is necessary.

FOLDING A LETTER One need not worry about which edge of a letter is inserted first into the envelope, but—if you wish to be strictly proper—insert the open, or unfolded edge, first. It is sufficient that the paper be folded neatly—once, of course, for the envelope that is as deep as half the length of the paper, and twice for the envelope that is a third as deep. The paper that must be folded into thirds is used only as personal stationery for men or for business purposes. Women's personal letter paper should fold only once and fit into its envelope. Notepaper is the same size as the envelope and goes into it flat with only the original fold.

The envelope

Write the name and address on the envelope as precisely and as legibly as you can. If your writing is poor, print.

When you are writing to someone in a North American city with a zip code, write it on the envelope, as it is an essential part of the address. Zone numbers are used in many foreign cities, and are an integral part of the address.

The address may be written with each line indented a few spaces or with a straight margin on the left. The two forms are shown below. Both are equally correct.

Mr. Harvey S. Simpson
4 Hillside Lane
Clinton
Ohio 20567

Mr. Harvey S. Simpson
4 Hillside Lane
Clinton, Ohio 20567

CORRECT USE OF "ESQUIRE" "Esquire" has virtually gone out of general use in the United States—except among the conservative members of the older generation and among lawyers and justices of the peace. Its correct use, furthermore, is confusing. For example, engraved invitations are always addressed to Mr. Stanley Smith on both invitation and envelope. Handwritten invitations, as well as all other personal letters, may be addressed to Stanley Smith, Esq.

A WIDOW AND HER HUSBAND'S NAME   No note or social letter should ever be addressed to a married woman—even if she is a widow—as Mrs. Mary Town. Correctly and properly a widow keeps her husband's name, always. If her son's wife should have the same name, she becomes Mrs. James Town, Senior. Or, if there is no other in her community with the same name, she becomes simply Mrs. Town.

YOUNG PEOPLE   Young ladies are addressed as "Miss" from the very day they are born. Both the first and last names are used on envelopes—the only time a girl is addressed as "Miss Taylor" is on the inner envelope of a wedding invitation.

Boys may be addressed as "Master" until they are six or seven. After that they are addressed without title until they graduate from high school at approximately eighteen. At that time they take the adult title of "Mister."

"Messrs." may not be used to address a father and son. It is correct only in writing to unmarried brothers.

"PERSONAL" AND "PLEASE FORWARD"   Because in writing to someone at his home address you properly assume that no one else will open the letter, it is rude to write "Personal" on it. But if you are writing a social note to a friend's business address, it is entirely correct. "Please Forward" is correct if you know a former address but not the current one.

RETURN ADDRESS   It has always been customary to place a return address in the upper left-hand corner on the face of a business envelope. When it was necessary to use one on a personal letter, it was put on the flap. Whatever the real reason for making this distinction, it did separate the two types of letters in our mail.

Today (in response to requests made by the United States Post Office) it is preferable to put any return address on the face of the envelope. If handwritten, it should be very small. Remember that zip codes are a part of the return address.

UNSEALED LETTERS   Properly, any letter given to a person (other than a commercial messenger) for delivery by hand is unsealed. Customarily, the person who will carry it seals it immediately in the presence of the writer, but this is not obligatory.

Exceptions may be made, of course, should there be a heavy or particularly valuable enclosure that might slip out after the time of writing. In this case, it is polite to explain why the envelope has been sealed.

5

Social notes
and invitations

There are occasions when everything must be just right, and perhaps the happiest of these are engagements, weddings, balls, and parties. In the pages that follow you'll learn the ins and outs of announcements, invitations, acceptances, and regrets for these important and festive social events.

All wedding invitations are worded in the third person, and their answers of acceptance or regret are invariably written by hand in this same form. The words must be placed on specified lines and centered as evenly as possible. Names of hosts belong on the first line, the "request the pleasure of" on the second, the name of the guest on the third, and so on.

Invitations to the largest and most elaborate of weddings consist of an invitation to the church ceremony, a "pew card," and an invitation to the reception. But many variations are possible and perfectly correct, as we shall see.

When a guest is expected to attend the church service only, no invitation to the reception is enclosed.

If the wedding is to be in a very small church or chapel and the reception in a very big house or club, then many will receive invitations to the reception and few to the ceremony.

If it happens that not only the church but also the reception is limited to a small number who are sent handwritten invitations or are given oral invitations, then engraved announcements may be sent in place of invitations to the friends who could not be included, as well as to acquaintances who would have been invited to a larger wedding.

The invitations to a large wedding are sent three weeks beforehand; those to a simpler wedding can be mailed as late as ten days before the wedding day.

CORRECT STYLE OF WEDDING INVITATIONS

Correct invitations to any wedding, whatever its size, are engraved on the first page of a double sheet of heavy paper, ivory or white, either plain or with a raised margin called a plate-mark or panel. The engraving may be in whichever lettering style the bride prefers. The invitation may be about 5½ inches wide by 7⅜ inches deep, or slightly smaller, and it is folded once for insertion into its envelope. Or it may be about 4⅜ by 5¾ inches and go into the envelope without folding.

Two envelopes are used with wedding invitations. The inner envelope has no mucilage on the flap and is addressed to Mr. and Mrs. Brown with neither first name nor address. It is put into an outer "mailing envelope," addressed side toward the flap. This envelope is then addressed by hand.

The names of children under thirteen are written on the inner envelope, "Joan, Robert, and Frederick," and inserted in an envelope addressed to "Miss and the Messrs. Greatlake" or "Miss Joan Greatlake" and below "Robert and Frederick Greatlake."

In all formal correspondence it is incorrect to abbreviate the address. Neither does one use initials for the first name—"Mr. and Mrs. Harold T. James" is correct rather than "Mr. and Mrs. H. T. James." When the middle name is known, that should be written out also: "Mr. and Mrs. Harold Taylor James."

When every member of a family under one roof is included in the invitation, the envelope may be addressed:

Mr. and Mrs. Joseph Truehart and Family

A daughter's name may be written below her parents'—"Miss Helen Truehart," or "The Misses Truehart." Boys over twelve or thirteen, however, are more correctly sent separate invitations.

A girl may properly ask a bride if she may bring her fiancé to the wedding, if it will cause no inconvenience. If the bride has plenty of invitations, she should obtain the man's name and address and send him a separate one. If she has a limited number or cannot get his address, she may write his name below that of his fiancée on the inner envelope and enclose it in an outer envelope addressed to the girl only.

This would also be done if the bride has told some of her friends to "bring an escort."

Although it may seem unnecessary, it is thoughtful to send invitations to members of the bridal party as mementos. These invitations are addressed exactly as they are to the other guests.

There are three excellent reasons for placing a return address on a wedding invitation, and certainly there is no very valid reason for omitting it. First, the Post Office Department requests that all first-class mail carry a return address. Second, it provides the wedding guest with a definite address to which to send a gift. Third, it also provides an address to which the guest may send a reply, especially when no R.S.V.P. is found on the invitation. Very often the only address in evidence is that of the church, or the club or hotel at which the reception is to be held. More information is usually welcome.

FOLDING AND INSERTING

When preparing to send out the invitations, address all the envelopes first. An envelope-sized invitation is inserted in the inner envelope, folded edge down, with the engraved side toward the flap. An invitation designed to fit an envelope half its size will require a second fold, which should be made with the engraving inside. This is then inserted, folded edge down, into the envelope. With the unsealed flap of this filled inner envelope away from you, insert it in the mailing envelope. If the invitation is folded, all insertions (such as the reception card or pew card) are placed inside the second fold with the type facing the flap of the envelope. If the invitation is not folded a second time, the cards are inserted in front of it (nearest you), with the reception card next to the invitation and any smaller cards in front of that.

CORRECT WORDING OF WEDDING INVITATIONS

The wording of the wedding invitation varies as little as the conventions governing its size and mailing. For example, the invitation to the ceremony itself should always request "the honour"—spelled with a "u"—of your "presence" and never the "pleasure" of your "company." It is the invitation to the reception that requests the pleasure of your company. But it is perfectly proper for communicants of the Roman Catholic Church who so wish to use a form in which the phrase "at the marriage of" is replaced by "at the Marriage in Christ of"; and where appropriate there is added beneath the name of the bridegroom the lines "and your participation in the offering of the Nuptial Mass."

In the examples of correct wording, spacing, and styles of engraving that will be given, it is important to note the omission of punctuation, except after abbreviations and initials, and when phrases requiring separation by punctuation occur in the same line.

The wording of an invitation to a house wedding gives a house address in place of the name of a church, and R.S.V.P. is added at the bottom left corner of the invitation. (R.s.v.p. is equally correct form.)

Here is an example of correct wording, spacing, and style for a wedding invitation.

Mr. and Mrs. Charles Robert Oldname

request the honour of your presence

at the marriage of their daughter

Pauline Marie

to

Mr. John Frederick Hamilton

Saturday, the twenty-ninth of April

at four o'clock

Church of the Heavenly Rest

New York

Occasionally, when every guest is invited to both ceremony and reception, the invitation to the reception or to the breakfast is included in the invitation to the ceremony.

Mrs. Alexander Oldname

requests the honour of your presence

at the marriage of her daughter

Barbara

to

Mr. James Town, junior

Tuesday, the twenty-first of October

at three o'clock

Church of the Resurrection

Ridgemont, New York

and afterwards at the reception

Bright Meadows

R.s.v.p.

When the bride's own father is not living and she has a stepparent, or her mother has divorced and remarried, the invitations are worded:

Mr. and Mrs. John Huntington Smith
request the honour of your presence
at the marriage of her daughter
Mary Alice Towne
etc.

If the bride's mother is giving the wedding alone:

Mrs. Bertram Jones
requests the honour of your presence
at the marriage of her daughter
Helen Jeffrey Jones
etc.

Invitations are issued by the parents of the bride even when the wedding takes place at a house other than their own. The names of the parents at the head of the invitation means that *they* are giving the wedding but not in their own house.

Mr. and Mrs. Richard Littlehouse

request the honour of your presence

at the marriage of their daughter

Eleanor

to

Doctor Frederic Robinson

Saturday, the fifth of November

at four o'clock

at the residence of Mr. and Mrs. James Sterlington

Tuxedo Park, New York

R.s.v.p.

When the bride's parents are divorced, the wedding invitations are issued in the name of the parent who pays for and acts as host at the reception. In the event that relations are so friendly that they share the expenses and act as co-hosts, both names should appear.

Mr. and Mrs. Henry Smith
(or Mrs. Jones Doe, if she has not remarried)
and
Mr. and Mrs. Robert Doe
(or Mr. Robert Doe)
request the honour of your presence
at the marriage of
Mary Doe
to
William Hughes, etc.

The bride's mother's name, whether she has remarried or not, appears first. If neither parent is remarried the wording would be:

Mrs. Jones Doe
and
Mr. Robert Doe
request the honour of your presence
at the marriage of their daughter
Mary
etc.

It is important to remember that good taste ordinarily does not permit "Miss" as a title before the bride's name, but the case that follows is an exception. If the bride has no relatives and the wedding is given by friends, the wording is:

Mr. and Mrs. John Neighbor
request the honour of your presence
at the marriage of
Miss Elizabeth Orphan
to
Mr. John Henry Bridegroom
etc.

Invitations to the marriage of a young widow or divorcée are sent in the name of her parents exactly as were the invitations for her first wedding, except that her name, instead of being simply "Priscilla," is now written "Priscilla Banks Loring," thus:

Doctor and Mrs. Maynard Banks
request the honour of your presence
at the marriage of their daughter
Priscilla Banks Loring
to
etc.

A more mature woman, or one whose parents are dead, may send out her own invitations:

The honour of your presence
is requested
at the marriage of
Mrs. John Kerr Simons
to
etc.

The same woman would drop the "John" and use "Mrs. Kerr Simons" if she were a divorcée.

The fact that the groom has been divorced does not change the invitation to, or announcement of, his new bride's marriage.

On the wedding invitations, the name of a bridegroom in the armed forces whose rank is below Lt. Commander in the navy or Captain in the army is given this way:

John Strong
2nd Lieutenant, United States Army

or

Robert Todd
Ensign, United States Navy

The title of higher ranking officers precedes their name, and the service may or may not be included on the line below.

Colonel John Spring
United States Air Force

The name of a noncommissioned or an enlisted man in the armed forces is engraved "John Strong," and "Signal Corps, U.S.N.R.," or "Coast Artillery, U.S.A.," or whatever his particular designation is, in smaller type directly beneath the name on the wedding invitations. Or if the bride chooses to include "Private First Class, U.S.A.," or "Apprentice Seaman, U.S.N.R.," she may do so.

The name of the bride who is in the armed forces is engraved:

marriage of their daughter
Alice Mary
Lieutenant, Women's Army Corps

When the bride's father is in the armed forces and absent on duty, his name appears as follows:

Major (overseas) and Mrs. John Jones
request the honour of your presence, etc.

An officer in the reserves does not use his title unless he is on active duty.

High-ranking regular officers continue to use their titles and include their service on the line below with "retired" following the service.

General George Harmon
United States Army, retired

When the young bride comes as a stranger from abroad, or from a distant city, without her family, the bridegroom's family may give the wedding and send the invitations in their name. This is another of the rare cases where the title "Miss" is used.

Mr. and Mrs. John Henry Pater
request the honour of your presence
at the marriage of
Miss Marie Mersailles
to
their son
John Henry Pater, Junior
etc.

The bride's own family may later send announcements, but it should not send invitations.

The most flattering wedding invitation possible is a note personally written by the bride. Even though she is sending engraved invitations to most of the guests, she may, as a special gesture of affection, send a few handwritten ones to those she cares most about. Such a note should be brief, sincere, and personal.

Dear Aunt Jane,
Dick and I are to be married at Christ Church at noon on Thursday the tenth. We hope you and Uncle Dick will come to the church and afterward to the reception at the home of our friend, Mrs. Tilden, at Two South Beach Street.
With much love from us both,

Affectionately,
Helen

This type of note is also written when the wedding is to be very small, or when it is held on short notice. In these circumstances, telephone invitations are also perfectly correct.

It happens on occasion that the date of the wedding must be changed after the invitations have already been engraved. To order a new set of invitations would involve an enormous and unnecessary expense. Instead, the bride may enclose a small printed card saying, "The date of the wedding has been changed from . . . to . . ." or, if the number of guests is small, she may write the same information by hand on a small card.

When a wedding must be postponed indefinitely after the invitations have been mailed, it is necessary to send the news out as fast as possible. If it is possible to have cards printed in time, that is the best solution. If not, the bride and members of her family and bridal party who can help must send out handwritten notes at once. The wording, depending on the cause, would be:

Owing to the sudden death of
Mrs. Henry Miller
The marriage of her daughter
Sarah
to
Mr. Robert Sage
has been postponed

WORDING OF INVITATIONS TO THE RECEPTION

The correct form for the invitation to a wedding reception depends upon the combined plans for wedding and reception. That is, the invitation sent to guests who are also invited to the church differs from that used when the ceremony is very small and invitations are sent out only for the reception.

The invitation to the breakfast or reception following the church ceremony is usually engraved on a card to match the paper and engraving of the church invitation. The most commonly used form is this:

Reception

immediately following the ceremony

Essex County Country Club

West Orange

The favour of a reply is requested
Llewellyn Park, West Orange

INVITATION TO THE RECEPTION ONLY

When the ceremony is small and a big reception follows, the invitations to the ceremony are given orally, and general invitations to the reception sent out for a later hour. The size and style of these invitations are exactly the same as those to the wedding itself. The wording follows this form:

> Mr. and Mrs. John Huntington Smith
> request the pleasure of your company
> at the wedding reception
> of their daughter
> Millicent Jane
> and
> Mr. Sidney Strothers
> Tuesday, the first of November
> at half after twelve o'clock
> 55 Clark Lane
> Hillsdale

R.s.v.p.

A RECEPTION FOLLOWING A HOUSE WEDDING

When the reception follows a house wedding, it is not necessary to send any sort of separate invitation as it is assumed that those attending the wedding will stay on.

ENCLOSURES

To the family and those intimate friends who are to be seated in specially designated pews, a card (approximately two by three inches) may be enclosed, with "Pew No." engraved and the number filled in by hand. The style matches that of the invitation.

The more usual and less expensive custom is for the mother of the bride and the mother of the bridegroom each to write on her personal visiting card the number of the pew that each member of the family and each intimate friend is to occupy.

Pew No. 7

Mrs. John Huntington Smith

600 East Fifty-Seventh Street

WRITE BETTER, SPEAK BETTER

If the bride and groom want their friends to know what their address is to be, an At Home card is included with the invitation. These cards have traditionally followed a form similar to this:

At home

after the fifteenth of November

3842 Olympia Drive

Houston, Texas

Wedding announcements

When the number of guests who can be accommodated at the marriage service or the reception is limited, announcements are sent to those friends of both families who would otherwise have been invited to be present. They require no gift or acknowledgment except what your own

Mr. and Mrs. John Fairplay

have the honour of

announcing the marriage of their daughter

Madeleine Anne

to

Mr. George Followes Highseas

Ensign United States Navy

Tuesday, the twenty-seventh of March

One thousand nine hundred and sixty-five

Washington, D. C.

interest and impulse suggest. Announcements are never sent to anyone who has been invited to the wedding or the reception.

CORRECT STYLE AND WORDING

The form of the wedding announcement resembles the form of the wedding invitation in almost everything except wording. The note paper, the styles of engraving, the two envelopes, the manner of addressing the envelopes are all the same.

The standard wording is shown at the left.

"AT HOME" NOTICES

When announcements are sent, the At Home notice may be engraved in the lower left-hand corner.

After the first of December
25 Elm Street, Greattown

Or cards in the same form as those used with wedding invitations may be enclosed.

Mr. and Mrs. John Newlywed
will be at home
after November twelfth
25 Elm Street
Greattown

Other formal invitations

Formal invitations are engraved or printed on white cards—either plain or plate-marked like those for wedding receptions—or written by hand on personal notepaper. The size of the card of invitation depends upon personal preference. The most graceful proportion is three units in height to four in width or four high by three wide.

The lettering is a matter of personal choice, but the plainer the design the safer. Punctuation is used only when words requiring separation occur on the same line, and in certain abbreviations, such as R.S.V.P. The time should never be given as "nine-thirty" but as "half past nine o'clock" or, the more conservative form, "half after nine o'clock."

If the dance or dinner or other entertainment is to be given at one address and the hostess lives at another, both addresses are always given.

The replies are addressed to the person, or persons, from whom the

AN INVITATION TO A PRIVATE DANCE

Mr. and Mrs. Harold Gilding

request the pleasure of

Miss Sally Waring's

company at a small dance

Monday, the first of January

at ten o'clock

400 Lake Shore Drive

R.s.v.p.

AN INVITATION TO PRESENT THE DEBUTANTE AT AN ASSEMBLY

The Committee of the Westchester Cotillion

invites

Mr. and Mrs. David S. Williams

to present

Miss Penelope Williams

at the Cotillion

on Friday, the ninth of September

at ten o'clock

Shenorock Shore Club

Rye, New York

60

invitation comes. The full first name, rather than initials, is used, and the name of the state is also written out in full. A return address should appear on the back flap of the envelope.

BALLS AND DANCES

The forms most commonly used for private dances and debutante assemblies are shown on the opposite page.

Even when a private dance is given for a debutante daughter, her name need not appear. The invited guest's name is written in, as shown in the sample. The expression "small dance" is often used for a private function regardless of its actual size.

INVITATIONS TO RECEPTIONS AND TEAS

Invitations to receptions and teas differ from invitations to balls in that the cards on which they are engraved are usually somewhat smaller. The time is limited to a definite period indicated by a beginning and a terminating hour. Also, except for very unusual occasions, a man's name does not appear. If the tea is given for a debutante, her name is put under that of her mother, and sometimes under that of her sister or the bride of her brother.

When a reception is held in honor of someone, "In honor of Mr. and Mrs. Robert Fuller, Jr." may be written by hand at the top of the invitation. This is true whether the rest of the invitation is fully engraved or is a fill-in "card of general invitation" (see page 62).

An invitation to a tea dance:

> *Mrs. Grantham Jones*
> *Miss Muriel Jones*
> *at Home*
> *on Tuesday, the third of December*
> *from four until seven o'clock*
> *The Hilton Hotel*
> *3751 Wildwood Boulevard*   *Dancing*

Or to a tea for a debutante:

> *Mrs. James Town*
> *Mrs. James Town, Junior*
> *Miss Pauline Town*
> *will be at home*
> *Tuesday, the eighth of December*
> *from five until seven o'clock*
> *850 Fifth Avenue*

For an evening reception:

To meet the Honorable George Stevens
Mr. and Mrs. James Town
at Home
Tuesday, the eighth of December
from nine until eleven o'clock

THE CARD OF GENERAL INVITATION

Invitations to important entertainments are nearly always specially engraved so that nothing is written except the name of the person invited. But the hostess who entertains frequently will find a card that is partially engraved with spaces left to be filled in by hand very helpful. These cards may serve for dinner, luncheon, dance, or any other occasion. Cards of general invitation like the one shown below do not need to be specially ordered but can be purchased from an engraver or stationer. Hence they also save the user the expense of having the full form engraved.

Mr. and Mrs. Harold Foster Stevens

request the pleasure of

company at

on

at   o'clock

Two Knob Hill

INVITATION BY MORE THAN ONE HOSTESS

There is no rule about the order in which the names of two or more hostesses should appear, but the one at whose house the party will be is usually placed first. Or if one is a great deal older, her name may head the list. The invitation should make very clear where the event is to take place and where the acceptances and regrets are to be sent. For example, if the luncheon is to be at Mrs. White's house, the correct form would be this:

Mrs. Walter David White
Mrs. Henry Edward Black
Mrs. Theodore Jamison Gray
request the pleasure of your company
at luncheon
Tuesday, the tenth of November
at half after one o'clock
123 Sutton Place

R.s.v.p.
Mrs. Walter David White

If, on the other hand, the luncheon is to be at a club or hotel, the invitation must clearly show where acceptances and regrets should be sent. The form is this:

Mrs. Walter David White
Mrs. Henry Edward Black
Mrs. Theodore Jamison Gray
request the pleasure of your company
at luncheon
Tuesday, the tenth of November
at half after one o'clock
Hotel Carter

R.s.v.p.
Mrs. Walter David White
123 Sutton Place

HANDWRITTEN INVITATIONS

When the formal invitation to dinner or luncheon is handwritten instead of engraved, plain white or cream notepaper or paper stamped with house address or personal monogram is used. The wording and spacing must follow the engraved models exactly. The invitation may not be typewritten. The illustration on the following page shows the correct form for a written invitation to a dinner party.

If the letterhead does not contain your address, it is important to write this below the hour. It is never proper to include a telephone number on a formal invitation.

Mr. and Mrs. John Kindhost
request the pleasure of
Mr. and Mrs. Robert Geldings Jr's
company at dinner
on Tuesday, the sixth of December
at eight o'clock

A WRITTEN INVITATION TO A DINNER PARTY

Informal invitations

Except for invitations sent to out-of-town guests or those for formal occasions, the invitation by note is seldom used today. Informal invitations may be extended over the telephone, in person, or on commercially designed invitations. Be sure you are perfectly clear about the date and hour and leave your guests in no doubt about what kind of party you are giving.

If you feel that a handwritten invitation is needed, you have a choice of several possibilities. However, as is true with more formal invitations, the informal one should not be typewritten.

VISITING-CARD INVITATIONS

For an informal dance, a tea to meet a guest, or bridge, a lady may use her ordinary visiting card. Because the Post Office will not accept very small envelopes, a practical size should be ordered for visiting cards or other small-size cards. They should be written, if possible, in black ink. Examples are shown on the next page.

INFORMALS

Informals (small folding cards engraved with your name) may also be used for invitations. The invitation is written as shown at right.

On informal invitations it is correct to put "regrets only" instead of R.S.V.P. if you prefer.

64

To meet
Miss Millicent Gordon

Mrs. John Kindhart

Tues. Jan. 7
Dancing at 9 o'clock

1350 Madison Avenue

Wed. Jan. 8
Bridge at 2 o'clock

Mrs. John Kindhart

R.s.v.p.   **1350 Madison Avenue**

TWO EXAMPLES OF VISITING-CARD INVITATIONS

Cocktail Buffet

Mr. and Mrs. Allen Burns

Sunday, June 9th
6:30 o'clock
10 Haverstraw Rd.

AN INVITATION WRITTEN ON AN INFORMAL

HANDWRITTEN NOTES AND ANSWERS

Informal invitations are written in the second person and follow a fairly definite formula.

January 2

Dear Mrs. Steele,
  Will you and Mr. Steele have dinner with us on Thursday, the seventh of January, at eight o'clock?
  Hoping so much to see you then, I am

Very sincerely,
Caroline Robinson Town

Dear Phyllis,
  Will you and John lunch with us this coming Saturday, at one o'clock?
  Looking forward to seeing you.

Affectionately,
Caroline

Here is an example of a handwritten note of acceptance:

January 5

Dear Mrs. Town,
  We would be delighted to have dinner with you on Thursday the seventh at eight o'clock.
  Thank you for thinking of us,

Sincerely yours,
Leah Steele

And here is an example of one declining an invitation:

Dear Caroline,
  We are so sorry that we cannot accept your kind invitation for Saturday because of another engagement.
  Thank you for thinking of us, and I hope to see you soon.

Sincerely,
Phyllis

RECALLING INVITATIONS

If invitations have to be recalled because of illness or for some other reason, the following forms are correct. They are always printed instead of engraved—there being no time for engraving. In an emergency the message may be handwritten or given by telephone.

Owing to the sudden illness of their daughter
Mr. and Mrs. John Huntington Smith
are obliged to recall their invitations
for Tuesday, the tenth of June

When an engagement is broken after the wedding invitations have been issued:

Mr. and Mrs. Benjamin Nottingham
announce that the marriage of their daughter
Mary Katharine
to
Mr. Jerrold Atherton
will not take place

Acceptances and regrets

The form of acceptance or regret depends upon the form of the invitation received, for the degree of formality or informality must be the same. On the telephone, of course, this presents no problems, but for the handwritten answer there are definite formulas. Once learned, the formal reply is easiest to write, because no changes or embellishments are necessary other than in the names and the dates.

THE FORMAL ACCEPTANCE OR REGRET

Whether the invitation is to a dance, a dinner, or whatever, the answer is identical, with the exception of the pertinent word—that is, the following form may be used with the substitution of "a dance," etc., for "dinner."

Mr. and Mrs. Donald Lovejoy
accept with pleasure
the kind invitation of
Mr. and Mrs. William Jones Johnson, Jr.
for dinner
on Monday, the tenth of December
at eight o'clock

Also used but not quite so formal is this form:

Mr. and Mrs. Donald Lovejoy
accept with pleasure
Mr. and Mrs. Johnson's
kind invitation for dinner
on Monday, the tenth of December
at eight o'clock

Note that in the first form the full name, including "Jr." when appropriate, must be used, whereas in the second, "Mr. and Mrs. Johnson's" is sufficient.

THE FORMULAS FOR REGRET:

*Mr. and Mrs. Timothy Kerry
regret that they are unable to accept
the kind invitation of
Mr. and Mrs. Harvey Brent Smith
for Monday, the tenth of December*

*Mr. Sidney Hartford
regrets that he is unable to accept
Mr. and Mrs. Worldly's
kind invitation for dinner
on Monday, the tenth of December*

If the names of two or more hostesses appear on an invitation, the envelope is addressed to the one at whose house the party is to take place; or if it is to be at a club or hotel, to the name and address indicated below the R.S.V.P. (Without such indication, you must address it to all of them at the hotel or club.)

When you write your answer, repeat the same order of names that appeared on the invitation.

*Mrs. Donald Lovejoy
accepts with pleasure
the kind invitation of
Mrs. White and
Mrs. Black and
Mrs. Grey
for Tuesday, the tenth of November
at half after one o'clock*

REPLY TO A WEDDING INVITATION

An invitation to the church only requires no answer whatever (except when the wedding is so small that the invitation is a personally written note). The answer to an invitation to the reception or breakfast is written on the front of a folded sheet of full-size letter paper or on fold-over notepaper; and although written by hand, the words must be spaced as though they were engraved.

ACCEPTANCE:

*Mr. and Mrs. Robert Gilding, Jr.
accept with pleasure
Mr. and Mrs. Smith's
kind invitation for
Tuesday, the first of June*

REGRET:

*Mr. and Mrs. Richard Brown
regret that they are unable to accept
Mr. and Mrs. Smith's
kind invitation for
Tuesday, the first of June*

COMBINATION ACCEPTANCE AND REGRET:

Mrs. John Brown
accepts with pleasure
Mr. and Mrs. Smith's
kind invitation for
Saturday, the tenth of June
but regrets that
Mr. Brown
will be absent at that time
(or
"will be unable to attend")

REPLIES TO INFORMAL INVITATIONS

When an invitation is sent on a visiting card or an informal, the reply may be telephoned or written briefly on your own card.

VISITING-CARD REPLIES:

Accepts with pleasure!
Wednesday at 4

Mrs. Robert Gilding, junior

14 Water Street

Sincere regrets
Wed. Jan. 8

Mr. and Mrs. Henry Osborn

INFORMALS In replying on an informal, you use the same degree of formality as was used in the invitation.

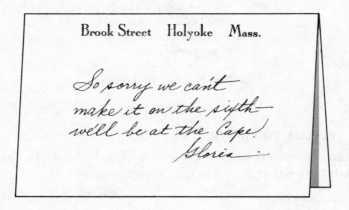

If your informal is engraved as a visiting card, you may write:

WHEN IT IS NECESSARY TO CHANGE YOUR ANSWER

If for any reason you find you cannot attend a function which you have already accepted, let the hostess know immediately. In most cases a telephone call is best, as it is quick and gives you a chance to explain your problem and express your regrets. If you prefer, however, and there is ample time, you may write a short note, giving the reason and your apologies.

Sometimes you may refuse an invitation for perfectly legitimate reasons and then find that circumstances have changed and you can attend after all. If the affair is a party involving a limited number, such as for bridge, a theater party, or a seated dinner, it is best not to say anything. The hostess will surely have filled your place, and it would only embarrass her if you asked to be "reinstated." However, if the party is a large reception, a cocktail buffet, a picnic, or any affair at which another guest or two would not cause any complications, call the hostess, explain the situation, and ask if you might change your regret to an acceptance.

Birth announcements

The first announcement of the birth of a baby is usually made to the nearest and dearest friends and relatives as soon as the proud father or delighted grandparents can get to the telephone. Announcement cards are sent to their own friends and those of the grandparents who are close to the family.

One of the nicest types of birth announcement consists simply of a very small card with the baby's name and birth date on it, tied with a white or pastel ribbon to the upper margin of the "Mr. and Mrs." card of the parents.

A large variety of commercially designed announcement cards with space for the baby's name, date of birth, and parents' names to be writ-

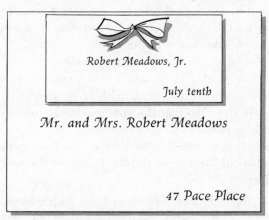

Robert Meadows, Jr.

July tenth

Mr. and Mrs. Robert Meadows

47 Pace Place

71

ten in by hand are also available. Those which include such data as the baby's weight and length and foolish phrasing or coy designs are better left on the rack. The simplest card is the best.

In the week following the birth, the father may send a release to the local newspapers announcing the event: "Mr. and Mrs. Robert Meadows of 202 Park Avenue, New York City, announce the birth of a son, Robert, Jr. on July 10, 1984, at Doctors' Hospital. They have one daughter, Jane, 4. Mrs. Meadows is the former Miss Mary Gilding." Or "A daughter, Mary Jane, was born to Mr. and Mrs. John Phillips of 19 Maple Avenue, Hillsdale, on February 9 at St. Joseph's Hospital. Mrs. Phillips is the former Miss Mary Star of New Haven, Connecticut." The same announcement may be sent to the editor of the church newsletter or bulletin.

Engagement announcements

Usually a few days—perhaps a week—before the formal announcement the engaged couple notify close relatives and friends of their engagement, usually by phone or letter.

The formal or public announcement is made by the parents of the bride-to-be. This is done either by notes or at the engagement party, and then publicly through the newspapers. Engraved announcements are never used.

The newspaper announcement of the engagement with all the pertinent information is sent by the bride's parents to the society editor of all the papers in which it is to be printed. You may include a picture if you wish. If you live in the suburbs of a large city or in a small town, a copy should be sent to the local paper (which may be a weekly). Others go to the paper of your choice in the nearby city and to the paper suggested by the bridegroom's family in their locality.

The announcement should be sent to the papers a week or more in advance of the date on which you wish it to appear, and that date should be clearly stated so that the announcement comes out simultaneously in all the papers. If the couple wish to keep their engagement a surprise until it is announced at an engagement party, the newspaper announcement should appear on the day following the party.

The usual form is as follows:

Mr. and Mrs. Herbert Coles Johnson of Lake Forest, Illinois, announce the engagement of their daughter, Miss Susan Bailey Johnson, to Dr.

William Arthur Currier, son of Mr. and Mrs. Arthur Jamison Currier of Atlanta, Georgia. A June wedding is planned.

Miss Johnson was graduated from Bentley Junior College. She made her debut in 1980 at the Mistletoe Ball in Chicago, and in May will complete her nurse's training at Atlanta General Hospital. Dr. Currier was graduated from the Hill School, Yale University, and the Yale Medical School. He completed his residency at the Atlanta General Hospital and is now in practice in that city.

In unusual situations, the information as to schools and employment remains the same although the identification of the bride and bridegroom and their parents may vary.

When one parent is deceased: The announcement is worded the same whether made by the mother or father of the bride.

Mrs. Herbert Coles Johnson announces the engagement of her daughter, Miss Susan Bailey Johnson, to Dr. William Arthur Currier . . . etc. Miss Johnson is also the daughter of the late Herbert Coles Johnson. . . .

If the parents are divorced: The mother of the bride usually makes the announcement, but the name of the other parent should be included.

Mrs. Jones Farnham announces the engagement of her daughter, Miss Cynthia Farnham. . . . Miss Farnham is also the daughter of Mr. Henry Farnham of Worcester, Mass. . . .

If the parent with whom the bride lives is remarried:

Mr. and Mrs. Samuel Harvey announce the engagement of Mrs. (or Mr.) Harvey's daughter, Miss Jane Barber Cutler (Harvey) to. . . . Miss Cutler (Harvey) is also the daughter of Mr. David Soames Cutler (or Mrs. James Little) of Menlo Park, Calif.

If divorced parents are friendly: On occasion, divorced parents may remain good friends, and their daughter's time may be divided equally between them. If this is true, they may both wish to announce the engagement.

Mr. Gordon Smythe of Philadelphia and Mrs. Howard Zabriskie of 12 East 72nd Street, New York City, announce the engagement of their daughter, Miss Carla Farr Smythe. . . .

If the bride is adopted: If the bride has been brought up since babyhood by her foster parents and uses their last name, there is no reason to mention the fact that she is adopted. If she joined the family later in life, however, and has retained her own name, it is proper to say:

Mr. and Mrs. Warren La Tour announce the engagement of their adopted daughter, Miss Claudia Romney, daughter of the late Mr. and Mrs. Carlton Romney. . . .

Older women, widows, and divorcées: A woman of forty or more, even though her parents are living, generally does not announce her engagement in the newspaper, but instead calls or writes her relatives and friends shortly before the wedding. A widow or divorcée announces her second engagement in the same way.

Death notices

Notices of death should go to morning and evening papers in a large city, and to the local paper (daily or weekly) in towns or suburbs. They usually contain the date of death, names of immediate family, place and time of funeral, and, frequently, a request that a contribution be given to a charity instead of flowers sent to the deceased. When this is done, the sum is sent to the charity with a note saying, "This donation is sent in loving memory of Mrs. Roy Haskell, of 10 Park Place, Mount Vernon." The address of the sender should appear on the note. The charity sends a notice of the contribution to the family of the deceased, and an acknowledgment to the donor. The latter in no way takes the place of a thank-you note from the bereaved family—one of whom must write in person to express their appreciation. The notice may be telephoned to the paper by the person making the funeral arrangements, but often the funeral director handles it as part of his services.

CONSTANTINE—Mary Phillips, on March 19, 1982. Beloved wife of Henry S. Constantine, devoted mother of Henry S. Constantine, Jr. and Barbara Constantine Franklin, sister of Dorothy P. Hill. Reposing at the Frederick Carter Funeral Home, Farmingdale, Mass., Monday and Tuesday, 2:00 P.M.–9:00 P.M. Funeral Wednesday, 11:00 A.M., at Christ Church, Farmingdale. In lieu of flowers, please send donations to the New York Cancer Fund.

Occasionally the notice reads "Funeral private" and neither time nor place is given. Very intimate friends are given this information, either by telephone or on the personal card of the relative or friend in charge: "Mr. Brown's funeral will be at Christ Church, Monday at eleven o'clock." Others are not expected to attend.

When the notice reads "Please omit flowers," this wish should be strictly followed.

test your skills

SOCIAL NOTES AND INVITATIONS

1. *Write a negative and an affirmative reply to the invitation below:*

Mr. and Mrs. Arthur Grave

request the honor of your presence

at the marriage of their daughter

Gillian Lucy Grave

to

Mr. Ian Courtney Vault

on Saturday, the twelfth of September

at four o'clock

Church of the Atonement

and afterward at the reception

Broken Arrow Country Club

2. *True or false:*

a. You may telephone an invitation to a christening.

b. It is acceptable to type your answer to a formal dinner invitation.

c. Relatives and close friends should be notified prior to the announcement of an engagement in a newspaper.

d. Wedding announcements should not be sent to those who have attended the wedding.

e. You should write an acceptance note for a wedding invitation even though not invited to the reception.

3. What is an At Home card and how is it used in a wedding invitation?

Answers to this quiz appear on page 700.

HOW TO ADDRESS IMPORTANT PEOPLE

The correct form of envelope address for business and social correspondence, the proper formal salutation and close, and the title by which the dignitary is introduced are given in this table.

TITLE	ENVELOPE ADDRESS	SOCIAL CORRESPONDENCE
The President	The President The White House Washington, D.C.	The President and Mrs. Washington The White House Washington, D.C.
The Vice President	The Vice President United States Senate Washington, D.C.	The Vice President and Mrs. Hope Home Address
Chief Justice, Supreme Court	The Chief Justice The Supreme Court Washington, D.C.	The Chief Justice and Mrs. Page Home Address
Associate Justice, Supreme Court	Mr. Justice Katsaros The Supreme Court Washington, D.C.	Mr. Justice Katsaros and Mrs. Katsaros Home Address

Cabinet Member	The Honorable
	  Gary George Gussin
	The Secretary of the Treasury
	Office Address
		The Honorable
		  The Secretary of the Treasury
		  and Mrs. Gussin
		Home Address

Former President	The Honorable
	  Alfred Edward Work
	Office Address
		The Honorable
		  Alfred Edward Work
		  and Mrs. Work
		Home Address

United States
Senator
	The Honorable
	  John Wandzilak
	United States Senate
	Washington, D.C.
		The Honorable
		  John Wandzilak
		  and Mrs. Wandzilak
		or (for a woman senator)
		Mr. and Mrs. John Row Doe
		Home Address

Member of the
United States House
of Representatives
	The Honorable
	  Henry Cobb Wellcome
	United States House of
	  Representatives
	Washington, D.C.
		The Honorable
		  Henry Cobb Wellcome
		  and Mrs. Wellcome
		or (for a woman member)
		Mr. and Mrs. John Knox Jones
		Home address

FORMAL OPENING OF LETTERS	FORMAL CLOSE OF LETTERS	TITLE OF INTRODUCTION
Sir:	I have the honor to remain, Most respectfully yours,	*Only the name of the person being introduced is spoken.*
Sir:	Very truly yours,	The Vice President
Sir:	Very truly yours,	The Chief Justice
Sir:	Very truly yours,	Mr. Justice Katsaros
Sir: *or* Dear Sir: *or* Madam:	Very truly yours,	The Secretary of the Treasury *or* The Attorney General *or* The Postmaster General
Sir:	Very truly yours,	The Honorable Alfred Edward Work
Sir: *or* Dear Sir: *or* My dear Mr. Wandzilak: *or* Madam:	Very truly yours,	Senator Wandzilak of Alaska
Sir: *or* Dear Sir: *or* My dear Mr. Wellcome: *or* Madam:	Very truly yours,	Representative Wellcome of Nebraska

(*continued*)

HOW TO ADDRESS IMPORTANT PEOPLE (*continued*)

TITLE	ENVELOPE ADDRESS	SOCIAL CORRESPONDENCE

Ambassador of The United States	The Honorable
	   John Wilson Smith
	The Ambassador of the
	   United States
	American Embassy
	London, England
		The Honorable
		   John Wilson Smith and Mrs.
		   Smith
		*or (for a woman
		   ambassador*)
		Mr. and Mrs. Leeds Walker
		Home Address

Consul of The United States	Mr. John Smith American Consul Rue de Quelque Chose Paris, France	Mr. and Mrs. John Smith Home Address

Ambassador of a Foreign Country	His Excellency
	   Juan Luis Ortega
	The Ambassador of Mexico
	Washington, D.C.
		His Excellency
		   The Ambassador of Mexico
		   and Señora Ortega
		Home Address

Minister of a Foreign Country	The Honorable
	   Carluh Matti
	The Minister of Kezeah
	Washington, D.C.
		The Honorable
		   Carluh Matti and Mrs. Matti
		Home Address

Governor of a State	The Honorable
	   Joseph L. Marvin
	Governor of Idaho
	Boise, Idaho
		The Honorable
		   Joseph L. Marvin
		   and Mrs. Marvin
		Home Address

State senators and representatives are addressed like United States senators and representatives.		
Mayor	His (*or* Her) Honor the Mayor City Hall Easton, Maryland	His Honor the Mayor and Mrs. Lake *or (for a woman mayor)* Mr. and Mrs. L. T. Wayne Home Address

Judge	The Honorable Carson Little
	Justice, Appellate Division
	Supreme Court of the State of
	   New York
	Albany, New York
		The Honorable Carson Little
		   and Mrs. Little
		Home Address

Bishop, Protestant	The Right Reverend John S.
	   Bowman
	Bishop of Rhode Island
	Providence, Rhode Island
		The Right Reverend John S.
		   Bowman and Mrs. Bowman
		Home Address

FORMAL OPENING OF LETTERS	FORMAL CLOSE OF LETTERS	TITLE OF INTRODUCTION
Sir: *or* Madam:	Very truly yours,	The American Ambassador *or (if necessary)* Our Ambassador to England
Sir: *or* My dear Sir:	Sincerely yours,	Mr. Smith
Excellency:	Very truly yours,	The Ambassador of Mexico
Sir:	Very truly yours,	The Minister of Kezeah
Sir:	Very truly yours,	The Governor *or (if necessary)* The Governor of Idaho
Sir: *or* Madam:	Very truly yours,	Mayor Lake
Sir:	Very truly yours,	The Honorable Carson Little, Judge of the Appellate Division of the Supreme Court
Right Reverend Sir:	Respectfully yours,	Bishop Bowman

(*continued*)

HOW TO ADDRESS IMPORTANT PEOPLE (*continued*)

TITLE	ENVELOPE ADDRESS	SOCIAL CORRESPONDENCE
Clergyman, Protestant	The Reverend David Dekker *or* (*if he holds the degree*) The Reverend David Dekker, D.D. Address of his church	The Reverend David Dekker and Mrs. Dekker Home Address
Rabbi	Rabbi Paul Aaron Fine *or* (*if he holds the degree*) Paul Aaron Fine, D.D. Address of his synagogue	Rabbi (*or* Dr.) and Mrs. Paul Aaron Fine Home Address
The Pope	His Holiness Pope Paul VI *or* His Holiness the Pope Vatican City	
Cardinal	His Eminence Alberto Cardinal Vezzetti Archbishop of Baltimore Baltimore, Maryland	
Archbishop, Roman Catholic	The Most Reverend Leo Lowen Archbishop of San Francisco San Francisco, California	
Bishop, Roman Catholic	The Most Reverend Matthew S. Borden Address of his church	
Monsignor	The Right Reverend Monsignor Ryan Address of his church	
Priest	The Reverend John Matthews (*and initials of his order*) Address of his church	
Member of Religious Order	Sister Angelica (*and initials of order*) *or* Brother James (*and initials*) Address	
University Professor	Professor Robert Knowles *or* (*if he holds the degree*) Dr. Robert Knowles *or* Mr. Robert Knowles Office Address	Professor (*or* Dr. *or* Mr.) and Mrs. Robert Knowles Home Address
Physician	William L. Barnes, M.D. Office Address	Dr. and Mrs. William L. Barnes Home Address

FORMAL OPENING OF LETTERS	FORMAL CLOSE OF LETTERS	TITLE OF INTRODUCTION
Sir: *or* My dear Sir:	Sincerely yours, *or* Faithfully yours,	Mr. (*or* Dr.) Dekker
Dear Sir:	Sincerely yours,	Rabbi (*or* Dr.) Fine
Your Holiness:	Your Holiness' most humble servant,	(*By audience only*)
Your Eminence:	I have the honor to remain, Your Eminence's humble servant,	*One is presented to* His Eminence, Cardinal Vezzetti
Your Excellency: *or* Most Reverend Sir:	I have the honor to remain, Your Excellency's humble servant,	*One is presented to* The Most Reverend, The Archbishop of San Francisco
Most Reverend Sir:	I have the honor to remain, Your obedient servant,	Bishop Borden
Right Reverend and dear Monsignor Ryan:	Respectfully yours,	Monsignor Ryan
Reverend Father:	I remain, Reverend Father, Yours faithfully,	The Reverend Father Matthews
My dear Sister: *or* My dear Brother:	Respectfully yours,	Sister Angelica *or* Brother James
Dear Sir:	Very truly yours,	Professor (*or* Dr.) Knowles
Dear Sir:	Very truly yours,	Dr. Barnes

6

How to write for information

Here are the simple, basic rules for writing letters of inquiry that won't waste your time or the recipient's. Learn how— and how not—to keep these letters short, clear, and direct, and how to be sure you get an answer. And learn to answer inquiries fully and efficiently.

There isn't much of a trick to writing a letter of inquiry. You simply decide what you want to know and write it down as concisely and clearly as possible. Sounds simple, doesn't it? Yet every business-man, public official, or frustrated customer can testify to the amount of confusion and wasted time and money that results from poorly written letters of inquiry. What can go wrong?

Unless you get straight to the point—don't be vague, please—several things could happen:

1. Your letter won't be read.

2. The reader might have to write back and ask you what you meant; this is sometimes embarrassing, sometimes insulting.

3. The answer might give far more detail than you wanted, because the respondent is guessing what you want.

None of these results is good. Each wastes time and causes delays. So make things simple:

■State in the opening sentence the subject of your inquiry.

■For each item of information you want, use a separate paragraph.

■Unless you're asking for confidential information, and need to justify your request, don't overplay why you want the information. Few people care what your reason is for making the request or how you plan to use the information. Explanations just irritate them. Here's an example of how *not* to do it:

Dear Sirs:

Just the other day my neighbor, Mrs. Myrtle, mentioned how nice a table would look on my patio. Not just any table, she said, but a nice wooden one. Of course, wood would be necessary to go with the siding of the house and all the trees in the yard.

My husband planted those trees years ago—about twenty, I guess. It's so sad he didn't live to see them grow.

My patio isn't terribly big, so the table shouldn't be large—just a medium-size one would do nicely.

And of course I wouldn't want to spend too much on it. Herman's pension and insurance left me nicely taken care of, but one mustn't be extravagant.

Do you have something nice that you think I might like? I hope so. Mrs. Myrtle and I would like to have the table soon so we can have coffee outside during the warm weather.

Sincerely,

The sales manager will have a great time with that letter asking for a medium-size wooden table that doesn't cost too much. It would be interesting to know what he did, but he won't tell.

Letters that got results

Here are some better letters:

Dear Mr. Manager:

Would you be willing to share your experience as founder and editor of a quarterly magazine?

Specifically, I'd like to know:

what objectives the magazine is designed to meet,

the editorial policy which has been set, and

your method of evaluating the success of your magazine.

Any information you can give us will be a tremendous help in planning a magazine we hope to launch here.

Many thanks for your time and help.

Appreciatively,

Dear Mr. Gordon:

I'd appreciate your help in preparing an article about marketing by major corporations.

The article will deal with shifts in advertising strategy over the past five years—shifts to meet changes in consumer attitudes, preferences, and buying power.

If the information is available for publication, I'd be interested in knowing how your advertising strategy—the copy platform, media mix, and frequency—has changed over the past five years, and the reasons for the changes.

Since the article will be illustrated, it would also be helpful if you could send reproduction proofs of different ads that illustrate both your current campaign and that run five years ago.

We'll certainly appreciate any information you can give us.

Many thanks,

One important point to remember in writing letters of inquiry is to avoid being negative—it's okay to be polite, but don't be totally humble. That is, don't say things like:

I know I shouldn't take your valuable time.
I don't want to inconvenience you.
I realize I'm imposing, but. . . .

Phrases like that are a red flag; they offer the reader an excuse not to do what you want him to do.

Now that you've seen how to write a letter of inquiry, you'll want to know how to answer one—especially one that is like the vague inquiry about wooden tables.

Letters of inquiry come from three basic sources:

People who are seriously interested in your product or services.

Those who are interested but are shopping around.

Those who are sort of interested but mostly just curious.

When you don't know what prompts the inquiry, you must assume the person is interested but shopping. Therefore, your answer should go out before the competition's, and it should sell.

FOUR RULES FOR ANSWERING INQUIRIES

■ *Be prompt.* If someone is interested enough to write for information, he can be sold. Make sure you get your answer out quickly. Anyway, even if you don't want to sell anything, it's rude to keep people waiting for answers.

■ *Be specific.* Answer the questions—if you can figure out what they are —and give enough detail to convince the person that your product or service is the best available. If you want to include more detail than you can comfortably handle in a letter, enclose a catalog or specification sheet and refer to it.

■ *Be polite.* True, many inquiries are not well thought-out. But the person who made the inquiry didn't know he was vague, and if he knew

THE INQUIRING STUDENT

ONE FORM of correspondence that bulks large in company files consists of letters from students, requesting information for class projects. Here are some samples of good inquiry letters from high school and college students. Note that all of them identify the writer and explain the reason for the request: This is important because (a) companies are sometimes reluctant to release information about themselves unless they know how it's going to be used, and (b) knowing the age level of the writer helps guide them in sending the appropriate literature.

Gentlemen:

I am a student in the Retail Merchandising class of Newtown High School. Our teacher has suggested that each of us write to a company and find out how it conducts business. Can you tell me:

1. How long have you been in business?
2. How many branches do you have?
3. Approximately how many machines do you sell each year?
4. What kinds of machines do you sell?
5. How many people do you employ?

If you can send any other information that would give me a better understanding of your company, I would appreciate it.

Truly yours,

Gentlemen:

I am the editor of the *Clarion*, North College's student newspaper.

In a forthcoming issue, we are planning an article on electronic translating machines. The article will stress recent developments in the field, particularly in its applications in colleges.

Can you send black-and-white photographs to illustrate the article? We plan to use three to six pictures. We will, of course, be happy to return the pictures, if you wish, along with a complimentary copy of the issue. Naturally, we will credit your company as the source of any pictures we use.

Since the deadline for the article is August 20, we would appreciate receiving the pictures by August 12.

Very truly yours,

WRITE BETTER, SPEAK BETTER

as much about your business as you do, he'd be in it. So, assume the
questions are in good faith and be patient.

■ *Say "thank you."* Inquiries represent a great source of business. Obviously, not every inquirer will buy something, but how do you tell in
advance? You can't lose if you assume everyone will buy and treat them
as if the sale were about to be made. Isn't it natural to say "thank you"
to someone who has bought something from you?

DON'T INSULT THE CUSTOMER

Here's an answer to a letter of inquiry that is so unfriendly and condescending in tone it's guaranteed to lose a customer:

> Dear Mr. Davis:
>
> I assume that what you really want to know is the cost of our consulting services when you are seeking a new job. I say "assume" because,
> frankly, your letter was vague and I can't be sure.
>
> The attached sheets explain our service in detail. I suggest you read
> them and if you are still interested, call my secretary and she will try
> to make an appointment for you.
>
> I would like to point out that our fee is payable when we are contracted, and not when you find a new job.
>
> Sincerely,

That letter was written by a guy who's had it all his own way for too
long. Otherwise, he'd have written it this way:

> Dear Mr. Davis:
>
> We'd be delighted to talk with you and work out a strategy for finding you a new job.
>
> At this point it's hard to say what the cost would be, because the fee
> is based on a combination of what you presently earn and the type of
> position you hope to attain.
>
> I've tentatively put you down for an appointment on Thursday of
> next week at noon. I realize how hard it is to search and be discreet,
> so lunch hour is usually the best time to chat. If that isn't convenient for
> you, please call me and we'll set another time.
>
> Thanks very much for contacting me. I'll look forward to meeting
> and talking with you next Thursday.
>
> Cordially,

Here's another good reply:

> Dear Mr. Dalton:
>
> We do, indeed, have a punctureproof tire. They're available in a size
> to fit your Ford wagon and the price is only $25 per tire.

86

I've enclosed a brochure which describes how these tires are made, and the mileage and safety advantages for you and your family. Also enclosed are the names of dealers in your area.

We believe that these tires are the best available anywhere. When you've driven on them we know you'll agree.

Thanks for writing.

Happy Motoring!

There may be times when you have to refuse information—for competitive and other reasons. When that happens, be honest. Don't make excuses. Just say you can't release the information and tell why:

Dear Mr. Frost:

I'm terribly sorry we won't be able to give you the marketing information for your article.

As you know, this is a highly competitive industry. If the information you requested became public, it would prove very valuable to our competitors and seriously hamper our sales efforts.

We do appreciate your desire to include us in your article. If you need other information—of a less sensitive nature—we'll be glad to provide it. I'll await word from you. Good luck with your project.

Cordially,

It may be that the information requested doesn't exist in your records. If so, you might mention what you do have:

Dear Mr. Harrelson:

I regret to say it, but the information you requested isn't available.

Our safety department records the number and cost of accidents, but we don't know the man-hours lost and their cost in lost productivity.

Sorry I can't be of more help.

Cordially,

In Bear Creek Orchards, Oregon, Harry and David are owners of The Fruit-of-the-Month Club. They answer inquiries in such interesting ways, it makes you want to ask a question just to get their answer!

Recently a customer's monthly fruit package had been broken into before delivery. The fruit that had not been taken was spoiled. She wrote asking what could be done about it.

Harry and David wrote:

It's sort of a left-handed compliment,
Mrs. Smith,
that by the time your gift package reached you it had proved just too tempting to someone along the way.

We're sorry and embarrassed, of course.

Since the shipping season for peaches has ended, we'll send Crisp Mountain Apples at Thanksgiving in replacement.

We hope this will make up for the disappointment expressed in your letter.

Best wishes,

There isn't any trick to writing or answering letters of inquiry. Determine what you want to know, or tell; *then*—write it down.

test your skills

HOW TO WRITE FOR INFORMATION

1. *Fill in the missing blanks:*
In writing a letter of inquiry, you should decide what you want to know and write it down as _____ and _____ as possible.

2. *Underline the right answer:*
a. You (should, should not) state in the opening sentence the subject of your inquiry.
b. Each item of information you want (need not, should) be set off in a separate paragraph.
c. Common courtesy (demands, does not require) that you explain why you want general information.

3. In as clear, concise, and direct a way as possible, write a sample letter asking the Denver, Colorado, Chamber of Commerce for information you might need if you were considering a move there. You must make a decision at once, so you will emphasize your need for a prompt reply.

Answers to this quiz appear on page 701.

AND DON'T FORGET

When you write a letter of inquiry, or any other business letter:
1. The heading (your own address and the date) should appear in the upper right-hand corner of the letter, not crowded in. If you want an answer, be sure it is clear, complete, and legible.
2. The inside address (name and complete address of the person you're writing) should appear on the left above the salutation.
3. If possible, keep a carbon or other copy for your records.

7

How to complain
and get action

You feel you've been gypped and you want justice. But to whom should you write? What should you say? Is it wise to sound angry? Should you threaten the company? These pointers and sample letters will show you the best way to handle written complaints and get the results you want.

Most reliable companies pay close attention to customer mail, particularly mail from dissatisfied customers. But writing letters to a company is one thing; getting the company to do what you want is another. And it requires a certain amount of know-how to persuade a manufacturer to repair your broken toaster or make an adjustment on your mishandled airplane reservation.

First, you must observe certain principles that have nothing to do with letter writing. The most important is that you must deal with a reliable company. Let's say you've spent $15.00 on a gold-plated hand-warmer which won't work. If you bought it from a fly-by-night retailer who bought an odd lot from a fly-by-night wholesaler who bought the hand-warmers from a fly-by-night manufacturer, you can resign yourself to having thrown away $15.00.

Second, if the product carries a guaranty or warranty, be sure that you understand its terms. If there's a one-year warranty on the picture tube of your television set, the manufacturer will probably not make good if it breaks down after thirteen months. There's a legitimate reason for this. As one spokesman for a large company put it: "It costs us a certain amount to make a warranty, because we know that in a year's time, we're going to have to pay a certain amount on repairs. We figure this out before we sell the product, and it's included in the price. In other words, the warranty is an insurance policy, and the customer pays for that insurance when he pays for the product."

The same man did add, however: "If a product becomes defective a few weeks after the warranty has run out, we may make the adjustment for the sake of good will."

When in doubt, write

In other words, if you're dissatisfied with the product, it doesn't hurt to write a letter. If it's a good letter, the company may help you out even if the warranty has expired.

Now, let's assume that you feel you have a legitimate grievance about a product you've bought. Let's also assume that the store from which you've bought it refuses to give you satisfaction. You're immediately faced with two problems:

Whom should you write to?

What should you say?

Unfortunately, there is no simple answer to the first question because almost every company is organized differently. In some large companies each major product is handled by a product manager, who's responsible for making all decisions concerning his product. In other cases, a central customer service bureau will handle all correspondence.

Perhaps the best way to handle the problem is, first, to look at the user's manual you received with the product—assuming that (a) you received one and (b) you've held on to it. This will probably tell you where to write in case of trouble. (If you haven't held on to it, shame on you! In the future, remember to file these manuals away where you can get them quickly.) If the manual doesn't tell you, the store where you bought the product may be able to give you the manufacturer's address. Another source is the item itself, which will invariably carry the manufacturer's name and usually the city where the company is located.

If the street address isn't given, however, and the manufacturer isn't a large one, the Post Office is likely to return your letter for lack of sufficient address. But all is not lost. You can learn the address of almost any company in the country by using your telephone. Call Directory Assistance of the city in question (dial 1 plus the area code plus 555-1212) and ask for the telephone number and address of the company

90

you want. In many areas, the operators will provide this information to their customers. If the operator gives you a choice of several different addresses—for example, the executive office, the service office, or the sales office—ask for the executive office. The executive office will generally know where to forward any letter sent to it. When you can only get the telephone number, however, you can, if you wish, call the company directly and secure the information yourself.

Should you write to the company president?

There is one school of letter writers which firmly believes that the way to get fast action from a company is to write directly to the president. This, however, is not always the best course. In many cases, the president will never see complaint letters addressed to him. His secretary will simply route them to the proper department. And you've wasted a couple of days while the letter is in transit to the correct department.

In other cases, however, the president does take a close interest in complaint mail. The head of the correspondence department of one large public utility explained what happens in his company: "The quickest way to get a response is by writing to our president. Although usually he won't answer it himself, he insists that we file a report on the disposition of the case. You can be sure that we handle his letters more promptly than the routine ones. We even have a couple of expert correspondents who handle mail which he wants answered."

As a general rule, then, the following may be sound practice: If you're not in a great hurry for an answer, write to the president of the company. If he doesn't see the letter, all you've lost is time. But he may take an interest in customer correspondence and, in that case, you may get a more satisfactory answer.

Should you be angry?

Again, there are two schools of thought. Some effective letter writers feel that the only way to budge a company is to write an explosively angry letter, letting the company know in no uncertain terms that you're disgusted with its product or service. Undoubtedly, this tactic can sometimes achieve the desired end.

Unfortunately, people who write in anger sometimes forget to include important information that the company needs in order to correct the situation. If that information is lacking, all the anger in the world will get you nowhere. The company will simply write back asking you coolly for the information it needs.

A calm, reasoned letter that presents all the facts will probably get the same or better results than an irate one.

What about threats?

With a few exceptions, threats do not frighten companies. Most of them want to keep their customers happy, but they will not be especially worried if you tell them you'll never buy their product again, or if you warn them that you'll tell your friends about your bad experience. These problems crop up in the mail regularly, and the company knows' that your complaints will probably not make too much difference in its over-all profit picture.

A significant exception is the public utility, which is hemmed in by state and federal regulations. Here's what the spokesman for one public utility admitted: "If a customer threatens that he'll complain to the state Public Service Commission, we'll generally pay closer attention to him. This is because when the PSC steps into a case, it usually wants a whole raft of information. It's a nuisance for us to collect, and it takes up a lot of our time. Therefore, we handle these letters with extra care so that we can avoid the headache."

By extension, when dealing with any company which is subject to extensive government regulation, it may help if you threaten to report the complaint to the authorities. Public utilities, railroads, truckers, and insurance companies fall into this group.

How long the letter?

The single most-often-voiced complaint companies have about customers' letters is that they're too long. "So often," said one company correspondent, "we have to wade through a couple of pages before we can find out the problem. And then we have to wade through a couple

> **I** have made this letter long only because I did not have the time to make it shorter. —*Pascal*

more before we can find out what they want us to do about it. In the end, we're irritated, and we're less inclined to be as helpful." In short, be short.

What information should you give?

In order to take action on your complaint, the company has to know some simple factual data. When a product is involved, include the following information:

1. The model number or a detailed description of the product.
2. The name and address of the store from which you bought it.
3. The date of your purchase.
4. A copy of the bill of sale, plus a copy of paid invoices for any service rendered on the product since you bought it.
5. A *brief* description of the problem.
6. An indication of whether you're writing for the first time. If not, give the dates of your previous correspondence—the date of your last letter to the company and the date of the last letter you received from them—as well as the name of the person who wrote you.

If you're writing in answer to a letter from the company, include the company's filing number, if there is one. This usually will appear near the top of the letterhead, and often will be preceded by some such notation as "Reference" or "Ref." or "Account No." Some companies even say quite clearly at the tops of their letters: "When replying, please refer to File No. 000." This enables even the most poorly trained filing clerk to locate your correspondence.

Sample complaint letters that got action

AN ANGRY COMPLAINT LETTER

The XYZ Bicycle Company received this angry blast one morning:

Attention: Parts Division
Reference: 16″ Two-Wheel Bicycle
Model A32

Gentlemen:
I am angry, disgusted, and will never believe anyone who sells or represents the XYZ Company. I need not tell you that the best way to lose future sales is to misrepresent a product; and I'll also tell you that

if I could get my hands on the salesman who sold this bike to me, I'd hit him.

When I bought the bike from the Anderson Department Store, Main Street, Jonesville, in March of this year, I was told that this was the best bike on the market, and that parts would be easy to obtain.

As you will note, there is a box along with this letter. Inside the box is the broken part, which is the cause of all the trouble. [Note: If you know the name of a broken part, mention it.] After having talked to seven repair shops in my city, I am furious at being told: "The company doesn't have replacement parts," and "The big stores sell this bike, and we repairmen get the gripes. It shouldn't be on the market."

I am asking that you either replace the enclosed part, or send me a replacement bike. I've never begged, borrowed, or cheated in my entire life, and I have absolutely no feeling of guilt in making this request.

Mary Jones Warner

The company sent back a replacement part, along with a letter explaining that the model had been discontinued; that was the reason the customer had been unable to obtain a replacement locally. It is doubtful that Mrs. Warner's anger helped her get better service, but it certainly made her feel better—and this is one of the legitimate reasons for writing an angry letter.

Incidentally, Mrs. Warner did a very nice—and a very smart—thing after receiving the replacement. She wrote a gracious thank-you note to the company. If she ever has trouble with the bicycle again, the company will probably go out of its way to help her. Here is what she wrote to the man who sent her the company's apologies:

Dear Mr. Johnson:

Thank you for your letter of June 5, and the new sprocket and rear wheel assembly. These parts have been a perfect replacement.

You people certainly restored my faith in your company, and have made us very happy. I do hope that you won't think me an old shrew for my letter of July 31, but sometimes people just won't take the time to help one another. Your company and you have proved me wrong, and I shall speak of your firm with pride.

Yours very truly,
Mary Jones Warner

A CALM COMPLAINT LETTER TO A MANUFACTURER

Dear Sirs:

In the fall of 1980 I bought a Jones Typewriter, Portable Special Model, at ABC Store in Jonesville. I had used it only a few days when the space bar broke.

We took it to a local repair shop; they told us that it was a factory defect and suggested that we take it back to ABC. ABC accepted the machine and sent the part in. We waited three months, and since your company did not send a replacement, they let us have the space bar from another typewriter.

Now, six months later, it has broken again. We took it back to ABC. They are no longer carrying your typewriter, but they assured us that the guarantee is still good and suggested that we write you for further instructions as to what steps to take.

The guarantee was registered in my name, at the address below.

I will appreciate anything you can do to help us on this matter.

Respectfully,
James Christopher

A POLITE COMPLAINT LETTER AND ITS SEQUEL

Gentlemen:

I am aware of your reputation for quality products plus reliability; consequently I do not hesitate to write to you.

For the past two years, my two sons, ages eight and ten, have enjoyed your Electronic Hockey Game. The other day, a welded joint gave way and rendered the game absolutely useless. It was the joint that connects the side to the top of the game, and without it the playing area is too unstable for the kind of action the game generates.

The purpose of this letter is to ask your permission to send you the set for rewelding.

Rainy days become quite dull for them without that game, so I trust I shall hear from you soon.

Very truly yours,
Howard Gerber

The company's parts-and-service manager, apparently charmed by Mr. Gerber's letter, answered that Mr. Gerber need not send back the game; the company would send a new frame if he could give the model number listed on the instruction sheet. Mr. Gerber replied:

Permit me to thank you for your prompt and considerate reply. My sons were delighted to know that you cared.

Since the instructions are long since gone, I am enclosing a snapshot of my sons playing the game. If possible, please send the picture back; it is the best one my wife has ever taken of the youngsters, and we would like very much to keep it.

I regret that I can find no identifying numbers on the game itself, but perhaps this information will help you :

The frame is red. It measures 2' by 4' by 6" high.

Again, my sincerest appreciation of your kind attention.

Sincerely,
Howard Gerber

The approach in both these letters was courteous and friendly. And Mr. Gerber got his frame.

A FIRM, IMPASSIONED LETTER

A man with a methodical mind sent the following letter to a nationally known firm after his method had been reduced nearly to madness. It is a good letter because it states the problem clearly and succinctly and at the same time shows his strong indignation:

Dear Mr. Blank:

Last October I signed a contract with your company for the installation of dry walls and the renovation of a bathroom in my home at the above address. I am now appealing to you to have this work completed in a satisfactory manner.

I have spoken to your Quincy, Mass., store manager on several occasions, to the plumbing department manager, to your maintenance people, and to anyone else who seemed to be in a position to assist in completing the work. I have received considerate responses followed by service people trying to do the necessary work.

Nevertheless, I have had expensive broadloom rugs badly stained; I have had water pour through my kitchen ceiling at least six times after your people left my home with everything supposedly in order; and I now again have leaks, grout falling out, and other defects.

I have experienced nothing but trouble with your workmanship and materials from the outset. I will illustrate with details—an incomplete list—which your records should confirm.

1. An expensive vanity was delivered with doors assembled upside down and door catches not functioning properly.

2. The dry wall work was left in such rough condition that your installers had to return several times. In some areas sanding was overlooked; in others, dry wall taping was not used, and molding was left incompleted.

[The next few paragraphs listed additional defects.]

Mr. Blank, I had your service people come to the house at least six times because of leaks from the bathroom to the floor below. There were denials of responsibility. Children were blamed, etc. And in each case, it was finally established that the installation was faulty. At this writing, water is again leaking to the floor below when the shower is used.

Frankly, I believe I have reached the point of no return in dealing with your local staff.

I now want to have my bathroom completed in a workmanlike manner, even if it means removing the entire installation. In the event that any removal is necessary, I will not accept a patched-up finish.

For a job that costs about $2500, your performance has been outrageously bad. I expect the courtesy of a prompt reply from you, and the necessary inspections and corrections from qualified personnel.

Sincerely yours,

The president did send various executives to view the shambles, and some corrective measures were taken. As this paragraph is written, some two years after the letter was written, the work has still not been completed satisfactorily, but it is considerably further along, and with one or two more letters, this man may eventually achieve a completely satisfactory job.

Sample request and adjustment letters

REQUESTING REPLACEMENT PARTS

When an item breaks or wears out and you want a replacement, a simple, short letter will best serve your purpose. If you still have descriptive literature that came with the product, see if it contains information about reordering. If the literature includes a price list for parts, send along a check or money order. Otherwise, ask the company to bill you or to send the item C.O.D. If you don't know whom to write, send it to the Order Department.

Gentlemen:
    Please send me Part No. 21—the heating rod—for your broiler unit, Model 23.
    You may bill me or send it C.O.D.

Sincerely,

Gentlemen:
    I should like to order the following items of glassware from your Sven Hagstrom smoked crystal set:
        three old-fashioned glasses
        one piece of stemware
        two snifters
    Please bill my charge account, No. 20–321.

Sincerely,

When you're not sure of the model or the serial number, give any other details that might help to identify it:

Gentlemen:
    Can you supply me with a cutting-blade unit for your Quik-Shear Lawn Mower?
    The mower is about thirty years old. The cutting blades are thirty-

six inches long, and are both welded and bolted to the mower frame.
If the part is available, please send it C.O.D.

Sincerely,

Gentlemen:

Can you send me Item No. 57, the lock-nut washer for your Tripod
Model Mark II?

The item was left out of the carton in which the tripod came.

I purchased the tripod on March 3, at the Community Camera Store,
45 Main Street, Centerville, Oregon.

Sincerely,

Dear Sirs:

Please send me a handle for your four-cup percolator.

I ordered the percolator from your factory, and it arrived with the
handle broken.

May I suggest that you examine your shipping carton with an eye
to providing more padding adjacent to the area of the handle. I suspect the skimpiness of the padding accounted for the breakage.

Sincerely,

COMPLAINT ABOUT NONDELIVERY

If a store fails to deliver an item, you'll probably call first to find out
why. If you get no satisfactory response, a letter to the store manager
may help. Include any information that will enable the store to track
the item down, including:

1. Your sales slip number.

2. A detailed description of the item.

3. The department from which you ordered it (this should appear
on the sales slip).

4. Your charge-account number, if the item was charged.

Dear Sir:

Your store failed to deliver the order described below, which was
scheduled for delivery to our home on January 17.

Items ordered: 54″ mattress; 54″ bed spring; bed frame

All items ordered from Dept. 66

Sales Slip No. 325–45

Revolving Charge Account 101–12

Please take the following action:

Arrange to have your truck deliver the merchandise to our home on
Friday, January 31.

Confirm, either by mail or phone, that you have received this letter
and will take the action requested. You may call me at 617–3224, any
day between 8:00 and 12:00 A.M.

Sincerely,

Here's a letter about a delay in delivery of mail-order goods:

Dear Sir:

On April 15, I ordered an oven rack (Part No. 587) and a broiler pan (Part No. 586) from you. I requested that you bill me for the items.

They have not yet arrived, although more than a month has passed. Will you please send the items, or explain the delay.

Sincerely,

UNJUSTIFIABLE OVERCHARGES

When you feel you have been overcharged, write to the top man at the store. Give him as many details as are needed to explain the situation, but try to be brief and factual.

The following letter is one which a customer sent to a store when he felt he had been unjustly overcharged. The important things to note in this complaint are:

It reviews the problem.

It requests specific action, i.e., a request for a refund.

It provides relevant documentation.

Dear Mr. Jones:

I hope you will be able to correct a large overcharge.

On June 16, I spent $600 in your store on a range, a refrigerator, and a washing machine.

They were to be delivered to my home in Poughquag, N.Y.

Your salesman, Sam Casey, told me that shipping charges would come to about $17. He suggested that the order be sent express collect by truck. I agreed and paid immediately for the merchandise.

A couple of days later, he called to ask if it would be all right to ship by Railway Express. He assured me that the charges would be about the same. Again, I agreed.

You can imagine my feelings when the Railway Express agent called from Brewster, about twenty miles from Poughquag, to tell me that the items had arrived, and that shipping charges would be $22. Further, that if I wished them delivered to my house, I should have to get a trucker and pay *his* charges, also.

I obtained a trucker who charged me $38 more.

You will agree, I'm sure, that I should not be forced to pay for Mr. Casey's error, particularly since I permitted him to make precisely the arrangement he wanted.

I'm willing to pay the Railway Express charges of $22.93, although they are about $6 more than Mr. Casey estimated.

However, I feel that your store should reimburse me for the $38 extra I had to pay because of your salesman's miscalculation.

Sincerely,

THREE THINGS TO DO
WHEN YOU CAN'T PAY A BILL

IF THE BILL you've run up is so high that you've given up trying to pay it, then it's time to take yourself in hand. If your delinquency is due to a temporary inability to make payments, send a letter of explanation.

Perhaps the best way to handle this situation is to make a firm resolution to pay back a certain amount each week or month—no matter how small. Then you might send a letter in which you:

1. *Apologize for your delinquency*. A sincere apology will make the credit manager feel that you're as worried as he is, and that you're just as determined that you do the right thing as he is.

2. *State that you expect to pay regularly*. This is terribly important to credit managers. If they're receiving regular payments, they can handle your account with no additional work. If the payments are irregular, the manager will have to set the card aside in a special file, or flag it with a special tab designed to remind him that he hasn't done a very good job of screening credit risks.

3. *Enclose your first payment*.

In an effort to encourage regular repayment by delinquent customers, some stores will send them a form which states that the signer agrees to repay a certain amount regularly, plus a small interest charge. Unless you need this club over your head in order to force yourself to repay the bill, don't sign it—at least, not without the advice of a competent lawyer. You have nothing to gain, and you'll lose the interest. The following letter will serve as a model:

Dear Mr. Smith:

Your records will show that I have been in arrears on my account for five months.

I am sorry about this delinquency. Certain personal affairs have until now made it impossible for me to pay what I owe.

However, I now want to pay this debt as soon as possible. Therefore, I plan to send you $3.00 a week until the debt is cleared.

I enclose the first payment. And I again apologize for my tardiness. It will not be repeated.

Sincerely,

P.S. For verification, I am enclosing photostatic copies of your invoice and those of Railway Express and the trucker.

Interestingly enough, the customer received no answer. The next letter which he wrote explains why:

Dear Mr. Smith:

Several months ago, when I decided to write you about a serious overcharge, I asked the salesman with whom I dealt, Sam Casey, for the name of the store president. He gave me the name of Joseph Jones.

On June 29, I wrote to Mr. Jones. I have never received an answer.

Recently, I called your headquarters. The switchboard operator told me that you, rather than Mr. Jones, are the president. Mr. Jones, she told me, is responsible for out-of-town shipments.

Thus, I assume that Mr. Jones was probably responsible for the overcharge, which may account for the fact that I did not hear from him.

I am enclosing a copy of my letter to Mr. Jones. I trust that you will send me the $38 which I have requested.

Sincerely,

This letter achieved the results. The customer got the refund. The moral? Don't give up until you've exhausted all the possibilities.

When you want to charge it

ESTABLISHING AN ACCOUNT BY MAIL

In opening a charge account by mail, two courses are open: You can request a charge-account application form in a brief letter to the store's credit department:

Gentlemen:

Please send me the forms necessary for opening a charge account at your store.

Sincerely,

Or, you can send in the information the store will probably require, and let the store fill out the form. You will probably want to do this when you're also ordering an item from the store.

Include the following information in your letter:

1. The names of other stores where you have charge accounts, and the serial numbers of those accounts.

2. The name of at least one bank with which you do business.

3. One other credit reference, such as a Diner's Club or American Express Credit Card.

4. The names and addresses of your and your spouse's employers, and the length of time you've been employed.

5. Your telephone number.

Gentlemen:

I should like to order the plant holder—item 32G—advertised in your Spring Catalog.

I should also like to open a charge account with your store, and have this item billed to my account.

I have charge accounts with the following stores:

Smith Brothers	Armand's Clothiers
Centerville, N.J.	Smithtown, Pa.
Account No. 317	Account No. 628–43

For further credit references, you may check with the following:

First National Bank	American Express
of Centerville	Credit Card Division
35 Main Street	770 Broadway
Centerville, N.J. 07281	New York, N.Y. 10009
Account No. 42,876	Account No. 040 428 641 2

My husband, Martin Cline, has been an employe of Smith's Dry Cleaners, 32 Auburn St., Medford, N.J., for three years. I have worked for Dr. John Cleves, 83 Main Street, Medford, N.J., for eight years. My telephone number is 323–6146.

Sincerely,

WHEN A STORE FAILS TO RECORD PAYMENT

If a store's monthly statement fails to record a payment you've made, give the following information in your letter asking for a correction:

1. The date of your payment. This is quite important. If the store knows approximately when your payment arrived, it will be able to check its records more accurately and more quickly.

2. The name under which you sent the payment. For example, if you're a married woman your account may be under your husband's name, but you may have paid by check, signing your own first name. Or you may have endorsed your paycheck over to the store. If the name on the check differs from that on your charge account, the store may not have given you proper credit.

3. The amount of the check.

4. Your charge-account number.

Gentlemen:

I believe your statement of March 3 is in error.

If you examine your records, I think you will find that I paid you

$75 by check on April 25. I signed the check "Mary G. Cline." Please send me a corrected statement.

Sincerely,
Mary Graham Cline
(Mrs. Martin Cline)
Account No. 456 890

WHEN A STORE FAILS TO CREDIT RETURNED MERCHANDISE

If the store has failed to record a credit for merchandise which you've returned, include:

1. The serial number on your credit slip.
2. The name or number of the department which granted the credit. (This usually appears on the credit slip.)
3. The date the credit was issued.

Dear Sirs:

I believe your statement of March 3 should include credit for a sweater which I returned on February 25. The amount of credit was $16.
The credit slip number is 567–23. The department number is 43.
Please send me a corrected statement.

Sincerely,
Mary Graham Cline
(Mrs. Martin Cline)
Account No. 456 890

test your skills

HOW TO COMPLAIN AND GET ACTION

1. Which of the following methods are the most effective in getting action?
    a. Write an indignant letter that criticizes company policies.
    b. Threaten to warn your acquaintances against buying the firm's products.
    c. Appeal to the president's obligations to the customer.
    d. Write to the Better Business Bureau and demand immediate action.
    e. Write a reasonable, polite but firm letter to the company (preferably addressed to the president) explaining your grievance (briefly and clearly) and stating what you want the company to do about it.

2. Pretend that you bought a new Howitzer III car from the World Motor Company. It has a whine in the engine, but the dealer insists that it is just "in your mind" and he refuses to do anything about it. Write a sample letter to the president of World Motor Company that you think would get results.

Answers to this quiz appear on page 701.

8

Writing your
public officials

Elected officials all agree that mail from constituents is important in forming their opinions. But they also agree that it's the quality of the letters, not their quantity, that influences them more. These practical guidelines will help make your letters effective.

How can you, as an independent citizen, get answers to your questions, or action on your complaints, or an ear for your opinion, from elected public officials?

Five representatives and senators have provided detailed answers to questions on how best to correspond with them. The first question was: *Do you read all the mail sent to you by voters, or does your staff screen it and route only the most important letters to you?*

Most replied that an administrative assistant either screens their mail and briefs them on its contents, or else goes over it with them. Here is one typical response: "I read most of the mail sent to me by voters. I receive a minimum of fifteen hundred letters a week and I try to skim all of them. All carefully written letters, important gripes, letters from friends, and letters that 'say something' are, of course, put at the top of the pile and, of course, I read those with care."

Note the four categories of letters to which the congressman pays the most attention. Later, we'll explore these in some detail.

Are elected officials influenced by the volume of mail on a subject? Two questions were asked:

Does the quantity of the mail you receive on an issue ever influence your thinking or your efforts in regard to that issue?

Are you influenced to any extent by write-in campaigns, or so-called inspired mail, on an issue—specifically, large numbers of letters, all expressing the same opinion in identical, or nearly identical words?

The answers boiled down to Yes and No, respectively.

One senator said that letters are very useful. He wrote: "Let me point out that my state has dire need for federal aid in many fields, such as operation of schools, construction of public works projects, planning of transit systems, and the like. My attention has been directed to possible shortcomings in pending legislation relative to such matters because informed officials and private citizens have taken the time and trouble to write me setting forth basic facts meriting consideration."

Another senator, in answer to the first question, said: "It is the quality of the letters. By that I mean the person *who gives the reasons* [italics the editor's], for his position is definitely more helpful. . . ."

Said a congressman: "Quantity of mail is important, but quality is of far greater importance. Much quantity mail can be inspired mail. *The least effective kind is a form that has obviously been received from someone else by the sender or which is clipped from a newspaper* [italics the editor's]. Nevertheless, quantity is important on a given issue as it indicates that large numbers of people may be affected one way or another by governmental position or by a vote."

Two other congressmen indicated that the volume of mail will cause them to explore an issue more closely. Said one: "I think the quantity of mail influences my political thinking about an issue only slightly. It ordinarily, however, will not alter my judgment or decision about how I shall vote on a particular issue. It might well keep me from pursuing a given matter more aggressively or it might tend to temper my opposition to a piece of legislation."

The other said: "Quantity of mail causes me to give the matter a 'second look,' but doesn't necessarily change my position. *The source is more influential than quantity.*"

Six characteristics of an effective letter

Congressmen were asked what they considered to be the characteristics of a good letter. Here are the individual qualities mentioned:

1. Individuality and a creative approach.

2. Questions framed so as to evoke an individual response rather than a form response.

3. Evidence that the writer has some knowledge of the issue.

4. Expression of a personal viewpoint to distinguish his letter from an inspired form letter.

5. Legibility.

6. Brevity.

SEVEN MISTAKES TO AVOID

When asked what were the most common flaws in mail from constituents, the congressmen's answers were:

1. The writer states his position on legislation, but doesn't explain the problem in his community, or how the law would affect his business, or give other reasons for the position he takes.

2. The most common flaws are oversimplicity and triteness, especially in dealing with very complex issues.

3. Hostility in the writer's attitude constitutes a bar or a defect in communication.

4. Representative's name is misspelled and incorrectly addressed.

5. Confusion between a bill in Congress and one pending in the State Legislature is shown.

6. Letter lacks a reply address.

7. Signature is typed rather than signed.

What a congressman looks for in your letter

Let's summarize the congressmen's answers in order to understand how best to get a quick, informative answer from them, and to ensure that they pay attention to your letter.

1. If you're making an inquiry you should:

a. State your request in the first paragraph.

b. Explain the reason for your request. This will help the representative give you a more precise answer.

2. If you're expressing an opinion on an issue or a bill, you should do the following things in order to give it more weight:

a. State your position in the first paragraph; be quite specific about the measure to which you're referring. If it's about a bill up for consideration, give the number of the bill if you know it.

Finally, when the legislators were asked whether they preferred that mail be sent to their offices or their homes, without exception they preferred their offices.

Sample letters to elected representatives

LETTERS ABOUT SPECIFIC BILLS

The writer of the letter below gives a good, personal reason for his position. He might have bolstered his argument, however, by describing his income in greater detail. A little drama never hurts.

> Sir:
> I strongly urge you to assist in having Bill H.R. 1811 passed.
> It would be of considerable help to those, like me, who are handicapped, to have a $600 tax exemption. My income has been reduced considerably, even though I have tried to keep as busy as is physically possible.
>
> Respectfully,

It may be useful to remind the representative of the effects of legislation on his constituents.

> My dear Mr. Smith:
> Passage of the Wheat-Cotton Bill (H.R. 6196) would in effect be

b. Explain the reasoning behind your position in the next paragraph or two.

c. Avoid copying a form letter provided by a club or association. You might use it as a basis, but put your letter in your own words.

3. Regardless of the reason for your letter, you should:

a. Keep it short. Congressmen are reluctant to wade through more than a single page.

b. Make it legible—a typed letter is easiest to read. If you don't have access to a typewriter, be sure your handwriting is clear.

c. Include your return address. It goes without saying that your signature should be easily readable.

d. If you have an official position in an organization interested in a measure or an issue, mention it, either listing your title below your signature or incorporating it into the body of the letter.

equivalent to a tax on bakery products, since it would mean an increase in wheat and flour prices.

I feel that such increases would result in further hardship for the needy, and would render a disservice to all your constituents as well. I respectfully urge you to vote against it.

Very truly yours,

A little humor can make a letter stand out from the run of correspondence. Avoid, however (as this letter does), sarcasm. Cutting humor makes representatives bleed, and a bleeding congressman is an angry congressman.

Madam:

I am opposed to the recent action of the House Health and Safety Committee in approving H.R. 4731.

This bill will repeal a section of the 1906 Food, Drug, and Cosmetic Act which keeps candymakers from using "non-nutritive ingredients" in their products.

I do not wish to eat talc when I eat candy. Maybe talc has some nutritive value, but being a conservative, I don't like getting used to it.

While normally I vote Republican, I voted for you in the last election because I felt that you had a slight edge over the Republican incumbent.

I trust that you will continue to follow through with the admirable work you have done. And I am confident that you will do what you can to keep candy adulteration from becoming legal.

Very truly yours,

LETTERS ABOUT GENERAL ISSUES

The letter following is a beautiful example of simplicity and clarity. The writer is restrained, informal, and direct. If you were a congressman, wouldn't you be proud to have constituents who could write like this? You'd be very inclined to listen to them.

My dear Mr. Smith:

I have been very interested in the Peace Corps and have followed its progress with pleasure. Noting the success of this program in other countries, I would like to suggest a "Domestic" Peace Corps. Our young people could help the American Indians, the itinerant workers, and the people who live in depressed areas.

I'm sure the problem has already been called to your attention, but I should like to add my concern.

Sincerely,

The personal touch in the following letter certainly helps its effectiveness. The congressman's wife probably has the same kind of complaint.

Sir:

I feel that Air Pollution Control is one of the most important issues facing us today.

It is more dangerous than such diseases as lung cancer and heart disease because it affects not just many thousands, but millions of people.

My venetian blinds, window sills, floors, etc., have to be swept and washed with soap and water daily. Inhaling this soot *must* be detrimental to our health.

Won't you please see what can be done to eliminate this serious condition? It is vitally important.

Sincerely,

The next letter enclosed a newspaper clipping about the writer's topic. This is an effective way of dramatizing a letter. If the clipping is a small one, paste it to a separate sheet of paper so that it doesn't get lost, and put it behind—not in front of—your letter, so that the representative doesn't get distracted by the clipping before he reads your letter.

My dear Mrs. Jones:

I should like to call your attention to the enclosed article, which appeared in the Centerville *Journal* July 3.

I cannot understand why former Attorney General Biddle insists on pushing the slab design of the Franklin D. Roosevelt Memorial down the throat of the Washington Fine Arts Commission.

Both the Commission and the House seem to feel, as I do, that the slab design is unsatisfactory.

I object to these gigantic "idiot cards" and I object to Mr. Biddle's bullying. I hope that you will support the Fine Arts Commission at the proper time.

Sincerely,

ADAPTING A FORM LETTER

As noted earlier, elected representatives will pay less attention to a form letter than to an original composition. If an organization to which you belong suggests that you send a letter to your congressman, and provides a model, adapt it so that it comes out in your own words. Here, for example, is a letter that was published by the National Restaurant Association as a model for its members. Wisely, NRA offered the letter merely as an aid, so that its members could send their own versions:

Sir (or Madam):

I am writing because a bill presently before your committee contains a provision which would seriously harm my business if enacted.

I know you don't want to do anything to hurt the restaurant business but, believe me, this Tax on Tips bill would do just that.

I run a small place (twenty-five employes) and we all get along fine. My waitresses don't want to tell anybody their tips and they will resent having to do so. If I give them tax receipts instead of paychecks, they are going to quit. I won't be able to convince them that I have to do it.

I run my own place and keep my own books but I've got all I can handle. If I have to do all the government's bookkeeping, I'll have to hire a bookkeeper at least three days a week. My profits are too low to permit this. I'd do it now if I could. My payroll taxes last year were more than my profit. Please don't raise them now.

Please eliminate the Tax on Tips.

Very truly yours,

GUIDELINES FOR ADAPTING FORM LETTERS

Before giving some alternative samples, here are the suggestions that the National Restaurant Association offered its members. They're an excellent guide in adapting all kinds of form letters:

1. Tell your congressman/woman why you are opposed to the measure. Use your own words.

2. Give examples based on your personal experience.

3. Tell him or her what you would do if the legislation were to become law.

4. Don't just oppose. Give your reasons and give another solution if possible. For example, NRA's alternative solution to the problem of giving employes credit for tips toward social security benefits is to treat tips as self-employment income.

ALTERNATIVE LETTERS

My dear Mr. Smith:

The Tax on Tips clause in H.R. 1 will do severe damage to my business, and I hope you will oppose it.

As the owner of a small chain of restaurants in this city, I operate on a profit margin of 3 percent. According to my own calculations— and this has been confirmed by my accountant—the profit margin will drop to 1.5 percent if the Tax on Tips bill becomes law. In short, my already narrow margin of profit will be cut in half.

As you know, this is a profit level at which it is almost impossible to conduct a business. For this reason, I suggest that you eliminate the Tax on Tips clause from the bill, and let stand the present method of treating tips as self-employment income.

Sincerely,

That letter emphasizes the profit-margin problems, but it expresses the same idea as the model letter. The next sample emphasizes the effect the bill would have on employes:

My dear Mrs. Jones:

On behalf of my waiters, I should like to express my opposition to Section 205 of H.R. 1, the Tax on Tips clause.

Smith's Restaurant, of which I'm the owner, has seven people waiting on customers. I have explained to them how the clause will affect their tips. Six of the seven said they were opposed to the measure because they feel it's none of my business how much money they make in tips. And, as one of them said, "I think that the tax is one more government grab for power. Why do they have to pick on the little guy?"

As far as I'm concerned, the tax would be a burden; as far as my employes are concerned, they would resent it. I hope that, as our representative, you'll take our feelings into account when you vote on this measure.

Sincerely,

The final alternative letter emphasizes why the writer thinks a different method of handling the measure would be superior.

My dear Mr. Smith:

Section 205 of H.R. 1, the Tax on Tips bill, is a poor way of achieving a worthy end.

I speak as one who owns a restaurant with seventy-five employes, fifty of whom serve the public.

The weakness of Section 205 is that it will seriously damage the relationships between employers and employes. While I sympathize with the government's need for money, I feel that it shouldn't be done at the expense of good human relations. This is an unsound way to run either a government or a business.

A superior way of collecting this money would be to lay the burden of payment on the employes rather than on the employers. This is the way it is now done in a number of other areas, for example, with court reporters who sell transcripts of trials. They, and not the courts, must report this extra money.

Don't you agree that it's unfair to single us out for special treatment? I hope that you will vote against this measure because it is discriminatory to our type of business.

Sincerely,

SHORTENING THE LONG LETTER

When we're very excited about an issue, we tend to talk about it. When we write letters about an issue that concerns us very much, we tend to do the same thing, and will often write two or three pages to get our point across. In writing to congressmen, this is cutting our own throats. They simply don't have time (and, some would argue, the powers of concentration) to wade through a long letter. Therefore, if you want to get something off your chest, by all means put it in writing—and then trim the letter down to its essentials. You'll get a much better hearing.

To the ABC's of letter writing we discussed in chapter 2, add a knowledge of the issue you're writing about, an individual approach, and a clear statement of what you want your elected representative to do and why. You'll have a letter that can get results.

test your skills

WRITING TO PUBLIC OFFICIALS

Read the following letter as though you were a senator or congressman who had received it from one of your constituents. Then, regardless of whether you personally agree or disagree with the writer's point of view, evaluate the letter in terms of the five questions that follow.

My dear Mr. Jones:
   I believe the Civil Rights bill is unconstitutional.
   The Thirteenth Amendment states that "neither slavery nor involuntary servitude, except as a punishment for crime whereof the party shall have been duly convicted, shall exist within the United States. . . ."
   The Civil Rights bill will make a barber cut a specific person's hair, force a woman to give a massage to a specific person. This, I believe, is certainly a form of involuntary servitude, and, hence, it would be unconstitutional.
   There are many other reasons for opposing the bill: It doesn't define many important terms, such as "discrimination" or "race," and it would subject us to more federal power.
   Because of these reasons, I hope you will vote against the bill.
                                                          Sincerely,

1. Is the letter written effectively?
2. Does the writer support his stand with evidence?
3. Does he give a specific example of how he thinks the proposed bill would violate the individual rights of citizens?
4. Does he reinforce his stand with additional arguments?
5. Does he conclude by telling his representative exactly what he wants from him?

Answers to this quiz appear on page 702.

9

Writing to newspapers, magazines, and TV

You may want to air an opinion, inform your neighbors, or just see your own words in print. You may want a television network to change its programing. Whatever your reasons, this chapter shows you how to write letters that editors will want to publish and broadcasters will listen to.

Every day of the week, you are bombarded by thousands of words and images from the gigantic communications media. Newspapers and magazines try to influence you to believe one thing or another; television and radio programs are largely designed to induce you to buy the product of the company sponsoring the program. In short, you, the reader, the viewer, the listener, are a target.

Must you be a target? Does it do any good to try shooting at the hunters? It does. The mass media welcome letters from the public for a variety of reasons. Sometimes it's even possible to turn the tables and exert a bit of influence on them.

Magazines value letters from readers because letters are one of the few ways in which the editors can tell whether they are doing a good job. Just how important some magazines consider reader mail can be judged from *Time* magazine's issuance of a small book for its own employes who answer reader mail. A few lines from the introduction to the *Time* manual will explain how they handle correspondence:

"Of the hundreds of letters received by the editors every week, *Time* publishes only twenty-five to thirty in the Letters column. These few are chosen for a variety of reasons, but primarily for their interest and readableness. Letters on significant issues, especially those written by qualified authorities, get first consideration. Letters that question . . . *Time*'s handling of the news get particular attention because the editors sometimes like to publish them with a note to explain what *Time* sources were, to clarify misinterpretations, to answer questions, to correct errors. Bright, amusing letters are always welcome, of course, to give the column balance, and to indicate the kind of bright, intelligent readership which *Time* has."

Four ways to get your letter published

You'll increase the chance of getting your letter published if you observe a few rules of good correspondence.

Keep it brief. Magazines have only a limited number of pages to give to letters. The editors of the letters columns look for mail that expresses in a few sentences the meat of the argument. One editor says, "One of our favorite correspondents was the author, Upton Sinclair. He used to write us regularly, sending just two or three handwritten sentences, letting us know exactly what he thought in no uncertain terms. And because he was always brief and clear, we published his letters frequently."

Keep it relevant. This is related to the rule of brevity. If you disagree with an article, say so at the beginning, and tell exactly why in as few words as possible. A letter which wanders all over the lot will stand less chance of being published than one which sticks to the subject. As one editor said, "Some correspondents seem to think they can bully us into publishing their letters by writing at great length. It just isn't so. We don't get bullied, we just get bored."

Be reasonable. A letter which says, "You're all wet," will not receive nearly as much attention as one which says, "You're all wet. Here's why," and then gives the reasons. As one editor said, "You should say what you think in the first sentence, and why in the second sentence."

If possible, use a light touch. Time's statement that "bright, amusing letters are always welcome" is echoed by the editors of other magazines. Editors like to make their letters columns as readable as the rest of the magazine, but they're often hard put to do it because most letters are serious, even heavy-handed. If you can insert an amusing phrase, the editor will jump at it like a fish at bait. It will help to brighten his page and keep other readers interested.

Several other points mentioned by editors as being helpful in letters from correspondents are:

1. Don't write a vague letter of praise in the hope of getting it published. While magazines, like anyone else, enjoy praise, they don't like to publish letters which say, "I wanted to tell you how much I enjoy your magazine. I've read it for years." As one editor said, "When we do put in one of these letters, we're always uncomfortable about it. It sounds too much like a puff—as if one of our own editors wrote it."

2. Get your letter off early. Often, good letters have to be rejected for publication because they've arrived too late for inclusion. For a monthly magazine, try to send your letter out within the first week or two after you get your copy. For a weekly, if you live any great distance from the editorial offices, send your letter airmail.

3. Don't worry too much about the form or the spelling. Editors read everything legible, whether it's typewritten or handwritten in pencil or pen. One editor recalls receiving a letter written on a paper bag. Naturally, a neat letter is more attractive, even to editors.

4. Address your letter properly. Check the letters-to-the-editor column to see if it lists a name and address to which you should direct your correspondence. Otherwise, address your letter directly to the editor, at the magazine's editorial office. Use the editor's name if it's listed.

HOW EDITORS SHORTEN LETTERS

Here is a long letter received by a national magazine:

> When I read _____'s article, "Why I Love America" in the January issue, my eyes brimmed with emotions of pride and shame.
> Pride for my native land, which I too, love dearly.
> But shame, that so many of us "natives" should have to be reminded by an adopted friend of the glories to be enjoyed, of the rights we have, to live, speak, and dream in freedom. He has made me want to shout, "Look Americans! Look about you at the opportunities we so casually acknowledge. Look in wonder, look in love, look in peace."
> To your author, I extend a hand warm with friendship and love, and say "thank you" to him for helping me to take a new view of my own land—My America!

Here is how the editors shortened it for publication:

> I read _____'s article with pride and shame—pride for my native land that I, too, dearly love. But shame—that so many of us "natives"

should have to be reminded by an adopted friend of the rights and glories that we have.

The article made me want to shout, "Look Americans! Look about you in wonder, in love, in peace!"

To your author, I extend a hand in friendship and in gratitude.

Keep it brief and relevant, and add the light touch. The editors smiled when they read this one:

> In your January issue, on page 15, an Iowa dentist is shown putting steel tooth caps on cows. I've lived in that hard grass country, and will admit that it really would be helpful to cap the cow's teeth with something that will stand the wear.
>
> But I was a farmer and stockman for "nigh on to 50 years" and I never saw a cow with front teeth on her upper jaw. Where did your artist find her? I want to go and see her. I know this new age is faster than I was accustomed to, but I'll still bet you don't have upper teeth in front on anybody's cow. How about it?

The editors shortened this letter for publication, giving just the high point of the humor:

> I was a farmer and stockman for nigh on 50 years, and I never saw a cow with front teeth in her upper jaw. Where did your artist find her? I want to go and see that cow for myself!

Writing to newspapers

In general, everything that holds true for letters to magazine editors holds true for letters to newspapers. Usually, brevity is important.

Most newspapers restrict the length of their letters to three or four sentences. A few of the larger papers will give readers more leeway. *The New York Times,* for example, has a maximum rule of eight hundred words, which is more than a full-sized column. A letter of this length, however, is usually printed only if it is by someone who's a known authority in the field about which he's writing.

Most newspapers have certain taboos—subjects which they will not touch in the letters columns. As outlined by one editor, they are:

1. No personal messages, such as "Will that nice boy I met on the beach call me."

2. No poetry.

3. No lost-and-found.

4. No advertising, no matter how subtly disguised.

5. No personal attacks. (This point has to be loosely defined. Public

figures such as the President and members of Congress are usually considered fair game for adverse criticism on public issues.)

Some newspapers try to make their letters columns exceptionally lively. Says the letters editor of one successful daily: "We like mail if it's violently opposed to an editorial stand that we've taken. A letter that begins, 'How stupid can your editors be?' is more exciting, more likely to be published, than one which says, 'May I take the liberty of disagreeing with your position.'"

THERE'S STRENGTH IN NUMBERS

There are times when newspapers can serve as a powerful weapon for alerting the public to injustice. Let's take an example of an urban renewal plan which threatens to wipe out a section of a community. The newspaper may have covered the stories in its news columns. It may even have sent out feature writers to tell in depth how the people affected feel about it. But how much more powerful will the voice of the people be if it makes itself heard through the letters column!

Here's what one editor said about the strength-in-numbers policy: "If we receive a few scattered letters on a subject, we'll be less likely to publish them than if we receive four or five or a dozen or more. If we were to receive a lot of letters from the residents of an area that was about to be demolished, we'd be likely to print a lot of them, because we'd feel that this is something of widespread interest. On the other hand, if we receive only a couple of letters, we may or may not publish them. It's a case of the squeaking wheel getting the grease."

Therefore, if you feel strongly about an issue, particularly a local issue which will affect you and your neighbors, urge your friends to write their own mail on the subject.

Don't send it all in on the same day, for it will seem too much like a rehearsed campaign, and it will lose some of its effectiveness. But a dozen or two dozen letters spread out over a week or two can be amazingly effective.

Six keys to the "letters" column

John Illo is a young, earnest college instructor, an independent thinker. His name cropped up during a search by the author for samples of good letters to the editor. Over a period of several months, his name was signed to a number of letters in *The New York Times*. It seemed evident that anyone with such a high batting average might have some useful suggestions about how to get letters published.

He did, indeed. When contacted, he said that letter writing to publications was one of his avocations. And he offered a number of suggestions which are printed here, because they are valid whether you're planning to correspond with magazines or with newspapers.

1. Choose a periodical whose views are not radically different from yours. Disagreement is published in letters columns, but disagreement within limits.

2. If the letter is topical, write promptly. A stale letter is like stale news, and editors have little interest in either. Letters to a daily paper should be sent within a day of the story or column that provoked it.

3. The beginning of your letter should refer succinctly to the story or topic that occasioned it: "Mr. Abe believes that fluoridation of public water supplies is a violation of free, individual choice (Newark *Courier-Telegraph*, May 15, 1963)."

4. All letters should be sober and rational for their best effect. The letter of commendation should not gush, the letter of protest should not rage, the letter of complaint should not whine.

5. If you can bring some specialized knowledge to your letter, it will be more authoritative, and hence, more likely to be published. One way to acquire this knowledge is to set up a file of subjects in which you're interested, and to put in it items that will help you in composing your letters.

6. After writing your letter, let it cool overnight. And then ask yourself: Will I want to see this over my name in print next week?

Sample letters to the newspapers

COMPLAINT ABOUT A MUNICIPAL FACILITY: Note that this first letter has a lively beginning; it registers a complaint, gives a very factual documentation, then calls for action.

Sir:
The condition of the subway in summer is a disgrace to this city.
On July 15, at 5:00 P.M., the weather on the street was pleasant, even cool. But when I entered the subway, a thermometer I had with me registered 99 degrees.

HOW TO HIT THE EDITOR HARDEST

OVER A GOOD MANY YEARS as editor of a farm magazine, I have received all kinds of letters. Some have been commendatory, more haven't, and that's to be expected. Those who disagree with the editor's views, or with something else appearing in the magazine, are more likely to write and say so. They have as much right to their opinion, and to express it, as the editors have. And that's fine. It's great that we live in a country where it's that way.

But if you do write a letter of disagreement, I'll tip you off as to how you can hit the editor hardest:

1. Write in a reasonable "tone of voice," even if you're boiling mad. If you're writing just to tell off the so-and-so, go ahead if it makes you feel better. The letters that have some thought to express, and that do it in a calm, unshrill way, are the ones that penetrate the editor's hide and really "get to" him. A sincere letter like this can have more impact on us than you might ever guess—whether or not it winds up in print in the Letters column.

2. Disagree all you want with a statement, an idea, or a point of view, but don't attack the editor's motives. You only get his defenses up when you attack his motives; and you certainly won't influence him that way.

3. Make the letter reasonably brief. The three-page, single-spaced kind is just too much to expect anyone even to look at in the hectic days common to any lively editorial office. It will get more attention if when the editor picks it up he sees it is of moderate length. Besides, in such length you'll probably state your views more effectively anyhow.

Editors like mail from readers. The more, the better. That's one of their ways of keeping touch with what their constituency thinks. Besides, there are some mighty good ideas in that mail, some of the best that editors come across anywhere. There's stimulus there, too, and we need it daily.

So please write, even oftener—we love it. All I'm trying to do here is help you "register" when your letter arrives, and I assume that's what you want. More power to you.

—*Carroll Streeter, Farm Journal*

I think that in this age of progress, it ought to be possible to find a way to ventilate this subway at a cost within the city's budget.

Sincerely,

COMPLAINT ABOUT GOVERNMENT POLICY: The writer of the next letter was obviously indignant, even outraged. And he bases his outrage not on a purely personal emotion, but on a statement issued by a civic organization. This lends his letter greater weight and impact:

> Your newspaper reports that the St. Louis Citizens Committee for Nuclear Information says that three thousand children in Utah and Nevada have received excessive radiation doses and that about a dozen will have thyroid cancer.
>
> The federal government explodes the bombs. The federal government establishes radiation controls. But the people of the United States, who have paid taxes for the bombs and controls, do not protest.
>
> It is a matter of common sense: You can't explode nuclear bombs without people feeling some effects at least a few hundred miles away. And what about us who live in other parts of the country. Do we protest? No. What's the use? Parental common sense has little weight in the face of scientists, and the Atomic Energy Commission has reassured us that all is well.
>
> Now nuclear tests in the air are banned, but, for many children, it is too late. The tragedy is that people are helpless before their governments, and when they are not helpless, they are defrauded.

Writing to television and radio stations

The television industry spends millions upon millions of dollars to entertain you, to inform you—and to sell you. It is a rich giant and, perhaps because of its riches, sometimes a sensitive giant. It is a giant that is loath to offend, eager to please.

For this reason, you, the viewer, can talk crossly to the giant, and there is a good chance that he will listen. He may not hear the actual words you speak, but he will get the tone of your voice, and he may be moved.

Your letters to the networks *are* read, and they *are* heeded. Your letters have saved a few programs from going off the air; your lack of letters have sent others into oblivion.

In order to understand how to get the most mileage from your letters, you should understand a bit about how networks handle their mail.

All mail comes into the mail room, where it's sorted according to addressee. If it's addressed to an individual, it goes directly to him.

(This can be an important point to remember for certain types of letters, which will be discussed further on.) If it's addressed to the network, or to a specific program, it will, in most cases, go to an office generally known as Audience Information.

Audience Information usually consists of a tactful, experienced person who's been with the network for several years, and knows her way around well enough to answer most letters intelligently and to route the others to the departments that can handle them effectively.

IT DOES PAY TO WRITE

Unless you're a very important person, it is unlikely that letters which you address to a network executive about a program or a commercial will ever reach him or her. A secretary in all probability will send them off to Audience Information to be answered.

However, while the television executive may never see your letter, this doesn't mean that he may not be influenced by it. The networks have set up machinery for getting viewers' opinion through to the top brass. The machinery consists of periodic reports from Audience Information on the nature and number of letters commenting on different aspects of programing.

For example, whenever ABC receives five or more letters on a given subject in a month, that information goes into a report sent to top executives, with excerpts from most of the letters. NBC executives receive a statistical report. It makes no mention of letters about specific programs. Instead, it breaks letters down into the subjects about which they're written.

Thus, under Commercials, the report lists the following categories: Beer and Wine; Excessive Length and Frequency; Offensive-Bad Taste;

Television's Garry Moore devised a system for coping with vicious and insulting poison-pen letters. He mailed the offending missive right back to the sender with this note of his own: "The enclosed letter arrived on my desk a few days ago. I am sending it to you in the belief that as a responsible citizen you should know that some idiot is sending out letters over your signature. Cordially. . . ."

—*Bennett Cerf in This Week Magazine*

Sound Levels; Tobacco. It is interesting to note that in one summer month, out of a total of twenty-seven comments on radio and television commercials, eighteen—two out of three—fell in the "Excessive Length and Frequency" and "Offensive-Bad Taste" categories.

Under Programs, the categories range from "Children's Viewing Hours" and "Color" to "Taste" and "Technical." One month not long ago, 70 percent of the mail was devoted to just four subjects: "Scheduling and Discontinuance of Certain Series," "Practices," "Taste," and "Personalities." By far the largest grouping was "Scheduling and Discontinuance."

Now, since these statistical breakdowns make no mention of which programs the viewer is commenting on, a television executive would have to be a seer in order to know how the viewers are reacting to specific programs. Nevertheless, when there is a great volume of mail on a given subject, the Audience Information department will sometimes make a special call or send out a memo to alert the executives to it. For this reason, it does pay to write.

CATEGORIES OF NETWORK MAIL

Mail to the networks generally falls into one of five broad categories. Here is a list of them, along with suggestions on how you, the viewer, can make your letters in these groups most effective.

PROGRAMS This is the largest class, consisting of complaints and compliments about specific programs. When writing a complaint letter, be as specific as possible, listing the name of the program, when you saw it, on what station it appeared, and the nature of your complaint.

TICKETS FOR PROGRAMS If you'd like tickets for a specific network show, write to the Audience Information Bureau at network headquarters as far in advance as possible. If you don't particularly care which show you see, but you do want to see some programs on certain days, tell them so. If you do have program preferences, list them in order of preference. Also, don't forget to say how many tickets you want.

PHOTO REQUESTS With few exceptions, the networks will not send out photographs of performers. However, there is a simple solution to this problem. Always send your photo requests to the person whose picture you want, in care of the program on which he appears. Send the letter to your lócal station or the national network. There letters will be passed on to the people responsible for getting out the pictures.

MUSIC Requests for the names of theme songs or other musical material can be sent directly to the network's Audience Information Bureau. They'll dig up the information and send it to you.

EDUCATION The networks receive many requests from teachers and students for various kinds of information about television and radio, and will generally send out simply a few brochures or a reference bibliography. NBC, incidentally, is generally reputed to have the best selection of brochures on the television industry and television as a career.

MISCELLANEOUS The American public seems to feel that the networks are a reliable source of general information, and the networks have responded by doing their best to oblige. They are constantly receiving —and answering—such queries as: "Where can my daughter learn reweaving?" and "How do you get the effect of fog on a theater stage?"

Here, incidentally, is a moneysaving tip. There's no need to enclose stamps or a self-addressed envelope when you expect an answer. The networks will pay the postage on their own mail, even when they're doing you a favor.

Sample letters to television stations

EDUCATIONAL REQUESTS Here are two letters asking for program material for educational and research purposes:

Gentlemen:

We are conducting a Reading Workshop for selected high school teachers from the state of Alabama and are collecting materials for distribution to the group. The number of participants is thirty.

Will you kindly send us sample copies of available materials on reading or related literature where possible.

Yours truly,

Gentlemen:

I would be greatly interested in reading the script to a program televised yesterday evening (over your station in San Francisco) which reported on a convention in Chicago of pilots who had participated in the raids on Hiroshima and Nagasaki in August 1945.

I missed seeing this program myself, but I feel it would be most useful to me, as I am engaged in research that bears on problems of the psychology of nuclear armament.

I would be glad to reimburse you for the expenses that this request might entail.

Sincerely,

FOUR WAYS TO PRESSURE THE NETWORKS

WHILE NETWORK EXECUTIVES are admittedly sheltered from viewer mail, they do feel the effect of a volume of mail on any given subject. The following suggestions will help increase the weight of your complaints or compliments on specific programs or commercials and make it more likely that the network will respond.

1. State your credentials. If you hold any executive title in your company, or in your town or city government, or even in a reasonably well-known organization, get it into the letter. If you are a member of an organization, church, synagogue, club, etc., mention this. A routine letter of complaint signed by a member of a Kiwanis chapter or church group will probably receive more attention than a good letter signed by someone they may consider a "nobody."

2. When a show is sponsored by only one or two companies, send a copy of your letter to the sponsor. Individual sponsors have little control over what goes into a program supported by several companies; but if they are the sole or the sharing sponsor, they are much more sensitive to viewers' comments.

3. When writing a letter of complaint or comment to a network show, send a carbon to the local station. They usually like to know what the local viewers are thinking, and if they get enough comment on one side of a question, they'll add their pressure to yours.

4. Make sure that you know what you're talking about. It is not unusual for the networks to receive letters complaining about shows that have appeared on other networks.

One final point is worth mentioning. Networks and stations, for all their faults, are not utterly spineless. They do have some sense of responsibility to the public, and when they are bold enough to step into an area of controversy, they will usually not be intimidated by threats of boycotts, nor will they be influenced by vituperative letters. If you see a television show which you think is in bad taste, or unfair, or poor for whatever reason, by all means let the people responsible know about it. But remember that your letter will have greater weight if it is rational and thoughtful, not just angry.

Note: Be certain to include your return address when you expect a reply to your letter.

Note: The request for scripts of programs is a fairly common one. In some cases the networks can supply them; in some cases, they cannot. The author of the letter above, not knowing the name of the program, wisely wrote the network. If, however, you know the name of the program, write to it directly, in care of the network.

MUSIC REQUEST Broadcasters frequently receive letters like this, asking about music played on television shows:

Gentlemen:

I would appreciate some information concerning your television program "The Match Game."

I would like to know the name of the theme song, and where I may obtain the music in sheet form or on record.

Sincerely yours,

CONGRATULATORY LETTER Most welcome of all are letters that show favorable public reaction to a program or a performer:

Dear Sirs:

I congratulate you on the excellent presentation by Frank McGee on the Supreme Court decision last Monday night.

Not only was the narration well written, but the presentation was completely objective, allowing the viewer to make his own decision for or against the Supreme Court's decision.

I felt that the closing quote by the United States senator summed up the situation ideally.

Congratulations again on this type of public service programing by your Public Affairs department.

Sincerely,

Letters like this help to keep such shows on the air.

CRITICAL LETTERS This was written to the producer of a well-known children's show by an irate mother:

Dear Mr. _____:

Your program is the sole television program permitted in this house for our three-and-one-half-year-old daughter. As you must know, your word is almost law. Just your having said something makes it so.

On occasion, I sit with Elizabeth and we enjoy the hour together. I have always objected to several of the commercials on the show. Candy of any sort, and chewing gum of all kinds should, I think, be mentioned at the discretion of parents or physicians or both, not dangled enticingly from the TV screen.

I know you have to have a sponsor, but it seems to me that you ought not to need to stoop to unhealthy foods, and certainly unnecessary ones. (I am not a food nut, incidentally, but I feel that sweets should not be emphasized unduly.)

Sincerely,

The producer of the show sent an answer explaining that he does not have control over commercials as long as they are in good taste and not truly harmful.

Here's a letter protesting poor programing practices, sent to the owner of a local television station:

Dear Sir:

May I protest the avalanche of family-comedy programs you have been showing in the evenings during the past two months.

I counted twenty-three last week alone.

Your station has a responsibility to serve all members of the community, and certainly there are not many who can digest this tiring repetition night after night.

As the comptroller of the XYZ Company, I am in frequent contact with leading Centerville businessmen. In private conversations, many of them have expressed feelings similar to mine.

We look to you for more diverse programing. If it is not forthcoming, some of us will simply turn to other stations. Others will protest to the Federal Communications Commission when your license is due for renewal.

Will you please give us fare that is worthy of our intelligence?

Sincerely,

And here's one protesting a program that the writer felt showed poor taste. It was sent to a network president.

Sir:

On February 25, your local affiliate, in Centerville, Mass., broadcast the network program "Burlesque Again."

As a responsible parent and as the chairman of the Centerville Youth Group, I protest the shoddiness of this show. The leers, the double entendres, the overstuffed and underdressed girls, and the questionable comedians, all left a very bad taste in my mouth.

I suspect it is not a show of which you, personally, are proud. And while I cannot expect you to censor every program, I can hope that you will encourage your staff to be a little more intelligent, a little less sleazy. We look to you for entertainment and information; you gave us cheapness.

Please do whatever you can to see that this sort of program is not repeated in the future.

Sincerely,

And finally, here's a plea to save a program. Chances are slim, but enough like it might cause a network to review its decision:

Dear Sir:

My family and a multitude of my friends have enjoyed Lily Smith's program, "It's Your World," for many years.

And so, it came as a great shock when we read that her show will end in two more weeks.

Mrs. Smith is one of the most intelligent and perceptive interviewers that have ever appeared on television in this area. Her frequent involvement in controversy has made her that much more interesting.

Television offers my friends and myself little enough that is worth watching. Mrs. Smith is always an exception.

I write not only for myself, but also for many of my acquaintances. Please keep her with you—and with us.

Sincerely,

test your skills

WRITING TO NEWSPAPERS, MAGAZINES, AND TV

1. From the salutations below, select the one you think best for a letter to the editor, and tell why:
a. Dear Sir:
b. To The Editor:
c. Dear Mr. Streeter:
d. Dear Erring Friend:

2. Why is it better to write in a reasonable "tone of voice" than to write a rip-snorting angry letter?

3. Is it a good idea to attack the editor's motives? Why or why not?

4. Below are two lead-in paragraphs to letters to the editor. Which do you prefer, and why?
a. Dear Sir:
   As one of your loyal readers, I follow every issue and for a long time now I have been vitally interested in the debate on the farm problem. I have some interesting ideas that I would like to present for your considered opinion. . . .
b. Dear Sir:
   It seems to me that a reasonable solution to the farm problem would be to change the federal parity formula along the lines suggested by the Ad Hoc Committee referred to in your issue of June 6.

Answers to this quiz appear on page 702.

10

Applying to schools
and colleges

Getting into school or college can be a difficult proposition
these days, but you can smooth the way for your child or
yourself with clear, well-organized letters of inquiry and application. Here, in detail, are the special considerations and
procedures you need to know.

If you're the parent of a child whom you hope to send to a
private school or to college, you'll probably have to write quite a few
letters and fill out a seemingly inexhaustible number of applications.
Good letters can help your youngsters gain admission.

If you plan on sending your youngster to a private school, you are in
one of two situations: either you know which school you want to send
him to, or you don't.

If you're not sure which one would best suit his needs, hie yourself to
the public library and pick up a copy of either *Private Independent
Schools*, published by Bunting & Lyon, Inc., Wallingford, Connecticut,
or *The Handbook of Private Schools*, published by Porter Sargent, Boston, Massachusetts. These thick manuals list most of the boarding
schools, day schools, and military schools in the country. They also tell
a bit of the history and describe the buildings and equipment, the
faculty and staff, the size of the student body, admission requirements,
costs, and other pertinent information.

Having selected a number of schools you'd like to know more about,
your next step will be to write them for catalogs. The catalogs will give
you the same information you found in the manuals, but in greater detail. Keep this inquiry letter brief; there's no need to go into detail about

128

your child at this point, since the letter will, in all probability, be thrown out as soon as the catalog is sent. You can send the letter to the school, or to the headmaster if you prefer.

A simple, one-sentence letter like this should do the trick:

Gentlemen:
Please send me the current catalog for your school.

Sincerely,

After you've gone over the catalogs and selected schools to which you'd like to apply, it's time to send a more detailed letter.

Three points to consider before you write

■*Timing:* Write for your application as much as a year in advance. Many schools will start interviewing applicants around January or February of the year before they enter. Therefore, if you write for an application form in August or September and return it by October or November, you'll be adequately protected.

■*Child's Age:* Include the age of the child if he's quite young. Most private schools with a first grade have a minimal age at which they'll accept a beginning youngster.

■*Scholarships:* If you're planning on asking for scholarship help, mention it in the letter so that the school can send you a scholarship application form. Failure to do this may delay matters later.

SAMPLE REQUESTS FOR APPLICATION FORMS

Here are several letters that you might adapt.

Dear Sirs:
My daughter will graduate from the eighth grade at Centerville Public High School this spring, and is interested in attending a private, coeducational high school in the city.

We would appreciate it if you would send us an application form. My daughter would like to enter in the fall of 1985.

We should also like to visit the school and see its facilities. Will you tell us the procedure for making an appointment?

Sincerely,

Dear Sir:
We would like to apply, on behalf of our son, Richard, for the seventh grade for September 1985. Richard is now in the sixth grade at Centerville School.

129

Please send us the proper application forms and any other relevant information for parents of prospective candidates for admission.

Very truly yours,

Dear Sir:

We are applying to your school because of its outstanding reputation. We are a family of very limited means. However, we feel that we have an unusual child who would be an asset to any school. We therefore would also like to request scholarship information, with a view to major assistance.

Yours truly,

The headmaster who provided the last letter commented that "it makes a favorable impression because it's simple and straightforward."

If your youngster is old enough, you might encourage him to write for the application forms himself. This is not an unusual procedure, and it's a good way to get him involved in his own future. Fundamentally, the child need do no more than ask for the application form. But he may want to add a few flourishes. Don't discourage him; they won't hurt his chances. Here are letters that youngsters have sent to schools:

Gentlemen:

I should like to obtain application forms for your school.

I am presently in the eighth grade at the Centerville School. Will you please send me your entrance requirements and examination dates.

Very truly yours,

Dear Sirs:

I am interested in attending the Centerville Private School next year.

I am a ninth-grade student in the Gifted Student Program at Midville School, Midville, Kansas.

Last year, I was elected to the school's honor society. This year, I'm editor of the school yearbook.

I would like to go to Centerville because it emphasizes learning and minimizes competition. I also feel that Centerville will provide me with greater opportunities to participate in extracurricular activities such as dramatics and writing.

Please send me an application, and information about your scholarship program, since I would need financial aid.

I would also appreciate an appointment for an interview. I can visit your office any Saturday.

Respectfully yours,

The application form which the school sends you may cover only one sheet of paper, or it may go on for three or four. Different schools will ask different questions, and their decision about accepting your child will depend on factors peculiar to that school. The most sensible course to follow in filling out the forms is to be honest. One headmaster told me, "Some parents lie about their child having had psychiatric help. There's not much point in trying to conceal it because sooner or later we find out about it, and it doesn't make the parents look very good."

Applications to colleges

Basically, correspondence with college is similar to that with private schools. But a few suggestions are in order about avoiding unnecessary words. Here are some thoughts from college admissions executives:

1. When requesting an application, keep the letter short. One official put it this way: "Too many parents write long letters telling us about their kids, and at the end, they ask for the application. It doesn't do any good to tell us how good your child is—we assume you're biased and we don't read it; we simply don't have the time or the interest."

2. Limit yourself to asking one or two major questions, if you have any. "Many people," said one admissions executive, "ask us a tremendous number of detailed questions about the school. Usually, this is information which they can get from our catalog, and so we frequently don't even bother to answer the questions. We simply send them the catalog."

3. Make sure that you're writing to the right school. Arnold Goren, director of admissions of New York University, gave this example: "We'll sometimes get applications intended for the State University of New York. This, of course, just wastes everyone's time."

4. Remember that a college is an educational institution, not a vocational guidance center. Youngsters will sometimes write to a college saying, "I think I may want to be a doctor. Tell me what a doctor's life is like." Schools are rarely equipped to handle this type of inquiry. If your child wants information about a career, have him discuss it with the high school's guidance counselor, or check the library for books on the vocation he is interested in.

5. In requesting an application, don't try to impress the school with your importance or your important contacts. Generally, it carries little weight. Said one admissions officer: "We have to be like Caesar's wife—

131

MOTHER GOES TO COLLEGE

IF YOU ARE a woman and are planning to resume your education and seek a career after marriage and children, you will need to write letters of application to schools and colleges. One of the following examples covering several typical situations may be used as a guide. When writing to request an appointment, always address a specific person by name. Faculty and staff members are listed in the college catalog which you should obtain beforehand.

Here's a simple request to your former college, asking for a transcript of your record. Don't forget to include your maiden name.

Mr. James Brown, Registrar
College of the Plains
Farview, Nebraska

Dear Sir:
 Please send me a transcript of my work at the College of the Plains. I was a member of the class of 1960, and was a student from 1956 to 1960, registered under my maiden name, Anne Hudson.
 Enclosed is my check for $2.00.

Thank you,

The letters that follow are written to the college or university you hope to enter. They prepare the college officials for your call and give information about your previous academic background and the course of study you hope to follow.

Mr. Able Cooper
Director of Admissions
Venerable College
Riverton, Massachusetts

Dear Mr. Cooper:
 Fifteen years ago, I left the University of Centralia in my junior year to marry. I would like to find out if it is possible for me to complete my degree at Venerable College. Enclosed is a transcript of my previous college work.
 My major at Centralia was English. However, my interests have changed somewhat, and I think I would like to work in the area of psychology and counseling.
 I will call your office in a few days for an appointment.

Thank you,

132

The first of the following letters gives pertinent personal details; the second mentions career experience related to your studies:

Mrs. Ralph Tomes
Director, Center for Continuing Education
Fuller College
Urbana, New Jersey

Dear Mrs. Tomes:

I am interested in returning to school to prepare myself for a career in teaching, probably at the secondary level, and would like an opportunity to talk with you about certification requirements and the programs open to me at Fuller College.

As my three children (aged four to twelve) still require considerable attention, I am not free at present to attend school on a full-time basis. However, I would like to begin as soon as possible if a part-time program can be arranged.

I am a graduate of Brookcroft, class of 1970, where I majored in French and minored in mathematics. My choice of teaching field would probably be one of these two subjects.

Enclosed is a résumé of my background and experience. I will call your office in a few days for an appointment.

Thank you,

Dr. Hugo Arbitrage, Chairman
Department of Economics
Allstate University
Big Valley, California

Dear Dr. Arbitrage:

I am interested in graduate study in economics, with the eventual goal of teaching at the college level, and would like to talk with you about the requirements of your department.

After my graduation from Venerable, in 1972, I worked for several years before my marriage as a stock analyst for the firm of Long and Short. During that time I completed three graduate courses at Open University, but did not finish my master's degree. A résumé of my background and experience is enclosed.

I could probably manage almost a full schedule if necessary. However, I would prefer to begin on a more limited basis if this could be arranged.

I will call your office in a few days for an appointment.

Sincerely,

above suspicion. We just can't afford to show favoritism to one student because his family may know somebody."

THE APPLICATION

Colleges prefer that the student himself, rather than the parent, fill out the application. An admissions officer told me, "The youngster is going to be on his own in school, and we want to get as good an idea as possible of what he's going to be like. Until he arrives on campus, his application form will represent him, and so he ought to make as good an impression with his application as he would if he were coming for an interview."

Judging from the criticisms of many admissions officers, prospective students aren't too careful about this. Admittedly, when a youngster's grades are high, it's not going to count very strongly against him when his application form looks as if it were used to wipe a windshield. On the other hand, if he's an average student it may have an effect on the admission department's overall evaluation of him; the prudent student will try to have everything possible working for him, not against him.

STEP-BY-STEP PROCEDURE

Keeping these points in mind, you should now pay very close attention to the following paragraphs. They are adapted from instructions prepared by New York City's excellent private institution, Columbia Grammar School. The suggestions were drawn up under the direction of Headmaster James W. Stern for the guidance of Columbia's students. Because they constitute an extremely knowledgeable and sensible approach to the process of college application, and because it is broadly applicable to students in both public and private schools, much of it is reprinted verbatim.

FILING INFORMATION Set aside a drawer at home specifically for college information, applications, etc. Keep all materials in folders. Set up a system so that you can easily find what you are looking for. Instruct well-meaning parents, maids, brothers, sisters, etc., not to "clean out" the drawer or throw away any mail from the colleges.

WRITING FOR APPLICATIONS AND CATALOGS Once you have determined the list of colleges to which you will apply, write immediately to each for its catalog and for its "Application for Admission." You may type or write the letter.

Use your own phrasing, but cover all of the following points:
- High school.
- When you plan to enter college.
- Request for Application for Admission.
- Request for catalog.
- Your name and home address.
- Address the letter to Director of Admissions or Admissions Office.
- Keep the letter short and direct.

CHECKING THE APPLICATION

As soon as you receive catalogs and applications for admission, read each catalog carefully, paying particular attention to requirements for admission and admission tests required.

Before you write one single word on the application for admission, read it over carefully to familiarize yourself with what is requested. Check carefully for:

1. Deposit required, if any, or application fee required.

2. Can you type the application or are you requested to use your own handwriting? If not specifically stated, you may do as you wish.

3. Is a photograph required? How many? Always write your name on the back of the picture in case it is detached.

4. If essay-type questions are asked (autobiographies, compositions, why you have selected that particular college, etc.), write your answers first on scratch paper. Make all corrections before you transfer the final draft to the application. Save your original draft; you may want to read it over before you go for a college interview and you may be able to use all or part of it for another application.

5. Since all College Board test scores will be reported to the colleges in your senior year—no matter when you took the tests—don't hesitate to discuss them at any interview.

6. Your nationality or citizenship.

7. When asked to list secondary schools you have attended, this refers only to high school years unless otherwise stated.

Don't hesitate to consult with your school's college guidance counselor if you're not clear about an application question.

135

After completing each application, jot down on a separate sheet of paper the important information you have supplied. File this or photo-copy the application; you may be able to use it on another application, or you may want to go over it before an interview.

It is your own responsibility to handle the applications for admission. No one at school will keep after you to finish them or get them mailed. If you are mature enough to go to college, then you are mature enough to handle this responsibility.

THE SCHOOL RECORD FORM

Each college will require the school to complete certain forms concerning your application for admission. These forms, usually called "The Secondary School Transcript" or "Record" are sent to the school in one of several ways.

The college may send it to you when it sends you the application form. If it is separate from the application, look it over to see whether you, personally, have to answer any questions on it. Then turn it over immediately to your school. Don't hold it until you've completed the application form.

The college may send it to you attached to the application form, and instruct you not to detach it. This means you must complete your part first, and then turn the *entire* application over to the school. In this case, the application will not be returned to you. Your school will mail it to the college.

The college will send the school record form directly to the school when the college has received your application. In this case, you do not have to turn in anything to the school.

RECOMMENDATION FORMS

Certain colleges will send you forms to be filled in by teachers who have taught you or know you well. It is your responsibility to select the teacher or teachers whom you want to recommend you.

When a graduate student suddenly applied for a scholarship at his university, he was asked why he needed the assistance. In a letter to the dean he explained, "My wife and I are now separated, and this leaves me as my sole means of support." — *Wall Street Journal*

136

Before giving the teacher the recommendation form, ask him if he will be willing to recommend you. If he is, hand him the form and a properly addressed envelope with a stamp on it. When he has filled out the recommendation, he will mail it directly to the college.

If you are asked to list teachers who will recommend you on the application, be sure to ask their permission before putting down their names. The college admissions office will write them.

COLLEGE ADMISSIONS TESTS

It is your responsibility to take the proper college admission tests at the proper time for each college to which you are applying. What the tests are, and when they are required, can be found in each college's catalog, or in an "Information to Candidates for Admission" guide which some colleges send along with the application, or in both.

All information on the College Board Examinations appears in three publications of the Board: the "Bulletin of Information," "A Description of the College Board Scholastic Aptitude Test," and "A Description of the College Board Achievement Tests." The principal of your school, or the school's college adviser, should be able to supply you with these.

It is also your responsibility to complete the registration form required for each College Board Examination testing program. You can probably obtain these from your principal or college adviser.

The registration form must reach the College Board by a certain date. The deadline for each testing date is listed in the "Bulletin of Information" which you have received.

It is wise to make up a "college calendar" on which you note all deadlines, including those for applications, interviews, registration, dates of College Entrance Examination Board exams, etc.

Certain colleges require the American College Testing Program (ACT) examination. Check the college catalog. If you must take this examination, see your principal or college adviser for a registration form and information concerning the tests.

COLLEGE SCHOLARSHIP

If you must receive financial assistance from a college in order to attend, it's a good idea to discuss this with your principal or college adviser. He will probably be able to offer good, specific suggestions and tell you about special or regional scholarships that are available.

Most colleges are members of the College Scholarship Service (CSS).

137

This is a central clearinghouse for scholarship information and does away with having to file a separate financial statement for most colleges to which you are applying.

The CSS form must be filled out by the parents, not the applicant. The school probably has a supply of these forms, or you can obtain them by writing directly to: College Scholarship Service, Post Office Box 176, Princeton, N.J. 08540. Since the forms change each year, be sure to ask for the form valid for the academic year in which the student is entering his first year of college.

Parents should retain a work copy for their own files in case information supplied to the CSS is needed for other forms during the applicant's senior year.

COLLEGE INTERVIEWS

Consult each college catalog to determine if a personal interview at the college is required, suggested, or not required. Many colleges send representatives to various cities around the country to interview applicants who cannot afford a trip to the campus.

A good procedure to follow is: visit and arrange for an interview at as many of the colleges to which you apply as you possibly can. For details on the interview, see pages 460–461.

FIRST-CHOICE COLLEGE

As soon as you and your parents have come to a final decision about which college is your first choice, tell your principal or college adviser. This information will be noted on your school transcript and sent to your first-choice college.

You should also write to your first-choice college informing them of your desire to attend.

Never tell a college—on the application or in an interview—that it is your first choice if it is not. *Remember: it is not necessary to select a college as your first choice.* Most applicants do *not* indicate a first choice, and it does not in any way affect their chance for admission. They do not make up their minds which college to attend until they hear from all to which they have applied. On the other hand, once you have told the college and your school about your first choice, you must attend that college if you're accepted.

Approximately 165 colleges agree to "The Candidates' Reply Agreement Date" which is about May 1 each year. Applicants who receive notice of acceptance by these institutions need not reply with their decision to attend or to accept financial aid until the agreement date. This enables candidates to consider all available opportunities. Check each catalog to see if that college is a member of the agreement-date group, and consider this in your planning.

COLLEGE ACCEPTANCES

Let us assume you are applying to four colleges—A, B, C, and D—and you prefer A and B to C and D.

If you are accepted to B before you hear from any of the others, then write to C and D and thank them for their consideration of your application; inform them that you are withdrawing your application because you have made other plans for your education.

Do not wait to do this just to collect college acceptances: you may be keeping another applicant from being accepted. (See page 142 for an example of a withdrawal letter.) If you still prefer A over B, then hold B's acceptance until you hear from A. If A accepts you, then write to B saying that you are flattered to have been accepted, but have made other plans.

If you hear favorably from D first, then hold the acceptance only until you hear from another institution on your preference list. Write a withdrawal letter as soon as you hear from a more preferred college. If you do not hear from another college, then you can still say Yes to D.

Remember, *all acceptances are conditional,* based on your completing the senior year with grades comparable to those submitted for three or three and one-half years of high school work. Many seniors feel that the second semester is the time to let down their efforts. This is not true; students have had acceptances turned into rejections because their final grades for the senior year took a noticeable drop.

CRITERIA FOR COLLEGE ADMISSION

Most colleges use the following criteria, in approximately this order of importance, to select their candidates:

1. secondary school record
2. school's recommendations
3. College Board scores
4. character and personality
5. extracurricular participation

SHARPEN YOUR STYLE

Keep your letter opening crisp, positive, and precise.

BAD: I'm thinking about entering your college next year, and I wonder what information you could send me.

GOOD: I plan to apply for admission to Ivy College in the fall of 1986. Please send me a catalog, application form, and information about your entrance requirements.

Sample letters to colleges

REQUEST FOR A CATALOG AND APPLICATION FORM

2424 Merit Road
Centerville, Calif.

Dear Sir:

Please send me a catalog and an application for admission.

I am now a junior at Centerville High School, and plan on entering college in the 1986–87 academic year.

Sincerely,
William C. Smith

REQUEST FOR AN APPOINTMENT FOR AN INTERVIEW

Dear Sir:

I should like to make an appointment with your office for an interview concerning admission to Centerville College.

I am a junior at Centerville High School, and plan to enter college in the fall of 1986.

Any time on Friday, November 15, or Monday, November 18, would be convenient for me to visit you.

Sincerely,

The foregoing letter is perfectly adequate, and will do the job nicely. You may, however, want someone to guide you around the school. In this case, you may write:

Dear Sir:

On December 14 through 17, I shall be visiting Centerville, and would like to become better acquainted with your college.

I would be grateful if you could arrange for me to have an interview concerning my admission. Any time from the 14th through the 17th will be satisfactory. I should also appreciate it if you can have someone guide my parents and me on a tour of the college. Again, any time during that period will be satisfactory.

Sincerely,

LETTER TO A STUDENT GUIDE When writing to a student for help on a tour of his college, you should include:

1. When you'd like to have him guide you.

2. Whether you'd like to visit any particular part of the campus.

3. A reference as to how long it might take, so that neither of you will feel obligated to spend more time than he desires on the tour.

Dear Joe:

I'm planning to visit Centerville on Saturday, October 14, and hope to spend some time touring the college. As you know, I'm graduating from Midville High this coming June, and Centerville is one of the colleges I'm applying to.

Can you spare an hour or two during the day to act as my guide? I'd be especially interested in seeing the laboratories, because I hope eventually to work in biology.

If you can act as my shepherd, please let me know what time I should meet you, and about how long you think we should spend together.

Sincerely,

THANK-YOU LETTER FOLLOWING AN INTERVIEW

Dear Mr. Smith:

Thank you for spending time with me last Friday when I visited Centerville University.

I enjoyed our discussion, and found it most useful for getting a clearer idea of what Centerville expects from its students and of the many advantages it has to offer them.

I hope that we will have a chance to meet each other again.

Sincerely,

APPOINTMENT REQUEST FOR YOURSELF AND A FRIEND

Dear Mr. Johnson:

On January 13, a classmate of mine, Jane Smith, and I will be visiting Centerville University. We would appreciate it if you could arrange to have a college interviewer see us during the day.

We would prefer to have separate interviews.

Both of us are in our third year at Midville High School.

Will you be good enough to let me know what time I may have an appointment? Also, will you send Miss Smith a letter telling her the time of her appointment? Her address is: 23 Mason Terrace, Midville.

Sincerely,

141

LETTER OF ACCEPTANCE TO A COLLEGE

Dear Mr. Johnson:

Thank you for your letter of May 16, telling me that Centerville College has accepted me as an entering student in the 1986 academic year.

It goes without saying that I'm delighted, and that I do expect to attend.

Within the next few days, I shall be sending you the information you requested about my scholarship and about my dormitory needs.

Sincerely,

LETTER OF WITHDRAWAL TO A COLLEGE

Dear Mr. Johnson:

Thank you for your letter of May 16, telling me that Centerville College has accepted me as an entering student in the 1986 academic year.

Although I am grateful for your acceptance, I shall be unable to attend Centerville because I have made other plans for my education.

Sincerely,

test your skills

APPLYING TO SCHOOLS AND COLLEGES

1. In writing for information about possible admission to a college, which of the following points are relevant for you to mention?
   a. your high school
   b. religious affiliation
   c. when you plan to enroll
   d. hobbies
   e. ultimate goals
   f. request for admission application
   g. request for catalog
   h. housing requirements
   i. name and address
   j. references

2. Write a letter to a college requesting the following:
   a. admission application
   b. catalog
   c. appointment for an interview
   d. tour of the campus (You would especially like to see the science laboratories, as you plan to be a biologist.)

Answers to this quiz appear on page 702.

11

Writing and your college career

At school or college the ability to write well is essential to your success. New demands will be made on your ability to express ideas and communicate information as clearly and concisely as possible. Your achievement is measured by how accurately you express what you have learned.

Your room at college can be the loneliest place in the world, especially in those early hours of the morning, when you are screwed into the chair at your desk, the light glaring down on the blank page in your typewriter. It's the sixteenth sheet you've rolled into the machine. You've crumpled up the first fifteen and tossed them into your wastepaper basket; and you still don't know how to get started on that paper due for your English seminar or for your science class.

You may be a plane fare away from home, and there are no parents handy to turn to for advice. You're on your own. At no other time of your life have your writing skills, your ability to write well and effectively, been so crucial to your success or failure.

And your reliance on these writing skills will not diminish with time; on the contrary, as you move up from class to class toward that ultimate cap and gown and the coveted sheepskin, the demands on your writing skills and techniques become more critical. The instructors and professors become less lenient with your writing. They want to see evidence of original thinking in your research papers, a précis which is concise, and examination papers that show your mastery of style and content.

You undoubtedly appreciate this concern with how you handle your written assignments, and you try to meet this high standard. But people tend to develop the writing skills demanded of them by way of trial and error; and this can prove a time-consuming and often costly method of learning for the college student.

"Your report lacks organization," writes your instructor at the top of the report which took weeks of sweat and sleepless nights as well; and the grade you receive seems hardly worth the effort you invested.

"Where did you get your facts?" demands your learned professor in the margins of your report on the history of the American tariff; and there goes another unsatisfactory notation into his little black book.

"Your ideas are muddy!"

"I asked for a précis, not for your profound observations!"

"Your writing is sadly lacking in clarity."

You may slap the returned papers down on your desk, and mutter some dire threat, some heartbroken protest, but no one sees you and no one hears you. What is even more painful in such moments is the knowledge that these criticisms by the earnest members of the faculty are eminently correct.

You know, as a matter of fact, that nothing is going to help you write that acceptable book report, précis, or that admirable science report except study and practice of the techniques of good writing. And you know that different kinds of reports require different skills.

"WHAT SHALL I WRITE ABOUT?"

That's the first question you put to yourself, when you've been asked to produce a research paper for your history class, your English class, art, science, or any other class.

"What's a good topic?"

Friedrich Nietzsche, that ailing, pessimistic philosopher of the past century, said that selection, too, is an act of creation. The creative element is perhaps the most important element in any kind of writing you may do, in or out of school.

Think about that topic. Is it something to which you can bring a new slant, a new viewpoint? Will it be of interest to your fellow classmates, to your instructor? Are you sufficiently interested in the topic yourself? Do you think you can give it all the time and energy it will need? Think about it.

Once you've made your decision in this most important initial step, you'll begin to jot down thoughts and ideas. You'll have some notion of the facts and figures, names, places, dates necessary for the report, but you know, too, you'll have to do some considerable research in the area you've selected. The thing to do now, of course, is to dig up, not the research material itself, but the sources for such material.

GETTING THE FACTS TOGETHER

For anyone planning a research paper there are two principal types of sources, primary and secondary. Primary sources include original manuscripts and documents, transcriptions of speeches, and first-hand observations; secondary sources consist of reports, analyses of documents, and scholarly comments on texts as well as any second-hand treatment of a subject found in books, articles, and encyclopedias.

As a student you will probably stick with the secondary sources you find in the college library, but if primary source material is available, you would be wise to use it. In either case, you must become familiar with those reference books which can supply you a road map for the specific books, items, and articles you will need for the substance of your report.

You must know how to select the more important data from all the reading you cover in your research. You can learn how to study old facts and develop your own new conclusions. You can learn to take old material and give it a new interpretation in the light of your own, modern outlook or to utilize your own experience to offer a fresh and novel viewpoint. You must know how to write yourself cogent notes, and how to file them for quick and easy reference. You must be able to develop an outline from your notes and use these references in your footnotes and in whatever bibliography you supply with your paper.

Chapter 12 is an invaluable guide to writing good research papers. It shows you how to tackle and solve the problems we've mentioned.

Chapter 13 covers that frequently requested précis. It tells you exactly what a précis is, and what it is not. It offers you numerous examples of the précis, ways of planning it, improving it, developing it, cutting it down to the essentials. It also spells out for you the more common faults which creep into the précis, and how to avoid them.

Chapter 13 also takes up the book report and the science report. It describes the main elements in a good book report and helps you develop guidelines as well as answers to all the questions you put to yourself about the book. It will tell you exactly what to look for in a novel, in a biography, in a book on some particular chapter of history, in a book of essays. It also describes the techniques involved in writing a one-paragraph review. You will learn the steps necessary in the writing of a science report: the gathering of data, analysis, and conclusion.

"Taking Written Examinations" deals with the skills and techniques of writing good answers to exam questions and how to take much of the fear and trembling out of the process. It tells you how to allocate your time so that you don't find yourself with two or three unanswered questions when the final bell rings. It explains the best way to read the examination questions, defining for yourself exactly what is required in their answers. It shows you how to plan your answers by taking the time to organize your thoughts before you put word to paper and by writing out a short outline for your answer. And of course, it tells you how to prepare yourself for your exam.

AFTER GRADUATION

Then, looking beyond the boundaries of the campus, there is a most important chapter on how to write an application for a job. It may be a summer job you want because you are tired of loafing on the beach, or because you would like a little more money in your pockets this next school year, or because you must help with tuition costs. And, of course, there is the career job you will have to find after graduation from high school or college.

You will be expected to write a résumé of your background and education, the traveling you have done, the languages you speak and write, the jobs you have held in the past. There are examples of such résumés in this chapter, along with suggestions for describing your scholastic and athletic honors, your fraternity or sorority, and on how to bypass the red tape of personnel departments.

You may have little or no experience in the type of job for which you are applying. This chapter will tell you how to cope with such a contingency. It will also give you advice about what to write if you are already out of school and were fired from your last job.

It will also tell and show you how to answer a want-ad and how to write that difficult shot-in-the-dark letter to a company or organization which hasn't advertised any openings; how to make much of your interests and impress with your potential.

Whether or not you are a student, there is much you can glean from the next four chapters. But for the college man or woman who knows he still has something to learn about the writing skills and techniques and who is willing to learn, these chapters are required reading.

12

How to write
a research paper

**Your biggest written assignment will be the research paper
or term paper. This chapter tells you where to find information, how to set up a bibliography, how to take notes on your
reading, how to plan and organize your paper, prepare footnotes, and write your final draft.**

The research paper draws its material from many sources. Its
aim is to assemble facts and ideas and by studying them to draw new
conclusions as to fact or interpretation, or to present the material in the
light of a new interest. For instance, a military historian who wanted to
understand why General Lee lost the Battle of Gettysburg would study
the written records of orders and events, the correspondence and memoirs of witnesses, the actual terrain, and the interpretations of other
historians. In the light of that evidence, he would try to frame an explanation. Or a literary critic who wanted to understand why a certain
novelist often used certain themes would study the facts of the novelist's life as found in sources (letters, memoirs, public records, biographies), the kind of education he received, the kind of ideas current in
his particular place and time, and so forth. Such material would be his
evidence. The researcher might discover new facts, and new facts can
easily upset old theories. Or he might have to depend on facts that were
already available in scattered sources. Then his task would be to collect
those facts into a new pattern of interpretation.

The difference between the book written by the professional historian
or literary critic and the term paper written by a student may appear so
great that they seem to have no relation. But the basic method should

be the same: to collect the facts and interpret them. The term paper can be intelligent, well informed, interesting, and original in its conclusions, and the student should try to make it so. But first of all he should try to make his work systematic. If it is not systematic it will probably not have the other qualities.

Finding information on your subject

The first step toward making your paper systematic is to learn how to investigate your subject. The historian going to the order book of a general, the documents of a politician, the terrain of a battlefield; the anthropologist observing the Indian tribe; or the literary scholar studying the manuscripts or letters of an author is using what are called primary sources. He goes to original sources of information for his facts. But the college student must usually use secondary sources. He reads the report of the anthropologist or he studies an edition of a poet prepared by a scholar. Even here he should try to use material which is as close as possible to the original source of information. He should not depend on digests or commentaries of the anthropologist's report, but should go to the report itself. He should not merely read what has been said about a novelist, but should read the novelist's actual work. He should not rely on interpretations of the Declaration of Independence, but should study the actual text. Get as close to the facts as possible. No matter how good your reasoning is, it is useless if the facts on which it works are not dependable.

The research paper, we have said, draws its material from many sources. It is not a digest of one book or article. But how do you get at the useful sources?

Special reference books give a good starting point, standard encyclopedias and dictionaries, and such compilations as the *Stateman's Yearbook* and the *World Almanac*. In addition to such general reference works, there are those devoted to special fields, for example, the *Dictionary of National Biography* (limited to the British), the *Dictionary of American Biography, Who's Who* (British),*Who's Who in America,* the *Encyclopedia of the Social Sciences,* the *Catholic Encyclopedia,* the *Cambridge History of English Literature,* the *Cambridge History of American Literature,* the *Oxford Companion to English Literature,* the *Oxford Companion to American Literature,* Bartlett's *Familiar Quotations,* and the *Reader's Guide to Periodical Literature.* Other helpful reference works include: *An Encyclopedia of World History*, the *Dictionary of American History, Facts on File*, and the *Harper Encyclopedia of Science*. Reference books are so numerous and sometimes so specialized that it is often helpful to consult *How and Where to Look It Up*, by Robert W. Murphy, to know where to go in the first place.

The reference book will give an introduction to a subject and certain basic facts. Best of all for the student, it will usually offer a list of other works, books, or articles less limited in scope than the treatment in the reference book itself. With this as a starting point the student can make up his own *working bibliography* for his subject. As he reads into his subject he will encounter references to other works, and can gradually extend the range of his working bibliography. The subject catalog of the library will also provide new items.

Your working bibliography

The working bibliography should be kept on convenient cards of uniform size, with only one entry to a card. This allows the student to arrange them in alphabetical, or other order (by topics, for example), according to his need. The entry on the card should contain all the basic

ENTRY FOR
A BOOK

Strachey, Lytton, <u>Elizabeth</u> <u>and</u> <u>Essex</u>, London, Chatto and Windus, 1928.

ENTRY FOR
AN ARTICLE

Barrington, Margaret, "The Censorship in Eire," <u>Commonweal</u>, XLVI, August 15,1947, 429-432.

WRITE BETTER, SPEAK BETTER

information about a book or article: the author's name with the last name first, the title of the work, the volume number if any, the place of publication, the publisher, the date of publication. If the work appears in a periodical or collection, that fact should be indicated with volume number, the date, and the pages occupied by the work.

This form is to be retained in making up the final bibliography to be attached to your finished paper. There the order will be alphabetical by authors. Your final bibliography may be shorter than your working bibliography, for the final bibliography should contain no entry from which you have not taken material for the actual paper, whereas certain items in your working bibliography will be dropped as more valuable items come to light.

The professional scholar may want to work through all the material on his subject, but the student preparing a term paper scarcely has the time for such a program. And many items in the bibliographies you encounter are antiquated or trivial. So to save time and energy, try to select the items which will best repay your attention. There is no rule for this. Selected bibliographies sometimes appear in textbooks and other works. Sometimes an author will refer with special respect to another work on his subject. And as a student you can always take your working bibliography to an instructor for comment.

Taking notes on your reading

Unless you take notes on your reading you will probably not be able to remember much of the relevant material and will certainly not be able to organize it well when you come to write your paper. If you have taken your notes carefully, you will be able to lay out before you the whole subject and put it in order. The paper will almost write itself. But if the notes are to give you the most help, they must have a convenient mechanical form.

Notes can be put on note cards (usually 3″ by 5″), on small or half sheets, or on full sheets. What you use does not much matter, so long as the size is manageable and uniform. Not more than one note, however brief, should be on a single card or sheet. You should strictly adhere to this rule, even when notes are on the same topic; for when you take the notes, you cannot be sure in what order you will eventually use them. Only if each note is independent can you arrange them in the order you want when you come to write your paper. Each note should carry

150

at the top, at left or toward the center, some indication of the precise content, not the general subject of your investigation, but some sub-topic. And at the top right, or at the bottom, the note should carry an adequate reference to the source from which it is drawn. Presumably the full bibliographical information about that source is already in your working bibliography, so some skeleton notation will be adequate here. (When you are taking notes not from your working bibliography but from general reading, you should record full bibliographical information with the note.) Below is a specimen card or sheet:

```
American success worship    Chesterton, What I Saw
                              in America, pp.107-10.

American worship of success not materialistic.  Fact
of worship means a mystic rather then a materialist.
Frenchman who saves money to retire and enjoy his
omelet more of a materialist.  American does not work
for the enjoyment of things, but for some ideal vision
of success.  He does not want the dollar for what it
will buy but as a symbol.  Phrase "making good" il-
lustrates the fact, carries a moral connotation by
a "sort of ethical echo in the word" good (p. 108).
Not necessarily an admirable morality, but a morality
implied, and idealism of a kind.
```

When we look at the actual note on the card we see that several other phrases might have been used to indicate the topic discussed. For instance, "American business mysticism," or "American materialism." All that is needed is a word or phrase that will remind the note-taker of the content. We notice, too, that after the direct quotation there is a parenthesis with the page number. The note-taker apparently feels that this is a telling phrase worth remembering and perhaps using. If he quotes it, he will want the exact page reference.

As for the bibliographical indication at the upper right, he might have reduced it simply to "Chesterton" if there was no Chesterton other than G. K. Chesterton on his bibliography and no other book by that author. This entry is for his own convenience and need tell him only what he has to know to identify the source.

So much for the mechanics of note-taking. As for the process, you should make your notes relevant, accurate, and clear. To make them relevant keep constantly in mind the main purpose of your investigation.

HOW TO USE THE LIBRARY

AFTER CHECKING your library's general reference books, you should find out whether the library has any specific books that would give you helpful material on the subject you're researching.

Every book that the library owns is listed on an index card. These index cards are assembled in the *card catalog*. (The librarian will tell you whether the book is on the shelves or has been borrowed.)

How can the card catalog tell you where to look for the book on the shelves?

The Dewey Decimal System. This system of organization divides library books (except works of fiction and biography) into ten classes with numbers which identify them on the shelves.

000–099	General works (reference books, encyclopedias, bound periodicals, almanacs)
100–199	Philosophy, psychology, conduct
200–299	Religion, mythology
300–399	Social sciences, economics, government, law
400–499	Language (includes dictionaries, grammars)
500–599	Natural sciences (mathematics, biology, etc.)
600–699	Useful arts (includes agriculture, engineering)
700–799	Fine arts (includes sculpture, painting, music)
800–899	Literature (includes poetry, plays, essays)
900–999	History (includes geography, travel)

Each of these classes has subdivisions. For example, literature is divided into:

800–809	General
810–819	American literature
820–829	English literature
830–839	German literature
840–849	French literature
850–859	Italian literature
860–869	Spanish literature

There are additional subdivisions, so that under literature we have special numbers designating poetry, drama, fiction, etc. By the use of decimals, the numbers are broken down further. Early English Drama 1066–1400, for instance, is 822.1. These numbers are called the *class numbers.* They are combined with the initial of the author's last name to give the *call number,* by which a book is classified.

Some libraries use a system of their own or the Library of Congress system. Whichever system is used, the most important key to the location of any book in a library is the call number.

Small libraries keep their card catalogs as simple as possible. Some libraries have an *Author Card,* a *Title Card,* and a *Subject Card* for each book they own. In the upper left-hand corner of these cards is the call number.

Author card. If you know the author's name you can locate the title of any of his books, listed alphabetically, that are in the library.

Title card. If you do not know the author's name, but you do know the title of the book, you can find both title and author on the title card. Title cards are placed in alphabetical order according to the first word of the title of the book, except for the articles *A, An,* or *The: Last Days of Pompeii, The.*

Subject card. Though many libraries do not cross-refer the cards in their catalogs under general headings, some do.

Cross-reference card. If the topic you are researching is limited, you may not easily find specific books that would help you. In that case, look in related fields. Cards which say "see" or "see also" will guide you in directions that may prove fruitful.

The magazine file. After researching the card catalog, look next into the *Reader's Guide to Periodical Literature* which lists magazine articles. Are there any articles that might shed light on your topic? Check with the librarian to learn whether the magazine containing those articles are available. Make a careful record of unavailable magazines because you might find them in another library or at home, or be able to borrow them.

Newspaper index. The New York Times Index, available in many libraries that subscribe to the paper, offers a complete index to articles that have appeared in *The New York Times.*

You are studying a particular subject with particular limits. You are not concerned with anything only casually associated with the subject. If, for instance, when your subject is the economic background of the American Revolution, you are reading a general history of the period, you should not be distracted by military strategy of the French and Indian Wars or an analysis of Puritan theology. Your job is to follow your main purpose through a body of various materials, and often what is major for you will be minor in the work you are investigating.

Some note-taking may be premature. It is always best to become acquainted with a work before you take notes from it. In your first reading indicate material for possible notes, and pass on. When you have finished the work, or those parts relevant to your interest, you can better assess it for notes. In this way you will get from any particular work only the most pertinent notes, and you will avoid duplication.

The note itself may be a direct quotation or summary. If it is a direct quotation, it is sometimes valuable to record the context of the quotation. What leads the author to make his statement? What point does he try to establish by it? You do not want to misinterpret your author by implication. For instance, suppose a critic should write:

> Although Herman Melville has created in Captain Ahab of *Moby Dick* a character of intense interest and monumental proportions, he has in general little sense of the shadings of personality and motive. Most of his creations are schematic, mere outlines without flesh. He lacks that basic gift of the novelist, a sense of character.

If you, assembling material for a paper on Melville as a novelist, should merely quote, "Herman Melville has created in Captain Ahab of *Moby Dick* a character of intense interest and monumental proportions," you would have a misleading note. An accurate note would run something like this:

> Even though William ———— believes that Melville in general lacks a sense of character, he admits that Captain Ahab is a "character of intense interest and monumental proportions."

This principle of context holds good for the note by summary as well as the note by quotation.

The kind of summary you use depends on the special case. If the author's method of reasoning is very important, the form of the summary should indicate the logical structure of the original text. Where only facts or scattered opinions are relevant, the summary merely records them. As for the scale of the summary, there is no guiding principle except the note-taker's need. Try to forecast what you will need to write your paper, not merely what you will incorporate in the paper but what you will need to understand your subject fully when you write.

Organizing your notes

Once your notes are taken, how do you use them? This also depends on your subject. Some subjects suggest a chronological order, others a logical order. For instance, if you are doing a paper on Keats's development as a poet you might first arrange your notes chronologically—notes on early poems, notes on middle poems, notes on late poems. But if your subject is an analysis of the themes of Keats's poems, you might try to arrange your notes by themes, running various classifications until you have one that seems to make sense. Or you might find, sometimes, that two levels of organization are necessary. For instance, certain themes of Keats's poems might be characteristic of certain periods. Then having established one type of classification (by theme) you might run another type (by chronology). Notes are flexible. You can use them as a device to help your thinking as well as to help you organize your material.

Notes record questions and issues. The different authors you have consulted have had individual approaches to the general subject, different interests, different conclusions. As you work over your cards you can locate these differences and try to see what they mean to you in your special project. Ask yourself if there is any pattern of disagreement among the authors you have consulted. List the disagreements. Are they disagreements of fact or of interpretation? Compare the evidence and reasoning offered by the authors who are in disagreement. Can you think of any new evidence or new line of reasoning on disputed points? Can you think of any significant points not discussed by your authors? What bearing would such points have on their conclusions? Again, use your notes as a device to help your thinking.

Planning your paper

By working over your notes and thinking about ideas suggested in them you will probably strike on some vague general plan for your paper. But do not commit yourself to the first plan that comes into your head. Consider various possibilities. Then when you have struck on the most promising, try to work up an outline on that basis. You will undoubtedly

155

start with a rough, suggestive outline, the barest shadow of the paper you want to write. By checking back on your material you can begin to fill in the outline and determine the relation among the facts and ideas you wish to present. So you will arrive at a more fully organized outline. A topic outline may serve your purpose, but at some stage making a sentence outline will help you to state exactly what you mean.

Once you have an outline prepared, you can begin the actual composition. Use your outline as a guide, but do not consider yourself bound by it. As you write, new ideas will probably come to you, and if they are good ideas you should revise your outline to accommodate them. The outline is not sacred. Like your notes, it is simply a device to help you think. And remember that your paper should be a fully rounded composition, unified and coherent, emphasizing matters according to the scale of their importance. The outline is only a start toward creating a balanced, fluent, well-proportioned discussion.

Your paper should be more than a tissue of facts and quotations from your notes. It should represent your handling of a subject and not a mere report on what other writers have said. Naturally, a large part of your material will be derived from other writers, but you should always ask yourself just what a fact or idea means in terms of your own purpose. It should find a place in your pattern, and if there is no proper place for it, it should be excluded. In the end, you will always find that some of your notes are not usable. A writer who has studied his subject always has more material than he can use well.

Citations and footnotes

Give full credit for the source of every fact or idea derived from another writer. In your own text you will want to acknowledge any important item as a help to your reader. It is easy to introduce a statement or a quotation by a clear explanatory phrase or sentence. We are all accustomed to such introductory remarks as these:

Charles A. Beard has proved that . . .
An excellent statement of this view is given by James Truslow Adams in his *Epic of America:* . . .
On the other hand, such a liberal as Henry A. Wallace holds that . . .

Factual information that is general knowledge need not be cited in your text or in a footnote.

Exactly what demands a footnote? First, every direct quotation is

156

identified in a footnote. Second, every statement of fact that is not general knowledge is referred to its source in a footnote. Third, every opinion or interpretation drawn from another writer should be referred to its source in a footnote, *even if the opinion or interpretation is one which you have independently come upon in your own thinking.* In cases where a group of facts or opinions treated together in one paragraph are drawn from the same source, one note at the end of the paragraph will serve for all the material. Where more than one source is involved for a single item in the text, one note will serve to acknowledge the several sources.

Variation in certain details is permissible in the form of footnotes *but not* in the same paper. Learn one of the standard forms and use it consistently in all your work. Here are a few general principles:

1. The author's name appears in direct form, not with the last name first, as in the bibliography.

2. The title of a book or periodical is underlined in typescript or writing. This corresponds to italics in print. Even a relatively short piece of writing which has independent publication is considered a book. Sometimes a piece of writing, a poem for instance, first appears independently as a little book and is later included in a collection of the author's work. Practice varies in treating such items, but it is permissible to treat it as a book.

3. The title of an item in a periodical appears in quotation marks.

4. When an item is first mentioned in a footnote full bibliographical information is given. Later references use a brief identifying form, to be described later.

FOOTNOTES FOR BOOKS

Here are examples of various types of footnotes. Observe carefully the form of punctuation, the nature of the material included, and the order of the items presented.

ONE AUTHOR:

1. Gerald G. Walsh, *Dante Alighieri: Citizen of Christendom,* Milwaukee, Bruce Publishing Company, 1946, p. 17.

But the punctuation might be handled in this fashion: Gerald G. Walsh, *Dante Alighieri: Citizen of Christendom* (Milwaukee: Bruce Publishing Company, 1946), p. 17.

MORE THAN ONE AUTHOR:

1. James L. Steffensen, Jr., and Lawrence Handel, *Europe This Way,* New York, Atheneum Publishers, 1968, p. 20.

TRANSLATION:

1. Anton Chekhov, *The Party and Other Stories,* tr. Constance Garnett, London, Chatto and Windus, 1919.

FOOTNOTES FOR ITEMS FROM COLLECTIONS

1. Wendell L. Willkie, "Freedom and the Liberal Arts," in *The Humanities after the War,* Norman Foerster, ed., Princeton, Princeton University Press, 1944, p. 5.

Here the abbreviation *ed.* is for editor: Norman Foerster is the editor of the collection.

FOOTNOTES FOR ITEMS FROM PERIODICALS

1. Henry Albert Phillips, "The Pith of Peru," *National Geographic,* LXXXII, August 1942, 169.

Here the Roman numerals give the volume number of the periodical.

Abbreviations in notes and bibliographies

There are a number of abbreviations found in notes and bibliographical forms. You will not find a use for all of them in your own writing, but sooner or later you will encounter them in works which you read. Some of the Latin abbreviations are now replaced by English forms or may be omitted altogether (as with *op. cit.*). The main thing is to use Latin or English abbreviations consistently.

c. (*circa*)   About a certain date (to indicate an approximate date).
cf. (*confer*)   Compare (English form: see).
ch. or chaps.   Chapter(s).
col. or cols.   Column(s).
ed.   Edited by, or edition, or editor.
et al. (*et alii*)   And others (when a book has several authors, the first, with *et al.,* may replace the full list).
f. or ff.   One or more pages following the page indicated.
ibid. (*ibidem*)   In the same work (referring to a work cited in a note immediately preceding).

The last number, 169, is the page reference. Notice that the abbreviation *p.* is omitted for periodicals after the volume number.

1. Loren Eiseley, "Science and the Unexpected Universe," *The American Scholar*, XXXV, Summer 1966, 423.

For a quarterly magazine, as in this case, the season instead of the month is given, if that is the practice of the magazine itself.

FOOTNOTES FOR ITEMS FROM THE BIBLE

1. Psalms 23:6–8.

Here the first number is for chapter, the others for verses, inclusive.

1. II Cor. 6:9.

Here the abbreviation *II Cor.* is for Second Corinthians. Certain books of the Bible have such standard abbreviations.

All the forms given above indicate the first reference to a work. For subsequent references, three forms may be used. When the source in a footnote is the same as that indicated in the footnote immediately preceding, the abbreviation *ibid.* (for *ibidem:* in the same place) is

---

infra   Below (indicating a later discussion).

l. or ll.   Line(s).

loc. cit. (*loco citato*)   In the place cited (when there is an earlier reference to the source).

MS.   Manuscript.

n.d.   No date (when publication date cannot be determined).

no.   Number (as when listing the number of issue of a periodical).

op. cit. (*opere citato*)   In the work cited (used with author's name to indicate source already referred to).

p. or pp.   Page(s).

passim   In various places (when the topic referred to appears at more than one place in a work cited.)

q.v. (*quod vide*)   Which see (English form: see).

see   Used to suggest that the reader consult a certain work referred to.

seq. (*sequentes*)   Following (English form: F. or ff.).

supra   Above (when the topic referred to has already been discussed).

tr., trans.   Translated by, translator, or translation.

vide   See (English form: see).

vol. or vols.   Volume(s).

used, with a new page number reference, if that is needed. For example:

1. Loren Eiseley, "Science and the Unexpected Universe," *The American Scholar*, XXXV, Summer 1966, 423.
2. *Ibid.,* 424.

When the reference repeated does not immediately precede, either of two basic forms may be used. If the author has only one work referred to in the footnotes, his last name may be used, followed by the page reference, or his last name with the abbreviation *op. cit.* (for *opere citato:* in the work cited), with the page reference. The first practice is simpler, and is becoming more common than the other. For example:

1. Arthur Mizener, "The Desires of the Mind," *Sewanee Review*, LX, Summer 1947, 462.
2. Wendell L. Willkie, "Freedom and the Liberal Arts," in *The Humanities after the War,* Norman Foerster, ed., Princeton, Princeton University Press, 1944, p. 5.
3. Mizener, 464.

If the author has more than one work referred to in the footnotes, then his last name will not be enough, and an abbreviated title will be necessary.

1. Mizener, "Desires," 464.   *Or:*   1. Walsh, *Dante,* p. 19.

Notice that the abbreviations *p.* is omitted in the Mizener reference, for the reference is to a periodical, while it is used in the Walsh reference, which is to a book. In other words, the short form follows the practice of the long form in this respect.

When material is not drawn directly from its original source but from some intermediary source, acknowledgment should be made to both sources. For instance, the following note indicates that the writer has used a quotation from Stephen Spender which appeared in a book by Moody E. Prior:

1. Stephen Spender, *The Destructive Element,* Boston, Houghton Mifflin Company, p. 11, quoted by Moody E. Prior, *The Language of Tragedy,* New York, Columbia University Press, 1947, p. 343.

Your final bibliography

After you have prepared a draft of your paper and established all your footnotes, you are ready to set up your final bibliography. This may differ from your working bibliography, in that it contains only items which are actually referred to in your paper, not items which have been consulted but not used.

The form for such a bibliography permits certain minor variations. For instance, the place without the publisher is sometimes given; and there may be differences in punctuation. For example, the following entry can be punctuated in two ways:

> Barnes, Harry Elmer, *The Genesis of the World War*, New York, Alfred A. Knopf, 1926.
>
> Barnes, Harry Elmer. *The Genesis of the World War*. New York: Alfred A. Knopf, 1926.

But in all variations the author's name comes first, with the last name first, followed by the full title of the work, the periodical or series if any, the place of publication, the publisher (if this form is used), and the date of publication. The items may be listed in either of two ways: (1) in a straight alphabetical order, according to the last name of the author or, if there is no author, by the main word of the title; (2) alphabetically within certain groups determined by the material dealt with: "Books," "Periodicals," "Documents," and so forth. Here are some examples of entries in the bibliography of a paper on Woodrow Wilson:

PERIODICAL: Baker, Ray Stannard, "Our Next President and Some Others," *American Magazine*, LXXIV, June 1912, 131–143.

BOOK: Barnes, Harry Elmer, *The Genesis of the World War*, New York, Alfred A. Knopf, 1926.

DOCUMENT: *Congressional Record*, XLIX–LI, Washington, 1913–1914.

DOCUMENT: *Legislative Manual, State of New Jersey, 1912*, Trenton, 1912.

BOOK: McAdoo, Eleanor R. W., *The Woodrow Wilsons*, New York, Macmillan Company, 1937.

BOOK: Wilson, Woodrow, *The Public Papers of Woodrow Wilson*, Baker, Ray Stannard, and Dodd, William Edward, eds., New York, Harper and Bros., 1925–1927.

PERIODICAL: Wilson, Woodrow, "Democracy and Efficiency," *Atlantic Monthly*, LXXXVII, March 1901, 289–299.

COLLECTION: Wilson, Woodrow, "Leaderless Government," in *Report of the Ninth Annual Meeting of the Virginia State Bar Association*, Richmond, 1897.

Notice that an overall alphabetical order is given, by author when an author is specified, and by leading word when there is no author ("Congressional" and "Legislative"). In this short bibliography all types of sources are grouped together—books, collections, periodicals, and documents. In a long bibliography such types might be set up as distinct groups, each item within a group in alphabetical order.

Nine things to check in your final draft

At this stage you should have an outline and a draft of your paper, with all quotations properly inserted, all acknowledgments for facts and opinions (either quoted or summarized) indicated in footnotes, and a final bibliography attached for all works actually referred to in your footnotes. Now is the time to check carefully to see if there is any need for revision. Try to answer the following questions:

1. Does my paper have a guiding purpose? That is, is there a subject properly fixed and limited? Have I stated it clearly?

2. Is my paper really a discussion of the subject and not a mere tissue of quotations and summaries? Does it go somewhere? What is my own contribution to the discussion of the subject? Have I offered evidence and arguments for my point of view? Have I indicated how my point of view differs from the points of view held by other writers? If my paper is primarily exposition, have I added new facts to the discussion, or have I made the pattern of facts clearer than before?

3. Is my paper well organized and proportioned? Is there a clear introduction? Does the discussion really constitute the main body of the paper? Is my conclusion an accurate statement of what I have accomplished? Is it brief and pointed? Are my transitions clear? Have I introduced irrelevant material?

4. Is my style clear and grammatical? Are my paragraphs well organized? Is my punctuation correct?

5. Is my outline a satisfactory one for my paper as it now stands?

6. Am I sure that all my quotations and summaries are accurate?

7. Am I sure that my footnote references are accurate?

8. Is my final bibliography accurate?

9. Are my footnotes and bibliography in the proper form? Is the form I have used consistent?

If your paper is deficient on any of these counts, revise it. In checking on the paper or in making revisions, don't try to do everything at once. Take one question and follow it through the whole paper. You will get your best results by concentrating on one point at a time.

13

Précis, book reports, and project reports

From time to time you will be asked to write these special kinds of report. Each has its own special requirements. The step-by-step explanations of these forms in the pages that follow will make it easy for you to produce top-quality papers with a minimum of agony.

In school or out of it, you may be asked to write a brief, accurate summary of something you have read. It might be a speech, a short story, a report, a poem, or a whole novel. Anything that isn't already written "tight"—in clear but very concise form—can be summarized in a shorter version.

Writing a précis is an excellent exercise in careful reading and accurate writing. You must, first of all, understand completely what you have read. Then you must state your understanding in the most skillful way you possibly can.

A précis is a *brief summary of a longer piece of writing expressed in your own words*. It is a condensed version of the essential thought of the original material. It is usually only one-third, perhaps only one-fourth, as long as the original. (The word précis is pronounced *pray*-see. Its plural form, also spelled précis, is pronounced *pray*-sees.)

A précis is *not a paraphrase of the original writing*. It is not just saying in different and simpler words exactly what the original said.

When you paraphrase a selection, you may write a version that is as long as the original. The précis is not as long as a paraphrase.

A précis contains no comment or opinions of your own. It contains no details, no examples, no illustrations. Its language is shorn of unnecessary words. Its whole purpose is defeated by literary frills. It should be the shortest possible description of what you have read.

The six steps in writing a précis

1. Read the selection carefully. Read it again and again until you are quite sure you understand completely what the author is saying. Search for the writer's main idea. Go through sentence after sentence until you have located the topic sentence. Analyze it closely. Should there be any words or phrases that you do not quite understand, look them up in the dictionary.

2. As you read, take brief notes on points that seem important to the author. When you have finished reading, read your notes. Do any of them now seem unimportant in view of the main idea? Those will be the points to omit in your précis.

3. Now write that main idea in your own words. Make it as concise as you can. Do not include ideas or opinions of your own.

4. Revise your writing to be sure that your version is accurate.

5. Check your version to be sure that the sequence of facts or thoughts is exactly the same as the sequence in the original.

6. Reread your précis with a view to cutting its length in half.

HOW TO SHORTEN YOUR PRÉCIS

You could write a précis that is just one sentence long. But you might not be doing justice to the material you are summarizing. You can, however, cut the extra words from your writing to make your final draft concise yet still clear.

Change clauses to short phrases:

EXAMPLE: *When he finally reached* the restaurant he found *that his friend had already arrived.*

CUT TO: *At* the restaurant he found *his friend waiting.*

EXAMPLE: *Since he could not* meet her at the train, he sent his friend *to replace him.*

CUT TO: *Unable to* meet her at the train, he sent his friend *instead.*

EXAMPLE: *If you take* the steak from the freezer now, it will *be thawed out in time for dinner.*

CUT TO: *Taking* the steak from the freezer now will make it *thaw by dinnertime.*

Change clauses and phrases to single words:

EXAMPLE: After *he has graduated,* he will go into the army.
CUT TO: After *graduation,* he will go into the army.

EXAMPLE: My friend *who is a native of Brazil* is coming for a visit.
CUT TO: My *Brazilian* friend is coming for a visit.

EXAMPLE: She entertained her sorority sisters *in a gracious manner.*
CUT TO: She entertained her sorority sisters *graciously.*

As you can see, there is more than one way to say the same thing. In précis writing, the shorter the version, the better. The very meaning of the French word *précis* is "exact," "terse."

SAMPLE PRÉCIS—GOOD AND BAD

Here is a reading passage followed by four student précis. Three of them are incorrect, inadequate, unsatisfactory. One of them is satisfactory. Read the passage and each of the précis and decide which of the rules were broken, and why the satisfactory version meets all the requirements of a successful précis.

The great artists of the past, despite the love lavished on them by the scholars and esthetes, are becoming more and more remote and unfamiliar. They are not replaced by others because we are moving into a world of non-art. One has only to compare the world of the long sea voyage, sunsets, leisure, complete works of so-and-so, with the still mildly esthetic world of the train and then with the completely incurious existence of the air passenger with his few reassuring leaflets issued by the company, his meals wrapped up in cellophane in a cardboard box, his copy of *Time* in case the sleeping pill doesn't work. This unseeing, unreading traveler is a symbol of the new public. Poetry for this civilization may well cease to exist, for no one except a few professors will possess the necessary ear to follow its subtleties. Reading aloud is almost extinct and the poet who wrestles with his subtle tone-effects secures his victories for himself alone. The hopeless are the irresponsible, the irresponsible are the lazy. We must accustom ourselves to a reading public which is both too slothful and too restless to read until a sense of values is restored to it. (205 words)

PRÉCIS 1

The great artists of the past are not being replaced because these days we don't need them. Nobody has time any more for taking long sea voyages, looking at sunsets, or reading everything somebody wrote. We're too busy flying in all directions. Speed is our motto. We're hurrying too fast to take time to read. (55 words)

PRÉCIS 2

In our day there are no great artists and writers as there were in olden days when artists had rich patrons to support them. The public isn't interested in looking at paintings or reading books any more. People are too busy flying around in all directions to care about art any more. So painters and poets are going out of business. (61 words).

PRÉCIS 3

The great artists of the past are becoming remote and unfamiliar and are not being replaced by others because we are moving into a world of non-art. One has only to compare the mildly esthetic days when people traveled by train and had time to read with modern days of airplane travel. Nowadays there is only time to read a few leaflets and skim through *Time* before you are at your destination. Poetry, for instance, may well cease to exist because only a few professors live quietly enough to have the necessary ear for hearing what a poet writes. The reading public is too lazy and too nervous to care. (111 words)

PRÉCIS 4

Great artists of the past are not being replaced by comparable modern artists. Our world of non-art is symbolized by the difference between leisurely travel in the past and the rapid, nervous travel of today. The poet finds no large audience to appreciate the fine points of his work. Reading is not the discriminating art it once was, nor will it be again until a sense of values is restored to an irresponsible, lazy reading public. (77 words)

As you read, could you put your finger on the rules that were broken in these précis?

1. Though this précis was short enough, it missed the main point and emphasized unimportant details.

2. This précis is also short enough, but the writer injected his own ideas and comments into his writing.

3. This précis commits two errors. It is too long—over half as long as the original material. It also lifts sentences from the original. A précis must be written in one's own words.

4. This version is the right length, gets the main point, and summarizes the author's ideas in different words. It is a successful précis.

How to write a book report

A book report is half fact and half fancy. The facts are the author's, the fancy is yours. Unlike a précis, a book report should reveal your own feelings and opinions. It is not enough to describe details of the book.

You must express your reactions and your judgment. Your report should be written from your own point of view.

THE SKELETON OF YOUR REPORT

Following a simple outline, like the one below for a novel, will help you to include all the necessary elements in your book report.

1. Introduction
   A. Who is the author? (*This is fact.*)
   B. What type of book is it? (*Also fact.*)
2. Plot
   A. Briefly, what is the story about? (*Fact.*)
   B. How does the story develop? (*This is your opinion.*)
3. Characters
   A. Who are they? (*Fact.*)
   B. How are they portrayed? (*Your opinion.*)
4. Setting
   A. Where, when? (*Fact.*)
   B. How is it described? (*Your opinion.*)
5. Style
   A. General characteristics. (*Facts.*)
   B. How did it appeal to you? (*Your feelings.*)
6. Summing-up Impression. (*Your opinion.*)

As you can see, the way you feel about the book is as important as the factual account of its details. We will discuss, first, expressing your feelings and ideas so that the reader of your report will understand its appeal to you.

CAPTURE YOUR FIRST REACTIONS

When you have closed a book on its last page you have strong feelings of satisfaction, indifference, or letdown. Don't let this moment of strongest reaction escape you. It is the best time to jot down a few random notes summing up your feelings about the book.

You may not have time or even want to write your review then and there. It might be wiser to let your thoughts simmer for a few days before tackling the job of writing your complete report. But while your relationship with the book you have just finished reading is the closest, put some of your thoughts on paper. It may be difficult to recapture them if you wait too long.

Whether you liked the book or it left you feeling dissatisfied, it is important to get your sensations on paper when your feelings are sharpest. Those scribbled notes of yours may give you a pleasant surprise when you settle down seriously to your report. You will find that you have a head start. Your notes may give you a complete introductory paragraph or an excellent summarizing conclusion.

HOW TO JUDGE A NOVEL

Rereading your notes will sharpen the overall impression of the book that has been "jelling" in your mind. Now is the time to ask yourself some questions as you prepare to evaluate the book:

What is the theme of the book? What message is the author trying to send you? Is the theme clearly expressed and successfully proved? Or does the author present several conflicting themes without proving any of them?

Does the plot make sense? Do the incidents follow each other logically and realistically? Are you convinced that such things could happen to these particular characters?

Do the characters seem like real people to you? Do you care what happens to them? Are they all beautiful and good? Or do they show their weaknesses and their bad points? Can you believe that each character would really behave as the author shows him behaving? Or does the author move his characters around as though they were puppets on strings? What have you learned about human nature in general as a result of meeting these characters?

Does the dialogue sound real? Does it tell you about the people who are speaking? Does it reveal their personalities? Do the conversations help to move the story forward and keep it moving? Or does the talk go on and on, getting nowhere?

Does the setting—the time and place—of the story come to life for you? Can you picture the scenes in your mind's eye? Are the descriptions clear and vivid? Or are they long-winded and dull enough to make you want to skim them to get on with the story? Does the author give enough colorful detail to make this other place come to life?

Does the style suit the plot and the theme? Is it clear and simple? Light and amusing? Serious but straightforward? Heavy and wordy? Full of effective figures of speech?

As you answer these questions, take notes. Do not be afraid to be critical, but don't criticize for the sake of sounding smart. Note especially one important incident so the reader of your report can sense the flavor and tone of the book. Note a quality of a character—good or bad —that will make your reader feel your enthusiasm or your antagonism toward that character.

Take notes, too, on the "fact" parts of your basic outline. Identify the book and its author. Then arrange your notes in the correct outline form. Have you included too much? Remember, you are not rewriting the book nor giving a blow-by-blow summary of the plot. Your job is to judge the elements of the book and to evaluate it as a whole. One test of a good book report is your success in choosing *significant* details to comment on.

After double-checking your outline and filling in the necessary material, write your first draft. Begin with the factual introduction and wind up with your personal impression of the book as a whole. Revise and polish your first draft carefully to be sure you've included only what should be there and left out nothing important.

HOW TO JUDGE A BIOGRAPHY

In writing a report on the study of someone's life, the facts are important, but so too are your answers to the following questions:

Is the book's subject presented as an ideal person who is always good and right? Or do his bad as well as his good qualities show?

Do the times and the places come to life for you? Are there enough details to make the setting seem authentic?

Do you understand how the subject related to his times?

What influenced the growing up of the subject—his family, his education, his friends, his experiences?

Is the subject admirable, despite his weaknesses?

Did he face up to his trials and conflicts and solve them, or did he sidestep them?

Are the conversations believable and in character?

Does the author's style contribute to your pleasure in the book, or did you keep reading just to find out what happened?

Would you like to know more about the subject of the biography or any persons portrayed in the book, or was your curiosity satisfied?

> All good books are alike in that they are truer than if they had really happened and after you are finished reading one you will feel that all that happened to you and afterwards it all belongs to you; the good and the bad, the ecstasy, the remorse and sorrow, the people and the places and how the weather was. —*Ernest Hemingway*

HOW TO JUDGE HISTORY AND CURRENT EVENTS

Does the author present only one viewpoint? Does he examine various aspects of the background of events, or does he give one simplified explanation?

Is the background material clear and logical, or does it confuse you?

Does the author give a new perspective on the events he describes? Did your attitude change as you understood better his point of view? Or were you unconvinced?

Did the author give all the facts? You can't tell without checking with other authors' accounts of the same events. Did he distort facts to suit his purpose, or omit important details that would have changed the picture entirely?

Does the author distinguish clearly between the facts and his interpretation of the facts? Were you able to recognize the differences between them?

Were you impressed or displeased with the author's style?

Was the author qualified to write about these events or this period? Was he an expert? What was his education and experience?

HOW TO JUDGE A SCIENCE BOOK

Did you understand the material easily? If not, was it because the author didn't write clearly? Or was it because you didn't have enough background to make the material understandable?

Did the author seem to be writing down to you? Was the material too simplified? Or did he succeed in explaining complicated material clearly enough for you to grasp it?

Did the author bring material to life for you by presenting it in terms of human interest? Did he relate science to your everyday life? Or did he make it seem remote and unreal?

Are the author's facts accurate, so far as you know?

Does he supply helpful diagrams, charts, and illustrations to clarify material?

What are the author's qualifications for writing this book? Is he an acknowledged expert in the field, or did he have the help of experts?

Writing your report

Having read your book and recorded your impressions while they were fresh in your mind, you are ready to assemble your notes. You will have the factual material on hand, and your answers to the questions you asked yourself. These answers may be lengthy. They may emphasize one phase and not another.

Arrange your notes in basic outline form. Include all necessary information; omit details that add little to the picture. Sum up your general impression in the conclusion.

Now write your first draft. Check it thoroughly for correct grammar, usage, spelling, and punctuation. Polish your first draft by writing in your corrections. Read it over and over. Does your enthusiasm or dislike for the book carry through to you as it should to the reader of your report? If your report plods along, try to introduce some color and emotion so that your reader will be tempted to investigate the book.

HOW TO WRITE A ONE-PARAGRAPH REVIEW

You may be asked to write only a few full-length reports at school. But you may be required to submit many one-paragraph reviews.

Offhand, a one-paragraph review sounds like something you can toss off without much thought. In two or three sentences you can identify the book and say whether you liked it or not. But that isn't enough.

Being able to write a closely packed summary paragraph will help you in many writing chores—science reports, examinations, business letters, committee reports.

When you have a concise review to write, keep in mind the answers to all of the check-list questions, but plan to use only *some* of the answers. The trick is to select the questions most appropriate for this particular book. Eliminate all but the most important comments.

The success of a one-paragraph review depends on the compactness of your thoughts and your sentences. Every idea and every word must count. There is no room for details, descriptions, and dialogue. Your comments must be brief, positive, concrete, and put together in simple, direct sentences.

Arrange your notes in outline form. Study them coldly. Which details are vital to your report and which ones are less important? Can two important details be included in the same sentence? Try it. Can you express your feelings about the main theme in one sentence? Try it.

Write your first draft as compactly as you can. Go over it word by word to see if you can't condense it even further. Aim at leaving only the gist of the matter intact. Ruthlessly cut out the rest.

Make a clear, clean copy of what is left. Does it make one paragraph? Have you left out something really vital? If you put it back in, will it upset the whole paragraph? Try it.

When you are satisfied that you have written the tightest, yet clearest paragraph possible, make a final copy and hand it in.

How to write a science project report

Knowing how to write clearly and with authority is just as important for the scientist as it is for the journalist or the scholar. There are two reasons why you should learn how to write good reports of your science projects. First, by putting your work into words you will gain a better understanding of your project. Second, knowing you are going to write a report and what should be included in the report will help you plan and conduct the project. You will have to apply to writing the same scientific method—planned, orderly procedures—that you use in your science work.

The form and content of a science report will vary with the kind of project you are reporting on. Not all of the following items must be included in every report. For example, if a project did not involve an experiment, the report would not include the items about experiments.

THE TITLE

A good title will distinguish your project report from all others which have to do with the same general area of study. Titles of scientific reports should convey important information rather than show off the author's cleverness. Thus, the title, "Snakes Are Our Friends," would not be a suitable title for a research project on snakes. It doesn't tell enough, specifically, about the contents of the report. A better title would be, "The Diet of the North American Garter Snake." This title tells exactly what the report is about.

ABSTRACT OF THE REPORT

A 100- to 150-word summary of the report should follow the title. This summary should include in one paragraph a statement of the purpose of the project, general methods of procedures used, and principal findings and conclusions. The purpose of an abstract is to give the reader enough information for him to decide whether or not to read the whole report.

BACKGROUND INFORMATION

This section of the report should give the reader enough information to be able to understand the history and the importance of your problem. It will often include a review of other people's findings. If well written, this section will explain your motives for undertaking the project and will stimulate the reader. Background information may contain references to books and articles, indicated by footnotes. This section is often called simply "Introduction."

THE PROBLEM

If your report is based on the study of a specific problem, the problem should be clearly stated or defined. You should tell whether you are searching for or testing hypotheses, suggesting a theory, or merely reporting some observations made under clearly specified conditions. While discussing the problem, you may often want to show its relationship to other problems. The best reports include a discussion of the relationship of the problem to existing theories.

HYPOTHESES TO BE TESTED

If one or a series of experiments is being reported, all hypotheses being tested should be stated. This section may also include a discussion of what the possible experimental results will mean in terms of accepting or rejecting the hypotheses.

PROCEDURES

Anyone who reads your report should, with the proper materials and facilities, be able to repeat your experiment or observations and obtain

HOW TO PREPARE YOUR FINAL COPY

ONCE THE PRELIMINARY DRAFT of your paper is finished, all that remains to do is make a clean, clear copy of everything you've written. If you must submit a handwritten report, take plenty of time over it, so that every page is neat. If you can possibly type your report, do so. It will be more readable and attractive to look at.

Here are some tips on typing your paper:

1. Double-space the text of your report.

2. Leave a one-line space between footnotes. Single space a two-line footnote. Indent the first line and run the second line flush with the left-hand margin.

3. Leave one space after a comma or a semicolon.

4. Leave two spaces after any punctuation mark that ends a sentence, e.g., period, exclamation mark.

5. Leave two spaces after a colon when the next word or sentence begins with a capital letter.

6. Paragraphs are usually indented three or sometimes five spaces. Leave an extra space between paragraphs.

7. Center the main heading; use all capital letters.

8. Minor headings can be centered or run flush with the left margin. Capitalize the first letter of each word (except for articles, prepositions of four letters or less, and conjunctions like *and* and *but*). Underline the heading.

9. Number the pages in the upper right-hand corner.

Here's another valuable tip if you do type your report. It pays to type all footnotes on a separate sheet before you start the body of your paper, so you will know exactly how much space they take up. You can allow for this space by marking off the line that will divide the text from the footnotes. You can thus make sure that every numeral in the text has its corresponding footnote below.

Give yourself time to proofread carefully for typographical errors, slips in punctuation, or minor mistakes in spelling. After correcting them, put your pages together inside a folder or stiff paper cover. Label the cover with the title of your report and the name of its author—yours.

similar results. Therefore, you must describe in detail all of the equipment and conditions (temperature, pressure, or any other environmental factors which could affect the outcome). Photographs and drawings can be used as well as words. Every step in your procedure should be carefully explained. If you discover that some method of doing something will not work, mention it so that others will not repeat your mistake.

DATA OR OBSERVATIONS

Numerical data such as measurements and other statistics are best presented in the form of tables. Observations—i.e., descriptions of flowers or of the behavior of animals—should be reported in a simple, logical manner. Frequently such observations are recorded chronologically, in the form of a diary.

ANALYSIS AND INTERPRETATION OF DATA

In simple, short reports, this section may sometimes be included with the preceding one. The analysis of numerical data may include graphs and diagrams. Statistical methods may also be used to discover relationships. Nonmathematical observations should be analyzed and interpreted in terms of the hypotheses that were being tested. Put more simply, if the experimental data support or confirm your theory, you should organize them in the way that most clearly shows this support or confirmation.

CONCLUSIONS

In this section, each hypothesis should be reexamined and rejected if the data show it to be wrong. Hypotheses which are supported by the research can be tentatively accepted for further testing. You will seldom be able to fully accept a hypothesis. This section should also, when appropriate, discuss the effect of rejecting or accepting the hypotheses on the theories previously discussed.

IMPLICATIONS OR RECOMMENDATIONS

This section is sometimes devoted to "generalizations." In this next-to-last section of your report, you should discuss any meaning your research may have for a better understanding of a broad area of science. You should also include a discussion of any new problems (or revisions of hypotheses) that have been suggested by your study. Never try to draw illogical connections between your research results and unrelated areas of interest and study. For example, it would be silly to say, "Some foolish people kill our valuable snakes," in a report about "The Diet of the North American Garter Snake."

SUMMARY

Always conclude a scientific report with a brief summary of the principal results of your investigation. It is often convenient and desirable to do this by means of a simple opening statement such as "The principal findings of this study were:" and then list the findings.

HINTS ON STYLE

When writing a scientific report, avoid the use of words that add no scientific understanding to what you are saying. Uncommon words and names should be defined. Use the third person as much as possible (that is, do not use the words "you" and "I"). When in doubt about a word, use a dictionary.

test your skills

WRITING PRÉCIS, BOOK REPORTS, AND PROJECT REPORTS

1. What is a précis?

2. Put *1* before each statement that applies to a précis and *2* before those applying to a paraphrase:
   a. _____ Saying in simpler words what the original said.
   b. _____ Condensed version of the original material's essential thought.
   c. _____ In French means "exact," "terse."
   d. _____ May be as long as the original version.

3. Re-read the section, "How to Judge a Novel," and pages 164–166. Then write a précis of the material in "How to Judge a Novel."

4. a. A book report is unlike a précis in that _____
_____.

   b. The best time to make a few notes on your feelings about a book is _____.

   c. In writing a concise review, the best method is to select _____
_____.

Answers to this quiz appear on page 703.

14

Taking written examinations

Don't let exams frighten you! As in other forms of writing there are simple rules you can follow when you are faced with a written examination or an essay question. Here are tips on evaluating the questions, managing your time, and organizing and writing good answers.

No matter what kind of test you are taking, there are some general rules which you should always follow. You should use your time wisely, and you should read test directions and test questions carefully to avoid needless errors. In addition, there are some guidelines for "reasoning out" the correct answers to questions. Because these principles are applicable to all examinations, it is important that you understand them fully.

Almost all tests have a time limit. Some tests are essentially power tests; you will have a liberal amount of time to complete these. Other tests are essentially speed tests; you will have to work quickly through them and pace yourself to make optimum use of your time.

Know how long you have to complete the test. Make a mental note of the number of minutes you are allowed to work on the test questions; if you have any doubt, ask the examiner. On standardized tests, the time allowed is frequently indicated on the direction page.

Look over the entire test before you start to answer any questions. Only by getting an idea of the test's scope—how many and what type of questions there are—will you know how fast you must work through the items. The minute you spend in surveying will help you make better use of time and thereby improve your test performance.

Set up a schedule for progress through teacher-made tests. Determine how far you should be at the end of a specified number of minutes. This should not be too difficult if you know the total number of minutes you have to complete the test, and the number and types of questions. Leave some time at the end to go back to complete any skipped items and to check some completed items. Periodically check on your progress to maintain proper speed. You should wear a watch to the examination unless you are sure the room has a clock which can be seen easily.

Setting up a time schedule on *standardized tests* is *not* necessary. Move along at the fastest rate at which you can function well, as the main idea is to get as many items right as possible.

Begin to work as rapidly as you can with reasonable assurance of accuracy. Have your paper and pencils and your mental framework all set to go before the test begins. If directions are given before the timed portion of the test is begun (as in many standardized tests), be sure you understand them ahead of time.

Omit or guess at items which stump you. If the test is primarily one of speed and you seriously doubt that you will have time to reconsider an item later, then make a guess and go on to the other questions. If you do find time to get back to an item, concentrate on it and make the best answer you can.

Work fast on those items which will yield the most points in a given amount of time, unless instructed otherwise. Get the most points in the shortest time possible. In tests consisting of relatively few essays or problems you should answer the easiest questions first. When a test consists of a large number of objective items, it is usually best to work the items in sequence.

Use the time remaining after completion of the test to reconsider and improve your answers. Stay in the examination room for the full time allotted. Do not give up; there is evidence that persistence pays off with higher scores. If time permits, check all your answers. Do not be afraid to change answers if it seems desirable.

Read directions and questions carefully

Testing involves precise communication between test maker and test taker. The test maker, in carefully worded directions and questions, tries to find out the extent of the test taker's understanding, knowledge, and skill in certain areas.

The test taker's task is twofold. First, you must be able to understand with precision what the test maker wants; second, you must be able to communicate what you know. The second task will be dealt with later; the first will be the focus of this section.

Students tend to underestimate the importance of carefully reading directions and questions. A perfectly "correct" and well-written answer to a question not asked will receive no credit. Frequently, understanding the question may be more difficult than the idea being tested for.

Become familiar with test directions ahead of time. Information about the types of questions in many standardized tests (such as those taken in connection with college and job applications) is frequently available to the prospective test taker. A thorough understanding in advance of the types of questions you will encounter on the test will save time and prevent your misunderstanding complicated directions.

The College Entrance Examination Board publishes a booklet called "A Description of the College Board Scholastic Aptitude Test," [1] which every student should read as well as copies of old examinations.

Pay particular attention to those parts of the directions which most influence how you will take the test. The directions provide the information you need to make good decisions concerning which questions to answer, what kind of answer to make, how fast to work, and so forth.

WHAT TO LOOK FOR WHEN YOU READ DIRECTIONS

Time limit. The time you are permitted to spend taking the teacher-made test will guide you in determining how fast you should go through the questions and how complete your answers should be.

Aids. Are textbooks, notes, slide rules, scrap paper, or other aids permitted? Be sure you know what you can and cannot use.

Order of answering. Is there a special order in which you must answer the items? If so, follow this order, not only because you may be penalized if you do not, but also because you are most likely to do your best when you take the test in the manner planned. If there is no restriction about the order in which you must answer the items, work first on those items which will yield the most points in a given time.

Number of questions you must answer. Do you have to answer all the questions, or are you permitted a choice? If you do not have to answer

---

[1] College Entrance Examination Board, Publications Order Office, Box 592, Princeton, New Jersey 08540. There is no charge for the booklet.

every question, it is foolish to waste time answering questions that will not count toward your score.

Type of answer required. Do the directions specify what kind of answers you should give and what form they should be in? Are calculations and other preliminary steps required, or only the answer? Is the maximum number of words you can use specified? Are you supposed to circle, cross out, or mark on an answer sheet the correct answer? Do you have to copy the question over as part of your answer? (Do not, unless you have to. It takes valuable time.) For true-false statements, do you have to correct the false statements? On matching items, may words in the answer list be used more than once? These are just a few of the many possible kinds of directions.

Scoring. Whenever possible, try to determine ahead of time how the test will be scored. This will help you plan the distribution of time; you will probably spend more time on questions that count most.

Take the practice questions seriously. At the beginning of many tests you will find an exercise or two to practice on. The correct answers are usually given. These exercises give you a chance to make sure that you and the test maker are communicating. If you do not understand the directions, you may find this out when you attempt the practice questions; so do not peek ahead to see what the given answer is.

If there is an explanation of why a particular answer is correct, study this explanation. Even though you may have answered the question correctly, a study of the test maker's reasons will often help you in thinking through other, more difficult questions.

Another reason for seriously attempting the problems for practice is that they give you a running start. When the actual test begins, you won't have to overcome inertia.

Keep the directions in mind when answering the test items. Often the instructions direct you to choose an *incorrect* answer from among several correct ones. For example,

A famous English playwright:
   a)   Christopher Marlowe
   b)   William Shakespeare
   c)   William Congreve
   d)   Washington Irving

This item appeared on a test in which the directions were: "Each of the following items contains three correct and one incorrect answer. Choose the incorrect answer." Because Marlowe, Shakespeare, and Congreve were all English playwrights the correct option is Washington Irving. William Shakespeare will be chosen by the student who does not keep the directions in mind when answering the questions.

Cream is heavier than milk.
Cream is found at the bottom of a quart of milk that is not homogenized. (True or False)

A student who answers this question without first carefully reading the instructions that accompany it will be in trouble because the directions state that he is to assume the first statement is *true* and then to judge whether or not the second statement would be true on the basis of the first. With this set of directions, you can see that the proper answer is *true*. If cream *were* heavier than milk (and you are told to assume that it is), then cream would indeed be at the bottom of a quart of milk. This type of test item is used to measure reasoning ability, not factual knowledge.

The moral of these two examples is: Do *not* depend upon the questions in the test to tell you the nature of the directions.

WHEN IN DOUBT—ASK

Ask the examiner for clarification when necessary if you are permitted to. It is important to understand the directions before you begin.

On most standardized tests the examiner is instructed not to help students with the questions themselves. The directions, in such a case, will include something like this: "Once the test begins do not ask any questions." If the test is in progress, it is better that you spend your time trying to figure out for yourself what is being asked rather than wait for the examiner to come to your seat and tell you he cannot help you. Of course, it is a different matter if your question concerns the mechanics of taking the test, such as where to record an answer or where to sharpen your pencil.

There is no rule that a teacher cannot help interpret questions on his own classroom tests. You should realize that no matter how experienced the teacher is as a test maker, it is still likely that he will occasionally construct ambiguous items. It is very reasonable for you to ask such questions as: Would you define this word for me; should we interpret this to mean such and such.

Remember, the worst the teacher can do is refuse to answer. In fact, if the teacher listens to your questions and will not help, it may suggest that he feels you do not have a valid point.

Be alert to read the questions as they are, not as you would like them to be. We frequently see what we want to see. When you encounter an easy, familiar-looking item, don't jump to the conclusion that you know what it is. Read the question carefully to make sure it is indeed the question you thought it was. Many good teachers will test for a point which was emphasized in class or in the textbook but in a slightly different way. Changing just one word in a question can alter the answer; read every word.

Pay attention to the "key terms" in the questions. Every word in a question is important. If you mistakenly read *ounces* for *pounds* or overlook a *not,* you will answer the question incorrectly. Because of such careless errors we have all missed test questions we should have answered correctly. But for each question missed because of *misreading* there are several other questions answered incorrectly because of *misinterpretation.* Those words upon which an accurate interpretation and an appropriate response depend are the question's "key terms."

Circle the key terms in this example taken from a standardized test in American history.

Show *two* different ways in which democracy was extended during the Jacksonian period.

We did not circle the words *two* and *Jacksonian.* Like most words which are underlined or italicized or relate to proper names, *two* and *Jacksonian* are important words and to misread them would be unfortunate, but there is nothing subtle about these terms; there is little interpretation required.

We did, however, consider *show* to be a key term in the question. Demonstration with evidence and not just description is required.

Another key term in the above example is the word *extended.* The

---

A question in a college exam read, "What steps would you take to find the height of a building, using an aneroid barometer?"

One student, short on knowledge but long on ingenuity, replied: "I would lower the barometer on a string and measure the string."

—*The Wall Street Journal*

---

answer should contain evidence of how democracy was increased and not just how it was preserved.

Circle the key terms in the introductory line of this multiple-choice question:

The outbreak of World War I was a direct result of the
  a) sinking of the *Lusitania*
  b) assassination of the heir to the throne of Austria-Hungary
  c) rise of nationalism in Europe
  d) imperialism of England and France and the subsequent jealousy of Germany
  e) attack on Pearl Harbor

If you circled *World War I* or just the *I*, you identified an important word, because to read *II* for *I* could have led you to choose (e), the wrong answer. We circled the term *direct* (or *direct result*) because keen interpretation is involved with this term. Options (c) and (d) are clearly underlying causes of World War I, but *direct* alerts us to look for an immediate activator—a triggering event.

Use any remaining time after you complete the test to check your *interpretation* of directions and questions. Many open-ended questions (e.g., essay questions) contain several subquestions, and it is these questions and complicated directions which are most likely to be misinterpreted.

How to use good reasoning techniques[1]

There are many questions or parts of questions which you can answer correctly if you are willing to work at them. In this section we shall suggest ways to help you "reason out" what the correct answers to problems should be.

Naturally, problem-solving techniques cannot serve as a substitute for the basic knowledge of subject matter. Nevertheless, you can often reason out an answer, even with a limited background. Reasoning is important.

Make a sincere attempt at every question. Do not avoid questions that look complicated and involved. One research study showed that the willingness of test-wise students to tackle longer questions was a

---

[1] Much of the material presented in this section is adapted from Benjamin S. Bloom and Lois J. Broder, *Problem-Solving Processes of College Students: An Exploratory Investigation,* Chicago, The University of Chicago Press, 1950.

factor that differentiated them from unsophisticated students. Don't give up on questions that seem to require extracurricular knowledge or contain references to things that seem unfamiliar to you. These things may be unessential for determining an acceptable answer. You may be able to figure out the answer anyway.

Of course, it is usually foolish to spend too much time on any one question. If you do not seem to be making any progress, try another question. But before you give up, satisfy yourself that you have made a sincere attempt to figure out an answer.

Think through the questions. The emphasis of this principle is on the word *think*. Think—use your head—to obtain an acceptable answer. Do not rely on your impressions or feelings unless you have to or are told to do so. Think through each problem on the basis of what is stated in the question; do not merely put down a suitable-sounding answer you remember from your textbook, class notes, etc. The answer to a similar, but not identical, question may be misleading. (Trying to remember an *approach* you used to answer a similar question can be helpful.)

Be aggressive in your attempt to answer questions. Interrogate yourself. Keep asking yourself questions like: What is the question I am trying to answer? What are the key terms? What is my best guess on the meaning of this unfamiliar word? What are the elements or parts of the problem? What are the concepts that apply in this case? What does my own experience tell me that might help in answering the question? Are the instances from my experience relevant? What kind of answer is needed here? Can I break the question down or translate it in some way to make it easier to answer?

Translate material in a question to a different form. Do not expect that just looking at a question will make the answer pop up. It is sometimes helpful to change the problem into language that is easier to handle. For example, make the question more concrete. In a numerical problem, this might mean substituting numbers for abstract ideas or symbols; in a history problem, it might be advantageous to change dates to events. Long and involved problems can profitably be broken down into parts, and by working to find the answers to these smaller parts, you will be able to answer the entire question.

Evaluate your answer. Does it deal with the question asked? Is it the kind of answer you think is needed? Have you, by translating materials as suggested above, distorted the question and thus come up with an inappropriate answer? Be sure that the alternative you have selected or the essay you have written is pertinent to the question.

If stuck, go on to another question. This principle is not really in conflict with those mentioned earlier which, basically, advised you not to give up too quickly but to do your utmost to work out the answer. But when you have tried the procedures described here and have attacked the question from a variety of approaches without success, go on to another question. "Changing the scene" helps to free your mind from any blocking that may have made you forget important material and may save valuable time. While you are working on another problem, the question that resisted solution often remains suspended in your mind, ready for you to reattempt a solution which may be suggested by other questions.

Essay questions

An essay question requires the test taker to compose his own answer, which may vary in length from a mere sentence or two to a lengthy discourse. And the content of the answer may vary from the mere recall of a specific bit of information to a well-organized, critical evaluation of a philosophical position.

The ideal answer should show that you (a) understand the question, (b) know the relevant material, (c) can present the material in an organized manner, and (d) can state your ideas clearly. The objective of this section is to help you write such answers.

Remember the general principles of test taking. In addition, keep in mind these points which have a direct bearing on essay questions:

Be prepared. There is no substitute for "knowing your stuff." No amount of test-taking technique can make up for a deficiency in knowledge. No amount of proficiency in stating, developing, and evaluating ideas can take the place of facts.

After you learn the "raw" facts and ideas, together with their supporting material, finish off your studying for essay examinations by testing yourself for flexibility. To do this, form questions on the basis of key words and terms appearing in your notes, i.e., choose several of the outstanding ideas and then try to compare, contrast, differentiate, analyze, relate, criticize, evaluate, and interpret them.

Record some facts and formulas you have memorized on the back of a teacher-made examination. Do this even before you read the questions. It helps prevent blocking and inertia. The minute you take to jot down a few facts is usually a good investment.

If, however, you are instructed not to write or make calculations except in a designated area, you should comply with the directions.

Read the question carefully. One of the most common comments on returned examination papers, often written in bold handwriting to show the instructor's emphasis and impatience, is "Read the question!!" Make sure you understand what is being asked before you begin to write your answer. Answer exactly what the instructor intended.

To be sure you do, circle key words and terms. Do not write a three-page answer if a paragraph or a sentence is requested. Many essay questions contain several parts or subquestions; be sure to address your answer to all of them.

Try hard. If you find that you are unprepared to answer most of the questions, do not give up or make a half-hearted attempt. Instead, work harder than ordinarily to put together an outline of plausible ideas; then, write neatly and forcefully. It is often surprising to see the string of ideas you can pull out of your mind once you catch hold of even one idea, however fragmentary.

Use time wisely. It is easy to lose track of time when you are answering a question on a topic about which you know a great deal. Allocate your time among the questions, saving more time for essay questions which carry greater weight and require longer answers.

If you do have some time remaining, read over your answers. Frequently additional ideas come to mind. At the very least, you can correct misspellings or insert words to clarify an idea.

JOT DOWN YOUR FIRST IMPRESSIONS

Read all the essay items, jotting down beside each question the points that occur to you. By following this principle *before you begin writing your answers,* you will have a chance to unburden your mind of those fresh, important first impressions.

There are several reasons why this time will be well spent. First, by reading all the questions at the start you will have a chance to think over some of them, perhaps subconsciously, while answering others.

Second, because your mind follows chains of associations, ideas you have at the start of an examination may be lost if you don't write them down. The effort expended in answering one question in depth can block out ideas pertaining to another question. Third, the points you write down can serve as the beginning of an outline for your answers.

At this point, work fast. Do not linger over any questions waiting for additional ideas. However, do not jot down your ideas so sketchily that when you come back you cannot reconstruct them.

Here is an example of an essay question with marginal notes (based on immediate recall) recorded.

Competition bet
countries led to
nationalism
No need for
other countries
for trade

Minerals
(coffee, spices, etc)
Wanted money
and land
War
Cortez + Aztecs

The fifteenth- and sixteenth- century voyages of exploration produced lasting changes in the political and social structure of Western Europe. Would you say that these voyages tended to hasten or to delay the growth of national states? Explain.

You are now ready to begin answering a question. We suggest that you work first on whichever question seems easiest for you, being sure to number your answer plainly.

ORGANIZE YOUR ANSWERS

Organize your answer before writing. After rereading the question carefully to make sure you understand precisely what is being asked, add to the list of points already jotted down beside the question during the preliminary reading any additional points or details which may occur to you.

If only a one-paragraph answer is expected, proceed directly to write your answer. But when longer answers are expected, you should arrange your points in a logical sequence.

Here is a suggested procedure:

1. Go through and place a check mark alongside each major idea.
2. Look over the major ideas and decide how you will order them in

your essay, and write alongside each major idea the numbers 1, 2, 3, etc.

3. To support each major idea, use the remaining notes and designate them as 1a, 1b, 1c (for those points which will be used to support the first major idea), or 2a, 2b, 2c (for the points to be used in support of the second major idea), and so forth.

4. During the ordering of ideas, if you should see any gaps in either the major ideas or their supporting materials, simply insert a brief notation into the outline.

Do not spend too much time on your outline trying to make it elaborate and in exact form. An outline serves as a flexible guide, not as a rigid mold.

Reproduced below is the example from principle 2. The check marks, numbering system, and new points are added in accordance with the procedure described above.

> 2/ Competition bet
> countries led to
> nationalism
> 3√ No need for
> other countries
> for trade
>   3a. Break Venetian
>   Trade Rts.
>   3b Italy
> 2b. Minerals
>   (coffee, spices, etc)
> 2a Wanted money
>   and land
> 1√ War
> 2e Cortez + Aztecs
>   1a Unity fostered
>   2d from
>   danger within

The fifteenth- and sixteenth- century voyages of exploration produced lasting changes in the political and social structure of Western Europe. Would you say that these voyages tended to hasten or to delay the growth of national states? Explain.

When you have finished organizing the points for your question, begin writing the answer. When you have finished writing your answer to one question, organize your answer to another. Work your way through all the questions using this procedure.

Three rules for a clear, direct answer

Write to the point. After you have completed your brief outline, you must add muscle and skin to this skeleton. Do not, however, add unnecessary fat. Write the essentials. Your essay should be lean and alive, not fat and slow. Your task is to be explicit, giving ample supporting material to make your outline have substance but including no irrelevant facts which may distract from your main theme.

■First, in the opening paragraph write a direct answer to the question. For example, if you were given the question, "Why does Whitehead appeal to the poets for evidence concerning the nature of the objective world?" you should begin by writing "Whitehead appeals to the poets for the following four reasons . . ." This approach directs your answer to the specific question asked, and precludes your shifting the answer to an area about which you may have more information.

■Second, devote all subsequent paragraphs to supporting, amplifying, and modifying every point made in the first paragraph. Explicitly state relationships, causes, and effects, giving, where appropriate, dates, names, examples, and exceptions.

■Third, make your answer clear. Lead the reader neatly through the paper by well-chosen "transitional" and "directional" words. For example, if you are making an amplification, write, "to amplify . . ."; if an exception, write, "the exception is . . ."; if comparing, write, "on the one hand . . . and on the other . . ." Leave nothing to chance. Tell the instructor exactly what you are doing.

If you know your material but write like a person who is bluffing, how is the examiner expected to know the difference? He may, if he is not too tired, notice that the paper contains facts scattered about, but could those facts have been mentioned just by chance? If you know your stuff, convey this message to the examiner by adhering to the three suggestions stated directly above.

RELEVANT OR IRRELEVANT?

One practical question students frequently ask is: Should I include in my answer some facts which I know even though I am not sure they are relevant to the question? If you feel the material has a reasonable chance of being relevant, it is usually wise to state it briefly to make the instructor realize that you are familiar with it. You could footnote it to minimize its interference with the logical flow of your answer.

Write something for every essay question you are asked to answer, even if you do not know your stuff. It is rare that the instructor will ask you a question about which you know absolutely nothing. Since almost all instructors give partial credit on essay questions, it is worth

TWO ANSWERS TO AN ESSAY QUESTION

Here are two different answers to the same essay question. Marginal comments point out their respective strengths and weaknesses.

A GOOD ANSWER starts with a direct answer to the question;

preoutlines the topics and order;

starts one of the reasons;

transition;

specifics given;

specifics given; adds a sentence . . .

adds a phrase to show relevance of the point to the question;

adds an afterthought to make sure the relation of the point to the question is clear;

amplifies with an example;

transition;

a new point which came to mind during the writing of this answer.

The exploration of the 15th and 16th centuries *hastened* the growth of national states. The reasons have to do with ~~war, money~~ *danger, wealth* and trade, and ~~prestige~~ *pride*.

One of the prime ingredients for the beginning of national states was a common danger from the outside. Because countries went to war over the right to control certain colonies and trade routes, they had to unite *within*, in order to fight off aggressors.

Other forms of competition between one country and another contributed to the growth of national states. ~~One country was eag~~ Competition for land and wealth was fierce. The resources of the new lands (such as coffee, spices, minerals) were considered valuable. Each country was eager to gain land because the products of the land meant more wealth, as when Cortez conquered the Aztecs. A united country could best succeed in this form of competition.

brought about by the new discoveries These resources increased the power of mercantilism. With the opening of new trade routes, the Northern and Western European states were able to break the Venetian and Arab trade monopoly with the Indies. The colonization led to a system involving a state-controlled market between the colony and its mother country. This permitted the nations of Europe to become economically ~~separate units,~~ ~~with no common market existing between them.~~ *a condition which fostered nationalism.* It is interesting to note that Italy, which did very little exploration, took longer to become a united nation than did the other countries of Europe.

Another feature in producing national states was the ~~prestige~~ *national pride* these voyages tended to produce. The voyages were financed by a national government. Any new discovery was associated with the sponsoring government and added to the spirit of nationalism.

A POOR ANSWER This answer was retyped to correct mechanical errors. The instructor's comments appear in the left-hand margin.

Interesting, but what relevance does this have to the question.

But how does all this strengthen nationalism?

No reason given. Only a conclusion is being stated

Competition, wealth trade and pride are all suggested—but their relation to the development of nationalism is hard to see.

The voyages of exploration is a rather ambiguous term because actually there was no sudden burst of interest in exploring the world around them--they just were looking for easier trade routes to the Orient. This so-called age of exploration if it was indeed exploring was quite by accident.

When the first countries colonized the "New World" every other country now wanted to get in on it. However, to make voyages in the first place, knowledge was needed in shipbuilding and navigation. Henry the Navigator bettered the conditions of European states by contributing to navigation, maps, etc. He also began a school for navigation. Great effort was now put forth to build more and more ships and for each country to go and colonize for itself.

So the voyages of exploration didn't delay the growth of national states. The voyages were all a part of the national states. The explorers who reached other lands claimed their find for their countries. These many voyages induced the growth of the national states.

I think these voyages of exploration bound a nation together. The reason for this is that anything a group of people do together, and this was done by a whole country not just its leaders, tends to unite them. Many times newly discovered lands brought great wealth to the mother country and new places for people to settle and raise families. Then when trading was carried out with the newly found places this again helped to unite the nation. People were also united in a common cause, this being to beat other countries to these places, for trade and colonization. The lands that were claimed, and the prestige and trade that followed these voyages, affected all the people of the country.

your time to marshal the fragments you do know into an answer, though you may not be able to write a complete one.

Perhaps the best way to indicate how this can be done is with an illustration. Notice in the following example that the student was not familiar enough with the writings of Coleridge or Tennyson to back up either choice with solid, detailed evidence. Although this gap precludes his receiving a perfect score (or possibly even a good score), it is unlikely that he would receive a zero—the score he would be sure to get if no answer whatever were written. Notice how the student was able to make effective use of his ability to analyze his deficiency. Also, there is hardly any padding or bluffing, which often irritates the grader.

QUESTION. *Would you say that the poetry of Coleridge or Tennyson was more in the tradition of "romanticism"? Give evidence to support your answer.*

ANSWER. Tennyson's writings are considered to be in the Victorian tradition, whereas Coleridge is regarded as a major romantic poet. On this basis, I would answer Coleridge. A more complete answer would make liberal use of examples from each of their writings to justify this choice. Since I am not able to quote from their works, I cannot provide that kind of answer.

If I were to have samples of their writings before me, I would look to see which ones had those characteristics more nearly resembling those ascribed to romantic literature. These include the tendency toward the supernatural, the love sentiment, the extravagant incident, and the picturesque description. Perhaps its most revealing attribute is its disposition to exalt imagination, feeling, intuition, and emotional truth—often at the expense of reason and judgment. My guess is that these characteristics are found more often in the poetry of Coleridge.

Answer in outline form if time does not permit a complete essay answer. If in spite of your good intentions you run short of time, put down the main points of your intended composition. An answer in good outline form is far superior to an answer in fragmentary form or one that is left blank. Many teachers will grade you on the number of actual ideas or points you make rather than on the amount of verbiage that surrounds any one idea or point.

Write legibly. Make sure the instructor can read what you write. Contrary to popular belief, most graders do not give the student the benefit of the doubt when they cannot read what is written.

For neatness' sake double-space your answers, using generous side margins, and leaving extra space between answers. This will permit you to insert new material without messy cramming.

15

Applying for
a job

Once you're out of school or college your writing skills are more important than ever—and particularly when it comes to finding a new or a better job. Here's what you should put in a résumé, how to answer a want ad, model covering letters, even what to say if you were fired from your last job.

$\mathbf{P}$robably nobody ever won a job solely through a letter of application, or a printed résumé of his experience. But a well-written presentation of your work history can help to point out your qualifications to an interested employer. What's more, when you're competing for a job opening, a good written presentation can create a strong impression that may prejudice the interviewer in your favor.

First, we'll discuss job résumés, since they're usually essential when you're applying for a job. A résumé should be accurate, brief, and clear. It should put your best foot forward, tell the most important things about you that a prospective employer might want to know; and it should do these things fully but with no padding.

The most common type of résumé is the chronological form that gives a list of your previous jobs, starting with the most recent and going backward in time to the beginning of your working life. Most detail should be given to your recent jobs, since employers are less likely to be interested in what you did ten years ago.

If you haven't had much working experience, and can fit everything on one page, then do so. But if you've had four or five years of work, and a considerable amount of experience behind you, it may be quite worthwhile to go on to a second sheet.

Let's take a look at a good standard résumé from a man who has had a fair amount of professional experience.

James C. Cartwright
333 Centerville Street
Centerville, La.
Telephone: (918) 898–7274

RÉSUMÉ OF WORKING EXPERIENCE

1980 to present Eastern Regional Sales Manager
ABC Electronic Corp.
Centerville, La.

Supervised sales force of 25 men selling radio and TV components. Responsible for recruitment, training, and the establishment and fulfillment of sales goals. During this period, region's sales rose an average of 30% annually, compared to previous rise of 18%.

Presently employed by the firm, but family ownership prevents rising any higher in the foreseeable future.

1975–1980 Field Salesman
DEF Sales & Service Co.
Waco, Texas

Sold hardware to stores and supermarket chains. Opened up new territory after six months on job and built it to second largest in company.

Left to assume better-paying job with ABC Electronic Corp.

1973–1975 GHI Engineering Co.
Los Angeles, Calif.

Designed machine tools for the aircraft industry. In last six months of work, became a customer engineer. Left in order to become a full-time salesman.

EDUCATION

College: Boston University, Boston, Mass.
B.S. (Engineering), 1971
High School: Boston High School, Boston, Mass.

PERSONAL

Age: 35
Married: 1973
Children: Three, ages 3, 5, 8
Health: Excellent
Height: 5'9" Weight: 160
Affiliations: Sales Executives Club of Centerville; Kiwanis

Civic: Member, Centerville School Board; Chairman, Center-
                ville Muscular Dystrophy Fund Drive

SERVICE

1971–1973   U. S. Army
                Enlisted as Pfc, honorably discharged as Staff Sgt.
                Overseas duty in France, Germany

REFERENCES

Available on request

That résumé is by no means the only acceptable type but it will provide a good model and serve as a target for comments and criticism.

The ten parts of a successful résumé

Let's study this résumé line by line for its ten key components.

Name, address, telephone: This information should always go at the top where it can immediately be seen, on the left or right side. If you want to put your name on the left and your address on the right, that's all right, too. It seems simpler, however, to keep all this data together.

Title: "Résumé of Working Experience" is one of several alternatives. "Résumé," alone, is satisfactory, too. (Incidentally, "résumé" is a French word, pronounced ray-suh-may, with all syllables equally accented.)

Some authorities suggest that this title be placed above the name, and that below the name there should be inserted:

JOB OBJECTIVE
Regional Sales Manager
(or whatever job you are seeking)

There's nothing wrong with this suggestion. In many cases, though, it's probably unnecessary, since the person to whom you're applying for a job will know quite well what position you're applying for. You will have mentioned this in a letter that you sent along with the résumé, or in the interview.

Date listings: The usual format is to have the dates stand alone in the left margin. This makes a neat appearance.

Also, it's customary to list your most recent position first. The reason is that a prospective employer will be most interested in your latest experience.

195

Job data: List first your title, and then the name of the company. This helps the prospective employer place you in time and space.

Job description: This is the most difficult part of your résumé, and the most important. It is worth spending quite a bit of thought on before you write the final draft. Your goal is to present yourself in the best possible light, playing up your strong points and playing down your weak ones. (In the section "Special Situations" we'll discuss some deceptions that you may want to use in case your best possible lights aren't very good.)

In preparing the job description, ask yourself: What did I do in this job that would impress a prospective employer? Or you might ask: If I were hiring somebody for the job I want to get, what sort of experience would I look for? This is the kind of information you should try to get into your job description.

Here's a checklist that may help you in composing your job description most effectively:

■ Can you indicate any unusual responsibility you've been given?
■ Can you give any examples of having helped the company grow?
■ Can you show how you saved money for the company.
■ Can you show that you were promoted rapidly?
■ Did you receive any other form of recognition that would show your ability? (For example, if your salary increased substantially within a year or two or three, you might give this in terms of percentage to show your achievement dramatically.)

When explaining why you're looking for a new job, or why you left your previous job, consider whether it's to your advantage to do so. If you left because of "personality clashes" don't say so. To a prospective employer, this indicates that you may be a troublemaker, and you'll have one strike, or possibly two, against you. Think hard and you'll probably be able to come up with some other reason, such as a company reorganization leaving your position uncertain.

In describing the jobs you held prior to your most recent one, try to avoid repeating duties that you've mentioned. An employer is likely to favor an applicant who's had some diversity of experience in related areas, giving him greater flexibility.

Education: Give the name and location of your college, the degrees you've earned, and the dates you earned them. If you didn't go to college, give the date of your high school graduation. Unless you're a relatively recent graduate, there's no need to go into detail about your college activities. (See next page.)

Personal: The information listed in the model is what's usually expected. If you've been divorced and have remarried, there's no need to tell the employer about it unless he asks. You might want to eliminate the "Married" entry, and insert instead: "Marital Status: Married, three children."

If you'd just as soon not mention that you have children, leave it out and don't mention it unless you're asked.

If you prefer to be discreet about the fact that you're divorced or widowed, you might write: "Marital Status: Unmarried."

Service: List the branch of service, and if you had substantial promotions, your beginning and leaving ranks. Mention any overseas duty. It will make you feel better, and may add a dash of color to the résumé.

References: There's not much point in listing references in the résumé, since the prospective employer won't use them until he's talked to you, and he may not want to talk to the references you put on your résumé. Come prepared, however, to give him the names of people he can call who will give you a good recommendation.

Salary desired: Notice that no mention is made of this point. The reason is, it's irrelevant. If you list a salary and it's less than the man is willing to pay, you're selling yourself short. If it's more than he's willing to pay, you're automatically disqualifying yourself before you have a chance to let him talk to you. If you're good enough, and he wants you strongly enough, he may be willing to come up in his salary. But let him talk to you, first.

A note on style

There are three possible styles of language in writing a résumé, the first-person style: "I did this, I worked as that, etc."; the third-person style: "He did this, he worked on that, etc."; and the impersonal style: "Did this, worked on that, etc."

The first-person style is apt to sound a bit egotistical, because you'll find yourself putting "I" into almost every sentence, and if you've a sense of modesty, you'll begin to feel uncomfortable with it.

The third-person style tends to pomposity. The reader knows that you prepared it, and cannot avoid wondering, "Why does he pretend that somebody else prepared it?"

The impersonal style is the easiest to read and quite easy to write.

How to handle special situations

There are a number of "special situations" that require special résumés. Let's consider the most common ones.

YOUNG JOB SEEKERS

If you're a young man or woman with little job experience, your problem will be to impress your employer with your potential, rather than with your past. To do this, you'll have to make the most of your scholastic and extracurricular activities. The first step is to list on a worksheet everything that might impress a prospective employer.

If you're fortunate, you'll have done some work—perhaps full-time during the summer, or part-time during the year, or both. Make a list of these jobs and give a brief description of them.

If you've majored in any subjects at school which you think may help you in your work, put those down.

If you've won any scholastic or athletic honors, or have achieved any meritorious recognition, put it down.

List the extracurricular activities in which you've engaged. If you achieved any positions of prominence on teams or other organizations, list them.

If you're a member of a college fraternity or sorority, put it down. You may be fortunate enough to hit an employer who belonged to the same organization.

An employment office was checking on an applicant's list of references. "How long did this man work for you?" a former employer was asked.

"About four hours," was the quicky reply.

"Why, he told us he'd been there a long time," said the caller.

"Oh, yes," answered the ex-employer, "he's been here two years."

—*The Wall Street Journal*

When you've put down everything, you can arrange it in a résumé that follows the format below. This is a résumé for someone who's just graduated from college and is seeking her first job.

Résumé of
Marjorie B. Major
120 Main Street
Centerville, Ky.
Telephone: MA 1–2345

OBJECTIVE
Laboratory Technician

SCHOLASTIC RECORD—COLLEGE

1979–1983 University of Chicago
Chicago, Ill.
B.Sc., 1983
Majored in Chemistry
Scholastic Average: B plus
Minored in Mathematics
Scholastic Average: B plus
Scholarships:
1979–1980: Half-tuition scholarship
1980–1983: Full-tuition scholarships

Working Experience:
1981–1982 Laboratory Assistant, Chicago Downtown Hospital. Work involved blood, urine analyses; record-keeping. Average 10 hours per week during the school year. Worked full-time during summers of 1981 and 1982.
1979–1980 Clerical Assistant, Chemistry Department, University of Chicago. Maintained records of Ford Foundation project on the body chemistry of twins.

Extracurricular activities:
1979–1980 Chemistry Club; Treasurer 1980
1979–1980 Women's Tennis Team; co-captain 1980
Sorority: Alpha Alpha Alpha, Honorary Society of Chemistry Department

SCHOLASTIC RECORD—HIGH SCHOOL

1975–1979 Centerville High School
Centerville, Ky.
Scholastic Average: A minus
Scholastic Recognition:
In 1979, won the Kentucky Science Fair prize for an exhibit on the spectroscopic analysis of the stars.

Extracurricular activities:
    Tennis Club; 1975–1979
    Orchestra; 1975–1976
    Glee Club; 1977–1979

PERSONAL

[Follow model of previous résumé]

REFERENCES

School, working, and personal references available

AUTHOR'S NOTE: If the résumé is for a young man, he will probably have to put down his draft status. To leave it out will only make the prospective employer wonder why he has.

WHEN YOU'VE BEEN FIRED

This is sometimes a difficult matter to handle in a résumé. Here are several ways to deal with the problem:

If you were discharged because the department was reduced, explain it with a simple sentence: "Reason for leaving: Lack of business resulted in elimination of all but two senior employes." Or, "Reason for leaving: Company reorganization eliminated department."

If you were discharged because your work was unsatisfactory, put as good a face on it as you can. One method is to state that this was simply not the proper slot for you. One useful cover-all statement: "Reason for leaving: Position required different skills than I possessed."

This leaves unspoken the fact that you were fired, and is broad enough to encompass everything from incompetence to the fact that your boss didn't like your face.

WHEN YOU'VE BEEN UNEMPLOYED FOR A LONG TIME

Prospective employers like to think that the person they're hiring has been keeping busy. It makes them uncomfortable when they consider hiring somebody who hasn't been keeping his nose to the grindstone.

If you're not exactly the grindstone type: If you've taken a sabbatical for a year or two, if you've looked for work for quite a while and haven't been able to find it, or if personal affairs prevented you from working, then it may be a good idea to conceal this fact—or, at least, not to call attention to it.

How?

Several solutions are possible, depending on your position in life.

HOW TO ASK FOR A RAISE

AFTER YOU'VE WORKED successfully at a job for a while, you will begin to think about a promotion or raise. As soon as the situation comes to a head, you are faced with a dilemma: If I ask and get turned down, will I have to quit? How can I ask for a raise and show I mean it, and yet not be so aggressive as to create antagonism toward me?

The answer is to avoid a threat unless you are prepared to leave. Appeal to fairness and the fact that a raise will help you work better. Avoid such irritating comments as "Joe gets more than I do for the same work" or "I have been doing my work well for a year."

Similarly, when you're asking for a promotion, don't let your employer think you assume that your seniority in the job automatically entitles you to advancement or that you're guaranteed to follow your co-workers up the promotion ladder. Show the extra work you are doing or the new responsibilities you have taken on that deserve extra pay or a promotion. Remember an employer expects you to push your salary up, not pull it up after you.

Dear Mr. Cortland,

As you know, I have been working in the shipping department at Continental for more than a year. In that period, the department has lost two men, only one of whom has been replaced.

One of the men who left was the head of the department, Jerry Whalen. Since I have had more training than the rest of the men, I automatically assumed most of his duties. This has entailed more work and responsibility for me, and I have often worked late to catch up on my regular duties.

Needless to say, I enjoy my work and the new responsibility it involves. I think I am doing a good job, and I get the satisfaction that comes from this knowledge.

However, I feel that in view of the added responsibility and work, an adjustment in my pay is indicated.

Would you be kind enough to investigate and see if you don't agree with me?

Respectfully yours,

If you're an upper-echelon executive, or somebody who's had ten or fifteen years of working experience, you might consider using the consultant gambit. It's not unusual for someone who's been working for others for quite a while to try to strike out on his own. And it's not unusual for someone who's tried to strike out on his own to fail. The world, after all, is made up of 99.9 percent failures, and nobody really holds that against anyone, since we're all pretty much in the same boat.

Here are two different versions of a "consultant" entry:

1981 to present Independent consultant.

1981–1983   Independent consultant. Experience showed I was better suited for working within the structure of a company than as an independent entrepreneur.

This second, amplified version subtly tells the prospective employer that you've learned your lesson and are ready to settle down and be the good employe he desperately needs.

Of course, if you actually have tried operating independently, and can describe some of your accomplishments in reasonably glowing terms, by all means do so.

Another gambit that you might use to cover a gap in your career is: "Supervised personal investments."

This is an impressive-sounding and satisfactorily vague explanation that can mean almost anything you want it to mean. It will work best if you really do have some substantial personal investments in securities or real estate; for then you can explain in the interview that personal affairs kept you too busy to hold down a full-time job.

If you're a middle-management person, or if you're a relative newcomer to the job market, your absence from work may not need too elaborate a disguise.

Whatever your explanation, don't apologize. You've done what you've done because you believe it was the right thing to do.

For example, suppose you became fed up with the rat race and decided to become a farmer. You chucked your job, started raising chickens, and lost your shirt. Now you're back in the market for a job again. How do you describe this in a résumé?

One solution is to be vague about it, if you think that you can tell the story in person more effectively. In this case, you might simply say:

1982–1983 Spent one year in independent enterprise—to be explained in interview.

Another solution is to be quite frank about it, but in terms that reflect credit upon your spirit:

1982–1983   Personal requirements dictated spending a year away from chosen career. At the end of this period, recognized that my greatest abilities did lie in my career field.

You don't, of course, need to explain everything—leave some of the details to the interview.

Covering letters for résumés

A covering letter sent along with a résumé can, if properly written, do a good job of selling your abilities and calling attention to your strong points.

A good question to begin with is: "What's the main point I want to get across?" Your answer might be, "My experience," or "My fast rise," or "My general sales ability." Whatever it is, this should be a major point to emphasize in your covering letter. Call attention to it near the beginning, because the prospective employer may be so harried that he won't have time to read anything except the first paragraph or two before he turns to the résumé.

Again, as with all of your other correspondence, keep the covering letter short.

Some sample letters appear below.

REPLYING TO A WANT AD

Read the ad carefully to try to get a feeling for what kind of experience the employer is most interested in. (The sample letter immediately below, for example, answers an ad which stressed the employer's interest in somebody with a broad background in production and with supervisory experience.)

It's a good idea to identify the date and newspaper in which the ad you're answering appeared. The employer may have placed more than one ad.

For the same reason, it's also a good idea to mention the kind of position for which you're applying.

Dear Sir:

Your advertisement for a production manager in the May 12 *Journal* interested me because your requirements closely parallel my working experience.

As the enclosed résumé indicates, I've had more than ten years' experience in all phases of production. For the past eight years, I've supervised a work force of at least a dozen people.

I'll be happy to tell more about my experience in an interview. You can reach me during the day at WW 1–2345, and in the evenings at WW 2–9876.

Sincerely,

Dear Sir:

The sales job which you describe in your advertisement in the *Mirror* of April 19 is one for which I think I can show you some excellent qualifications.

You ask for a "go-getter with proven experience." As you'll see from my résumé, I've turned in an above-average sales record for the past five years, ever since entering the sales field.

While I'm quite happy in my present work, the description of your job sounds even more appealing. I'd enjoy discussing my qualifications with you at your convenience.

Sincerely,

If you're applying for a job for which your qualifications are poor, then your letter might stress your personal qualifications, your zeal, and your willingness to learn:

Dear Sir:

If an ability to take direction well, and to carry out orders faithfully, is important to you, then I may be a good man for the job you advertised in the *Chronicle* of August 15.

The job sounds particularly interesting because it is precisely the kind of work I have wanted to do for many years. My working experience thus far has, I think, given me the attitudes and the understanding that would enable me to learn the details of the position you've advertised.

I'd very much appreciate the chance to talk to you, and to get your opinion on whether my background and inclinations would be suitable for the job you offer.

I can be reached by telephone at 398–4123.

Sincerely,

General covering letters

When you're sending résumés to prospective employers, you're at a disadvantage if you don't know exactly what their needs are. In this case, you'll have to take your chances, by trying either an all-purpose letter which calls attention to your availability, or else a more specific letter emphasizing the areas in which you think you're strongest.

The latter choice is preferable. You only live once, and you might as well spend your working hours doing a job for which you feel best qualified. If you emphasize only a couple of points about yourself, you'll lose the interest of some prospective employers who may have a job for you which isn't down your alley, but you'll probably attract the attention of an employer who detects in you a prospective employe who knows what he wants. (And there are certainly few enough of those around.) It will also help you to get a hearing if you express some enthusiasm for the employer's line of business. He would obviously prefer to hire someone who is interested in his field, so let him know how you feel about it.

One preliminary word before writing your application letter. Presumably, you'll be writing to a company which you think will have a job of the type you want. Try to get the name of the president, and write your letter to him. He may or may not do the interviewing, but even if he doesn't, he'll pass the letter on to the person who does—and a letter coming down from upstairs always carries a bit of extra prestige.

test your skills

APPLYING FOR A JOB

1. The basic purpose of a résumé is to _____.

2. A résumé should include what basic information?

3. What is the function of a covering letter?

4. A covering letter should include these essential points: _____.

5. Below are four openings to covering letters. Which do you think is the most effective and why?

a. Reference is made to your ad in *The Courier Journal News* of Jan. 3 for a sales manager with a "proven track record."

b. I note with interest your ad of Jan. 3 in *The Courier Journal News* that your company wants to hire a sales manager of demonstrated competence.

c. Would you consider a man with annual sales of $250,000 for each of the last five years to have a "proven track record"?

d. I'm your man!

Answers to this quiz appear on page 703.

16

Good writing is good business

In business, words are as important as figures. Words make sales and create good will, win new customers, and hold old ones. Words can obtain credit, get bills paid, report on new ideas and products, launch sales campaigns. So success in writing is a key to success in business.

How do you say No to the best customer you ever had? How do you reply to a just complaint (the washing machine that doesn't rinse, the shrinkless shirt that shrinks)? How do you inquire about a prospective customer's credit? How do you tactfully refuse credit to a firm whose business you'd like to have? How do you begin a sales letter which will really sell? How do you write a collection letter which won't offend, but at the same time will bring you that long-overdue payment?

The skills involved in writing are never as important as they are to your business. Your enterprise may be large or small, an old established company, or one just getting up off the ground. You may be dealing with the ordinary day-to-day transaction or with the problem situations which crop up in the normal course of events.

A skillful writer will cement and develop relations with an old customer. A well-written letter will open the way for the development of a new customer and for increased business. A carefully worded letter can heal wounds, avoid a break in communications, prevent the loss of sales. A smartly written letter can break through into areas you haven't reached before, carry your sales records to new highs.

And if you are the man or woman responsible for letters which keep old customers happy, bring in new customers, and increase the volume of business, then you are certain to attract the attention of your superiors in the company. You will be in line for those promotions and salary hikes you want and have earned.

In the next chapter you will learn ways to picture the people with whom you correspond. There are sample letters you may study and emulate and a checklist of eleven imperatives to help you create in your mind the person who is to receive your letter.

Plan your correspondence

Once you are satisfied with the picture you have created, you can plan your correspondence. Planning is important for almost any kind of letter, but especially for the business letter.

List the details your letter must cover, its purpose or purposes (sales, inquiry, follow-up, response). Then outline the order in which you will write about these details, keeping in mind always the reason you are writing.

Plan to be concise, direct, and easy to understand. Remember that the ultimate aim of every business letter is to develop in your reader the sense that his dealings with you will bring him profit and perhaps pleasure.

In Chapter 18 you will find guidelines for planning whatever business letter you must write, a variety of sample plan sheets for the variety of business situations you meet on a day-to-day basis, as well as an analysis of their separate values.

Of course some letters are more difficult to plan and write than others, as in the following examples.

An irate customer writes, "Not only have I not received the merchandise I ordered; you haven't even acknowledged the order."

A young man writes, "I've lost my job and I can't continue the payments on the television set I bought from you."

Your landlord sends you an unexpected notice informing you that your building is going down and that you'll have to move your business in thirty days. That's scarcely time enough to find another place.

How do you assuage your irate customer? How do you meet the problem of the young man out of work? How do you get a little more time from your landlord to relocate your shop?

Difficult situations of this sort are always cropping up in the course of the business day. In each case, we want to maintain a friendly busi-

WRITING A LETTER OF RESIGNATION

IF YOUR JOB in an organization is not an important one, a verbal resignation is all that is expected. However, if your job holds some responsibility or if you have held a position for a long time, it is a good idea to explain in writing why you are leaving. This provides you with an opportunity to create good will.

A letter of resignation should do the following:

1. Give notice that you intend to leave at a specific time.

2. Express appreciation for the opportunity, experience, courtesy, and pleasant time you have had. You may modestly mention some of your achievements as a reminder to your employer if you plan to ask later for a letter of recommendation.

3. Explain why you are leaving.

4. Suggest methods of replacement, if it will be difficult for the company to replace you.

5. Leave the door open for your employer to call you in and offer a better arrangement.

A letter of resignation should be rather formal, and written "for the record." Here is a good example:

Dear Mr. Cortland:

After serious consideration, I have reached a definite decision to resign from the company, effective September 30. You will readily understand my decision in view of my personal financial obligations. I feel that greater opportunities would be available to me in a larger company.

My two years with the Cortland Company have been pleasant and have provided a stimulating challenge. I enjoyed working with you, and I regret very much the necessity of leaving because of extreme economic pressures.

I hope that the new methods I introduced into the accounting department proved that I was worthy of the confidence you placed in me.

I will, of course, help in training the person you select to fill my position. If at any future time a problem should arise, I shall be happy to assist in any way I can.

Respectfully yours,

ness relationship; in some cases we may find ourselves asking for special consideration. Whatever the circumstance, each demands a carefully planned, tactfully worded response.

Chapter 21 deals with some of these delicate situations, and suggests ways to meet them. It contains many sample letters and explains why and how each letter works and the result you might expect from it.

At the head of the list of delicate situations come the times when you have to say No in your letter.

You have been asked to extend credit to a customer and you can't do it. You have been asked by a shopkeeper for the exclusive right to sell your product and you can't give it to him. A large chain of drug stores wants a special price from you on a huge purchase of your merchandise, but in fairness to your other customers you can't give a special discount.

In each case, you'll have to write that big No. But how do you do it with a smile, with a thank you and the hope that your letter won't drive off business, current or future? In Chapter 20 we discuss how to plan an effective response; how to plot it; what to keep uppermost in mind when writing your No; what to avoid.

EVERY LETTER IS A SALES LETTER

Nothing, of course, helps business more than the effective sales letter. Actually, every letter which leaves your office is in one way or another a sales letter. Whether it is an inquiry, a response to an inquiry, a letter acknowledging an order, or even a letter asking for payment on an order, it carries the stamp of your firm, its personality, its approach to business, its approach to its customers, present or future. It creates an atmosphere about your company and its products; it makes for good will and confidence; it makes for sales.

The sales letter itself is the direct "pitch" and warrants special analysis and care in the writing. Its aim is obvious, but the elements which will bring the desired results—sales—are not always so apparent.

The sales letter, its planning, its organization, and the results you might expect from it, are explored in depth in Chapter 19.

Finally, Chapter 22 deals with business reports which, you will discover, differ very little from the reports you wrote at school.

You are asked to write a report on the public preference for small cars, as opposed to medium-sized and large cars. You are asked to develop a report on the potential sale of frozen fish foods in New England, or on the possibilities of housing developments in Alberta.

To begin your reports on these business activities or proposals, you would examine your company's files, the company library, and other libraries. You might arrange a series of interviews or, sometimes profitably, mail out a mass questionnaire.

You will take notes, as you did with your school report, analyze your data, draw up an outline, before you get down to your actual writing. You will check your data (this is especially important in the business report) and make sure that your work is readable, concise, and clear. If you are expected to include your own judgments, as is often the case, you might well be constrained in your negative views, and be in control of your enthusiasms. Your recommendations may involve huge sums of money, as well as your reputation and future with your company.

Not all business reports are of such scope and depth. You may be asked for a report no longer than a one-page memorandum. Nevertheless, you will have to give it as much care and attention as you would its bigger brother. The smaller report, however, may allow for an informal, almost conversational, form. The larger report is always formal, and generally presented in that manner, sometimes to the great number of people who own some stock in the organization.

In either case, clarity, conciseness, and readability are essential; the format will depend on where and to whom the report is delivered.

This chapter will help you decide on the form you choose, as well as the extent of the research expected of you, and the significance of your conclusions and judgments in each instance. It also provides guidelines for the writing of each part of your report, as well as a sample outline for the report and suggestions which should help you achieve the conciseness and clarity you desire.

Remember that whether you're asked to turn out a letter, a memo, or a full-scale report, your ability to communicate in writing is vital to the success of your business career.

One of the most tactful men he ever knew, a California manufacturer says, "was the man who fired me from my very first job. He called me in and said, 'Son, I don't know how we're ever going to get along without you, but starting Monday we're going to try.'"
—*Gene Sherman in Los Angeles Times*

17

Picture the people you are writing to

Learning to talk the reader's language is the prime secret of success in business-letter writing. The case histories in this chapter will show you how some creative businessmen have learned to stop answering letters and start answering people—just by observing ten simple rules.

A good business-letter writer must be creative. A letter is supposed to give somebody information. That's why it is written. It's almost impossible to write a letter that fails to convey *some* information. Even a child can do that, but only when you give a letter added duties and qualities do you become creative.

Your letters of reply to inquiries may be designed to win new customers, to keep old customers, to accept or refuse credit, to handle adjustments, or to win the cooperation of suppliers. In any of those letters you are trying to accomplish something. You are trying to create a good feeling about your organization, and that creates a problem.

You are selling. Let's face it, no matter what kind of letters you write, if you aim to make people feel that your organization is a fine one that deserves their high regard, you are selling.

If you have taken courses in salesmanship or read books and articles on the subject, one of the first things you learned was that star salesmen have one thing in common. Before they call on a new prospect they do some digging. They learn all they can about the man—his name, his occupation, his marital status, the number and ages of his children, his income status, hobbies, likes and dislikes, and lots more.

Your language must be the reader's language. Armed with all the facts he can gather, a salesman is able to approach a prospect with confidence. He can talk the prospect's language. Once he meets the man, he picks up additional advantages. He sees what the prospect looks like, absorbs the physical surroundings, sizes up his personality, his disposition, his current mood, how his associates and employes act in his presence. All these observations are trail marks. The alert salesman follows that trail to reach his prospect's interest and win his confidence. Those facts and observations are vital to successful selling.

Certainly no good salesman would talk in identical terms to a farmer and to a bank president. A superior salesman wouldn't talk in exactly the same terms to the bank president and the first vice president.

When responding to letters of inquiry you are a salesman. Therefore, you have to school yourself to do all the things other salesmen have found are essential to success. There's one difference. No letter can do as thorough a selling job as a flesh-and-blood individual engaged in face-to-face selling. For that reason, when selling by letter you have to be even more painstaking and thoughtful. You have to compensate for the disadvantages.

Stop answering letters and start answering people

The mind is a delicate instrument. It will travel in any direction with just a gentle prod. Your mind follows brain boulevards you have established through habit. To change the direction, you must change some habits. Most business people think, "I must answer this letter."

At the office you think, "I must answer this letter," but if you get a letter at home—a letter from a friend—you say, "I have to answer Bill."

There is a world of difference in the way the two letters are written. When the signal to the letter-writing department of your mind is, "Answer this letter," you do just that. You write to a piece of paper with markings on it. When the control room says, "Write to Bill," the letter you write is a warm, human document, full of personality and catering to Bill's viewpoint.

Bill gets pleasure and satisfaction from the letter he receives. The originator of the *letter* you answer gets cold, colorless information.

Form a new habit. Say, think, and feel, "Let's answer Bill Jones." Stop saying and thinking, "Let's answer this letter."

Know whom you're writing to. That's not easy. A great number of your letters are written to people you've never met. You can't be the direct salesman running around or phoning people who know the man. He's a name and a number on a letterhead or a ledger card—an unknown who wrote a letter of inquiry.

This you do know: He is an individual, filled with all the hopes, the doubts, the fears, the human warmth, the failings, and the prejudices you'll find in all individuals. But with each individual the quantities vary. That's what makes them individuals.

A LETTER IS A VERY PERSONAL DOCUMENT

While he was in the army George Riley made a lot of new friends— fellows from all over the country. At Christmas time, each year, he hears from a number of them. And because it is the only time of the year that they correspond, most of those cards have something more than the standard holiday greetings. There are a few handwritten lines bringing him up to date on what they are doing, how many kids they have, and so on. It's up to him to write to each of them and tell them what his personal status is these days. Last year he heard from seven of his army friends.

When George replied he had the same information to give to each friend, but he found it necessary to write seven entirely different letters. He knew these folks. He knew how they differed. A letter that might have been fine for one of them would have been all wrong for the other six.

The uniform letter would have made Dick feel George was getting dumber. It would have made Barney think he was showing off. It would have made Herbie think he'd lost his sense of humor. It would have made Lowell think he'd become shallow—and so on.

When you stop to think about that in terms of the letters you write to people unknown to you, it's frightening, isn't it? Only one out of seven would have been right. You can't afford to write business letters that have so low a batting average.

What can you do to compensate for not having met or heard anything about the folks you write to?

HOW TO BE A LETTER DETECTIVE

If you have read detective stories, you've come across cases where a letter from an unknown party turns up. The crime-detecting technicians analyze the paper and the ink. A handwriting analyst makes his study. The detective hero, often a psychologist, makes his deductions.

By the time all the reports are assembled the sleuths could recognize the writer on a dark night, lying face down in a pitch-black alley. They know where he came from, what he does for a living, and when he had his tonsils removed.

You don't need to set up the counterpart of a crime-detection laboratory. But you should learn to be a detective.

All inquiries tell you something about the writer. Any letter you receive—even a filled-in coupon from a magazine ad—can tell you something about the writer. The part of the country it comes from tells you a lot—big city or small town. The envelope, the stationery, the handwriting or typing, the manner of expression, the spelling and punctuation, even the name, tell a story. What he says, how it's expressed, the question asked, the method of payment are all parts of a big jigsaw puzzle. Your job is to put it together.

Letter detecting is not a time consumer. True, you'll take some extra time when you first tackle this fascinating job. But if you give it your full attention for a few days, you'll soon find yourself doing it automatically. As you pick up a letter, certain features will jump at you; you will absorb the telltale marks at a glance. In seconds you'll have some knowledge of the writer.

You won't always be right. In some cases a further exchange of letters will give you an entirely new picture of the writer. In other cases you'll never find out you were wrong. But you will often hit the bull's-eye. You will be right and you'll be writing far more effective letters.

As you perfect yourself as a letter detective you'll be pleasantly businesslike with Joe Blowe and folksy with Oscar Zilch. You'll spell it out for John Jones and summarize for Paul White. You'll see the need for flattering Tom Green and for laughing with Harry Johnson.

THE GREATEST SECRET OF ALL: TRANSPOSE

And here's the greatest secret of all in writing the right kind of letters to individual people. Once you've made your analysis and have determined the kind of a person your correspondent is—*transpose!* You've met thousands of individuals. Some made vivid impressions on you and have remained in your memory. They represent many types.

When you read fiction, consciously or subconsciously, you associate the characters in the story with people you've known. They become flesh-and-blood individuals to you. If someone says, "bookworm," you get a mental image of a bookworm you know pretty well. If someone says, "playboy," up comes another picture of somebody you know. It is hard to think of a descriptive term that fails to produce some kind of image.

That same reaction will take place once you've put a label on the person who wrote the letter you're answering. But that isn't enough. It isn't strong enough. Let the old friend you remember *become* the person who is to get a letter from you.

Write to a friend. The mental picture you have formed of the man who wrote to you makes you think of your friend Horace. Sharpen your memory of old Horace and mentally start your letter, "Dear Horace." Keep Horace in there working for you. Talk to Horace all through the letter. He's somebody you really know. You understand a great deal about Horace. You'll be talking his language. As you write with Horace on your mind, your letter will come to life.

Bald Eagle Airlines writes to a "friend"

Here's a letter received by the Washington office of Bald Eagle Airlines:

Gentlemen:

I'm 82 years old. I've never flown in a plane and always promised myself that maybe some day I would. My boy Harry will be 50 this July 8th coming and since he lives down in Dallas now I thought maybe this is the time to keep that promise to myself.

Now I will tell you frankly a man my age gets nervous thinking about things like being air sick and I hear you have to be strapped down the whole time and another thing, I do not think I like the idea of nothing but cold things to eat and though I hear it's done, I can't see how you can safely cook in an airplane.

You send me the rates and let me know how long it takes and if you have anything to say about those other things I would like to know about them.

Respectfully,
Martin Grimes

Can you picture Martin Grimes? Mental images of him may vary, but take his handwritten letter and see what kind of portrait you can draw. No youngster, of course. He might be a spare man with a few strands of pure white hair. There's a bit of a twinkle in his eye and a good crop of well-embedded smile wrinkles in his face. He's sentimental. He likes to talk. There's a good measure of the sport left over from his younger days. He likes life and likes people. He realizes that, at his age, he should take care of himself and feels just a little foolish about taking his first flight at eighty-two. He's hoping that all of his fears and doubts will be wiped out by the answer he gets from the airline. He's mighty anxious to fly.

This answer is in step with the reader:

Dear Mr. Grimes:

I envy you, Mr. Grimes. There's nothing I can think of quite as wonderful as a first flight. And this will be a first flight in one of Bald Eagle's 727 or 747 luxury liners. I'm excited about it myself. The things I'm going to tell you make me feel that I'm the one bringing you and your son together for this fine occasion.

I don't think you have any reason to worry about motion sickness because reliable studies have proven that fewer people experience discomfort or illness when flying than when riding in cars or trains. And you can forget about being strapped down. For a few minutes when the plane takes off and again when it lands your stewardess will ask you to fasten your seat belt. During the rest of the flight you can get up, move around, do whatever you want.

And here's another happy surprise. You'll be served a fine hot lunch while in flight. This is possible because of the specially designed vacuum containers and electrical heating elements that were created for this very purpose. Hot coffee and cold milk are yours for the asking at any time.

The flight you would find most enjoyable leaves Washington National Airport at 8:55 on the morning of July 8th. Two hours and forty-five minutes later, which is 10:40 Texas time, you'll be in Dallas, refreshed and happy, saying "Happy Birthday" to your son. The round trip fare is $250.00 first class and $200.00 economy class, which includes all taxes, and you pay nothing extra for the fine luncheon you'll enjoy while in the air.

Here's what I've done. I have reserved a seat for you on that plane and I'm holding it here at my office. Please call me, at your convenience, so that we can take care of the details of your return flight and I'll explain, at that time, how you can pick up your ticket and make arrangements for limousine service to National Airport. The phone number is EXecutive 3–2080.

And when you see your son in Dallas, Mr. Grimes, please give him my warm wishes for a happy birthday too.

Cordially,
Herbert Pflaum
Sales Manager, Washington Office
Bald Eagle Airlines

Mr. Pflaum is a fine salesman. He has a feeling for people. When he wrote to Mr. Grimes he could visualize the man. The attitude he adopted created a letter that blended with his mental image of his potential passenger. Had he been face to face with Mr. Grimes he would have used the same language he put on paper.

A cold letter and a warm reply

There will be times when the letter you receive is cold and formal. The writer of any letter is a human being even though his manner of writing business letters may fail to reveal his human qualities. Far too many charming individuals have the unfortunate notion that business correspondence should be devoid of warmth and color.

When replying to such letter writers you can't afford to gamble on being as free and friendly as Mr. Pflaum was in his letter. If you want your reply to be rich with personality and the suggestion that you must be good people to deal with, however, you will avoid the temptation to follow the writer's style.

As publisher of the weekly newsletter *Television Digest,* Martin Codel received this letter:

Dear Mr. Codel:

This is to acknowledge receipt of your form letter of recent date soliciting my subscription to your weekly newsletter, the *Television Digest.* I have heard of your publication on numerous occasions but have never seen a copy. The facts that have come to my attention and the literature forwarded to me by your office lead me to surmise that the weekly issues may bring to my attention timely news of the industry.

In consideration of the fact that I am immensely busy and the nature of my duties requires an exceptional amount of reading I am reluctant to burden myself with additional matter. If, therefore, your publication is not in excess of a single letter-size sheet this is your authorization to enter our subscription for a one-year term.

Very truly yours,
J.M.L.

The letter, from a large manufacturer of television equipment, was signed by the president. The newsletter averaged about twelve pages. This was Mr. Codel's reply:

Dear Mr. L.:

When a busy man like you takes time out to express his interest in *Television Digest* I am deeply gratified. Thank you, Mr. L.

In your letter you have summarized the very reason why *Television Digest* was created. It was brought into existence because the leaders of this dynamic industry are immensely busy—because the day-to-day requirements of keeping themselves fully informed demand a vast amount of reading and research.

Television Digest is not additional reading matter. The editors of the weekly newsletter do your reading for you. They take long articles and reports and condense them to a few brief sentences—sentences that give you the facts you want and need. Add to this the frequent reports of significance originated by the *Digest*.

The *Digest* reports on every facet of the television-electronics industries. The areas it covers require more than a single letter-size page, *but the parts you will select for reading will average a page or two per issue*. As you will see when you examine the sample copy I'm giving you with this letter, each issue displays a "Summary-Index of the Week's News" at the top of page one. At a glance you'll see which articles you want to read. The rest of the issue will make no demands on your time.

There is no need for you to take the time to reply to this letter, Mr. L. Because the *Digest* will enable you to cut down on your weekly reading time, and because you will not have more than a page or two of important facts to read, I'm taking the liberty of entering your annual subscription unless I hear from you to the contrary.

My warmest thanks.

Sincerely,
Martin Codel

Trade on the writer's likes and dislikes. That's exactly what Martin Codel did in his letter of reply. Mr. L. had concealed his personality behind an iron curtain of flutter-butter, old-fashioned language. But he gave publisher Codel a break. He told him what he liked and didn't like. In his reply Mr. Codel was a personable human being telling, in clear, compelling terms, why *Television Digest* would give Mr. L. just what he wanted.

Adopting the writer's viewpoint

During one of its annual campaigns the Tuberculosis Association of Washington received this letter from a prominent businessman:

Dear Mr. F.:

In this morning's mail I received your appeal for a contribution to this year's campaign. Your letter suggests that my firm increase its customary contribution.

As a businessman, as you can appreciate, I am called upon to contribute to every campaign that comes down the pike. While we try to play an active role in community activities and to allocate funds for charitable purposes judiciously, the demands are greater than the means.

In light of the well-publicized advances that have been made in the conquering of TB I fail to see any justification for an increased donation. Recent articles in the local press have shown where both deaths and the demand for hospital beds have decreased. I therefore feel we are justified in reducing the sum to be given to your campaign.

If I am mistaken in my conclusions I shall be glad to review your counterclaims.

Respectfully,
J.D.B.

Mr. F. replied:

Dear Mr. B.:

Your November 17th letter demonstrates why you have reached the height you have attained in the business world. Despite the fact that your present views put our fund requests in a bad light I am sincerely pleased that you have given our appeal that much thought. It leads me to believe that you will give this reply equal consideration.

The impressions you have gained from the articles about TB control are understandable and intelligent. The facts you read are true. But beneath those facts there are many unseen currents.

Yes, the new miracle drugs and improved treatment techniques have pulled the death rate down dramatically and have sharply cut the number of hospital beds needed.

The grim truth, however, is that we have more known cases of TB, right here in our own community, than ever before. This could be because we are more actively looking for the disease, or because more people are being infected. In either case the situation is serious. The seriousness is enhanced by the additional fact that the majority of new cases being detected have reached the active stage where the victim is capable of spreading the disease to others.

The great cuts in death and hospitalization bring on other problems. The people who survive need years of home treatment. They need rehabilitation in order to become useful members of society again.

When we take these several considerations together and examine them, I know you'll appreciate the need for ever-increasing funds. More efforts must be made to detect the disease quickly before it becomes active. More must be done to help TB sufferers get the home care they must have, and the mental and vocational training that will enable them to become self-supporting and not lifelong recipients of public assistance.

These are the reasons why we appeal to community leaders, like you, to set the example for the citizens of this area by making a contribution this year that reflects an understanding of the increased needs.

My warmest thanks for giving me the opportunity to fully explore the problems with you.

Sincerely,
E. F.
Executive Director

Mr. F.'s letter reveals his proper mental picture of this civic-minded businessman. His letter is devoid of tugs at the heartstrings. It is devoted entirely to the *business* viewpoint of the problem. His letter resulted in an increased contribution.

The technical made simple and clear

Let's look at one final example of a letter correcting a misunderstanding and reflecting the writer's mental picture of a person he has never met. This letter was received some years ago by a mortgage loan firm in Washington, D.C.

Dear Gentlemen,

My wife and I are talking about buying a home. Last week we went to the Home Show and at your booth we got a copy of your booklet, "How to Borrow Money to Buy or Build a Home."

Now we have got our eye on a house and we are worried about the finances and that is why we were so interested in your book. In the book I notice that you talk about these FHA loans and you say that if we want an FHA loan we have to come to you or somebody like you, and you talk about the fees we pay when you get the loan for us.

Well we pay taxes and if the government is putting up money to lend people who want houses I do not see why we should have to pay you for getting us that money. I have plenty of free time and can go down there to the FHA offices myself and work things out with them which is what I guess you would do to earn that fee. But I called them up and got a real run around and a lot of fancy talk I didn't understand. That is why I am writing to you. Please be honest with me and tell me who I should see at FHA so that I can arrange for the loan from them myself and save those fees which I sure can use.

Very respectfully,
William T.

Writing about technical subjects to uninformed prospects: The letter the mortgage company received was handwritten. As a letter-writer detective you should have little trouble seeing this man. He's a solid, straightforward, plain-talking citizen. Perhaps he hasn't had a great deal of formal education, but he's made his way in the world. He has saved enough to be thinking of a home and, since he has lots of free time and his writing is somewhat shaky, it's a safe guess that he probably is no youngster.

Mortgage loans can become pretty involved and difficult to understand to the man who never has dealt with them. The folks at the loan company, to answer Mr. T. properly, had to create a good mental image of him first. With that image in mind they had to reply to his questions in terms he would understand, but they had to do so in a manner that would not give him the feeling that they were laughing at his lack of knowledge about mortgage loans.

Here is the answer William T. received:

Dear Mr. T:

You have asked a very good question, Mr. T. I'm more than glad to give you the honest answer you want.

The financing of homes is pretty complicated. Those of us who are in the business deal with the problems every business day. We get so close to it we often forget that certain language we use is not familiar to folks like you who may have reason to deal with mortgages just once in a lifetime.

FHA, the Federal Housing Administration, doesn't lend money to everybody. Back in the early thirties, when money was mighty hard to find, there were many families who wanted and needed homes, but they couldn't find anyone willing to risk lending them the money needed to buy or build. Congress saw the importance of correcting this condition. They passed an act that resulted in the creation of FHA. Congress told FHA that it was their job to help people who wanted homes by offering to insure the money advanced by private lenders.

Right now you have a house in mind. Very few people are in a position to pay all cash for such a big purchase. First you'll come to us or to some other mortgage loan company. Give us the address of the house and tell us the price and how much of a cash payment you can make.

The next step is for us to ask FHA to send inspectors out to look at the house. They will examine it carefully and tell us how much of a loan they are willing to insure. If the amount of cash you are prepared to pay and the loan FHA will insure add up to the price the owner wants we're ready for the next step. Our people go to private lenders. One of them will accept the FHA-insured mortgage and, through us, advance the money to you.

That's the way it works and that's how we earn our fees. Like most businesses, the mortgage loan business is very competitive. Competition protects you because our fees must be as reasonable as we can make them if we hope to attract clients. You'll find them very reasonable.

I have asked Mr. Nichols, one of our mortgage loan specialists, to give you a ring to see if he can give you any further help. Thanks so much for letting me explain how we can help home buyers.

Sincerely,
G.W.D.
President

A full, understandable answer wins confidence. The president of the company took the time and trouble to make a highly complicated subject completely clear. He did it with understanding and with warmth. He spared the reader any feeling of inferiority by saying for him that most folks deal with the complexities of a mortgage only once in a lifetime. He could see the man behind the letter and he spoke as a man to a man in explaining this common problem.

Ten golden rules

You have seen how four different businessmen applied the principle of picturing the people they were writing to and produced creative personal letters to meet problem situations. Now you will want to apply the system yourself. Here are the main considerations you should keep in mind when picturing the people you write to.

1. Start with the attitude that you must create confidence and a warm feeling about your company.

2. Keep in mind the fact that you are selling and must think as a salesman.

3. To influence people a good salesman must be able to talk the reader's language.

4. To talk his language you must stop answering letters and start answering people.

5. If you are to answer the person you are writing to in language he'll understand and appreciate you must be a letter detective.

6. Form the habit of studying every inquiry for clues to the writer's nature and personality.

7. Transpose. Form a picture of the writer and then think of a friend with the same characteristics.

8. Write to *your friend.*

9. When answering a cold, formal letter, dig a little deeper till you find something that represents the writer or, at least, his basic interests.

10. When the writer reveals a lack of knowledge of your business take extra pains to make your reply to him nontechnical and full of understanding.

test your skills

PICTURE THE PEOPLE YOU ARE WRITING TO

Below are letters from three persons making the same complaint. Analyze the letters, giving a picture of each writer. How would you reply?

1. Dear Boatbuoy:

What kind of business do you run? When I went on vacation two weeks ago I ordered the paper discontinued. Today I came back to find 14 papers piled up outside my door. Your people must be idiots. It's practically an announcement that nobody's home. It's a wonder I wasn't robbed. I'm not going to pay for those papers. If you have any sense you'll fire the jerk who kept on delivering them.

Sincerely yours,

2. Dear President Boatbuoy:

Truly I'm in awe of your organization. It's so efficient that nothing can turn it off. Before going on vacation I told you to discontinue my paper. But I came back today to find all of them in front of my door. That's what I call real intelligence. It takes a genius not to figure out that nobody's home and it could attract thieves. I reject these treasures, Boatbuoy. Call for them at your leisure and add them to your personal collection of priceless artifacts.

Devotedly yours,

3. Dear Mr. Boatbuoy:

Despite my order to stop delivery of the paper during my vacation, it was delivered every day. That was both wasteful and dangerous. The outdated papers are useless to me, and their presence could have attracted thieves. I do not feel that your deliveryman showed good judgment, and I do not expect to be billed for this period.

Yours truly,

Answers to this quiz appear on page 704.

Disraeli, in conversation with a friend, disclosed the secret of his ascendency in royal power. "When talking with the queen," he said, "I observe a simple rule of conduct: I never deny; I never contradict; I sometimes forget." The inevitable contrast with his great rival came in when he added: "Gladstone speaks to the queen as if she were a public department. I treat her with the knowledge that she is a woman." —*Lucy, Chamber's Journal, January 30, 1915.*

18

Plan your letters
before you write

**Every letter you write offers you an opportunity to make a
good impression on others. Don't pass these chances up! Two
business writing experts designed these Plan Sheets to help
you organize your thoughts before you put words on paper—
for extra clarity and impact.**

$\mathbf{H}$abit may well be one of the most powerful forces on earth.
When you take a busy man who has a thousand things to do, twice that
many to think about doing, and give him a letter to write, it's going to
read with all the excitement of a telephone directory. He'll lean on
phrases he has used before, write words he's not fully concentrating on,
get the job done as quickly as possible and forget it.

And there is a pretty good chance the person getting the letter written
under those circumstances will forget it too. That is, assuming he reads
it at all!

Too many people treat letters like those "bad pennies" that keep turning up even when you concentrate on avoiding them. It's a shame, because letters offer a beautiful opportunity to make a good impression
on other people—and have them think well of both the writer and the
company he works for.

But making that kind of impression takes thought; it won't just happen automatically when the letter is finished and mailed. Once you
have established a pattern of thinking out a letter *before* you start writing, your letters will improve—and writing will be more fun and take
less effort.

Here are some guidelines for writing a better letter:

Five guidelines to good letter planning

Make sure you have all the details about the situation your letter will cover.

■Know the main reason you're writing. Sound stupid? Well, consider: Is your letter to cool off an angry complainer, to quote a price, to say No to a request? Whatever the main reason, have it firmly in mind *before writing;* aim at getting it into the letter as soon as possible; and *make it clear.*

■Is there another purpose the letter should accomplish? If you quote a price, should you also make a bid for the order? If you turn down a request, should you suggest an alternate course of action? And an angry complainer has to be won back as well as cooled off. Know how the situation is to be handled before you write the first word.

■If your letter is to lead to direct action, be sure you say what it is, and how soon it should be taken.

■Before you do anything, set aside a specific time for handling your correspondence—a time when you will not be interrupted. Good planning requires concentration. We suggest the first hour in the morning. Phones seldom ring, guests seldom visit that early. And your thoughts are sharper first thing; they haven't yet been cluttered with the day's problems.

■Write notes to yourself when you plan, but don't write the letter until you've phrased it in your mind. That way you'll avoid using words and phrases that are unnatural.

THE PLAN SHEET METHOD

In developing a letter-writing training program one of the largest life and health insurance companies used some simple Plan Sheets. They act as a guide to the thoughts you should have clear in your mind before you get one word on paper.

The company studied hundreds and hundreds of letters, and discovered a surprising thing. You write really only three different kinds of letters: one that you originate; a reply to another; and a follow-up. So they designed three Plan Sheets.

Once you have filled out your Plan Sheet, your letter is practically written—and you are not in danger of forgetting anything that should be included.

PLANNING A GOOD REPLY

For instance, the insurance company has just received this letter from an applicant, and it is your job to answer it:

> Gentlemen:
> Although I address this letter "Gentlemen," I'm not so sure you are. When I find out that you have had men talking with my neighbors, my bank, probably even my tailor to find out what kind of guy I am—I doubt seriously that you are gentlemen.
> I filled out all the questions your agent asked—and truthfully. Why do you have to check up with everyone else about me?
> You had better have a good explanation—or else you can tell your agent he can keep the policy. I don't want it.
>
> Joseph Street

Angry? You bet. And your job is to write Mr. Street. Certainly you wouldn't want to tackle this answer without having planned it well! But because you may not be familiar with insurance practices, here is some background you would need before filling out the Plan Sheet for replies.

1. On large policies, most life insurance companies conduct investigations into the financial, physical, moral, and family background of the applicant.

2. The purpose is to confirm the facts given by the applicant; be certain the risk is a good one; be sure the applicant can carry this amount of insurance without a problem.

3. By insuring the best prospects insurance companies can keep costs for insurance down, and pay better dividends.

4. In this instance, Mr. Street applied for $20,000 and he did pass the inspection. Now the company is ready to issue the policy.

OK? Let's work out the Plan Sheet. (See opposite page.)

Now, putting all those points together, here's our reply:

> Dear Mr. Street:
> Since every life insurance company must protect its insured and their investment, most of us investigate applicants in advance and eliminate those who are poor insurance risks. Your application has been processed, and we find you to be a preferred risk. Our apologies for any concern our inquiry might have caused.
> Your doctor, Sherman Acton, M.D.; your banker, William R. Graham;

PLAN SHEET FOR
REPLY TO A LETTER

1. WHAT IS PURPOSE OF MY LETTER?

Get Mr. Street to accept policy

2. WHAT DOES WRITER WANT TO KNOW?—OR HAVE US DO?

Why we checked on him.

3. CAN WE GIVE READER THE INFORMATION—OR DO AS HE ASKS?

Yes

4. WHAT POINTS SHOULD I COVER IN MY LETTER?

1) *Reasons for investigations*

2) *Common practice*

3) *Results of our check-up*

4) *Hope he'll take policy*

5) _____

5. IS THERE ANY WAY THE READER BENEFITS?

*By insuring only better ap-
plicants, we keep costs lower
and dividends higher.*

6. WHAT APPROACH SHOULD MY LETTER TAKE?

Admission of Guilt	(Apologetic)	Appreciative
Arouse Curiosity	Ask for Help...Cooperation	
Ask Question	(Awareness of Reader's Problem)	
(Complimentary or Congratulatory)		Good News
Humorous	Personal	Positive vs. Negative
Regretful	Sense of Urgency	Sympathetic

and other persons who know you best are all in agreement that you are an excellent prospect for insurance.

Thanks to your friends, we know you better and look forward to welcoming you as one of our nearly 2 million insureds.

Cordially,

How Plan Sheets help the writer

Never realized difficult letters could be written so easily, did you? And so effectively, too.

Using Plan Sheets, you can make sure that your letter accomplishes what you've set out to do. Here are some ways they help:

- Letters will be easier to understand.
- They will contain *all* the important points.
- All questions will be answered.
- Messages will invariably be shorter.

Their greatest value is when you're dealing with a complicated problem —or a lengthy subject. Here they can be invaluable in helping you organize, sort, and analyze your thoughts before you begin dictating or putting words on paper. There's another plus—planning ahead can help set the right tone to accomplish your purpose.

PLANNING A FORM LETTER

How about trying this same system to originate a letter?

THE PROBLEM: 1. Your company is one of the largest department stores in the country. Consequently, the list of charge-account customers is tremendous. While you enclose return envelopes with bills, they are not stamped.

2. During any given year, you receive hundreds of letters from customers asking why such a large organization can't put a stamped envelope in with its bills.

3. Management has decided to prepare a standard letter which can be used to answer all such inquiries.

AND, SOME BACKGROUND: 1. Your store mails approximately 3 million bills a year.

2. At 20¢ an envelope, it would cost approximately $600,000 to stamp the envelopes. To offset this additional cost, prices on your merchandise would have to be raised.

Let's work through our Plan Sheet for Letters Originated.

PLAN SHEET FOR
LETTERS ORIGINATED

1. WHAT IS PRIMARY PURPOSE OF MY LETTER?

Advise reader of our policy on stamped envelopes

2. IS THERE A SECOND PURPOSE?

Keep his business and good will

3. WHAT DO I WANT THE READER TO KNOW—OR DO?

We won't put stamps on return envelopes

4. WHY?

Costs too much over year

5. HOW CAN READER BENEFIT?

Keeps cost of merchandise down

6. POINTS TO BE COVERED IN MY LETTER:

1) *Won't put stamps on envelopes*

2) *How many envelopes in year*

3) *What total cost would be*

4) *Effect on customers*

7. WHAT APPROACH SHOULD MY LETTER TAKE?

Admission of Guilt	Apologetic	~~Appreciative~~
Arouse Curiosity	Ask for Help...Cooperation	
Ask Question	~~Awareness of Reader's Problem~~	
Complimentary or Congratulatory		Good News
Humorous	Personal	Positive vs. Negative
~~Regretful~~	Sense of Urgency	Sympathetic

Now, putting all those points together, here's our reply:

> Twenty cents isn't a big amount, Mr. Smith—we'd be the first to agree. That is why we can readily understand your asking us to include a stamped return envelope with your charge notices.
>
> But when you take the cost of putting a 20¢ stamp on each return envelope and multiply it by the more than 3 million bills that go out in a year, you have a figure of over $600,000! And when you consider that our operating costs must be calculated when we set our prices, you can quickly see why, in these days of soaring costs, we don't want to saddle our customers with any extras.
>
> We do want you to know how grateful we are for every suggestion that would enable us to give our customers better service. We appreciate you taking the time to send us yours.
>
> Thank you,

Another tough assignment handled with a minimum of trouble. Are you convinced these sheets save you work?

PLANNING A FOLLOW-UP LETTER

Ready to handle the third—and last—type of letter? This should be a lot easier now that you're getting the knack of it.

THE PROBLEM: 1. You've enlisted in the air force—and the only thing holding up your acceptance is a medical report that was requested of your personal physician.

2. Twice you've written. Twice there's been no reply. And time is running short for you. This letter has to do the trick. Here's where the Plan Sheet will help.

Would you send those records, if you received this follow-up?

> Dear Doctor:
> Is my heart bad?
> Do I have an ailment I'm not aware of?
> Medically, don't I meet the air force requirements?
> These are just a few of the questions going through my mind, Dr. Melvin, since I haven't received the medical report I asked for. Won't you put my mind at ease, and also help me get into the air force?
> You must be very busy, but if the air force doesn't have my medical record by next Friday, they won't accept me.
> Please, take just a few minutes now to have your nurse put my records in the mail. I'm anxious to get in the service and do my part.
> Thank you,

Let's be realistic. Planning this way takes time—and you wouldn't make out a Plan Sheet for every letter you needed to write. Just the

PLAN SHEET FOR
FOLLOW-UP

1. WHAT DO I WANT READER TO DO?

Send medical report

2. WHAT LIKELY REASONS WOULD READER HAVE FOR NOT HAVING DONE THIS?

Too busy – away – Didn't receive previous request

3. WHAT APPEAL CAN I MAKE TO GET ACTION?

Might lose my chance to get in Air Force
Show concern about my medical record

4. HOW CAN I PHRASE MY APPROACH TO MAKE IT MORE ATTENTION-GETTING? WHAT TECHNIQUE COULD I USE?

Ask questions = show concern

5. POINTS TO COVER:

1) *What I need from doctor*
2) *Why I need it*
3) *How fast I need it*
4) *Please send it*

6. WHAT APPROACH SHOULD MY LETTER TAKE?

Admission of Guilt   Apologetic   Appreciative

Arouse Curiosity   Ask for Help ... Cooperation

Ask Question   Awareness of Reader's Problem

Complimentary or Congratulatory   Good News

Humorous   Personal   Positive vs. Negative

Regretful   Sense of Urgency   Sympathetic

difficult ones. But it may pay dividends to plan all your messages this way while you're trying to school yourself.

It won't take long before you have these questions established firmly in mind, and automatically you'll ask them before you begin to dictate. Then you can reserve filling out such sheets for those really complicated messages or those that require considerable tact.

Having done all the things we've talked about, put yourself into the shoes of the person you're writing to and test your reaction. If you still wear a smile when you're done, you have probably written a darn good letter.

Just remember, as with everything successful in life—*plan first!*

test your skills

PLAN YOUR LETTERS BEFORE YOU WRITE

Below is a letter written to a man who was furious because a department store had made several errors in his account. Read it and explain the writer's "plan."

Dear Mr. Friendly:

Our records show that you returned the dozen pairs of socks on January 23, as you stated in each of your letters to our accounting department. It is inexcusable that we continued to bill you after you returned the merchandise and wrote three letters explaining the circumstances.

I make no effort to minimize my own concern and dismay over such inefficiency on our part. I have tried to track down the reason for this error, but it seems to be one of those mysterious things that happen in an age when men are dependent on machines, when employes are sometimes not as conscientious as we would like, and when we must keep accounts straight for 279,483 charge customers. This, I am sure you will agree, requires a lot of bookkeeping, and inevitably we do slip up—as we did in your case.

Our only defense is that we try to streamline our methods in order to reduce overhead and continue to give the lowest prices possible. I do hope you will forgive us and let us continue to serve you. We value your patronage and good will and regret the inconvenience we have caused you.

Sincerely,
George Gorgewell
Customer Representative

Answers to this quiz appear on page 704.

19

How to write
sales letters

Here's a formula for successful sales letters, whether you are selling doorknobs or battleships. Scores of examples show how other businessmen have captured the reader's attention, created a desire for the product, persuaded the purchaser of its value, and wrapped up the sale—all in a letter.

Practically everything that can be sold—from smoked hams to swimming pools—is now sold directly by mail. Some companies do all their selling by mail; others depend on letters to develop leads for their salesmen and aid in various phases of their selling operations.

Like a good advertisement, a good sales letter must compel reader attention by enthusiasm, vitality, originality, and a thorough understanding of the specific sales situation. Since a sales letter, more than any other type of letter, has to overcome reader resistance, it must be keyed to the prospect's needs, problems, and interests. To overcome reader resistance, a sales letter usually follows this well-established formula:

1. Arouse interest.
2. Describe, explain, and convince.
3. Stimulate interest to the point of closing a sale.

But many successful letters ignore or adapt such a formula to stress sincerity, spontaneity, and credibility.

Long experience has shown many pitfalls in writing sales letters. Avoid the following: being patronizing or condescending; writing over the head of your reader; using complex, trite, or exaggerated words and phrases; claiming too much for the product and emphasizing too many points in one letter. Understatement is often more effective than wild claims and high pressure. Never assume that your prospect knows about your product or remembers what you said in a previous letter. Also, your letter should aim at creating a mood—an atmosphere conducive to obtaining the results you want.

There is one infallible test of the effectiveness of a sales letter—the number of sales it brings in. As one professional letter writer said: "Make your letter so convincing that the prospect would rather have the product you are selling than the money he must part with to buy it."

The start of a sales letter

Only a few of every hundred circular letters that reach the average executive's desk are read. With these odds against you, it is easy to see why your letter has to have an interesting and exciting beginning.

The most important sentence in a sales letter is the first one, because in a large percentage of all letters it is the only sentence that is read. The first sentence has one key function: to attract enough favorable attention to get the reader to continue. A short opening paragraph—indeed, short paragraphs throughout the letter—invite further reading.

Arousing favorable attention requires a pertinent thought, a thought that can be tied in to the body of your letter without too much explanation. It may be:

1. A striking statement:

Would you like an extra $65 each week—in addition to your regular pay?

Honestly, I've got the easiest job in the world!
All I have to do is convince you that you are in line for some husky profits when you take on . . .

We have the answer in CASH for you!

This is a letter to warn you against MONOCLE, a new monthly magazine of political satire.

If, despite this warning and your own better judgment, you return the enclosed card, a *free copy* of this dangerous magazine will find its way into your home. Then you will be really sorry because . . .

Save 42% on the electric bills for
YOUR NEON SIGN! . . . without a penny's cash outlay from you!

We have stumbled upon a treasure that we must share with you.

You may never win a prize for knowing—

What President's hat was held by his defeated rival while the victor read his inaugural address?

What President applied for a patent on a flatboat he invented? (It had air chambers for floating over shoals.)

Will YOU Be Ready for the Boom Years Ahead?

The next few years will see the biggest boom this country has ever known. And with it—inflation.

This is still hard for many people to accept. But the fact remains that those who DO prepare for the boom times ahead will reap big dividends for their foresight—and avoid the blunders others will make.

2. An anecdote or joke:

A Reader's Digest letter once quoted an ancient Persian poet: "If thou hast two pennies, spend one for bread. With the other buy hyacinths for thy soul."

One time when Lady Astor was making a speech, she admitted: "We women DO talk a lot, but even then we don't tell half we know!"

This is a story of a SUCCESSFUL CHALLENGE . . .

A *Let's Have Better Mottoes Association* member who signs himself "Anonymous," and who takes umbrage for reasons not specified, proposes the motto:

"Money can't get you friends but it can certainly bring a better class of enemies."

I'd like to tell you about a teacher who built a fortune of one million dollars in the stock market, yet who never made a salary of more than $6,000 in his life.

How did he do it? Not by any hit-and-miss method, but by carefully searching for investments with "special" features that others had overlooked. When he found one that satisfied him, he invested some of his savings and waited for it to "work out."

Here's the story . . .

Recently I had the privilege of visiting a community in the San Joaquin Valley of California where a modern miracle has taken place. If you had been with me, I am sure you would have agreed that it was an experience not easily forgotten.

3. A startling fact:

$100 grew to $20,000
$100 grew to $17,000
$100 grew to $ 8,000

That's right! Had you invested a *total of $300* in just three common stock warrants in 1962, your investment would have *grown to $45,000* by 1966.

$10 billion in security values were lost in one week in June!

4. An analogy:

There's a firm in Ohio no larger than yours that secured 104 new accounts and made $19,500 in two months from a $5.87 business investment. And did it, mind you, without any special offer of any kind.

Men have much in common besides tonsils.

5. A startling offer:

Special Offer to ————— Subscribers Only!
Here's a book we consider so important that we'll send you a copy to read for 5 full days—*entirely at our expense!*

A NEW IDEA—
and I guarantee you'll like it!

HERE IS A SECRET THAT WILL HELP YOU MAKE MORE MONEY IN 1972 THAN IN ALL YOUR LIFE BEFORE . . . .

We are in an excellent position to save you money.

Maybe I can help you better yourself—by telling you about a magazine that's helping others.

WIN A FREE NEON CHANGEOVER ON YOUR SIGN . . . IF YOUR NEON SIGN IS THE OLDEST IN YOUR BOROUGH!

Invest $500 a Year in These Growth Stocks

Retire with $50,000 in 10 to 15 Years

Here's a bargain in good reading for the whole family that I don't think you'll want to pass up.

If you haven't yet met HORIZON, we invite you now *to see* a magazine made like a quite spectacular illustrated book;
to sample its extraordinary range of contents: arts and ideas from the ancient to the avant-garde, from civilizations familiar and foreign; and
to subscribe on exceptional terms, available for a short time only: *$6 less* than usual.

Dear Reader,
Once or twice in a reading lifetime, a book comes along which is so important, so enthusiastically praised by the experts, and so outstandingly successful that no well-informed person would wish to miss the opportunity of reading it.

We take special pleasure in calling your attention to such a book, which we have the honor of publishing.

6. A gift or free booklet—a "bribe for listening":

Here is your new KOLORITE Guide!

"KOLORITE" is Weber's way of expressing a sincere interest in your office planning problems, Doctor—and so we are pleased to enclose our popular color folio.

It took our editors two years to gather the material for this handbook. You get it FREE—by just returning the enclosed card today.

You get over 100 inspiring sales promotion ideas that have paid off brilliantly for industrial advertisers during the past two years.

THE ENCLOSED RESERVATION

—made out in your name entitles you to a FREE copy of the first edition of a new book which shows . . .

A copy of "————," one of the most popular and provocative little business booklets in print, is yours for the asking . . . absolutely free and with no obligation involved. We ask only that you read it carefully.

21 PAGES OF TIMELY IDEAS FOR *YOUR* BUSINESS

For you . . .

a transparent plastic letter opener–magnifying glass FREE. As a magnifying glass, it will come in handy for the hundred little things you want to look at more closely around the house. And as a letter opener, it is something you will want to keep handy on your desk.

We want you to have this letter opener–magnifying glass for the opportunity it will give us to let you know something about ———— services and how they save you time, trouble, worry, and money.

The editors of ———— Magazine have just put together a remarkable new booklet entitled "16 Ways to Save Money on Your Phone Bill." It contains information that can help you to *cut your phone bill in half*.

It will take you less than a minute to fill out and return the enclosed postage-paid card entitling you to a free copy of "Forging Ahead in Business." BUT, IT WILL TAKE AT LEAST AN HOUR TO READ THE BOOKLET AND ABSORB ITS CONTENTS.

We are reserving in your name a valuable booklet entitled "————
————." Your copy will be delivered to you promptly upon receipt of the pull-out card in the window of this letter.

7. The "you are special" approach:

It has taken a while, perhaps, to achieve your own measure of success in the world of business. But when you analyze your present position in terms of the progressive steps you have taken, your ambitious cultivation

237

of opportunities, and your overall dedication to your career, you realize, suddenly, you *are* a success.

This letter is for the smartest girl in your office (part of the inside address).

This letter is addressed to the top man in a closely held corporation. If you're the man we're talking about, you should immediately become familiar with 8 tested ways to increase travel and entertainment expense deductions that command top-executive attention everywhere.

You are invited to be
an opening night critic . . .
. . . when the curtain goes up on an important and widely heralded premiere.

My dear wealthy friend:
Any one of these eye-opening money facts may bring thousands of dollars your way.

Dear Reader:
You have been selected to receive a free copy of Volume I, Number 1, of SHOW BUSINESS, the exciting new magazine of the performing arts.

Do you realize what an important man you are to Haverford? You hold the key to success in her Development Program. You represent the difference between a credible and a distinguished level of alumni support.

If you're the kind of man this letter was written for, you like the idea of finding new ways to do things better, and you like saving money, too. And if that's the way you like to do business, you very probably count on some kind of appointment book or desk calendar to help you keep track of appointments, meetings, dates, and all the other things you can't afford to forget.

There are certain people whom we are glad to welcome as charge customers . . . and you are one of them.

This is important.
You probably are one of the more than eighty-four million people in the United States who own life insurance. You own life insurance because you recognize the obligation you owe to your loved ones.

You are part of a group of teachers and dealers to whom we are offering—FREE—an issue of the ———— ———— Plan.

"Dear Sir:"
which starts this letter in lieu of your name doesn't have the personal impact of several other no-name salutations: "Dearest," for instance, or "Greetings." But what I have to say, and to sell, is nevertheless in-

tended for a man who has a quality of mind and a range of problems and aspirations similar to yours.

A VITAL MESSAGE TO EVERYONE WHO WANTS TO HOLD ON TO HIS MONEY

8. The selection of an individual by definition:

In every company there is one man to whom others come when decisions must be made. This letter is addressed to you as the man in your company who carries this responsibility.

To the man who really wants to cut down maintenance costs . . .

Because of some distinctly complimentary things ABOUT YOU that we have learned, your name is included among those who should find this letter particularly interesting.

If you were just a name and a street number to us and we knew nothing of your interests, there would be no point at all in asking you to accept what amounts to two issues of ———— FREE!

WHY are we writing to *you?*
Because we think you're the sort of person who believes in getting the most out of being alive. Because we think you want the greatest thrill, pleasure, and convenience every second you sit behind the steering wheel of a car!

If you are looking for a way to "Get Rich Quick" by speculating in the stock market, this letter is not intended for you.

9. Asking or offering a favor:

May I ask a favor of you—the kind of favor I would not mind doing if I were in your place?

May we take a moment of your time this morning? We should like to have you look around your office, Doctor. A good look, with new eyes. Is your professional home attractive? Is your operating room constructed for maximum convenience with a simple, easy-to-work-in arrangement of space and equipment? Does your reception room induce patient relaxation—or is it coldly clinical? Are your methods and your outlook modern, or do you find yourself practicing with outmoded equipment?

Will you help us to help you?

I want to do you a favor. A favor that can put you on the threshold of the greatest *profit*-making opportunities of your lifetime.

10. Asking a question:

A question can be an effective way of drawing the reader closer to you. *What do you think, Mr. Brown?* immediately makes Mr. Brown part of your letter. The question may be used in the opening to create attention, to convince, to emphasize a point, or to get action.

Isn't that right, Mr. Brown?

Don't you agree, Mr. Jones?

What would you do in a situation like this?

Will you please do this for me, Mr. Brown?

Mr. John Doe	Please return this
30 Church Street	opinion page.
New York, N.Y. 10007	Thank you.

I hope you will permit us to call you for your advice concerning a publishing suggestion that has been made.

As publishers of the nationally famous annual guide, INCOME TAX ADVICE, we are aware that many accountants, attorneys, controllers, trust officers, and other business advisers use this book to prepare tax returns for clients.

What do you say to a kid who can't walk?
You've seen her, haven't you? She lives down the street, or around the corner on the way to the mailbox.

HOW MUCH PROFIT DO YOU WANT?

How much could you have made (or saved) had you known that the market would turn bearish in February and that prices would fall.

IS THERE DANGER
In a "Wait-and-See" Policy?

Can you answer these questions:
Are *you* being cheated by social security?
How can you borrow money—and save?
When are honeymoons dangerous?
Can you build your *own* job security?

Are you uncertain about what's going on or unsure about what will happen next?

Did you ever stop to question HOW a certain record is being written in your office and WHY it is written that way?

WOULDN'T IT BE WONDERFUL
IF YOU COULD LAUGH
THIS SUMMER
at every customer who walks in your office and gasps:
"It's the heat—it's the humidity—it's unbearable!"
You can have your laugh, because your office will be COMFORT-ABLE . . . THANKS TO A _____ ROOM AIR CONDITIONER.

DO YOU HAVE A DIRTY TOWEL ON YOUR CONSCIENCE?

11. Appeal to nostalgia:

Nostalgia can be used effectively to convince, to capture attention, or to set an emotional tone. It is an appeal to something in the reader's experience that will arouse his interest and make him receptive.

Remember the dreams we used to dream as youngsters, when we paged eagerly and excitedly through the mail-order catalog?
High adventure, indeed!
That's the feeling we hope you will recapture as you leaf through our catalog pages.

Is there any music you'd rather hear this evening than your boy's voice ringing out "Hello, Daddy."

Do you remember the smell of new-mown hay?

Have you ever met someone just once and later wished that you could get to know him better—have him for a friend, perhaps?

"Why Didn't I Think of That Myself!"

Dear Doctor:
The title *Doctor* sounds good, doesn't it? You worked hard for it; you have every right to be proud of it—and it's still kind of new. You'll probably find some other things new to you in the months to come as you start to establish yourself in your profession and build a practice.

May we say "Welcome!"
Going into business is a big step. We know because when we went into business 34 years ago we had a lot at stake, too. We weren't too sure then that we'd be around now to write you this welcome note.
But we are, because, like you, we offer a high-quality, dependable product to the most discriminating and hard-to-please buying audience in the world—the American retailer and businessman.

12. A strong negative thought:

On rare occasions a negative approach has been used successfully, although it is usually fraught with failure. Here are a few successful examples:

Don't be embarrassed!

Don't risk an infection!

"A SALESMAN CAN'T INFLUENCE ME," SHE SAID.
Yet her whole life and her family's are influenced by salesmen.

241

LETTERS YOU DON'T HAVE TO WRITE

A RECENT SPEECH by Maxwell C. Ross, a well-known sales promotion expert, listed fifteen ways letters can be used to create good will—and, eventually, sales. "There's just one prerequisite," he said; "the person using them has to be a nice guy, courteous, friendly, and above all, sincere."

Each is simply a friendly, personal letter that you send on some occasion when you would not be expected to send a letter at all. Such letters don't have to be written, but they create a tremendously favorable impression.

1. *You can use a letter to follow up a salesman's call.* You could start something like this: "John Smith told me today of the pleasant visit he had with you about your insurance program. I know that John will do a fine job for you." Then finish off in your own words.

2. *You can use letters to make appointments.* You say, "It's about time for me to sit down with you, Jim, and go over your insurance in the light of the new tax changes. I suggest that we get together late Friday afternoon. How would four o'clock be?" You don't need to say much more, but you'll be surprised at the nice reception you get when you arrive.

3. *Whenever a customer or client has been promoted or has changed jobs,* it's a nice gesture to send a letter like this: "Congratulations on your appointment to District Sales Manager. This is fine news, and I know you'll do a great job."

4. *When a customer is ill* all you need to say is: "I'm certainly sorry to hear that you are laid up. I hope it won't be many days before you're back at your desk."

5. *When there is a death in the family.* If it's tactfully done a short message of sympathy can mean much.

6. *When a daughter or son gets married, or a new baby arrives.* These letters make no tangible effort to sell; they're simply good-will builders—the kind that some day will bring something nice to you because you went out of your way to do something nice for somebody else.

7. *When people buy a home,* write to them. Your letter doesn't need to be long or fancy. Perhaps: "I hope you are enjoying getting

settled in your new home." If you have something to sell, tell these folks you'd appreciate a chance to call when things are squared away. In some cases, an inexpensive gift like a small rosebush or a young tree helps to create good will.

8. *When a customer has a birthday.* Quite a few successful salesmen make a practice of keeping birthday lists and sending cards or letters. If you use a card, write something in longhand on it.

9. *When people move to your town* a letter of welcome is an excellent source of new business. They don't know where to go for dry cleaning, laundry, milk—what service station to trade with, where to do their banking, or the nicer places to eat. So you write: "Welcome to Centerville. We know you'll like it here. If there is any way we can help you get settled, please let us know."

10. *When you read about a customer in the newspaper,* send him a letter. Clip the article, send it to him, and say: "I don't know whether your children keep a scrapbook of the nice things that happen to you, but just in case they do, here's an extra copy."

11. *When a customer is elected or honored in some way,* perhaps you would say: "I've heard some nice things about the work you've done for the Chamber of Commerce, so I was not surprised to see that you have been elected vice president."

12. *When someone has done you a favor* he will appreciate a note from you. "Thank you for those two extra tickets. I hope I can repay the favor soon."

13. *When some product or service pleases you,* take time to write about it. "I wanted you to know how pleased I am with our new floor furnace, and with the courteous and efficient way your men installed it."

14. *When a serviceman comes home* write to him or to his parents if he lives at home. That's a small way to show your appreciation of all he has done for your and his country.

15. *Thank new and old customers for their orders* with letters. In Des Moines, a filling station operator sends a post card to new customers. All the card says is, "It was nice of you to stop at our station. I hope you'll come back often."

SHE SAID, "I wouldn't have an automatic washer."
"I WOULDN'T EITHER," I answered . . .

1. UNLESS it was fully automatic, no tubs to empty—nothing to clean.
2. UNLESS I wanted to live longer, better, and with less work.
3. UNLESS it was guaranteed five years by a well-known company.
4. UNLESS it would wash curtains and feather pillows.
5. UNLESS I could starch, dye, bleach, and blue in it.
6. UNLESS my husband was a crank and wanted me to work myself to the bone.
7. UNLESS I was a crank and believed there was no better way of doing anything than the way I did it.

The body of a sales letter

Once you have aroused reader interest by the beginning of your sales letter, you must go on to convince the prospect. This is the job of the body of the letter. Although sales points vary with the product, the basic objectives are to explain what the product can do for the reader and to convince him that your claims are true. If you know and believe in your product thoroughly and sincerely, the body of the sales letter will be the easiest part to write. Before you tackle it, make certain that you know not only your product's virtues but also its faults. Then sell yourself on what you are selling. When the reader finishes a good sales letter, he should feel that the writer really believes in the product he's selling and the company he represents.

Here are some examples of paragraphs that effectively carry the burden of explaining and convincing:

Briefly, ———— cuts down time by enabling a clerical worker to do three jobs at once:
Posting to customer's statement, ledger card, and sales register, all in one operation.
Wage statement on employe's check or cash pay slip, on earnings-record card, and on payroll summary sheet, all in one operation.
Accounts-payable check, remittance advice, journal entry, all in one operation.

You've Seen It Yourself . . .
The wholesome fun *your* youngster has whenever an issue of ———— arrives.
You've seen how he enjoys the page after page of stories . . . pictures . . . games . . . riddles . . . jokes . . . news and good comics that are in every issue of this first complete newspaper for children.

You've watched how eagerly he follows the sport tips from the experts
. . . the latest scientific findings . . . the do-it-yourself experiments.

You've noticed how he learns about hobbies . . . different occupations . . . pet care . . . musical instruments . . . good books and culture from other lands.

Yes, by bringing —————— into your home, you're giving your youngster a great deal of wholesome, educational pleasure.

When you look over the enclosed Reply-O-Letter samples, note how
easy they make it for your customers and prospects to say "Yes!"

There's nothing to sign—no postage to pay—and the card *stays* with
the letter until the receiver is ready to act.

The address automatically becomes the "signature"—that's part of
the magic of Reply-O-Letter.

You immediately sense the value of having the reply card *with* the
letter. That way it can't be misplaced. It is always at the receiver's
fingertips, ready to be rushed on its way back to you.

Stated simply—make it easy for people to act and you get better results!

The secret's in the scale. Now typewriter margins can be set *before*
paper is inserted in the machine. Now your typists can center headings
with ease and perfection. Absolutely no "margin math" is ever needed.
Nor is it necessary to move the typewriter carriage.

With the perfect positioning scale there's no fumbling . . . no figuring . . . no time-wasting retypes . . . no inaccuracies, because your
typists will be able to center letters correctly the very first time.

CREATING CREDIBILITY

Today's customer is a skeptic who wants everything proved to him. As a
result sales letters make a special effort to prove their point. This may
be done by any of the following devices.

1. The guarantee:

But that's not all we offer. If for some reason the prepared material
doesn't cover your particular situation, our advertising department will
be glad to apply its skill and experience to *your* promotional problems.
There is no charge for this personalized advertising service. It is one of
the many extra services we have set up for you.

2. Free sample:

Will you please tell us the name of the person in your organization
who is responsible for the methods you use in writing, routing, and
supervising office and factory records?

245

We'd like to mail him a special portfolio of manufacturing forms. This portfolio is a handy filing folder containing . . .

Several samples of ————— are enclosed. Look at them, try them, test them. We're sure you'll like them.

3. Free trial:

Read this book at my risk and expense. Don't send a penny now. Just your permission to send it on to you to read for ten (10) whole days.

If at the end of the 10 days, you feel that ————— is not the answer to your financial problems, return it and no questions asked. If, however, you wouldn't part with it for love or money (and we don't believe you will), just send $3 in any convenient form and the book is yours to keep, to own, and to use as a ready reference.

The ————— has to be seen to be believed. Without seeing it, you can't realize how many applications it will have to your particular office routine. Without seeing it, you can't appreciate how easy it is to use and how economical it is to operate. You have to see it—and we want to show it to you. Like its many satisfied users (General Motors, Continental Can, and Du Pont, among others), we know that you won't do without it once you have seen what it can do for you.

4. Testimonials:

"I do not usually write testimonial letters," says Mrs. Hugh Kerr of Cincinnati, Ohio, "but I do want to thank you for Lawn Care and to report the astounding results from the use of Scott's Seed and Turf Builder. This is my first experience with Scott's and I am delighted."

We just received a report from a satisfied owner . . .

Read what others say who are sorry now that they did not start sooner. Our many satisfied users are our best advertisement. For example, Mrs. Fluelleh writes . . .

Mr. and Mrs. Edward Heyman, of Sachsonville, Illinois, were driving around the city one evening.

"We saw a lawn," wrote Mr. Heyman, "that was in a class by itself. Neither unusual heat nor almost complete lack of rain appeared to have affected it. I made bold to go to the house and ask for an explanation. The owner replied tersely, 'Scott's Seed and Turf Builder.' That seemed to him to tell all."

5. Reputable user or sponsor:

The value of ————— is acclaimed by the country's most progressive dealers in gift merchandise. Join the more than 16,400 subscribers who attest to the value of this magazine by reading it month after month.

The Upsilon Co., of St. Louis, has carried subscriptions for 30 or more of their men for years. And their history has been one of continually increasing sales volume.

S. T. Coleridge's of Janesville, Ohio, started years ago with a handful of subscriptions. Now they provide ————— for 47 of their men . . . and in the meantime have grown to be one of the most successful houses in that area.

A.B.D. carries 41 subscriptions for the salesmen in their branch offices on the West Coast. They've been doing this as a "group subscriber" since 1932.

6. Statistics of acceptance:

More than 10,000 sales managers have found these books active sales aids to the men on the road. Wouldn't it be a good investment to get ————— for all your salesmen to help them plan for more effective selling and better results?

Over sixteen million owners attest to the fact that Ronson is truly The World's Greatest Lighter.

7. Reference to the receiver's experience:

When you received this letter, you felt something inside the envelope. You consciously or unconsciously asked yourself, "What can this be?" So—you opened it.

8. Reference to the writer's experience:

If I could arrange for you to meet, in person, the Editorial Staff of —————, you'd be as impressed as I was this afternoon. I have just come from an editorial meeting. I sat there fascinated, watching these men and women judging material received from our representatives who cover the markets and news centers.

9. Tests of the product in use:

Here are a few examples of its durable qualities:
Ran a month on wearing-apparel unit without padding or flannel.
Formerly changed padding, flannel, and cover every week.
Ran 27 days, 243 hours, 16,250 shirts—on a swing bosom press.
Ran 25 days on collar press, 21 days on sleeve press, 23 days on bosom press, 17 days on body press—actual working time.

10. The reason why:

Because of quality production, we are able to offer you these forms made on the best-grade Bristol board at the following low prices.

11. Offer of comparison:

The unusual thing about the special services that you get is the fact that they cost you no more. Compare prices: ——————— costs far *less* when you consider the extra wear (not tear!) you get from all your washables!

12. The case history:

We had *two* calls this morning for young ladies to stay in homes where they can *earn* their room and board . . . and we have not run an ad for places in many weeks. The time of year is now approaching when people are making their plans for fall and winter.

13. Description of the raw material:

Here are a few interesting facts about the last issue you received:
To produce it for you, our 16 traveling editors consulted more than 200 plants, interviewed more than 300 key men in industry, and covered over 8000 miles!

Ending the letter

The last part of a sales letter is the clincher, the extra deciding point that will turn the reader into a customer. This may be a special bargain offer, a time limitation, or merely a summary of your previous arguments. If a letter deals with several points, it is wise to recapitulate before you make your final appeal. Here are a few endings that have been used successfully:

1. Limited-time or limited-quantity offer:

THIS OFFER WILL POSITIVELY BE WITHDRAWN NOVEMBER 29, 1985.

Do this today. Mail the postage-free card in the window of this letter. Get it in the mail now so that these THREE GREAT HOLIDAY BONUSES can be yours without a penny's cash outlay! Don't wait—put your best foot forward for the Holiday Bonuses. You'll be glad you did. Because only a limited number of these new aids is available, it's impossible for me to send more than one to each teacher. So please do not order more than one for yourself. As soon as more become available, I'll see to it that you get as many as you need. There's no obligation for this helpful service, of course.

This unusual offer must necessarily be LIMITED.
You may now enroll in ——————— for the low fee of $1.00. Your ONE

DOLLAR brings you every feature of my complete course, training, and service. This offer is available through September.

2. Time urgency:

Time is growing short, so send today for your free-of-charge booklet and folder. There's no obligation for them or for any further information you may require. Just mail the attached card now.

Now is the time to lay in your spring supplies. Use the enclosed order blank to tell us your needs. We'll do the rest. Send no money until you get the invoice. Specify later shipment if you like. Do it now while you have the urge. You'll thank us many times next year for suggesting it.

But do it today—the croup season is here . . . now!

3. Premiums, special services, or combination offers:

A special offer should be made to stand out. This can be accomplished by using indentation, a contrasting ink, a different type face, etc.

Our director wants so much for you to have the benefits of this course now that she has arranged a *special gift* for you *if* you enroll promptly.

Fill out the enclosed order form.

Drop it in the mail BEFORE SATURDAY, MAY 5th—and we will send you *your own personal copy* of this lavishly illustrated annual.

4. Increase in price:

The low prices, effective till December 31, are listed below. You'll notice they give you a 10 percent saving if you send your check with your order.

5. Personal pride:

Be the first in your community to have one of these new lawn mowers . . .

6. Making response easier:

This may be accomplished by enclosing stamped or business-reply cards or envelopes, permitting telephone response, or requiring no cash at the time of ordering.

A self-addressed envelope that requires no postage is enclosed for your convenience. You may use the back of this letter for your reply. We will appreciate it if you will let us hear from you soon.

Naturally, the brochures won't cost you a penny. And there's no obligation, either. So you'll have them that much sooner, please send us the card right now.

The above card requires neither postage nor signature. Just drop it in the mail and you will receive full information about the plan *and* the very useful tax facts booklet.

Jot your name on the card above right now—then drop it in the mail. I'll see that you get this timely, helpful information—without any cost or obligation on your part.

7. Salesman's call:

Call me today for a free demonstration. We will send a representative at your convenience.

You will hear from our nearest division office in a few days . . .

8. Buy at retail stores:

Get a bottle of ———— from your favorite grocer today and discover how it brings out the hidden flavor of all good foods.

Thorough as this folder may be, you can't really see the full value of ———— until you see it "in the flesh." Our representative at your neighborhood A.B.C. store will be happy to show you his display . . .

For the convenience of people living in your area we maintain an office located at . . .

9. Delays and apologies:

If your dealer happens to be temporarily sold out because of the ever-increasing public demand, leave an order with him: it will pay you to wait for a genuine Ronson lighter.

The unprecedented demand for our booklet during the past few months has exhausted our supply. We are taking the liberty of enclosing a leaflet . . .

Closings that can lose you sales

Some closings irritate. They may negate the effectiveness of an otherwise convincing sales letter. Avoid the following:

Just sign on the dotted line.　　　　Don't pass this up . . .
Trusting this will be satisfactory . . .
Beg to remain . . .　　And oblige . . .　　Yours while they last.
Don't miss this opportunity.
You'll be sorry if you don't order now.

20

How to say No
with a smile

When you have to say No to a customer, must it mean losing his business? The answer is No! You can turn down unreasonable or impossible requests and still build good will for the future by learning to make the three-part "sandwich" letter of refusal described here.

There are times when we must say No to friends, customers, and prospects. Obviously it is good business to say Yes whenever you can, but it is also good business to say No on many occasions.

"The customer is always right" is a brave statement that makes good reading and telling but it is not a true statement. The customer is often in error—sometimes to his own disadvantage. A successful businessman rephrased the motto to read: "The *right* kind of customer is always right." That comes closer to the truth but is filled with danger. It requires you to judge customers and say, "This one is the right kind of customer. This one is not."

Perhaps in personal contact selling, where we meet our customers on frequent occasions and have the opportunity to assess them, we can pass such judgments. For letter writers such opportunities are rare.

But even the right kind of customer must be told No on some occasions. Your job is to decide when and how to do that.

Your attitude writes the letter. Most often you are faced with the possibility of having to turn someone down when you've received a letter of complaint, a letter asking for adjustment, a letter asking for credit, or a letter asking for something extra. The attitude you take when you have read such a letter determines the nature of your answer.

251

If the letter you read makes you indignant, scornful, suspicious, or unhappy and you retain that attitude while writing the reply, you will write a bad letter.

HONESTY IS MOST PEOPLE'S POLICY

Most people are fair and honest. Not all, but most.

Here is one example. Some time ago a wholesale supplier of furniture, bedding, carpeting, and furnishings to hotels, tourist courts, and large institutions had a meeting with his advertiser. They discussed the fact that virtually no effort had been made to bring the firm's name to the attention of the motel and tourist-court field. They would map out a mailing campaign to make the name of the firm well known to all tourist-court and motel owners in their trading area. To get the ball rolling quickly, their first piece had to make an indelible impression.

The company had a big supply of metal floor lamps that it had bought at a very low price. It was the type of lamp that the prospects could use to good advantage.

Here's what was done. A giant mailing card was prepared which featured an illustration of the lamp and this headline: "You can have as many of these sturdy metal floor lamps as you want for *whatever you care to pay*. Do not pay more than $3.50."

Within two weeks the entire stock of some 2500 lamps was sold at an average price of $3.00! Sure, a few people took advantage and bought lamps for 25¢ each, but the vast majority paid a fair price.

That example offers a basis for your considerations when you receive a letter containing what might seem like an unwarranted beef or an unreasonable demand.

People want admiration. They want to appear fair, honest, and generous. All of us enjoy being admired. If anyone tells you, "So-and-so said you're a good person to deal with," your chest puffs up. You are susceptible to that kind of flattery; so are the people who write to you.

When anyone gets worked up to the point that he feels impelled to sit down and write a letter of complaint, or to demand something, he passes up the opportunity to pose as the big, openhanded sort. He becomes a complainer, which belittles and discomforts him. He does it only because a stronger emotion has taken control. He is angry. He is hurt. He feels that something that belongs to him has been denied.

And people are lazy. People don't take the time and trouble to write letters of complaint or adjustment unless they are moved strongly.

Weigh the human values before saying No. Taking these factors into consideration, you can't escape the conclusion that most angry letters are written because the writer has a powerful conviction that he's right.

Sure, there are the chronic troublemakers, the people who spend the better part of their lives writing letters to the editor and to city hall. But they're a small minority. You can't afford to view your correspondent as one of them. The safest course is to assume that everyone who writes you is convinced that his cause is just. Most often you'll be right.

And then turn to the Bible—"A soft answer turneth away wrath."

Perhaps you should say Yes. If you are genuinely sympathetic to the writer's viewpoint you are capable of writing a refusal that reflects that sympathy. Such a letter strikes a responsive chord. So the first thing to do when you receive a letter with a seemingly outlandish request is to consider sympathetically how and why the writer came to his conclusions. That puts you in a position to explain the reasons why it can't be done from his standpoint. It's just possible that some of the requests you normally would turn down should be granted. If that is the outcome of your reasoning both the complainant and your company gain. Even if the request or complaint is out of the ordinary, if you decide that it is just, you make the customer happy and you advertise the fact that your organization is fair and unselfish.

But often there is no getting around it: you have to say No.

When you say No, make a sandwich

The top layer consists of something the reader wants to know—something pleasing. *The middle layer* is a fat meaty filling of the reasons why you must refuse. *The final layer*, like the first, is something pleasing—something you will do.

In a moment we'll elaborate on that sandwich. First let's put the "poison" label on some of the common faults of refusal letters.

SAY NO NICELY

There is no need to offend. And be careful to avoid statements like "I'm sorry, but it is against the company's policy to do what you ask." You might just as well say, "Me, I'm a nice Joe, but the heels I work for have some cockeyed rule that says you can't have it."

Don't say, "You claim," or "You state," or "According to you," or anything else of that nature. It can and will be interpreted as "You're a liar." "I don't believe you." If the writer says that he received something with several parts missing and you have cause to restate the case in your reply, which of these sounds better to you: "You claim that several parts were missing" or "I understand that several parts were missing?"

SUGARCOAT THE PILL

Start your letter with something good. Now we've returned to the sandwich. You've read and reread the letter and have decided that you must refuse the request. Think: despite my refusal, is there anything I can do, anything I can offer, anything I can say that will please this person? There's always something. Start your letter with the best of those somethings. Now you come to that big, ugly No.

You can say No and make most people like it by a full explanation, demonstrating that a request was given great consideration.

Explain a refusal in detail. Your explanation should take into account the reader's viewpoint. Show that great consideration was given his individual request, that it wasn't lumped with issues raised a long time ago and then established as general policy.

Finally, you end up with that bottom layer of the sandwich: something you will do or something very pleasing. The end of your letter is always the part remembered longest. Leave the reader with a good taste in his mouth. In some cases you may have nothing more pleasing to offer than the item you used for the top layer—the opening of your letter. In that case, restate it, rephrase it, remind him of it.

Refusing long-term credit

Let's try a test case. Here is a letter received by the National Radio Institute. They offer home study courses in radio, television, and electrical appliance repair.

Dear Mr. Paul:

Well, I've just signed the lease and I'm opening my own radio and TV repair shop. Even though I haven't finished half the course yet, the practical experience I had before I started and what I've learned from you folks so far makes me feel I can make a go of it.

I guess that gives you some idea why I've gotten a little behind in my payments. I think I owe you for three months right now. It takes a lot of money to start a shop, fix it up and get all the tools and equipment.

Everybody's been very nice to me. The companies I approached have all agreed to give me credit even though I'm new and never did any business with them before. Well, you folks have known me for nearly six

*months now and until recently I've always paid on time. You know what
can be made in this business and from the good grades and reports I've
had on my assignments I think you know I have what it takes to make
this business a success.*

*So I'm asking you to do what the people who don't know me have
done. I want to complete the course just as fast as I can. The more I
know the better I can do, but I want you to give me credit. I want to
finish the course and pay you when the shop starts earning money.*

*Maybe six months from now, I'll have an easy time paying. In the
meantime keep me going and you can count on getting your money
when I'm through. I've got to hold on to all my money for working
capital.*

I'll appreciate your cooperation.

Very truly yours,
John Johnson

The Institute has no financial arrangements that would make it possible for them to okay such a request. This was their reply:

Dear Mr. Johnson:

You are absolutely right. The assignments I've received from you,
and the experience you have had, give me great faith in the success of
your new enterprise. And don't worry at all about being behind on your
last payments.

After reading your letter this morning I took it to Mr. Smith's office
and we discussed it at some length. We're both very pleased with your
progress, your ambition, and the bright future you face. It was our conclusion, however, that we'd be doing you a great disservice if we did the
easy thing and said Yes to your suggestion. We've seen lots of students
start businesses of their own. Many made good but there are some who
didn't. We want to see you make good.

It is never a good idea to start a business in debt. Credit is fine and
useful. But normal credit generally means that you pay what is owed in
thirty days' time. If we agreed to your plan, you would be building up
a debt for six months or a year. In time, despite how well your business
might be doing, that debt would become a burden. It is not a healthy
way to start. You are far better off if you keep yourself current, knowing what your fixed expenses are each month and meeting them. When
you consider that, I'm sure you'll agree that it is the only sound way to
launch your new career.

Of course we know what a burden it is to start a new shop. For that
reason, and because we want to help in every way we can, I have told
the bookkeeping department to adjust the books so that you are on a
current basis. The three months you owe for now can be paid for at the
end of the course. That gets you off to a fresh, new start.

To give you some additional help I'm enclosing one of our folders,
"How to Open Your Own Shop." This is always sent to our students

MARK TWAIN SAYS NO

WHEN 1364 sweeter and better people, including the author, have tried to dramatize Tom Sawyer and did not arrive, what sort of show do you suppose you stand? That is a book, dear sir, which cannot be dramatized. One might as well try to dramatize a hymn.

Now as I understand it, dear 1365, you are going to re-create Tom Sawyer dramatically, then put me in the bills as father of this shady offspring. Sir, do you know that this kind of compliment has destroyed people before now? Listen.

Twenty-four years ago, I was strangely handsome. I was so handsome that human activities ceased as if spellbound when I came in view, and even inanimate things stopped to look—like locomotives and district messenger boys.

Upon one occasion, when I was traveling in the Sonora region and stopped to rest, all the town came out to look. A Piute squaw named her baby for me; other attentions were paid me. Last of all arrived the president and faculty of Sonora University and offered me the post of Professor of Moral Culture and Dogmatic Humanities. I accepted gratefully and entered upon my duties.

But my name had pleased the Indians, and in the deadly kindness of their hearts they went on naming their babies after me. The University stood it for a couple of years, then felt obliged to call a halt, although I had the sympathy of the whole faculty. The president himself said to me, "I am as sorry as I can be for you, but you see how it is: there are 132 of them already, and 14 precincts to be heard from. The circumstance has brought your name into most wide and unfortunate renown. It causes much comment, some—by patrons who know only the statistics without the explanation— offensive and even violent. Nine students have been called home. The trustees of the college, growing more and more uneasy—along with the implacable increase in your census—have charged me with the unpleasant duty of receiving your resignation."

I know you only mean me a kindness, dear 1365, but it is a most deadly mistake. Please do not name your Injun for me.

Hartford, Sept. 8, '87

(*This letter to No. 1365 was never mailed.*)

when they've completed the course, but I thought you'd find it helpful now. The best of good luck to you!

Cordially,
Harry Paul

The strongest statement in this letter is, "After reading your letter this morning I took it to Mr. Smith's office."

When John Johnson is told that his request was considered important enough to warrant an executive conference you've made a friend even though you do turn him down. Look for the sandwich in the letter. Weigh the understanding and sympathy it reveals. Johnson may have been disappointed, but he would be an unusually hardheaded man if he were angry after reading Mr. Paul's considerate reply.

How to keep a customer while refusing credit

You can refuse with a smile. The credit manager of a women's apparel shop received a letter asking for a charge account. A routine check showed that the applicant had accounts at several other local stores and was not meeting her obligations. The manager had to refuse the application but wanted to sell his store. Some day the customer may be a good credit risk. In the meantime she can be a cash customer.

Dear Mrs. Applier,
You've paid us a high compliment in applying for a charge account. You've given us your confidence and have shown that you like our selections. I have something I'd like to give to you.

Dealing with people—their finances and their budgets—day after day, makes me a little bit of an expert I suppose. Many, many times I've had the real pleasure of helping people who have become tangled up in financial problems.

When your application arrived we asked the local credit bureau for the usual report. I have just spent quite a while carefully reviewing the report and I am convinced it would not be wise for you to take on added obligations now. That's why I'm making this letter an invitation.

Why don't you visit with me the next time you're in the store, Mrs. Applier? Perhaps, from the variety of experiences I have had helping people with money matters, I might be able to give you some thoughts that could prove valuable to you. I'll be delighted to be of assistance and I'm sure the store shares my feelings.

Sincerely,

A credit manager is in an excellent position to give individuals a great deal of sound advice about budgeting. Perhaps he will see where a troubled person with many delinquent bills would be better off consolidating her debts by securing a personal loan. But whether Mrs. Applier accepts his invitation or not, it is logical to assume she will have a warm feeling toward the store that offers a sympathetic, helping hand.

Any time the credit manager devotes to such counseling can bring untold dividends in good will, customer loyalty, and priceless word-of-mouth advertising.

Saying No to a juicy prospect

A large manufacturer of drug products, with its own salesmen situated in the major cities, had a letter from the head of a big chain of drug stores. The chain never had bought from this concern. The current salesman and the man who had handled the territory before him had made many efforts to win the account but every one of their attempts had failed.

Now the president of the drug chain had written. He said he would like to take on the manufacturer's full line for all his stores, but he wanted to buy direct, bypassing the salesman. If the manufacturer agreed, the chain would expect lower prices since there would be no sales commission to pay.

The offer was tempting, for the volume would be considerable. But this company protected its salesmen. They knew that they would be establishing a bad precedent if they agreed to the proposal. They would undermine the confidence and morale of their entire sales force. They had to refuse. This was the letter they wrote:

Dear Mr. P.:

Every time Boston has been mentioned in these offices somebody has sighed and wistfully talked about your great chain of modern drug stores. You must be immensely proud of the progress you have made, for I know that the entire drug industry is grateful to you for the manner in which you have raised the prestige and public acceptance of our contribution to society.

As you know we have made many overtures over the years. It has been our ambition to count you as one of our distributors. For these reasons your letter found a warm welcome.

I think you'll be particularly interested in the observation made by our national sales manager when I called a meeting this morning to discuss your proposal.

Mr. Osgard said, "The proposal would be far more tempting if we didn't know our own salesmen so well. We have built this business and it continues to grow not only because we are so careful about the uniform high quality of our products and the popular demand we have created with national advertising, but because every field man we have has been trained to help our retail customers to make extra profits.

"If we accepted this offer and eliminated the salesman we could reduce the prices but we'd be reducing Mr. P's turnover and profits too. These people are wonderful merchandisers but our men are specialists. They have never failed to show retailers how to make the most of our products, our promotions, our in-the-store merchandising. Our agreement to their offer would give them a surface advantage but would deprive them of a bigger, more important advantage. We'd be doing them a serious disservice."

What Mr. Osgard said is abundantly true. One additional consideration is that our business has been built on loyalty and good faith. We cannot violate those with our salesmen any more than we can with our customers.

Your business is so much to be desired it is difficult for me to reject you on any terms. If it suits your convenience I am planning to catch an early morning flight to Boston next Tuesday. I'll be delighted if you'll see me and our local man, Mr. Hammond, at ten o'clock that morning. The timing is particularly appropriate for we have news of a dramatic new national promotion about to be launched. When you hear the details I know it will appeal to your fine merchandising sense and you will see the broad opportunities for your own organization.

If the date I have mentioned is not convenient I'll appreciate your suggestion for a more suitable time.

My sincerest thanks for your letter.

> Cordially,
> Claude Snow, President

Mr. Snow got his appointment. He did not make a sale at that meeting, but did win the chain's business within the year. The letter quoted above was an important factor, for it led the drug chain's president to the inescapable conclusion that Mr. Snow's company stood for outstanding integrity.

Accentuating the positive

The following is a "No sandwich" with a fat filling of meat and a tempting aftertaste. The letter does much more than say No. It takes the negative, turns it completely around, and makes the reasons for the refusal into powerful sales arguments.

Kalb, Voorhis & Co., a New York Stock Exchange firm, produces a service for investment firms throughout the country. The service supplies the dealer firms and their salesmen with advertising and sales training materials. The firm offers a basic subscription to the dealer plus supplementary kits for each of their salesmen. One morning's mail brought this letter from an organization that employs an exceptional number of salesmen:

Gentlemen:

Thank you for sending me samples of your MSS service. It looks quite interesting and I can see where we could use it to excellent advantage. We are considering taking a basic subscription plus eighty-six salesmen's kits.

If we do take the service we will make full use of it. In other words we will be using your newspaper mats and sales letters and literature extensively. We cover our territory thoroughly and I would want your assurance that we will be given exclusive use of your material for this area before we enter into any agreement with you.

I look forward to your reply.

Sincerely yours,
R. M. A.

Kalb, Voorhis & Co. does not offer the service on an exclusive basis. They answered Mr. A's letter in this manner:

Dear Mr. A.:

Your interest in the MSS service is as fine a tribute as we could hope for. There are few retailing organizations in the country who have won and merited the reputation for progressiveness you enjoy. My sincerest thanks for your stamp of approval.

Your request that you be given an exclusive on MSS services for your area has been given a great deal of study. Your reasons for requesting it are clear and certainly make good sense. If you'll follow me through the reasons why this is impractical, however, I think you'll agree that it would not give you any true advantage.

The way to convince another is to state your case moderately and accurately. Then scratch your head, or shake it a little, and say that is the way it seems to you, but that of course you may be mistaken about it; which causes your listener to receive what you have to say, and as like as not, turn about and try to convince you of it, since you are in doubt. But if you go at him in a tone of positiveness and arrogance you only make an opponent of him.

—Benjamin Franklin

If we were to accept subscriptions on an exclusive basis we would have far fewer subscribers. The only antidote for that, naturally, would be a considerable increase in the annual fees. The subscription price would be multiplied by four or more. Even that might be acceptable to you until you weigh the advantages against the additional costs.

You undoubtedly noticed, when reviewing the sample issues, that we do not send our subscribers the mats for the newspaper ads. We send prints of the ads. If a subscriber wants the mats he requests them and they are sent to him without charge. There's a reason for this. It enables us to watch for requests for identical mats coming from more than one dealer in a specific city. When this occurs we caution both dealers. They check with each other and thus eliminate the possibility of identical ads appearing over two different firm names in the same city. In five years this situation has come up only twice. The number of ads we offer makes it unlikely that two dealer firms will choose the same ads at the same time.

The only other possibility of overlapping is in the use of our suggested sales letters. Here the chances are even more remote. MSS brings you fifty to sixty suggested letters a year. The average firm may use five or six. The chances of two dealers in one city selecting the same letters and sending them to the same people are so extremely unlikely we have not a single instance of its happening even though we have as many as seventy subscribers in some cities.

The sales kits your salesmen will get, as you have seen, give them fresh, compelling approaches, sound answers to objections, prospecting methods, telephone technique, practical information on tax-savings, and many other direct aids. Here there need be no fear of overlapping at all. Each man takes these lessons and applies them in his own manner.

Summing it all up, don't you agree that the vastly higher fee we'd be compelled to ask for an exclusive on MSS would fail completely to bring you commensurate advantages?

And there's one thing more, Mr. A. When you subscribe to MSS you have the privilege of coming to us with requests for any special newspaper or direct mail advertising you want prepared for your individual use. Here you do have an exclusive. There's no charge for these services. We're delighted to do these things for you.

Since MSS does represent to you a sound tool for adding to your sales, and to the strength of your advertising and sales training, I hope that I have answered the one objection that came to mind in a manner that opens the doors for this great flow of invaluable services. They can start next week if you'll phone me collect or air mail your acceptance today.

Cordially,

Consider each of these examples of letters of refusal and you'll find in the background a uniform attitude, a genuine desire to help.

The ten things to remember when you say No

1. Your attitude writes the letter, so avoid anger and indignation.
2. First put yourself in the other fellow's shoes.
3. Look for logical reasons for a complaint or unusual request even if they were not expressed.
4. Agree if you can.
5. Say No with care and thoughtfulness.
6. Avoid expressions that may create anger.
7. Start out with something the reader will like.
8. Take a lot of space and time to give your reasons for refusal.
9. Explain your rejection from the standpoint of the reader.
10. End your letter with something you will do for him or something pleasant to him.

test your skills

HOW TO SAY NO WITH A SMILE

1. Why is your attitude important in writing a letter in which you must say No?

2. Name two ways attitude can be shaped.

3. Below are two letters that achieve the same purpose, but one is better than the other. Tell which is better and why:

a. Dear Mr. Fazeby:
   Reference is made to your letter of Mar. 12 requesting long-term credit for a shipment of bolt oars. Periodically we receive such requests, but any extension of credit beyond the regular 90-day allowance is against company policy. We regret that we can't accommodate your request, and look forward to continuing to serve you as we have in the past.

b. Dear Mr. Fazeby:
   I know that it is difficult to start a new company and I sympathize with you in your economic difficulties. New firms, such as yours, frequently find themselves overextended and short of cash. Several have asked us to extend their credit, but we learned long ago that we can help our customers more by keeping a firm 90-day credit schedule, which enables us to offer lower prices. Although we, regretfully, can't extend your credit, we would be glad to help in any other way possible. If you would like, we will have our district manager call on you; possibly he could make some marketing suggestions that would stimulate your sales and increase your profits so that you can get on your feet faster.

Answers to this quiz appear on page 704.

21

How to handle
delicate situations

This chapter is a challenge. Here are six tough problems in business-letter writing: situations that will demand all your tact, understanding, and powers of persuasion. Think them through, write your own answer, then compare your letter with the solution proposed by the experts.

You've now read some effective letters of response to inquiries being used with success by a number of well-known companies. You've seen that there is an almost endless number of ways to create a sales letter that will bring results. You've learned that you can refuse credit and still keep a friendly customer. You have seen that you can admit to an error graciously—meanwhile reaffirming your company's honesty and efficiency. You've discovered that with a little thought and ingenuity you can sweeten your refusal of a request with an offer of an unasked-for favor. You can see that once you have learned some methods of approach, planning, and organization, business-letter writing is usually a surprisingly simple job. In this chapter we'll look at the problem of writing responses that are really tough.

First, suppose you see how much you've learned, how well you are doing. Here are six letter-writing problems. Read the problems. Study them carefully. Think about them. Adjust your mental attitude and then write the letters of reply.

After you have written your letters—not before—turn to the sample replies on the pages that follow. Read the letters and the analysis of each and measure your letters against the samples. See if you are satisfied that you have thought of every point. Tell yourself whether or not your letters were as strong and as effective as they might have been. If they were not, see what you can do to improve them.

PROBLEM NO. 1—WRONG NUMBER

You are in the mail order business. Twice a year you produce a catalog of household and gift items. You mail the catalog to old and prospective customers. A good customer has just received your Christmas catalog. He is a business executive who has been selecting his firm's Christmas gifts from your catalogs for a number of years.

You get a letter from him ordering 100 desk clocks. But he has made an error. The clock he has specified is not in your catalog. It is featured in a competitor's catalog. You have a similar clock. Your clock sells for $13 a unit. The competitor's clock is $12.50.

Your agreement with the manufacturer of the clock you handle does not permit you to lower the price. The only advantage your clock has over the competitive brand is that it features a radium dial and swivels on its base, whereas the other has a plain dial and is in a fixed position. Write to your customer. (Sample reply on pages 267–268.)

PROBLEM NO. 2—WHERE, OH WHERE?

You work for a manufacturing plant. This letter comes to your attention. It's your job to find out what happened to the order, to take whatever action is needed and then to answer the letter. (Sample reply on page 269–270.)

Gentlemen:

More than three weeks ago I saw your ad in the PDQ Trade Journal. In response to the ad I wrote to you, enclosing my check for $142.78, a copy of the ad, and a covering letter ordering one gross of your Model 0021, to be shipped to me express collect.

I have not received the merchandise. You haven't even had the courtesy to acknowledge my order. If you are not prepared to ship the ordered merchandise immediately return my check at once.

Sincerely,

O. P. Hattery

PROBLEM NO. 3—STUDENT TROUBLE

You conduct a correspondence school in typewriter cleaning and repair work. Students make a down payment of $50 and then pay $10 a month for sixteen months while taking the course. Joe Typer has been taking the course for seven months. His assignments and payments have come in promptly. His work has been excellent. Now you get a letter from him instead of his completed assignment:

Gentlemen:

I have bad news. The whole time I've been taking your course I've been working and doing the lessons at night. My wife has been working too. Now she's broken her leg. The right one.

Now I have to work at night too. I fix the dinner. I wash the dishes. I do the laundry. I clean the apartment. I help the kids with their homework and put them to bed and I have to tend to my wife too. I'm too tired to do anything else. I quit.

Yours very truly,
Joe Typer

When Joe started the course he signed a binding contract. He is legally liable for the balance of the payments whether he completes the course or not. This is your own school. What you say to him is up to you. Write to Joe Typer. (Sample reply on pages 270–271.)

PROBLEM NO. 4—THE LANDLORD

The insurance agency you head occupies half a floor of a large but old office building. You have been in the building for twelve years. Two years ago the building was sold. Mr. Clay, the new owner, resides in a distant city. You have never met him. He has refused to renew leases for any of the building's occupants. You are on a month-to-month basis. This morning you had a letter from the owner. He tells you he has decided to completely modernize the building. In order to do so in the least expensive and most efficient manner he is giving all tenants thirty days' notice to move.

Office space is difficult to obtain and you are in the midst of your busiest season. Write a letter to the owner. (Sample reply on pages 272–73.)

PROBLEM NO. 5—OUT OF CASH

You are Harry Elect. You own and operate a retail outlet for electric appliances. Business has been fairly slack, but you count on good volume during the Christmas season. You stock heavily. Business is good, but not as good as you had hoped. Right after Christmas some new merchandise of various types comes on the market. Heavy national advertising by the manufacturers builds up a healthy demand.

You order the new merchandise in. You know you have to do some local advertising to let people know what you have. The combination of these conditions puts you in bad shape for current finances. Your bank has loaned you as much money as it will. Your resources are beginning to press you for payment.

A letter arrives from the sales manager of your biggest supplier. He tells you he is unable to ship the goods you just ordered because his credit department advises him that you are behind in your payment for previous shipments. Your greatest hopes were based on your offering of his goods. Your advertising, already being printed, features that merchandise. There is nothing you can do about sending his company a check now. Write to him. (Sample reply on pages 274–275.)

PROBLEM NO. 6—GET RICH QUICK

You are an investment dealer. Mrs. Bowers, an elderly widow, is one of your clients. She has sufficient capital to produce the income she needs provided that she lives carefully and that none of her capital is touched. You have taken great pains to invest her money in highly conservative securities that give her the income her situation requires.

Today you get a letter from Mrs. Bowers. She is visiting friends in a distant city. She tells you that she met a salesman for an investment firm there. On his advice she wants to sell a number of her current securities and use that money to buy stock in the CDQ Mining and Exploration Company. The man she met has assured her that she can double her money within six months.

You look up the CDQ stock and you see that it pays no dividends at all; that the value of the securities is highly questionable; that Mrs. Bowers is more likely to lose her money than double it. Write to her. (Sample reply on pages 275–276.)

How businessmen solved these problems

Have you written your letters of reply? Go over them carefully. Edit them. Picture yourself talking on the telephone, using the words you've written. Do they sound right? Warm? Do they take the other fellow's viewpoint into consideration? Do they cover all essential points? Does each one start with a statement that will lure the reader into wanting to know what comes next? Does each start with a tone that will help the reader to feel well disposed toward you? Has each letter an ending that pinpoints the action you want and makes it as easy as possible for the reader to take action?

Are your thoughts presented in logical order? Have you sidestepped the use of tired, worn-out expressions? Are your words and sentences simple and clear? Does each letter flow smoothly, avoiding abrupt, puzzling shifts of thought?

Does each letter show that you formed a sharp mental picture of the person you've written to? Where you had to refuse a request did you show that great consideration had been given to the proposition before you turned it down? Did you start and end your letters of refusal with something the reader would enjoy reading?

If you are satisfied that your letters are as good as they should be, read the sample answers. Compare them with your own letters. See if the analysis of each sample letter could apply to your own efforts.

REPLY TO PROBLEM NO. 1—WRONG NUMBER

Dear Mr. Obermann,

Although thousands of orders come in at this time of the year, the ones that get the warmest greetings are those from loyal customers, like you. You've given us your Christmas order for many years. Every transaction we've had with you has been exceptionally pleasant.

Undoubtedly, at this time of the year you are snowed under with catalogs from many mail order houses. It would be nice to think our catalog was the only one that claimed your attention, but of course that wouldn't be good business on your part. Evidently you read at least one other catalog this year. The desk clocks you specified are not carried by us.

I've done some checking for you. The clock you ordered is offered by Joe Stow & Co., 212 98th Street, in Keokok, Iowa. If you feel that the Stow clocks will serve your purposes best, that's where they are.

But, Mr. Obermann, I hope you will take another look at the desk clocks on page 131 of our catalog. You'll be particularly interested in Model 41. Model 41 is almost identical to the clock you selected, with two exceptions. Our clock has a radium dial, giving it extra utility. It also features a swivel base, giving your customers added convenience. The prices of the two clocks are almost the same. The two additional values in Model 41 add only 50¢ a unit to your cost. In case your copy of the catalog has been discarded I'm enclosing another one for you.

Desk clocks seem to be unusually popular this year and Model 41 has been selling immensely well. To be certain that your needs will be covered I'm putting aside the 100 you want. I'll hold them until I hear from you.

After you've read this letter, please phone or wire me collect to tell me whether you want the folks on your Christmas list to have Model 41. Your clocks are sitting on the shipping room "hold" counter, all prettied up in their sparkling Christmas wrappings. They're ready to go to you the moment you say, "Okay." I'll be grateful if you'll give me your decision by Friday of this week.

Sincerely,

Analysis:

■ SETTING THE ATMOSPHERE. The opening paragraph performs several useful functions. In a warm, friendly manner, the first sentence reminds Mr. Obermann of the order he placed. The balance of the paragraph creates the mental atmosphere needed under the circumstances. He's reminded of his "loyalty"—of the fact that he's given this firm his Christmas orders each year and that all transactions have been "exceptionally pleasant." The desirability of dealing with this mail order house has been implanted in his mind firmly and with flattering courtesy.

■ STATING THE SITUATION. The second paragraph tells of the error that was made. Great tact has been used to avoid the possibility of Mr. Obermann's feeling foolish and ill at ease. He is even complimented on his good business judgment in looking at competitive catalogs.

■ EXTREME SERVICE. In the third paragraph the writer caters fully to Mr. Obermann's interests. Although he wants the business he spells out the fact that he went to the trouble to learn where Mr. Obermann can get the competitive item if he wants it above all others. This is extreme service and consideration. It cannot fail to make a deep impression on Mr. Obermann. The writer is so immensely fair and helpful that the desire to do business with him soars to new heights. What he has done is unusual enough to be remembered for years. Mr. Obermann can become a great spreader of good will for the company.

■ MAKING THE SALE. The fourth paragraph makes a strong and logical bid for the order. Without deprecating the competitive article the writer builds up the greater desirability of his own. He makes it completely easy for the buyer to examine it by telling him precisely where to find the illustration and description in the catalog. To be sure that no chance is lost he even encloses a duplicate copy of the catalog. In telling of the higher price, he presents it in the most desirable manner. First he tells what the extra qualities are and then he quotes the price in the lowest denominator. He speaks of 50¢ a unit—not $13.00 a unit.

■ PRELUDE TO ACTION. The fifth paragraph starts the drive for the desired action. Without seeming to put undue pressure on Mr. Obermann, it makes clear the need for fast action. Model 41 is going fast. Fine service to Mr. Obermann is manifest again—the writer is protecting his customer's interest by holding the needed quantity for him.

■ACTION. Now, in the final paragraph, the wanted action is detailed. It is made cost-free and simple. An additional advantage is piled on. Mr. Obermann is given a mental picture of the attractive Christmas wrappings. Speed of delivery is held before him as still another benefit. The letter ends by requesting action by a specific date.

REPLY TO PROBLEM NO. 2—WHERE, OH WHERE?

Dear Mr. Hattery:

One gross of Model 0021 left here by Air Express this morning, twenty minutes after your letter arrived. By this time you've had my telegram advising you of the shipment.

My warmest thanks, Mr. Hattery, for writing and bringing this inexcusable delay to the surface. You've been very patient.

The moment your shipment was out of here and the telegram sent I started an investigation. Until you've had some more experience with us you'll find it hard to believe, I'm sure, but this is far from our normal method of handling orders.

The rule here is that an order is acknowledged the day it arrives and, if humanly possible, the goods are shipped that same day. The longest we normally take to make a shipment is forty-eight hours, unless we have no inventory of the item requested. That's why your well-justified complaint constituted a serious mystery here.

I didn't have to look far. The first place checked was the accounting department. Your order and check went there first to be entered on the books and to permit them to search the files to see if you were a new customer or not. They found that you had placed one previous order nearly three years ago. And that's where it happened. When the old folder was returned to the file your new order went in the file too. That's where it was found this morning.

No heads rolled. Nobody was fired. The folks working in that department are good. They handle thousands of details each week and they make amazingly few errors. But they are human and mistakes will happen. We had a little meeting and showed them what had occurred in your case. It put everyone that much more on his toes to safeguard against a similar slip in the future.

So, we owe you more than a deeply sincere apology, Mr. Hattery. We owe you a vote of genuine appreciation. The incident will make us even more efficient in the future.

I do hope that the delay didn't cause you any serious inconvenience. Please accept our warmest thanks for your business. I look forward to hearing from you again so that we'll be able to demonstrate the far more normal courtesy and speed with which your orders will be handled. Although your letter specified that the merchandise should be sent express collect we have prepaid the shipment, to demonstrate our desire to make amends.

Sincerely,

Analysis:

■ TELL HIM AT ONCE THE ACTION TAKEN. Mr. Hattery's greatest interest is to find out what you're going to do. The opening paragraph, therefore, gives him that information without frills or prelude.

■ UNRUFFLE HIS FEATHERS. With good cause the customer was upset. The second paragraph pours some oil on the troubled waters and the following paragraph adds to the desired effect. It lets Mr. Hattery know that his letter caused deep concern and instant investigation. That's flattering.

■ FULL EXPLANATION. The second item of importance, after you've filled the order, is to establish that this type of handling is highly unusual in your plant. A full explanation is essential. The fourth and fifth paragraphs tell the story. The story is complete and it is believable.

■ THIS ISN'T NORMAL HERE. The explanation may tell how it happened, but you have another important job to perform. You have to convince the customer that, despite his experience, you have an efficient organization. Paragraph six tackles that job, and number seven ties the bow on the package.

■ SOMETHING EXTRA. The final paragraph makes a bid for future business and gives the customer a bonus to make amends for the discourtesy and the delay. It is bound to leave Mr. Hattery thinking, "Aren't they nice people!"

REPLY TO PROBLEM NO. 3—STUDENT TROUBLE

Dear Mr. Typer:

I don't blame you a bit. If I had the problems that are sitting on your shoulders right now the chances are I would have written the same letter you just wrote to me.

Of course you can't find time to carry on your home assignments, and give them the concentration they deserve, with all those troubles and duties at home. I wouldn't expect or want you to.

You've been doing a fine job up to this point. Seven months ago you saw an opportunity to do something that would lead you to a real career. You made your decision and went to work. You've worked well—

unusually well—and the realization of your ambition is not far off. Now there's been a disruption. But this present condition won't last forever, Mr. Typer. You'll still reach your goal.

I'm putting your papers in a special file on my desk. On top of it I've written, "Hold in suspense for three months." That means that you won't have to do any assignments or make another payment for three months. You're being given a leave of absence until your home situation is back where it was before your wife's unfortunate accident.

All of us here hope that Mrs. Typer makes a quick and painless recovery. The only thing I'm going to ask you to do right now is to return the postcard I'm putting in with this letter. Three months is my guess as to the length of time you'll need. If you think the time should be shorter or longer, or if you agree with my guess, just tell me on the card and drop it in the mail. That way I'll know when to send your next lesson.

Good luck and thanks for letting me know the circumstances.

Cordially,

Analysis:

■ YOU'RE RIGHT! Joe Typer's letter makes it clear that he's disturbed and unhappy. He's in a state of rebellion. He has told you that he's quitting. Undoubtedly he expects you to write back telling him he can't or shouldn't quit. He's mentally prepared for that, and he's prepared to resist you. The opening paragraphs of this letter take the wind out of his sails. The school agrees with him. He's told he's right—that he's doing what anybody would do. Joe's mental resistance to the expected onslaught melts away.

■ AMBITION REKINDLED. Seven months ago Joe Typer had a vision. The vision was strong enough to impel him to put up his hard-earned money and devote a lot of his spare time to make that vision a reality. Those are strong motivations. Deep down inside of Joe a good percentage of that vision and determination must exist today. They've been buried by immediate problems. The writer, recognizing this, uses the third paragraph to trade on these elements. He rekindles the ambition. In doing so he reminds Joe that his work with the course has been unusually good. This is pleasing and it adds glitter to the promised career.

■ UNDERSTANDING IS GOOD BUSINESS. While the earlier paragraphs indicate sympathy and understanding, the fourth paragraph puts them on a practical basis. The school's action shows Joe the way out of his troubles without giving up his career ambitions. The offer makes it easy for him to make the decision that he can and will complete the course.

Not a word is said about his contractual obligation to the school. The tone of the letter is that the writer wants to help a friend. You don't talk to a friend about helping him in one breath and then threaten to sue him in the next. You don't even hint at a possibility. If Joe fails to accept this generous offer it may become necessary to use pressure in some future letters. In this first one, however, it would be completely out of order.

■ASK FOR ACTION.   At a casual glance it may not seem necessary to ask for any kind of action now. Actually the need is urgent. If the action request is absent the chances are that Joe will not respond. The school, under those circumstances, will have to wait for three months before they know whether Joe is going to continue or not. That is bad. During that period they could have been writing additional letters to him giving other reasons why he should not drop out. Learning that he is still determined to quit, after three months have passed, represents a far more difficult job of reselling and a greater danger of financial loss.

On the other hand, if Joe returns the requested postcard now, saying that he will start again when his home life returns to normal, he has made a mental and moral commitment. The chances are he'll see it through. The postcard is essential.

REPLY TO PROBLEM NO. 4—THE LANDLORD

Dear Mr. Clay:

Sincerest congratulations on the progressive move you are about to make. You have a fine building here. The location is one of the best in the city. Now you plan to make the building as modern and as desirable as any of the new buildings that have grown up around us. It's a splendid plan.

When your letter arrived this morning I canceled all my engagements for the day. I have phoned or visited nearly a dozen office buildings and real estate offices in an effort to make satisfactory arrangements that would enable me to comply with your request. So far I've found nothing that will come close to meeting my needs.

The half floor we've been occupying for the past twelve years is a lot of space. Finding an equal amount of space in any office building in town, I've learned, is going to be a real problem. Immediate occupancy is what makes this difficult. In several buildings, there will be adequate space available in three to six months, but not sooner.

What is the best way for me to cooperate with you, Mr. Clay? As you know, our offices are on the second floor. How long do you think it will be before your workmen reach my part of the building?

At this time, Mr. Clay, I would like to apply for a long-term lease in your renovated building. Perhaps, if your plans call for the completion of the upper stories first, I can stay where I am until one of them is completed and then move right into that part of the building. I'll phone you Thursday morning at 10:30 to discuss this idea with you.

Cordially,

Analysis:

■SURPRISE. Perhaps there are as many as 100 tenants in your building. On the morning you received your letter, identical letters reached everyone else. There's little doubt that, within forty-eight hours, Mr. Clay's desk was piled high with red-hot answers. Letter after letter would start out by pouring abuse on his head. Many of them would drip with tears as the writers told their sad stories. A good percentage would cry out about the long years they had paid their rent month after month—and then to be treated like this!

Out of this heap of bitterness, anger, self-righteousness, and self-pity Mr. Clay would find few, if any, who looked at the problem from *his* viewpoint.

Paragraph one actually pats him on the back. It recognizes his progressiveness. It makes him feel wise and enterprising. Here's a letter he can read with pleasure and with an open mind.

■COOPERATION. In the second paragraph Mr. Clay gets his second happy surprise. This tenant actually dropped everything and made a real try to comply with the request that he get out in thirty days.

The third paragraph develops this theme further and reveals some of the inescapable problems involved.

The fourth paragraph elaborates on the cooperation theme and sets forth a possible solution to the difficulty. The writer has taken the initiative in suggesting a way out. He has not written saying he can't do it. *He* has done the thinking.

■TEMPTATION. Mr. Clay will have to find tenants for his reconstructed building. Here's an offer to take a half floor. Coupled with the offer is the suggestion of how Mr. Clay and the writer can work out a plan that will be mutually beneficial.

■ACTION. The writer spells out what action *he* will take. He doesn't leave the next step up to the harassed Mr. Clay, but takes the bit in his own teeth.

In a situation of this type it is quite possible that the cantankerous landlord will not do anything for anybody. It is also possible, however, that his reconstruction plans will permit him to forestall the need for some occupants to move as quickly as others. Abuse and chest-pounding have little chance of winning you whatever dispensation Mr. Clay can hand out. The sample letter shown here creates an atmosphere that would encourage Mr. Clay to give you the utmost consideration. It is simply a matter of looking at every problem from the other fellow's viewpoint.

REPLY TO PROBLEM NO. 5—OUT OF CASH

Dear John:

If I were your credit manager I'd do exactly what he did. I am behind in my payments right now and that's what he has to watch. He's on his toes.

But, John, while he watches credits you watch business and you watch the people you sell to. I'm only one of your many customers, but I believe you know how we went all out with your line this Christmas. As an alert sales manager you know, too, that Christmas business was not what any of us expected.

Your Christmas goods—a fair part of them—are still here and I haven't called on you to take any of them off my hands. You have wonderful merchandise and I know we'll sell it, given enough time. And now you've proven again what great merchandisers you are by bringing out your new line and backing it up with equally great promotion.

The demand is here. Folks are asking for your items and I'm spurring that interest by doing a big local advertising job on your new lines.

If you and I were sitting in your office or mine, right now, and you were the president of your company, I know perfectly well you'd back me up. And I know what a top salesman you are, John. As a personal favor to me, and for the broader distribution of your own goods, I'm asking you to sit down with your credit man and sell him Harry Elect.

My business is sound. I need time and I need help to get out from behind my over-heavy inventory, which I will do. My bills will be paid and your house will be the first to know it—with checks—when those consumer dollars come in.

I'll call you Friday morning.

Cordially,
Harry Elect

Analysis:

■THE MAN'S RIGHT. As Harry Elect, the normal, immediate reaction to the bad news from your supplier would be indignation, bitterness of past loyalties being forgotten, deep disappointment. But the expression of any of these emotions is not calculated to get you what you need and want. On sober second thought you can, with complete honesty, appreciate the credit problems faced by a big manufacturer. To the credit office you are no more than a ledger card. Right now that card doesn't look too good.

The first paragraph says that you know he's right. You compliment him on his alertness. This gets the letter off to a fine, interesting start. It does something more. You are asking the sales manager to go to bat for you with the credit man. You've put a beautiful tool in his hands. He can show your letter to the credit man and what you said can only help —cannot hurt—your cause.

■FLATTERY. The second and third paragraphs express sincere appreciation for the sales manager's capabilities and admiration for the company and its products. The words you've used about the sales manager appeal to his ego and to his business judgment. They make him *want* to understand and appreciate your current problem.

The fourth paragraph lets him know that his company has your full loyalty and support. You are devoting your advertising to the promotion of *his* merchandise.

■CHALLENGE. On the dual basis of helping his company and you, the fifth paragraph goads the sales manager with a friendly challenge to display his sales ability, his knowledge of people and of markets, by going to bat for Harry Elect.

■CONFIDENCE. Without exaggeration or too much stress, the sixth paragraph builds confidence in the basic soundness of Harry Elect and his store. It promises, too, that payment will not be long in coming.

■ACTION. Taking the action on his own shoulders, Harry Elect accomplishes two vital objectives. He eliminates the need to sit and worry while waiting for a reply. He also places the sales manager in a position where he cannot put off doing something about Harry Elect's request, no matter how busy he may be. That phone call is coming on Friday morning and he must have an answer by that time.

REPLY TO PROBLEM NO. 6—GET RICH QUICK

Dear Mrs. Bowers:

Of course you would like to double your money. I understand exactly how you feel. The hope that such a thing will happen for them is what pulls hundreds of thousands of people to the race tracks and to the gambling tables every day. But there's one great difference between those people and you. When they place a bet on a horse, a card, or a number, they do so with the full realization that the money they put up will bring them no dividends or interest, and, if they happen to be wrong, the money is gone forever.

Mrs. Bowers, you and I have had some long sessions together. You have been frank and open with me, trusting me as your counselor, and I know how important it is to you to preserve every bit of your capital. You've shown me the vital need to keep that money working for you so that it can produce the income you need for your living expenses.

I would be doing you a serious disservice if I did not warn you, as emphatically as I know how, against the step you are considering.

As soon as your letter arrived I investigated the CDQ Mining and Exploration Company. The reports and statements I read were long, but the information boils down to a few simple facts. At the present time there are no facts to give you, or anyone else, the assurance that the CDQ Company will have anything of practical commercial value. The future welfare of the company is based on pure chance. The company has nothing capable of producing any income on your investment today. In my opinion, the chance of losing whatever sum you invest is far greater than the chance of realizing a profit.

Your money and your securities, Mrs. Bowers, are your property and, of course, you have liberty to do with them as you will. As your counselor, and as a friend, I urge you not to go into this proposed venture, but the final decision is yours and I'll do whatever you request.

Sincerely,

Analysis:

■THE TEMPTATION IS UNDERSTANDABLE . . . BUT. While this letter starts with a measure of sympathetic understanding, it quickly shifts to a shocking contrast. The writer, knowing Mrs. Bowers and her financial circumstances, realizes that she would never consider taking her precious capital and gambling with it at the track or roulette table. The opening of his letter puts her on notice that she is contemplating a move that is equally reckless.

■SECURITY . . . NOT WEALTH. Mrs. Bowers is reminded of her true needs and goals. At her age she needs security far more than sudden wealth. This portion of the letter reminds her of that basic fact. At the same time it serves to reestablish the shared confidence of the relationship between her and her investment counselor—an important reminder at this time.

The writer shows that he took the time and trouble to investigate the CDQ Company, for her benefit. He strips the situation down to the essential truths so that she can see, for herself, the great risk she is taking.

276

■ You have a free choice. The last paragraph of the letter puts the power of final decision in Mrs. Bowers' hands. He is not dictating to her. He is giving her counsel and allowing her the face-saving opportunity to say, "*I* have decided not to take this big risk."

Your attitude is showing

How well did you do? Are you satisfied that the letters you wrote handled each of the six situations as fully and as understandingly as the sample replies?

This exercise is less a test of writing skills than a test of *attitudes*.

Compare the attitudes your letters reflect with the attitudes displayed in the sample letters. Are you satisfied that the approach you took, in each case, is calculated to lead the reader to take the action you want? Are your letters stripped of irritants? Has each of the letters taken full recognition of the reader's point of view?

If you are *not* satisfied that your own letters did all the things they should do, look for the missing elements; search for the sour notes. See what you *could* have done to make your own letters—your own action requests—as easily acceptable as the samples.

What you are seeking is *not* a way to write these particular letters. You are looking for the key to a winning attitude in all of the letters of reply you write from this day on.

Special parts of a business letter

Business letters may contain these special elements:

1. Reference number. This line, usually referring to a numbered file, may appear at the upper right directly below the date line.

2. Attention line. This line is used when the letter is addressed to an individual but may be passed on to others. It appears below the inside address and above the salutation in this form: "Attention: Mr. Harold Feldspar." When an attention line is used, the salutation under it should read, "Gentlemen:".

3. Enclosure line. This appears at the lower left and enumerates enclosures described in the body of the letter, such as checks, invoices, and the like. The form is, "2 Encl."

22

How to write business reports

When you are assigned to write an important business report, how you perform can mean a lot to your career. Here's what you need to know about what is expected in various types of reports, how to set them up, gather information, organize your material, and write a successful presentation.

A business report is an orderly presentation of facts about a specific business activity or program. Although it consists mainly of facts, it often contains the writer's interpretation of the information with conclusions and recommendations. Reports may be oral or written. The oral report saves the time of the reporter, but the written report may save the time of many executives. This is because executives have to listen to every word of an oral report, but they may read or skim the written report at their convenience. The written report—because it is a permanent record—has other, more important, advantages:

1. It compels the reporter to be complete and accurate.

2. It is less likely to be distorted as the ideas in it are transmitted directly from one person to another.

3. It can be referred to in its original form again and again.

Although individual firms classify business reports in many ways, they are most importantly grouped according to purpose and according to format and style.

As to its purpose, a business report is either informational or analytic.

INFORMATIONAL REPORT. An *informational report* contains facts. It presents a situation not as it should be, but as it is, or as identified individuals or agencies say it is. The writer does not include his own opinions; nor does he offer his conclusions and recommendations. Examples of informational reports are: a foreman's weekly report of production in his section, a salesman's expense sheet, a management consultant's report of employes' daily work habits, and a buyer's report of coat styles being worn in certain parts of the country. Such reports are usually valuable for their facts alone, although they may later be used—perhaps in combination with other reports—as the bases for decisions by the managements to which they are submitted.

ANALYTIC REPORT. Like an informational report, an *analytic report* contains facts, but it also contains an analysis of the facts and the writer's conclusions or recommendations. The analytic report is frequently the basis for an important company decision. Thus, the writer shoulders great responsibility. An analytic report might call for the writer's recommendations on how a new product could be successfully marketed, on how a company's assembly line could be speeded up, or on how hiring and firing provisions should be altered.

Two styles of business report

THE INFORMAL REPORT

The informal report may range from a short, almost fragmentary statement of facts on a single page to a more developed presentation taking several pages. Usually, the informal report is submitted in the form of a letter or memorandum. The informal report rarely if ever carries a cover, table of contents, or any special display except for necessary tabulations, as shown in the example below. In style, the informal report is personal and relaxed.

August 27, 1985

Memorandum to Mr. Norton:

I have been in touch with L. M. Crewes Associates about the terms under which they will revise our form letters. The fee is a flat $10,000.00 for one year's service, including the following:

1. Reviewing and rewriting where necessary the form letters of all departments.
2. Preparation of a Correspondence Manual for use by all those who dictate. (The cost of printing is not included in the fee.)
3. A series of six one-hour discussion meetings for all letter-writing personnel.

4. Distribution of the *Crewes Better Letters Bulletin* every two weeks to all persons included in the program. A sample is attached.

After one year, continued service will be provided for $2,000.00 per year. This fee will include review of all new form letters, three group meetings, and continued distribution of the *Crewes Better Letters Bulletin* every two weeks.

Mr. Draper, with whom I spoke, said his company could begin at any time upon one month's notice. He mentioned the Standard Bank and Trust Company, the Amalgamated Oil Company, and the Universal Mining Company as recent clients.

Robert Griswold

Robert Griswold: WF
Enclosure

THE FORMAL REPORT

The formal report usually includes any number of the following: cover, title page, table of contents, introduction, letter of transmittal or presentation (see below), center and side headings, and statistical tables, charts, and other types of visual aids. It may also contain detailed appendices and an index. It is sometimes printed and bound in hard covers, like a book. Because the formal report is ordinarily the result of intensive investigation, it tends to be long. When it is very long, a brief summary of its main points may be included immediately after the introduction.

In style, the formal report is relatively impersonal and restrained. For objectivity's sake the writer de-emphasizes his own point of view. Generally, he does not refer to himself as *I* or *we,* but uses third-person references such as "the writer," "the investigator," "it was learned," and "investigation disclosed."

THE LETTER OF TRANSMITTAL

As a rule, formal reports are accompanied by a letter of transmittal or presentation. As the name suggests, a letter of transmittal serves merely to transmit the report from the writer to the reader. It consists of a short message, almost perfunctory in nature. Although it is routine in tone and style, a letter of transmittal performs several important functions, such as providing a permanent record of transfer, showing the date on which the report was submitted, stating the name and position of the writer of the report, and showing when and by whom the report was authorized. The letter may also invite the reader's comments and suggestions. For example:

September 15, 1985

Mr. Ralph C. Jones, President
Kaycee Products Corporation
459 South Street
Paterson, Oregon

Dear Mr. Jones:

In accordance with your request of June 29, I have made a survey to determine the advisability of establishing a warehouse in Chicago. The results of my investigation, as well as my conclusion and recommendations, are embodied in the accompanying report.

When you have had an opportunity to go over the report, I should appreciate your comments. Should you wish to discuss the report with me, I shall be happy to be at your office at any time convenient for you.

Respectfully submitted,
John Phillips
Controller

THE LETTER OF PRESENTATION

The letter of presentation not only transmits the report but also emphasizes its importance. Besides containing the same information as the letter of transmittal, it usually states the purpose and scope of the report, refers to the writer's sources of information, and highlights special features. Occasionally, material that is normally included in the letter of presentation is put instead in a more formal "Introduction" to the report. A typical letter of presentation might read:

September 15, 1985

Mr. Ralph C. Jones, President
Kaycee Products Corporation
459 South Street
Paterson, Oregon

Dear Mr. Jones:

In accordance with the instructions contained in your memorandum of June 29, I have made a survey to determine the advisability of establishing a warehouse in Chicago. The results of my investigation, as well as my conclusion and recommendations, are embodied in the accompanying report.

In addition to the careful study given to our markets in the Middle West, this report has sought to embody the thinking of our major competitors who recently announced similar plans for branch warehouses.

Although the bibliography included in this report is self-explanatory, special acknowledgment should be made to Mr. Benjamin Petty of the Sales Department for the market information he supplied. The Trade Publishing Company of Chicago was also very helpful. This firm opened to us their news files which have for many years meticulously reported the activities of our competitors in the Chicago area.

Respectfully submitted,
John Phillips
Controller

There are many other ways in which companies describe their reports: *routine, operational, inspection, periodic, annual, sales, statistical, record, progress, special, examination,* and so on. Actually, the name applied to the report is less important than the writer's complete understanding of what is wanted and needed for the particular circumstance.

Selecting the type of report you want

Before a writer embarks on any research or determines the type of report he will write, he must consider: What kind of report has been requested or is expected? When is the report due? What is the purpose of the report? Who will read the report?

The reporter may be instructed to make a specific kind of report or he may have a precedent to follow. In the majority of instances, however, he must decide for himself what type of report is required and along what lines the content, format, and style should be planned.

The length of time the writer has to prepare the report should guide him as to the type of report expected. If a very short time is allowed, it might be almost impossible to prepare a formal report and, thus, an informal report would be acceptable. But if enough time is allowed for considerable research, the report will inevitably be formal in style and will include the writer's conclusions—perhaps even specific recommendations. For example, if an office manager must in one day prepare a report on the preceding month's absenteeism among clerical personnel, he cannot be expected to produce more than a brief tabulation, probably in memorandum form. If, on the other hand, an office manager has two weeks in which to prepare a report on the same subject, his research will be more penetrating. He might study the conditions which influenced attendance during the month, compare that month's record with the corresponding month a year ago, or compare the records of other companies to determine the significance of his firm's figures.

The writer also should be able to determine from the subject or the purpose of the report what kind of report is desired. For example, should the writer be asked to prepare a report to help decide whether

his company should merge with another firm or continue as now constituted, he would be making a serious mistake if he drew up a short, informal report. If, on the other hand, a salesman were asked for a
weekly report on the new accounts he had called on, it is unlikely that
the company would want him to spend many hours on the project.

A report intended for public consumption is usually formal in format
and style. A report prepared for an associate or co-worker may be informal. The more the writer knows about the reader, the better able he is
to adapt his style and content to that person. Remember, however, that
a report may be read by more people than the one to whom it is directed. For this reason, when the writer is in doubt, the safe course is
to prepare a formal report.

Five steps in preparing your report

After the writer has a clear idea of the kind of report he is going to produce, he begins the actual work of research and composition. This task
entails five distinct steps:

1. investigating the sources of information

2. taking notes

3. analyzing the data

4. making an outline

5. writing the report.

The extent of investigation depends on the length and importance of
the report. Thorough research frequently involves examination of the
company files; personal observation, interviews, and letters; questionnaires; and library research.

COMPANY FILES. Much of the information the reporter needs may already be in the company's possession. Hence, early in his research, he
should examine the files for other reports, correspondence, and sales,
financial, and operational records that may be pertinent to the subject
he is investigating.

PERSONAL OBSERVATIONS, INTERVIEWS, AND LETTERS. Even after studying library materials and company files, the writer may need to talk
with others or write personal letters to obtain information. In a report
that is dependent on the opinions of certain persons, for example, the

283

writer must interview those persons or communicate with them by letter. On-the-spot observation of conditions may also be necessary for a
complete report.

QUESTIONNAIRES. When it is necessary to canvass a large number of
people, a questionnaire may be the only feasible method of research. A
questionnaire should be brief and should not have any leading questions. Such a question as "Do you serve Miracle Bread in your home?"
may not elicit as truthful a response as questions framed as follows:

1. Do you serve a packaged bread in your home? _____ Yes _____ No
_____ Every day   _____ Often   _____ Occasionally
2. If the answer to question 1 above is Yes, please state name of bread
served _____. If you have no brand preference, check here _____.

An addressed postage-paid return envelope should be provided with
the questionnaire. If the results of a questionnaire are incorporated in
the report, a copy of the questionnaire should be included.

LIBRARY RESEARCH. Relevant background material on almost any
subject can be found in a good general-purpose library. Selecting *what*
to read is the difficult task. In some instances, the most current books
on a particular subject should be consulted. In other cases, the works
of particular authors should be read. Under still other circumstances,
only certain parts of selected books must be examined. The card catalog file at a library provides a quick reference to the sources of information available there.

Standard reference works, newspapers, trade publications, and magazines should not be overlooked. Past issues as well as current issues of
periodicals may provide valuable information.

In the course of investigation, the writer makes notes of anything that
appears related to his subject. Seldom does he take time then to analyze
the way each fragment of information will serve him in the finished report. After taking notes, the writer requires a period of assimilation during which he will again give careful thought to the purpose of his report
and try to establish a logical relationship between his seemingly far-
flung facts. At first there may be no semblance of order, but as the writer
keeps turning the data over in his mind, a pattern evolves. This pattern
may be of the most general nature, but it provides the writer with at
least a starting point, directional signs, and a few important stopping
places on the way to a conclusion.

In the analytical process much of the collected data will have been

284

IN PRAISE OF MEMOS

THE MEMO, properly used, can be a powerful communication device to make your time more effective and work more efficient.

A memo tends to take the fuzziness out of communications. It's in writing, and it has your name on it. Memos establish a record and contribute to more effective business relationships. With a memo you can be absolutely sure that a request and due date are as clear as possible. You can avoid lengthy, time-consuming conversations by clearly stating the facts in advance. If the receiver of a memo has questions, he can come back to you. The purpose of a good memo, however, is to preclude questions through careful thinking in the first place.

Assuming you are like the rest of us, your mind is splintered into a number of areas of concentration. How are you going to get all these things done? Precision is one answer. Knowing precisely what is required of you through a memo can help you move swiftly and effectively to fulfill the demand.

As a record of your activities, memos can be especially valuable. They are particularly handy when a new man comes on, or with a new supervisor, or even a new client. Here is a ready record which quickly brings the new person up to date.

The memo has another important function: accountability. If something goes wrong, chances are someone "goofed." This is not always true—only 99 percent of the time. Memos, properly used, thus establish accountability 99 percent of the time when things don't work out as originally intended.

More and more businesses are places where "getting along" with people is not only nice—it's essential. The memo can be helpful where you must deal with people who, no matter how hard you try, just don't seem to be your type. A memo limits that danger area of personal contact, while at the same time giving others all they require from you in a usable form.

In the last analysis, of course, how memos help you get ahead hangs on how good they are. They don't have to be literary gems. But they do have to be clear, understandable, to the point. The best memo clearly states its purpose—why it was written.

thrown out, the need for new data may have been revealed, and perhaps the writer's preliminary ideas about the form of the report or its content will have undergone considerable change.

THE OUTLINE—ESSENTIAL NOT OPTIONAL

Once the general pattern of the report has taken shape in the writer's mind, a written outline is the most effective—and most often the only —way of organizing the details.

Most analytical reports are evolved inductively: The writer lets his facts lead him to his conclusions and recommendations. In drafting the outline, the writer will therefore put his facts first—at least tentatively. When he reaches his conclusions and recommendations, however, he has the choice of putting them at the end of the outline or going back and inserting them at the very beginning.

Since an outline is prepared solely for the guidance of the writer, strict formality in wording and numbering of topics is not required.

MAKE SUBHEADINGS SPECIFIC. Within reason, heads and subheads should be specific. On the other hand, putting too much detail in the outline defeats the purpose of the outline and wastes the writer's time.

The last step in making a report is writing it. This task involves a constant shuttling between outline and notes and constant attention to the qualities of all good reports.

THE OUTLINE AS A GUIDE. In the report, the writer follows the same order as in the outline, all the time referring to his notes for the necessary details. This step gives the writer the opportunity to test the completeness of his information and to question its validity or accuracy. If the records he has collected are well documented, he can always go back and consult his original sources. At times, he may see the need to investigate additional sources for data relating to topics in his outline.

Ingredients of a good business report

A good report has these qualities: factual accuracy, clearness, conciseness, restraint in language, and convenience to the reader.

1. If a report is to be of any value at all, the facts in it must be accurate. Accuracy demands completeness as well as correctness. The omission of important facts is nearly as dangerous as the inclusion of erroneous data. Even when the writer's recommendations are not favorably received,

the report is of considerable value if the facts are correct. At least, the reader is able to draw his own conclusions on the basis of the data presented.

2. The principles of clearness that apply to business letters apply to business reports as well. To insure clarity, the reporter should first take care that he has investigated his subject thoroughly and outlined it logically. He should then write or dictate his report, keeping the paragraphs and sentences varied in length and the words as simple as the subject permits. The selection of exact words and their orderly arrangement within the sentence, plus accurate punctuation, are essential.

3. A business report should be concise. This does not mean that a long report is always undesirable, but it does rule out the wordy report. An executive must do an extensive amount of reading and usually insists that any report prepared for his attention be confined to the essentials. Irrelevant ideas, too much detail, and unnecessary words waste the reader's and the writer's time.

4. Since the value of a report lies largely in its objectivity, the writer should present his findings in a conservative manner. Insofar as possible, he should allow the facts to speak for themselves. The reporter should not permit his prejudices to warp his judgment or color his report. He should employ restraint in his selection of words. Superlatives and other extravagant expressions are inappropriate in all but the most informal reports. Compare the probable effect of the two sets of phrases below on a reader who is trying to arrive at the truth.

EXTRAVAGANT	CONSERVATIVE
Conditions in the bookkeeping department are appalling.	Conditions in the bookkeeping department are in need of improvement.
The workers are lazy and incompetent.	The incidence of lateness among the workers is higher than the average in other departments. The criteria for selection and the methods of training are not in accord with modern personnel practice.
I would certainly recommend a change in methods.	A change in methods would be desirable.
You could then be absolutely sure of 100 percent efficient operation.	Increased efficiency would be the result.

5. The writer makes his report more convenient for the reader to use principally through its mechanical display. Center and side headings are particularly helpful in providing points of reference. Lists, tables, graphs, diagrams, and even photographs may clarify and shorten the text material and save time for the reader. Wherever possible, the illustrative material—clearly labeled—should be adjacent to the related text. In long reports a table of contents and occasionally an index may prove beneficial.

Many business executives expect that the report will be prefaced by a short résumé, usually labeled "Summary" or "Conclusion." In this way, an executive is able to grasp the main points of the report immediately and to leave the details for a closer examination at another time.

test your skills

HOW TO WRITE BUSINESS REPORTS

1. Mark the following statements true or false:
   a. A business report can be informational or analytical but not both.
   b. Only facts appear in an informational report.
   c. Facts should not appear in an analytical report.
   d. An analytical report may not include the writer's recommendations.
   e. A report is categorized as informal or formal on the basis of format and style.

2. List the steps necessary in preparing a report.

3. What qualities are included in a good report?

4. What is the primary difference between a letter of transmittal and a letter of presentation?

5. Listed below are several functions performed by both a letter of transmittal and a letter of presentation, and some that are performed only by a letter of presentation. Which three apply only to a letter of presentation?
   a. Provides a permanent record of transfer.
   b. Shows date on which report was submitted.
   c. States purpose and scope of the report.
   d. Refers to writer's sources of information.
   e. States name and position of the writer of the report.
   f. Highlights special features.
   g. Shows when and by whom report was authorized.
   h. Invites reader's comments and suggestions.

Answers to this quiz appear on page 705.

PART TWO

The tools
of the
trade

23

Good craftsmanship
pays dividends

In Part One you explored many ways you can make your
writing clearer and more persuasive. But just as important
as the techniques you have studied are the basic nuts and
bolts of English: vocabulary, grammar, punctuation, and
spelling. Here's a chance for you to polish up.

If you have ever tried to change a tire without a jack, or replace a washer in your kitchen faucet without a screwdriver, then you
know the importance of tools. Any craftsman, amateur or professional,
needs tools. There is no substitute for the right tool for the job, and the
good craftsman, whatever his trade or profession, makes certain that he
carries it in his kit.

In writing and speaking you carry a kit, too. It is not as visible as
your television repairman's metal box or your doctor's little black
leather bag. But it is there—in the words you use in your correspondence, in the grammatical structure of your sentences, in your spelling
and punctuation. The better your verbal tools and the greater the precision with which you are able to use them, the better will be the letter
you write, the talk you give, whatever form of communication you use
in the course of your business and private affairs.

A larger and richer vocabulary is of primary importance in making
your writing easier and more effective. How often has your pen fal-
tered, your hand fumbled at the typewriter, as you probed your brains
for that suitable word, that suitable phrase? A delicate situation calls
for precision in your vocabulary. Is it "sympathy" or "consolation" you
want to say? "Blemish" isn't exactly what you want to indicate; is it

"scar" or "damage" or "imperfection"? The English language is perhaps the most subtle of all languages. The nuance of a word and its connotations often are of utmost importance in the communication of an idea, a thought, or even a fact. You don't say "credible" when you mean "credulous." "Guaranty" and "warranty" are used interchangeably in speech, but there is a subtle difference between the two words and you want precision in the contract you write.

In addition to a good vocabulary, the know-how to use it concisely and clearly is equally essential. The tool required for this ability is grammar. You probably learned most of what you need to know about grammar in school. Perhaps you did some more advanced work in the mechanics of the English language later on. You've learned, too, in your daily experience, that poor grammatical structure in a memo, letter, or report will rub you the wrong way and give you a negative impression of the writer. None of us is absolutely free of uncertainties about grammar.

Is it "these kind of cars" or "this kind of cars"? How can you always tell when to use *who* and when to use *whom?* Should you say "If I were you" or "If I was you"? Rather than guessing at or avoiding such problems in grammar, how much better to review some of the basic rules so that your writing may flow more easily and work more effectively.

Spelling and punctuation are the two remaining tools in your verbal kit. Now in English spelling presents certain problems. In most other languages a word is spelled exactly as it sounds, but we know that this very often is not the case with our language. "Lake" is spelled with an "a-k-e" so why not "ache"? "Lose" has one "o"; "choose" has two. "Hoarse" is a condition of the voice and "horse," an animal. No wonder so many people have difficulty in learning to spell properly.

But the recipients of your correspondence *will* take note of your spelling if it is poor, just as they will react unfavorably to incorrect punctuation or grammar. The rules you will find in chapter 32 can help you avoid the most troublesome spelling mistakes.

A knowledge of punctuation is an important tool because improper punctuation may change your intended meaning. Many of us tend to be careless in this area. A misplaced comma, the absence of a necessary period or semicolon, and the misuse of quotation marks may prove misleading or embarrassing.

The chapters in this section will give you the opportunity to improve these very important basic communications skills.

24

Seven modern steps
to word power

**The old-fashioned approach to vocabulary building was to
sit down and memorize lists of words and their meanings.
But experts now agree that you can increase your word
power faster and gain a more useful vocabulary learning
words by the inductive method—the modern way.**

This vocabulary-building section is not a memory course.
Memorizing lists of words by rote happens to be the slowest and most
difficult way to learn them. You will find that you have forgotten most
of the list by the next day.

What, then, is the correct procedure?

Just this.

Look at the word first in its context: in the paragraph where it appears. The sense of the paragraph will give you an inkling of the significance of the word—even if you have never seen it before. You naturally become eager to know the definition of the word in order to
understand the sentence in which you have seen it: your approach,
then, is *indirect and psychological,* because you wish the information,
not as an end in itself, but as a means to an end. You realize that if you
learn the meaning of the word you will comprehend the sentence. You
are using what is called the modern *inductive* method, in that you first
discover the word at work, you are challenged by it, you guess at its
meaning, and you then confirm or correct your guess by referring to
the dictionary.

When you use this modern method, words become living entities,
charged with action and emotion. They then become hard to forget.

Let's be specific. We will discuss thirteen adverbs and two adverbial phrases and try to prove how much easier it is to learn by the *indirect, inductive and psychological* route.

MEETING NEW WORDS IN CONTEXT

■I. Give your careful attention to the following sentences in Groups A, B, C, D, and E. In each sentence you will find an adverb in italics. If the word is new to you try to guess at its meaning and keep it in mind. You are going to be asked about it.

GROUP A

1. He complained *acrimoniously* (ack-ri-mo'-nee-us-lee).
2. We argued *acrimoniously*.
3. They mocked each other *acrimoniously*.

(You can feel the unpleasant overtone of this word, can't you?)

GROUP B

1. He completed the operation *adroitly* (a-droyt'-lee).
2. He drove *adroitly* through the maze of traffic.
3. *Adroitly* she knitted the complicated stitch.

(This word obviously applies to some manual action.)

GROUP C

1. He moved slowly and *circumspectly* (sir-cum-spect'-lee) through the range of fire.
2. Fearing a trick, he answered all questions *circumspectly*.
3. By walking *circumspectly* he avoided an ambush.

(There's a feeling of watchfulness about this word.)

GROUP D

1. These two building leases ran *concomitantly* (con-com'-i-tant-lee).
2. Living and learning go on *concomitantly*.
3. Rain, snow, and sleet, all came down *concomitantly*.

(You probably know why two or more things *must* be involved in these actions, even if you happen never to have seen the word before.)

GROUP E

1. He examined the plans *cursorily* (cur'-so-ri-lee).
2. He ran through the pages *cursorily*, then threw the novel down in disgust.
3. He did his homework so *cursorily* that he flunked his examination.

(This word should carry an impression of superficial haste.)

Remember your ideas of these meanings and of the meanings of the words in italics in Sections II and III as you are going to have a test on them in Section IV.

MORE NEW WORDS IN CONTEXT

■II. Now you are ready to tackle five more words. Examine (but not cursorily!) the following statements and come as close as possible to figuring out the meanings of those that are new to you.

1. Teachers are apt to talk *didactically* (dye-dack'-tik-a-lee).
2. Extremely modest persons usually speak of their own accomplishments *disparagingly* (dis-par'-a-jing-lee).
3. People with extremely facile and ready tongues can talk *glibly* (glib'-lee).
4. The person who is looking for sympathy talks *plaintively* (plain'-tiv-lee).
5. Pessimists usually speak *ominously* (om'-i-nus-lee) of the future.

GUESSING THE MEANING FROM THE SENTENCE

■III. Are any of the following words strange to you? If so, please guess at their meanings as best you can.

1. Man cannot break the laws of nature *with impunity* (im-pyoo'-ni-tee).
2. He placed his hand on the hot radiator *inadvertently* (in-ad-vert'-ent-lee).
3. He was a disagreeable old man who answered every question *irascibly* (i-rass'-ib-lee).
4. Inasmuch as the plans were executed *sub rosa* (sub ro'-za) the stockholders realized too late how completely they had been mulcted.
5. He never gave up quietly. He always complained *vociferously* (vo-sif'-er-us-lee) if he thought he had been treated unfairly.

TEST YOURSELF: FITTING THE WORDS TO MEANINGS

■IV. Now see if you can write each of the words that you have had in Sections I, II, and III opposite what you believe to be its correct meaning in the list below.

1. Expertly; dexterously; with skillful use of the hands or mind. . . . .
2. Accompanying; occurring together. . . . .
3. Like a teacher; as if teaching a lesson. . . . .
4. In a manner of smooth ease and fluency; without much thought. . . . .
5. In a heedless manner; without care; inattentively. . . . .

HOW TO READ A DICTIONARY ENTRY

WHEN IT COMES to learning new words or checking the meanings or pronunciation of familiar ones, a good dictionary is your basic tool. To use it most effectively, you should know the common elements of a dictionary entry described below. The various parts of some typical entries from the *Reader's Digest Great Encyclopedic Dictionary* are illustrated on the facing page.

1. *Main entry.* The main entry word is printed in bold face type set slightly to the left. Main entries appear in alphabetical order and show where the word is divided into syllables and where it may be broken.

2. *Pronunciation.* The proper pronunciation is shown in parentheses or slashes immediately after the main entry. Consult your dictionary's pronunciation key for interpretation of the symbols. Preferred pronunciation is given first; other acceptable forms of pronunciation follow.

3. *Part of speech.* An appropriate abbreviation (such as *n.* for noun, *v.t.* for transitive verb) shows the part of speech. Frequently more than one part of speech is covered in a single entry.

4. *Definitions.* The definition tells what the word means. In entries for words with several meanings, definitions are numbered with the most common meaning coming first. Related meanings are shown by letters.

5. *Labels.* These abbreviations in italic type indicate that a word is limited in use to a certain area, profession, or situation. *Obs.* means a word is obsolete, *Med.* that it is a medical term, *slang* that it is slang usage, and so forth.

6. *Illustrative phrases and usage notes.* Frequently sample phrases or comments on correct usage will clarify the meaning or use of a word in various situations. See the examples opposite.

7. *Etymology.* Material in brackets gives information about the word's origin. In some dictionaries, the etymology appears right after the pronunciation. Check your dictionary key for meanings of symbols.

8. *Inflected forms and derivative words.* The past tense, past participle, plural, and other inflected parts of verbs and nouns are shown if there is any irregularity in the form. Words derived from the main entry word are also listed.

9. *Synonyms and antonyms.* Lists and discussions of words with similar or opposite meanings frequently appear at the end of the entry.

SAMPLE DICTIONARY ENTRIES

MAIN ENTRY

WORD
DIVISION

RELATED
DEFINITIONS

PRONUNCIATION

PART OF
SPEECH

ETYMOLOGY

PARTS OF
SPEECH

ILLUSTRATIVE
PHRASE

CURRENCY
LABEL

DERIVATIVE
WORDS

DEFINITION
NUMBERS

INFLECTED
FORMS

LEVEL LABEL

LOCALITY
LABEL

SYNONYMS
AND ANTONYMS

NOTE ON
USAGE

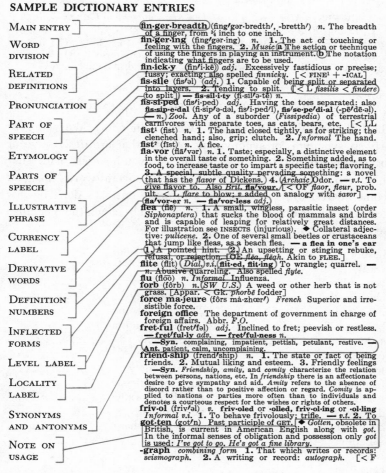

fin·ger·breadth (fing′gər·bredth′, -bretth′) *n.* The breadth of a finger, from ¾ inch to one inch.

fin·ger·ing (fing′gər·ing) *n.* **1.** The act of touching or feeling with the fingers. **2.** *Music* **a** The action or technique of using the fingers in playing an instrument. **b** The notation indicating what fingers are to be used.

fin·ick·y (fin′i·kē) *adj.* Excessively fastidious or precise; fussy; exacting: also spelled *finnicky.* [< FINE[1] + -ICAL]

fis·sile (fis′əl) *(adj.)* **1.** Capable of being split or separated into layers. **2.** Tending to split. (< L *fissilis* < *findere* (to split) — **fis·sil·i·ty** (fi·sil′ə·tē) *n.*

fis·si·ped (fis′i·ped) *adj.* Having the toes separated: also **fis·sip·e·dal** (fi·sip′ə·dəl, fis′i·ped′l), **fis·se·pe′di·al** (-pē′dē·əl). — *n.* *Zool.* Any of a suborder (*Fissipedia*) of terrestrial carnivores with separate toes, as cats, bears, etc. [< LL

fist[1] (fist) *n.* **1.** The hand closed tightly, as for striking; the clenched hand; also, grip; clutch. **2.** *Informal* The hand.

fist[2] (fist) *n.* A fice.

fla·vor (flā′vər) *n.* **1.** Taste; especially, a distinctive element in the overall taste of something. **2.** Something added, as to food, to increase taste or to impart a specific taste; flavoring. **3.** A special, subtle quality pervading something: *a novel that has the flavor of Dickens.* **4.** *Archaic* Odor. — *v.t.* To give flavor to. Also *Brit.* **fla′vour.** [< OF *flaor, fleur,* prob. ult. < L *flare* to blow; *n* added on analogy with *savor*] — **fla′vor·er** *n.* — **fla′vor·less** *adj.*

flea (flē) *n.* **1.** A small, wingless, parasitic insect (order *Siphonaptera*) that sucks the blood of mammals and birds and is capable of leaping for relatively great distances. For illustration see INSECTS (injurious). ◆ Collateral adjective: *pulicene.* **2.** One of several small beetles or crustaceans that jump like fleas, as a beach flea. — **a flea in one's ear** **(1.)** A pointed hint. **(2.)** An upsetting or stinging rebuke, refusal, or rejection. [OE *flea, flēah.* Akin to FLEE.]

flite (flīt) *(Dial.)* *v.i.* **(flit·ed, flit·ing)** To wrangle; quarrel. — *n.* Abusive quarreling. Also spelled *flyte.*

flu (flōō) *n.* *Informal* Influenza.

forb (fôrb) *n.* *(SW U.S.)* A weed or other herb that is not grass. [Appar. < Gk. *phorbē* fodder]

force ma·jeure (fôrs mà·zhœr′) *French* Superior and irresistible force.

foreign office The department of government in charge of foreign affairs. Abbr. *F.O.*

fret·ful (fret′fəl) *adj.* Inclined to fret; peevish or restless. — **fret′ful·ly** *adv.* — **fret′ful·ness** *n.* —**Syn.** complaining, impatient, pettish, petulant, restive. — **Ant.** patient, calm, uncomplaining.

friend·ship (frend′ship) *n.* **1.** The state or fact of being friends. **2.** Mutual liking and esteem. **3.** Friendly feelings —**Syn.** *Friendship, amity,* and *comity* characterize the relation between persons, nations, etc. In *friendship* there is an affectionate desire to give sympathy and aid. *Amity* refers to the absence of discord rather than to positive affection or regard. *Comity* is applied to nations or parties more often than to individuals and denotes a courteous respect for the wishes or rights of others.

friv·ol (friv′əl) *v.* **friv·oled** or **·olled, friv·ol·ing** or **·ol·ling** *Informal v.i.* **1.** To behave frivolously; trifle. — *v.t.* **2.** To

got·ten (got′n) Past participle of GET. ◆ *Gotten,* obsolete in British, is current in American English along with *got.* In the informal senses of obligation and possession only *got* is used: *I've got to go. He's got a fine library.*

-graph *combining form* **1.** That which writes or records: *seismograph.* **2.** A writing or record: *autograph.* [< F

297

6. Forebodingly; in a way portending evil.   . . . .
7. In strict confidence; privately.   . . . .
8. In a loud-voiced manner; vehemently; noisily.   . . . .
9. Expressing sadness or melancholy.   . . . .
10. Angrily; irritably; in hot-tempered fashion.   . . . .
11. With freedom from punishment or injurious consequences.   . . . .
12. Slightingly, in a way to undervalue and discredit.   . . . .
13. Hastily and superficially, without due care and attention.   . . . .
14. Cautiously with watchfulness in all directions.   . . . .
15. With sharpness and bitterness.   . . . .

ANSWERS: (*Also serving to explain the sentences in Groups A, B, C, D, and E to Sections II and III*):

(1) adroitly   (2) concomitantly   (3) didactically   (4) glibly   (5) inadvertently   (6) ominously   (7) sub rosa   (8) vociferously   (9) plaintively   (10) irascibly   (11) with impunity   (12) disparagingly   (13) cursorily   (14) circumspectly   (15) acrimoniously

TEST YOURSELF: MATCHING WORDS AND SYNONYMS

■V. The following drill will be well worth your effort. We will give you forty-six synonyms or synonymous phrases that are descriptive of the thirteen adverbs and two adverbial phrases you have just had. That is, each adverb will have to be written opposite several words that you think come nearest to its meaning. If you make mistakes don't be discouraged. The whole object of this device is to help clinch the meanings of these words in your mind.

1. hastily   . . . .
2. warily   . . . .
3. teacherlike   . . . .
4. cholerically   . . . .
5. in a way foreboding evil   . . . .
6. sadly   . . . .
7. covertly   . . . .
8. loudly   . . . .
9. inauspiciously   . . . .
10. testily   . . . .
11. dexterously   . . . .
12. cautiously   . . . .
13. slightingly   . . . .
14. easily   . . . .
15. caustically   . . . .
16. heedlessly   . . . .
17. at the same time   . . . .
18. angrily   . . . .
19. prudently   . . . .
20. with exemption from punishment   . . . .
21. smoothly   . . . .
22. stingingly   . . . .
23. thoughtlessly   . . . .
24. deprecatingly   . . . .
25. conjointly   . . . .
26. without harm   . . . .
27. bitterly   . . . .
28. fluently   . . . .
29. depreciatively   . . . .
30. ingeniously   . . . .

31. irately ....
32. portentously ....
33. sorrowfully ....
34. without punishment ....
35. rapidly ....
36. like an instructor ....
37. mournfully ....
38. privately ....

39. clamorously ....
40. blatantly ....
41. noisily ....
42. instructively ....
43. confidentially ....
44. in a melancholy way ....
45. belittlingly ....
46. superficially ....

ANSWERS:
(1) cursorily (2) circumspectly (3) didactically (4) irascibly (5) ominously (6) plaintively (7) sub rosa (8) vociferously (9) ominously (10) irascibly (11) adroitly (12) circumspectly (13) disparagingly (14) glibly (15) acrimoniously (16) inadvertently (17) concomitantly (18) irascibly (19) circumspectly (20) with impunity (21) glibly (22) acrimoniously (23) inadvertently (24) disparagingly (25) concomitantly (26) with impunity (27) acrimoniously (28) glibly (29) disparagingly (30) adroitly (31) irascibly (32) ominously (33) plaintively (34) with impunity (35) cursorily (36) didactically (37) plaintively (38) sub rosa (39) vociferously (40) vociferously (41) vociferously (42) didactically (43) sub rosa (44) plaintively (45) disparagingly (46) cursorily

TEST YOURSELF: PICK THE WORD FOR THE SITUATION

■VI. Choose and write in seven of the adverbs or adverbial phrases you have been studying that you think will best fit the situations:

1. You are a burglar. You have just entered a wealthy home through an unlocked window. All is dark, and alas, you have forgotten to bring your searchlight. What's more, you can't find the electric switch. How will you move around in this room until you can get your bearings?
....

2. You are an irritable, touchy old man, and as you walk along the street on this cold, raw morning you feel nothing but enmity toward the whole world. A beggar stops you for a coin. How do you refuse?
....

3. A friend has been importuning you for weeks to look over a novel he is writing and give him your criticism. Knowing your friend you are certain that the novel is bad even before you read it; besides you are a very busy man. Rather than give your friend a blunt refusal, however, you take the manuscript home one evening. How do you examine it?
....

4. Your small son wishes to know why it snows. You are well versed in the natural sciences and have made it a habit to answer all your son's questions as clearly and accurately as possible. How do you answer him?
....

5. You have influence with the chief of police and, furthermore,

your wife is the mayor's daughter. Consequently, you never trouble to obey traffic laws. In fact, you can break them . . . .

6. A woman has broken your heart purposely. It takes you years even to begin to get over it. And then one day you meet her again. She is gay, debonair; she has obviously forgotten what she has done to you. This angers you and you intend to sting her when you remind her of her cruelty. In what fashion do you speak to her? . . . .

7. You are a very modest person. Rather than praise anything you have done, you prefer to take as little credit as possible for your accomplishments. How do you usually speak of yourself? . . . .

ANSWERS:
(1) circumspectly (2) irascibly (3) cursorily (4) didactically (5) with impunity (6) acrimoniously (7) disparagingly

TEST YOURSELF: CHANGING THE FORM OF THE WORDS

■ VII. One of the quickest ways of improving and increasing your vocabulary is to practice turning words into other forms. Can you change the adverbs in this chapter into their noun forms?

1. acrimoniously	. . . .	8. glibly	. . . .
2. adroitly	. . . .	9. plaintively	. . . .
3. circumspectly	. . . .	10. ominously	. . . .
4. concomitantly	. . . .	11. inadvertently	. . . .
5. cursorily	. . . .	12. irascibly	. . . .
6. didactically	. . . .	13. vociferously	. . . .
7. disparagingly	. . . .		

ANSWERS:
(1) acrimony (2) adroitness (3) circumspection (4) concomitance (5) cursoriness (6) didacticism (7) disparagement (8) glibness (9) plaintiveness (10) ominousness (11) inadvertence (12) irascibility (13) vociferousness

Occasionally you may feel that these exercises are time consuming. But we urge you never to let the lack of time stand as an obstacle to your work. Thomas Carlyle, the great philosopher, claimed that there is time in every man's life for a career within a career. Even so-called geniuses are largely geniuses because they are willing to use the time that others throw away. It was Michelangelo who said: "If people only knew how hard I work to gain my mastery it wouldn't seem so wonderful at all." And Alexander Dumas, the French novelist, confessed: "Infatuated, half through conceit, half through love of my art, I achieve the impossible working as none else ever works. . . ."

Careers are not had by wishing and hoping. They are *bought* with work and enthusiasm.

25

Learning words by the "unfolding process"

There is more than one way to approach the definition of a word, especially when it has many shades of meaning. This in-depth study of fifteen vocabulary words will teach you how to unfold all the nuances of the new terms you encounter in your reading and conversation.

Let us now approach the problem of word development from a slightly different direction. We will still rely on the indirect method: that is, the method that shows you a word first in its context, rather than flashing it on you alone and away from its meaning in a sentence.

Even if you have never seen a word before, you can usually get some idea of its meaning from the way it is used. Try to sense the meaning of the italicized words in these sentences.

The *taciturn* old man only grunted in answer to our questions.
The speaker's *polemic* aroused the people against the dictator.
The young man's *fatuous* giggle was extremely irritating.

If you guessed that the old man in the first sentence was not the talkative type, you're right. Taciturn means "habitually silent or reserved." Did the speaker in sentence two criticize the dictator? He did indeed; polemic means "an attack on another person's opinions or principles." And if you think the young man in the last sentence was acting rather silly, you're right again. Fatuous means "foolish."

The meanings and uses of the following group of difficult words will be revealed by what we might call the "unfolding process." As you meet each word, even though it is for the first time, its meaning will be partially shown to you by the context, and its full meaning will gradually unfold before the chapter is over.

GETTING A FEELING FOR THE WORDS

■I. Please read out loud each of the sentences given below, so that you may get at least a feeling for the italicized words. You may still be completely in the dark as to the meaning of a few of them.

1. He lives a severe and *abstemious* (ab-stee′-mee-us) life.
2. That is a *chimerical* (ki-mair′-ik-al) and wholly unfounded fear.
3. The mental alertness you acquire is an important *facet* (fass′-et) of improved vocabulary.
4. Honesty is a *fetish* (fe′-tish) with him.
5. The *Machiavellian* (mack-ee-a-vell′-ee-an) moves of the dictators are astounding.
6. *Ochlocracy* (ok-lock′-ra-see) is one dangerous result of war.
7. Only God in his wisdom is *omniscient* (om-nish′-ent).
8. Since John's treachery was discovered, he has become a *pariah* (pa-ry′-a).
9. The employe received a *peremptory* (pair-emp′-toe-ree) dismissal.
10. The refugee painted a *poignant* (poyn′-yant) picture of his sufferings.
11. The wife of Socrates was sour and *querulous* (kwair′-ul-us).
12. That is the most ridiculous and *specious* (spee′-shus) argument I have ever listened to.
13. The war fever in 1941 was *ubiquitous* (you-bick′-wi-tus).
14. He is so *unctuous* (unk′-choo-us), I cannot bear him.
15. That *vainglorious* (vain-glo′-ree-us) and pompous general annoys all who know him.

TEST YOURSELF: SELECTING THE RIGHT SYNONYM

■II. Some of these words may already be old friends of yours, and an actual part of your speaking vocabulary. With others you may be only partially acquainted, and some could easily be entirely unfamiliar to you. The following exercise will be another step toward a clarification of the unfamiliar ones.

Let's start with the first. Directly after "1. abstemious" you will find

---

Synonym: A word used when you can't spell the word you want.
—*Chicago Daily Tribune*

---

three words identified with the letters "a," "b," and "c." Check which-ever word you think is a synonym for "abstemious." Continue the process. Refer back to Section I when you wish to.

1. *abstemious*	a. licentious	b. miserly	c. sparing
2. *chimerical*	a. monstrous	b. fanciful	c. difficult
3. *facet*	a. side	b. tap	c. point of view
4. *fetish*	a. shoe	b. object of worship	c. love
5. *Machiavellian*	a. kingly	b. politically cunning	c. angelic
6. *ochlocracy*	a. dictatorship	b. mob-rule	c. democracy
7. *omniscient*	a. omnipotent	b. rare	c. all-knowing
8. *pariah*	a. outcast	b. invisible	c. traitor
9. *peremptory*	a. tardy	b. fearful	c. decisive
10. *poignant*	a. piquant	b. painfully moving	c. bitter
11. *querulous*	a. questioning	b. complain-ing	c. fretful
12. *specious*	a. remarkable	b. cunning	c. subtly false
13. *ubiquitous*	a. ecstatic	b. omnipres-ent	c. pestiferous
14. *unctuous*	a. dirty	b. uncon-cerned	c. making a bland pretense of spirituality
15. *vainglorious*	a. silly	b. boastful	c. fastidious

ANSWERS:
(1) c (2) b (3) a (4) b (5) b (6) b (7) c (8) a (9) c
(10) b (11) b (12) c (13) b (14) c (15) b

Please recheck your answers and correct your mistakes if you have made any. Also go back to Section I on each of your mistakes and note how the sentences have new meanings once you properly understand the word.

TEST YOURSELF: TURNING THE TABLES

■III. Now we are going to ask you to think *in reverse*. The more angles from which you approach these words, the more the words will become fixed in your mind.

It is only fair to warn you that this will be a difficult exercise, one in which the most alert mind can easily be tricked.

Below you will find in italics the fifteen words you have just covered. After each master word there are three words lettered "a," "b," and "c."

Three words follow: "1. abstemious": "a. miserly, b. prodigal, c. phil-anthropic." One of these three words is directly *opposite* in meaning to abstemious. Check the one that you think is the antonym, or opposite in meaning, and repeat this process with the whole list. We have put in some synonyms to fool you, but don't be trapped by them!

1. *abstemious*	a. miserly	b. prodigal	c. philanthropic
2. *chimerical*	a. harmless	b. real	c. ghastly
3. *facet*	(This word has no antonym.)		
4. *fetish*	a. amulet	b. object of hate	c. rosary
5. *Machiavellian*	a. noxious	b. happy	c. naïve
6. *ochlocracy*	a. rule by one	b. rule by the rich	c. rule by the intelligent
7. *omniscient*	a. all-seeing	b. ignorant	c. religious
8. *pariah*	a. leper	b. hero	c. idol
9. *peremptory*	a. debatable	b. temporary	c. slow
10. *poignant*	a. sharp	b. dull	c. immature
11. *querulous*	a. calm	b. satisfied	c. peaceful
12. *specious*	a. general	b. authentic	c. hesitant
13. *ubiquitous*	a. found nowhere	b. found everywhere	c. humorous
14. *unctuous*	a. crude	b. suave	c. ignorant
15. *vainglorious*	a. modest	b. boastful	c. plaintive

ANSWERS:
(1) b (2) b (3) no antonym (4) b (5) c (6) a (7) b (8) c
(9) a (10) b (11) b (12) b (13) a (14) a (15) a

TEST YOURSELF: MATCHING MEANINGS

■IV. The unfamiliar words may now be getting more under your control. In the exercise that follows try to write the proper word (saying it aloud as you do so) next to each of the synonyms or synonymous phrases:

1. dictatorial ....
2. mob rule ....
3. outcast ....
4. shrewdly cunning ....
5. all-knowing ....
6. object of worship ....
7. painfully touching ....
8. everywhere ....
9. one face of a gem ....
10. complaining ....
11. temperate ....
12. true only in appearance ....
13. boastful ....
14. foolishly fanciful ....
15. pretending spirituality ....

ANSWERS:
(1) peremptory (2) ochlocracy (3) pariah (4) Machiavellian
(5) omniscient (6) fetish (7) poignant (8) ubiquitous (9) facet
(10) querulous (11) abstemious (12) specious (13) vainglorious
(14) chimerical (15) unctuous

TEST YOURSELF: SUGGESTIVE PHRASES

■V. Which word does each of the following phrases remind you of?
Write the correct word at right.

1. Reign of terror during French Revolution. . . . .
2. An object of worship among savages. . . . .
3. An absurd creation of the imagination. . . . .
4. A leper. . . . .
5. A dictator's methods. . . . .
6. The arguments of a demagogue. . . . .
7. He seemed to be everywhere at once. . . . .
8. The suffering of a refugee. . . . .
9. Boastfulness was a characteristic of Napoleon. . . . .
10. A complaining wife. . . . .
11. Women who are on a reducing diet. . . . .
12. A diamond. . . . .
13. God. . . . .
14. A martinet's order to an underlying. . . . .
15. A smooth appearance of sanctity. . . . .

ANSWERS:
(1) ochlocracy (2) fetish (3) chimera (4) pariah (5) Machiavellian (6) specious (7) ubiquitous (8) poignant (9) vainglorious (10) querulous (11) abstemious (12) facet (13) omniscient (14) peremptory (15) unctuous

TEST YOURSELF: THE RIGHT WORD FOR THE CONTEXT

■VI. "Toujours la pratique" say the French—"Always the practice."
Let's turn these words a new way, for unless you are absolutely sure of
them you will never use them publicly. We have split the words into
four groups of five each so that you can check your results as you go
along. Several words are repeated. Write in each blank space the one
word among those you are studying that best fits the meaning.

GROUP 1

1. The refugees painted a . . . . picture of their suffering in
Germany.
2. You may insist that everybody hates you and avoids you, but I
assure you that's a . . . . of your diseased imagination.
3. That teacher makes a . . . . of discipline.
4. He is a glib, ... person; I do not trust him.

5. Your .... schemes to win the nomination will get you nowhere; already your name is anathema to most of your constituents.

ANSWERS:
(1) poignant (2) chimera (3) fetish (4) unctuous (5) Machiavellian

GROUP 2
1. At Christmastime, the .... Salvation Army lassie reminds a selfish public of people for whom the season may not be merry.
2. That is a .... argument; but possibly you may get a number of unthinking people to believe it.
3. I admit you have done a lot for your country, but this absurd quality of .... will not make you popular.
4. Invalids and crotchety old men and women seem peculiarly addicted to the quality of ....
5. There are so many .... to the international situation that it is difficult to guess what the future holds.

ANSWERS:
(1)ubiquitous (2) specious (3) vainglory (4) querulousness (5) facets

GROUP 3
1. No one knows what is going to happen in the world. Things are in such an imbroglio. One would have to be .... to know.
2. Poor people, through lack of money, are forced to be ....
3. Lynching is an excellent example of ....
4. Sometimes it is necessary for an author to know what is going on in the minds of his characters. This is called ....
5. After murdering Lincoln, John Wilkes Booth became a ....

ANSWERS:
(1)omniscient (2)abstemious (3)ochlocracy (4)omniscience (5)pariah

GROUP 4
1. Some mothers make their commands so .... that they antagonize their children.
2. He is winning you over to his side with .... reasoning.
3. His .... machinations make him the most feared and the least trusted man in America.
4. In the spring the color green may be said to be almost ....
5. Some housewives make an absolute .... out of neatness.

ANSWERS:
(1)peremptory (2)specious (3)Machiavellian (4)ubiquitous (5)fetish

■VII. Defining some words is incredibly hard. Just think, for instance, of writing a definition of "sky" in such a way that a blind man will get a clear idea of what you mean. But your very attempt to define the fifteen

words that are listed below will force you to think intensively about
them and will hammer and clinch their meanings in your mind in a way
that nothing else could. When you have finished please check your answers with the dictionary definitions. Your wording, of course, will be
different, but if your definitions contain the main elements, you may
certainly consider that you have substantially mastered the words.

Word	Definition	Word	Definition
1. abstemious	. . . .	9. peremptory	. . . .
2. chimerical	. . . .	10. poignant	. . . .
3. facet	. . . .	11. querulous	. . . .
4. fetish	. . . .	12. specious	. . . .
5. Machiavellian	. . . .	13. ubiquitous	. . . .
6. ochlocracy	. . . .	14. unctuous	. . . .
7. omniscient	. . . .	15. vainglorious	. . . .
8. pariah	. . . .		

ANSWERS:

(1) Eating and drinking sparingly; self-denying in the indulgence of the
appetites and passions.

(2) Merely imaginary; fanciful; fantastic; visionary. The noun means a
frightful, vain, or foolish fancy.

(3) One of the small surfaces cut upon a diamond or other gem. By extension, a part, aspect, or point of view of any large subject.

(4) A material object believed to be the dwelling of a spirit that will protect the owner from harm; any object of devotion or blind affection.

(5) Of or pertaining to the Florentine politician Niccolō Machiavelli, or
to a system of political trickery.

(6) Mob rule.

(7) All-knowing or all-wise.

(8) A social outcast.

(9) Positive in judgment or opinion; dogmatic; dictatorial.

(10) Severely painful or acute to the spirit.

(11) Disposed to complain or be fretful.

(12) Appearing true or plausible, but not so.

(13) Seeming to be everywhere at once; omnipresent.

(14) Characterized by affected emotion; hence unduly suave.

(15) Excessively proud of one's own attainments, accomplishments, or
performance, as shown in undue elation, boasting.

PLAIN AND FANCY WORDS

This chapter has contained a few long and somewhat unusual words,
and this leads us to a warning that we can't repeat too often. When
we speak of the value of a large vocabulary we don't mean a vocabulary
of *large* words. A large word has its place. Sometimes it will crystallize
a meaning that otherwise might require a whole phrase to express. Fine.
Use such a word then. It will make for brevity and clarity. It is much

WRITE BETTER, SPEAK BETTER

simpler to describe a man as a "monogamist" than to have to say that "he is the type of man who believes in marrying only one wife." But never use a long word when a short one will do. Never try for fancy phrases. Persons who do that are not being "literary." They are merely being stuffy and are attempting to parade their knowledge. Don't say, "I reside in my domicile." Say, "I *live* in my *house.*" You don't commence; you *begin.* You don't pass away, or go to your reward; you *die.* A conflagration is a *fire.* And you don't retire; you just plain *go to bed.*

The highest art is usually the simplest in form.

Add to your word collection

Collecting lists of synonyms (words with similar meanings) is a productive, and often entertaining, way to enlarge your vocabulary. Any good dictionary includes listings and often brief discussions of hundreds of synonyms. When you look up a word, carefully study the treatment of those synonym entries which sometimes follow the word's definitions. If you do this, you may be able to choose a more exact and effective word for the occasion.

For example, once you are aware of synonyms, you won't necessarily have to write that the girl is *cute,* the game *exciting,* the idea *interesting,* the dress *pretty.* Instead you can choose among a variety of adjectives like *graceful, exquisite,* or *dainty* for the girl; *hairraising, dramatic,* or *suspenseful* for the game; *engrossing, sublime,* or *provocative* for the idea; *smart, stylish,* or *chic* for the dress.

A study of synonyms for *old* might add to your vocabulary these, among other words: *immemorial, aged, ancient, aboriginal, decrepit, antique, hoary, elderly, patriarchal, venerable, passé, antiquated,* and *antediluvian.*

Similarly, studying antonyms (words with nearly opposite meanings) will improve your understanding and also contribute to vocabulary growth. For example, seeking antonyms for *praise* may add to your vocabulary such words as *vilify, stigmatize, lampoon, abuse, censure, blame, deprecate, condemn, impugn, denigrate, disparage,* and *inveigh against.* Not all the antonyms you discover will prove directly useful but all will add to your own word supply.

26

Quick vocabulary builder: words from Latin and Greek

Knowing the most important roots, prefixes, and suffixes from Latin and Greek will help you increase your vocabulary quickly and easily, for these are the building blocks from which many of our words are formed. Here's a review of some of the most useful of these word elements.

Our English speech is a reservoir of the classical languages. It has taken over to itself and absorbed for its own use more than one quarter of the entire Greek language and more than 50 percent of the entire Latin language. A knowledge of Greek and Latin stems or roots (the terms are used interchangeably in this chapter) is invaluable in any program of vocabulary building.

You will find it excellent practice to keep a weather eye out for these roots and for their various and varied combinations in your daily reading. There are so many that tracing them becomes a fascinating sport. There is the Latin word *signa,* or "sign," which gives us in*sign*ia, the *sign* you wear; *sign*al, a sign; *sign*ify, make a sign; as well as de*sign,* *sign*ature, in*sign*ificant. We also have the Latin term *portare,* "to carry," which leads to *port*er, one who carries; *port*able, able to be carried; re*port*er, one who carries news back; de*port,* carry away; im*port,* carry in; and ex*port,* carry out.

A knowledge of Latin and Greek roots is a splendid vocabulary stretcher. In the pages that follow you will learn a few of the most common. If you read the etymological notes in your dictionary when you look up a word, you'll soon become acquainted with many more.

In the exercises ahead we will take English words apart and will show

how you can easily identify and define hundreds of words that you may never have seen before.

THE *GAMOS* WORD FAMILY

■ I. The Greek stem *gamos*, which literally means "marriage," usually appears as an ending in English in the form *gamy*. This has given rise to a large word family.

(1) *Monogamy* (mon-og'-a-mee): Our people practice monogamy and are a monogamous (mon-og'-a-muss) nation. This means the practice of having only one wife or husband at a time. The term comes from two Greek words: *monos*, "one" and *gamos*, "marriage."

(2) *Bigamy* (big'-a-mee): A "bigamist," as you remember, is a person who marries any other person while having a legal spouse living. Here we have a combination of two languages: *bi* means "two" in Latin, and combined with *gamos* gives us "two marriages."

(3) *Polygamy* (po-lig'-a-mee): This means several spouses to one person, as formerly practiced by Mormon males in Utah and by females in Ceylon, New Zealand, and elsewhere. Such married people were *polygamists* (po-lig'-a-mists). *Poly* in Greek means "many."

(4) *Misogamy* (miss-og'-a-mee): This term means hatred of marriage, and a person who holds this view is known as a *misogamist* (miss-og'-a-mist). *Misos*, translated from the Greek, means "hatred."

NEW WORDS FROM OLD STEMS

■ II. Now notice how the above Greek and Latin stems will branch out and lead to still more new words.

(1) *Monotheism* (mon'-o-thee-izm, *th* as in *think*): This is the philosophy of the *monotheist* who believes in one god: Greek *monos* combined with *theos* signifying "god."

(2) *Bicuspid* (bye-cuss'-pid): A tooth with two prongs on the lower end of it. You have already learned the translation of *bi; cuspid* is from the Latin *cuspis* meaning "point."

(3) *Polyglot* (pol'-ee-glot): *Glotta* is Greek for "tongue" or "language." So the polyglot is one who speaks many languages.

(4) *Misanthropy* (miss-an'-thro-pee): *Anthropos* in Greek means "man." We have, then, the hatred of man or of mankind. A *misanthrope* (miss'-an-thrope), therefore, is anyone who has a morbid aversion to, or distrust of, his fellow men.

BRANCHING OUT STILL FURTHER

■ III. Still more discoveries can be made with the roots that you have learned.

(1) *Theology* (thee-ol'-o-jee, *th* as in *think*) is the knowledge of God and religion. To *theos* we add the Greek ending *-logia* which means "knowledge." The usual way that *-logia* appears in English words is in the form of "logy."

(2) *Philanthropy* (fil-an'-thro-pee) is the direct opposite of misanthropy. Philanthropy means the love of mankind; the word *anthropos*, which you already know, is combined with the Greek word *philos* meaning "loving; friend." The word and the concept of philanthropy originated among 16th-century humanists.

NINE IMPORTANT ROOTS

■ IV. Now, if we are to combine the two new stems in the above section, we have:

(1) *Anthropology* (an-thro-pol'-o-jee), which you can now interpret as the "knowledge of man" or the history of the human race, and

(2) *Philology* (fil-ol'-o-jee), which should mean "love of knowledge," which is what it did mean in Greek. Later it came to mean more especially the love of words and the study of language, and is usually used today in that sense.

You now have an ownership in nine important Greek or Latin stems, which, in their usual English forms, are:

MONO—one	MISO—hatred of	ANTHROPO—man
BI—two	GAMY—marriage	PHILO—love of
POLY—many	THEO—god	LOGY—knowledge, study of

BE A WORD DETECTIVE

■ V. Can you qualify as a good word detective? Keep in mind the nine stems we have just discussed and try to arrive at the meanings of the following words. Guess intelligently, and only refer back to the roots if you have to. Write your meaning in the blank.

1. Many Englishmen wear MONocles (mon'-o-kluz) . . . .
2. He delivered an interesting MONOlogue (mon'-o-log).
   . . . .
3. He has a MONOpoly of the trade (mo-nop'-o-lee). . . . .
4. He lives in a MONastery (mon'-ass-tair-ee). . . . .
5. He is riding a BIcycle (bye'-sickle). . . . .
6. Man is a BIped (bye'-ped).
7. France and England made a BIlateral (bye-lat'-er-al) agreement.
   . . . .
8. A rectangle is a POLYgon (pol'-ee-gon). . . . .
9. A MISOgynist (miss-oj'-i-nist) shuns the company of women.
   . . . .

10. Romans practiced POLYtheism (pol'-ee-thee'-izm, *th* as in *think*).
. . . .

11. The apoTHEOsis (ap-o-thee'-o-sis, *th* as in *think*) of Hitler was effected by the German people. . . . .

12. The President's wonderful stamp collection was the envy of PHI-Latelists (fi-lat'-el-ists). . . . .

13. The ANTHROPOid (an'-thro-poyd) apes are similar in appearance to humans. . . . .

14. BioLOGY (bye-ol'-o-jee) is a fascinating science. . . . .

15. England is a MONarchy (mon'-ark-ee). . . . .

ANSWERS:
(1) lens for ONE eye (2) speech by ONE person (3) control by ONE person of the market (4) place where people live ALONE (5) vehicle of TWO wheels (6) creature with TWO feet (7) TWO-sided (8) MANY-sided figure (9) HATER of women (10) belief in MANY gods (11) raising to GODhood (12) LOVERS, hence collectors, of stamps (13) MANlike (14) STUDY of life (15) country where ONE person rules.

A REVIEW OF NINE ROOTS

■VI. It will be good practice to check over and pronounce *out loud* the words you have learned:

1. GAMY—marriage
monogamy
bigamy
polygamy
misogamy

2. MONO—one
monotheism
monogamy
monocle
monologue
monopoly
monastery

3. BI—two
bigamy
bicuspid
bicycle
biped
bilateral

4. POLY—many
polygamy
polyglot
polygon
polytheism

5. MISO—hatred of
misogamy
misogynist
misanthropy

6. THEO—god
theology
monotheism
apotheosis

7. ANTHROPO
—man
misanthropy
anthropoid
anthropology
philanthropy

8. PHILO—
love of
philology
philatelist
philanthropy

9. LOGY—knowledge,
study of
biology
theology
philology
anthropology

WORDS FROM THE LATIN *ANIMA*

■I. There is the simple word "animal." Why particularly do we use the word "animal" instead of some other combination of syllables?

"Animal" is from the Latin word *anima*, meaning "breath," "soul," or "spirit"; and animals, as opposed to minerals or "inanimate" objects, do breathe and do possess that mysterious something that gives to them a life not found in "inanimate" things. The stem *anim* is found in a host of common English words:

*anim*alcule—an animal of microscopic smallness, as the ameba
*anim*ate—to breathe life into; to inspire
equ*animity*—equal or placid spirit or mind
magn*animous*—of large or noble spirit
un*animous*—of one mind
in*anim*ate—not alive
*anim*osity—vehement enmity
pusill*animous*—fainthearted; cowardly
*anim*advert—to turn the mind to; to notice; to criticize

COMBINATIONS WITH *ANIMA*

■II. In many cases, English words are formed by combining parts of two or more Latin words. Thus "equanimity" is a fusion of *aequus*, "equal," and *anima*. You will recognize this new stem in such words as "equation," "equality," "equity," "iniquity." "Magnanimous" combines *magnus*, "large," with *anima*. Engage in a little etymological exploration, if you will, and see what other words you can turn up with the stem of *magnus*, "large."

1. . . . . a person large in importance, as in an industry
2. . . . . to make large
3. . . . . splendor; grandeur
4. . . . . speaking "big" or in pompous or flowery style
5. . . . . bigness or greatness
6. . . . . a large bottle (2-quart) for champagne or wine
7. . . . . a great work; a major literary or artistic work

ANSWERS:
(1) magnate   (2) magnify   (3) magnificence   (4) magniloquent   (5) magnitude   (6) magnum   (7) *magnum opus*

WORDS FROM THE LATIN *UNUS*

■III. "Unanimous" combines *unus*, "one," with *anima*, "mind." Can you think of some other English words which contain the stem of *unus*?

1. . . . . make into one
2. . . . . a fabulous animal with a single, straight horn
3. . . . . of one form or kind
4. . . . . the state of being united

KNOW YOUR PREFIXES AND SUFFIXES

WITH ROOTS or stems, prefixes and suffixes are among the most important building blocks of words. A study of them will be of great value to anyone who wants to increase his vocabulary. A prefix is an element placed before a word or root to make another word of different form or meaning. A suffix is an element that is placed after a word or root to make a word of different meaning or function. Here is a list of some of the most common prefixes and suffixes, with their meanings and examples of their use.

PREFIXES

ante-	before	antedate
anti-	against	antisocial
hyper-	beyond the ordinary	hypersensitive
il-		illiterate
im-		impossible
in-	not	inaccurate
ir-		irreligious
poly-	many	polysyllable
post-	after	postseason

SUFFIXES

-ful	characterized by, or as much as will fill	beautiful spoonful
-hood	state, condition, character	childhood falsehood likelihood
-less	without	faultless
-ly	like	saintly
-meter	measure	thermometer
-polis	city, or resident of	metropolis cosmopolitan
-ship	condition, character, skill	friendship statesmanship
-some	tendency	meddlesome

5. . . . . the only one of its kind
6. . . . . harmony; also a joining together

ANSWERS:
(1) unify or unite   (2) unicorn   (3) uniform   (4) union   (5) unique
(6) unison

EIGHT MORE LATIN STEMS

■IV. Continuing our etymological exploration, let us next consider the word benevolence. Its meaning—a feeling of good will toward others or a charitable action for the benefit of others—can be understood better when we analyze the two Latin roots that have been welded together to form the word: *bene*, "well," and *volens*, "wishing." Benevolence means, literally, "wishing others well." *Bene* is found in other words. Here are a few:

*bene*fit   *bene*ficiary   *bene*diction   *bene*factor

The stem of *volens*, "wishing," also appears frequently:

*vol*ition   *vol*untary   *vol*unteer

If we now dissect two of the words containing *bene*, we will discover that new Latin stems can easily be added to our repertoire: "benediction," a blessing, is, literally, a "saying well." The stem *dic* is from the Latin *dicere*, meaning "to say" or "to tell." You can see it in the following words:

*dic*tate   *dic*taphone   *dic*tion
in*dic*t   pre*dic*t   male*dic*tion

Again, "benefactor," literally "well-doer," contains *fac* (from the Latin verb *facere*), meaning "to do" or "to make." Watch how this stem is employed in the following words:

*fac*tor   *fac*tory   manu*fac*ture
*fac*t   *fac*totum   *fac*tual

Thus, the study of a few of these simple words brings to light eight new stems. Here are the Latin words with their meanings and with the part that serves as a stem in italics. Can you think up an English word using each stem and write it in below?

STEM	MEANING	EXAMPLE
1. *anima*	soul, spirit, mind	. . . .
2. *aequus*	even, equal	. . . .
3. *magnus*	large, big, great	. . . .
4. *unus*	one, single	. . . .

315

5. *bene*   well   . . . .
6. *volens*   wishing   . . . .
7. *fac*ere   to do, to make   . . . .
8. *dic*ere   to say, to tell   . . . .

A REVIEW OF EARLIER STEMS

And now can you recall to your memory the other Greek and Latin stems that you have had in this chapter? In the chart below you will find a list of them, each with an example. Can you fill in the English meaning of each stem, starting with *mono?*

1. mono (monocle)   . . . .
2. bi (bicycle)   . . . .
3. poly (polygamy)   . . . .
4. miso (misogyny)   . . . .
5. gamy (bigamy)   . . . .
6. theo (monotheism)   . . . .
7. anthropo (anthropology)   . . . .
8. philo (philatelist)   . . . .
9. logy (philology)   . . . .

ANSWERS:
(1) one   (2) two   (3) many   (4) hatred of   (5) marriage   (6) God
(7) man   (8) love of   (9) knowledge, study of

Building words from numbers

In this section we will explore several roads that branch off from the simple numbers *one, two,* and *three.* You may find that we will repeat some etymological roots that we have already had.

WORDS BASED ON *MONOS*

■ I. The Greek word *monos,* "one," appears in English words as *mono* or *mon.* Thus a "monocle" is a glass for *one* eye. "Monogamy" is *one* marriage. A "monogram" is a combination of two or more letters arranged to represent a single unit.

Try to write in each of the spaces below a word containing *mon* or *mono* that will fulfill the description that follows:

1. . . . . a treatise on *one* subject
2. . . . . a speech uttered by *one* person
3. . . . . mental derangement confined to *one* idea
4. . . . . an airplane with *one* pair of wings
5. . . . . exclusive possession or control of any *one* thing

6. . . . . a word of *one* syllable
7. . . . . belief in *one* god
8. . . . . uttered in *one* unvarying tone
9. . . . . government in the hands of *one* ruler
10. . . . . a dwelling place where each person under religious vows lives as *one*
11. . . . . the inhabitant of the place described in item 10

ANSWERS:
(1) monograph (2) monologue (3) monomania (4) monoplane
(5) monopoly (6) monosyllable (7) monotheism (8) monotone,
monotonous (9) monarchy (10) monastery (11) monk

If we analyze some of the words in the previous exercise, we will discover that a number of new stems have appeared.

1. In *monograph,* we have *graph,* a stem meaning "to write." Other examples:

graphic—written; hence, vivid
graphite—the black material in a lead pencil
autograph—one's own signature
chirography—handwriting
telegraph—writing at a distance

2. From *monologue* we can isolate the stem *logue* or *logy,* which is a Greek root meaning "knowledge" or "discourse." We have learned a body of words, containing this root: entomo*logy,* philo*logy,* embryo*logy,* etymo*logy.* Others are:

dialogue—discourse by two people
eulogy—discourse in praise of someone
biology—knowledge or science of life
trilogy—discourse in three parts

3. *Monomania* reminds us of other words containing the same root, *mania,* "derangement":

dipsomania kleptomania pyromania
nymphomania megalomania

4. *Monotheism* gives rise to other words containing the Greek root *theos,* "god":

polytheism theology theocracy atheism

WORDS BASED ON *BI*

■II. *Bi* is a prefix from the Latin, and denotes "two." Thus, "biannual," twice a year; "bicameral," with two chambers, as the Senate and the

317

House of Representatives in the U.S. Congress, or the Senate and the House of Commons in Canada; "biceps," a muscle having two heads of origin; "bicuspid," a tooth ending in two points. Can you write in the following spaces ten other forms with *bi?*

1. .... a vehicle with *two* wheels
2. .... occurring every *two* years
3. .... eyeglasses having *two* kinds of lenses
4. .... *second* marriage while the first is still in effect
5. .... every *two* months
6. .... something used for *two* eyes
7. .... an animal with *two* feet
8. .... something cooked *twice;* i.e., a cracker
9. .... cut into *two* parts
10. .... a marine animal with *two* shells, as an oyster

ANSWERS:
(1) bicycle (2) biennial (3) bifocals (4) bigamy (5) bimonthly
(6) binoculars (7) biped (8) biscuit (9) bisect (10) bivalve

A brief examination of the above words will introduce us to still other stems. For instance, we have:

1. *bicycle*—(*cycle,* "wheel")—tricycle, cycle
2. *bigamy*—(*gamy,* "marriage")—monogamy, polygamy
3. *binoculars*—(*ocul,* "eye")—oculist, monocle
4. *biped*—(*ped,* "foot")—pedal, quadruped
5. *bisect*—(*sect,* "cut")—insect, section

WORDS BASED ON *TRI*

■ III. *Tri* is a Latin prefix meaning "three." Thus (in music) a "triad" is a chord of three notes; a "triangle" is a figure of three angles; a "tricolor" is a flag of three colors. Now fill in the ten spaces with the proper words made up of *tri:*

1. .... a vehicle of *three* wheels
2. .... having *three* sides
3. .... made up of, or pertaining to, *three* languages
4. .... a series of *three* literary or musical compositions
5. .... every *three* months
6. .... the union of *three* persons, as the Father, the Son, and the Holy Ghost
7. .... *three* people who sing a song
8. .... consisting of *three*
9. .... *three* children born simultaneously from the same mother
10. .... a *three*-legged stand, as for a camera

318

ANSWERS:
(1) tricycle   (2) trilateral   (3) trilingual   (4) trilogy   (5) trimonthly
(6) trinity   (7) trio   (8) triple   (9) triplets   (10) tripod

In the above words we can separate two more useful stems:

1. *later*, "side"; as in bi*later*al, a two-sided object, and quadri*later*al, a four-sided object.

2. *pod*, "foot"; as in *pod*ium, the small raised platform on which the conductor of an orchestra stands; chiro*pod*ist and *pod*iatrist, the professional names of the doctors who take care of your feet. Incidentally *pod* is the Greek form of the stem which appeared in the Latin form *ped* earlier.

TEST YOURSELF: A FINAL REVIEW OF ROOTS

The following roots have been brought to your attention. In order to fix them in your mind, try to fill in the spaces allowed for each number with two words based on the indicated root.

1. *mono,* one
   a. ....
   b. ....
2. *graph,* write
   a. ....
   b. ....
3. *logue,* discourse
   a. ....
   b. ....
4. *mania,* derangement
   a. ....
   b. ....
5. *theos,* god
   a. ....
   b. ....
6. *bi,* two
   a. ....
   b. ....
7. *cycle,* wheel
   a. ....
   b. ....

8. *gamy,* marriage
   a. ....
   b. ....
9. *ocul,* eye
   a. ....
   b. ....
10. *ped* or *pod,* foot
    a. ....
    b. ....
11. *sect,* cut
    a. ....
    b. ....
12. *tri,* three
    a. ....
    b. ....
13. *later,* side
    a. ....
    b. ....
14. *volens,* wishing
    a. ....
    b. ....

If you are uncertain as to any of your answers please refer to the various sections of this chapter to check your results.

It is hardly necessary to point out how swiftly a student's vocabulary will expand if he will train himself to watch for Greek and Latin roots, to follow them up, and to learn their meanings.

27

Two keys to clarity: grammar and usage

"Dull rules and duller drills" expresses the attitude that many of us bring to grammar study. Yet grammar, with a precise vocabulary and proper usage, is one of the great keys to good writing and speaking. It is the game of putting words together so they work—and it can be fascinating.

Grammar lessons in school were a bore for many of us, if not an outright bugaboo. Yet this is strange since, more than any other subject we studied as children, grammar has almost all the qualities of a game. Here's how it goes:

In grammar we split up the sentence, take it apart, then put it together again (the same sort of thing we do with a jigsaw puzzle). The pieces of the game are the parts of speech (noun, verb, adjective, adverb, etc.), and we are required to place the pieces properly to put together a recognizable picture. We become detectives, discovering the relationship between words and phrases and clauses. We become lawyers, arguing the logic of our cases as to the use of a specific word or the structure of a sentence.

Grammar can be fun. Young people who show no interest in the rest of their schoolwork sometimes become completely involved in this game of grammar. But this happens only when they recognize it as a game, and not as a series of dry-as-dust rules and definitions to commit to memory.

We may have been taught that a verb "shows action or state of being," but did our teachers explain that "state of being" is expressed by some form of the verb *to be* (am, is, was, will be, and so forth)? Did they illustrate the difference between a *noun* ("the name of a person, place, or thing") and the person, place, or thing, itself? In many cases the answer is No, and if we were bored by grammar we will have to put the blame where it probably belongs—on the way we were taught.

Actually, grammar involves relatively few rules. What it does require is the ability to analyze, to make judgments, and to act on your decisions. If you can follow the instructions that come with a dress pattern, if you can trace the route of some old wiring and revitalize an electrical outlet, then understanding grammar should be no problem at all.

ERRORS THAT EMBARRASS

Our writing and speech are normally free of grammatical error. Still, even an occasional error may prove embarrassing. If you say "don't" at a dinner party when you should say "doesn't," your hostess may feel, with some justification, that she has invited you for the wrong evening. If you say "between you and I," talking very confidentially, when you should say "between you and me," you may erode the respect and confidence you've so carefully built up in your business colleague or customer or date.

You may not wince when a star quarterback announces, in a television interview, that his team played "good." You hear that kind of thing so often. But you had better not say that your desk-model mini-computer works "good," if you're trying to sell that machine to a young executive.

Good usage for good communication

The importance of correct usage in business and in our personal lives is self-evident. The better our grasp of grammar, the better we use the language we speak and write, the clearer and the more precise our communication will be.

Colloquial usage in our language, it is true, tends sometimes to disregard strict grammatical rules, yet is still generally accepted. The most common example is the use of "me" instead of "I." For some reason which appears to have no logic, we almost inevitably answer the question: "Who is it?" with "It is me." Now, strict grammarians would maintain that this is absolutely incorrect. The grammatically correct form, as everyone knows, is: "It is I." Yet no one seems to be particularly bothered by this lapse in usage.

Still, when our speech is transferred to the written page, we will say, and wisely, "It is I who am responsible for this department," not "It is me who is responsible . . ."

Usage, of course, involves something more than the basic rules of grammar; it often depends on the sense and meaning of a word, and we must be sensitive to these when we use any word in an expression.

We are not "liable" to have dress shirts in stock. We are "likely" to have them in stock. *Liable* means susceptible to risk, injury, or damages; *likely* indicates probability.

You say, "Let me do it," not "Leave me do it."

You say, "Leave me alone," not "Let me alone."

You are more likely to hear these errors than to read them, because people tend to be more careful with the written word. But writing carries its own crop of faulty usage.

"I'm coming over your house tomorrow."

Sharpen your style

The late William Strunk, Jr., made his advice to students brief and cogent. Among his most important maxims was "omit needless words." Another, equally useful, was: "Use definite, specific, concrete language." The examples below illustrate the merit of his suggestions for achieving a crisp, accurate style.

WEAK: The business suffered a series of damaging misfortunes within a short period of time.

BETTER: In one month the company's warehouse burned down, the treasurer absconded with the funds, and the competition lowered prices.

WEAK: Unexpectedly high attendance made it impossible to accommodate all those who wished to enter.

BETTER: Six hundred people were turned away at the door.

WEAK: He was visibly chagrined at the teacher's corporal rebuke.

BETTER: He cried when the teacher slapped him.

WEAK: The fact that one acts in a hasty manner is bound to result in an inefficient use of one's time or goods.

BETTER: Haste makes waste.

By plane, helicopter? How long do you expect to stay in that suspended position?

"I've got a product which is different than any other product on the market."

The writer means "different from." True, "different than" is acceptable in some instances and H. W. Fowler, that supreme authority in usage, writes that it is correct to say "different than" instead of "different from that which" as in "The results of the survey were different than they expected." But in most cases "from" is the preferred usage.

MASTERING THE RULES OF USAGE

There are some areas in usage, however, in which there is no dispute at all. For example, you never say "full with"; you always say "full of." You divide the apples "between" two; you may divide the apples "among" four. You don't "refer back" to some item in your sales letter; you simply "refer" to the item; "refer" implies a looking back. You never say, "I plan on being in the office at nine in the morning"; you say, "I plan to be in the office."

A mastery of usage involves so many different words and expressions that it requires reading, listening, and checking meanings throughout a lifetime. But this can be enjoyable and fascinating. As a handy reference, a brief dictionary of usage appears on pages 648–698.

Spot your grammar problems

On the two pages that follow you will find two grammar tests with which you can test yourself. Your scores in these will give you a good indication of what you remember of grammatical structure and its rules, and what you may have forgotten. In this way you eliminate guesswork and concentrate on your weak spots. The tests are followed by a chapter on the basic rules of grammar, and grammatical terms are fully explained and defined.

In the elementary test on the next page, a score of 90 percent or better will indicate to you that your speech is free of the type of error that is a hallmark of illiterate usage. In the advanced test, a score of 80 percent or more will signify a better-than-average grasp of the fundamentals of good speech. In checking your choices in both tests, be guided solely by what you generally say or would be inclined to say, not by what you believe to be "correct."

ELEMENTARY TEST

1. You (was, were) not present at last night's meeting.
2. (Them, Those) hats are very becoming.
3. I (seen, saw) an interesting sight yesterday.
4. She gave Mary and (I, me) some candy.
5. Crazy people speak to (themselves, theirselves).
6. We (can, can't) hardly hear him.
7. We won't go there (any, no) more.
8. He must (of, have) walked around the block ten times.
9. Have you (et, eaten) all the watermelon?
10. I (stood, stayed) at the farm all summer.
11. He took my best pencil (off of, from) me.
12. We (done, did) all we had to.
13. (Leave, Let) me do it for you.
14. (This here, This) book is the one I need.
15. He (don't, doesn't) do anything I ask him to.
16. We work (good, well) together.
17. Did you (learn, teach) him how to skate?
18. We want you and (she, her) to go.
19. All his money was (robbed, stole, stolen).
20. We (began, begun) early and finished early.
21. Give it to (us, we) girls.
22. (We, Us) boys are going out tonight.
23. (Him and me, Him and I, He and I) had a terrible fight last night.
24. The dog licked (its, it's) chops.
25. He is (happier, more happier) because of what happened.
26. Have you (drank, drunk) your milk?
27. (Set, Sit) down for a few minutes.
28. The sun has (rose, risen).
29. He (ain't, isn't) my friend anymore.
30. Don't (ever, never) do that to me.
31. Have you (wrote, written) the letter yet?
32. The man (drowned, drownded) before we could save him.
33. I'll do it (irregardless, regardless) of what you say.
34. Did you get an (invite, invitation) to her party?
35. We (did, done) the work and went home.

ADVANCED TEST

1. He (lay, laid) asleep for an hour.
2. Please (lay, lie) your hand on mine.
3. John is (lying, laying) down.
4. Have you (laid, lain) on the grass this morning?
5. How (is, are) your mother and father today?
6. What kind (of, of a) man did she marry?
7. Everything he (prophesied, prophecized, prophesized, prophecied) came true.
8. How has the war (affected, effected) your business?
9. The (principal, principle) street of most towns is called Main St.
10. (Beside, Besides) your interest, I also want your help.
11. Is this the man (who, whom) you claim defrauded you?
12. Everyone but (he, him) is accounted for.
13. All except (she, her) have turned in their papers.
14. Neither of the girls (are, is) here.
15. (Has, Have) either of the men returned?
16. George as well as John (is, are) on our side.
17. One of us (is, are) always here.
18. The captain or the lieutenant (is, are) always on hand.
19. He's a lot older than (I, me).
20. I am (uninterested, disinterested) in lectures on ancient art.
21. The memoranda (is, are) on your desk.
22. The murderer was (hanged, hung) at daybreak.
23. Do it (as, like) you were instructed.
24. So that's (who, whom) you thought it was!
25. (Your, You're) going to get the surprise of your life.

ANSWERS to Elementary Test: (Credit 3% for each correct choice)
(1) were (2) Those (3) saw (4) me (5) themselves (6) can (7) any (8) have (9) eaten (10) stayed (11) from (12) did (13) Let (14) This (15) doesn't (16) well (17) teach (18) her (19) stolen (20) began (21) us (22) We (23) He and I (24) its (25) happier (26) drunk (27) Sit (28) risen (29) isn't (30) ever (31) written (32) drowned (33) regardless (34) invitation (35) did.

ANSWERS to Advanced Test: (Credit 4% for each correct choice)
(1) lay (2) lay (3) lying (4) lain (5) are (6) of (7) prophesied (8) affected (9) principal (10) Besides (11) who (12) him (13) her (14) is (15) Has (16) is (17) is (18) is (19) I (20) uninterested (21) are (22) hanged (23) as (24) who (25) You're.

28

Good grammar
in a nutshell

Sometimes a problem in expression can only be solved by going back to the book. So here, for review and reference, is a brief distillation of the basic rules of grammar, covering parts of speech; simple, compound, and complex sentences; and other aspects of sentence structure.

Grammar, wrote Samuel Johnson, maker of the first great dictionary of our language, "is the science of speaking correctly; the art which teaches the relations of words to each other."

Many modern grammarians base their studies primarily on the spoken language in preference to the written. Intonation and context are as important as formal rules of structure. Then too, in recent times, knowledge of the formation and change of all modern languages has advanced greatly. What appear to us today as "rules" are understood by grammarians as the state of current usage. And while rules are characteristically inflexible, usage bends and changes with time and the needs of the users. Only a few decades ago the subjunctive mood was far more familiar than it is today. Now one never says "If I be here tomorrow," but uses the present indicative "If I am here tomorrow," which was once considered not proper formal English writing style, and hence not acceptable in educated speech.

For practical everyday purposes, Samuel Johnson's definition still expresses the need for a current grammar to guide the speaker and writer. At the same time, it is well to keep in mind that language is living, that expression has not remained the same over the generations. In the following pages "the relations of words to each other" are described. An understanding of them provides a better "feel" for the structure of the language. And once this understanding is achieved, words can be used with greater ease and confidence. Your communications, both written and spoken, will be clearer and more effective.

The sentence

Words are, of course, most meaningful in relation to each other. Place a word in a sentence and a sentence in a paragraph and they will always mean much more than when standing alone. A word by itself—with no relation to any others—means little. Apples. Sky. Logic. Uranium. The first two words make clear images. The third brings to our minds a thought process. And, unless we have scientific knowledge, "uranium" perhaps evokes the hazy vision of a bomb blast shaped like a mushroom.

Phrases say more, of course. Bushel of apples. Dark sky streaked by lightning. Logic of events. Uranium, a metallic chemical element. Such phrases, in varying degrees, add to these *subjects*. But if *verbs* and *complements* are added to them their meanings become comprehensive, complete; they become *sentences*.

> *A bushel of apples costs $1.25.*
> *A dark sky streaked by lightning greeted us on our arrival in Boston.*
> *The outcome was dictated by the logic of events.*
> *Uranium, a metallic chemical element, is important in the field of atomic energy.*

A sentence is complete; it has a subject and it tells something about that subject. It is meaningful by itself. Making a full sentence is no more than putting the subject, verb, and complement together—grouping words to express a complete statement. In conversation, a single word or phrase may replace a full sentence, because the complete sentence is understood. If someone asks, "When will you arrive?" the reply may be, "Early tomorrow." It means, "I'll arrive early tomorrow." Part of the sentence is understood.

The parts of speech

The different kinds of words that make up full sentences are known as *parts of speech*. These terms come up frequently in the study of the sentence; they fall traditionally into eight categories—conventional "filing drawers"—into which the words of our language have been gathered for more than four hundred years. You studied, probably memorized, these parts of speech in school but here is a list of them and their usual definitions to jog your memory.

1. A *noun* names something.

   cloud, Shakespeare, biology

2. A *pronoun* takes the place of a noun.

   you, her, I

3. A *verb* expresses action or refers to an event or a state of being.

   is, fight, amaze, show, seem

4. An *adjective* qualifies—tells us something about—a noun or a pronoun.

   beautiful, angry, strange, green, small

   ("The," "a," and "an" are special adjectival forms called *articles*.)

5. An *adverb* qualifies a verb, an adjective, or another adverb.

   cleverly, ago, very, usually, angrily

6. A *preposition* shows a relation between a word and a noun (or a pronoun) that follows it.

   from, in, at, with, of, among, behind

7. A *conjunction* connects words or groups of words.

   and, but, although, or, yet

8. An *interjection* expresses emotion, acts as a signal, or adds a conversational touch.

   Hey!   Wow!   Hello.   Well!   Oh!   Say!

We just heard about a little boy who said to his teacher, "I ain't got no pencil."

She corrected him at once: "It's 'I don't have a pencil.' 'You don't have a pencil.' 'We don't have any pencils.' 'They don't have any pencils.' Is that clear?"

"No," said the bewildered child. "What happened to all them pencils?"   —*Peggy Lee, quoted by Leonard Lyons*

A word can act as several parts of speech, depending on its purpose in a particular sentence. Some words may be nouns as well as verbs, such as "escape," "telephone," and "fight." Some may be adjectives and nouns, such as "blue," or even an adjective, a verb, an adverb, and a noun, such as "last."

Kinds of sentences

The parts of speech are the building blocks of language and are combined in different ways to make sentences. However, there are only four kinds of sentences that result from these combinations: *simple, compound, complex,* and *compound-complex.*

SIMPLE SENTENCES

The most rudimentary sentence consists of a *subject* and a *verb* or *predicate.*

> *Smoke rises.*

The noun "smoke" is the subject; the verb "rises" is the predicate.

The classification of a sentence as simple, however, has nothing to do with brevity. This, also, is a simple sentence:

> *A good newspaper editor has a talent for stripping long, verbose paragraphs of unnecessary detail, a knack of writing arresting headlines, an ability to select the most graphic pictures for his front page, and a fantastic memory of the middle initials in the names of the town's leading citizens.*

Among all the nouns in this sentence, only "editor" is the subject, about which something is being said, and only the verb "has" is the predicate, which says something about the subject. All of the other elements of the sentence are complements. Whatever the intricacies of a sentence, its structure can easily be mastered once the subject and the predicate have been determined.

These sentences are also simple, though each of them has compound elements.

1. *Smith and Jones play tackle on our first-string football team.*
2. *Franklin is offensive guard but also plays linebacker.*
3. *Walters, the quarterback, mixes up the plays boldly and excitingly.*

Example 1 has two nouns (a compound subject): "Smith" and "Jones." Example 2 has two verbs (a compound predicate) telling us something about Franklin's place on the team: "is" and "plays." Example 3 has two adverbs modifying the predicate "mixes up": "boldly" and "excitingly."

Although the elements of these sentences are compound, the sentences are simple; each one is a simple, independent whole.

COMPOUND SENTENCES

Two sentences put together by a *coordinating conjunction* make a compound sentence. That is to say, a compound sentence consists of two or more independent clauses, each of which could, by definition, stand alone as a sentence. (A clause is a group of words containing a subject and a predicate whether or not it stands alone.)

> *Everyone knows that Joe DiMaggio was one of the best hitters of his day, but some experts say he was the most graceful center fielder in the history of baseball.*

Put a period in the place of the comma, take out "but," and capitalize "some," and these two independent clauses could stand alone. They would not, however, provide the dramatic contrast that they do when combined into a compound sentence, as above.

A compound sentence may also be formed with punctuation.

> *The stock market turned upward today; it was the first rally after a week of declines.*

The *semicolon* takes the place of the coordinating conjuction, but there should also be a connection in sense; the ideas of the sentences should be related.

COMPLEX SENTENCES

Who, what, when, where, how, and why? The answers to these are a fair description of what goes into the *dependent clauses* which combine with an independent clause to form a complex sentence, contributing information that makes the independent clause more precise, more meaningful.

> *Seniors* who wanted to study astronomy *had to walk a mile to the observatory.*
> *We often held our meetings at Fitzgerald's restaurant,* where we could be sure we would get good service.
> When the English explorers came to America, *they discovered and took back to Britain the tobacco plant.*
> *The team* which finished last in 1963 *won the championship two seasons later.*

HOW TO DIAGRAM A SENTENCE

TEACHERS and students of English grammar have often found it useful to represent the parts of a sentence in pictorial form. This process is called diagramming a sentence. It is not necessary to be able to diagram a sentence to have a complete command of grammar, but because many people find it entertaining and useful, here are the basic principles of sentence diagramming.

On a main horizontal line the subject is placed first, followed by a vertical line which crosses the horizontal line, then by the verb, then by another vertical line which does not cross the main line but separates the verb from the direct object. A single-word modifier slants downward from the word it modifies. An indirect object is shown on a horizontal line attached to the verb by a slanted line. EXAMPLE: Joe threw the ball.

EXAMPLE: Joe threw the pitcher the ball.

Many sentences, of course, have a compound direct or indirect object. EXAMPLE: Beethoven composed sonatas and symphonies.

A predicate nominative is separated from the verb by a slanting line. EXAMPLE: Ralph Waldo Emerson was a famous lecturer.

If you want to explore sentence diagramming, complete instructions can be found in any standard grammar.

The teacher wrote on the blackboard: "I ain't had no fun all summer." Then she asked a youngster in the front row, "Harry, what should I do to correct that?"

"Mebbe—get a boyfriend?" he suggested helpfully.

COMPOUND-COMPLEX SENTENCES

The fourth kind of sentence consists of a compound sentence (two or more independent clauses) and one or more dependent clauses. The compound-complex sentence has all the ingredients of the other three kinds of sentences, as well as some new elements.

> *Most novels which win the critics' praises are ignored by the public; although the sale of film rights to Hollywood redeems some, most of these books are commercial failures.*

The sentence above contains two independent clauses and two dependent clauses.

INDEPENDENT:
1. *Most novels . . . are ignored by the public . . .*
2. *. . . most of these books are commercial failures.*

Example 1 is put together with the following parts of speech:

Most (adjective) *novels* (noun) *are ignored* (verb) *by* (preposition) *the* (adjective) *public* (noun).

Although "most novels are ignored" would stand by itself as a complete sentence, the pertinent meaning of the clause comes with the addition of "by the public." "By the public" is a *prepositional phrase*—that is, a group of words beginning with a preposition and ending usually, as in this case, with a noun or pronoun. "Public" is here the *object* of the preposition "by." Prepositional phrases do not stand alone (except in special instances, such as shortened commands like "At ease!" or in titles like "In the Mood"). They are usually modifiers acting in the manner of adjectives or adverbs, depending on their use. The way to tell the difference is to determine whether the phrase gives us information about the subject (*adjectival*) or about the predicate (*adverbial*). "By the public" is an adverbial prepositional phrase because it adds information about the predicate.

The independent clause, Example 2, has the following parts of speech:

. . . *most* (noun) *of* (preposition) *these* (adjective) *books* (noun) *are* (verb) *commercial* (adjective) *failures* (noun).

This clause begins with the same word as Example 1: "most." Here the word is a noun, rather than an adjective. ("Most" can also be an adverb, as in "most disturbing," where it modifies an adjective.) The way to tell that "most" is the subject is simply to take apart the sentence—that is, to analyze it. If the prepositional phrase "of these books" is mentally eliminated, it is easier to detect that "most" is the subject of the clause and "are" is the predicate.

In the words "commercial failure" we meet an example of the *complement*. Together, this adjective and noun tell us something about the subject; they complement it. (Complements are of several kinds, and are discussed below under "Other Parts of Sentences.")

There are also two dependent clauses in our example of a compound-complex sentence:

3. . . . *which win the critics' praises* . . .
4. . . . *although the sale of film rights to Hollywood redeems some* . . .

Example 3 is easy to identify. It is an *adjectival clause*—it tells us about (modifies) "most novels."

Example 4 is an *adverbial clause;* in total, it is a modification of the verbal action expressed in the independent clause to which it is subordinated. The conjunction "although" is sometimes called a *subordinating conjunction,* because it links a dependent clause to an independent clause.

Other such conjunctions are:

after, as, as if, as long as, as though, because, before, if, in order that, provided that, since, so that, than, though, unless, until, when, whenever, where, wherever, while

Word agreement

It may seem needless to say that a singular subject takes a singular verb, while a plural subject takes a plural verb. However, in conversation and writing people frequently make a grammatical error when a phrase or other element comes between the subject and the verb and the agree-

WRITE BETTER, SPEAK BETTER

ment may not be clear. It's hard to tell which noun the verb belongs to.

The small table *around which the children play* was *in the hall.*
The small tables *owned by the church* were *in the hall.*
The men, as well as the nurse, were *aghast at the sight.*

Similarly, a pronoun should always agree in person and in number with its *antecedent* (the noun it represents). If the antecedent is singular, the pronoun is singular; if the antecedent is plural, the pronoun is also plural.

The boy *did* his *best in the contest.*
The boys *in the school did* their *best.*
The boy *and the* girl *did* their *best.*
Neither one *of the boys did* his *best.*

The following words are generally considered singular and take the singular form of the verb:

each, either, neither, one, everyone, anyone, someone, no one, everybody, nobody, somebody, anybody, none, much

The following words are plural and take the plural form of the verb: *both, few, many, several.*

Other parts of sentences

A fundamental principle of knowing grammar is largely a matter of understanding how the *predicate* (verb in its full form) suits the subject. As already shown above, there are many instances in which the verbs, as well as the subjects, require other elements to make them clear and to make them say all that we want them to say. Once these mainstays of grammar—the subject and verb—are recognized, the other grammatical "supports" that may accompany them can be more easily singled out.

The *complement* mentioned in the discussion of dependent clauses

> Language most shows a man: speak that I may see thee. It springs out of the most retired, and inmost parts of us, and is the image of the parent of it, the mind. No glass renders a man's form, or likeness, so true as his speech. —*Ben Jonson*

above is a major one of these parts—a word or group of words—that completes the sense, or thought, of a sentence.

A complement is related to either the subject or the verb. Where its relation is to the subject, we will find a rather colorless verb *linking* the complement and the subject. Here are some examples:

She (subject) *is* (verb) *beautiful* (complement).
It (subject) *grew* (verb) *colder* (complement).
She (subject) *became* (verb) *a nurse* (complement).

Depending on the context, these verbs may also be used as *linking verbs:* look, grow, get, prove, taste, remain. There are many others.

TRANSITIVE AND INTRANSITIVE VERBS

When *action verbs* have complements, called *direct objects,* they are also transitive (*trans* means "across"). The direct object receives the action of the verb (in a grammatical sense).

He (subject) *threw* (verb) *the ball* (direct object).
John (subject) *loves* (verb) *Mary* (direct object).
The company (subject) *manufactures* (verb) *washing machines* (direct object).

An action verb which has no direct object is called an *intransitive verb* (meaning "not transitive"), because it does not carry across to anything.

The runner stumbled.
The couples danced.
The policeman frowned.

Many action verbs can be both transitive and intransitive.

The children played (intransitive).
The children played a game (transitive).

Linking verbs are also intransitive and usually do not express action.

ACTIVE VOICE AND PASSIVE VOICE

Verbs have both *active* and *passive* voices. When the action of the verb is performed by the subject, the verb is in the active voice. When the subject is acted upon, the verb is in the passive voice. In some instances, the passive voice serves us better by putting the main idea foremost.

The ball hit John (active).
John was hit by the ball (passive).

When a transitive verb appears in the passive voice, the performer or doer of the action is not always indicated.

He was expelled.
The books were burned.

INDIRECT OBJECT AND OBJECTIVE COMPLEMENT

Transitive verbs may also be associated with two other elements of a sentence: the *indirect object* and the *objective complement*.

The indirect object goes before the direct object, and usually tells to whom or for whom the action expressed by the verb is being done.

They (subject) *gave* (verb) *him* (indirect object) *the prize* (direct object).
Her (pronoun) *tact* (subject) *won* (verb) *her* (indirect object) *many friends* (direct object).

In a sentence such as "He gave to it his best effort," the use of "to" makes "it" the object of a preposition. Here "it" is not an indirect object. Such a prepositional phrase usually appears after, not before, the direct object, and there is then no confusion between a prepositional phrase and the indirect object.

The objective complement relates to the direct object and may be either a noun or an adjective; it completes the meaning of a sentence in which the direct object has not done so.

Our protest made the agreement invalid (adjective).
Everybody considered him intelligent (adjective).
They elected General Grant President (noun).
As always, events proved him right (adjective).

Appositive

The appositive is a noun or pronoun which usually follows another noun or pronoun to identify or describe it.

His father, a bricklayer, *built their house.*
He lost track of his cousin Fred.

Verbals

All the major elements of the sentence have now been mentioned except three, which have names so formidable that they discourage many from even approaching grammar. They add greatly to the richness of the language, and anyone who wants to enrich his own speech or writing should make use of them. These are *participles, gerunds,* and *infinitives,* all verb forms known as *verbals.*

The *participle* is used as an adjective, in the present tense by adding -*ing* to the verb form, and in the past tense usually by adding -*ed*.

> *They saw the animal* suffering.
> *The mayor,* ridiculed, *left the platform.*

The *gerund* is used as a noun by adding -*ing* to the verb form.

> Traveling *is educational.*

The *infinitive* is used as a noun, adjective, or adverb if preceded by "to" (though sometimes the "to" is omitted).

> *He wanted* to argue (noun).
> *He had a match* to win (adjective).
> *He is difficult* to convince (adverb).
> *He would not dare* [to] flinch ("to" omitted; infinitive used as an adverb).

All verbals may take complements (or modifiers) and form verb phrases; in addition, the infinitive forms clauses.

Participial phrase:
> *He found another student* going his way.

Gerund phrase:
> Crowning a king *is the greatest pageant of modern times.*

Infinitive phrase:
> *The boy was asked* to develop color pictures.

Infinitive clause:
> *The father asked the boy* to develop color pictures.

("The boy" is subject of infinitive "to develop.")

The following paragraph contains examples of the use of a number of these verbals:

> *The* burning *(participle)* wreckage of Jones's car challenged the contestants to continue *(infinitive as adjective modifying "contestants").* Driving *(gerund)* was difficult. Those who tried hardest to win the lead *(infinitive adverbial phrase)* guided their cars between the flames and the infield guardrail. Defying death *(participial phrase),* they gained precious yards over their less intrepid pursuers in the fiercely contested championship race.

29

Why spelling and punctuation are important

Don't underrate good punctuation and spelling! These "little" skills are basic tools in the writer's constant quest for clarity and accuracy. And, what's more important, they can make all the difference in whether your writing makes a favorable or unfavorable impression on others.

Let's take three little words, in the same order, and punctuate them differently:

"What a girl!"

"What, a girl?"

What a difference punctuation can make! Now let's look at a more businesslike situation:

He announced I have a new sales device to demonstrate.

He announced, "I have a new sales device to demonstrate."

The first of these two sentences is not clear. Who is going to do the demonstrating? The "he" and the "I" are confusing. But the addition of a comma and quotation marks take care of the confusion and make the statement perfectly clear.

The instructions on how to operate some new gadget you've bought read, "Grip the right knob pull to release the liquid."

After a split moment of hesitation, you realize that gripping the "right knob pull" will release nothing: that you have to grip the knob, then pull.

Someone has omitted an important punctuation mark.

How much clearer it would be if the directions read, "Grip the right knob, pull to release the liquid."

Proper punctuation lends a precision to your writing, gives it clarity, conveys to your reader exactly the meaning you intend.

"Before leaving the girls clean up the office."

Is this an order to clean up the office before leaving the girls? Or is it a simple statement that the girls clean the office before leaving?

You can't tell without the proper punctuation.

Punctuation can make the difference between the understanding of a communication—business, social, or any other kind—and the absence of that understanding.

There are some thirty punctuation marks we use in the English language. Each of them is of considerable importance to our writing, its clarity, and its effectiveness. In the next chapter, you will find a complete list of these punctuation marks and a thorough explanation of how to use each one properly.

THE ECCENTRICITIES OF ENGLISH SPELLING

The rules for punctuation are relatively few and easily mastered. But the story is quite different when we begin to hunt for the rules and regulations which govern the art of spelling.

For example, there is no rule which guides us in the spelling of such similar sounding words as *lief* and *leaf*, *peace* and *piece*, or *flower* and *flour*. The English write "honour" and "centre" and "theatre"; we write "honor" and "center" and "theater"; and there is no rule in spelling to govern this difference.

A person from a foreign country who is learning English finds our spelling an almost impossible task. The truth of the matter is that we, native-born, English-speaking people, don't find it much simpler.

George Bernard Shaw, that great and ornery English playwright, was irked by much of the world he saw around him, but nothing irritated him more than our English spelling.

"I need not repeat familiar arguments," he wrote, "about the waste of teachers' time, and the difficulties thrown in the way of English children trying to learn their own language; or the fact that nobody without a *visual* memory for words ever succeeds in spelling conventionally, however highly educated he or she may be."

He even went so far as to leave a huge sum of money in his will to endow the development of an English alphabet which would make English spelling logical, at least as he saw it.

Until that alphabet comes along, however, we'll have to make do with the one we have; and let us not minimize for a moment either the difficulty of that task nor its importance.

The commonest cause of poor spelling is sheer laziness. We just don't apply ourselves to the task of learning to spell correctly. And this is rather strange since we know the importance of proper spelling in both our business and social correspondence.

Poor spelling in a sales letter will diminish the customer's confidence in our products, and may lose us that possible sale. Poor spelling in letters to our friends, acquaintances, and other correspondents certainly doesn't improve their opinion of us.

Is it "discrete" or "discreet" you wish to write in the private communication you are putting into the mails? Is it "stationery" or "stationary"? "Principle" or "principal"?

It's "access*ible*" and "debat*able*"; "allegi*ance*" and "differ*ence*," and "exp*ense*." It's "nurs*ery*" and "element*ary*."

Are there any simple rules to govern these differences in spelling or to guide us in the use of *ible* or *able, ance* or *ence* or *ense,* or of any of the other countless varieties of peculiarities we meet in this English spelling of ours? The answer is No.

Nor are there rules to cover such oddities in our spelling as *though, enough, thought, photograph, sign, schedule* (we begin to see Mr. Shaw's point of view—and here is another word spelled without apparent logic, *view,* unless we know that the word is derived from the old French).

How to master the art of spelling

Nevertheless, for all the seeming lack of reason, there are a number of spelling rules which may be learned to good purpose, and there is a consistency in these rules which makes them helpful.

Chapters 31 and 32 define these rules and tell you how to employ them. You will also find in these chapters a number of tried and proven methods for sharpening your spelling abilities. There are quizzes that will help you determine both your weaknesses and strengths in spelling; and lists of words frequently misspelled, with drills and tests to aid you in mastering them.

Spelling may be one of the more difficult elements in our English language, but it is an element which cannot be neglected if our business and social communications are to be understandable and effective.

30

Punctuation pointers

Clarity, clarity, and clarity are the three main reasons for punctuation. Punctuation marks are signposts that guide your reader through the sentences you have built and bring him out understanding what you've said. Here's a review of the most important punctuation marks and their uses.

The sole purpose of punctuation is to make the meaning of the written word clear to the reader. Punctuation adds clarity to the writer's words, but it is not a panacea for a poorly constructed sentence. Sentences that are difficult to punctuate or that require a great many commas are usually weak and should be rebuilt.

The chief marks of punctuation are given on the following page. Although there are more than thirty marks listed, only eleven of them are regularly used in everyday writing. These are indicated by italics, and their uses are explained in the chapter. (Many of the others, such as the hyphen, actually concern the spelling of words not the construction of sentences.) A quick glance will tell you that you are already familiar with all the important punctuation marks. The problem is not ignorance of the punctuation marks themselves but their correct use—at the right time and in the right place. Too much punctuation is as undesirable as too little, and a misplaced comma often creates absurdities. You should therefore make sure you know how to use punctuation marks intelligently. Fortunately, the rules of punctuation are governed mainly by common sense, not by the whims of grammarians. So it is easy to master them, particularly if you keep constantly in mind the principal object of punctuation is clarity.

Punctuation marks

´	Accent, acute	° ° °	Ellipsis (or . . .)	
`	Accent, grave	!	*Exclamation point*	
'	*Apostrophe*	-	Hyphen	
°	Asterisk	. . .	Leaders	
{ or }	Brace	¶	Paragraph	
[ ]	*Brackets*	( )	*Parentheses*	
^	Caret	.	*Period*	
‚ (ç)	Cedilla	?	*Question mark*	
^	Circumflex		(*Interrogation point*)	
,	*Comma*	" "	*Quotation marks*	
:	*Colon*	§	Section	
†	Dagger	;	*Semicolon*	
—	*Dash*	~	Tilde	
¨ (ö)	Dieresis	___	Underscore	
‡	Double dagger	/	Virgule (Slash)	

Apostrophe

POSSESSIVES. Use the apostrophe to indicate the possessive case of nouns. Do not use the apostrophe to indicate the possessive case of pronouns.

John's   Jones's   its

CONTRACTIONS. Use the apostrophe to show a contraction or omission of letters. Place the apostrophe where the letter or letters are omitted.

it's for *it is*	*ass'n* for *association*
haven't for *have not*	class of '64

But omit the apostrophe in contractions formed by dropping the first letters of a word if the contraction has come into common usage.

phone   plane   varsity

LETTERS AND SYMBOLS. Use the apostrophe to form the plurals of letters and symbols.

p's and q's   5's   #'s   the 1920's

WORDS. Use an apostrophe to indicate the plural of a word referred to as a word, without regard to its meaning, but use the regularly formed plural if a meaning is attached to the word.

> There are three *but's* in the sentence.
> The *yeas* have it.
> There are eight *threes* in twenty-four.

ABBREVIATIONS.   Use an apostrophe to denote the plural or some other form of an abbreviation.

three O.K.'s   O.K.'d   V.I.P.'s

Comma

APPOSITIVES.   Use a comma to set off an appositive, that is, an expression that explains or gives additional information about a preceding expression.

> The president of our company, *Mr. Edwards,* is in Europe.

But do not separate two nouns, one of which identifies the other.

> The conductor *Bernstein* returned to America today.
> The witness *Jones* testified that he saw the defendant.

CITIES AND STATES.   Separate the name of a city from the name of a state; also, separate the name of the state from the rest of the sentence.

> Brown Company of Auburn, *New York,* has reduced turnover 50 percent.

COMPOUND PREDICATES.   Compound predicates are not usually separated by commas.

> The total number of children in high school is increasing *and* will continue to increase for several more years.

COMPOUND SENTENCES.   Separate the independent clauses of a compound sentence by a comma, unless the thoughts expressed require a more emphatic separation than the comma. (See SEMICOLONS.) The comma precedes the conjunction.

> We appreciate very much your order of July 16, *but* we are unable to accept it because of our established merchandising policy.

The comma may be omitted before *and* if the clauses are short and closely connected in thought.

> The radios were shipped yesterday *and* the televisions will be shipped tomorrow.

DASH AND COMMA. Do not use a dash and comma together.

DATES. Separate the day of the month from the year by a comma. If no day is given do not separate the month from the year by a comma. The trend is to omit the comma after the year, unless the construction of the sentence requires punctuation.

. . . payable March 12, 19— to stockholders.
. . . as of March 19— the stockholders . . .

ELLIPSIS. Use a comma to indicate that one or more words, easily understood, have been omitted. (A construction of this type is known as an *ellipsis.*)

The employer contributed 60 percent; the employes, 40 percent.

ESSENTIAL AND NONESSENTIAL PHRASES AND CLAUSES. A restrictive phrase or clause is one that is essential to the meaning of the sentence and is not merely descriptive or parenthetic; it should not be set off by commas. A nonrestrictive phrase or clause is one that adds an additional thought to the sentence but is not essential to the meaning of the sentence; it should be set off by commas.

The lawyer *who argued the case* is a close friend of the defendant.
The rule against lateness, *which has been in effect many years,* is strictly enforced.

INTRODUCTORY WORDS. Use a comma to separate an introductory word from the rest of the sentence.

Yes, the meeting will be held as scheduled.

INSEPARABLES. Do not separate words that belong together and are interdependent, such as a verb from its subject or object or predicate nominative, or a limiting clause from its antecedent.

In the following examples the commas in brackets come between such inseparables and should be omitted.

The rapid advancement of the company to its present enviable position in the publishing world [,] is attributable largely to the acumen and energy of its founders. (The comma separates the subject "advancement" from its verb "is.")
The revision combines with the first edition's thoroughness [,] a constructive viewpoint, a wide range of practices, and up-to-date methods. (The comma separates the verb "combines" from its objects "viewpoint," "range," and "methods.")
The leeway allowed the defendants in this trial, as in all others [,] where justice prevails, is in sharp contrast to the treatment accorded

defendants in totalitarian countries. (The "where" starts a limiting relative clause modifying "others." See ESSENTIAL AND NONESSENTIAL PHRASES AND CLAUSES.)

NAMES. Do not use a comma between a name and *of* indicating place or position.

Brown Company *of* Auburn, New York
Mr. Edwards *of* Robinson & Co.
Mr. Nash *of* counsel

Place a comma between a name and *Inc., Sr., Jr., 2nd, III,* etc.

Lever Brothers, Ltd. Mr. R. G. Jones, Sr.

NUMBERS. Use a comma when writing figures in thousands, *but not* in street, room, post office box, and telephone numbers.

$15,800.65   3,820   1381 Vinton Avenue
4,000   P.O. Box 4671 GR 5–4251

O, OH. Use a comma after *oh* if other words follow it, but do not use a comma after the vocative *O*.

Oh, he returned the manuscript yesterday.
O Shepherd, speak!

PARENTHESES AND COMMA. Use a comma after a closing parenthesis if the construction of the sentence requires a comma. Never use a comma before a parenthesis or an expression enclosed in parentheses.

You need tea, sliced lemon, sugar (preferably lump), cream, and assorted cookies.

PARENTHETICAL WORDS AND PHRASES. Use commas to set off parenthetical words or phrases like *I believe, for example, however,* unless the connection is close and smooth enough not to call for a pause in reading.

Furthermore, credit obligations may be paid out of capital items.
The economic condition of the country, *I believe,* has been gradually improving.
He was *perhaps* busy at the time.
That make of car is not expensive and *therefore* appeals to potential customers in the low-income brackets.

But distinguish between words used parenthetically and the same words used as adverbs.

However, I shall follow your advice. (Parenthetical)
However early he arrives at his office, his secretary is always there before him. (Adverb)

345

Thus was a fortune built from nothing. (Adverb)

Thus, the assignment does not represent the substitution of one liability for another. (Parenthetical)

PARTICIPIAL PHRASES. Do not separate a participle from the noun it modifies when the noun is not the subject and the participial phrase is not closely connected with the rest of the sentence.

WRONG: The operators, *having agreed to arbitrate,* the union called off the strike.

RIGHT: The evidence *being merely circumstantial,* the jury acquitted him.

RIGHT: The operators, having agreed to arbitrate, went back to work.

PHRASES WITH A COMMON ELEMENT. Place a comma before a word or words that are common to two or more phrases but are expressed only after the last phrase. In the following examples the commas in brackets are frequently *omitted in error.*

The report was documented with references to many, if not all [,] of the recent court decisions on the question of interlocking directorates. (The words "of the recent court decisions" are common to "many" and to "all.")

The sales manager's reports are clearer, more concise, more accurate [,] than those of the advertising manager. (The words "than those . . ." are common to "clearer," "more concise," and "more accurate.")

Note: If the phrases are connected by a conjunction, the comma is not needed.

. . . are clearer, more concise, *and* more accurate than those . . .

QUOTATIONS. Set off direct quotations by commas.

"I am interested," he said, "in anything you have to say."

His reply was, "I am not interested in the matter."

"I am not interested in the matter," he replied.

But if a question mark or exclamation point is needed at the end of the quotation, do not use a comma.

"What is the lowest price you can quote?" he inquired.

"How dare you interrupt me!" she cried.

QUOTATION MARKS AND COMMA. Place the comma on the *inside* of quotation marks.

When he spoke of "overtime," I thought he meant over forty hours.

SERIES. Separate words and phrases in a series by a comma. Although it is optional, most book publishers use the comma before the conjunction connecting the last two members of a series. (See the use of a semicolon in a series, pages 355–356.)

Thus, we speak of buying goods on credit, of a merchant's credit, *and* of making a payment by credit.

Its membership comprises manufacturers and wholesalers of silverware, watches, diamonds, *and* semiprecious stones.

But do not use a comma between two parallel constructions joined by a conjunction.

This amount is equal to the covered loss less (1) the coinsurance deduction *and* (2) the normal loss.

He can ask for changes in the estimate *or* for a completely revised estimate.

Colon

INTRODUCTION TO LISTS, TABULATIONS. The most frequent use of the colon is after a word, phrase, or sentence that introduces lists, a series, tabulations, extracts, texts, and explanations that are in apposition to the introductory words.

The following is an extract from the report: The cause of crime is social.

These conditions must exist: adequate heating, plastered and painted walls, locked front doors.

But do not use a colon to introduce a series of items that are the direct objects of a preposition or verb or that follow a form of the verb *to be*.

WRONG: The requirements of a good secretary *are*: ability to take rapid dictation and to transcribe it rapidly; ability to spell correctly and to use the dictionary to the best advantage; familiarity with . . . (Omit the colon.)

Note: A colon may precede a formal tabulation even when the tabulated words or phrases are the objects of a preposition or verb or follow a form of the verb *to be*.

The requirements of a good secretary are:
Ability to take rapid dictation and to transcribe it rapidly
Ability to spell correctly and to use the dictionary to advantage
Familiarity with . . .

TIME. Use a colon to indicate clock time, unless the time indicated is exactly on the hour.

4 A.M.   9:30 P.M.

FOOTNOTES. When reference is made to a publication in a footnote, some writers use a colon to separate the name of the city of publication from the name of the publisher. A comma is also acceptable.

Gavin A. Pitt, *The Twenty Minute Lifetime,* Englewood Cliffs: Prentice Hall, Inc., 1965, p. 20

BIBLE REFERENCES. Use a colon to separate the verse and chapter in biblical references.

Matthew 10:4.

DASH AND COLON. Do not use a dash with a colon.

Dash

PRINCIPAL USE. The dash is used principally to set off explanatory clauses, to indicate abrupt changes in the continuity of expression, and to set off a thought that is repeated for emphasis.

When I last spoke to John—it must have been two days ago—he was willing to sign the petition.

SERIES. A dash may be used before or after a clause that summarizes a series of words or phrases, but a colon is more common *after* it.

Wage and hour, arbitration, union contracts—these are only a few of the services in our Complete Labor Equipment.
Our Complete Labor Equipment includes six services: wage and hour, employe relations, union contracts, labor relations, state labor law, and pension and profit sharing.

DASH AND OTHER PUNCTUATION MARKS. A dash may be used after an abbreviating period. If the material set off by dashes requires an interrogation or exclamation point, retain the punctuation before the second

---

IT'S A PROBLEM

Although they are often confused, *its* and *it's* are two completely different words. *Its* is a possessive pronoun meaning "belonging to it." *It's* is a contraction of "it is," with the apostrophe substituting for the missing *i*. The words are used correctly in these examples:

The dog is in its pen.   I'm afraid it's too late.
It's fun to go skating.   The tree has lost its leaves.

dash. Do not use a dash with a comma or semicolon. Do not use a dash and colon together before a list of items.

The check is now O.K.—he made a large deposit.

The head of the personnel department—is his name Donovan or O'Donovan?—said he thought there would be an opening next week.

Ellipsis

When you are quoting and want to omit words, use three consecutive asterisks (***) or dots (. . .) to indicate an omission of words. If a period would ordinarily follow the words omitted, you will then have three dots followed by a period (. . . .).

Exclamation point

EXCLAMATORY SENTENCES.   Place an exclamation point after a startling statement or a sentence expressing strong emotion.

How incredible that he should take that attitude!

EXCLAMATORY WORDS.   Place an exclamation point after exclamatory words or interjections.

Hurrah!   Zounds!   Good grief!

FOR EMPHASIS.   If not used to excess, an exclamation point is a good device to lend emphasis or to drive home a point.

Buy now!   The closed shop is out!

Parentheses and brackets

BRACKETS.   If your typewriter has a bracket key, use brackets to enclose comments or explanations in quoted material, to rectify mistakes, and to enclose parentheses within parentheses; otherwise, use parentheses for these purposes.

EXPLANATORY EXPRESSIONS.   Use parentheses to enclose parenthetical or explanatory expressions that are outside the general structure of the sentence. Parentheses indicate a stronger separation than do commas or dashes.

The place at which an incorporators' meeting (sometimes called the first meeting of the stockholders) is to be held is determined by statute in most states.

349

FIGURES. Enclose a figure in parentheses when it follows an amount that has been written out in words, and when the American equivalent of foreign currency is given.

> Under the will he received £ 100,000 ($250,000).
> Seven thousand five hundred (7,500) dollars.
> Seven thousand five hundred dollars ($7,500).

Note: If the figure is written before the word "dollars," do not use the dollar sign; if the figure is written after the word "dollars," use the dollar sign. This rule also applies to the percent sign.

QUESTIONS AND ANSWERS. In testimony (question-and-answer material) use parentheses to enclose matter describing an action and, also, to indicate a person who has not previously taken part.

> Q. (By Mr. Smith) Will you identify this handkerchief? (handing the witness a handkerchief).

ENUMERATIONS. Enclose in parentheses letters or numbers in enumerations run into the text.

> Stock may be divided broadly into two kinds: (1) common stock and (2) preferred stock.

SINGLE (CLOSING) PARENTHESES. Parentheses are usually used in pairs, but a single closing parenthesis may be used instead of a period to follow a letter or small roman numeral in outlines and in lettering and numbering paragraphs.

PUNCTUATION IN PARENTHESES. Commas, periods, and similar punctuation marks belong within the parentheses if they belong to the paren-

---

WHEN TO USE THE APOSTROPHE IN PLURALS

The apostrophe plus s ('s) normally shows possession. There are only a few special cases in which 's should be used to form a plural. These are: 1. plurals of numerical figures; 2. plurals of letters; 3. plurals of signs; 4. plurals of words referred to as words. Here are some examples of plurals correctly formed by adding 's:

> He gives more +'s than —'s.   She used three *because*'s in one
> Add two 4's and three 5's.   sentence.
> The 1890's were gay.   He should mind his *p*'s and *q*'s.

thetical clause or phrase. They are outside the parentheses if they belong to the words of the rest of the sentence. See also PERIODS AND PARENTHESES, below.

The boy ran as if a ghost (and, indeed, he may have been right) were following him.
He reported the action at once. (He has a strong civic sense of responsibility.)
He turned in a perfect examination paper. (What an example for the rest of the class!)

Period

SENTENCES.   Place a period at the end of a declarative or imperative sentence.

The contract was signed last week. (Declarative)
Hold the shipment until next month. (Imperative)

INITIALS AND ABBREVIATIONS.   Place a period after initials and abbreviations. There are a few exceptions to this rule. Preferably, the periods are omitted between initials standing for organizations.

Ph.D.   C.O.D.   ibid.   Chas.   Thos.   R. E. Smith   UNICEF

OUTLINES.   Place a period after each letter or number in an outline or itemized list unless the letter or number is enclosed in parentheses or followed by a closing parenthesis.

OMISSIONS.   Omit the period after:
Contractions

ass'n   sec'y

Roman numerals, except in an outline

Vol. II   *George V*

Shortened forms of names and words in common use

Ed   Will   ad   memo   percent   photo

Letters identifying radio station

WOR   NBC

PERIODS AND PARENTHESES.   When an expression in parentheses comes at the end of a sentence and is part of the sentence, put the period outside the parentheses; if the expression is independent of the sentence and a period is necessary, place the period within the parentheses.

> The creditor can get a judgment against him and garnishee his wages (see page 384).
> The creditor can get a judgment against him and garnishee his wages. (The law of garnishment is discussed at page 384.)

But do not use a period when a complete declarative or imperative sentence is enclosed in parentheses *within a sentence.*

> The honorary chairman of the board (he retired from active duty several years ago) addressed the Quarter-Century Club.

PERIODS AND QUOTATION MARKS. Always place the period *inside* the quotation marks.

> Please explain what you meant by "without reservation."

Question mark (interrogation point)

INTERROGATIVE SENTENCES. Place a question mark after a direct question but not after an indirect question.

> Have you heard the decision that was made at the conference? (Direct)
> Mr. Rogers asked me, "When will the book be ready for publication?" (Direct)
> Mr. Rogers asked me when the book would be ready for publication. (Indirect)

REQUESTS. Do not place a question mark after a question that is a request to which no answer is expected.

> Will you please return the signed copy as soon as possible.

QUERIES. A question mark enclosed in parentheses may be used to query the accuracy of a fact or figure. Other punctuation is not affected by this use of the question mark.

> The treaty was signed September 5(?), 1945.

SERIES OF QUESTIONS. A question mark is usually placed after each question in a series included within one sentence, and each question usually begins with a capital.

> What will be the significance of man's landing on the moon if men still cannot get along with their fellows? If man's cultural endeavors have been sacrificed? If world peace is still unstable?

But the question mark may be omitted in a series of questions in a construction like the one in the following example.

Who is responsible for (a) copyediting the book, (b) the art work, (c) the production schedule?

QUOTATION MARKS WITH QUESTION MARKS. See PLACEMENT OF QUOTATION MARKS.

Quotation marks

DIRECT QUOTATIONS. Enclose the exact words of a speaker or writer in quotation marks, but do not enclose words that are not quoted exactly. The quoted material may be a word or several paragraphs in length.

On the 15th he wrote, "Please consider the contract canceled if the goods are not shipped by the 10th of next month."
On the 15th he wrote that we should consider the contract canceled if the goods were not shipped by the 10th of next month.
He wrote that he was "no longer interested" in the proposition.

But do not use quotation marks when the name of the speaker immediately precedes the quotation or in question-and-answer material.

Mr. Edwards: In my opinion the machine is worthless.
Mr. Roberts: Upon what do you base that opinion?

PARAGRAPHS. When quoted material is more than one paragraph in length, place quotation marks at the beginning of each paragraph but only at the close of the last paragraph.

DEFINITIONS. Use quotation marks to enclose a word or phrase that is accompanied by its definition.

The party against whom garnishment proceedings are brought is called the "garnishee."
"Bankruptcy insolvency" means that a debtor's total assets are less than his total liabilities.

UNUSUAL WORDS OR TRADE TERMS. Use quotation marks to enclose an unusual word or phrase or one used with a special trade meaning the first time the term is used. It is not necessary to use the quotation marks when the term is repeated.

This "pyramiding" was carried to an extreme in the public utility field.
In "spot" markets, commodities are bought and sold in specific lots and grades with a definite delivery date specified.

TITLES AND NAMES. Use quotation marks to enclose the titles of:

articles	paintings
chapters or parts of books	plays, motion pictures, sketches
brochures, pamphlets	poems
operas	songs

Do not use quotation marks with:

names of periodicals and well-known publications, such as Who's Who and dictionaries;

the Bible or names of its books or other parts of it;

movements of a symphony, concerto, or other compositions, or names of numbered compositions.

Note: In letters or advertising material, the title of a book may be capitalized for emphasis. In printed material the title of a book is usually italicized; therefore, in preparing material for the printer, you should underline the title of a book.

SINGLE QUOTATION MARKS. Use single quotation marks to enclose a quotation within a quotation.

Rachel said, "Anna asked me, 'Well, do you like my play?' and I answered, 'I'll produce it.' "

THE IRRESISTIBLE QUOTATION MARK

To the do-it-yourself sign painter and poster letterer, quotation marks are a fascinating and irresistible mystery. There is no accounting for the way in which these artists reach for quotation marks at the slightest, even at no, provocation: "Special 'Mother's Day' Dinner"; "Prices Slashed for Our 'Fire Sale' "; " 'No Trespassing.' " And the card that graces (or graced) the knick-knack shop in Palm Beach: "Brow 'z' ers Always Welcome." Somebody had something cute in mind, but what?

Actually the legitimate uses of quotation marks are fairly few: to enclose the exact phraseology of spoken or written language that is being cited; to set off titles of books, chapters and the like, when italics are not so used; to mark a word or phrase being used in a special way, and sometimes to disclaim responsibility for the words of someone else. —*Theodore Bernstein*

354

PLACEMENT OF QUOTATION MARKS.   Always place a period or comma inside quotation marks.

> The account was marked "paid," but he never received a receipt.
> The check was marked "canceled."
> Many thanks for sending me a copy of Dr. Jones's article, "The Trade of Nations."

Always place colons and semicolons outside quotation marks.

> Turn to the chapter entitled "Consideration for Stock"; the reference is in the first paragraph.

Interrogation and exclamation points come before or after the quotation marks, depending upon the meaning of the text.

> Who is the author of the short story, "Curfew Shall Not Ring To-night"? (The entire question is not quoted.)
> He shouted, "I will never consent to those terms!" (The exclamation is part of the quotation.)

Semicolon

COMPOUND SENTENCES.   A semicolon may be used to separate the parts of a compound sentence when the comma and conjunction are omitted.

> The adjustment has been made; the file has been closed.

LONG, INVOLVED CLAUSES.   Use a semicolon to separate long, involved clauses.

> A low rate of interest usually reflects easy conditions and a rather inactive industrial situation; a high rate, money stringency and industrial activity.

PUNCTUATED CLAUSES.   Use a semicolon to separate clauses that are punctuated by commas.

> On the other hand, if the turnover is low in comparison with the normal figure, it shows just the opposite; that is, weaker sales policy, and poorer purchasing ability and stock control than the average.

SERIES.   In enumerations use semicolons to separate the items unless they are short and simple; also, to separate items that contain commas. (See the use of a comma in a series, pages 346–347.)

> The three classes of long bills are (1) bills drawn in ordinary business operations; (2) long bills arising from the making of foreign loans; (3) finance bills.

The most important of these services are published by Moody's Investors Service, Inc.; Standard & Poor's Corporation; and Fitch Publishing Co., Inc.

BEFORE A CONJUNCTIVE ADVERB. Use a semicolon before an adverb that serves the purpose of a conjunction. The conjunctive adverbs are *accordingly, also, besides, consequently, furthermore, hence, however, indeed, likewise, moreover, nevertheless, otherwise, similarly, so, still, therefore, thus.*

He telephoned that he did not plan to leave until next week; *therefore,* I did not consider it necessary to send the report to him by airmail.

QUOTATION MARKS AND SEMICOLON. Place the semicolon *outside* quotation marks.

PARENTHESES AND SEMICOLON. Use a semicolon after a closing parenthesis if the construction of the sentence requires a semicolon. Never use a comma or semicolon before a parenthesis or an expression enclosed in parentheses.

test your skills

PUNCTUATION POINTERS

Following the rules outlined in this chapter, punctuate the following sentences:

1. Its plain to see said she there are too many ands in that sentence
2. The artist Marat will open a show in Richmond Virginia on Wednesday April 27
3. The suggestion which had arrived too late was held for the next meeting
4. However you do it get here by the first of the month
5. However I would like to see you earlier if possible
6. Jim Browne hes a friend of yours isnt he called today
7. Cans made up 60 percent of the litter bottles 40 percent
8. Did the company destroy its image he mused
9. Will you please send the five hundred dollar $500 withdrawal as quickly as possible
10. Yes the concert will be played over Station WXYZ at 130
11. Hurry deliver the package to the following address 6672 Schnefel St Kansas City Mo
12. The businessmens assn was formed in the early 1940s

Answers to this quiz appear on page 705.

31

How to become
a good speller

You can't expect to become a good speller overnight, or by learning a secret gimmick. But these commonsense pointers will help you tackle the job in the most interesting and efficient way, knowing that you will succeed—because good spellers are made, not born.

Aristotle, the great Greek philosopher, was tutor to the future king, Alexander the Great. One day they were doing a lesson in mathematics which required many calculations. Alexander, always impatient, suddenly threw aside his work and exclaimed: "Why must I go through all these little steps? Why can't I get the answer immediately? I'm the future king!"

"There is no royal road to knowledge," answered his tutor.

There is no royal road to knowledge. There is no short cut to any branch of learning, and that is especially true for spelling. We had trouble with spelling in America long before Noah Webster published his famous speller. No perfect speller was ever born. Spellers are *made*.

Every person who writes a letter, research paper, press release, or short story without making a mistake in spelling has reason to congratulate himself. At some time in his life, he spent the time and made the effort to become a good speller. Spelling may seem to come easier to some people than to others, but no one is an intuitive speller. However, everyone can become a good speller by following scientifically prepared steps. Some have learned the spelling of every word they met painfully and slowly. That was a waste of nervous energy. Time and nerve-power will be conserved, and success will be assured if you will follow the steps enumerated below. This is a prescription for good spelling that has rarely failed. Why not give it a trial?

Tricks that help you spell

Try to discover little devices of your own that will help you to remember the spelling of words that have no rules. For example *principal* means the head of a school or the main thing; *principle* means a rule or a truth.

Much slaughter on the battlefield of spelling has been caused by these two enemies of peace of mind. And yet one simple device will remove forever the confusion caused by them.

A princip*le* is a ru*le*. Both of these end in *le*. Now you have the whole secret. If it means a ru*le*, spell it with the *le;* the other meaning must be spelled princi*pal*. You may remember it another way. If your principal is a fine fellow, he was a PAL to you. And there you have the second sure way of remembering these two spelling demons.

STATIONARY VS. STATIONERY

These two have been fighting on our literary battleground ever since we can remember. You think you have the correct spelling when suddenly the other one butts in and then you're lost again.

How can you be certain? Easily. Take a lett*er;* yes, a lett*er*. That's what stationery is used for, and you'll notice that *letter* ends in ER. Now station*ery* ends in ERY.

The other word means *standing* still. Think of the *a* in st*a*nding and you'll remember the ARY in station*ary*.

SEPARATE

The word sep*a*rate has long been a trouble spot.

Think of the word PART. When you sep AR ate, you take things a PART. That will tell you to be sure to spell the word with AR.

These three devices you may use. But the best tricks are the ones you think up yourself. When you discover a way to spell a word that has always given you trouble, you will be so overjoyed at the discovery that you will never forget the spelling. All laws of psychology teach us that we seldom forget anything we learned with pleasure. Therefore, try to be a spelling discoverer; enjoy your latest discovery and one more spelling demon will be eliminated.

Here is a good way to prevent confusion in spelling *their* and *there:*

$$\left.\begin{array}{l} \text{here}\ldots\ldots\ldots \\ \text{(w)here}\ldots\ldots\ldots \\ \text{(t)here}\ldots\ldots\ldots \end{array}\right\} \text{place}$$

The personal pronoun must, by elimination, be *their.*

Remember! Form your own memory devices.

Consult the dictionary

The dictionary is probably the most valuable book in your library. You should form the habit of consulting it the moment you are confronted with any spelling difficulty. Don't delay. When a word bothers you, and no rule or device will help, look it up while the annoyance is fresh. This is good psychology. The sooner you remove the cause of the annoyance (the doubtful word), the more certain will you be of its disappearance as an annoyance.

The dictionary is an authority that cannot be challenged. It is much more reliable than the memory of ordinary mortals. Why worry about the spelling of a word? A glance into the dictionary will answer your question. Sometimes the same word may be spelled correctly in more than one way, and the dictionary will help you with this. For example, U.S. spellings of *labor, favor,* and *armor* are paralleled in England by the spellings: *labour, favour,* and *armour.* The British prefer the spellings: *connexion, deflexion,* and *inflexion* to the North American *connection, deflection,* and *inflection.*

The British (and many Canadians) spell these words with RE: *centre, metre, theatre.* The U.S. spellings are: *center, meter,* and *theater.*

In all these instances, and many more, a good college dictionary will indicate these differences. For this purpose the special section on "Spelling" is especially useful.

Remember! Consult the dictionary.

Make your own spelling list

Make a list of your difficult words. Find opportunities to use them. Mark Twain, the American humorist whose principles of writing deserve the respect of all who would learn, said, "Use a new word correctly three times, and it's yours." Use a word that has given *you* trouble three times correctly and you should not have any difficulty.

The important thing is to use it *correctly*. Misspelling a word a number of times only fixes the misspelling more firmly. There is a popular expression to the effect that "Practice Makes Perfect." But that really should be "Practice Makes Permanent." If we always make the same mistake, no amount of practice will do anything to improve our knowledge. Remember to use a word correctly the first time.

Listen

Develop the art of listening carefully. Many people whose hearing shows no organic defect are poor listeners. They do not pay attention and consequently they don't really hear what is being said. The more cultured the topic, the more alert must the listener be. These days there is much talk in the field of economics. Terms like *government, security, conservation* are heard repeatedly. Do you hear *gover n ment* or *guvment? Scurity* or *security? Consivation* or *conservation?*

It is true that sometimes the speaker himself is at fault because his enunciation is not perfect. That does not excuse the listener, however. If a word does not seem quite clear to you, you owe it to yourself to consult the dictionary as soon as you are near one. Thus you will firmly establish that word in your mind.

Remember! Listen attentively; look up a doubtful word; let no time be wasted.

Learn to spell any hard word

Here are steps to follow in learning a word that gives you trouble. Don't take short cuts. Follow the instructions to the letter!

1. *Look* at your word. Be sure to *pronounce* each syllable carefully: *in de pend ent.*

2. *Close* your eyes or turn away and form a picture of the word in your mind. If the letters are not clearly before you, look at the word again, until you see it with your eyes closed.

3. *Pronounce* the word and write it at the same time. If you are not sure, try to picture the word. Be certain that you write it correctly the first time.

4. *Write* the word a second time, using it in a sentence.

5. The next day write the word down as someone else reads it to you.

32

The simple rules
of spelling

Mastering the basic rules of spelling—and the exceptions to them—will give you the solid foundation you need to be a good speller. Careful study of the rules, word lists, and exercises in this chapter will enable you to spell all but the most unusual words without looking them up.

It is possible to consult your dictionary every time you are in doubt about the spelling of a word. The knowledge of a few helpful rules, however, will make that unnecessary. As is true of almost all rules in English grammar, there are some exceptions to the rules in spelling. Therefore, it is necessary to master the exceptions as well as the rules. Study the rules, do the exercises, and try using some of the words you have studied as soon as possible.

Remember that your ultimate aim in spelling is to be able to spell every word you want to use without wasting time sounding it out or looking it up in the dictionary.

This chapter will give you a few of the most useful and important spelling rules and help you solve problems like these:

How many times have you been puzzled about doubling a consonant?

Does *beginning* have two *n*'s in the middle?

Does *omitted* have two *t*'s?

Why has *benefiting* one *t,* while *admitting* has two?

What's the correct plural of *ally?* Of *alley?*

These and all other questions are easily answered if you will remember a few scientific rules. There are very few rules in English as sure to help you as these.

Remember, though, that English spelling is idiosyncratic at best. You must master the exceptions as well as the rules if you are going to be a consistently good speller. In some cases, as with the *-ance, -ence* words, you must simply rely on practice and memory.

Doubling final consonants

RULE 1: When a one-syllable word (run) ends in one vowel (u) followed by one consonant (n), that consonant is doubled (nn) before a suffix beginning with a vowel (er).

Now discover for yourself what would happen to the final consonants of these words:

WORD	+ ER	+ ING
hit	hiTTer	hiTTing
spin	spiNNer	spiNNing
wrap	wraPPer	wraPPing
trim	triMMer	triMMing

The following words have more than one syllable but they follow the same rule as the words just described. They *double* their final consonant before a suffix beginning with a vowel.

WORD	+ ER	+ ING	+ OTHER SUFFIX
admit		admiTTing	admiTTedly
begin	begiNNer	begiNNing	
compel		compeLLing	
confer		confeRRing	
control		controLLing	controLLable
commit		commiTTing	
equip		equiPPing	
omit		omiTTing	

These cases are all covered by another simple rule.

RULE 2: A word of more than one syllable (occur) ending in a single vowel (u) and a single consonant (r), which has the accent on the final syllable, doubles that consonant (RR) before a suffix beginning with a vowel (occuRR ing). Remember the accent must be on the last syllable.

oc cur'   ad mit'   per mit'

Unless the final syllable has the accent, there will be no doubling of the consonant. Thus, *benefit* will not double the *t*, because the accent is on the first syllable. *Ben' e fit ing.*

Study the suffixes to the following words. Each word satisfies three conditions:

1. It has more than one syllable.
2. The last syllable has the accent.
3. The last syllable ends in *one* vowel and *one* consonant.

WORD	+ ING	+ ED	+ OTHER SUFFIX
abet	abe TT ing	abe TT ed	abe TT or
abhor	abho RR ing	abho RR ed	abho RR ence
admit	admi TT ing	admi TT ed	admi TT ance
allot	allo TT ing	allo TT ed	allo TT ance
annul	annu LL ing	annu LL ed	annu L ment (one L because the suffix begins with a consonant)
commit	commi TT ing	commi TT ed	commi T ment
confer	confe RR ing	confe RR ed	confe R ence (one R because the accent is on *first* syllable)
concur	concu RR ing	concu RR ed	concu RR ence
defer	defe RR ing	defe RR ed	defe R ence (only one R because accent is on *first* syllable)
dispel	dispe LL ing	dispe LL ed	
excel	exce LL ing	exce LL ed	
infer	infe RR ing	infe RR ed	infe R ence (one R. Why?)
occur	occu RR ing	occu RR ed	occu RR ence
omit	omi TT ing	omi TT ed	
rebel	rebe LL ing	rebe LL ed	rebe LL ion
recur	recu RR ing	recu RR ed	recu RR ence
refer	refe RR ing	refe RR ed	refe R ence (one R. Why?)
regret	regre TT ing	regre TT ed	

Special case: Words ending in *C* add *K* before a suffix beginning with *e, i,* or *y,* in order to retain the hard *c* sound before the vowel.

picnic + *ed* = picnic K ed
traffic + *ing* = traffic K ing
panic + *y* = panic K y

EXERCISE 1. Below is a list of verbs of one syllable. Add ING to each of them. Some will double their final consonant. Some will not. Why?

Remember Rule 1. There must be only *one* vowel followed by *one* consonant for you to double.

cramp	. . . .	nod	. . . .
drum	. . . .	rain	. . . .
grin	. . . .	rest	. . . .
hit	. . . .	rig	. . . .
look	. . . .	scrub	. . . .

Six out of the ten doubled their consonants. The remaining four did not because they had a vowel and two consonants (cr a m p) or two vowels and consonant (l oo k).

Look at the words below and notice how the meaning is determined by the single or double consonant. This is why correct spelling is so important to convey your meaning.

bar	He *barred* the door.	plane	The carpenter *planed*
bare	He *bared* his arm.		the wood.
din	The teacher *dinned* it	scrap	The two dogs *scrapped*.
	into John's ear.	scrape	Walter *scraped* his new
dine	We *dined* at four.		knife on the cement
pin	Mary *pinned* her dress.		floor.
pine	Mary *pined* away.	wag	He *wagged* his head
plan	They *planned* a happy		solemnly.
	life.	wage	He *waged* a bitter war.

Notice these few exceptions to the rule:

bused	*transferable*
chagrined	*transference* (but *transferring*)
gaseous (but *gassed*)	*facility*

EXERCISE 2.   Write correctly the words formed:

defer + ed	*deferred*		
refer + ence	. . . .	tire + less	. . . .
shop + ing	. . . .	swim + er	. . . .
suit + able	. . . .	trim + er	. . . .
hit + ing	. . . .	occur + ence	. . . .
singe + ing	. . . .	commit + ed	. . . .
control + ing	. . . .	equip + age	. . . .
repel + ant	. . . .	excel + ing	. . . .

EXERCISE 3.   Write the present participle (ing) and past participle (ed) of the following verbs. Some will double the final consonant; others will not. When in doubt, refer to the rules on doubling final consonants.

WORD	PRESENT PARTICIPLE	PAST PARTICIPLE
admit	*admitting*	*admitted*
adapt	. . . .	. . . .
cramp	. . . .	. . . .
design	. . . .	. . . .
conceal	. . . .	. . . .
congeal	. . . .	. . . .
blot	. . . .	. . . .
stop	. . . .	. . . .
crush	. . . .	. . . .
excel	. . . .	. . . .
defer	. . . .	. . . .
envelop	. . . .	. . . .
extol	. . . .	. . . .
flutter	. . . .	. . . .
happen	. . . .	. . . .
hum	. . . .	. . . .
level	. . . .	. . . .
quarrel	. . . .	. . . .
rub	. . . .	. . . .
signal	. . . .	. . . .
retreat	. . . .	. . . .

EXERCISE 4. By adding the various endings, make new words. In some instances, the final consonant of the original word will be doubled. When in doubt, refer to the rules about doubling final consonants.

Form an adjective of the word *puck* by adding *ish*.   puck + *ish* = *puckish*

Form an adjective of *wit* by adding *y*.   . . . .

Form a noun from the verb *spin* by adding *er*.   . . . .

Form a noun from the noun *blot* by adding *er*.   . . . .

Form a noun by adding *er* to *design*.   . . . .

Form an adjective by adding *al* to *comic*.   . . . .

Form a noun by adding *er* to *shut*.   . . . .

Form a noun by adding *er* to *slip*.   . . . .

Form a noun by adding *eer* to *profit*.   . . . .

Form a noun by adding *ing* to *meet*.   . . . .

Add *able* to *inhabit* to form an adjective.   . . . .

Add *er* to *toil* to form a noun.   . . . .

Add *er* to *put* to form a noun.   . . . .

Add *ment* to *develop* to form a noun.   . . . .

Add *ment* to *defer* to form a noun.   . . . .

Add *er* to *rub* to form a noun.   . . . .

Add *er* to *develop* to form a noun.   . . . .

Make the feminine of *god*.   . . . .

Name the man who sells you drugs.   . . . .

Add *er* to *trap* to form a noun.   . . . .

The final *E*

RULE 1: When a word ends in *E,* drop the *E* before adding a suffix that begins with a vowel:

move + *ing* = moving   advise + *able* = advisable

use + *age* = usage   tribe + *al* = tribal

RULE 2: Keep the final *E* before a suffix that begins with a consonant:

pave + *ment* = pavement   use + *less* = useless

care + *ful* = careful   bare + *ly* = barely

Caution! When a final *E* follows a soft *C* or *G,* it is usually retained before a suffix beginning with *O* or *A,* to prevent a change in pronunciation: couraGEous, notiCEable

The final *Y*

Why should the final *Y* cause so much trouble? Two simple rules will take care of all such words. Notice these words:

SINGULAR	PLURAL
abb(ey)	abbeys
journ(ey)	journeys
monk(ey)	monkeys

THE *Y* PRECEDED BY A VOWEL

RULE 1: When a word ends in *Y* preceded by a vowel, the *Y* remains unchanged. Here are some examples:

1. The letter *s* is added to form the plural.

alley + S = alleys   pulley + S = pulleys

attorney + S = attorneys   trolley + S = trolleys

chimney + S = chimneys   turkey + S = turkeys

donkey + S = donkeys   valley + S = valleys

medley + S = medleys   volley + S = volleys

2. The suffix *ing* or *ed* is added.

allay + ED = allayed;   + ING = allaying
annoy + ED = annoyed;   + ING = annoying
buy   + ING = buying

3. The suffix *er* meaning *one who* is added.

buy + ER = buyer   employ + ER = employer

4. The suffix *ance* is added.

convey + ANCE = conveyance

Can you add other words?

5. The suffix *al* is added.

portray + AL = portrayal

EXERCISE 1.   Spell the following words correctly.

1. *tourney* in plural   . . . .
2. past tense of *allay*   . . . .
3. past tense of *volley*   . . . .
4. *alley* in plural   . . . .
5. past tense of *survey*   . . . .
6. present participle of *portray* . . . .
7. past tense of *journey*   . . . .
8. past tense of *relay*   . . . .
9. plural of *delay*   . . . .
10. past tense of *parlay*   . . . .

THE Y PRECEDED BY A CONSONANT

So far we have studied the final Y preceded by a vowel. This did not change when you formed the plural or added a suffix.

RULE 2: If a word ends in Y preceded by a consonant, change the Y to *I* and

a. add *ES* to form the plural of a noun:

academy	academies	ally	allies
actuary	actuaries	cry	cries

b. add a suffix:

beauty + FUL = beautiful   busy + NESS = business
mercy + FUL = merciful   cozy + NESS = coziness
pity + FUL = pitiful   icy + NESS = iciness

airy + LY = airily
angry + LY = angrily
clumsy + LY = clumsily

c. to form the third person singular of a verb add *ES;* to form the past tense of a verb add *ED*:

Verb	Third person singular	Past tense
carry	carriES	carriED
dignify	dignifiES	dignifiED
marry	marriES	marriED

Caution! There is only one case in which the *Y* is retained when it follows a consonant. That is before *ing*—in other words when you form the present participle of a verb.

carry + ING = carrying
dignify + ING = dignifying
marry + ING = marrying

EXERCISE 2.   In the space to the right put C if the spelling is correct. If it is incorrect, write the proper spelling.

merciful	....	surveyor	....
beautiful	....	portraying	....
cozily	....	pitying	....
attornies	....	busied	....
valleys	....	merryly	....

EXERCISE 3.   Write the correct spelling of the following words with the suffix added.

pretty + ness	....	duty + ful	....
petty + ness	....	ready + ness	....
steady + ing	....	carry + ed	....
ready + ed	....	hurry + ing	....
bully + s	....	copy + er	....
airy + ness	....	sloppy + ness	....
pity + ed	....	lively + hood	....

Plurals of nouns

Most English nouns add S to form the plural.

cat + S = cats   hat + S = hats   house + S = houses

The plural of nouns ending in *O* preceded by a vowel is formed in the regular manner by adding S: studios, radios, cameos, trios. *But* the plural of nouns ending in *O* preceded by a consonant is formed by adding *ES*:

buffaloES   calicoES   potatoES   vetoES

368

Caution! A few nouns ending in *O* preceded by a consonant are made plural by adding merely *S*. Most of these have to do with music:

altOS	pianOS
sopranOS	solOS
contraltOS	dynamOS
egOS	silOS

Certain nouns ending in *f* or *fe* form the plural by changing *f* to *v* and adding *S* or *ES*. Each word must be studied individually.

SINGULAR	PLURAL	SINGULAR	PLURAL
calf	calves	loaf	loaves
elf	elves	sheaf	sheaves
knife	knives	thief	thieves
leaf	leaves	wife	wives
life	lives	wolf	wolves

These words may be learned in groups according to the sound of the vowel before the *f*.

ee SOUND		ĭ SOUND		el SOUND	
leaf	leaves	knife	knives	elf	elves
sheaf	sheaves	life	lives	self	selves
thief	thieves	wife	wives	shelf	shelves

Following are groups of words ending in *f* which add only *S* for the plural.

IEF		OOF	
belief	beliefs	hoof	hoofs
brief	briefs		(rarely hooves)
chief	chiefs	proof	proofs
grief	griefs	roof	roofs
handkerchief	handkerchiefs	goof	goofs

EXERCISE 1. Write plurals for the following words:

reproof	. . . .	slough	. . . .
reprieve	. . . .	basso	. . . .
sieve	. . . .	mambo	. . . .
halo	. . . .	surf	. . . .
gulf	. . . .	trough	. . . .
coif	. . . .	stiletto	. . . .
albino	. . . .	sheaf	. . . .
shelf	. . . .	radio	. . . .
puff	. . . .	calf	. . . .
muff	. . . .	sylph	. . . .

To form the plural of nouns ending in Y, see "The final *Y*," page 366.

Compound nouns add S or *ES* to only the principal word to form the plural. In the *in-law* series, the principal word is son, brother, etc.

brothers-in-law   mothers-in-law

A few compound words are practically single words and add the S at the end. This explains such cases as:

spoonfuls   cupfuls   bowlfuls   handfuls

A long time ago the English language had quite a list of words whose plurals do not end in S. Only a few are left today, but they never give any trouble because they are learned in the very early grades of school.

child	children	deer	deer
brother	brethren	sheep	sheep
ox	oxen	swine	swine
foot	feet	louse	lice
tooth	teeth	mouse	mice
goose	geese	man	men
cannon	cannon (or S)	woman	women

NAMES OF PEOPLE

As a general rule add S or ES to form the plural:

All the Johns in the school.
Who can keep up with the Joneses?
How many Agatha Christies have you read?

LETTERS, SIGNS, FIGURES

These form their plural by adding 'S.

Cross your *t*'s.
Mind your *p*'s and *q*'s.
Underline the *3*'s in the line.

FOREIGN WORDS

Foreign words act differently when their plurals are formed. Since many of these foreign plurals are from the Latin, the Latin plurals are used.

Many Latin words ending in *us* form their plural by changing the *us* to *i*. The most familiar of such words is

alumnus (a graduate of a school)   alumni (graduates)

Other Latin words that form the plural by changing *us* to *i* include:

fungus	fungi
focus	foci
radius	radii
bacillus	bacilli
terminus	termini

Some Latin words ending in *um* change it to *a* to form the plural. A familiar word is *datum, data* (the facts in the case).

medium	media
addendum	addenda
bacterium	bacteria
candelabrum	candelabra
curriculum	curricula
desideratum	desiderata
erratum	errata
stratum	strata

Latin has a group of nouns ending in *is* singular, *es* plural. A familiar case is *crisis, crises*.

amanuensis	amanuenses
analysis	analyses
antithesis	antitheses
axis	axes (center)
ellipsis	ellipses
hypothesis	hypotheses
oasis	oases
parenthesis	parentheses
synopsis	synopses

The Greek language has given us a few plurals. These are from the ancient Greek:

automaton	automata (or automatons)
criterion	criteria

From the French have come these strange plurals:

beau	beaux (or beaus)
tableau	tableaux (or tableaus)
chateau	chateaux
portmanteau	portmanteaux (or portmanteaus)

These familiar words are all Italian plural forms:

spaghetti	banditti
confetti	ravioli

EXERCISE 2. Form the plurals of the following nouns:

t	. . . .	flurry	. . . .
Mary	. . . .	sulky	. . . .
anniversary	. . . .	surrey	. . . .
dromedary	. . . .	inequity	. . . .
kerchief	. . . .	satellite	. . . .
4	. . . .	functionary	. . . .
court-martial	. . . .	avocado	. . . .
bay	. . . .	dynamo	. . . .

EXERCISE 3. Have someone dictate the following passage containing many singular nouns for which you will write the plurals.

Mother sent Mary to the Grand Union to purchase some *grocery* _____ for the long weekend. Among the *thing* _____ she wanted to obtain were: *tomato* _____, *potato* _____, and *avocado* _____. She also asked for three *quart* _____ of milk, two *pound* _____ of butter, several *piece* _____ of cake, and a pound of caramel-filled *chocolate* _____.

After making these and other *purchase* _____, Mary started to return home. Some interesting *adventure* _____ occurred on the way. She met one of the best *soprano* _____ in the church choir. Mary herself was usually placed among the *alto* _____. After wandering up and down several narrow *alley* _____, she ended one of the most interesting *journey* _____ by finding a bundle of *key* _____ which she had lost six *day* _____ before. Mary will not forget these *event* _____ for a long time.

How to handle confusing suffixes

WORDS ENDING IN *ABLE, IBLE*

When you are able to add *able* and *ible* correctly, you have an ability that is to be envied. If you learn how to use *able* correctly, then *ably* and *ability* follow naturally.

With this particular spelling difficulty, the best advice is: *Observe carefully.* There is no hard and set rule. But if you master a few key words, the others will come easily.

Our most familiar words add -*able* to form the adjective. This list contains most of the words in ordinary use:

eat + ABLE = eatable	talk + ABLE
laugh + ABLE = laughable	drink + ABLE
comfort + ABLE = comfortable	read + ABLE
regret + ABLE = regrettable	unthink + ABLE

Now study the words that end in -*ible*. You will notice that the words in the following group have a double -*ss* before the -*ible*.

acces*sible*	admis*sible*	compres*sible*
repres*sible*	pos*sible*	permis*sible*

Each of these words, except *possible*, has a noun ending in *ion*. That is another sure way to recall their spelling.

acces*sion*	acces*sible*	admis*sion* admis*sible*

Few writers make mistakes in spelling the noun *permission*, and you should not have difficulty with the adjective if you associate the suffix -*ion* with *ible*. How would you tell the spelling of a word like *kiss*? It ends in *iss*. But it has no noun in -*ion* (*kission*) and hence no ending in -*ible*, but has the form kiss*able*.

You can apply this -*ion* -*ible* test to many doubtful words, and you will be able to think of the correct form that way.

Notice! The following words all end in *ion:*

apprehension	reversion	corruption
combustion	coercion	division
destruction	comprehension	perception
expansion	digestion	reprehension

Now the simple rule in all of these words is: Drop the *on* and add *ble*.

apprehension − on = apprehensi + ble

This removes the whole problem of *a* or *i* in forming the suffix.

Practically all other adjectives ending in *ble* have the form *able*.

Adjectives which also end in -*ible* but do not have an -*ion* form can be remembered in this way: The *ible* is necessary to preserve the sound of soft *g* or *c*. Thus the word *tangent* has the adjective *tangible*, because an *able* would change the pronunciation of *g* from its present *j* sound to the sound of *g* in *gum*. Other words in this class are:

dedu*cible*	produ*cible*	redu*cible*
condu*cible*	corri*gible*	incorri*gible*
eli*gible*	ineli*gible*	iras*cible*
intelli*gible*	invin*cible*	le*gible*

Be sure that you remember the three reasons for adding -*ible*, not -*able*:

1. It follows double *ss* and comes from a noun ending in -*sion* (permission).

2. The noun ends in -*ion* (coercion).

3. The ending keeps the *c* or *g* soft (deducible, eligible).

EXERCISE 1. Add *able* or *ible* to each of the fifteen words on this list:

account	depend	market
avoid	detest	perish
comfort	discount	return
companion	fashion	review
credit	favor	season

Did you add *-able* to each of these? Then you were 100 percent correct. Now add *-able* or *-ible* to the roots of these words:

abomination	*abominable*	conformation	. . . .
commendation	. . . .	appreciation	. . . .
admiration	. . . .	consideration	. . . .

Did you add *-able* to each of these words? You were 100 percent correct. You can accept as a basic fact: A noun ending in *-ation* will have an adjective in *-able*.

Add the endings *-able* or *-ible* to the roots of the following words:

demonstration   *demonstrable*

derivation	exportation	notation
duration	habitation	refutation
estimation	imagination	separation
execration	irritation	taxation

Did you add *-able* to the roots of each of the words (after dropping the *-ation*)?

EXERCISE 2. Have someone dictate the following passage which contains many words ending in the suffixes *ible* or *able*.

The prosecuting attorney protested that the evidence by the defendant about his *taxable* income was *inadmissible*. In the first place, it was not easily *accessible*. In the second place, although the evidence was originally *acceptable* in a lower court, the decisions in such courts are *reversible*.

The defendant's attorney objected that such reasoning was *unsupportable* and *intolerable* and that it was *reprehensible* on his opponent's part to bring up such a claim. The tension was increasing *perceptibly*. If this continued, the defending attorney might have to be ejected *forcibly*, or be *eligible* for disbarment. However, the atmosphere soon cleared and the case proceeded to its *inevitable* conclusion.

WORDS ENDING IN *ENSE*

There are only a few words ending in *ense:*

defense	immense	pretense
expense	offense	suspense

WORDS ENDING IN *ANCE, ENCE*

There are no simple ways of learning when to add *ance* or *ence*. It is best to study each of the following lists, using the words as often as possible until you habitually spell them correctly.

Common *ance, ant, ancy* words are:

abundant	descendant	important	remembrance
abundance	elegance	inheritance	remonstrance
acquaintance	elegant	irrelevancy	repentance
appearance	endurance	irrelevant	repentant
assistance	entrance	lieutenant	restaurant
assistant	entrant	maintenance	sergeant
balance	grievance	nuisance	significance
brilliance	guidance	observance	significant
brilliancy	hindrance	observant	stimulant
brilliant	ignorance	pendant	tenancy
clearance	ignorant	perseverance	tenant
countenance	importance	pleasant	tolerance

Common *ence, ent, ency* words include:

absence	convenient	experience	penitent
absent	correspondence	government	permanence
abstinence	correspondent	impertinence	permanent
abstinent	deference	impertinent	persistence
adherence	(deferential)	imprudence	persistent
adherent	dependence	imprudent	pestilence
antecedent	dependent	independence	precedence
apparent	difference	independent	preference
coherence	diffidence	indulgent	present
coherent	diffident	inference	prominence
coincidence	diligence	influence	prominent
concurrence	diligent	insistence	providence
concurrent	divergence	insolence	provident
conference	divergent	insolent	reference
confidence	efficiency	intelligence	repellent
confident	eminence	intermittent	reverent
conscience	eminent	magnificence	residence
consequence	essence	magnificent	resident
consequent	(essential)	occurrence	sentence
competence	equivalent	opponent	sufficient
competent	excellence	patent	superintendent
complement	excellent	patience	tendency
compliment	existence	patient	violence
convenience	existent	penitence	violent

375

EXERCISE 3. Insert *a* or *e* in the space indicated for the following words:

complim_nt	exist_nce	magnific_nt	guid_nce
remembr_nce	descend_nt	brilli_nce	consci_nce
consist_nt	acquaint_nce	complem_nt	coincid_nce
superintend_nt	griev_nce	conveni_nce	appar_nt
depend_nt	perman_nt	abund_nce	consequ_ntial

THE ADVERBIAL SUFFIX LY

In forming adverbs from adjectives ending in *AL*, simply add *LY* to the original word.

Adjective + ly = adverb.

$$verbal + ly = verbally$$

EXERCISE 4. Form the adverbs of the following adjectives:

accidental	incidental	professional
critical	intentional	real
elemental	ironical	typical
equal	logical	usual
exceptional	mathematical	verbal
final	practical	global

WORDS ENDING IN ARY, ERY

There are more than 300 words ending in *ary*. There are only two commonly used words ending in *ery:*

cemetery   stationery

It may help you to remember that in ceme*tery* only *e*'s are used. Recall that statio*nery* is used to write a let*ter*.

Some common words ending in *ary* include:

auxiliary	honorary	secondary
boundary	imaginary	tertiary
centenary	infirmary	tributary
dictionary	library	vocabulary
elementary	revolutionary	involuntary
evolutionary	secretary	

WORDS ENDING IN ISE, IZE

There are no hard and fast rules to differentiate between the words ending in *ise* and *ize*. Perhaps the best procedure would be to master

376

the list of *ise* words and then remember that all others are spelled *ize*.

advertisement	despise	supervise
advise	disguise	(supervision)
adviser	enterprise	surmise
arise	exercise	surprise
chastise	franchise	reprise
compromise	merchandise	(reprisal)
demise	revise (revision)	

WORDS ENDING IN *IZE*

agonize	emphasize (but emphasis)	neutralize
antagonize	familiarize	ostracize
authorize	fertilize	patronize
(authorization)	generalize	pulverize
baptize (but baptism)	generalization	realize
burglarize	humanize	recognize
capsize	hypnotize	solemnize
centralize	idolize	specialize
characterize	itemize	symbolize
(characterization)	legitimatize	tantalize
demoralize	localize	terrorize
dramatize	modernize	visualize

In some instances the British spelling is *ise*.

realise   criticise   penalise

There are only two words ending in *yze*:

analyze   paralyze

WORDS ENDING IN *OUS*

The suffix *ous* means *full of* and occasionally gives some people difficulties because they tend to add an *i*. Another difficulty may arise with nouns which end in *e* and then add *ous*.

The following words add *ous* to the noun to form the adjective:

Noun	Suffix	Noun	Suffix
danger	+ ous = dangerous	mountain	+ ous = mountainous
hazard	+ ous = hazardous	murder	+ ous = murderous
humor	+ ous = humorous	peril	+ ous = perilous
libel	+ ous = libelous	poison	+ ous = poisonous
marvel	+ ous = marvelous	riot	+ ous = riotous
moment	+ ous = momentous	slander	+ ous = slanderous

377

The following adjectives are based on nouns that end in *e*. Because the suffix begins with a vowel, the final *e* is dropped.

adventure	+	ous	=	adventurous
analogue	+	ous	=	analogous
desire	+	ous	=	desirous
trouble	+	ous	=	troublous

The following adjectives are based on nouns ending in *f*, which changed to *v* when the *ous* was added:

grief	+	ous	=	grievous
mischief	+	ous	=	mischievous

Be especially careful not to insert an *i* which was never at the end of the word.

Occasionally the final *e* is retained before *ous* for phonetic reasons, i.e., to retain a soft *c* or soft *g*.

courage	+	ous	=	courageous
advantage	+	ous	=	advantageous
outrage	+	ous	=	outrageous

WORDS ENDING IN Y PLUS *OUS*

Common sense will tell us that when *beauty* adds *ous*, the sound *sh* can enter (as would happen with *tio*). To prevent this, the *y* is dropped and an *e* is added, as in:

beauty	+	ous	=	beauteous
bounty	+	ous	=	bounteous
duty	+	ous	=	duteous
pity	+	ous	=	piteous
plenty	+	ous	=	plenteous

EXERCISE 5. Write the correct adjectives of the following nouns by adding *ous*.

advantage	....	plenty	....
courage	....	adventure	....
dolor	....	bounty	....
peril	....	danger	....
mountain	....	grief	....
beauty	....	humor	....
desire	....	outrage	....
pity	....	duty	....
trouble	....	libel	....
mischief	....	poison	....

33

Can you read
what you write?

Your letter may be beautifully organized, well expressed, perfectly punctuated, and superbly spelled—but if no one can read it, so what? Here writer Robert O'Brien explores some of the pitfalls into which illegible handwriting can lead us, and suggests a few remedies.

In Washington, D.C., a truck driver misread a carelessly formed "4" for a "7" in a handwritten order, and pumped 385 gallons of fuel oil through a disconnected intake—into the basement of the wrong house. In Connecticut a housewife dashed off a note asking the milkman to leave three quarts of chocolate milk. Next morning, neatly stacked at the back door were eight cartons of cottage cheese. In a New England city, a man stepped up to a bank teller's window and shoved a note under the wicket. In bold scratchwork it said, "Wug I thiie a www cxzllmnhd!" The jittery teller kicked his alarm button, bells clanged, police converged on the bank and nabbed the man. They discovered that he was a respectable businessman with laryngitis. What the note said was, "May I have a new checkbook?"

Bad handwriting doesn't always have results this bizarre. Still, illegibility on a national scale piles up astonishing statistics. The Handwriting Foundation, established by the nation's leading pen and pencil manufacturers to promote better handwriting, estimates that illegible penmanship costs U.S. businessmen approximately a million dollars *a week* in scrambled orders, lost time, missent deliveries, clerical mistakes, and other forms of inefficiency. Automation in business offices by no means eliminates handwritten paper work. In a regional office of a large oil company, a card-punch operator misread a poorly penned numeral and fed the wrong rate into her machine. In a twinkling, 2,000 incorrect invoices shot out the other end.

Most Americans used to be pretty good penmen. What has happened? For one thing, penmanship is no longer stressed in most schools. The "push-pull" drills of the old writing methods have become almost as archaic as the McGuffey Reader and the hickory switch.

For example: In a small city in Pennsylvania, an elementary-school official explained that pupils from the first through sixth grades receive an average of only fifteen to twenty minutes a week of formal instruction in penmanship. After that, he said, the students are largely on their own.

But lack of sufficient training is not the only cause of poor handwriting. Until he reached college, a friend of mine wrote a commendable script. Under pressure of high-speed note taking, it broke up into a hieroglyphic shorthand.

A hotelman told me, "You can almost trace a man's career by his signature. When he starts out in life, it's clear and legible. The higher he climbs, the worse it gets." A graphologist, an expert who reads character from handwriting, offered this explanation: At the bottom of the ladder, the man is considerate, conscientious, hard-working, anxious to make a good impression—qualities reflected in his straightforward script. In the rough-and-tumble of competitive life, however, he has less time for such basic details. As a result, his writing becomes hasty.

LEGIBILITY PAYS DIVIDENDS

Handwriting improvement may even lead to self-improvement. Psychologists believe, for example, that if you make a conscious effort to be more considerate of others by writing more clearly, you may find yourself acting more courteously at home, in your job, on the highway. An aunt of mine wrote such a small, indistinct hand that I had a hard time deciphering her letters. Suddenly, though she still wrote small, I could read every word. She simply had the thoughtful idea of using a finer pen point and writing more distinctly. "Now," she writes, "I must keep a desk that lives up to my handwriting. It's never been tidier. For the first time in my life, I know where everything is!"

The rewards of readable handwriting are far from intangible. In a recent Handwriting Foundation survey of several hundred personnel directors, 88 percent regarded legible handwriting as an important factor in landing a job. Twenty-nine percent used it as a standard for promotion. The employment manager of a large department store put it in practical terms. He spread eight filled-in application forms across his desk. On all eight the penmanship was slipshod. "These applicants were turned down," he said. "Their illegible sales slips would create extra work for our accounting division, cause customer complaints, destroy good will, and lose business."

Some years ago, Philadelphia businessmen complained so about the deplorable handwriting of the city's high school graduates that school officials launched a drive for better penmanship. They came up with a new look in the alphabet, called the "Philadelphia Simplified Alphabet," and prepared manuals, wall charts, and teaching guides.

Much of the trouble, the educators found, was caused by fancy capital letters, so they pruned all unnecessary and potentially misleading "scrollwork." They insisted on such things as this: that *t*'s contain *no*

HOW CARELESS HANDWRITING LEADS TO TROUBLE

What the clerk wrote — *What was meant*
Result: embarrassing, wasteful confusion in billing.

Could the teacher tell that this extreme backhand slant on the left was part of the Gettysburg Address? Besides, the letters are all the same height, and there is not enough space between words. Some backhand slant (see right) can be readable.

How's that again? Forward slant on left is so extreme that loop letters have been closed. Letters are crowded, and too thick a pencil has exaggerated both errors. Slant on right is clear.

Here are examples of frequent sources of headache for postal and mail-order clerks. In each pair of letters, the one on the left was meant to be the one on the right.

loop and that they be clearly crossed (to avoid confusion with *l*'s); that the loop of an *e* be clearly kept open; that great care be taken to distinguish between potentially look-alike numerals such as *4*'s, *7*'s, and *9*'s; *3*'s and *8*'s; *6*'s and *0*'s. They insisted that a one-letter space be left between words, that all letters slant the same way, be uniform in size, and look as though they rest on a straight line whether there are lines on the page or not.

Today many of Philadelphia's public-school pupils are learning the new handwriting method. And from the samples I've seen, they're doing it well.

After seeing the difference these changes made, I went to work on my own capitals, numerals, and loops. With patience and practice, I trimmed out a dozen flowery kinks that had cluttered my handwriting for years. The result was a gratifying improvement in legibility, neatness, and writing speed.

IMPROVE YOUR WRITING STEP BY STEP

During the process, incidentally, I discovered that it's a mistake to try to revamp your handwriting all at once. Tackle a single letter at a time. When you've made its improved form an integral part of your style, start on another letter.

Remedial action has also been taken in the schools of New England. The New England School Development Council, with a membership of 150 school systems, appointed a Handwriting Committee which discovered that far too many elementary and high school pupils did not know how to sit properly, how to hold their pens or pencils, or how to tell what was wrong with the way they wrote. The committee drafted and distributed a teacher's guide, *Handwriting Today*, which has revitalized penmanship programs.

"Handwriting," says Lewis Mumford, "is an art open to any amateur, for the delight he gets from it himself and the further pleasure he gives to others." With a little care all of us can write more clearly, showing that we respect the written word and, above all, the reader.

A final word of advice: When you start your improvement program, tell your bank and credit-card companies what you're up to. My bank telephoned me a few days after I'd started to brush up *my* handwriting. "Better come in," the manager said. "I think we've got a forgery." I drove down and looked at the check. It was my new signature! The only difference between it and the old one was that you could read it.

PART THREE

How
to speak
better

Part three

34

Of cabbages
and kings

"The time has come," the Walrus said, "to talk of many things: of shoes—and ships—and sealing-wax—of cabbages—and kings—" And, like the Walrus, we talk of so many things, and how we talk about them is so important to us, that good speaking is an art we should all learn to master.

How important to you is the art of good speaking? It can be vitally important, a key factor in your success or failure.

Almost three hundred years ago, British author and politician Joseph Addison had this to say about it: "If the minds of men were laid open, we should see but little difference between that of the wise man and that of the fool. The difference is that the first knows how to pick and cull his thoughts for conversation . . . whereas the other lets them all indifferently fly out in words." And this is still true today. It is by what you say and how you say it that people judge you most often. That is how important your speech is.

Speech is perhaps man's greatest gift. It may be, as some people maintain, that animals, fish, birds, bees, even plants and flowers have particular speech of their own, but in no other species on earth is the art of audible sound more fully developed than in man. And the more advanced the society of man, the richer the language he speaks, the greater the variety of sounds he employs.

From the instant we wake with the alarm clock till we shut our eyes in sleep, we constantly use these sounds, making ourselves heard and understood through the medium of speech. It's "Good morning" before we sit down to our cup of coffee; and has it ever occurred to you to count the number of ways we say "Good morning"? Lovingly? Perfunctorily? Grumpily? Even angrily? And have you ever thought of the way that "Good morning" of yours has a very definite effect on the people to whom you address it?

A "Good morning" can relieve morning weariness, can brighten the entire office staff, can raise eyebrows, or lower them. It's amazing what speaking just two words can do or undo. But you know all this from your own experience. There is power in words, and particularly in the way they are spoken.

"IT'S NOT *WHAT* YOU SAY . . ."

"I need your help," says your immediate superior, walking up to your desk. Is he issuing a command or making a request? Is he delivering a routine order or is he paying you a welcome compliment?

"Please come in." Are you asking your milkman to step into the house, while you get the money to pay his bill, or are you joyfully welcoming a long lost friend?

These are simple phrases in simple situations; yet the way we speak them gives each a distinct emotional meaning. Now let us explore another area: the ambiguous phrase in a complicated situation.

Asked about his possible candidacy and reelection in 1928, Calvin Coolidge said, "I do not choose to run." Coolidge was known as a plain speaker, his remarks often on the dry side. Yet in a matter of the greatest significance to the people of the United States the President had delivered an enigmatic phrase. Was he really retiring from the political scene, or was he demanding that his party draft him as its candidate in the coming elections?

When President Lyndon Baines Johnson made a similar statement in 1968, he was careful to add that he would not run for reelection even if he were nominated by his party. This prevented the kind of confusion that followed the Coolidge pronouncement.

Now the words we use, and the way we use them, are not likely to

The difference between the right word and the almost right word is the difference between lightning and the lightning bug.

—*Mark Twain*

shake the nation. They may, however, have a considerable effect on our business, social, and family lives, and in our communities.

Each of us speaks many ways at different times. We have one way of speaking to the man behind the grocery counter, another when we speak to our employers or employes. We speak one way in a discussion group at the PTA meeting, another with the man who is examining our income tax statement, and still another when we entertain our good friends and relatives.

Our vocabulary and our tone also change with the different audiences and situations we encounter. Sometimes we find it necessary to be firm, sometimes tractable; sometimes harsh, sometimes gentle. At times we are amenable, at other times irritable. We presume, we hope, that we are *never* boring.

Just as nothing irks us more than the bore, nothing pleases us more than a good talk with a friend or business associate. Despite the omnipresence of the "idiot box," or because of it, the art of good conversation has become a more valuable asset than ever before. We are quick to recognize good talk and just as quick to appreciate it.

How do we define this art which arouses our interest, respect, and trust? More importantly, how do we develop this art in ourselves? Both of these questions will be explored and answered in the coming chapters.

How to be a good host

Good talk makes the good host: at that cocktail lunch with a prospective client, with your boss when he is invited to dinner at your home, at a party, at a school meeting. And good form is an essential element of good talk.

Do you know how to introduce a churchman to an army officer? How to introduce a celebrity, a widow, a divorcee? Do you know how to avoid the embarrassment of an unexpected guest, a party-crasher, or forgetting someone's name? Do you know how to get a conversation started among your guests? Do you know how to change the subject, diplomatically, when the talk becomes too heated? Do you know how to keep your guests comfortable, at ease, happy? And do you know how to say your farewells when the party is over?

You'll find all the answers to these questions in Chapter 36, "The Art of Being a Successful Host." There you will also find suggestions on how to talk with celebrities and with people in emotionally difficult situations. It is never easy, for example, to find the proper words to speak to someone who has lost a child, a husband, a wife, or a parent. Even when we think we have the appropriate words, we have trouble finding our tone.

We meet a friend who has just been divorced.

"Sorry," we say, perhaps a little too dolefully.

"Nothing to be sorry about," responds our friend, sometimes with a gaiety which puzzles us, sometimes almost belligerently.

The initial "Sorry" was hurdle enough. The response to the gaiety (real or affected) or the belligerency is even more difficult.

How do you speak with someone who is blind, or who suffers from some other physical handicap? The tendency is to be tender and overly sympathetic. This approach, of course, is all wrong. Handicapped people want their handicaps ignored, want to be treated like any human being. Unhandicapped persons may find this difficult, particularly at a first meeting; but they can unlearn this awkwardness.

How do you talk with bores, drunks, "wolves," quarrelsome people, gossips, foul-mouthed people, people who insist on discussing their embarrassing private lives? Chapter 38, "Ten Conversation Problems and How to Solve Them," steers you through the course.

Selling yourself—or your product

Most of us spend a lot of time talking on the phone. What we have to say and how we say it can be vitally important to us. All the time you speak on that telephone, the person at the other end of the wire is not only listening to the words you're saying, but is also getting a picture of your personality. You should be aware of this picture-making every time you dial a number, especially if you are calling someone for the first time.

Chapter 39, "How You Come Across on the Telephone" offers suggestions which will help you develop the telephone image you want and will make your words more effective than ever.

Another chapter focuses on the job interview. It tells you how to prepare for an interview with a potential employer.

Being able to speak effectively is very important in furthering your career in business. Whether you are making a sales talk to a prospective customer or presiding over an important business conference, your

ARE YOU A BORE?

IF YOU THINK you are, you're not. If it never occurs to you that you might be, there's a horrid chance that you are, for the outstanding characteristic of the bore is his unawareness of the fact. He is too self-satisfied to be concerned with his effect on others.

The variety of bores is enormous. One of the worst examples, to my mind, is the narrator who starts his story with its grandmother, explores every branch of its family tree, and ends up with remote descendants, while his listeners sit around in a state of polite, help-less petrifaction.

I also shrink from the Jokester Bore: You have only to lay eyes on him to see "Have you heard this one?" rising to the surface. We all know the Hypochondriac Bore who draws up symptoms from a bottomless well and is never happier than when giving a stitch-by-stitch account of that last operation. I dread too the male—it is almost always a male—who interrupts the mildest statement with a "now wait a moment" and proceeds to put the offender in his right place. And there is the Snob Bore who manages to inject famous names into every other sentence.

Most bores begin boring with "I remember" and a heavy accent on the "I." So it's a good idea, when you find yourself remembering too much too often—especially about your family—to lay off.

Not all bores are talkative; there is the Strong, Silent Bore. In his own household he glooms his family into an awestruck hush; at parties he never opens his mouth except to put something into it.

Can bores be cured? Yes, if we recognize our malady before it becomes chronic. We can watch ourselves for symptoms and, once alerted to the danger, we can take measures against it. One of the best is to stay alive and interested, not only in our own affairs but in the affairs of the world around us.

It is no accident that the man who expends himself most, even in a dull job, is the man who has most left to expend in his own home. Never bored himself, he never bores others.

In short, to be interested is to be interesting; to be alive yourself is to make others feel alive and grateful to you.

—*I. A. R. Wylie*

ability to speak so that others will not only be interested in your ideas but will be influenced by them as well, is one of the greatest assets a business person can have. And like any special skill, effective speaking can be learned.

Do you know, for example, how to make an introductory telephone call to a prospective customer? Do you know how to arrange the first meeting with a client? And what do you say when you walk into his office for the first time, with your attaché case in your hand? Once you've made the initial contact, how do you develop it? Should you be modest or forceful? Should you exude confidence? Should you strive to convince your client or allow him to convince himself?

Each occasion and each customer will call for a different approach, a different tone of voice, a different selling technique. Chapter 41, "The Five Steps to Successful Selling," gives you helpful pointers.

The ability to plan and run an effective meeting is a valuable asset. It is an ability which is quickly recognized and rewarded. A good chairman is a man who is respected not only for his organizational competence but also for the command with which he takes hold of a situation. Inevitably, such a chairman will discover himself in a position of leadership as a judge, an arbiter, a policymaker. And the skills you need to do the job right are few and easy to learn.

Do you know how to keep each member of the group to the main topic of the conference? Do you know how to sum up the meeting, how to present in capsule form the various opinions and ideas offered by the various speakers? Do you know how to close the meeting on a healthy, promising note? Chapter 42, "How to Run a Meeting," will provide the answers to these questions. It will show you how to develop the techniques essential to good chairmanship.

> "The time has come," the Walrus said,
>   "To talk of many things;
> Of shoes—and ships—and sealing wax—
>   Of cabbages—and kings—"

Lewis Carroll's Walrus wasn't really interested in talk at all; his mind was completely on the luscious oysters that had foolishly followed him and his friend the Carpenter. But the time "to talk of many things" is always with us, and our talk will invariably prove more interesting and more effective if we give time to developing the latent arts and skills in speaking that we all possess.

35

The secrets of good conversation

An interesting conversationalist is welcome anywhere—and you can learn to be one. Here are tips and helpful exercises that will give you more confidence in a group, show you how to start conversations on a variety of subjects, and tell you how to avoid common errors and embarrassing silences.

Conversation, in part, is self-expression. It provides us opportunities for asserting our individuality, telling the world just how we feel, or "letting off steam." Talk of this sort is pleasurable and valuable. It is like tinkering with a hot rod, or breeding tropical fish, or puttering around with painting or novel writing. It serves as a sort of safety valve and comes easily to almost everybody.

However, when conversation is entered into merely to "get something off your chest" it makes very bad conversation. It is too one-sided. No number of monologues ever add up to *real conversation*. When everyone wants to shoot baskets, the ball doesn't get passed around enough for a good game.

At its best, conversation means the pooling of information, the sharing of interests, the bringing together of ideas.

Conversation is a two-way thing, involving give and take, action and reaction. Indeed it is a many-way thing—the communication of many ideas among many people.

If you find yourself shying away from conversation, analyze your experiences in recent conversational situations. Try to remember in detail both the more and the less successful of these experiences. Then ask yourself the following questions:

> The wit of conversation consists more in finding it in others than in showing a great deal yourself. He who goes from your conversation pleased with himself and his own wit is perfectly well pleased with you.
>
> —*La Bruyère*

SIX WAYS TO SPOT CONVERSATION TROUBLE

■ Did I find it difficult to pick a *topic* for conversation? Did I cause embarrassment by talking on some tabooed topic?

■ Was adjusting to persons my problem? Did I get tongue-tied in the presence of certain individuals, or of certain *types* of individuals? Did I fail to give proper deference to older or more distinguished persons?

■ Was my general *attitude* at fault in dealing with people? Was I dogmatic, condescending, argumentative? Did I *adjust* well to the attitudes of *others?* To their *changes* in attitude?

■ Did I have trouble *starting* a conversation? Getting *others* to start?

■ Did I fail to keep a conversation *going?* Did I let it bog down? Could I have moved more smoothly from one topic to *another?* Was I clumsy in ending a conversation?

■ Was it some *mechanical* fault that made me ill at ease? Was it mispronunciation, forgetting names, overuse of slang?

On the basis of your analysis, give special study to sections of this chapter which most apply to you. Take up one area at a time and follow the suggestions for practice at the close of the chapter.

Prepare carefully for the more formal conversational situation. If you are to go into a business conference or an interview, become as well informed as you can about its subject. If you are to meet some new people, try to learn as much as you can about them. Even in casual meetings you can do this much planning—you can think before you speak.

But do not prepare and rehearse phrases to use on a specific occasion, for this is futile. You can never anticipate the exact turn a conversation will take. In using this chapter, moreover, you must not expect it to ease you over your very next conversational hurdle and all hurdles thereafter. No chapter, or book for that matter, can tell you what to say when your Aunt Matilda, aged seventy-five, arrives unexpectedly with her pet canary one gloomy Sunday and announces plans to spend three weeks with you. But armed with some principles, and some previous practice, you ought to be able to greet her or turn her away with more poise than apoplexy.

EXERCISE NO. 1

During the coming week take careful note of your conversations and their characteristics. What were your weak spots, your strong points? At the end of the week, decide what you need most to improve upon.

Each successive week, for a month or two, sit down at approximately the same time and repeat the process. Pick a time when your schedule isn't likely to be broken or interrupted.

Topics for people who don't climb mountains

If your difficulty seems to be finding suitable topics, your real problem may be thinking about topics in the wrong way. You may have some misconceptions concerning the things people talk about and what subjects make for interesting conversation.

One common misconception is that only the very unusual event is worth talking about. You ransack your mind for some preposterous coincidence, some tremendous achievement, some shattering experience, some hilarious situation.

Vastly exciting and amusing events do occur in this world, of course, and people enjoy hearing and telling about them.

But many an agreeable evening has been spent in small talk about the ordinary happenings and problems of everyday living—getting the children off to school, whether tomato plants should be staked or not, good places to spend the weekend.

So if you have never had quintuplets nor explored the upper Amazon, nor been forced at the point of a gun to prepare breakfast for four bank robbers, you need not remain silent. However simple the life you lead, it provides plenty of material for conversation. Remember that most other people are mainly interested in day-to-day events, too.

THE WEATHER—AND OTHER POPULAR TOPICS

Another misconception is that a topic must be literary, or abstruse, or very learned.

People do talk about the special theory of relativity, gambits in chess, and atomic fission, to be sure. But more often, they talk about life and love, and food and drink, and the weather. So do not feel that only topics you have studied for months are suitable for conversation.

WHAT TO TALK ABOUT

As a matter of fact, almost any topic is suitable for conversation. You can talk about basketball or badminton, knitting or crocheting, truth or honor, tea or sympathy, hitchhiking or door-to-door selling, the stock market or the chain store, or shoes, or ships, or sealing wax, or cabbages, or kings.

You can discuss books, plays, movies, television programs, news events, national policies, or local problems.

You can swap stories, anecdotes, observations, opinions. You can recall some idea from a magazine article, a newspaper column, a sermon. And your reaction to the idea may be more important to the conversation than the topic itself.

For one purpose of conversation is to enable other persons to compare their thoughts with yours. They hope you will prove enthusiastic about the same things they are; they find minor differences of opinion intriguing.

Conversation is a friendly art with a double pleasure—the warmth of sharing similar beliefs, and the stimulation of discovering differences.

So don't hesitate to express agreement, for fear of being thought unoriginal; and don't hesitate to express disagreement, for fear of being considered contrary.

If you can't rave about a best-seller like the others, don't think you must stay silent about it. If you think reporters are a nuisance at international conferences, say so. But remember to voice your dissent in such a friendly way that the conversation can continue. If you force your opinion as if you had a mission to convert others, you will not be contributing to the conversation, but stopping it.

Air your prejudices, too, if you want, provided you show by words or your tone that you know them to be prejudices; and provided, of course, that they are not offensive. If you can't stand calorie counting, or amateur psychoanalysis, don't hold back. On the other hand avoid becoming known as a person who "can't stand" things.

Some persons like to make challenging statements. To an admirer of Eugene Ormandy, they'll say, "Don't you think he plays everything too fast?" Such remarks may provoke stimulating discussion; they may also provoke discord. The challenge must be carefully handled, and you had better leave it till you are very sure of yourself and your company.

Before offering a topic, be sure you know something about it. This doesn't mean your knowledge must be encyclopedic. But be sure you are familiar with it. If you have had only a weekend of skiing you had better not tell how to execute a stem-Christy. There may be an expert present, and you will be much safer describing your first reactions to skiing, your first fall.

WHAT NOT TO TALK ABOUT

The wide variety of topics available to you is emphasized all the more by the relatively small number that must be avoided.

Parading your private life before strangers is taboo. So also is shaming your family or friends by describing their faults to a general company. Unless you aim to be an untouchable, you had better not tell the plots of books or movies or plays to those who haven't yet enjoyed them. Your chances of being invited again are slight if upon being introduced you promptly launch into a shady story.

Having only *one* topic for conversation is as bad as having none. We have all suffered from the bore who could only "talk shop," or who would never let anyone forget his aches and pains, or who chattered incessantly about the brilliance of her children.

If you think the variety of your topics is limited, find new ones.

How to find and develop topics

You read newspapers daily, probably subscribe to a magazine or two; you listen to radio programs or watch television; you hear stories from friends; you go to church and hear sermons; you attend the theater; you have a multitude of interesting experiences with customers, salespeople, colleagues, your family.

These are all topics for conversation.

When you come across a likely item in the newspaper, make a mental note of it. Circle it in pencil. Better still, tear the item out.

Fix in mind the idea you find in a magazine: "Americans are perfectionists. They have a naive faith that there is a best way of doing things, and they're going to keep on trying till they find it."

Remember the pungent phrase from the speech or sermon: "Every man is an unrepeatable experiment."

Out of such materials, build your own storehouse of topics. If your memory is not good enough to store such bits, keep a notebook or a card file.

Develop this material while it is still fresh in mind. Talk over an idea with family and friends. It may seem quite a different, certainly a fuller, one when you have examined and explored its possibilities.

If you keep on discovering and developing topics in these ways, you will never be at a loss for conversation.

IS IT TOPIC TROUBLE?

One possibility remains—that you haven't really got topic trouble at all. There may have been topics you could do well with, only you were too shy to speak up when they were mentioned.

You may have set your sights too high. You may have talked very well without realizing it.

Or you may have wrong goals. You may have been comparing yourself with someone who is a good conversationalist, but in a style not suited to you.

If that is the case start afresh. At the next occasion where you can do so, sit in, but only as a listener.

Use your silence. Listen carefully. Practice listening. Be able to report afterwards, to yourself or to others, what topics were covered and how they were discussed.

Compare the participants, their successes and failures. Evaluate their techniques.

At another time, though still making no direct contributions, ask questions. Try to draw people out. And evaluate what you hear.

At a meeting of Dale Carnegie fans, one man testified how he had applied the prophet's teachings to an encounter with a business prospect. "I did everything in the rule book. I started off by greeting him warmly, then I smiled at him and asked him about himself. I paid very close attention while he told me. I went out of my way to agree with his views on how wonderful he was. He talked for nearly an hour and when we finally parted company I knew I'd made a friend for life." The man paused for breath. "But, boy!" he concluded, "what an enemy *he* made." —*Maclean's Magazine*

At still another time use only single-statement contributions and questions. Evaluate the performances of others. Evaluate your own.

On the next occasion let yourself go. See how you do.

You may be very proud of the result.

EXERCISE NO. 2

Jot down a list of possible topics from your past reading and listening. Make a separate list of topics you have heard discussed in groups you were with during the week.

Do any topics occur on both lists?

Could you have used any other of the topics from the first list?

If so, why didn't you?

See it the other fellow's way

One may be able to talk about a great many topics, or at considerable length on some topic, and yet not be adept at conversation. One may tell some very good stories connected with the topic and yet provoke groans and boredom instead of laughter and interest.

For good conversation involves *two, three,* or *more* persons, not just one. It demands recognition of the knowledge and interests of the *other fellow,* of the *group.*

The good conversationalist tries to find topics the others *also* are interested in and *also* know something about.

The good conversationalist *slants* his contributions to his listeners, much as a magazine such as *Esquire* or *Seventeen* slants its stories and articles to the particular group of readers it seeks to serve.

If you meet a designer who has worked on the Whirlfast mixer which you have recently purchased, you can tell him so, you can praise the appliance or ask him about problems in designing it. But you wouldn't begin with a recital of defects you have found in it or with your notions of how he should have designed it.

Try to *stimulate* talking. Like Falstaff, be not only witty in yourself, "but the cause that wit is in other men." Try not to hinder the interchange of ideas. Try to keep the conversation moving. Try to keep it pleasant.

With old friends, this is no problem. We know their likes and dislikes. We enjoy talking about the same things. We feel at ease with them, even during long silences. If we didn't, we wouldn't be old friends.

But with strangers, difficulties arise. Discovering their interests may

397

HOW TO READ BODY LANGUAGE

ALL OF US communicate with one another nonverbally, as well as with words. We gesture with eyebrows or a hand, meet someone else's eyes and look away, shift positions in a chair. These actions we assume are random and incidental. But researchers have discovered in recent years that there is a system to them almost as consistent and comprehensible as language.

Every culture has its own body language. A Frenchman walks and moves in French. In talking, North Americans are apt to end a statement with a droop of the head or hand, a lowering of the eyelids. They wind up a question with a lift of the hand, a tilt of the chin, or a widening of the eyes.

The person who is truly bilingual is also bilingual in body language. New York's famous mayor, Fiorello La Guardia, politicked in English, Italian, and Yiddish. When films of his speeches are run without sound, it's not too difficult to identify from his gestures the language he was speaking. One reason English-dubbed foreign films often seem flat is that the gestures don't match the language.

Experts in kinesics—the study of communication through body movement—are not prepared to spell out a precise vocabulary of gestures. For example, when a student in conversation with a professor holds the older man's eyes a little longer than is usual, it can be a sign of respect and affection, or it can be a subtle challenge to the professor's authority. The expert looks for patterns in the context, not for an isolated meaningful gesture.

Kinesics is a young science—about nineteen years old—and very much the brain child of one man, anthropologist Dr. Ray L. Birdwhistell. But it already offers a smorgasbord of small observation.

One of the most potent elements in body language is eye behavior. Americans are careful about how and when they meet one another's eyes. In normal conversation, each eye contact lasts only about a second before one or both individuals look away. When two Americans look searchingly into each other's eyes, emotions are heightened and the relationship tipped toward greater intimacy.

Americans abroad sometimes find local eye behavior hard to interpret. "Tel Aviv was disturbing," one man recalled. "People looked me up and down. Finally, a friend explained that Israelis think nothing of staring at others on the street."

In the United States you are supposed to look at a passer-by just enough to show that you're aware of his presence. In parts of the Far East it is impolite to look at the other person at all during conversation. In England the polite listener fixes the speaker with an attentive stare and blinks his eyes occasionally as a sign of interest.

There are times when what a person says with his body gives the lie to what he is saying with his tongue. Thus a man may appear calm, self-controlled—unaware that his foot is beating the floor constantly, restlessly. Rage is another emotion feet and legs may reveal. Fear sometimes produces barely perceptible running motions—a kind of nervous leg jiggle. Then there are the subtle, provocative leg gestures that women use.

While children learn spoken and body language—proper postures, eye behaviors, etc.—they also learn a subtler thing: how to react to space around them. Man walks around inside a kind of private bubble, which represents the amount of air space he feels he must have between himself and other people.

Anthropologist Dr. Edward T. Hall points out that, for two unacquainted adult male North Americans, the comfortable distance to stand for private conversation is from arm's length to about four feet apart. The South American likes to stand much closer.

The American and the Arab are even less compatible in their space habits. Arabs may stand very close together to talk, staring intently into each other's eyes and breathing into each other's face. These are actions the American may associate with sexual intimacy and he may find them disturbing in a nonsexual context.

The amount of space a man needs is also influenced by his personality—introverts, for example, seem to need more elbow room than extroverts. Situation and mood also affect distance. Moviegoers waiting in line to see a sexy film will queue up much more densely than those waiting to see a family-entertainment movie.

Communication between human beings would be dull if it were all done with words. But words are often the smallest part of it.

take effort and time. We may even have grown shy of meeting and talking with strangers generally.

Are those your problems? If so, let us see what you can do to make
meeting and talking with strangers easier and more pleasurable.

YOU CAN TALK TO STRANGERS

When you know that you are going to meet strangers at some function,
try to find out something about them from mutual friends. Inquire
about their occupations and interests.

■ When you go into a strange house, be observant. Look for clues that
will help you to know the people who live there a bit better. What pictures, books, magazines do they live with? Do they read *Time* and the
New Yorker? Or do they enjoy *Life* and *Fortune?* If you don't like their
taste in bric-a-brac or lampshades, cross those topics off your list. Look
for things you can praise or that suggest a mutual interest.

■ At a large party, survey the several groups before you join one. Try
to spot one whose members at least *look* as if they might have something in common with you.

■ When you join a group, listen for a while for hints about the speakers'
personalities before making contributions yourself. It is better to hold
back a bit than to blunder. (If what you hear doesn't interest you, wander off to another group. And listen there for a while before joining in.)

■ Pay attention to the remarks made by the host or hostess in introducing you to the stranger. For example, with "Mr. Carr has just returned from the Near East" as a lead, you can comment on a current
news item about the Near East; or you can ask him about his mission, or his opinion on recent events there. Or you can merely express
pleasure in the opportunity to hear about that remote place at first
hand. In a few moments you will know much more about him.

■ Volunteer information about yourself. Mention what you do, or happen to have been doing just before you met him. This will probably
lead him to tell you something about himself.

■ Ask *personal,* but *not too personal,* questions. Obviously, one doesn't
ask a person's salary. But if one's host is with Bethlehem Steel, you can
certainly ask of a guest, "Are you with Bethlehem too?" If he is, you can
express interest or go on to further questions. If he isn't he'll probably
say what his work really is, and you can go on from there.

■ The stranger's first few remarks should give you clues to his interest.
If he says, "This rain is certainly good for crops," you know that his in-

terests are different from one who says, "If we have any more rain, the shops may as well close up."

■ The other fellow may be more ill at ease than you. Help him out. Talk about small matters to put him at ease.

■ Be on the alert for changes in mood and be ready to shift with them. Notice the other fellow's facial expressions, his hand movements, his stance. When does he perk up? When does he look distracted, vague or uninterested?

■ With strangers, especially, shun the argumentative approach, the challenging statement. Avoid politics and religion. You probably won't get far with such topics, and your host will certainly not thank you.

Check your attitude

A group of college students, asked what bothered them most in conversation, answered that it wasn't the topic, or the people as such, but rather the *attitudes* of people. They found it easy to talk with the *friendly* person, difficult to talk with the *dogmatic* person.

Is it your own attitude that you're uncertain about? Is your worry, not *what* you say, but *how* you say it? Do you think you might improve your attitudes, but don't know quite what to aim at?

Below are two lists, one of attitudes generally considered good in conversation, one of faulty attitudes. Run over both. If you think you have some of the good attitudes, strengthen and develop them. If you're afraid you have faulty attitudes, change them.

SEVEN WAYS TO BE A GOOD CONVERSATIONALIST

1. *Be interested.* Be interested in what's going on, what's being talked about, the other fellow, and what he's doing.

Be interested, not just in the one person you know very well, but in *all* the persons in the group. Let your gaze move from eye to eye. Pick out the person who hasn't said much, who looks ill at ease, and make a special point of talking to *him.*

2. *Be friendly.* Conversation withers if you are critical of the persons present, or are caustic about their contributions, or show, by your expression, that you don't think much of them.

Don't be so misled as to ape the trading of insults that goes on among professional comedians. Their feuds are carefully concocted by their gag writers, to spice up what might otherwise be a dull script.

3. *Be cheerful, good-humored.* Smile. Make it an interested, friendly smile. Show your good feelings in the way you say things.

Leave your tragic mask at home. Don't try to get people to gather round by exhibiting what a hurt, misunderstood soul you are.

4. *Be animated, and yet relaxed.* You're alive, so let your face and gestures show it. Time enough for immobility when rigor mortis sets in. (Of course, if on a particular occasion you don't feel up to being animated, beg off.)

But good conversation also has a certain calmness, a feeling of relaxation about it. It isn't work, strained and effortful. It is a play activity, a refreshing *rest* from work.

5. *Be flexible.* Topics change, and people, and moods. The good conversationalist changes with them. Tenacity is a quality we admire in a bulldog, and rigidity in a ramrod. But neither of these qualities has a place in conversation.

6. *Be tactful.* Follow the old saying, think *before* you speak. Think *first*, not *afterwards*. That is the essence of tactfulness.

If your neighbor's son has been expelled from school, stay far away from the topic of college requirements when chatting with him, or any talk about the irresponsibility of youth.

We can't help wounding people at times because we do not know all their sensitive spots. But we should try not to wound through mere thoughtlessness.

7. *Be courteous.* One could make a presentable case for the idea that good conversation is good manners. This does not mean merely remembering to say "Please," when asking for something, or thanking one's host for a pleasant evening upon leaving.

It does mean having a general attitude of consideration for others.

EIGHT BIG DON'TS IN CONVERSATION

1. *Don't be dogmatic.* Avoid the sweeping generalization, such as "All politicians are corrupt." Lord Acton took care to say, "All power *tends* to corrupt."

Moderate your statements. Avoid *all* and *always.* Swing over to *some* and *sometimes.* Use *a few, many, a great many, occasionally, infrequently,* whichever you think is warranted. Be careful too not to say *golfers* when you really mean *the golfers I happen to have met during my three-day stay at Oceanside.*

Learn the face-saving and argument-avoiding uses of: *perhaps; do you think; last week I heard someone say that; maybe I'm wrong, but.*

More important, avoid using a dogmatic *tone.* Some people manage to say, "It looks like snow," as if they were government meteorologists. Conversely, outrageous exaggerations can be gotten away with if you say them lightly and with a twinkle. "Fashion is spinach" didn't anger the couturiers overly—and perhaps turned them for a season or two to broccoli.

2. *Don't be condescending.* An attitude of being superior to everything and everybody will soon leave you in splendid isolation. There are better amusements than sitting alone looking down one's nose.

3. *Don't be argumentative.* Almost everybody likes a good fight—in the prize ring or the political arena. But almost no one is overjoyed to discover a battler in the living room.

Take the chip off your shoulder when you're going into company. The company will have a better time, and so will you. Do not argue for argument's sake. When you disagree, be, in Robert Louis Stevenson's phrase, an "amicable adversary."

4. *Don't be lifeless.* The other fellow expects to get some response from you to his witticism. Don't force him to carry the entire burden of the talking.

Moreover, make your responses something more than monosyllables. Conversation is a game which requires at least two players, and no game is fun if one player is halfhearted about it.

5. *Don't be insincere.* Praise people, but don't overpraise them. Don't gush, don't be fulsome. And praise the right thing. If your hostess serves excellent food on acceptable but undistinguished china, praise the food, not the plates.

6. *Don't be egocentric.* Express your opinions, certainly; state your re-

At a party one guest completely monopolized the conversation, much to the annoyance of the hostess's elderly mother. By the time he launched into a story of his experiences during the war, she was bored to the point of retaliation. "I was torpedoed in the Pacific," he began. "In fact, I lived for a week on a can of sardines."

"Really!" exclaimed the exasperated old lady. "Weren't you afraid of falling off?"
—*Eleanor C. Wood in Coronet*

actions; but without giving the impression that you think the universe revolves about you. Don't talk in such a way that your topics can be described as "the Pyrenees and me," "inflation and me," "the Taj Mahal and me," "the Supreme Court and me," "the decimal point and me," etc.

7. *Don't aim to be "the life of the party."* We admire the wonderful storyteller, the brilliant wit, the character whose infectious humor keeps the party convulsed with laughter. But we shouldn't let our admiration lead us into thinking that our every remark must be a joke, that the chief goal of conversation is laughter. Good conversation can be serious as well as gay.

If you wish, practice storytelling, read magazines such as the *New Yorker* for their humor, commit to memory prize bits of wit. These will help your conversation; and you'll have many chuckles as you read, say, Sydney Smith's "Bishop —— deserves to be preached to death by wild curates," or "he was very agreeable, but spoke too lightly, I thought, of veal soup."

But you will do better to try to find your own strengths in conversation. And you may discover yourself accounted the best conversationalist in town because you *listen* better than anyone else.

8. *Finally, don't be a mumbler.* Speak clearly. Speak up. Before a remark can be understood, before a question can be answered, before a joke can be laughed at, it must be heard, and it must be intelligible.

How to get conversations started

Some people sail briskly through the introduction stage, and then come to a dead halt.

Let's examine the basics of getting started in conversation (introductions are discussed in the next chapter).

The host, or whoever does the introducing, should also tell something about either or both the persons introduced that will help to start them off in conversation. Say: "Mrs. Green is president of our Woman's Club," or "Mrs. Green grows the best roses in town," or "Mr. Fitch is with the U.N.," or "Mr. Fitch does a great deal of sailing."

A play was recently produced on Broadway only because, some years previous, a host launched a playwright and a director in conversation with this remark: "You two ought to have something in common because you both have red hair and you both look discouraged."

Even at a large party, the attentive host will try to remain a few minutes with new guests to see that they are started off in conversation.

If you're uncertain about the other person's name, be sure to get it straight. This is insurance against the arrival of a friend to whom you will have to introduce the new acquaintance.

If the name is unusual, you may comment on this, or ask about the spelling, for some people are very proud of their names. But be cautious here. If the name seems bizarre, perhaps you'd better not show that you think it unusual at all. Osbert Thwistletick has probably suffered enough from his name already, without your comment.

A remark about the surroundings is a standard starter, and a good one. "It's a lovely party, isn't it?" will do; and so will pleasant comments about the house or the other guests.

DEVELOP THE LIGHT TOUCH

Keep to light, casual topics for a while: the occasion, the weather, the food, the difficulty of managing the egg nog, the hors d'oeuvres, the napkin. . . .

Keep the *tone* light at the beginning. A banker and an economics professor, upon being introduced, each adopted a bantering tone. "You're one of those fellows who tell us poor bankers what to think and do." "Well, you seem to like it. You're always stealing our best professors away to work for you." Several more smiling interchanges, and they settled down to serious talk of the state of the nation.

Asking the other fellow about himself and his work or interests or volunteering information about yourself is an excellent starter. "Do you come from this part of the country?" "Have you lived here long?" Or, if the host has mentioned his being an engineer, you can well ask whether he is a civil, electrical, or chemical engineer. But don't be too personal in the questions you ask.

And in volunteering information, be sure merely to mention what you do or what you're interested in. Don't launch into a five-minute description of your entire working-day routine.

Finding a mutually satisfactory topic to talk about, and the right tone, may take time and effort.

Sometimes two people click immediately. They spy each other across a crowded room, head for each other, and, somehow, are soon immersed in exchanging hints on the cultivation of mushrooms.

But sometimes half a dozen or more topics will be attempted and none will strike a spark. If this happens, don't give up. Keep trying.

Bearing in mind what you know of the other fellow, the group, keep throwing out the best ideas you can. All of a sudden, there it will be— the thing that two of you, or all of you, can have a very good time talking about.

How to keep the conversation going

There are many factors involved in keeping a conversation going, not the least being that the participants are willing to go on talking. Here are a few suggestions to help you.

Listening: Listen to what is being said. Don't let the talk flow over and past you like water over a stone. Focus on the ideas, focus sharply.

Listen actively. Let yourself react to what is said. Think about it. Feel about it. Show your reaction. Nod, smile. Don't be a jellyfish, floating passively with the tide.

Try to listen so well that you will be able to tell afterwards fairly accurately what was said.

Keep your eye on the ball, on the topic or the aspect of it that is being discussed *now*. Don't think ahead to what may be said two minutes from now. This may help you endure a boring speech; but conversation requires alertness. You don't want to wake up, suddenly, to find everyone waiting for you to answer a question you haven't heard. That *stops* the conversation.

Don't interrupt. Listen politely to the other fellow. Give him his say. Don't be so anxious to cut in with your idea that you disconcert the person talking. Learn to listen so well that you can tell when he *is* coming to the end of his contribution, so that you can come in with yours as a fellow contributor, not an intruder. Then you will have had your say, and you will have been a pleasant companion too.

Your contributions: These may be of almost any sort: forthright statements of fact, questions, expressions of opinion, mild disagreement, comments refining what has already been said to something that you think is closer to the truth.

But make sure that in your contribution, as in your listening, you are on the ball. Don't hark back to foreign sports cars when the group has left that topic ten minutes before and is discussing campers. And don't spend your time planning what to say when they get around to the Stanley Steamer. The planned bright remark usually sounds dragged in.

406

English historian George Macauley was noted for his garrulity as much as for his wisdom. An acquaintance once remarked, "He is certainly more agreeable since his return from India . . . now he has occasional flashes of silence that make his conversation perfectly delightful."

Try to make your contributions more than monosyllables. *Yes, no, perhaps,* are not stimulating. Give your fellow talkers something to work on. On the other hand, don't deliver orations, long discourses. Be crisp. Let your remark have a beginning and an end. You may have a lot to say on the topic. But the other fellow may have a few worthwhile ideas too. Give him a chance.

Remember the point made at the beginning of this chapter: conversation means give-and-take. The long contribution may stifle talk. The too-short one does little to help.

Transitions: The time comes when the best of topics seems to be exhausted. Interest wanes, contributions lag. That's the time to turn to a *new* topic.

One way to make the transition is to let the old topic die. Miss Frost says the last word on Florida oranges. Silence. Then, out of nowhere, "I met an interesting character last week. He grows worms." And you're off to interesting characters, worms, or odd occupations.

Another way is to pick up the last bit of talk on the old topic and shift by one or more steps to something new. When no one has anything to add on different types of mortgages you may remark, "Mortgages don't come into plays much anymore, do they? In the old days no self-respecting drama could do without one. The suspense was terrific, everybody wondering whether the old six-percenter was going to be paid off or not in the last act. But nowadays it's bigamy, and psychoneurotics . . ." So there you are, right in the middle of modern drama. Or bigamy. Or psychoanalysis.

A third way is to shift suddenly and sharply, making no pretense that you're doing anything else. "Well, we've about finished Hemingway, haven't we? If nobody has any objection, I'd like to ask about that picture over there. It's bothered me ever since I came . . ." Or more simply, "To change the subject."

WRITE BETTER, SPEAK BETTER

Try not to change the subject unwittingly. If the topic is wonder drugs, and someone is telling how her Aunt Martha was cured, don't latch onto the *Aunt* part and give your Aunt Emma's recipe for elderberry wine. If you must talk about aunts, restrict yourself to those who have swallowed aureomycin and lived.

And don't shift too soon. While the topic still seems to interest the others, don't let your waning interest lead you into pushing them around. Make a polite comment or two, or sit silent and try to look interested. A few coins of patience must sometimes be paid for the delight of good conversation.

Trouble: Sooner or later we all make a *faux pas*. In the excitement of talking, we momentarily forget the tragedy that has happened to some member of the group. Before we know it we have blundered, said something that hurts.

The way out depends on the individual situation. If you've blundered badly, and know the people well, perhaps you'd better say, "I'm sorry, Jane," and move on to another topic. But if you've only veered close to danger, then do your best to veer swiftly away. Do not make a scene by profuse apologies, and try not to become flustered. By staying poised yourself, you help the other person do the same.

When it's the other person who has blundered, do your bit to help. Become interested in the safe topic which she happens to think of, and talk about that. If she becomes flustered, supply one of your own.

End of conversation: There are times when conversation is out of place. The game of bridge doesn't require conversation, and some players prefer silence during the play, except for the bidding. We go to the theater to hear the play, not a neighbor's comments. (A converse suggests itself here: If you have friends in for the evening, ask if they'd like to see a particular television program before you condemn them to a watch night of silence.)

And the best of conversations must end. Start to go before the other

---

Conversation should be fired in short bursts; anybody who talks steadily for more than a minute is in danger of boring somebody.
　　　　　　　　　　　　　　　　　　　—Harlan Miller

fellow takes out his watch, don't dawdle over the coats and wraps, avoid starting new conversations at the door, pay your respects briefly to your host and hostess, and go.

Ending a conversation is also a way of keeping one going—the next one, the one you hope you'll be invited for.

Seven faults in conversation

The major faults in our conversation are, of course, the violation of any of its underlying principles, such as talking on topics which are taboo, or conversing without regard for the other fellow.

But there are also several mechanical faults which we should avoid. These result from carelessness, allowing ourselves to slip into a conversational rut, not thinking seriously about conversational techniques, not criticizing our own conversational efforts.

Do you have any of the faults below? If so, try to eliminate them by adopting the suggestions for correction.

Pet words: A common fault is to have pet words and to use them whether they are suitable or not.

Some people call all things they like or want to praise *cute*, or *darling*, or *exciting*, or *fabulous*. They describe all things they dislike or consider unsatisfactory as *ghastly*, or *weird*, or *dull*, or *queer*, or *putrid*. Sometimes a conversation seems to consist largely of *lousy* and *swell*.

Obviously, a mountain is not *cute;* and there are many other words for describing people, places, and books than *ghastly*.

The correction lies in learning to use those other words. Eliminate the pet words from your conversation for a while. Try to use terms which fit what you are describing. Refine your evaluations. Praise and blame with discrimination. Think first: Is it *excellent, good, fair, poor, completely lacking in merit?* Learn to use *admirable, deficient, awesome, spurious*. Build your vocabulary. Then, if you wish, return to *cute* and *ghastly*, but use them properly.

Superfluous words and phrases: Other persons add *naturally*, or *really*, or *actually*, or *literally* to most of their remarks. "Naturally, I told him to go, and naturally, he ——." Also overused are: *frankly, to tell the truth, so to speak, you see, you know, if you see what I mean, do you get the point*.

Eliminate such unnecessary words and phrases.

Fad words: Still other persons load their talk with fashionable words and phrases. They do not *dislike* things, they are *allergic* to them. At present *overall picture, contact, dynamic, process, basic, in terms of,* could well be used less often.

Too much slang: There's nothing wrong with slang itself. Even the college professor uses it, though he may confine himself to old forms now considered "acceptable." But much newly coined slang hardly lasts the year out.

Avoid too much slang. Use it occasionally and sparingly when you think it will lend vigor and color to your talking.

Affectations: Occasionally a person, after two years of French, wants people to know how well she has been educated. She sprinkles her conversation with *bête noire, accouchement, fin de siècle, amour,* etc. Don't join her ranks. Avoid using too many foreign words and phrases.

Also occasionally, we meet affectation with a reverse twist. The well-educated person decides to be "one of the boys." He slips tough-guy expressions into otherwise grammatical sentences. The result is ludicrous. In conversation, don't feel that adding a few very well-chosen words will make you something different from what you are.

Exaggerating: You must have heard a would-be wit proclaim his story beforehand as "the funniest story I ever heard," only to look crestfallen when the company didn't laugh quite as hard as he expected. Or you've heard an enthusiast describe the wonders of a gadget, and then have to back down when some more objective user listed its limitations.

Avoid embarrassment by avoiding exaggeration.

Your story may go over better if you introduce it with "I heard a funny story about that the other night."

Telling personal experiences awkwardly: An interesting personal experience can be ruined by too much dialogue, and by too much "so he said," "so I said," "and she said," "and they said." There's more apparatus here than story.

An interesting personal experience can be ruined by too much detail: "I went into this barber shop—it was the one on the corner of Maple Street and Knott—1516 the number was—closed up five years ago—anyway, I went into this barber shop—I had a dark blue suit on——." It's going to be a long while before anything happens in this story.

Good stories can be ruined by vagueness of detail: "Well, it seems there was this man and he went into this store and he asked for one of those, those what-d'ye-call-'ems. . . ." This man doesn't seem to know what "this" story is about.

Make up your mind what the point of your personal experience is. Give names or not as you please. Mention only the details that count, but be specific about those. Use dialogue sparingly, to advance the story or to reveal character.

Listen to good storytellers to improve your technique. And read stories for the help they can give. There's a very good one which begins: "Once upon a time there were three bears—a father bear, a mother bear, and a baby bear." A wonderful opening, for with fewer than twenty words, you're right into the story.

How to practice the art of conversation

There are very few practice *exercises* for conversation. One can rehearse the telling of a story. One can practice introductions. The best *practice* for conversation is conversation itself.

■ Practice at home with your family. If you feel your weakness is topics, talk about the play you have all seen (or the movie, or the television program). Try to keep the conversation going for a good while. Build conversations out of the events of the day as given in your evening newspaper. Bring half a dozen possible topics to the dinner table.

■ Practice with your friends. Invite a few over for the evening. In planning the evening don't let it be all bridge or some other game. Reserve part of the evening for conversation. If you feel that an innate friendliness is one of your strengths, and want to develop it, concentrate on an attitude of friendly interest in the talk of the others for that evening.

■ Practice with strangers. Try to put the principles you have been reading about here into practice. Be on the alert for hints that will help you. Adjust to the other fellow. Try to talk. Be an alive, an interested, listener and talker.

■ Most important of all, seek out conversation. Look for the situations in which conversations will develop. Cultivate a healthy, positive attitude toward meeting friends and strangers. Each opportunity to talk will provide practice. And as you improve, you will know more and more the stimulation and relaxation that good conversation offers.

411

36

The art of being
a successful host

Good talk is the essence of sociability, and the good host or hostess knows how to make it flourish. By observing a few simple procedures you can put your guests at ease and encourage the lively conversation and exchange of ideas that make any gathering memorable.

Hosting a successful party can give you a glow that will linger pleasantly for days—and it is a feeling that any of us can experience. It is easy to be a successful host and to guarantee a happy evening for yourself and your guests. A few simple precautions, a little imagination, and careful attention to detail are the whole of the recipe, whether your party is given to repay social debts, to help a charity, to pay a business obligation, or simply to have fun. If you follow that recipe, the party will be fun—for everyone.

The first ingredient for a successful evening is a well-chosen guest list. Do the same faces show up again and again at your parties? Are they likely to be a cross section of your country club membership, or of your business acquaintances? Can each guest tick off on his fingers in advance who the others are likely to be? If so, the chances are that the golfers will talk about their golf; the lawyers will talk law; the men will talk to the men; and the women will talk to the women.

"What's on the chair is more important than what's on the table," said W. S. Gilbert of dinner parties. Filling the same chairs with the same guests party after party, however engaging and stimulating they may be individually, is as unimaginative and palling as to serve truffles—or any other delicacy—as the only course at every meal.

Vary your guest list from party to party. Experiment. Bring in unfamiliar faces. Offer your guests the possibility of discovery.

If you must invite deadheads, at the very least leaven the lump with as many guests as possible who will be entertaining.

You may not always have a completely free choice of whom to invite. Some people may have to be invited for business reasons. You have to consider such matters as the balance between men and women; unattached men are much in demand, and you may not always be able to get your pick of them.

Don't feel you *must* ask good old Joe to every party you give, just because he is lonely and perhaps has no place else to go, or you are used to having him around. Indeed, a moment's reflection may show that you are inviting some people to your parties simply out of habit.

Five rules for introductions

Introduce your guests around as soon as they arrive.

Surprisingly, even sophisticated hosts often become confused and self-conscious about how to make an introduction. The basic guidelines are easily fixed in your mind:

1. The man is introduced to the woman if she is over eighteen:

"Mrs. Carillo, may I present Stephen Harding"; or less formally, "Mrs. Carillo, Stephen Harding."

2. The younger person is introduced to the older if both are of the same sex:

"Father, this is Joe White's son Robert"; or, "Father, Bruce Hackstaff."

3. Girls under eighteen are introduced to older people:

"This is Edna Dome, Mr. and Mrs. Alan Ross."

4. Either men or women are always introduced to a considerably older person, and often to a person of special distinction.

5. Some informal but correct introductions:

"Shirley Eder, do you know Lester Rondell?"
"Shirley Eder, have you met Lester Rondell?"
"Shirley Eder, I'd like you to meet Lester Rondell."

Try not to be flustered if in the tension of the moment a name you know perfectly well, and perhaps have known for years, disappears completely from your mind. Remember that everyone has had the same experience. Admit frankly, "I just got one of those awful name blocks on you, after twenty years. *You* say it!"

A useful device for preventing such a block, when introducing one person to a group, is to go from one name to another in a kind of easy rhythm, not giving the block a chance to surface.

Introduce newcomers all the way around, unless so many people are present that this is impracticable. Too many hosts, out of a compulsion to be on the move, abandon guests after a few introductions.

When you have to leave a new guest with a group he has just met for the first time, tell them enough about each other so that the conversation will have a starting point. "Roy is just back from the Pacific Northwest," you might say, "and he almost didn't make it. His engine conked out while he was crossing the Columbia River bar . . ."

Seating arrangements

The way you seat your guests at a formal dinner could make or break your party. Work this out carefully, well in advance, host and hostess comparing opinions. Then put the names on table cards, so that there is no possibility of your arrangements going awry. Juggle the cards in advance until the combination is exactly right. Mix and match.

Compare notes on each guest's interests, personality, conversational abilities. Should John, whose hobby is stamp collecting, be seated next to Alice, who is an expert on modern art? Is giggling Gladys a suitable table companion for booming Bill?

But do not cluster your guests simply according to the mutuality of their backgrounds or interests, putting all the pomegranates at one table and all the pears at another. On the contrary, upset the fruit basket. Having gone to the trouble of bringing a variety of people together,

---

Igor Cassini, the society columnist, asked Bernard Baruch how he arranged the seatings for all the notables who attended his dinner parties. "I never bother about that," Baruch assured him. "Those who matter don't mind and those who mind don't matter."

—*Bennett Cerf, Shake Well Before Using*

seat them so as to encourage conversational cross-pollination. Let each share the riches the others have to offer.

Usually you should not seat husbands and wives together—unless, of course, they are honeymooners and cannot be pried apart. You may wish to make exceptions also for possessive spouses who resent it if their mate, however faithful, is seated next to an attractive person of the opposite sex.

Sometimes a wife may be quite justified in wishing to keep within quick interrupting range of a husband with a roving eye (or *vice versa*). If you wish to play Solomon, separate that husband and wife but keep them in full view of each other.

Even the best-balanced seating arrangement cannot insure relaxed and enjoyable conversation. From where you sit, keep a weather eye on what is going on. If you see a table becalmed, you may have to go over and give the conversation a fresh start, even at a cost of leaving your own dinner unfinished. But don't bother them unless you are really needed. A good host, like a good waiter, does not get in the way.

Keep conversation-revivers in reserve: topics likely to arouse interest and discussion. A review of a book or motion picture in the morning paper, a local news item, or a diverting anecdote may turn the trick.

As a host, your responsibilities are not unlike those of the chairman of a panel discussion. You must pace the talk; spark it; see that all sides have a chance to get into the act.

Talk after dinner

You occasionally find a host who assumes that once dinner is over, his responsibilities are over too. He disappears into the television room, and that is the last anyone sees of him. The discourtesy is obvious. At a huge gathering, run by a trained staff, it may be possible for the host or hostess to disappear without damage, but not at a party given by you or me.

A generation ago, Lady Asquith held a reception in London. She received the guests graciously, and then retired upstairs to play bridge. Next day in a restaurant a woman at the next table said, "Lady Asquith, I was at your party last night." Lady Asquith smiled and bowed; but under her breath she murmured, "Thank God I was not."

A present-day host cannot permit himself such idiosyncrasies. When the guests settle down in the living room after dinner, your responsibil-

YOU CAN REMEMBER NAMES

"A PERSON'S NAME is to him the sweetest and most important sound in the language," wrote Dale Carnegie, the shrewd teacher of human relations, in *How to Win Friends and Influence People*. Many men and women who are leaders in their fields know this truth and practice it.

Not many of us share the ability to retain names. Indeed, name forgetting is so common that it is the subject of endless humor. But it is no joking matter. Failure to connect a name and a face can cost you a pleasant friendship or a lucrative business opportunity. At the least, it presents an embarrassing moment.

Dale Carnegie, long before his personality-improvement courses became big business, discovered that most of his pupils were plagued by this annoying mental block. He himself was bothered by it—and in his methodical way he set out to find a cure.

The experts he consulted didn't help much, and his own thinking and experimentation finally brought him to the conclusion that an accurate memory for names and faces was not necessarily a gift, but a skill that could be taught as effectively as arithmetic. He evolved a set of practical rules that are used today with great success. They are simple; they require concentrated effort and practice, but they work.

1. *When you are introduced to someone, get the name clearly.* If your host mumbles something that sounds like "Mr. Flamglm" or "Miss Plshmin," don't hesitate to ask the person who is being introduced what his name is. (But for goodness' sake, don't ask the host—he may have forgotten it.) The guest won't mind repeating the name correctly.

2. *The name must have a chance to sink into your mind.* The best way of achieving this, almost automatically, is to repeat the name aloud two or three times in the ensuing conversation, until it is indelibly registered.

3. *While you are getting the name, get the face.* Look at the person carefully. From his first day on the force every well-trained policeman has drilled into him the technique of remembering a face. This technique can be just as useful in ordinary life.

Start at the top—with the hair. Is it blond, dark, gray? Then the face: Is it round, oval, thin, heavy? Note the color of the eyes, the shape of the features. It is amazing how sharp the image will be and how long it will remain with you.

Hat-check girls who operate in large restaurants and night clubs without the use of markers, airline hostesses who never hear their charges' names, and a host of others whose livelihood depends on their ability to remember faces teach themselves to observe and register what they see. You can do it, too.

4. *With name and face in mind, you have to cement the two together.* Try to make a mental picture. You may be able to associate a man with his business: A carpenter may be named Sawyer, a contractor may be named Bridges. Mr. Mason—whether he is a mason or not—can be slotted quickly by picturing him in your mind's eye as laying bricks. Butler, Farmer, Fisher, and dozens of others also present immediate pictures.

You can sometimes find yourself using rhymes as memory props. "Mr. Fowler is a prowler" or "Mrs. Farnum should be with Barnum" is the kind of key that can be fashioned in seconds; by some psychological phenomenon it will stick with you for years.

Dale Carnegie's favorite system was to paint a mind picture of the person doing something that reminded him of the name. He made the picture as absurd as possible. One of his teaching manuals gives the following examples:

Hamilton. Picture Mr. Hamilton with a human head but a ham body. See him walk onto a platform scale. The weigher adjusts the balances and shouts, "You weigh one ton!"

Van Hatten. Picture Mr. Van Hatten driving a huge van. Instead of the usual top, the van is covered by a gigantic hat—van-hat-on!

Waclawski. Dress Mr. Waclawski in the uniform of a WAC. Under his arm he has a law book and he is wearing a pair of skis—wac-law-ski!

This procedure may seem silly, but, after all, you are the only one who knows you are using it. And, again with practice, you will find it extremely effective.

ity is still very much alive. By this time, most people will know whom they want to talk to; but it is up to you to see that no one is left out.

If the party is small enough so that everybody can sit, arrange your living room chairs in advance to facilitate conversational groupings, even at the expense of disarranging the decor of the room. If, by chance, there is one guest whom all the rest are sure to want to hear, go even further; arrange all the chairs in one arc or oval.

No matter how the guests arrange themselves, continue to be the quiet chairman. Move about, but don't interrupt. Supervise, guide, nudge, point, direct, but only as necessary—and then without seeming to. If someone's toes (conversational toes, that is) are being stepped on, rush to the rescue. If voices are beginning to sound irritated, create a diversion.

If someone is putting his audience to sleep with an endless story about his dog, give him the hook: ask the mother of five at his right whether she thinks sex in motion pictures has become too explicit, or whether she considers Beverly Sills as great a singer as Maria Callas.

"A host," said the Roman poet Horace, "is like a general; it takes a mishap to reveal his genius."

Sound like a strain for you? Well, in one way it is. A host can no more relax completely than a horseback rider can. At any instant the horse might shy. But if you have prepared your party carefully; if you have carried it forward with organization and consideration; if you have prevented the men from forming into one group and the women into another; above all if you have kept the conversation alive and lively—then when it is all over, you, as well as your guests, will have had a wonderful time. They will remember a sparkling evening—and you will be the one who put the spark in the sparkle.

That, sir or madam, is hostmastery.

POINTS TO REMEMBER

Take time to plan everything about your party with care. You'll find it's worth the trouble.

Vary your guest lists.

Don't slight introductions.

Mix and match your guests at the table.

Keep the conversation going.

Remember—the evening is not over until the last guest leaves.

37

When you meet
a famous person

A chat with the couple next door is one thing, but what if you find yourself seated next to a famous actor or a prominent politician? TV interviewer Barbara Walters gives sensible tips on how to see the celebrity as a human being and make the encounter a pleasure for both of you.

Celebrities didn't use to *mingle*, and no one expected them to. A young actress with a major role in a Clark Gable film asked him what she should call him. "For the time we'll know one another," he assured her, " 'Mr. Gable' will do fine."

That sort of regality is gone with the wind. These are the days of decentralized moviemaking in such unexpected locations as a New England village or a Minnesota airport. Glamorous people now are making lecture tours, sipping tea with the ladies in towns with unpronounceable names. And there are also the writers, actors, and musicians who travel because they are involved in causes: political, charitable, and protest. You'll meet them in campaign committee rooms, or at fundraising dinners, or when the cornerstone of a new children's hospital is being laid.

When the *Today* program has traveled to different cities or when I have been on a speaking engagement, I have sometimes been so impressed by new acquaintances that, with all sincerity, I ask them to call me if they plan to visit New York. And I think of busy women like Ann Landers, Mrs. Hubert Humphrey, and Mrs. Martin Luther King, Jr., who became my friends after only one day's meeting. We often drop each other notes about our work or families.

You have two choices when your turn has come to meet a celebrity. You can tell yourself you're such a worldly person that you won't bother him, which may mean that you're just plain shy, or else you can approach him gamely and say something. The latter alternative would be your favorite if only you knew of some opening remark so deft and delightful that the celebrity would be captivated by you. That kind of moment is the fabric of many a Walter Mitty dream, but it's not unrealistic at all. Celebrities have to talk to someone while they're waiting for their coffee to cool, and it might as well be you. And you might as well enjoy it.

How to approach a celebrity

You can safely begin a conversation with any famous person—or with anyone at all, for that matter—by indulging your natural impulse to express admiration. People tend to say flattering things to celebrities they don't even like, just to get a good look at them, and celebrities are well aware of this, but you're going to be different. Don't gush, don't take so long to say it that the smile begins to hurt his face, and try to avoid empty superlatives, such as *just loved, marvelous, fabulous, fantastic,* and *divine.*

If you're sincere, and absolutely certain of your ground, refer to the celebrity's achievement that most impressed you; he'll be charmed and grateful. But if there hasn't been an opportunity beforehand to confirm it and your recollection of the exact event is the least bit hazy, stick to generalities. Many a celebrity has been maimed by a well-intentioned fan who wanted only to be kind.

The most common mistake is the worst one: The fan has the wrong celebrity in mind. Composers get congratulated for scores they didn't write, authors for a best seller by someone else; actors are told that their performance in a movie they never made was unforgettable. It's a deflating experience for the celebrity and one that casts a pall over the rest of the exchange, which will be brief.

There's rarely any physical resemblance involved in the mixup. It comes rather from an inclination to file famous faces away under blurred headings, according to nationality or occupation. People will tell almost any English actor that he was splendid in *Lawrence of Arabia,* or any male singer with the exception of Andy Williams that *Moon River* is a beautiful theme, or they'll see Kitty Carlisle shopping in a department store and rush over to tell her how much they miss seeing her on *What's My Line?*

When in doubt, take the safe route of ambiguity and then gently change the subject—as in, "I've always appreciated your work so much. What are you doing in our town?"

Above all, don't ask him for clarification if you can't recall perfectly. It's essence of nightmare when a fan, beaming with bonhomie and quite impervious to the misery he is inflicting, insists on groping through his memory fragments for the name of that Broadway show he saw a few years back, the one with the terrific sets, or maybe it was just one set that turned, anyway the whole family saw it and you were just great, one of the *great* performances, if I could just remember the name . . . The hapless actor is obliged to catalog his entire New York career but he knows in his heart that it will turn out to be a play that starred Christopher Plummer instead.

"YOUR FACE IS FAMILIAR, BUT . . ."

There's something even more depressing than this sort of thing, when the fan's only grasp on reality is the celebrity's name, and that's when the fan doesn't have a name at all, not even a wrong one. He is not deterred by this a whit. He knows that the face is familiar, but he can't figure out why, and he reasons that he deserves an explanation.

What he usually says is, "Are you somebody?" Now that's a challenging question to answer; philosophers could maybe handle it, or theologians ready to develop the concept that we are all children of God. The abashed performer may try a modest, "No, not really," but the fan will persist. "I've seen you somewhere before, on television maybe? You *are* somebody."

NBC News correspondent Aline Saarinen told me of her all-time "Are you somebody?" experience. She was in Los Angeles reporting on the opening of a new art museum. With her was another NBC correspondent, Jack Paxton. As they were standing outside of the museum, a

> When I meet a man whose name I cannot remember, I give myself two minutes; then, if it is a hopeless case, I always say, "And how is the old complaint?" —*Benjamin Disraeli*

woman approached with joy of recognition written all over her face. "I just love your reports on the *Today* show," she told a complimented Mrs. Saarinen. "Your movie reviews are the best ever."

"Thank you," Aline responded graciously, "but I think you have me confused with Judith Crist."

"Oh, yes," said the lady, and she turned her attention immediately to Jack Paxton, *"But* I'd know you anywhere. You're John Chancellor!"

There's one other minor disaster area when approaching a celebrity who makes his or her living in front of a camera. *Never* indicate that he looks different from what you expected. It's astonishing how many otherwise sensitive people believe they are delivering a great compliment when they say, "The camera doesn't do you justice. You're so much better looking in real life," or that the celebrity looks younger in the flesh, or thinner. The inference is that the performer is deluded in his hope that he looks good on camera—and that's a blow at his professional survival. He must grit his teeth and say thank you, but some of his confidence leaks out. What is even worse is to tell him that he looks better on television than he does in person. Either way, you can't win. Nor can he.

Don't miss your chance to meet a celebrity

Don't assume from this that it would be a lot easier on all concerned to leave the celebrity strictly alone, thus avoiding all known booby-traps. People with famous faces expect to be noticed and have a stock of gracious responses to help you with the awkwardness you might feel. Most of them would be very disappointed if some sort of flurry of attention didn't accompany their travels.

Sometimes the problem is that we the public think the celebrity will be irritated by too much attention. I used to feel this way and the loss was mine. I remember attending a buffet dinner where Harry Belafonte was also a guest. The other women at the party swarmed around him so aggressively that I decided to reduce his burden by at least one female, and do him the kindness of remaining aloof. Besides, I thought I'd stand out that way and attract Mr. Belafonte by my cool indifference. I could have kicked myself afterward because I missed my chance to talk with one of the most interesting and intelligent performers of our time.

So by all means, take every opportunity that comes your way to exchange even a few sentences with a celebrity. But try to apply old-fashioned good manners in judging what are the proper limits.

LET GOOD MANNERS BE YOUR GUIDE

As an example of what I mean, my husband and I had dinner one night in a Baltimore restaurant with Johnny Carson and his teen-age son, and discovered firsthand why superstars are forced to become hermits. Other diners in the restaurant came over and interrupted our meal more than a dozen times to speak to Carson. Quite a number decided to stand a few feet away and just stare at him as he ate, and one boldly pulled up a chair and joined us. Johnny has told me that this is his idea of all-time rudeness.

My husband and I also remember an evening of such inconsideration that we talked about it for days. Shortly after our first astronauts landed on the moon, New York's Governor Nelson Rockefeller gave them a gala dinner in the grand ballroom of the Waldorf Astoria. Invitations were at a premium and the room was studded with the famous from every walk of life, not to mention the astronauts themselves. But Lee and I watched at first in fascination and then in disgust as person after person in this seemingly sophisticated group approached the table at which Frank Sinatra was sitting. When Sinatra wasn't being asked for autographs, he was being besieged by photographers and television cameramen. With bright lights continually flashing in his face, and strangers leaning over with their arms on him, he tried gamely to eat his dinner. He never lost his patience and I never felt more sympathetic or understanding of his plight. Sinatra's only choice would have been to have left the dinner completely, but then he would have missed the evening's remarks by the astronauts and that obviously was more important to him than his own comfort.

BE CONSIDERATE

What have I learned from all this? I'd make it a rule not to approach any celebrity while he is eating or relaxing at a private dinner. If you want to say something kind, or ask for an autograph, write a message and have the headwaiter deliver it.

(It's a minor point, but it makes a difference: before asking a celebrity for an autograph, please obtain a pen and a piece of paper. It's a nuisance for him to be asked to supply either.)

There's another kind of public encounter with a celebrity which also should be subject to the ordinary rules of politeness. It's when traveling by plane—you have fastened your seat belt preparatory for takeoff and looked around at your fellow passengers to discover that the one in the next seat is a celebrity. What to do?

Well, above all, be considerate. The celebrity may be in transit from one ordeal of putting out high-voltage charm to another that will be even more of a strain on his resources. Perhaps he has been counting on the peace and privacy of the flight to restore his energy and collect his thoughts. By all means speak to him, say something flattering and friendly—and then pick up a book and leave him alone. He'll be profoundly grateful to you if he's tired, and you've established an opening for a conversation when he feels like it.

CELEBRITIES ARE PEOPLE, TOO

Let us suppose that the celebrity you're with has some time to spend with you and seems disposed to chat. He's your lecturer of the day perhaps, and you're the official hostess; or you've met him at a party and for the moment you have his undivided attention; or he's waiting for an elevator too, and when it arrives you two are the only occupants. You've progressed safely past the opening courtesy of expressing your esteem

After the termination of the Seminole campaign, General Andrew Jackson visited Washington City, and during his stay there, having occasion to supply himself with a nether garment, employed a fashionable tailor named Ballard to make it. Ballard, who was a very pompous little fellow and very fond of being recognized by great men who had been his customers, a few days after he had finished the unmentionables, seeing the general in front of Tennison's hotel in conversation with some gentlemen, stepped up and spoke to him. The general, thinking him some distinguished individual, very cordially gave him his hand, but not remembering him, in a whisper inquired his name. To which Ballard replied, "I made your breeches." The general, deceived by the sound, immediately turned to the company and introduced him as Major Breeches—a title which poor Ballard was afterwards obliged to wear to the day of his death.   —*Harper's Magazine*, December 1852

and he has replied that he is touched by your compliment. Now it's your turn again.

Try something that demonstrates empathy with the celebrity as a flesh and blood person, subject to fatigue and wounds like any man. Chances are, in fact, that he is a more vulnerable person than you are, and basically shy as well. Don't expect that his real personality is exactly like his professional one; the confident, zany, or sexy image that the performer projects to the public is often a piece of fiction. Comedians in particular put on a glittering show while they're working, but may be withdrawn and despondent otherwise.

Most people who succeed in having really engaging conversations with celebrities stick to the areas that can be described as human interest. These have some promise of developing into a two-handed discussion, rather than that kind of agog question like "You have such a fascinating life, don't you?" which the celebrity can dispose of with one eye on the clock.

A journalist friend of mine, for instance, had a memorable five-minute chat with Queen Elizabeth at a cocktail party because she asked how the Queen's clothes had weathered the previous day's windy visit to an open-pit iron mine. The Queen bubbled as she described her amazed discovery that she had been dyed henna from head to toe, and went on to tell of attempts to brush her hat clean and her worry that her ensemble could be salvaged—"and it was brand-new, you know." By expressing her interest in a simple, practical matter, my friend gained a rare glimpse of the real woman under the crown.

The Queen herself is known to practice the same technique. Millions of television viewers saw her chatting with U.S. Ambassador Walter Annenberg when he apeared at Buckingham Palace to present his credentials. And what did the Queen ask as a conversation starter? She'd heard that the ambassador was redecorating the Embassy and asked how it was coming along.

LET YOUR EMPATHY SHOW

The saving quality in any question you ask a celebrity is empathy. I'm always won by people who want to know about my schedule—what time I have to get up in the morning (4:30 A.M.), or how I manage to get enough sleep (I don't)—because they show a thoughtfulness about me as a person, a woman who must function out of whack with normal working routine. I also melt at questions about our small daughter

425

Jacqueline. I think most people love to be asked about their children.

I broke the ice with the usually aloof Barbra Streisand by asking how she chose the right nursery school for her young son Jason. Mrs. Mamie Eisenhower relaxed before our long interview by talking of her favorite grandchild Susie. Former Vice President and Mrs. Hubert Humphrey enjoy talking of their grandchildren, and I spoke so often to them of my Jacqueline that they sent a candid photograph to my home, auto-graphed with affection, not to me but to Jacqueline. And finally, I know that actress Barbara Bel Geddes and I are soul mates although we have never met, because she recently sent me a beautifully illustrated chil-dren's book she had written some years eariler, with the inscription *To Barbara Walters, because she loves children as much as I do.*

I would make an exception in cases where the children are older and are conspicuously drug or divorce prone. In such cases, the subject of children is taboo. No matter how much publicity the unhappy facts of a celebrity's private life have received, no one has the right to poke into them, unless the celebrity brings it up.

Safe subjects for conversation

In most cases, though, children are a safe subject. You can ask how many a celebrity has, how old they are, where are they, is he satisfied with their schools. If you're a parent too, you have common ground under your feet and room to be expansive. You can tell him that your child is older, or about the same age, or whatever, and that you have mixed feelings about the length of his hair, or that she collects lame animals of assorted and smelly varieties.

Keep it light; don't open the closet. This is no place to tell about the time your daughter ran away and was brought back by the police, or what the psychiatrist said last week, or the night your son cracked up a car. It's too heavy, too sad, too personal; resist the temptation to keep the celebrity's attention by playing Peyton Place and dramatizing the misfortunes of members of your family.

HOBBIES AND CAUSES

Besides, there are so many more stimulating subjects to explore. Many celebrities today have deep commitments or unusual hobbies outside of their professional lives. Comedian Orson Bean has established an ex-perimental school and has some thoughtful ideas about education re-

426

form; Dean Rusk is an authority on Thomas Jefferson; Candy Bergen is an expert photographer; Steve McQueen has a reverence for the art of driving racing cars.

When you've had some advance warning that you'll be meeting a celebrity, you can find this sort of background information from library reference books and biographies, or from newspaper files, or—if he is coming to give a lecture or promote a film—from the tour director or publicity man.

I have a fabulous friend named Lola, and when I talk of her, I always think of the song, "Whatever Lola Wants, Lola Gets." Lola is by occupation a housewife. She has a tall and very handsome husband, four children, but no actual claim to fame except for her interest in people and the time she takes to nourish her friendships. As a result, she numbers among her very close friends such varied celebrities as Alan King, Sheila MacRae, Jack Valenti, and John Huston. Lola and I were recently at a party that Alan King and his wife Jeanette gave in their beautiful Long Island home to honor Ethel Kennedy on her birthday. I was seated at dinner next to Indiana's attractive Senator Birch Bayh. The senator was being mentioned as a possible Democratic candidate for President and we talked about both his and my views of that possibility. But Lola stole the show and the senator when she was introduced over dessert. "Tell me, Senator Bayh," she began, starting slowly, "how are the tomatoes coming along?" The senator laughed out loud and asked how on earth she knew that he used to grow tomatoes and still loved to. Lola, who now had his complete attention, explained that she knew that he was going to be at the party and that she'd looked him up in a reference guide she had at her house, much as she would study a libretto of an unfamiliar opera before going to see it. She also knew a good deal more about the senator and was so refreshing and complimentary because she had done this homework that I lost the senator for the rest of the dinner. But it was worth it for the experience.

TWO DON'TS WHEN TALKING WITH CELEBRITIES

Now, every celebrity doesn't grow tomatoes and besides, you might be much more familiar with his work than his hobbies. A few cautions. One is to avoid pretending to be an authority when you're not. If you fake a knowledge of painting, he's likely to leave you stranded at once with talk of acrylics and collages and the New York influence, and he's certain to discover that you're a fraud.

Another hazard of conversation about careers is that many people mention only the obvious. They stress the best-known contribution of the celebrity's lifetime, which may not be at all his best work or his favorite one. I'll bet that Somerset Maugham was pretty depressed by people who remembered only his very early triumph *Of Human Bondage.* And there's a story that Norman Mailer, discouraged that people spoke only of his first novel *The Naked and the Dead,* was ecstatic when John F. Kennedy was introduced to him and said he had liked *Deer Park.* Rachmaninoff, they say, hated his two most celebrated preludes and called them "very bad music."

A humanized and deliberately provocative question has fewer snares. Ask a painter what is the most beautiful thing he has ever seen. Ask a writer how he first broke into print. (And *never* ask how he gets his ideas; that's trite.) Or ask the celebrity where he lives and if he likes it, or where he'd live if he could live anywhere. Ask a musician if it is a waste of time to go to the symphony if the music seems meaningless. Ask him how to inspire children to appreciate music. Ask him if music is an acquired taste.

First thing you know, the celebrity will be talking to this person—you. And you won't just be listening, you'll be talking, too, and, most important, you'll be having a good time.

Seven problems with celebrities

■ *Two celebrities at once:* When two celebrities are standing together, as may happen at a cocktail party or dinner, don't fall upon the one who is your favorite and ignore the other; it will make both of them uncomfortable. Say, "I'm so pleased to meet you both," and if you're going to linger, make sure you have a three-handed conversation. If the person with the celebrity doesn't look familiar, and even when you're introduced there are no bells of recognition sounding, make the assumption that the unknown person matters. Put out the same warmth and friendliness toward him that you aim at the famous person.

Remember, too, when meeting one celebrity, not to put him down by asking about another more famous person he may have worked with. For example, when Mike Nichols was directing his first motion picture, *Who's Afraid of Virginia Woolf?* the poor man was up to here from answering questions about his two illustrious stars Elizabeth Taylor and Richard Burton. But he gave me one of my best interviews, I think, because I began by saying, "Mr. Nichols, I'm not interested in hearing about Elizabeth Taylor or Richard Burton. I want to know about you." And you know what else? Eventually, of his own free will, he got around to talking about the Burtons.

■ *The author whose book you haven't read:* Don't bluff that you have read it, and don't apologize for "not having time"—that's weak—and don't tell him you're on the waiting list to get it from the library (his royalties come from sales, not rentals). If there is time beforehand and the book is nonfiction, do what I often do when I must talk with five authors a week. If the book is nonfiction, I read the first chapter and the last, and a few in between. If there isn't time, or I can't get a copy in a hurry, I try to find a review of the book. It is no substitute for having digested the entire book, but it's better than no preparation at all. Sometimes the subject matter can be a springboard for a discussion. If you know the author has written about urban decay, for instance, ask his opinion of what is happening in your city.

■ *Celebrities who don't like to talk:* This includes, surprisingly, those outgoing, funny comedians who seem so approachable that strangers hail them by their first names. Buddy Hackett and Red Skelton are perfect examples of this. They give the impression that they are gregarious to a fault, but away from the stage, neither is very communicative except with close friends. Alan King is the rare exception to this generalization. He has a wide range of interests from politics to religion and loves nothing better than a stimulating discussion. But very often, highly creative people who work alone—painters, poets, fiction writers, and musicians—are almost unable to relax in a social gathering. Don't be offended and don't be hearty; be gentle and calm and considerate, as you would be with anyone acutely nervous.

■ *The celebrity is black:* Many white people have a tendency to assure a Negro celebrity at once that they are glorious examples of liberal thinking. They tell ancedotes whose main point is that they have Negro friends, or that their children bring Negro friends home to play, or that they have supported Negro causes since the Montgomery bus strike of 1955. Or they ask him his opinion of the Black Panthers, or tell him how shocked they were by the killing of Martin Luther King, or they congratulate him for being a credit to his race. It's all a dead giveaway as far as the celebrity is concerned. As he sees the situation—accurately, I think—he isn't being treated as a flesh and blood man at all but as a representative black confronting a white conscience. That's prejudice;

> Dorothy Parker, asked by an annoying guest at a party if she had ever had her ears pierced, murmured, "No, but I have often had them bored."
>
> —*Louis Sobol*

it's sneaky, but that's what it is. And don't presume because you have a tender heart and have read *Malcolm X* that you appreciate the difficulties of being black. Unless you are black yourself, you can't possibly imagine what his life is like.

I remember my own experience that taught me this lesson. I was filming an interview with the brilliant and strikingly beautiful wife of Black Panther leader Eldridge Cleaver. I approached Kathleen Cleaver with great warmth and empathy as if to convey to her that I was completely open-minded about her cause. I thought that this would lead to a more relaxed and ultimately more probing interview. But Mrs. Cleaver made it clear to me that she was having none of me and my good intentions. Her attitude said, "Just ask your questions and I'll answer them, but don't try to pretend that you have any knowledge of what I've actually gone through."

So keep to the same topics that would interest you if he weren't a Negro: Ask him if he finds celebrity tours a strain; if he would prefer talking to a male or a female audience; ask for tips on packing a suitcase; ask about the children. And don't go overboard with gracious charm. As in "Some of my best friends are Jewish," oversolicitude is patronizing—and sometimes bigoted.

■ *The celebrity is an athlete:* Most men have no difficulty in talking to athletes and many, in fact, depend on sports for their small talk. President Richard Nixon, for instance, is said to use the subject of sports as his ice breaker. To make strangers feel more comfortable in his presence, he begins by discussing the latest football or baseball game and even if the guest knows little about the game, the President's enthusiasm alone warms the atmosphere. But here you are. You can't tell a goal line from a shoelace but you want to talk to the hulking hero anyway. I've had this problem when the *Today* program, for reasons of whimsy or "let's shake them up a bit," sometimes will assign our resident sports expert Joe Garagiola to comment on a fashion show and me to interview a football star. But whether I meet the athlete in front of television

430

cameras or at a dinner party, the technique is the same. I begin by explaining that I know he's world famous at what he does, but I must apologize because I know nothing about his sport. Clearly I can't discuss the technicalities of the game, and I don't try, but I am interested in *him*. I can ask what is the excitement of the game for him, how does his family feel about his playing, does his wife worry about his being hurt, does the traveling across time zones upset him, do his children want to be professional athletes and how does he feel about that. And unless it's really terribly funny or in his field, I don't inflict on him the story about the time I got a stiff neck at the tennis matches, or my hilarious attempts to skate. I know he'll be bored rigid.

■ *Almost celebrities:* The near-great live precariously, never quite achieving the warm safety of real fame and always anxious that what little they have may slip away. Their inner fear may show itself as brashness, or quick fury over imagined discourtesies, or arrogance. However difficult the personality, put yourself out to be kind. Treat him with the deference he desperately requires. The lesser his fame the greater may be his need for affectionate treatment.

■ *The celebrity is fading:* I'm usually apprehensive when interviewing a formerly great star who is no longer in the limelight. I know that the viewer is curious to learn how the aging actor or athlete is accepting time's attrition, but no one wants to obtain this information at the cost of the guest's pride. The best method, on television or anywhere else, is to put the crucial questions obliquely in the third person. Don't ask Joe DiMaggio how he felt to be sitting in the stands idly while the crowd roared for a younger slugger. Ask him instead to comment on Mickey Mantle's gloomy observation on retiring, "From now on, it's all downhill." In answering that, he's almost certain to draw in his own experiences as illustration. Or ask a once-successful actress what she thinks of Brigitte Bardot's remark, "The best years of my life were when I was seventeen." The attitude you take is that the star is handling himself or herself magnificently, an example to all of how a gradual withdrawal can be accomplished with dignity and grace. You want him to explain why others accept this inevitability with so much bitterness and desolation; the reply will reflect his own insight and experiences in a natural, relaxed way, since he won't be feeling defensive. In interviewing Ingrid Bergman, for instance, I complimented her sincerely on her frankness in admitting her age and asked if she felt that beautiful women in general had a more difficult time than others accepting age. I remarked truthfully to Rex Harrison, "You seem very happy, very much at peace," and he told me that "getting out of one's cradle is a very nice thing," and that he thinks he gets better parts now that he is middle-aged, and that he enjoys growing older.

Keep it positive, avoiding such negative openers as "What do you do with your time these days?" or, "We miss seeing you on television. Where have you been?" or, "It must be hard to be away from the stage for so long." If you really must explore a sensitive area such as a former drinking problem or an old scandal, again be indirect. For example, I might ask an actor who has had more than his share of ups and downs, "How do you feel about the public, which seems to swing from criticism to adulation and back again so easily?"

When I wanted Judy Garland to talk about her difficult childhood, I asked her how young people in show business today compared to her friends in the days when she was starting in vaudeville. And I got an answer that still makes me feel sad every time I recall the interview. "We all started too young in those days," she said. And then she added with a tiny smile, "You know my mother was the stage mother of all time. She really was a witch. If I had a stomachache and didn't want to go on, she would say 'get out on that stage or I'll wrap you around a bedpost.'"

The point is that if you ask a performer not about himself but about others, you will very often find that he will respond by talking most personally about himself.

Another tip on the same subject: Don't attempt to probe in sensitive areas right after the introduction. Talk about less personal matters until you've built up some feeling of trust and liking. Until the celebrity, or anyone for that matter, feels comfortable with you, it's not likely that he will feel like disclosing anything more intimate than his hat size.

Clare Boothe Luce, former ambassador to Italy, tells about a big reception in Rome when the handshaking line suddenly stopped, leaving a flustered American girl standing in front of the ambassador. "Oh, Mrs. Luce," she said, "it's so wonderful to be over here in Rome seeing all these old, romantic ruins—and you, too."
—*Ray Josephs in The American Weekly*

38

Ten conversation problems and how to solve them

Conversation is not always a pleasure. You may feel uncomfortable about talking to the newly bereaved or the handicapped. You are annoyed by bores and drunks. Here Miss Walters shows practical ways to handle these and other difficult situations and avoid conversational disaster.

Even the poised conversationalist can be undone by (1) the bore whose single topic is his family's motor trip to Yellowstone Park, complete with daily mileage and road conditions, or (2) the drunk who gets you into focus by closing one eye and bellowing, "You think you're pretty smart, don't you baby," or (3) the haggard soul whose woes are required listening as a proof of friendship.

However clever we are, there will be times when we can't escape the bore, the drunk, the lecher. And however soft-hearted or cowardly we may be, we all have one day to face up to speaking to bereaved friend or a handicapped person.

I've drawn up some suggestions for the most commonly encountered problem people, but you'll discover that I'm not in favor of escape as a unilateral policy. There are painful, tedious people in abundance and some of them must be suffered kindly, maybe even until they run out of things to say. In the world today we are more and more driven to depend on one another's sympathy and friendship in order to survive emotionally. Most suicides occur when a person feels totally alone.

Furthermore, warm, sustaining relationships become especially important during those periods when we are our least lovable. People bursting with good will and an abundance of mental health are charming company; their need for ego-boosting is minimal. People sinking into self-pity and depression are dreary, but they can't get out of it by themselves. So every now and then, just sit there and listen, and listen, and listen. You're paying your membership dues in the human race.

The newly bereaved

I interviewed Mamie Eisenhower in Augusta, Georgia, not long after General Eisenhower had died. When I asked her what she wanted to talk about, Mrs. Eisenhower replied firmly, "The happy times." She was suffering from laryngitis at the time and was concerned that people would misunderstand and think that she was struggling to keep from crying. She didn't want that kind of sympathy, and I think this holds true for most newly bereaved people. There's a long period after a death when self-control is fragile. Pity smashes it flat and leaves the bereaved person feeling naked and mortified.

Shortly after Robert Kennedy's funeral I talked to Rose Kennedy on *Today*. She had buried three sons and a daughter, and I asked her what gave her the courage to keep going. I'll never forget her answer. It was, "I refuse to be vanquished."

My friend Kitty Carlisle Hart, widow of the playwright-director Moss Hart, has the same indomitable spirit. When I asked her what she liked best and least to have strangers say to her, she answered, "I hate questions on what its like to be a widow. It implies pity, and I hate pity— self-pity or any other kind."

HOW TO OFFER CONDOLENCES

When meeting a friend for the first time after there has been a death close to him, it's appropriate to offer condolences. Keep it very brief and simple, just enough to express sorrow that it happened, and then ask a question that will allow the friend to keep his composure. It can be related to the death, but not to his feeling of loss. Ask if he plans to move, or if most of the family were able to attend the funeral, or if he plans to go away for a while.

If you can't think of something sufficiently neutral, talk of something else entirely. A friend of ours whose beloved brother had died met a mutual friend on the street the next day. She was close to tears and dreaded talking to him for fear of making a spectacle of herself, but it couldn't be avoided. He looked at her somberly for a moment and said,

"It's a damn shame," and then briskly told her how he'd been able to figure out that zoning problem that had been bothering her. She couldn't digest a word he was saying, but she remembers that she listened in a haze of gratitude for his tact.

You're going to have to use your own tact to gauge whether talk is what the grieving person wants or not. If you have privacy, and if the death was recent, it's more likely that the person will want to talk of nothing else, will *need* to talk of nothing else. There's a Hebrew proverb about "wearing out" grief—if you bottle it up, you'll never soften it. "Give sorrow words," said Shakespeare. "The grief that does not speak whispers the o'erfraught heart and bids it break."

WHEN TO TALK AND WHEN TO LISTEN

Once the hyperexcitement and drama of the funeral is passed, sorrow sets in for a long, heavy stay. There's no way out of it but to endure it.

When you're with someone who has had a recent loss, and wants to talk of nothing else, you're going to have to compose yourself for patient, sympathetic listening. Life isn't easy; every conversation can't be a joy. And in later years, he'll remember gratefully that you listened when he needed you most.

All grief is not for the dead. People show the same symptoms of grief —lassitude, preoccupation with one topic, a general grayness—when they have been through mutilating surgery, or when a marriage or a love affair has ended before they were ready, or when they've just moved from a place where they lived long and happily, or when their self-esteem has been punctured by the loss of a job or failure to be chosen for an expected honor.

Be tender; let them tell you how rotten they feel, and what a lousy world this is. Don't argue and try to point out that they have no problems. Sometimes, as with teenagers, just sympathetically saying, "I know, I know," helps. And have no illusion that they'll be comforted to know you went through something similar—they couldn't be less interested. Also, it's unfair to all concerned to try to share the load by hailing someone over to join you. Psychologists say that one-to-one relationships require the most sensitivity and inner resources of which we are capable: look at the practice you're getting.

Eventually there comes a time when it seems reasonable, at least to you, that the period of mourning should be over. You've heard the same tale of woe twenty times and concluded that the person is being morbid. It's time for him to move on, but you don't want to be ruthless about it.

Try steering the conversation to the happy times, or comment, "Anyone who has gone through so much must have learned from such an experience. What would you say has been the most useful lesson?"

There's something else that might work. A friend told me this shaggy dog story when I was in my teens and desolated because the current love of my life had just made a date with the high school *femme fatale*. It's about a rich man who hears that there are four words which will explain the secret of life, but they are known only to a very old hermit who is almost impossible to find. The man is so desperate to learn the four magic words that he travels the world over and finally he climbs the highest mountain in Tibet and there, exhausted and penniless, he locates the old man. And the old man haltingly tells him the secret of life, "This too shall pass."

The handicapped

A former radio and television actor whose career was ended by Parkinson's disease, the affliction that used to be called "shaking palsy," remarked that handicapped people hate to leave the sanctuary of their homes because of the eyes. There are eyes everywhere, he said: eyes that slide away in revulsion or dislike, eyes that fill with that crippler pity, eyes that go blank, eyes that stare.

The sweetest encounter he ever had with a stranger occurred in England one evening when he was struggling along a country path. He met a schoolboy of about ten, who watched him with frank curiosity. "Is there something the matter with your leg?" the boy asked conversationally. "Yes," the man replied. "Oh, sir," said the boy, "I *am* sorry."

What the actor found endearing about that simple exchange was its honesty. Handicapped people can learn to cope with their affliction in time, but the embarrassment that their affliction causes others is almost unbearable.

The significant factor to keep in mind when talking to someone handicapped is he's *only* handicapped, not dying. Don't offer to help unless he asks for it, don't flutter and don't talk in hushed, mournful tones.

Perhaps the most difficult interview I ever had on *Today* was with a young man named Robert Smithdas. He was a remarkable person, deaf and blind, the only one with this multiple handicap since Helen Keller to get a master's degree. He went even further, obtained his doctorate, and now helps to teach others who are deaf and blind.

We communicated by his putting his thumb against my lips when I talked. His sensitivity was so acute that he could lip-read that way. Before the interview, his colleagues told me that I should treat him without embarrassment or pity, so I "chatted" with him until he felt at ease with me, and I with him, and then I was able to ask him many questions about his personal life and adjustment to his great handicap. I found he wanted me to ask these questions, wanted the public to understand.

I concluded by asking what he would most want people to know about his condition and he replied, "Please make it clear that we handicapped are not freaks, but feeling human beings."

In most circumstances where you are uncertain about your behavior, let the other person take the lead. Maybe he'd rather talk of trivialities while you both get your bearings, and maybe he's come to a time and place where he wants to unburden some of his agony. The choice is his, not yours.

We once had Mercedes McCambridge on *Today* and I was introducing her as a fine actress who in the past was an alcoholic. "Not *was* an alcoholic," she corrected me emphatically, "*is* an alcoholic." With that she began to talk about alcoholism and her long struggle with it in a moving monologue that I wouldn't have interrupted if I could. It went on for all the seven minutes of our allotted time, at the conclusion of which I opened my mouth for the first time since the introduction and said, "Thank you, Miss McCambridge." Letters from viewers subsequently confirmed my own feeling that it was one of the most effective "interviews" on *Today*.

In summary, the best advice I can give you is to treat the handicapped person with honesty, which means that you acknowledge that he has a handicap and make whatever adjustments are absolutely essential. But don't make the handicap more important than he is.

Relatives of the handicapped

It is wise and kind to stay away from the topic of a handicapped daughter or husband, or whoever, when you meet the relatives. If they don't mention the disability of their own accord, consider the subject forbidden. No matter how you think you can legitimize your curiosity by saying you have a friend with a similar situation, you're still taking liberties with private pain.

Increasingly, however, people have a healthy, open attitude about such matters as mental illness or mental retardation in their families. For centuries people had such intense shame about any variation from normal appearance or behavior that the victims were hidden in attics or institutions so relatives could pretend they didn't exist. Joseph and Rose Kennedy played a significant part in dispelling ancient superstitions and prejudices by refusing to hide the fact of their retarded daughter. Former Vice President Hubert Humphrey and his wife have also helped by their public acceptance and affection for their retarded granddaughter.

Muriel Humphrey spoke with me of this little girl on *Today* and impressed everyone with her lack of embarrassment or mawkishness. When I asked her about the child, Mrs. Humphrey answered, "Oh, she's just fine. I've been out in Waverly with her and we've had the grandchildren at the lake with us, and Vicky remembered how to swim from last year. And she's growing up to be such a nice young lady. She's seven and a half now and she's learning to read. So she has many possibilities ahead of her. She's doing very well."

Obviously, to discuss a relative's handicap is a decision that must be made within the individual, consulting whatever wisdom and courage is available. More and more people are making the decision I did, believing that they can ease some of the dark fears by sharing their experience. But many still can't bring themselves to talk about it, and I understand that too.

Never introduce the subject yourself, but if the person you're talking to is able to mention a mentally ill mother or a retarded child, don't flinch. Tell him that you think it is wonderful that he can be so open about it. Encourage him; if more people could stop feeling threatened by such family tragedies, all of society would give a sigh and relax a bit.

The bore

A bore has feelings. Very often he will interrupt something boring he is saying to comment that he is a bore.

If he is boring you, maybe it's your fault. "Being interested makes one interesting," Dr. Erich Fromm observed, to which I would add that you generally get out of a conversation what you put into it.

Regard the bore: He has fashioned for himself a social personality that he hopes will be a winner. He's afraid of awkward silences, afraid of being abandoned, afraid that if he stops talking he will have stopped existing. So he drones on, disgusted with himself but hopeful that this one time people will find him fascinating.

HOW TO SAVE A BORE FROM HIMSELF

You can bail him out by *insisting* that he be sprightly. The topic he has chosen isn't doing much for either of you, so change it drastically. There are subjects on which he can't be boring because he hasn't talked about them seventy-six times, hasn't even thought about them until you mentioned them. How about, does he think most men are uncomfortable with women? or, why is our society so concerned with hair—is it a sex symbol? or, what teacher helped him the most when he was a child?

You can also try whatever provocative subject is in vogue; there's bound to be one making the rounds, a guaranteed grabber. Pick whatever is current and choice, and ask the bore to comment on it. What he says may make you angry, but at least you won't be bored.

Is the problem that your particular bore talks so loud that he's giving you a headache? Lower your own voice to a near whisper. It has the effect of making him aware of his noise, in contrast to your softness. Night club singers use the same trick when audiences make too much clatter—they make themselves almost inaudible, and people quiet down to listen.

There are some desperation gambits when all else fails with the bore. If you're eating together, you can try talking about the hospital experiment in which volunteers can select any menu at all, but must eat exactly the same food in exactly the same amounts for thirty days. What would he eat? Ask him if people were colors, what color would he be? What color would his wife be? His boss? If he were an animal, what kind of animal would he be? Remind him that in George Orwell's *1984* the hero and heroine were broken because Big Brother discovered the one thing both dreaded most in the world. What is the one thing he couldn't stand?

Truman Capote has a natural gift that makes him a great guest at a dinner party: he is *always* interested in whomever he's talking to. One of the reasons Truman is always interested in people is that he won't allow himself to be bored. He told me that when he meets a truly crashing bore he asks himself, "Why am I so bored? What is it about this person that is making me yawn?" He ponders, "What should this person do that he hasn't done? What does he lack that might intrigue me?"

He catalogs thoughtfully the bore's face, his hair style, his mannerisms, his speech patterns. He tries to imagine how the bore feels about himself, what kind of a wife he might have, what he likes and dislikes. To get the answers, he starts to ask some of these questions aloud. In short, Truman gets so absorbed in finding out why he is bored that he is no longer bored at all.

The drunk

I'm afraid I don't suffer drunks gladly, even comical ones. There's one variety of drunk who is turning up more and more regularly on the social scene: the woman-hater. He's the kind of man who conceals his resentment of women when he is sober. His wife is washed out, his secretary harassed, and his mother hated him. As he drinks, he gets testier on the topic of pushy women, and when he is ripe he'll find one of the successful women in the crowd and tell her off.

The most graceful rescue I've ever witnessed happened one evening at a party Kitty Carlisle Hart had given. A drunken actor was taking off on me when Kitty suddenly appeared at his elbow. "Oh John," she said to him, beaming, "that's just how you used to insult me. You remember that time at Peter's when . . ." And she led him away, brightly recalling other days and other parties.

If there isn't such a resourceful angel to help you in such a situation, call someone over to join you and the drunk. Then either he will stop the personal invective or else the newcomer will come to your support. Try to move the conversation from the particular (you) to the general

A well-known bore was seated opposite James McNeill Whistler at a dinner party. During a lull in the conversation, he leaned toward the artist and said, "You know, Mr. Whistler, I passed your house this morning."

"Thank you," said Whistler quietly. "Thank you very much."

—*Mrs. Grace M. Warner*

(life); try to edge the drunk into a larger group. Whatever you do, slip away as quickly as you can and stay out of range for the evening.

If, on the other hand, the drunk is someone important to you, your boss or a close friend, and you don't want him to be contrite about his condition for the rest of your relationship, *you* pretend to be sick, and leave. The next day you telephone to apologize to him for having to slip away early.

When the drunk is a woman, a particularly unattractive situation, try to help. Tell her the noise of the party is getting you down and you'd like to slip upstairs to a quiet room for a cup of coffee, and would she please come with you? If you were about to leave, ask if you can drop her off and you'll have an opportunity to visit together on the way. Suggest you both find the powder room, and take the long route.

If she won't budge, and as a last resort only, suggest to her escort that he'd better take her home. In the case of a male drunk who is out of control, have his wife or a friend remove him from the premises. In either case, the light touch works best.

The Casanova

First of all, don't take him seriously. Unless you are alone on the sixth fairway at two in the morning—and how did you get there anyway? My own opinion is that there's far too little flirtation in our country as is. Most attractive males talk to most attractive women as if they were Rotarians comparing sales percentages in Des Moines. A European, on the other hand, or his rare American counterpart, breathes a little faster when talking to a good-looking woman. His eyes get brighter and some-how, for you anyway, the room gets brighter.

So be grateful. Even a man known to be on the prowl has *some* taste and he picked you.

If you are the object of a drunken pass, which admittedly is tasteless, don't get angry and tell him off, and don't bring it up the next day. It was annoying, that's true; but don't make a big thing of it.

Most verbal advances are the male's sniff of the wind. Is the girl available, or isn't she? He's entitled to one exploratory maneuver. If you're not available, *really not,* he is likely to feel the total lack of vibrations and drop the pursuit. If you're confused, or if you're feeling lonely at the time, or if you've had a fight with the man in your life and you're thinking of revenge, the Casanova will get the subliminal message that he can proceed. Then if matters get out of hand, it's hardly fair to play the outraged maiden.

Occasionally such men are so vain that they block out all the negative signals. Then I suggest you try scaring him to death. I knocked off a persistent knee grabber at a dinner party by looking into his eyes and purring, "You're right. We *are* meant for each other. Why don't you divorce your wife and marry me?" He has avoided me evermore.

The fighter

Into each life, alas, some verbal fists must fall. We all have had the experience, one time or another, of meeting someone whose conversational opener is a kick in the stomach. They start out with something like, "How are the peaceniks making out these days?" or, "You rich people really kill me." A friend of mine who helped to sponsor a youth hostel was asked by a stranger she'd just met, "Are you still hanging around with those long-haired freaks?"

The resultant conversation is not likely to be rich in human warmth. Don't waste your charm and logic on him; listen briefly to whatever destruction he stocks and then exit diplomatically by telling him that obviously he has given the matter a good deal of thought (a nice touch of irony there) and it was interesting to hear his views.

If, however, you're in a mood for a scrap when someone insults you, and you're sure you can keep your control, go ahead and defend your views. You can't possibly change his mind, but you'll sleep better.

The gossip

Gossip can be fun when it's gossip about famous people who'll never hear of your discussion and couldn't care less if they did. For me, gossip about Liz and Richard, or Jackie and Ari, is entirely fair, enormously interesting, and probably completely untrue. But gossip about people you know is not only morally wrong, it is also tactically wrong because it almost always gets back to the person involved.

And don't kid yourself into false virtue because you kept silent when others were lacerating someone's reputation. You're never just a spectator: Unless you put a stop to it, you're a participant. Change the subject in a firm voice; say, "I like Jane very much and I'm sure none of us here is glad that she's having problems. Let's talk about something else,

FIVE WAYS TO SAY NO

ALMOST EVERY DAY many of us are caught in positions where we should logically say No, but don't. However, there are several reasonable and friendly ways of saying No.

1. *Put it on an impersonal basis.*

One of the most serene housewives in town says she achieved her serenity when she licked the problem of saying No.

When a salesman knocks at her door, she is polite but firm: "My husband won't let me buy anything at the door."

2. *Make it clear that you would like to say Yes.*

Tim Gammon, at the Liberty Mutual Insurance Co., is in charge of adjusting claims. Gammon often has to say No. However, he always shows sympathy for the claimant. He explains that morally he may agree with him, but legally his hands are tied.

3. *Say No by helping the person say No to himself.*

One successful interior decorator claims he never says No to his clients' impractical ideas. Instead he educates them to say Yes to what he wants them to do. He tells about a woman who preferred an inappropriate flowery chintz curtain material. The decorator suggested: "Let's see just what you want your curtains to do." He talked about what fabrics would harmonize best with the modern décor. Soon the woman had completely forgotten chintz.

4. *In saying No, show what needs to be done to get a Yes.*

Dr. William Reilly, author of *Successful Human Relations*, advises business executives how to handle the man who wants a raise but doesn't deserve it.

"Yes, George, I understand your need for a raise. However, to give it to you we will have to make you more valuable to the company. Now let's see what we need to do. . . ."

5. *Most important, say your No in the nicest, warmest way you can.*

An effusive elderly woman who had decided to become pals with her young neighbor asked, "Cindy, would you like to come up to my house and play tomorrow?"

Cindy's face broke into a big warm grin as she said, "No." Her No was friendly and good-humored. But it was so unmistakably firm that the matter ended there.

like what I've been wondering about these past few minutes—who do you think gossips more, men or women?"

I guarantee that the resultant debate will be much snappier than the original gossip.

Of course, there's always the classic line when someone is running down a mutual friend. You look amazed and say, "Funny, she always speaks so well of you." I dare the gossip to go on after that, especially if you follow up your line with a compliment that the friend actually paid the gossip in your hearing.

Conversely, if you meet someone who you've heard has made a bitchy comment about you, try to be big about it. We all have said unkind things that we didn't really mean, tricked by something nervous in the situation or in ourselves. Sometimes people gossip just because they feel they must in order to be interesting.

If the gossip is someone you like and respect normally, tell her or him that you've heard he has a gripe about you and you'd like to straighten it out with him. Maybe it was a misunderstanding which can be cleared up then and there. Or maybe the criticism was deserved, in which case you can learn from it. There *is* such a thing as constructive criticism.

I once asked Mrs. Spiro Agnew on *Today* about personal criticism, wondering if it bothered her that her husband sometimes received so much of it. She replied serenely, "You can't have everyone love you."

Not many people have that much composure. Mrs. John V. Lindsay has a well-deserved reputation for being refreshingly honest. The first time I interviewed her on the *Today* show, I asked what she would do if someone seated her at a dinner party next to William Buckley, who had said cutting things about her husband during their mayoralty campaign. Said Mary Lindsay, "I'd get the flu."

People who reveal all

From the reporter's point of view, nothing could be finer than a President who replies to a question about his operation by pulling out his shirt and showing the scar. But the news value is absent when an acquaintance at a cocktail party wants to tell you about her alcoholic father or her concern that her husband is impotent.

It may be that the intimate disclosure is of a nature that touches on your experience and you can handle the conversation sympathetically.

Then your calm acceptance can be a big help. But keep in mind if you encourage her to talk about the problem that she may hate herself tomorrow morning because she was so frank, and she may blame you for her indiscretion.

If, on the other hand, you want to beat a retreat from the subject, don't fake understanding. Your discomfort will ultimately show itself and seem like righteousness or rejection. You must divert her at once. Find something positive to say, along the lines of, "I always knew that you were under some kind of strain and I guess almost everyone is, but I admire so much the way you handle your relationship with your children." Or how many activities she juggles without looking frazzled. Or what a helpful person she is, and how people respect her.

If the disclosure is about a marital problem or a falling out between two of your friends, *never referee*. They may forgive one another, but they'll never forgive you. At one point during our engagement, my husband and I decided to break it off. A friend congratulated him warmly, assuring him he was well out of that match. We still see that friend from time to time, distantly.

Tell the wailing one, "I love you both, but I won't let you tell me about this trouble because it hurts me too much." Or say, "I'm not a peacemaker. I'll just stay here on the sidelines and hold both coats."

The foul-mouthed

Obscene language at social gatherings as often comes from women as it does from men. I suppose the ladies see it as a mark of emancipation, catching the late comedian Lenny Bruce's technique but not his message. His use of four-lettered words was intended to force audiences to confront their stuffiness and prepare them to accept change. The underground press is still mired in the conviction that obscenity is change itself and the hallmark of the revolution.

Adults, however, can surely demonstrate that they are contemporary and liberal with better style. I pay no attention to an obscene word uttered once or twice—it could be a slip, and besides I've read better in books and heard worse in movies. But after the fifth time I say, "If you're trying to shock me, you're not. What you are doing by trying so hard, though, is offending me."

Dirty jokes also leave me unimpressed. I've confronted my own stuffiness, and I've decided to keep it.

39

How you come across on the telephone

Do you know the proper way to answer a home phone? An office phone? How do you place a business call? What's the best method of cutting off a long-winded caller? Learn the answers to these and other questions about what has become our most-used form of communication.

When you talk on the telephone, in your home or in an office, the quality of your voice and your ability to express yourself clearly and concisely are very important. The person at the other end of the line cannot see your facial expressions or gestures, and the impression he receives must depend entirely on what he hears.

The telephone is designed to carry your voice at its natural volume and pitch. It is not necessary to shout. In fact, raising your voice, especially during a long-distance call, will only distort it. The telephone mouthpiece should be held about one inch from your lips and the earpiece close to your ear. Speak clearly and distinctly, with the same inflections that you would use in a face-to-face conversation. If you must put the telephone down during the conversation, do it gently, and when you hang up, do not slam the receiver down. The person at the other end may still have the phone close to his ear, and the sudden sharp bang can be deafening.

The correct way to answer a home telephone is still "Hello." "Yes" is abrupt and a bit rude, but "This is Mrs. Jones's house" leaves the door standing open wide, and "Mrs. Jones speaking" leaves her without chance of retreat.

This is not nonsense. It is a really important aspect of modern telephone technique. In all big cities telephones are rung so persistently by every type of stranger who wants to sell something to Mrs. House-holder, to ask a favor of Mrs. Prominent, or to get in touch with Mr. Official (having failed to reach him at his office) that many people are obliged to keep their personal telephone numbers unlisted. The last thing that they want to do, therefore, is to announce, "Miss Star speak-ing." It is far more practical to say "Hello" and let the one calling ask, "Is Miss Star there? Mr. Director would like to speak to her." If she her-self answers, she simply says, "Yes, this is Miss Star speaking."

"WHO'S CALLING, PLEASE?"

When the telephone in the home is answered by someone other than the head of the household, the response to "May I speak to Mrs. Brown, please?" is usually "Just a moment, please." But if Mrs. Brown has told the maid, or a child, that she is very busy and cannot take any calls, the one who answers is correct in saying, "Mrs. Brown can't come to the phone just now; may I have your name, and she will call you as soon as she can."

If the caller should say, "I want to speak to Mrs. Brown personally," whoever has answered replies, "I'm sorry, but I can't interrupt Mrs. Brown. May I give her a message?" If the caller still refuses to leave a message or give his name, he can hardly expect Mrs. Brown to speak to him.

Some women instruct their maids or their children to ask, "Who is calling, please?" so that they are prepared when they reach the tele-phone. However, others feel that this gives an impression of prying and may prefer "Just a moment, please."

When a woman is alone in the house, she definitely *should* ask "Who is calling?" before giving out any information as to her husband's whereabouts or return. This is not only correct—it's a necessary safety precaution.

Whether to give your name with or without title is a frequent ques-tion. When talking with strangers, titles are always used, but in other situations usage may vary.

The following rules hold good: An older person announcing herself or himself to someone much younger says, "This is Mrs. Elder" or "Miss Senior" or "Mr. Elder."

A younger lady, whether married or single, says, "This is Marie Man-ners." To an older woman whom she knows socially she says, "Hello,

Mrs. Knox? This is Mary Bailey." Mrs. Knox answers, "Good morning, Mrs. Bailey!" (Or "Mary," if she knows her well.)

A gentleman calling a lady never, under any circumstances, announces himself to her as "Mr. Smart." Instead, if the call is social, he says, "This is George Smart."

If you are a young man calling a friend and the answering voice is that of a friend or a member of the friend's family, you say, "This is Jim Brown," or probably "This is Jim." If the voice is unfamiliar, you say, "This is Mr. James Brown. May I speak to Mr. Allen Gray?" or if the friend is the only man in the house, "to Mr. Gray."

Invitations by telephone

When Mrs. Jones issues an invitation by telephone, there is no long conversation, but merely:

Mrs. Jones: "Is that you Sally? This is Helen Jones." (*If she is much older* than Sally, she would say "This is Mrs. Jones.") "Could you and your husband (or John) dine with us next Tuesday?"

Sally: "I'm sorry we can't. We are going to the theater Tuesday night," or "We'd love to." And probably she repeats "Next Tuesday at eight" to be sure there is no misunderstanding of date or time. Before hanging up, she would add, "Thanks so much," or "We look forward to it."

It is not correct to preface an invitation with, "Hello, John. What are you doing Saturday night?" or, "Are you going to be busy Monday afternoon?" This maneuver puts John in the embarrassing position of saying "Nothing" and then wanting to refuse after being told that he is expected to dine with the Borings or to play bridge with the Revokes. On the other hand, if he answers, "I have an engagement" and is then told that he would have been invited to something he likes very much, it is disappointing not to be able to go—without seeming rude to the person he has at first refused. A young woman who says she has an engagement and is then told, "Too bad you can't come, because John Bril-

Small boy on telephone, as teen-age sister rushes to grab it: "You must have the wrong number. I don't have a beautiful sister."
—*Hank Ketcham in Woman's Home Companion*

liant was looking forward to meeting you," cannot change her mind and say, "Oh, then I'll get out of my dinner somehow and come." To do so would be the height of rudeness to all concerned.

In responding to a telephone invitation, it is very rude to say, "I'll let you know," unless it is immediately followed by an explanation such as "I'll have to ask John if he has made any commitments for that weekend," or "We have tickets for the high school play for that night, but perhaps I can exchange them for two on Friday." Without this sort of definite reason, "I'll let you know" sounds as if you were waiting for a better invitation to come along before saying Yes.

Three important don'ts

When you get a wrong number, don't ask, "What number is this?" Ask instead, "Is this Main 2–3456?" so that you can look it up again or dial more carefully the next time.

Don't answer and then say, "Wait a minute" and keep the caller waiting while you vanish on an errand of your own. If the doorbell is ringing and you can't listen at that moment, say "I'll call you back in a few minutes!" And do so.

Don't let too young a child answer the telephone. A lot of the caller's time is wasted trying to make the child understand a message and relay it to the right person. If there is a long silence, there is no way of knowing whether the child is hunting for Mother or playing with his dog.

Ending telephone calls

Under ordinary circumstances, the one who makes the call is the one who ends it. This is not a matter of great importance, but it is helpful to know if a call seems to be dragging on and getting nowhere. The caller simply says, "I'm so glad I reached you—we'll be looking forward to seeing you on the seventh. Good-by," or any appropriate remark.

We have all been trapped on the telephone by a long-winded caller —a determined salesman, perhaps, or a loquacious friend. When you have made several tentative efforts to end the conversation, which have been completely ignored, you may take more aggressive measures. At the first pause, or even interrupting if necessary, you may say, "I'm terribly sorry, but I simply must hang up—the baby's crying," or "My bath is running over," or even, "I'm late for an appointment now."

Another occasion on which a call should be ended quickly is when the person who receives it has a visitor—either in a business office or at home. It is very inconsiderate to carry on a long chat while your visitor tries to occupy the time and avoid listening to your conversation. When you answer the phone and find it is not a call which will be over in a moment or two, you should postpone it for a more convenient time. At home you might say, "Joan just dropped in for a visit, so may I call you back in a little while?" The businessman could say, "I have a customer with me at the moment. If you will give me your number, I'll call you back when I am free."

In either case, be sure that you do return the call as soon as you can.

The business telephone

When telephone calls go through a switchboard, the operator often answers the ring by giving the name of the company. Some firms, however, feel that a more friendly impression is made on the caller by the greeting "ABC Company, good morning," or "Good afternoon, ABC Company."

When the call goes directly through to an office or has been trans-

THE TELEPHONE COURTESY TEST

IF IT INTERESTS YOU to know how good your telephone manners may be, the number of times you can answer "Yes" to the following questions will give you your rating. If every one is "Yes," you deserve not merely a crown, but a halo!

1. Do you make sure of the correct number so as not to risk disturbing strangers by "calling from memory"?

2. Do you make sure that your conversations with busy people are as brief as possible?

3. When calling intimate friends who do not recognize your voice, do you resist playing a game of "guess who?" and announce yourself promptly?

4. Do you try to time your calls so as not to interfere with the occupations of those you call most often?

5. Do you make business calls well before the close of office hours,

ferred by the switchboard operator, the person answering should identify himself and his department: "Mr. Hugo, accounting department." If a secretary answers she should give her employer's name as well as her own: "Mr. Carlson's office, Miss Norton speaking." If her employer is not in, or if she wishes to protect him from unnecessary calls, she should then offer to help the caller if she can, or if not, take a message: "He's not available at the moment. May I take a message?" or "He's out of the office just now. May I have him call you?" or "He's attending a meeting this morning. Could I help you?" If he is in his office, she asks, "May I tell him who is calling?" Any of these phrases should elicit the necessary information without the abruptness of "Who's calling?" But if the caller is evasive, you may have to ask for his name more directly. "Who is calling, please?" is sometimes necessary.

PLACING A BUSINESS CALL

When placing a call, be sure that you have the correct number. Next to all business phones there should be a list of the numbers frequently called.

As soon as your call is answered, you must identify yourself; and unless the person you are calling knows you well, you must also name

especially if you are calling a person whom you know is a commuter?

6. In a business office, do you explain to personal friends inclined to talk at length that you will call them after hours?

7. Do you treat wrong-number calls as a mutual inconvenience and answer, "Sorry, wrong number," in a tone of polite sympathy instead of showing ill-tempered annoyance?

8. On a dial telephone, do you always wait for the dial tone?

9. When the number you are calling is not answered quickly, do you wait long enough for someone to lay aside what he or she may be doing and to reach the telephone? It is very annoying to have been disturbed just to pick up the telephone and find the caller has hung up.

10. When making a number of calls on a party line, do you space them so that others on the line may have a chance to use their telephones?

In the midst of a busy morning, the county agricultural agent got a call from a woman who said she was starting a chicken farm and wanted to know how long to leave the rooster with the hens.

"Just a minute," said the agent, who was busy on another phone.

"Thank you very much," said the woman, and hung up.

—*Bert Gustavson*

your organization. "This is Mr. Kramer of the Hobbs Company. May I speak to Mr. Hughes?"

It is not correct for a salesman to announce himself as Sam Sales to the operator or secretary who answers. He says, "This is Mr. Sales of the Blank Company." But when he reaches the person he is calling, he omits the "Mr." and uses "Sam."

Similarly, a young woman in business says, "This is Miss Caesar of the Wheel Tire Company," and with the person she is calling uses "Jane Caesar."

All names must be given as briefly but as explicitly and as clearly as is humanly possible.

The most discourteous telephone habit is that of the businessman who tells his secretary to call Mr. Jones and then is not waiting to take the call. For example, the secretary dials the number; a voice announces, "A. B. Jones Company"; the secretary says, "Mr. Frank Brown is calling Mr. Jones." Promptly Mr. Jones says, "Hello, Frank," but instead of hearing Frank's voice, he hears a secretary explain, "Mr. Brown is busy on another wire. He'll be with you in a moment." Mr. Jones listens good-temperedly a few seconds—and less patiently for more seconds. Mr. Brown is evidently unaware that seconds seem minutes to a busy person listening to a dead receiver.

The correct form for a wife calling her husband at his office is, "This is Mrs. Jones; is Mr. Jones in?"

Long-distance calls

When making a long-distance call, remember not to shout—amplifiers on the circuits will step up your voice all the way. On some overseas calls, it is also important to wait for the other person to finish speaking before you start. It can be a one-way-at-a-time circuit, and if both speak at once, both are shut off until one or the other stops talking. Keep on the tip of your tongue what you have to say, and say it promptly. If you have several things to say, write them down and read them off.

test your skills

HOW YOU COME ACROSS ON THE PHONE

Answer the following True or False:

1. A person calling a business office should announce himself to the secretary as "Mr. Hook of Brown and Smith," and when he gets the person he wants, say, "This is Bryce Hook."

2. A housewife properly answers the phone, "Sally Silt speaking."

3. It is improper to ask a caller to identify himself before answering his questions.

4. An older person calling a younger person introduces himself with his full name, "Wally Troll calling."

5. A woman who introduces herself as Mary Smith should not be addressed by the person she introduces herself to as "Mary."

6. It is a good idea to begin an invitation by checking a person's availability: "What are you doing Friday night?"

7. A person who gets a wrong number should apologize and say, "What number is this?"

8. It is never acceptable to end a conversation until the caller terminates it.

9. Democratic practice calls for introducing yourself to whoever answers the phone by your first name: "This is Jake Freely calling."

10. Because of the need for efficiency in offices it is permissible for a person to initiate a call on a second line after he has put in a call on the first line and to ask the person to "please wait a minute."

11. Women do not refer to themselves as Miss or Mrs. when using their full name: "This is Miss Mary Smith." "This is Mrs. Eve Adams."

12. When receiving a telephoned invitation it is proper to reply, "I'll let you know," before committing yourself, in case something better turns up.

13. An invitation should be preceded by a lengthy conversation.

14. As a simple precaution a housewife does not identify herself upon answering the phone.

15. Friends have an obligation to recognize your voice immediately so it is not necessary to identify yourself when phoning.

Answers to this quiz appear on page 705.

40

How to handle
an interview

You've learned to write résumés and letters of application. But equally important in getting a job is the way you conduct yourself at the interview. What will the interviewer be looking for? How will you sound to him? Here are pointers to help you put your best foot forward.

Just as the purpose of the résumé is to sell yourself to the point of an interview, so the purpose of the interview is to sell yourself into the job. The word "interview" is derived from words meaning "sight between" or "view between." In employment, the interview is a meeting between two people, the employer and the applicant. The purpose of this meeting is for the employer to get a view of the applicant, and for the applicant to get a view of the employer. The employer's aim during the interview is to find out if the applicant can be of service to the company; the applicant's aim is to find out if the company can be of service to him.

During your first interview for a position, your skills and abilities are in the background. The prospective employer knows that training for a specific job often requires a comparatively short time, but undesirable personal traits can take a long time to correct. Therefore, the employer prefers to hire people with positive, rather than negative, personal qualities—people he can depend on in their work.

The fundamental quality all employers demand of their employes is honesty. Honesty means that you not only refrain from stealing and lying, but also that you do a full day's work without supervision, are punctual, and have respect for the rights of others as well as a sense of justice and fair play in all your dealings. A prospective employer will not question you directly about your honesty, but he will look for signs of this trait in your attitude and conduct. Never lie on an application form or during an interview. If a prospective employer suspects you of dishonesty in even a small thing, he may disqualify you immediately, no matter how impressive your other qualifications may be.

The important qualities of consideration for others and a sense of responsibility are related to honesty. You must convince your prospective employer that you will fit harmoniously into his organization and will be a dependable and diligent employe. When an employer chooses a married man of thirty-five with a wife and children rather than a bachelor of the same age, it is usually because the employer expects that the married man with family obligations will have a greater sense of responsibility than will a single person accustomed to thinking only of himself. The bachelor, therefore, should draw attention to any of his activities that require cooperation with, and responsibility for, others. A married man, of course, cannot rely solely on his married status as proof of a considerate and responsible nature; he should also suggest these qualities by his general attitude and conduct.

Know your own goals

A prospective employer is interested in your sense of values and your attitude toward your work. What are you seeking in a lifetime job? What are your inner drives? Are you very ambitious or only moderately so—and why? What do you want to achieve through your work? Inner fulfillment through the use of your talents? Contribution to society? Fame? Political power? Position in society? Wealth? Home comforts? Ease in retirement? Job security? Travel? Before applying for a job, be sure you know why you want that job or a particular salary. The interviewer will try to find out. Do not answer his questions with, "Money," but go beyond that. Explain your motivation in terms of basic goals. Clarify these goals in your own mind first, so that you can talk about them intelligently and clearly when called upon to do so.

In addition to making certain of your soundness of character and basic motivation, an employer wants to know whether you have good judgment in matters relating to your work. This quality is sometimes referred to as "occupational intelligence." Employers know that it takes more than the mastery of certain skills to function successfully in a job.

455

They want people who are aware of the complexities of a job, understand the personal relationships it involves, and are resourceful in meeting new or difficult situations. An occupationally intelligent person knows the value of time—the time that belongs to him and the time that belongs to his employer. He is alert to errors and to new information that will improve his efficiency. If you are such a person, you have the qualifications that employers value highly.

An employer is always interested in any special talents or exceptional qualities that a job applicant may have, such as unusual creativity, imagination, analytical skill, or leadership and executive ability. If you have any one of these proficiencies to a marked degree, you should bring it to the attention of your prospective employer. If you reorganized a department in another company, thereby increasing efficiency, or if you won a prize for accomplishments related to your work, tell him about it.

Six keys to making a good impression

■ The most obvious of your personal traits are your physical appearance, deportment, and speech. We all form our first, and sometimes lasting, impressions of other people on the basis of these external features. If an employer's first impression of you is unfavorable, it will be that much more difficult for you to make an effective presentation.

The starting points for an attractive physical appearance are cleanliness and neatness. Do you spend a half hour in the morning and a half hour at night on personal grooming? Is your hair neat and becomingly styled? What about your attire? Find out early in life what type of clothing is right just for you, not anyone else; seek the advice of a professional in that field, if necessary. Wear the appropriate clothes for the occasion. For a job interview, you need business clothes, not those you would wear to a sports event. The interviewer will draw conclusions from your apparel before you have said a word. He will notice the cut and quality of a man's suit, the harmonious nature of a woman's outfit. Take a critical look at yourself in the mirror. If you see anything that can be improved, start at once. Let your physical appearance play a positive role in getting the job.

■ Good deportment should complement a pleasing physical appearance. Know the essentials of good manners and practice them with everyone until they become automatic. Good manners are unobtrusive.

They consist of behavior that is appropriate, considerate, and natural. To eliminate any irregularities in your deportment, study people with social charm and poise. Notice their behavior with men and women. Good manners will help you at all stages of your career.

■ Certain expressions and mannerisms invariably create a poor impression. You should know what they are so that you can avoid them. For example, in a personal interview do not try to show that you are at ease by using such unbusinesslike expressions as "between you and me," "I wouldn't tell this to everyone," "gee," or "My God!" Be friendly but not familiar. Avoid gestures that might distract the interviewer from the matter at hand. Do not play with your hair, clean your teeth with your tongue, examine your nails, scratch an ear, or fasten your gaze on a picture hanging a little to one side of the interviewer. Above all, do not haul out your cigarette pack, light up with a kitchen match, and seeing no ashtray, drop the ashes on the floor.

■ Are you a good listener? This quality is as important in business as it is in social situations. At work you will have to listen to other people constantly: to your subordinates, your associates, your superiors, and your clients or customers. What the other person is saying is just as important to him as what you say is to you. Think about what he is saying, and wait until he has finished before presenting your ideas. You must understand his statements in order to respond intelligently.

■ The best way to find out how your speaking voice sounds to others is to make a five-minute tape recording of yourself as you read a newspaper article. Choose a piece that contains many of the words you use in your daily conversations. Then listen to the tape very critically. Do you speak clearly, or do you slur your words? Is your voice pitched too high? Does it sound monotonous? If you are not satisfied with how you sound, concentrate on correcting one or two of your worst faults. Practice by reading aloud, and more important, practice in your daily speech. Later, make another recording to check your progress.

■ What you say, however, is even more important than a pleasant speaking voice. Make a habit of expressing your ideas correctly and clearly. To do this, you must think before you speak. Avoid slang, and never use profanity. Be polite and considerate of others in your comments, and avoid sharp, uncharitable remarks. Never downgrade others in an attempt to upgrade yourself. If you speak ill of a former employer or business associates to a prospective employer, he will expect the same treatment from you. The key to effective speaking is constant practice. Do not become complacent about your speaking skills; keep trying to improve them. One of your most important assets for a successful career is the ability to express yourself well.

How to prepare for the interview

Experienced interviewers plan every detail. They record the information they receive and their reactions to the interviewee. In like manner, the interviewee should prepare himself for the interview, planning every detail from entrance to exit.

Since the purpose of the interview for you, the applicant, is to find out about the job, you should plan beforehand all the questions you will ask about the company and the position for which you are applying. It is a good idea to list the duties or functions of the job, and to see how your idea of these responsibilities compares with that of the company. Often, the character of a job differs from company to company.

You should also be prepared to give an accurate account of your background, employment, education, and everything else that you have mentioned in your chronological résumé or personal-data sheet. Review each item on it before going to the interview, so that the facts will be fresh in your mind. Remember to take a chronological résumé even if you plan to present a different form of résumé to the interviewer.

While you will have some questions to ask about the company during the interview, you should learn beforehand everything you can about it. Such knowledge will indicate to the interviewer that you have a real interest in the company. If you can discuss the company's work intelligently with the interviewer, you will have a better rapport with him. You will also be able to devote most of the interview to the specifics of the job rather than to background information.

Dress appropriately for the interview. While there is greater acceptance today of brighter colors and a wider range of styles for business attire, your safest course is to lean to the conservative side.

Arriving for the interview

Be punctual. That does not mean that you must arrive far ahead of the appointed time. Appear five minutes before the appointed time so that the interviewer will know that you can be interviewed as scheduled. If you are late, he may think that you will not appear and take up other business, which he may not be able to leave when you arrive. If lateness is unavoidable, try to telephone. If, on the other hand, you are kept waiting fifteen or twenty minutes by the interviewer, you may ask the receptionist or secretary if perhaps it would be more convenient for the employer if you came at another time. Emergencies arise, and thoughtfulness is always appreciated. Never get angry if your interview must be postponed. Be gracious and set a time for another appointment. An applicant who loses his temper reveals many unfavorable characteristics, including a lack of understanding of the business world.

There is usually a coat-and-hat rack in the reception room. Remove your coat and hat, hang them up, and take a magazine while you wait. Do not expect the receptionist to entertain you.

If you happen to meet the interviewer in the elevator or hall, do not go along with him to his office wearing your coat or rain boots. Leave such things in the reception room, even though he wears his coat into the office.

What to do during the interview

Use the interviewer's name in your greeting when you enter his office. Say, "Good morning, Mr. Jones. I'm very glad to meet you," or express a similar friendly greeting. Do not sit down until he asks you to. Leave your cigarettes in your pocket. If the interviewer offers one, refuse it with thanks. You will have enough to occupy you without having to worry about matches and ashtrays.

Be ready to take the initiative in opening the conversation. What is the employer looking for in a job applicant, and how do you qualify? You may have said in your letter of application that you would like to work for the company. This is your opportunity to explain why you made that statement. You are the one who sought the interview. Of course, if the interviewer starts the conversation, pay attention to what he says and be ready to respond at the appropriate moment. Do not interrupt the interviewer. Listening is an art, and you will not be able to reply intelligently if you do not listen to what the interviewer is saying. Stop talking when he begins to speak, even if you have not finished what you wanted to say.

Your attitude is important. If you give the impression that you are not really interested, you will find that the employer is also not really interested. Be positive, and do not be afraid to express your enthusiasm for

459

HOW TO HANDLE YOUR COLLEGE INTERVIEW

A COLLEGE VISIT and interview serves a twofold purpose. It gives you an opportunity to see a school at which you may spend the next four years and to ask any questions you may have concerning that college. It gives a member of the admissions staff a chance to size you up and help determine whether this is a good college for you and what your chances for admission are.

Furthermore, if one or both parents go with you to a college, the family enjoys a common experience which can be discussed at home after the visit. Therefore, when it comes time to decide which college you will attend, you can all contribute opinions formed from firsthand impressions.

Parents are urged to visit colleges with their children; sometimes a parent notices and points out things to an applicant which otherwise may be overlooked.

Colleges do not like an applicant to appear for an interview without a previously arranged appointment.

You may arrange for an appointment by letter (addressed to the Director of Admissions) or by telephone. However, some colleges specifically request that all appointments be made by letter; check the catalog or "Information to Candidates" bulletin.

If you write for an appointment, give several dates on which you can appear. This may save correspondence if you cannot be seen on the date you select. (See pages 132, 140 for samples of appointment-request letters.)

Before visiting each college, reread the pertinent sections of its catalog and prepare several questions concerning points that are not covered in the catalog, or points that you would like expanded or clarified.

Be yourself during the interview. Don't be afraid to say, "I don't know," if you can't answer a question.

Subjects covered in an interview can range from A to Z. The entire discussion may center on you, your interests, activities, likes and dislikes, schoolwork, and so on. Then again, it may include current events, your opinions on world problems, a discussion of a recently read book.

Don't be disappointed if you travel several hundred miles for a ten- or fifteen-minute interview. The length of the interview does not determine your acceptability.

If you know a student who is in attendance at the college, it might be a good idea to write him that you will be visiting on a certain date, and ask him to show you around.

After you return home from the interview, write a thank-you note to the person who interviewed you. If you did not get the interviewer's name when called into his office, ask a secretary or an office worker for it after the interview.

If you visit a college with another applicant, do *not* arrange for an interview at the same time as his. This is *your* interview and should not be shared with another applicant.

Dress simply and neatly. Girls should not overdress or wear excessive make-up.

Your application for admission need not be in the hands of the college for you to have your interview. Ordinarily, you may have the interview at any time, but check the college's catalog to see if it stipulates otherwise.

All applications and interviews should be finished before the Christmas vacation. This is because you will start studying for mid-term examinations shortly after Christmas and also because most colleges start their admission selection work after February 1. Many colleges specifically state that they will not interview candidates after February 1 or March 1.

Note to parents: If you're present during an interview, remember that it is your child's interview, not yours. As much as you would like to have your child say more, or express himself better, or sit straighter, restrain your desire to make corrections or additions. Don't give the impression that your child depends on you to do his thinking and talking for him. College interviewers realize and take into account the fact that they are talking to nervous teen-agers who usually cannot handle themselves in an interview as well as adults can. By all means, participate in the interview if questions are directed to you.

the job and the company. While you are expected to have a mind of your own and need not agree with everything the interviewer says, you must remain calm and friendly throughout the interview. If you display temper or boredom, you can expect to have the interview suddenly cut short. You may be interviewed by someone who does not have as many college degrees as you have. Give him your full cooperation and respect. Try not to show superiority. In addition to giving an account of your qualifications, the interviewer must complete a reaction report. If you consider the other person during the interview and make it as easy as possible for him, his reaction is bound to be favorable.

Find out the essential facts about the job. Do not be afraid to ask questions about the job functions, the organization of the company, the standard steps of promotion, and similar relevant matters. The interviewer, of course, will ask you questions to find out whether you are the right man for the job. He will ask you about your most recent job and about other items mentioned on your résumé. Make sure you can talk intelligently and concisely about the various functions in your last job and your areas of competence. Be frank, but remember to avoid any criticism of your former company or co-workers. If you bear a grudge against your former employer, keep it to yourself. Mention only your pleasant and constructive work experiences. It is a good idea to have in mind certain incidents reflecting the high standards of your former company and to mention them, if the occasion arises. If you were discharged for incompetency, do not hesitate to say so. You are not unique. The interviewer will realize that your former employer may not have described accurately the functions of the job before hiring you. Make it clear that you want to avoid the same mistake and intend to know exactly what your next job will entail.

HOW TO DISCUSS SALARY

The question of salary can be a sensitive area. If the interviewer asks you, "What salary do you expect to get?" try to shift the burden of the question back to him by stating that you expect the standard rate of pay for a person with your experience working in that position. Know in advance what this standard rate is. Be accurate when questioned about your present or most recent earnings. If the employer enters into further negotiations with you, he will probably learn the exact amount of your salary when checking your references.

If you mentioned in your résumé that you have a portfolio of proof available, the interviewer may or may not ask to see it during the first interview. Bring the portfolio with you, but do not try to show it to the interviewer if he expresses no interest in it. Some employers believe that matters of proof and samples of work can wait until later, when the employer has decided whether the applicant has the basic qualifications to justify spending more time with him. Be prepared to give a concise explanation of each item in your portfolio of proof in case the interviewer does want to see your portfolio.

HOW TO END THE INTERVIEW

Rarely is a job offered at the end of the first interview. The employer usually has other applicants to see before he will make up his mind. Some companies administer tests to all promising applicants, and the interviewer may tell you that he will notify you when to appear for testing. References must be checked, even when an employer is fairly certain he wants to hire an applicant. Do not press for a decision or declare that you have another offer that you must decide upon by 4:45 P.M. Give the employer an opportunity to consider your application, and give yourself some time to decide whether this is the right job for you. You may realize during the interview that you do not want, or are not qualified for, the job described to you. Be straightforward. Say that you do not believe that you are the person they are looking for. To mention other offers, or say you want to "shop around," or offer similar excuses is a waste of time and indicates a lack of sincerity.

If you are an executive, you may terminate the interview. When it is time to leave, rise, shake hands, thank the interviewer for giving you his time, and say that you will look forward to hearing from him at an early date; or, if there is to be no further communication, say that you enjoyed meeting him. Be sure to take with you your portfolio of proof and any other belongings. Collect any belongings that you left in the reception room and, in leaving, thank the receptionist.

After the interview

As soon as you can, write a letter of thanks to the interviewer. Confirm your interest in the job if you are interested, and say that you look forward to hearing from him in the near future. Even if you do not obtain a job with the company at this time, you will have established with it a friendly relationship that may help you if you apply there again.

41

The five steps to successful selling

You've succeeded in selling yourself—the job is yours! And now your challenge is more important than ever: to sell your company's product or service. Master the five basic steps described in these pages, and you'll be well on your way to attaining sales success.

There are five steps in planned selling: the pre-approach, the approach, the presentation, overcoming objections, and the close.

The pre-approach is the step in which the salesman goes prospecting. Its keynote is constant alertness.

The alert retail salesman knows the specials for the day. He tries to build a core of steady customers by letting them know, in advance, about sales on items in which they have a special interest. He displays his stock in an attractive, attention-getting way. On the floor, he is ever watchful for the potential customer. He doesn't park his rear against the back counter and devote himself to chitchat with other salespersons. As he comes forward to serve a customer, he makes a preliminary analysis of the customer's appearance and actions.

The alert manufacturer's representative keeps in constant contact with dealers and purchasing agents. He strives for complete coverage. He works to please and keep his own customers. He explores to see if he can possibly capture some of his rivals' domains.

The alert realtor, or appliance salesman, or insurance agent keeps building his list of prospects. For material he draws upon present users, relatives and friends and their friends, acquaintances in clubs and social groups, the businessmen who serve him, and news items and listings. He also tries to attract prospects by demonstrations, exhibits, and contests. He makes himself known to his neighbors by doing community service.

He takes careful notes on whatever he can learn about these prospects: their personal characteristics; their likes and dislikes; their estimated income; members of the family; whether they are homeowners, etc. From his notes he decides whether they have a need for his services, which of them can afford a purchase, and whether other salesmen have an inside track. Where the prospect is an employe, he finds out whether he has the authority to buy for his company.

His ratings enable him to select the better prospects for immediate action and to eliminate deadwood or unlikely candidates. He keeps a tickler file on those prospects who are not available now, but who might be approached some weeks or months later.

The astute salesman does not attempt to build his list by obviously spurious means, like the roofer who, every three months, blankets the community with postcards reading: "While working near your home recently, I noticed that your roof needs repairs."

The approach

The salesman makes his approach when he establishes contact with the prospect, obtains further information about his needs, and confirms what leads he already has. He aims to establish a pleasant and positive contact and to attract attention and interest. He tries to obtain the information efficiently, unobtrusively, and accurately, making it clear that his purpose is to serve.

The retail salesman greets his prospect cordially and promptly. He regards all prospects as customers. If the prospect is looking at the merchandise, the salesman makes some pertinent remark about it: "This is a special for today." "This is a new design by Fowler." Only to those who look bewildered does he say: "May I help you?"

Through observation, trial questions, and the response to his opening, the retailer tries to discover what types of merchandise the customer is interested in and at what prices. He notices the appearance of the customer, remembering, however, that the well-to-do may dress plainly, or the poorly dressed person may be an enthusiast who spends every cent on phonograph records or tropical fish. If a second customer approaches, he greets him promptly with: "Good morning. I'll be with you shortly." But he doesn't leave his first customer unless the customer is having difficulty making a choice, and then only with permission.

If a representative makes his first contact by phone, he says with a smiling voice: "This is Arthur Jones. I'd like to speak to Mr. Barton." (Not, apprehensively, "Do you think Mr. -er- Barton has time to speak to me?") His request for an interview is direct, honest, and brief.

If this contact is made by letter, the tone is simple and vigorous and stresses the service angle. The hard-sell approach is not necessary, since you expect to make the sale in person later on.

When keeping the appointment, do more than announce yourself to the receptionist. Ask her a simple question, such as the correct spelling or pronunciation of your prospect's name. Be very pleasant and courteous here. It will pay to make a favorable impression. Receptionists and secretaries can be important helps or hindrances in your sales efforts.

If you drop in without appointment, try to pick a time when your prospect will not be too busy. But if he is, don't become impatient. Request a definite appointment at some future time.

The actual contact with your prospect may begin with discreet praise of him or his company, with some brief casual comment, or a direct plunge—some attention-getting, "headline" statement: "Mr. Barton, you're interested in the safety record of your employes." You will have prepared these and the sentences immediately following carefully, remembering that you are appealing to his needs and wants and also confirming your knowledge of them. You attempt to show him what a disadvantage he is at in not having these wants and needs satisfied. Thus, the auto insurance salesman, approaching a prospect who carries $25–$50,000 liability insurance, will stress the larger amounts recently awarded in accidents.

Avoid any resemblance to the "Help me through college" line. Direct your appeal toward a need which your product can satisfy. And stick to business. Your prospect may be active in civic affairs; but if you let him infer from your opening that you seek his aid in combating juvenile delinquency, he will be annoyed when you switch to selling machinery.

The presentation

This step, whether short or long, is the one toward which all your preparation has been heading. For here you show how your product or service *satisfies*. You turn your prospect from wanting a product to wanting your brand of that product.

The major ingredients of a successful presentation are:

■ *Be confident.* Believe in your product or service. Otherwise how can you expect your prospect to believe in it?

■ *Be clear.* Use a vocabulary adapted to the level of your listener: technical, if he is professional; simple, if he is a layman. Use short sentences. Restate points in several ways. Take up one thing at a time. Demonstrate before you describe. Think of your presentation as akin to the first paragraph of a good newspaper story, covering *who, where, when, how,* and *why.*

■ *Be as complete as is necessary for the particular prospect.* If he can afford only $16,000 for a house, it is foolish to show him $25,000 homes. If he is already half-sold, you may anger him by covering points on which he already agrees with you. Being complete, however, implies anticipating objections he may bring up.

Here are some additional pointers for improving your presentation:

1. During the presentation, strengthen the prospect's sense of need by referring back to points made during the approach.

2. Pave the way for a final *Yes* by asking questions which will bring a Yes response. "That's a heavy loss to incur, isn't it?"

3. Though, in general, assortments should be full, it is sometimes helpful to limit your items to those from which a choice is *most* likely to be made. The retailer, in dealing with children or a person who can't make up his mind, should whisk out of sight items which get a frown. By a series of choices he can whittle the possibilities down to a final choice among two or three.

4. When you demonstrate, let the article sell itself. Or rather, get the prospect to try it out and by so doing let him sell it to himself. Point out only distinctive features: "A very handsome set, at $25." "Our most popular set, $18."

5. People like to talk. Get your prospect to do so. He may talk himself into buying. And while he is talking, listen. He may disclose a need, a want, that you hadn't suspected. Conversely, if you do all of the talking, you will learn little about your customer, and may even talk yourself out of the sale.

6. Be prepared to shift ground. Your analysis may be faulty. Or your customer may think he knows what he wants until he sees the article, and then change his mind.

7. Avoid disparaging remarks about competitors. Your prospect may think highly of their product, and consider yours only on the basis of price or special services offered.

8. Be objective about your product. "All our pianos have a fine tone," may suggest to the customer that you lack discrimination.

Overcoming objections

Objections may arise at any point during the interview. When they do, meet them in one of the following ways:

If the objection is a serious one, use the "Yes, but ——" technique. Agree with the prospect, and even praise him for his perspicacity: "That's a very good question," "I'm glad you brought that up." Then show him how the disadvantage he has mentioned is counterbalanced or outweighed. The price is high, but the article has extra sturdiness, and promises fewer repair bills and longer life. Or balance the price against other features—greater safety or ease of operation.

If a strong objection is raised on a minor point, concede the point and do something about it. Offer extra service, replace or change a part, make a special concession or price. The new arm rest, cost $2, may sell the used car, price $1,095.

If the objection is too formidable, don't argue with the prospect. If the icebox won't fit, it won't fit. Shift to another article or offering.

If the objection is trivial, ignore it for the time being. The comment may only be a random one, soon forgotten or overcome during the general presentation. Deal with it only if it is repeated.

Deny an objection only when the customer is obviously misinformed. "We thought that for a long while, but recent research has shown that . . ." Be cautious and tactful in your denial, and use the objection as an opportunity to educate the customer. "The manufacturer advises that a carving knife be honed both before and after using."

Never try to overcome a legitimate objection by seeming to deny it. If the customer mentions a feature of some other brand, don't tell her that in all your twenty years of selling you've never heard of that brand. Similarly, avoid the cliché: "We don't have any call for that." This may be interpreted as a lame excuse for your own lack of alertness, or as a snub. The writer was once told this when asking for a 15-gallon fish tank, and the words had hardly been spoken when another customer came in and called out loudly, "Got any 15-gallon tanks?" It is much better to say: "We don't have that in stock right now, but I'll be glad to order it for you."

Be brief. Don't magnify the objection by spending much time on it.

Remember, the way to overcome objections is to anticipate them.

The close

The customer has reached his lowest level of resistance and is ready to buy. He needs just a little push to get him to sign on the dotted line. How does the salesman give that last little push?

Be sure to ask the customer to buy. Take the initiative, or the sale may be lost.

Ask him to buy when his interest is strongest. The article he comes back to, the one he looks back at while examining something else, obviously interests him. Judge his interest by the tone of his questions, the look in his eye.

Offer a series of minor choices. Blue or gray, disability waiver or not, this accessory or that?

Ask questions or make comments which suggest that the article is already sold. "Would you like delivery next week?" Have the order form on the desk and fill out part of it when you think he is really interested. If he isn't, he'll stop you; if he is, you'll have closed the sale.

Use a trial close. "If you bought this . . ." "Just let us deliver this to your home and . . ." The trial close may become the real close.

Summarize your arguments, with stress on the chief points of appeal. "Mr. Barton, we've agreed on point 1, that you . . . We've agreed on point 2, that we . . ."

If the facts warrant, dramatize the advantage of buying now. "Prices will rise on the first of the month." "We have only one of this type left." But remember that misrepresentation on this score is one of the easiest ways to lose a customer.

Use a reverse twist, so to speak. Suggest that perhaps the article is not the one the customer wants. "Are you sure . . . ?" This should be used, of course, only when you are quite sure that he *does* want it.

Get the pen into the customer's hand indirectly. Ease the asking for the signature by having him write something else, for example, the full name of a beneficiary.

If a sale is impossible, make your close an opening for a next time. "I'll call again in three months."

Seven common faults in selling

Certain faults in salesmanship are altogether too common, and deserve renewed attention:

■ *Not emphasizing needs and wants enough.* You make the sale only when the prospect knows his need, feels it strongly, feels that your product satisfies his needs.

■ *Emphasizing price exclusively.* Price is important, of course, but sales are not made on the basis of price alone. The person had a reason for buying a car before he started shopping around. Try to find that reason, and address your chief appeal to it.

■ *Failing to show an adequate assortment.* You must give the prospect a chance to choose the one thing that is right for him.

■ *Neglecting to explain the use and care of the article you sell.* For example, why risk having your customer get angry at your washing machine because you've neglected to tell him that it has a sand trap which requires regular cleaning.

■ *Forgetting that suggestion may sell.* Not all towns are taken by storm or a frontal attack. Call the prospect's attention to something. "This nail polish remover leaves the nails perfectly clean." Of course, suggestion selling is more than the stock "*And* something else?"

■ *Overcoming objections in an objectionable way, or not being alert enough to them.* Prepare to meet the challenge of the objection whenever it arises.

■ *Not taking the initiative in closing the sale.* What is the point of doing everything except sell the item or the service? A salesman's job is to sell, and the last step is as important as the first.

test your skills

THE FIVE STEPS TO SUCCESSFUL SELLING

1. What is the basic sales message you want to get across about any product or service?
2. List the five steps in selling and briefly outline what each entails.
3. Give three rules for a successful presentation.
4. What is the one absolutely essential ingredient of an effective close?

Answers to this quiz appear on page 705–706.

42

How to run a meeting

The man who can make meetings work is well on his way to success as an executive. Here's how the able leader understands his role and knows how to get the meeting started, how to keep discussion on the point, and how to bring it to a successful, decisive conclusion.

The leaders of today's business meetings do not just happen. They must learn to handle the complex job of resolving problems, controlling emotions, and passing information—and learn to do these accurately and expediently.

This is a job for specialists—specialists in a job that is never the same twice. The meeting leader must always remain flexible to the needs and demands of each specific meeting and adjust to those needs with ease and authority.

The leader, like the hub of a working gear, is the center around which all else revolves. He has to be alert to any change of pace. He must adjust to changes faster than any other part of the mechanism. Nevertheless, it is the members who provide the drive. The leader is never more than the guide.

There is no doubt that more than anyone else, the leader is responsible for the successful meeting. He is also responsible for most failures.

Make it clear to your meeting members, and to your whole organization, just what the leader is supposed to do. *He is supposed to lead.* He is the one responsible for the direction, temper, pace, and final decisions reached by the group. This may take some education. People feel they shouldn't appear to be too autocratic. The plain fact that the

471

leader must take his position behind the wheel is the most important concept for meeting members and prospective leaders to learn.

The leader has a clearly defined status: (a) He is not just another member. (b) He is *supposed* to have more authority than anyone else in the meeting. (c) He must be more conscious of time and the effectiveness of the meeting than anyone else.

After all, the leader is responsible to the other members and to himself for the productiveness of the meeting.

The meeting is an investment in time. It must be made to pay out.

Getting the meeting under way

With any meeting, the beginning is crucial. Follow these rules in opening your meeting to take advantage of every chance of success.

■ *Start on time.* Ask anyone who attends meetings frequently how many meetings start promptly as scheduled. This is probably the most violated of all meeting rules. And, paradoxically, the easiest rule for the leader to enforce. He has full responsibility and control over the opening of the meeting. Too often you hear this:

"Well, it's time to start, but Bill Carson isn't here. We'd better wait a few minutes."

Don't do it! Think of all the people who *are* there. If you wait for Carson, at the next meeting all the rest will be late. The leader who begins the meeting promptly will be immediately recognized and respected. He will stand out—there are so few like him. If you do nothing else to improve your meetings, this will be a big step. Remember, to start on time means you have a better chance to end on time.

■ *State the purpose of the meeting clearly.* Ordinarily, you will have set down in an agenda circulated earlier to those attending the subject and purpose of your meeting. Remember, however, that this agenda is probably at least twenty-four hours old. Many pieces of paper have passed over the meeting members' desks in the meantime. A restatement is essential. Your oral presentation will help to clearly define the problem for all present. It can easily clear up any last-minute confusions that may have arisen.

■ *Remember, state your ideas positively.* Nothing succeeds like success. Opening remarks that clearly say success is possible will immediately set the tone and direction of the remarks that will follow. Point out the importance of the problem. State the implications and effects of the decisions that will be made at this meeting. Show that the meeting is worthwhile, and give the members something to shoot for. *Don't be negative!*

■ *Use vivid words that will make your ideas sound interesting.* The crispness and vitality of your opening remarks will set the tone and pace of the entire meeting. Frame your ideas in colorful phrases. For instance, this is the type of statement that smothers meetings:

"We should try to appraise the possibilities of purveying the meat currently in inventory."

Try this:

"Gentlemen, this is a problem we *must* resolve. The meat is on the hooks. We've got to sell it or smell it!"

■ *Keep it short.* Limit your opening remarks to a minute and a half. The leader's job is to present the problem to the group clearly and fully. He must also communicate the urgency of the problem in order to move the group to action. Long-drawn-out openings take the edge off this urgency, and cause a misfire right at the beginning.

Making the meeting work

Leadership is an active force—it cannot be passive. It is a force which exerts itself to guide, direct, restrict, develop, contain, expand, elicit, repress, and generally stimulate the examining and developmental thinking of the group. The leader during the meeting is an active counselor, guide, administrator, compromiser.

The balance of how much and how little control the leader should exert during the meeting calls for a fine discrimination in judgment and a generous mixture of common sense. This balance cannot be outlined in a book. It can only be gained by a clear understanding of the duties of the leader and the goals of the meeting. And by doing.

GROUND RULES FOR EFFECTIVE LEADERSHIP

■ *Remain impartial if possible.* The leader functions best as the sorter, sifter, clarifier, and director in the meeting. Report facts, guide the discussion, watch for conflicts and personality flare-ups. Channel the group toward possible solutions. Emotions and facts must mix whenever people talk face to face. However, the emotional tone of the meeting will be better, and the meeting easier to handle, if you as leader can assume a neutral position.

SUGGESTION: If you must present a point of view or declare a personal position, try to do it through another member of your department. Or, draw a statement of your position from one of the other meeting members.

■ *Watch the pacing of the meeting.* Keep the meeting moving. Remember, in the platform speech, it is possible to time your ideas carefully, and to keep the thoughts marching briskly along. However, in the meeting you are dealing with perhaps a dozen people, and there is no script.

Think of the meetings you've attended when a sudden and deadly silence has set in and everyone sat waiting for someone else to make a comment. This unpleasantly awkward situation breeds tension. Tension is a direct road to conflict, dissension, and confusion.

Keep the ideas flowing. Once this flow flags it is difficult, often impossible, to reopen the tap. The leader must run herd on the group; keep nudging to maintain the pace.

SUGGESTION: Be alert to "silent periods." Move quickly to comment, question, or explain the moment you sense this silence settling in. When the ideas slow down, so does the urgency and the ability of the group to cope with the problem.

■ *Watch for emotional "build-ups."* Meetings are made up of people, and people are made of a little bit of logic and a *lot* of emotion. These are not the ingredients of "sweetness and light." It is the leader's job to maintain order and reasonableness.

The more the discussion stays in the realm of fact, the better the chance of success. Emotions don't solve problems or make rational decisions, and in the context of a meeting there is usually no answer to emotional conflicts.

SUGGESTION: Watch for the building of emotional tension between individuals or groups. Move in quickly to put out the fire. Change the direction of the meeting away from "tender" points. Use humor to lighten the air. Point out that both members could be right; that it all depends on where you stand, and how you look at it. When the tension has been reduced, you can turn back to a realistic look at the problem.

■ *Pull out all background information.* The natural human urge to drive directly to solutions is highlighted in the meeting situation. Although an admirable drive, it may lead to putting the motor on the boat before the hull is finished. Decisions and solutions can only be made on the information presented and discussed by the group. The major function of the meeting is to get all the facts out of the meeting members, and then to talk about those facts. Only then can the group hope to come to a logical and workable solution. Make your group do first things first. Make them consider all the facts. Don't let them become solution-minded *too* soon!

SUGGESTION: In your opening remarks, make it clear you want to go over the background material before you try to come up with the answers. Point out that if this isn't done, one person alone could replace the meeting as a decisionmaking tool. If one of the members rushes headlong to a solution, pull him back. This is part of the leader's control duty.

■ *Draw contributions from all members of the group.* There are silent members in almost every group. The meeting situation is designed to draw on the thinking of *all* members; to call out *all* ideas and mold them into a decision.

Be sure that everyone has a chance to make his offering. Encourage the member who shows signs of meekness. Be careful, however, not to put a reluctant member on the spot. Draw him into the discussion through an area you know is familiar to him. Then dig deeper for his position on the subject at hand. This will reduce the danger of post-meeting comments, which are usually made in the hallway outside the meeting room, such as:

"I just don't think I can go along with the decision made in the meeting." Or:

"That's all very well, but no one told Bill that my department just can't tool up for the job to meet that deadline."

These statements are important and pertinent. Unfortunately, they are being made at the wrong time and in the wrong place. They should have been made *in* the meeting for the enlightenment and consideration of all. Let the leader beware of these postmeeting comments. They usually mean another meeting must be called. The penalty is obvious— wasted time!

SUGGESTION: Be sure everyone gets in on the discussion and decisions. If you know of a particular meeting member who tends to postmeeting comments, pin him down *in* the meeting. Make him commit himself so definitely that he won't be able to say later he doesn't agree. You owe this to the group.

This is the type of leadership that can save many, many wasted hours around the meeting table.

THE ART OF ASKING QUESTIONS

No MATTER who we are or what our way of life, it has become increasingly important to discover what people feel and think—about almost every subject under the sun. When we hire someone or apply for a job, when we discuss our work with a boss or a subordinate, when we see our doctor or even talk to our family and friends, we interview and are interviewed.

How can we do this more successfully? Here are some useful techniques developed by experts:

Recognize that every encounter is "emotional." There is no such thing as an impersonal meeting of minds. Look inward: There's a human awareness, an exchange of feelings, with the waiter who takes your luncheon order, the unseen person at the other end of a telephone wire. But to enter into any real give-and-take we have to let down our defenses.

Make your purpose clear. "When you start asking questions," says the noted pollster Dr. George Gallup, "the other person immediately wonders, 'Why does he want to know?' Unless your purpose is clear, he may be reluctant to talk, or he may seize the opportunity to tell you all about his problems."

When you go to your doctor he can ask you intimate questions which you would resent from anyone else. In applying for a loan, though, you accept questions from a banker that you would resent from your doctor. It's a matter of defining the situation.

Respond to expressions of feeling. Instead of trying to reassemble the facts (who said or did what to whom) or to give specific advice, professional counselors listen for and encourage all expressions of feeling. Statements that begin "I feel" or "I wish" or "I don't care if," the interviewer acknowledges: "You feel very strongly about that, don't you?" or "Is that so?" Having such feelings recognized, without judgment or criticism, often has an almost magical effect in making a person open up.

Learn the art of open-end. Don't ask too many questions. Instead of the cross-examination approach, professional interviewers nowadays often start just by getting people talking—about the weather, sports, anything. And for depth interviewing they have developed the open-end question, which lets the other person assume the initiative and carry the conversation.

Don't tell the other person what to say. According to expert pollsters, "feedback" from the interviewer's own predilections or wishes is the greatest single source of error in public-opinion polls.

Watch your wording. Finding in the other person just what you expected to find usually means you are putting words into his mouth.

Because of this human tendency, "question building" for professional polls has become an art in itself. "Tricky or badly constructed questions can push or mislead others into giving completely false answers," says Stanley L. Payne, author of the book *The Art of Asking Questions.*

Protect the other person. Detective novels and courtroom dramas usually show an interview as a duel of wits in which the object is to probe for the other person's weak spots. In real life, those who have to ask for sensitive information generally follow the opposite rule—they lead to strength because recognizing a strength creates a bond between the questioner and the questioned.

Protecting the other person's pride is a vital part of getting information. As economist Stuart Chase points out, "Veteran interviewers in an unemployment survey would never ask, 'You're not working now, are you?' but rather 'Are you looking for a job right now, or waiting for a while?' "

Start where the other person is. "Beginners," says Dr. Leslie A. Osborn of the University of Nebraska College of Medicine, "often rush into an area of feeling where the other person is not yet ready to admit them." A worried heart patient, for example, may have to discuss the effects of his illness on his work and his family before he can plunge into an objective discussion of symptoms. It is up to the interviewer to find out what is on the other person's mind and start from there.

The successful interview, more like a good conversation than an interrogation, leaves the interviewed person feeling somehow heartened and uplifted. Why? To have concern for the other person, and show it, is the rule that makes all the others work.

■ *See that only one person speaks at a time.* There is no room in a meeting for a meeting within a meeting. Private discussions within the meeting group can only cause conflict and disunity. On this point, the leader *must* be firm! Don't allow the meeting to break up into smaller discussion groups. It's the leader's job to see that each member is heard by all present. If a splinter group persists, focus the attention of the whole group on it. Like this:

"Jim and Bill seem to have come up with something. Will you tell us about it?"

They'll get the idea.

■ *Pin down opposing points of view.* It would be naïve to think that all the varied ideas expressed during a meeting will mesh and support one another. There are bound to be strong differences of opinion. In fact, conflict is probably vital to the development of new thinking on a problem. It stimulates members to document and prove the ideas and points of view they present.

However, this is a controlled conflict—conflict controlled by the leader and used to help the group toward the ultimate solution of the problem under discussion.

SUGGESTION: Never disregard or attempt to hide conflicting ideas. Recognize them and point them out to the group. Bring them out into the open where they can be examined intelligently. Ask the conflicting members,

"Where do you stand exactly?"

Then,

"Why do you take that position?"

And finally,

"What do *you* suggest we do?"

No ideas are held as strongly as those *not* discussed!

■ *Stress cooperation, not conflict.* Most people come to the conference with a definite point of view. Good! They know other people will disagree. Good! They are determined to *force* the others to accept their position. Bad!

This results from a misunderstanding of what the meeting is designed to do. This point calls for some well-directed teaching.

The leader must lead the group to work together. Try to present the idea that this is a problem that demands the thinking of all present. No one can go it alone in the meeting. Point out that the meeting room is not a personal battlefield. Refer to the complexity of today's business;

to the growing need for specialists. Explain that the meeting is designed to draw together the thinking of all these *many* specialists. Draw out contributions by praising the group as a unit.

SUGGESTION: Conflict is always going to exist among people who think strongly. Take every opportunity to point out the advantages of "pooling" thinking. The feeling of cooperation will be stimulated by meetings that *work*. Successful, workable decisions are the most persuasive argument for cooperation in future meetings.

■ *Guide the meeting from problem to solution.* Move doggedly through the steps of the meeting from the presentation of materials to the final solving of the problem. Remember, the most common cause of poor meetings is lack of direction. This places the responsibility squarely on the head of the leader.

Each time a member speaks in a meeting, the direct line to the solution stands in danger of being derailed. The wrong emphasis, a misinterpretation of a contribution, a missed fact—any of these common happenings can send the group off the track. When you successfully lead a meeting, you are giving guidance and structure to the most complex of all speaking situations.

■ *Clarify contributions.* Be sure that what is said by one member is understood by all present. One of the most common misconceptions held by people is that there is a clear line from the speaker to the listener; that the listener always understands exactly what is said to him. Nothing could be further from the truth.

Here's how the leader can clarify issues in the meeting:

1. Ask questions in areas that may have been missed:

"There is one question we haven't asked: 'What is the marketing potential of this product?' Bill, what is your estimate?"

2. Pull out details needed to make each offering crystal clear:

"The one point we haven't covered is the cost of the advertising. How does this affect the plan?"

3. Define words that could lead to a misinterpretation:

"Al, when you say that this idea is 'critical' to the plan, do you mean that it wouldn't work without it?"

4. Ask members to elaborate:

"Jim, would you expand on that point?"

5. Rephrase statements you fear might not be clear.

"You feel that we should *not* advertise in national magazines. Is that correct?"

479

Psychologists tell us that we understand best those things we know or have experienced. Take advantage of this concept. Phrase difficult thoughts in simple, everyday terms. Use comparisons, analogies, similes, examples, contrasts, comparisons, stories, etc. Don't be afraid of being *too* simple. You can't!

■ *Use humor to reduce tension.* It is only human nature to hold strongly to your own ideas. It's difficult to retrack and admit that someone else has reached the right conclusion while you have been wallowing in error. It's difficult for the meeting member to admit he's wrong, but it's even more difficult for him to bow out gracefully. Often a member in a meeting would like to change direction or retreat from a stand, but finds it too awkward to do so. Be alert to this situation. Give him the opportunity to revise his position without seeming to "roll over!" Again, the leader can do this job better than anyone else.

SUGGESTION: Try using humor to open up this common meeting roadblock. When the tension is reduced and everyone is relaxed, it's easier for the reluctant member to step down. He can then do it gracefully—and save face.

■ *Make frequent summaries during the meeting.* Summaries report the progress of the meeting to all present. They are a running score card of the success of the group in attacking the problem. Summaries also serve to check on disagreements and point out to the members what conflicts demand their attention. Otherwise disagreements tend to get lost in the discussion, only to turn up at the end of the meeting, much to the dismay of all concerned.

WARNING! Keep your summaries under thirty seconds. This is plenty of time to do the job. Quick summaries will not interrupt the flow of the meeting. They will also serve as an example to the meeting group that you are very conscious of time, and that you plan to keep the ideas marching briskly along.

■ *Watch your time.* Nothing strikes as responsive a chord with the business person as time. He has been made very conscious of the time element by the fact that the day is too short for him to get all his work done. Any attempt to give him more time for his work will receive his warm appreciation.

Business meetings waste time indiscriminately. Make your meetings different. If you can reverse this trend, you will get broad support from the group. They will come better prepared. They will hold closer to the subject, mainly because they won't be worn out by endless, aimless talk.

As a result, they will move more directly to solutions and avoid wasteful tangents.

SUGGESTION: Keep the promise you made when you sent out your agenda. Keep to your stated time limit. If the meeting drags, move in quickly. Make it absolutely clear that you plan to work within the time you established. Nothing can make you more popular.

Wrapping things up

The closing of the meeting places special demands on the leader. Good guidance has brought the group to a solution of the problem. Now is the time to nail down the decision. Without a firm hand by the leader, the results can easily be lost or buried by misdirection.

At the close of the meeting the discussion is over. The leader now takes a position of complete authority. He reports directly the conclusions reached, the major disagreements, and most important, the future steps to be taken.

The following suggestions will help you fulfill completely your job as leader at the end of the meeting.

■ *Point out the decisions reached.* A clear statement of the decisions of the meeting recalls for the last time the agreements made. It gets the conclusions out in the open before the group.

The summary of decisions reached in the meeting will bring to surface any individual misunderstandings and disagreements. Naturally, this helps avoid additional unnecessary meetings.

■ *Point out differences.* Obviously, all meetings cannot be expected to end in complete agreement. The disagreements will be vital to future discussions. State them clearly. Evaluate the disagreements; indicate if they are small or great. Try to define them to the satisfaction of all present, particularly the minority group. Remember, you will have to deal with them in the next meeting!

■ *Point to future action.* State clearly the next steps to be taken. Announce if another meeting will be necessary. And when. Indicate how the decisions reached at *this* meeting will be used in the overall project. Thank the members for their help.

Follow up the meeting with a written confirmation of the decisions reached and the future action to be taken. This will serve as a reminder of the results to the meeting members and will inform others who are interested but not personally involved in this particular meeting.

481

43

"Me? Speak in front of a group?"

"You're next on the program." The words are almost guaranteed to bring a chill of fear to the uninitiated. But to the man or woman who knows how to go about it, public speaking can be both a rewarding and an exhilarating experience. And it's one you can share.

In a sense we have been public speakers ever since those long-forgotten days in early childhood when we rose to recite "Jack and Jill went up the hill" or "Little Bo-peep" to an enthusiastic audience of relatives and friends. So now that we have shown some ways in which you can talk better in social and business situations, let's see how you can develop that inherent ability to speak in public.

We all have a bit of the frustrated actor in us. To one degree or another, we all relish center stage. We delight in recounting an old family tale at a family gathering or dramatizing, in the clubhouse, the birdie we made on the fifteenth hole. We insist on speaking our piece at the P.T.A. meeting; we are flattered when we are asked to deliver a lecture-demonstration to our colleagues in the office or are invited to speak at a round-table discussion or on a business panel.

There is something about public speaking that enhances the ego, especially when we sense we are reaching our audience effectively. But there is another and more practical angle to our interest in public speaking. Whether or not we enjoy addressing an audience, we know that public speaking can be an essential part of our daily lives in our community and business affairs, and that a mastery of its techniques can be our key to success in both these areas.

The chapters that follow will instruct you in the skills and techniques of the art of public speaking. They will tell you how to choose an appropriate subject for your talk, how to organize your material and plan the speech, and how to deliver it in the most comfortable, impressive, and perhaps memorable manner.

The day arrives when you are scheduled to give a talk. "You're next," says the chairman of the meeting. And, likely as not, for all your love of the spotlight you suddenly stiffen up, your legs feel weak, your hands sweat, and an abrupt emptiness hits you in the pit of the stomach. You've got stage fright!

This is the most common of all afflictions the public performer experiences. There isn't an actor of any note who doesn't suffer from it. The greatest of them will readily admit to excruciating moments of terror, loss of memory, or sudden paralysis the very moment they are expected to make their entrances on the stage. The actor must invent ways to overcome this fright; and he usually succeeds. So can you. The next chapter, "How to Beat Stage Fright," will tell you how.

Fit your speech to your audience

Let us talk about the moment you were first asked to make this frightening public address.

"Jack, we want you to speak at our next Community House meeting."

"Why me? Who'll be there? What do you want me to talk about?"

Your response to the request is automatic, defensive; it also happens to be a good one. We'll forget the "Why me?" That's just asking for a compliment. But the answer to "Who'll be there?" is most important to the kind of speech you're going to make.

If the mayor of the town is to be the honored guest of the evening, you will want to talk on civic matters. If an astronaut is to be your guest, you might want to talk on the significance of space exploration. If it's "ladies night" in the auditorium, you're not going to talk about football. And you're not going to talk on how to bake apple pies if your audience is all male.

Your speech must be tailored to the interest of your audience. That's why you asked, "Who'll be there?" And the answer to that question will guide you in the selection of a topic and answer your second question —"What do you want me to talk about?"

Chapter 45, "How to Pick Your Subject," explores more fully the way to choose a topic. It offers you a number of categories from which to select the theme for your talk, as well as lists of specific subjects. It also provides you with a series of practice exercises which should prove helpful for your scheduled address.

Once you have selected the topic of your speech, you must start preparing it. Chapter 47, "Start With a List of Points," will tell you how to go about gathering the material for your talk: general information, pertinent data, facts, figures, and quotations. It will instruct you on how to develop the body of your speech, how best to begin your talk, how to build to a climax, and how to end it.

Other chapters will help you sharpen the effectiveness of your speeches. You will learn how to select the more important points and how to emphasize them in your delivery for a more effective address.

Learn to sell your ideas

And how do you persuade an audience? Do you ride herd? Are you a bulldozer of a speaker? Or do you lead, patiently, and wait for your audience to follow? Chapter 48, "How to Sell Your Idea," analyzes the various approaches of persuasion, as well as the value of each. It tells you how you can convince an initially friendly audience and explores the techniques for winning over the occasional hostile audience you may encounter.

Another way to help you develop the burden of your talk is to use visual aids to dramatize or emphasize a point. Chapter 49, "Use Visuals to Prove Your Point," offers a thorough discussion of techniques and equipment that can give your talk that additional visual punch.

Now that we have the speech and the mechanics of it all prepared, let's turn to the speaker himself. Have you given any thought to your appearance on the platform, and its possible effect on both your speech and your audience? Do you think casual clothes will be best for your talk at the Civic Club? Do you think business attire would be more suitable and effective? When is formal dress the proper wear? You know that, whether we wish it or not, the appearance of others affects our reactions to them. Your appearance will affect others equally. Do you have a tendency toward distracting mannerisms, such as pulling at an ear or fiddling with your glasses? Do you fill in pauses with "I-uh's" and "er's"? Such habits may be irritating to your listeners and they should by all means be overcome.

How about your attitude toward your audience? Does the occasion call for a familiar approach? Should you tell jokes? Or do you think it better, in this formal address, to keep some distance away from your listeners?

How about notes? Do you want a small outline in front of you to refer to from time to time? Do you think you might have some dates, names, places, on a card to which you can easily refer? What about the microphone in the room? the acoustics? How well will your voice reach your audience? Have you tested it? All these questions and problems are fully discussed in Chapter 50, "Preparing Yourself to Speak."

Finally Chapter 51 offers simple but important instructions on delivering a speech: how to keep calm and cool and make friends with your audience, how to follow the speech plan you've laid out for yourself, and how to finish on time. There are also a few words on how to talk on the radio and TV when those occasions arise.

With all this good advice from the masters in the art, and a little homework on your own part, public speaking should eventually become almost as easy as talking to your own family in your own home.

And after some practice it will be an activity you will enjoy.

Eight pitfalls to avoid

Edward Hegarty, a prominent teacher of public speaking, made the following list of reasons why speakers fail.

1. The speaker has nothing to say, nothing of interest, nothing new, nothing about people, no gossip.

2. He doesn't seem to know what he is talking about. This is perhaps because the listener doesn't understand.

3. He hasn't slanted his material to appeal to the listener.

4. He doesn't explain what he wants the listener to do.

5. He tells it all in the first minutes but then yaks on with etceteras and etceteras.

6. He assumes too much. He feels the listeners know more about the subject than they do know.

7. He shows no feeling for his subject, no feeling against it.

8. He doesn't make listeners want to follow him.

44

How to beat
stage fright

Stage fright afflicts just about everyone who's called on to speak in public—and there is comfort in that thought alone. In this chapter management consultant Stephen Price tells how he has helped scores of top executives turn panic into confidence on the podium.

Self-confidence is that wonderful, assured feeling you have just before you fall flat on your face—that was how one speech student felt about public speaking. Oddly enough, he was confident in other speaking situations.

The pain and frustration connected with public speech is difficult to imagine by those who have never lived through the experience.

There is a truism about speaking tensions: it only happens to the best people. Only the conscientious individual who is concerned about doing the perfect job suffers in anticipation of possible failure.

Winston Churchill, himself an experienced speaker, once remarked, "The maxim 'nothing avails but perfection' may be spelled paralysis."

The famous broadcaster Edward R. Murrow once mentioned what was obvious—that he was always tense before going on the air. He called it "the sweat of perfection."

Conscientious people feel less capable than they really are. The reason: there is a great disparity between the ideal self-image and that which is possible to accomplish. This criterion of self-evaluation makes any accomplishment seem small. It is a perfectionistic attitude which often inspires great deeds but also creates great frustration.

It is a false yardstick that depreciates any ability, however great. A review of past performances can sometimes bring a more realistic appraisal of what is expected and what is possible.

The circumstances and pressures that surround the speaking situation become a challenge to the ego. We are anxious about possible failure; we are nervous even about being nervous. Our normal reaction to all fear is either flight or fight. When we are giving a talk, we know that we are not going to fight the audience, and we are too responsible to run away.

Nevertheless, our system is prepared for violent physical action. We must find a way to release this nervous energy in constructive expression. If we do not, it tends to perpetuate the symptoms and sensations that bring distress and discomfort to the speaker.

The speaking pressures and tensions are released because our nervous system believes we need them. It is as if we set off a false fire alarm, and now we are stuck with the apparatus—energy that is seeking an outlet. Once it is given an outlet, we can return to a relatively normal physiological rhythm.

First, remember that every experience is different. The dissimilarities are greater than the similarities. What reminds us of the past is entirely different from the present. Rarely, if ever, do situations in life repeat themselves. There is always a difference: time, age, mood, audience, speaker, topic, results.

Next, we must remove the mystery labels from our feelings. Our feelings have no judgment. No matter how sophisticated we are, our feelings remain on "Primitive Standard Time." They respond when we need them or *think* we need them. Poise and control come with knowledge. The strange is fearful; the unknown brings apprehension. Conversely, with understanding comes control; with familiarity, comfort.

How you can break down mental barriers

One perfect example of how a psychological barrier kept people from accomplishment was the myth of the four-minute mile. For over a thousand years it was an accepted "fact" that it was humanly impossible to run a mile in less than four minutes. But in 1954 an Englishman, Roger Bannister, ran the mile in less than four minutes. Since that time, many other runners have run that mile and new records are being set.

Once we have understanding, we become selective and can choose to believe the reality and challenge the myth. We are then free to believe what is possible and to assume the attitude and the actions that help us change. We are ready to take on the outward manifestations attributed to a successful speaker.

There is a classic reference to this point written by William James:

> Common sense says, we lose our fortune, are sorry and weep; we meet a bear, are frightened and run; we are insulted by a rival, are angry and strike . . . the more rational statement is that we feel sorry because we cry, angry because we strike, afraid because we tremble. . . .
>
> Everybody knows how panic is increased by flight, and how the giving way to the symptoms of grief or anger increases the passions themselves. . . . In rage, it is notorious how we "work ourselves up" to a climax by repeated outbursts of expression. Refuse to express a passion and it dies. Count 10 before venting your anger, and its occasion seems ridiculous. Whistling to keep up courage is no mere figure of speech. On the other hand, sit all day in a moping posture, sigh, and reply to everything with a dismal voice, and your melancholy lingers.
>
> There is no more valuable precept in moral education than this . . . if we wish to conquer undesirable emotional tendencies in ourselves, we must assiduously, and in the first instance cold-bloodedly, go through the *outward movements* of those contrary dispositions which we prefer to cultivate. The reward of persistency will infallibly come, in the fading out of the sullenness or depression, and the advent of real cheerfulness and kindliness in their stead. . . .

LET YOUR TENSIONS WORK FOR YOU

A teacher of public speaking was called in to observe a speaker who was unusually lethargic in his speech and movements. He began with a molasses-paced, interminable walk to the speaker's stand. When he spoke, his pauses were so wide that the *Queen Mary* could have passed through with room to spare.

Critic Kenneth Tynan tells this story about a joint loss of memory by the incomparable acting duo of Alfred Lunt and Lynn Fontanne. An unexpected and unplanned silence developed in mid-scene during one of their London performances. After a moment's confusion, the prompter clearly whispered the next line. Mr. Lunt responded with his usual charming urbanity, "It's not that we don't know the line, old boy. We just can't remember which one of us says it."

When the man was interviewed, he admitted that he behaved as he did because he was very nervous about his speaking ability and wanted to hide it from the audience. He said, "I figured that if I could just slow myself down, I could lasso those shook-up feelings."

He had another talk to give in two months, so he went to work. His teacher demonstrated how unreleased tensions can create the impression of rigidity. The speaker learned to put his nervous steam to work. He learned the techniques of alert gestures, accelerated speech rhythms, energetic movments, and lively expressions.

During his next talk, he amazed everyone, including himself. From the moment he stood up and walked to the platform, he was like a man electrified. He packed so much power into his enthusiastic movements and energetic speech delivery that everyone in the auditorium sat up and took notice. Since he used visual aids in his talk, the microphone bothered him because he had to return to it every time. Like an old pro, he confidently pushed it aside. He noticed that the room was hot, took his coat off and invited everyone else to do the same. He swept through his presentation with an astounding aliveness.

Following the meeting, he said, "I know I was supposed to force the energy at first, until I got going. But for a minute, I didn't believe it would ever happen. Then when I saw them sit up and open their eyes!"

Do your homework

Eddie Rickenbacker, the World War I flying hero who later became president of Eastern Airlines, told of the time when he returned to a hero's welcome as the "Ace of Aces." At an important banquet in his honor, he stood up to a great ovation, opened his mouth to speak, and was terrified. He managed to mumble a few phrases in poor grammar and sat down.

He decided right there and then that this would never happen to him again. The next day he hired a speech coach, had Damon Runyon write a speech for him, and studied grammar. Then he arranged for a long lecture tour. Mr. Rickenbacker learned that each specialty requires its own preparation. A hero in battle can be a coward before an audience unless he is prepared.

If fear and tension do nothing else but stimulate the speaker to do his homework, they have performed their natural service.

Fear and tension should be considered a positive influence which sharpens our strategy so that we may do our best. We are always facing difficulties. We make progress by meeting the challenge and conquering our fears. In that way our emotions motivate greater effort—which invites growth and development.

Delivering a talk or a presentation does take time—time to prepare. Even the more experienced speaker, whether he admits it in public or not, profits from the perspiration of preparation.

Obviously, we cannot keep a secret from our nervous system. If our nerves are stirred up in anticipation of the event, they are more tranquilized by the very fact that we have done our best to make ready.

There is a military maxim which says, "When in doubt, attack." A prepared speaker never feels cornered. Whatever doubts he may have are swept aside when he behaves with the impetus of a man who knows what he is doing.

It is this knowledge which displaces his doubts with more confidence.

WAYS TO REDUCE PHYSICAL TENSIONS
Breathe in rhythm—slowly, deeply.
Yawn several times.
Gesture and move whenever possible.
Relax your throat, jaw, shoulders.
Loosen your arms.

DON'T BE PERFECT, JUST BE GOOD

Most successful people aim for perfection. Yet they know that perfection is its own worst enemy. So they balance the situation, not with sloppy effort, but by lowering their highest ideals a few notches.

They know that only a few people can swim the English Channel, but short of that, many can learn to swim expertly.

Perfection is a state of mind, not a reality. So the most we can ask of ourselves is to do the best we can. We can always do better next time.

Major Edward Bowes, who was famous as the originator of the

The human brain is a wonderful organ. It starts to work as soon as you are born and doesn't stop until you get up to deliver a public speech. —*George Jessel*

"Original Amateur Hour" during the 1930's, told about his first experience with public speaking.

> When I first came to New York, Mark Twain gave a dinner in my honor. There were many distinguished guests, and he noticed that I was getting panicky.
>
> When he asked, "You feel all right?" I said, "Frankly, I'm scared to death. I know that I will have to speak soon, and I don't know if I'll be able to get out of my chair. When I stand up, my mind sits down!"
>
> An experienced public speaker, Mark Twain replied, "It might help you, Eddie, if you keep one thing in mind. Just remember they don't expect much!"

When a man discusses his stress in anticipation of making a presentation, more often than not he will define his fears with such words as "I just don't want to make a fool of myself." The reply to that statement is that a fool doesn't go through all he is going through in trying to deliver a good talk.

If he has properly researched his topic and prepared himself in the best way he knows how, then he should be able to ride out any tensions, however unpredictable.

For the rest, he must have faith in his audience, knowing that they will appreciate his effort. With every important venture we run a risk —a risk of making fools of ourselves. And if, by earnestly performing as we do, we are labeled fools, then that's a chance we must take.

For it is that very courage to meet what comes that is written on the speaker's face and is respected by the listeners. Perhaps the first lesson of wisdom is to be willing to risk being taken for a fool—a conscientious, hard-working fool, of course.

Speak often, keep your momentum

To gain confidence, take up the challenge to speak at every opportunity. In that way you can develop a new tolerance for the stresses and toughen your reactions as muscles are toughened by activity. We all have a marvelous capacity to adapt to the external environment. Use it; speak often.

Throw away all your fine excuses.

When it comes to public speaking and presentations, use as a verbal talisman the potent words of Robert Frost, "The only way around is through."

45

How to pick
your subject

Unless a topic has been assigned, your first job will be deciding on a subject that will interest the group you've been asked to address. The tips and exercises in this chapter show you how to tailor your topic to the occasion, the audience, and the effect you want to achieve.

When you are asked to speak before a group, the program chairman may tell you what he wants you to talk about. You may know specifically what you must do in your speech: praise an associate who is retiring, nominate someone for office, or describe your firm's booth at a coming exhibit.

But sometimes the program chairman is vague, or the meeting is a routine one, and you must choose your subject yourself. That problem need not present difficulties. Once you have mastered a few simple principles, you should be able to decide easily what to talk about even at short notice.

The best choice is a subject that suits you, your audience, the occasion, and the length of time you have been allowed.

Choose a subject that suits you. You will talk best on a subject you know well, or in which you are deeply interested.

Remember, when you are talking you are an *authority*. You ought to know more about your subject than any member of your audience. This should be true if only because you are presenting your personal viewpoint and experience.

Therefore, consider as possible subjects: your job, hobby or interests, past experiences, beliefs and convictions, reactions to a book you've read; or some field of knowledge you've studied, an idea or process you'd like to explain, an issue you've discussed with friends, a project you're interested in, a desire or hope or wish of yours.

A personal list drawn up on this model might be: accounting; golf; baseball; gardening; trip across the continent; hitchhiking; better schools; sales taxes; tax laws; safer cars; safer driving; shopping centers; war and peace; the mature mind. Then there are the "how to" topics, by which you can give others the benefit of expert knowledge that you've acquired: how to prepare your income tax; how to buy a used car; how to acquire better reading habits.

PRACTICE EXERCISE
■ List ten subjects about which you think you have enough information to deliver a talk. List ten propositions which you would enthusiastically defend or attack.

Choose a subject that suits your audience. Audiences will listen more readily if your subject is one which vitally concerns them and is timely.

Certain subjects would appeal to parents but not to youngsters; others, to youngsters but not to parents; others, to both groups. Suburban businessmen might well be interested in parking problems, in meeting the competition of a branch store which a large city firm is going to establish in their midst, or in a "pet" charity.

Therefore, always think over what you know, or can find out, about your audience. Ask yourself the following questions:

What are they likely to be interested in as *individuals?*

What are they likely to be interested in as an *organized group,* that is, as health workers, engineers, members of a social club?

What are they likely to expect me to talk about?

PRACTICE EXERCISES
■ Jot down subjects you think might interest the groups mentioned above: health workers, engineers, members of a social club.

■ Go over the two lists you made in the preceding section (ten subjects about which you think you have enough information to deliver a talk, ten propositions which you would enthusiastically either defend or attack). From these, select subjects you think would interest: a group of Boy Scouts; the Ladies' Aid or Women's Guild of your church; a group of tourists visiting your city, school, or plant.

Choose a subject that suits the occasion. The demands of the occasion are so obvious that they would hardly seem to need mention. The Memorial Day Program demands a tribute to the dead and the ideals for which they gave their lives. The annual business meeting calls for reports on the year's activities and perhaps a look at plans for the future.

Yet all of us have been bored or annoyed by the speaker who disregarded this principle. He was so wrapped up in his own interests or wanted so badly to get something off his chest that he completely forgot the occasion. At a graduation ceremony a prominent doctor got very little applause for his excellent paper on "Diseases of the Liver." And at the initiation of new members into a society, a defeated candidate for office probably lost all chance of ever being elected by attacking the successful candidates and the election methods.

Keep your subject within the spirit of the occasion.

PRACTICE EXERCISE
■ What subjects would be suitable for: a Christmas party; the laying of a cornerstone; the fiftieth anniversary of a club, a business organization, or a college?

Choose a subject that suits your time allowance. That is to say, be sure your subject is one you can discuss *adequately* in the two, five, ten, twenty, or thirty minutes allotted you.

A talk on the "Causes of the American Revolution" can hardly be crammed into four minutes. But do not feel that you must give up this subject because you cannot treat it fully.

Narrow a broad subject, or limit yourself to some aspect of it. In this case, "The Stamp Act," "The Boston Tea Party," or "The Sons of Liberty" are relevant subjects which could be treated in a short time.

Conversely, if you merely must congratulate some teamworkers on the success of their charity fund drive, don't take half an hour at it.

PRACTICE EXERCISE
■ Assume that "Democracy at the Crossroads" is the theme of an hour-long radio program. List four subjects which might be discussed by as many speakers under this general heading.

Sometimes all four of the above factors will be of about equal importance in the choice of a subject. Sometimes one, such as the occasion, will be the most important.

Finally, if you are given a specific topic and find, after some thought, that you are not interested in it, suggest another topic that you feel would be more suitable, or refuse the invitation politely. There are times when it is better to remain silent than to speak.

494

PRACTICE EXERCISES

■ Assume that you are program chairman for the opening of a Youth Center in your town. The program committee has decided to include three short talks on the general theme of "Youth Today." What would you suggest as three subjects under this head?

■ A famous explorer returns from a trip. If he were as good a speaker as he is an explorer, how might he vary the subjects of a series of talks to fit: an explorers' club; a garden club; junior-high school assembly program; a reunion of his college classmates; a group of meteorologists?

■ Take the original lists of subjects you made out for yourself and see how you might adapt them to fit the various situations mentioned in this section.

The four main goals of public speaking

The speaker delivers his speech in order to get a response, a reaction, from his audience.

You will make a better speech, have a better chance of getting the response you want, if you define clearly beforehand both the *general* and the *specific purpose* of your talk.

On the basis of their general purposes, speeches tend to fall into four categories. Keeping your subject in mind, decide into which of the following your speech falls. You may wish:

To interest or amuse the audience. This is the general purpose of many after-dinner speeches, the chairman's or toastmaster's introductions, the preliminary talks before the main speech of the evening, the professional comedian's contribution, the popular travel or "culture" lecture, and indeed of many so-called educational talks.

In such cases speakers rely mainly on stories, anecdotes, and humor. These are successful when they keep the audience interested or amused.

To inform or teach the audience. This is the purpose of the classroom lecture, the business report, the training talk given to new or old employes by a manager or supervisor, the paper delivered at a convention by one specialist to other specialists, the "popular" lecture given by a scientist or expert to the general public.

Besides being interesting, this type of speech conveys information. It discusses, explains, or describes events or ideas, or teaches the audience how to do something. It strives for clarity and simplicity. It often uses audio-visual aids—charts, graphs, filmstrips, recordings, movies.

It is successful when the members of the audience, besides being interested or even amused, leave the auditorium with more knowledge, understanding, or skill than they had upon entering; and when at least some of the listeners remember the content of the speech long enough to put it to use.

To stimulate or impress. This is the purpose of many sermons, of the inspirational talk to salesmen or other businessmen, of the pep talk to athletes between halves or to workers in some cause at a rally, and of speeches made at "occasions"—Fourth of July and other holiday programs, memorial services, anniversaries, graduation and commencement exercises, reunions, induction and inauguration ceremonies, and other festive or solemn celebrations.

This type of speech does not attempt to change people's beliefs or get them to do something. Rather its general purpose is to strengthen existing beliefs, to get the auditors to do better or more vigorously things which, at the time, they are doing only adequately or half-heartedly. This is the speech that seeks to substitute earnest effort for lip service.

As such, it tends more to emotion than to logic, and may contain little or no information. It is frequently accompanied by other stimulants to the emotions: food, flowers, decorations, music, costumes, flags, lighting effects, processions, rituals. It is successful when the audience leaves feeling ennobled, stronger in its faith, eager to fight the good fight.

To convince or persuade. This is the general purpose of the speeches made by the courtroom lawyer, the candidate for office, the salesman, the legislator proposing a bill, the crusader, the reformer, the pleader for a cause, the scientist offering a new theory, the ordinary citizen getting up at a town meeting or public hearing to argue for something he says will benefit the community.

This type of speech seeks to change an audience's beliefs, to get them to take some specific action. Its appeal may be entirely intellectual and logical, or it may be strongly emotional. It organizes its arguments, backs up these arguments with facts and statistics, and frequently utilizes the methods of the stimulating and impressive speech.

It is successful when beliefs are changed, when, to some degree, the audience is more persuaded to do as you ask.

Obviously, a speech whose general purpose is to amuse will differ considerably in materials, tone, language, and structure from one intended to teach. Both will differ from speeches to stimulate or to convince. Knowing the methods and limitations of each will be a decided help in preparing your talks.

PRACTICE EXERCISES

■ On the subject of the weather, think of possible speeches you might make whose general purposes would be to interest, teach, impress, persuade your audience.

■ What were the general purposes of the twenty subjects on your original lists? Could you also deliver other speeches on the same subjects, but with different general purposes?

Spell out your purpose

After you've determined the general intent of your speech, the next step is to phrase as concisely as possible its *specific purpose*.

Think of the specific purpose variously as the main idea or central thought of your speech; the point you wish to make; what you want your audience to carry away with them; the special angle that you want to give your approach.

Boiling down your subject in this way will help you to concentrate your efforts, to eliminate related but distracting details.

Make sure your specific purpose contains one thought and one thought alone; that it is simple, easily understood, and easily remembered; and that it is calculated to arouse interest.

It may be phrased either as a sentence or as a question, or the sentence may be implied.

Vote for Thomas Brown for Town Clerk!
A high fidelity set will increase your enjoyment of music.
How does one cut a one-seam skirt?
It's about time Colford had a woman mayor.
(My specific purpose is to teach a group of Sea Scouts:) How to Tie a Bowline.

Avoid the complex, the lengthy or the indefinite topic.

Drug abuse.
How to start a store.
Lincoln as a young man gave little promise of his later greatness, but when we consider his background we can readily say . . .

If you want to talk about drug abuse, for example, you might limit your topic to, "What to Tell Your Children About Drugs."

SELL YOUR IDEA WITH QUOTATIONS

IN ONE SENSE, the speaker need never be alone on the platform. He always has strong friends he can call upon to back up the point he is presenting to the audience. These friends are called authority, testimony, and quotation.

Very often your audience will refuse to accept an idea with only your *own* authority behind it. Perhaps all they are looking for is a bit more convincing. Whatever the reason, the speaker has to reach into his bag of proof and come up with something that will help him sell his idea.

The use of authority, testimony, or quotation is simply the mustering of intelligent support for your position from people living and dead who have gone on record as agreeing with you.

Your listeners will recognize the stature and intelligence of the people standing behind your point of view, and they will find that they have to agree with what you say.

Authority and quotation are powerful forces for the speaker, *if* he uses them correctly!

Here are some guides for the use of this type of support:

1. Be sure your authority is recognized as someone who has the right to speak on the subject; someone who has a firsthand knowledge of the subject.

2. Choose an authority who will be accepted by your listeners as someone who is free of prejudice and doesn't have an ax to grind.

3. Recognize the difference in audience appeal between authoritative testimony by an expert and quotation from a book or by a historical figure. Testimony will usually support the speaker's point most effectively on questions of *fact;* quotation will usually work much more strongly to get an *emotional* acceptance of your viewpoint from the audience.

4. Stay away from hackneyed quotations whose triteness can only have a sickening effect on your audience.

5. Don't stretch a quotation all out of shape to make it fit into your speech.

Audiences never fail to respond to quotes by famous men; from literature; from the Bible; sayings which the speaker can use as supports for the idea he wants to drive home. If you are speaking on the need for executives to think out a problem carefully before they act, you might use this quote from Plutarch:

I do not think him a good shoemaker who makes a great shoe for a small foot.

Or, if you are speaking on the need for better communication in business today, you might quote Daniel Webster:

If all my possessions were taken from me with one exception, I would choose to keep the power of speech, for with it I would soon regain all the rest.

Perhaps the central theme of your speech is for greater dedication to the job and a stronger holding to beliefs. You could quote Abraham Davenport, adviser to George Washington, to whom a meeting adjournment was suggested because of the approach of the British. He answered:

The Day of Judgment is either approaching or it is not. If it is not, there is no cause for adjournment. If it is, I choose to be found doing my duty. I wish, therefore, that candles may be brought.

Where can you find these pertinent quotations to lend impact to your talk? Ever since Massachusetts bookseller John Bartlett published his *Familiar Quotations* in 1885, editors have been putting together collections of great sayings. Your local library will have a number of these books on its shelves. Most dictionaries of quotations are organized alphabetically by subject under such typical headings as *education, friend, patriotism*. But not every quotation related to the theme of your speech is going to be effective. It's up to you to apply the rules just set forth to make a truly appropriate selection.

The use of quotations trades heavily on several powerful forces of motivation: the strength of the source, the pertinence of the statement to today's situation, and the emotional impact which seems to encircle the glorious past. All these are subtle and effective pressures which move your audience to accept what you have to say, and help you sell your idea.

PRACTICE EXERCISES

■ What is wrong with the following specific purposes?
   a. The Washington Monument
   b. Hints for a long-distance call
   c. Savings banks, and investment funds, and stocks and bonds, and loans
   d. I want you to think about taxation

   Try to improve the statement of these specific purposes.

■ For a general audience, which of the following is the best specific purpose?
   a. Christmas and New Year's
   b. How to conduct an audit of a commercial bank branch
   c. I'd like to help you save a life

■ Assume you have to speak at (1) a party at an old folks' home, (2) an assembly program at a senior high school, (3) a meeting of members of a theatrical union, (4) a political rally. Which of the following subjects might be suitable? Guidance; Children's fears; Communism; Events in the news; Arbitration; Television; The spoken versus the written word; Basketball.

   Choose good specific-purpose sentences for those subjects you consider suitable. In the situations given what subjects would you choose to speak on? What would be your specific-purpose sentences?

How to analyze your audience

Once you have picked a subject that you think will interest a particular audience, *analyze* your *prospective listeners* and determine how the speech as a whole can best be *adapted* to them.

A speech in favor of lower real estate taxes might conceivably be made both to a group of tenants and to a group of landlords. But it could not be the same speech, with the same approach and arguments. What won applause in the one case might call forth hisses in the other.

A speech must be "pitched" to its particular audience.

Before you make a talk, decide how the answers to the following questions will affect your speech:

1. *Will the audience be a general or a specialized one?* A specialized audience, such as a group of doctors, requires slanting of the subject to its peculiar interests. The general audience needs a broader appeal.

2. *What will be the probable size of the audience?* With a small audience one can be more informal than with a large crowd.

3. What will be the age range of my listeners? How far back the experience of your listeners goes will affect your choice of material. With older folk, a mere reference to the Depression of the thirties will elicit an immediate personal response. But for teen-agers, those painful years will be known only at second hand.

4. Will the audience be male, female, or mixed? Material suitable for one sex might not be suitable for the other or for a mixed audience.

What is the educational and cultural background of the audience? It is as much a mistake to talk over the heads of the audience as to underestimate their capacities.

5. What social, political, and economic prejudices are my listeners likely to have? Try to find out beforehand the economic level of your audience, the sort of clubs they belong to, their social position. Liberal or conservative, management or labor, homeowner or apartment-renter —each tends to have firmly held beliefs. The skillful speaker avoids arousing needless hostility. In his arguments, he tries to show that his proposal ties in with principles they cherish.

6. What do they know about my subject? To cover in detail facts they already know will only bore them. To assume they have knowledge which they do not actually possess will leave them bewildered. The good speaker will investigate the extent of his audience's knowledge of his topic.

7. What will their attitude be toward my subject? Some members of your audience will be interested in your subject; others will be indifferent or apathetic; still others, if your specific purpose is to persuade, will be hostile. Adapt your speech chiefly to what you think is the predominant attitude with, of course, appreciation of the other attitudes.

The interested audience needs only to have its interest maintained. The most common fault here is to talk too long.

The apathetic audience must have its attention caught, its interest aroused and held. A strong opening, stressing early what the audience may gain from listening, and the steady, forward movement of your ideas will help achieve this end.

The hostile audience is, of course, the most difficult to handle. Many skilled speakers follow the practice of delaying for a considerable time any direct mention of their specific purpose. They show themselves to be friendly, modest, and good-humored. By their fair-mindedness they let it be known that they expect the audience to be as fair. They explore all the common ground they have with the audience; they return to points of agreement before venturing into areas of possible disagreement. In other words, they hope that if the audience gives a series of Yes responses, it will be less disposed to say No.

8. *What are they likely to know about me?* If the audience knows little about you, you may tell them some of your past accomplishments. But do so modestly. Whether they know you little or well, avoid the pitfall of boasting. Let the audience learn your worth from the competent way you handle your subject.

Answering the above questions should not be difficult when you are to speak in your local community. The important thing is to adapt your speech to your audience.

When you talk outside your community, your basic answers will come from the person or committee that invited you, supplemented by such information as you can gather from friends, associates, books. Professional lecturers often visit a town beforehand to look it over, talk with townspeople—the butcher, the banker, the farmer, the millhand—to get their views, test their reactions. Borrow this technique if you can, for it helps to show an audience that you know something of them and their special problems.

Keep on the alert, moreover, ready to change your adaptation to the audience up to the last moment. An important event on the afternoon of your talk may change the temper of your audience; the weather may dampen their spirits; or a preceding speaker may say something which you think will influence the audience against the opening you had planned.

Finally, watch the reactions of your audience, as you talk, particularly with regard to the special adaptations you have made for them. If you do not get a favorable response, take another tack.

PRACTICE EXERCISE

■ Select several subjects you might conceivably talk on and determine how you might adapt them to fit the interests and firmly held beliefs of audiences drawn from the following:

(1) Rotary Club (2) Elks (3) Taxpayers' Union (4) Knights of Columbus (5) Masons (6) Christian Endeavor (7) Zionist Organization of America (8) 4-H (9) Hi-Y (10) a country club (11) an electrical workers' union (12) a social fraternity (13) the National Association for the Advancement of the Colored People (14) the National Association of Manufacturers (15) Young Republicans (16) Young Democrats

46

How to prepare
your speech

Speech consultant Dorothy Sarnoff tells you how to plan and polish your material: the opening remarks that capture attention; the body of the speech that carries the message and the verbal tricks that bring it to life; the climax and the ending that leave your audience remembering.

First you must collect your material. Then you must organize it. Begin by jotting down what you already know of a subject. Add personal experiences or observations illustrating the points you wish to make. Interview people who have information you may lack.

Sometimes a telephone call to the library or to a specialist in your topic will bring out the facts you are after. Sometimes you will need a personal interview. If you require incontrovertible evidence of some arguable point, get it in writing.

Add to your information from newspapers, magazines, and books. Under no circumstances include as a fact any statement that is not backed by an unimpeachable source.

Your speech is divided into opening remarks, body, and conclusion. Let's look first at the opening remarks.

The varieties of introductions are as limitless as your imagination. Begin, if you wish, with a reference to the immediate locale—or the chairman—or the weather—or the train service. You may ask a question ("How many of you were caught in the New York blackout of 1966?"); you may make a dramatic statement; you may cite an incident from the day's news, history, or your own experience.

Quotations and anecdotes can make good introductions. "Quotations have great service for speeches," said Aristotle, "because audiences are commonplace. People are pleased when a speaker hits on a wide general statement of opinions that they hold in some partial or fragmentary form." But use them only if they are *appropriate*. Nothing is more pitiable than a story or joke dragged in, like a stray dog, by the scruff of its neck, and tied into your talk against its will.

Anecdotes and jokes told on the platform require a different form from those written for the printed page. Rehearse yours until you know you have the pacing and the punch lines right, or they will neither amuse your audience nor buttress your point.

Once you begin watching for quotations, you will find them everywhere. Dozens of books are fine sources of anecdotes, quotations, and jokes suitable for speakers, chairmen, and toastmasters. When you see a line worth quoting in a newspaper or magazine, file it on a card.

You may enjoy quoting *epigrams*—brief, witty commentaries on some particular circumstance, like this epitaph for Charles I of England:

> Here lies our sovereign lord and king
> Whose word no man relies on;
> Who never said a foolish thing,
> And never did a wise one.

Or you may prefer *aphorisms*—sentences which bring out universal truths. "The voice of the people is the voice of God" is an aphorism.

One of the most common, delightful, and dangerous introductions is *humor*. Nothing can warm up an audience like a good joke *well told*— but do not venture on a joke unless you know how to make it come off. Truly gifted raconteurs are few and far between.

A joke should be short, crisp, pruned. If your jokes fall flat when you tell them to your friends, do not delude yourself that somehow they will fare better when a hundred or a thousand people are listening. If you have a joke that seems appropriate, practice it aloud until you are sure you have the timing and punch line just right. Then try it on friends. If their laughter is perfunctory, file the joke in the wastebasket.

The body of the speech

At the beginning of a speech, you make friends with your audience and state your proposition. At the end, you nail down your proposition. But the body is the heart of your speech. It is there that you develop your theme and convince your listeners.

A speech should be organized as carefully as a sentence is parsed. The main idea and the supporting ideas should take their due positions and receive their due share of time.

Talks should be either *informative, persuasive, amusing,* or a little of each. An *informative* talk adds to the listeners' knowledge, but is not intended to change or strengthen their opinions. In effect it may be simply the extended and orderly answer to some factual question: "What can computers do to help a business?" "How do you make a candle from an empty milk carton?" "What will it be like to live on the moon?"

A *persuasive* talk, on the other hand, presents a problem, proposes solutions, and, through a progression of carefully reasoned steps, rouses the listeners to action.

Your talk should not go around and around like a leaf in a whirlpool, until it is finally sucked under. Make sure it has forward movement. See to it that each step reinforces the previous one and leads logically to the next.

It is natural to prepare, or at least organize, the body of the speech before deciding how to introduce it, since there is no point in developing an introduction before you know the idea you are introducing.

However, some people preparing a talk prefer to begin at the end. Somerset Maugham said he always wrote the end of his stories first; once he knew where to go, all he had to do was find a way to get there.

Prepare a talk, not an essay

Lincoln used to say that he liked a talk to be as personal and familiar as a chat between two people riding along in a buckboard. Though you should write out your speech to fix the organization and the key phrases in your mind, employ the familiar spoken language of person-to-person conversation. Make every sentence so plain that no listener can find an excuse for failing to get your meaning. Your listeners may never have heard of Disraeli, but by instinct they will agree with his statement that "I make it a rule to believe only what I understand." Emerson said: "Speech is the power to translate a truth into a language perfectly intelligible to the person to whom you speak." A speech, whether to thirty people or to three thousand, should have the quality of speaking not *at* or *to*, but *with*. Each time you rewrite, say the sentences aloud first to test them. Be sure they sound as good as they look.

505

Avoid technical language where it will not be understood. Use images that sharpen your point, not fuzz it. Use words that say exactly what you mean. Be colorful if you can. In any event, see to it that your listener goes away knowing exactly what your message was.

Be specific. "Any talk," said Louis Calhern, "without a specific example is weak." If you use a generalization, back it up with a specific the mind's eye can see. "Ten times the size of an office building elevator" gives you the picture faster than "640 square feet."

If your subject is abstract or complicated, take particular pains to present it in concrete terms, avoiding technicalities and statistics. Inflation comes to life for a listener not in billion-dollar terms but in terms of the cost of a loaf of bread or a quart of milk.

As Elizabeth Barrett Browning put it:

> A red-haired child
> Sick in fever, if you touch him once,
> Though but so little as with a finger-tip,
> Will set you weeping; but a million sick . . .
> You could as soon weep for the "rule of three,"
> Or compound fractions.

How to make your speech vivid

Skilled speakers cast magic spells through devices of rhetoric. The beginning speaker will profit by close attention to the choice of words and word structures in famous speeches.

I have just mentioned one of these devices—*concreteness*, which puts otherwise difficult concepts into terms that are familiar, easy, and often touched with emotion. *Simplicity* is itself a device.

A simple statement, however, does not always of itself evoke an emo-

---

Abraham Lincoln was resting with his managers in a hotel lobby. As usual the village dudes had congregated there, and one, bolder than the rest, remarked: "Mr. Lincoln, your speech was good but there were some points quite beyond my reach."

The simple Lincoln looked up and chuckled, "I'm sorry for you; I once had a dog that had the same trouble with fleas."

—*Edmond Tisdel*

tional response. It is strengthened if placed in *context:* "They drove to the village often for supplies and always stopped at the post office, a frame building that had once been a Catholic mission." Knowing that the post office (described by L. Woiwode in *What I'm Going to Do, I Think*) was a frame building, and that it once had been a Catholic mission, makes it seem more real to the reader.

APPEALS TO THE SENSES

Sensual images are highly effective: "Then they all left the room," writes Kafka; "the door was shut; the singing stopped; clouds covered the moon; the bedding was warm around me; the horses' heads in the open windows wavered like shadows." Note how one sense impression after another takes over: sound, sight, warmth.

Here is how Woiwode evokes smell:

"The smell was so toxic that when he held his face close to the stove, his eyes began to water, his nose and lungs burned, and he felt light-headed." And again: "The sheets . . . were damp and clinging and smelled of naphthalene. He'd fallen asleep to the smell and waked to it in the night and now, as he looked out at the meadow overlaid with moonlight, the smell seemed responsible for the silver color of the grass and the silver color of the trees encircling it, and for their unnatural stillness."

A sentence of O. Henry's shows what the imagination can do with sounds heard from a Manhattan hotel in summertime: "The pleasing distant roar of Broadway is transformed in the imagination of the happy guests to the noise of a waterfall filling the woods with its restful sound."

There are images, too, that evoke the sensations of physical activity, called *kinesthetic.* Ernest Hemingway was a master of kinesthetic images: "I slapped the Roman on the back and we went through the thumb-pulling again; me pulling his thumb too. I embraced the Wan-derobo-Masai and he, after a thumb-pulling of great intensity and feel-ing, slapped his chest and said very proudly, 'Wanderobo-Masai won-derful guide.'"

THE ARTFUL USE OF SLANG

Slang can add vividness to a talk, but must be used with great care, since it may either offend or baffle some listeners. "Attaboy," "do your thing," "that's his bag," "blew his top," "what a drag," "up tight," "don't put me down"—all are appropriate in some situations.

Inappropriate or exaggerated figures of speech can be laughable, as shown by these similes recommended in an Edwardian phrase book:
My heart is like a full sponge and must weep a little.
Her hair dropped on her pallid cheeks, like seaweed on a clam.
A book that rends and tears like a broken saw.

FIGURES OF SPEECH

Figures of speech, if not labored, add greatly to the color of a talk. We all use figures of speech, often without even realizing what we are doing; if you say "Wall Street is in trouble," you don't really mean a street, you mean the stock market in general.

There are many types of figures of speech.

A *simile* is a comparison of one thing to another: "My luv is like a red, red rose."

A *metaphor* is a comparison in which one thing is described as if it were another: "the starry canvas of the night."

Irony says one thing to convey another: "To prove his devotion, he beat her soundly."

Hyperbole is the use of exaggeration for emphasis: "He stood tall as a mountain."

OTHER SPEECH DEVICES

Rhyme ("courtly" and "portly"; "earning" and "learning," etc.) can tickle the ear, but should be used sparingly.

Anaphora is the repetition of words at the beginning of successive clauses or sentences, as in these lovely lines from Corinthians: "Charity suffereth long, and is kind; charity envieth not; charity vaunteth not itself, is not puffed up."

Balance can be equally effective: "Love beareth all things; believeth all things; hopeth all things; endureth all things."

Assonance is the deliberate repetition of a vowel sound, but in combination with a different consonant, so that it is not what is normally thought of as a rhyme: "old oak," "mad hat," "top notch."

Consonance is the repetition of final consonant sounds, as in "tip top," "knick-knack," "ding-dong."

Alliteration is the repetition of initial consonant sounds: "lonely, low-lying lands," "tried and true," "rhyme or reason," "sighted sub, sank same."

Word repetition pounds an idea home, as in this paragraph from President Kennedy's inaugural address: "There is an old Chinese proverb saying that each generation builds a road for the next. The road has been built for us, and I believe it is incumbent upon us, in our generation, to build our road for the next." Notice how the words "road" and "generation" are repeated for a harmonious integration of thought.

Cadence is rhythm combined with inflection, the melody of the phrases: "Give me liberty or give me death" and "I saw him wounded, bleeding, and dying."

There is much overlapping among these categories and terms, and the important thing is to grasp their function rather than to worry over what they are called.

The climax

The most popular climax is the strong conclusion. Arrange your ideas in a series that climbs to a crescendo. As in some symphonies, the talk should seem to build of itself. One instrument after another comes in until the entire orchestra is speaking. A speech on a great theme may deserve the rising thunder of such a finale as this:

"Others may hesitate, others may procrastinate, others may plead for further negotiations; but as for me, I am ready to act now. And for my action I am ready to answer to my conscience, my country, and my God."

The "dissolve" ending

An opposite, equally effective form of climax is the diminuendo, or dissolve ending. I call this "iris-ing out." Perhaps you've heard it in the last movement of a symphony where the orchestra diminishes and the instruments drop out section by section, even instrument by instrument, until the final passage ends with the cello on a single, drawn-out sigh.

In nightclub songs that involve deep emotions and end in low key, the song seems to fade away while the light on the singer shrinks gradually to a smaller and smaller circle until it lights only the face, then the eyes. Finally, it is a pinpoint, and disappears with the last note of music.

Here is a speech conclusion that iris-es out:

"I saw him bear the burden of a nation's destiny. I saw him implore divine guidance. I saw him wounded, bleeding, dying. For you . . . and for me." The final words fade like the spotlight, leaving the audience emotionally drained.

Climaxes, whether crescendo or diminuendo, require skillful handling. When overdone or inappropriate, they only make the audience uncomfortable and the speaker absurd. Say the sentences aloud before you put them down. Underact them in delivery. Rehearse until you know your cadence is right and your emotion convincing.

More hints for effective speaking

For closer communication, use the words "you" and "we"; balance statistics with graphic images; and pause for effect.

Questions can also strengthen a speech. They are of three kinds: those the speaker asks the audience to answer aloud; those he asks the audience and answers himself; and those which are entirely rhetorical, implying their own answers.

Be sparing with statistics and visual aids—charts, blackboards, slides. Use them judiciously to make your point clear, never allowing them to dominate your speech. Remember audience attention should focus on you the speaker; visuals can only illustrate or clarify your point.

If your speech requires a blackboard or easel, do not display the information on it until the time has come to use it. It distracts your listeners' attention.

If you are using a blackboard, don't scribble on it; write clearly, so that your audience will have no difficulty reading your words. Keep talking to your audience and eye-contacting them on your way to the board. Otherwise you are apt to cut off your connection.

If you are using slides, rehearse first with the technician, to be sure they are in focus. Be certain he understands your change-slide signal. Try to arrange for a screen with a mat finish, to avoid glare.

If you are using a projector, don't put it in the middle of the audience. That irritates. Put it in the back of the room.

Don't let your visuals get in the way of your message.

A chief petty officer was teaching about bulletin board displays in a navy instructor's training course. He held up a calendar bearing a stun-

BEATING THE "HO HUM ... SO WHAT?" BLUES

A GOOD FORMULA for organizing a speech is given by a public-speaking expert, Richard C. Borden. He classifies the four parts of a speech as:

Ho hum.

Why bring that up?

For instance. . . .

So what?

"Ho hum" suggests you are facing a bored audience who must be wakened to an interest in what you have to say. Mr. Borden says:

"Don't open your speech on safety-first by saying, 'My subject is the reduction of traffic accidents.' Say instead: 'Four hundred and fifty shiny new coffins were delivered to this city last Thursday.'"

If your speech is on civic improvement don't start, "I have been asked to tell you about the problems of our community." Rather say, "Eleven stabbings in twelve months at the Little Corner Inn have made some citizens aware of our civic problems."

"Why bring that up?" indicates that you must then tell your audience why it should listen to you. In the safety talk you might point out that one of those coffins may be for you or one of your friends, unless the warnings are heeded.

"For instance" of course means you should use plenty of lively illustrations and examples to clarify the points you are trying to make. On the subject of safety you could use actual cases depicting those daily hazards leading to injury or death.

Illustrative material may be found in incidents from the lives of your friends or of famous people in government, art, sports, and the like. Each example should be: illustrative—it should have a point; clear—meaning well expressed; specific—or definite; animated—with lift in it; timed—for climax.

"Why bring that up?" and "For instance" are the meat of the sandwich. They fit between the opening, which grabs attention, and the closing, which restates the theme and asks for action.

"So what?" means, Borden says, "The end of your speech should have a point." Tell your audience clearly what you expect them to do about what you have been telling them.

ning picture of a scantily clad young lady. After the class had had time to inspect it carefully, he put it away. Then he asked, "What was the month showing on the calendar?"

When no one could answer, the instructor drew this moral: "Don't make your teaching aids so attractive that they draw attention away from the message that they are intended to present."

How JFK did it

Theodore Sorensen in his book *Kennedy* gives us the guidelines by which he and the President prepared speeches. The relevant section is reproduced here, with important points underlined.[1] Note the basic principles the President followed: short speeches, short clauses, short words; points or propositions in logical sequence; simplicity and clarity; anecdotal emphasis tailored to the need of the speech. These principles will work for you too.

He would never blindly accept or blandly deliver a text he had not seen and edited. We always discussed the topic, the approach and the conclusions in advance. He always had quotations or historical allusions to include. Sometimes he would review an outline. And he always, upon receiving my draft, altered, deleted or added phrases, paragraphs or pages. Some drafts he rejected entirely.

The Kennedy style of speech-writing—our style, I am not reluctant to say, for he never pretended that he had time to prepare first drafts for all his speeches—evolved gradually over the years. Prepared texts were carefully designed for an orderly presentation of their substance but with no deliberate affectation of any certain style. We were not conscious of following the elaborate techniques later ascribed to these speeches by literary analysts. Neither of us had any special training in composition, linguistics or semantics. Our chief criterion was always audience comprehension and comfort, and this meant: (1) short speeches, short clauses and short words, wherever possible; (2) a series of points or propositions in numbered or logical sequence, wherever appropriate; and (3) the construction of sentences, phrases and paragraphs in such a manner as to simplify, clarify and emphasize.

1. Abridged from pp. 60–65, *Kennedy* by Theodore C. Sorensen. Copyright © 1965 by Theodore C. Sorensen. Reprinted by permission of Harper & Row, Publishers, Inc.

The test of a text was not how it appeared to the eye but how it sounded to the ear. His best paragraphs, when read aloud, often had a cadence not unlike blank verse—indeed at times key words would rhyme. He was fond of alliterative sentences, not solely for reasons of rhetoric but to reinforce the audience's recollection of his reasoning. Sentences began, however incorrect some may have regarded it, with "And" or "But" whenever that simplified and shortened the text. His frequent use of dashes as a means of separating clauses was of doubtful grammatical standing—but it simplified the delivery and even the publication of a speech in a manner no comma, parenthesis or semicolon could match.

Words were regarded as tools of precision, to be chosen and applied with a craftsman's care to whatever the situation required. He liked to be exact. But if the situation required a certain vagueness, he would deliberately choose a word of varying interpretations rather than bury his imprecision in ponderous prose.

"HE DISLIKED VERBOSITY AND POMPOSITY"

For he disliked verbosity and pomposity in his own remarks as much as he disliked them in others. He wanted both his message and his language to be plain and unpretentious, but never patronizing. He wanted his major policy statements to be positive, specific and definite, avoiding the use of "suggest," "perhaps" and "possible alternatives for consideration." At the same time, his emphasis on a course of reason—rejecting the extremes of either side—helped produce the parallel construction and use of contrasts with which he later became identified. He had a weakness for one unnecessary phrase: "The harsh facts of the matter are . . ."—but, with few other exceptions, his sentences were lean and crisp.

No speech was more than twenty to thirty minutes in duration. They were all too short and too crowded with facts to permit any excess of generalities and sentimentalities. His texts wasted no words and his delivery wasted no time. Frequently he moved from one solid fact or argument to another, without the usual repetition and elaboration, far too quickly for his audiences to digest or even applaud his conclusions. Nor would he always pause for applause when it came.

He spoke at first with no gestures, though he gradually developed a short jab to emphasize his points. Often his tone was monotonous. Often

513

his emphasis was on the wrong word. But often when his audiences were large and enthusiastic—particularly indoors, if the hall was not too vast—an almost electric charge would transmit vitality back and forth between speaker and listeners.

He used little or no slang, dialect, legalistic terms, contractions, clichés, elaborate metaphors or ornate figures of speech. He refused to be folksy or to include any phrase or image he considered corny, taste- less or trite. He rarely used words he considered hackneyed: "humble," "dynamic," "glorious." He used none of the customary word fillers (e.g., "And I say to you that is a legitimate question and here is my answer"). And he did not hesitate to depart from strict rules of English usage when he thought adherence to them (e.g., "Our agenda *are* long") would grate on the listener's ear.

"HIS SPEECHES SHOWED ERUDITION . . . NOT ARROGANCE"

The intellectual level of his speeches showed erudition but not arrogance. Though he knew a little French ("very little," he commented in 1957 after a somewhat halting telephone conversation with the King of Morocco on the North African situation), he was most reluctant to include any foreign words in his addresses.

He was not reluctant, however, particularly in those pre-1960 days, to pack his speeches with statistics and quotations—frequently too many for audiences unaccustomed to his rapid-fire delivery. While I learned to keep a *Bartlett's* and similar works handy, the Senator was the chief source of his own best quotations. Some were in the black notebooks he had kept since college—some were in favorite reference books on his desk, such as Agar's *The Price of Union*—most were in his head.

He would not always be certain of the exact wording or even the author of a quotation he wanted, but he could suggest enough for his staff or the Library of Congress to find it. Preparing his brief, effective statement against the isolationist Bricker Amendment to the Constitu- tion, for example, he told me, "Someone—was it Falkland?—gave the classic definition of conservatism which went something like 'When it is not necessary to change, it is necessary not to change.' Let's include the exact quotation and author."

He also liked on occasion—especially with college audiences which he enjoyed—to include humorous illustrations and quotations in the body of his speeches. An excerpt from a particularly abusive debate between earlier Senators and statesmen always delighted him, possibly because it contrasted so vividly with his own style of understatement.

Humor in the *body* of a prepared speech, however, was rare compared to its use at the *beginning* of almost every speech he made off the Senate floor. While here, too, he preferred historical or political anecdotes, both the quality and the sources of this introductory material varied widely. He believed topical, tasteful, pertinent, pointed humor at the beginning of his remarks to be a major means of establishing audience rapport; and he would work with me as diligently for the right opening witticism, or take as much pride the next day in some spontaneous barb he had flung, as he would on the more substantive paragraphs in his text.

Successful stories told by a toastmaster or by another speaker would be jotted down for future reference. Collections of Finley Peter Dunne and Will Rogers, current newspaper columns and quotations, the works of writers who liberally sprinkled their thoughts on history and government with amusing expressions or examples (such as Denis Brogan and T. V. Smith) were all carefully mined. Standard joke-books were never used, nor would he ever say, "That reminds me of the story of . . ." as a bridge to some irrelevant and lengthy anecdote, but many an old saw was adapted to modern politics and to a particular audience.

"NO LAUGH-GETTER . . . WAS EVER DISCARDED"

No laugh-getter once used or even considered was ever discarded. A large "humor folder" in my files grew continuously. Omitting all anecdotes from the texts that were distributed to the press usually avoided their being publicized, and thus made possible their use in another speech in another part of the country. Audiences watching him scribbling away during dinner often thought he was rewriting his speech, as at times he was. More often he was jotting down the opening lines most appropriate to that audience, working in many cases from a typewritten "humor list" of one-line reminders.

Except for joking about the political liabilities of his own religion, he avoided all ethnic references as well as all off-color remarks in public (although not in private). The only joke which backfired was told early in his Senate career. "The cab driver did such a good job rushing me to this luncheon," he told a Washington audience, "that I was going to give him a big tip and tell him to vote Democratic. Then I remembered the advice of Senator Green, so I gave him no tip and told him to vote Republican." The Associated Press solemnly reported the story as though it had actually happened, and a storm of letters from cab drivers and their wives caused the Senator to think twice about his choice of humor in the future.

He liked to poke fun at politics and politicians, his party, his colleagues and himself. He liked humor that was both topical and original, irreverent but gentle. In his eight years in the Senate no speech assignment worried him longer or more deeply than his role as Democratic jester for the Washington Gridiron Club Dinner in 1958. His successful ten-minute talk on that occasion was drawn from several hours of material gathered from many sources and tried on many "experts." Thereafter he tended more and more, except perhaps on the 1960 campaign circuit, to use that kind of political, more subtle and self-belittling humor, for it was naturally consistent with his own personality and private wit.

His best humor, of course, was spontaneous, and his increasing confidence on the platform brought increasing numbers of spur-of-the-moment gibes. Candor and humor, when combined, can be dangerous weapons politically, and at times he had to restrain his natural instincts in this direction.

In addition to the humor file, we kept a collection of appropriate speech endings—usually quotations from famous figures or incidents from history which, coupled with a brief peroration of his own, could conclude almost any speech on any subject with a dramatic flourish. On many of the hectic precampaign trips of 1957–1959, he would leave one community for the next with a paraphrase from a favorite Robert Frost poem:

> Iowa City is lovely, dark and deep
> But I have promises to keep
> And miles to go before I sleep.

He soon knew all these closings by heart; and while the standard closings, like the humorous openings, were almost always omitted from his released texts in order to facilitate their continued use elsewhere, his own reading copy (prepared in extra-large type) would have merely a word or a phrase to indicate the appropriate close: e.g., "Candles," "General Marshall," "Rising or Setting Sun."

> **A** man of mediocre intellect who had become a prominent politician in Ceylon once amazed Parliament with a brilliant speech. As he sat down amid thunderous applause, a single voice in the Opposition cried out: "Author! Author!" —*Amita Abayesekera*

Obviously the Senator was capable of selecting and remembering his own peroration without the help of these few words. But he looked upon his text and each part of it as insurance. Should the pressures of the moment or the fatigue of the trip benumb his brain as he stood on his feet, he wanted a complete text in his hands which he could follow or at least take off from. He would often deviate from his text or delete passages previously approved and sometimes discard it entirely. But— particularly in earlier days, when he knew his extemporaneous remarks were likely to be less organized, precise and grammatical than a more carefully prepared text—he wanted the reassurance a manuscript gave him.

A warning about ghostwriters

Many Presidents have employed a sizable stable of ghostwriters. Often each has an assignment, one specializing in humor, another in the poetic touch, a third in economics, a fourth in crime, and so on.

If you use outside help in preparing your speech, be sure to make your own decisions about what you want to say. Then work closely with your writer. Let the preparation be a mutual enterprise—but make sure the resulting speech reflects *your* thoughts and personality.

A ghostwriter who had been doing a series of articles for Samuel Goldwyn fell ill, and one of the pieces was written by a substitute ghost. Goldwyn, reading this article, expressed dismay: "This," he said, "is not up to my usual standard."

Some men come to their first speechmaking class and read speeches that obviously have been manufactured for them by someone else. Their talks fit their personalities about the way a man's golf shoes would fit his wife's feet. A speaker must choose a ghostwriter who understands him and will work closely with him.

517

Edit!

When the draft of your talk is ready, the time has come to edit, edit, edit. Check it against the following list:

1. Have I honored all requirements of the talk?
2. Have I researched the topic enough? Investigated all sources?
3. Have I taken into account the nature of the audience—its economic level, sophistication, culture, age, sex, experience, etc.?
4. Have I rechecked to make sure the talk fits the allotted time?
5. Have I "boiled down" the scope of the topic for the time allotted?
6. Have I constructed the talk so it has a clear purpose and makes a point at the end?
7. Have I enough strong ideas in the body and have I developed them sufficiently?
8. Have I arranged them in good order?
9. Have I asked questions, used "you" enough?
10. Have I an appropriate introduction?
11. Have I a strong conclusion?
12. Have I enough variety, specifics, and continuity?
13. Does my language appeal to sight, sound, smell, taste, and touch?
14. Have I used too many statistics?
15. Have I familiarized myself with the locale, its idioms, news, etc.?
16. Have I prepared the speech in *spoken*, not written language?

Harry Emerson Fosdick once commented that a half hour of writing time is needed for every minute of speaking time. Mark Twain said it takes three weeks to write a good ad-lib speech. Be sure you have taken all the time you need to prepare your speech well.

POINTS TO REMEMBER

Thorough preparation lessens nervousness.

Check the requirements of the talk: what your audience is like; the time limits; the proper clothing, etc.

Make sure you have something worth saying—and listening to.

Gather your material intelligently.

Prepare your introduction for immediate impact.

Convey your message in the body of your speech.

Make your conclusion memorable.

47

Start with
a list of points

Having trouble organizing your speech? Here's a sure-fire system for picking out the really essential points and arranging them to hold interest and stick in the listener's mind. You'll say exactly what you want to say in a way the audience will listen to and understand.

Most speeches start with this plan. The speaker says, "I have a number of points I want to make." Let's say you know the points you want to make. Now consider the devices you can use to present your points more effectively.

1. Make a list of the points you want to cover.
2. Use as few points as possible.
3. Analyze each point for interest to this group.
4. Arrange your points in the order best suited to hold interest all through the speech.
5. Number your points to help the group remember.

Here are some reasons for each of these bits of advice:

1. *List your points:* Take a blank sheet of paper and list the points you want to cover. Include every idea that comes to your mind. If you decide later that an idea doesn't belong, you can discard it. When your list is finished, check the three or four points that you think are the most important.

2. *Cut your list to as few points as possible:* The President's State of the Union speech illustrates the difficulty of holding interest throughout a speech with a large number of points. The message has to cover a large

number, and perhaps as a loyal citizen you should be interested in all of them. But no listener is going to be interested in any point because he should be interested. He has to see how it concerns him. Any speech will be better if you have just one point to make. The ideal is Cato's "Carthage must be destroyed." But if you have ten points on that list of yours, there are two devices for cutting: (a) forget some points; (b) combine minor points under the majors.

■ *Forget some points.* You are lucky if you have only three or four points on the first list you made up. Your listener has a certain span of attention. If you have more than four points, you'll lose his interest on points that have no or little appeal to him. You were told to include every idea on your first list, but in doing this you probably included points that you can now cut without any great loss to you.

Cut this type of point:

one of small importance to you;

one you don't believe has too much value;

one that calls for too much explanation;

one you consider padding, not germane to your objective;

one that calls for apology such as "This may not be of too much interest to you, but it is important in South America";

one that might start a controversy, unless you feel the controversy *should* be started.

Cutting these points gives you more time for the important ones.

■ *Combine minor points under the majors.* After you made a list of points, you checked three or four of them as your major points. Now check to see how many of those you didn't check can be used as sub-points under the majors. You may protest, "But all the points on my list are of equal importance, and I have fifteen." Assume this is true, but consider the listener. You want him to listen and to retain what you say. He can't listen through a dissertation of fifteen points; he can't remember fifteen points.

A speech-writing expert was working with a sales manager to get him to cut the list of points he was planning to make at a series of sales meetings. He claimed he couldn't cut to four; he had fourteen he just had to use. The expert suggested, "Cover your four main points; then open your meeting for questions and let your listeners ask about others they feel are important." He tried the advice in his first meeting, and the salesmen asked about three points he hadn't covered. A speaker can feel he has ten points that are important. The listener may feel that only three of them are important. Any cutting you do will help you get better attention and better retention.

■ *Three or four points are easy to remember.* This is the main reason for asking you to cut your list of points to three or four. To demonstrate to the students why it pays to use a small number of points, one public speaking teacher makes a speech on these three advantages of a plan:

First, it saves time.

Second, it saves labor.

Third, it saves money.

After he has stated the three points and has spoken for a few minutes, he asks, "How many points did I cover?"

The listeners answer, "Three."

Then he asks, "What was the first?"

They tell him, "Save time."

He follows with, "What was the second?"

They answer, "Save labor."

He continues, "What was the third?"

They reply, "Save money."

This demonstration proves that a listener can retain a small number of points. When you have a larger number, you may be asking too much of him. Your main interest should be in what listeners can remember, not in what you want to get over.

While speakers know that the small number of points is better, too few of them use what they know.

Remember all speeches are too long. Cato's line could be cut to "Destroy Carthage."

3. *Analyze each point:* Make each point on your list justify itself. Ask such questions as—

What is its appeal to this group?

How much explanation does it need?

Is it worth the time I have to give it?

What does it add?

What can I say about it that will make an impression?

What do I lose if I leave it out?

How many of these points will they remember?

Will they agree or disagree?

Don't mention any angle for any reason except that the audience will be interested in it. Be tough on your arguments. If the thought won't help, leave it out. If you don't think well of the point, leave it out. Your coverage of any point you consider weak will betray your attitude toward it. Judge every point on your answers to this question, "Why is this of interest to the listeners?"

4. *Arrange your points to hold interest:* From the time you made up your list of points, consciously or unconsciously you have been considering the order in which you will present them. You have such thoughts as "Should I present the big idea first or save it as a climax?" My advice is, "Think of buildup." Too few speakers understand this idea of buildup. Follow this plan, and you will have it.

Plan for presenting ideas:
    good ideas first;
    better ideas next;
    best points last.

One speech instructor used this similar plan to explain this formula for buildup.

Plan for presenting points:
    strong points first;
    stronger points second;
    strongest points last.

He claimed, "Your listener will be impressed with your strong point, he will be more impressed with the stronger one, and your strongest will strengthen the impression."

Either of these formula arrangements gives you a buildup as you speak. The same type of buildup helps with your subpoints. Under a main point "saves money," list the small savings first, the bigger savings next, and the biggest savings last. As you work over the arrangement of your points, you may feel you need to put one of your big ideas at the start of your speech for its shock value. Put it there, but don't use all your better material close to the start. Save some for the time when the listeners begin to tire of the sound of your voice. Think of buildup, and you won't be finishing with a string of etceteras. No listener likes the speaker who talks on after he has finished.

5. *Number your points:* Numbering the points you make is in line with the admonition of the old hymn, "Count Your Blessings." The numbers help the listener understand and remember, so that he may make those blessings his.

Tell your listener you are going to count the blessings you offer. These can be—
> three benefits.
> three advantages.
> three savings.
> three anything.

You follow that statement with:
> First, this—
> Second, this—
> Third, this—

■ *Why numbers help.* Numbers help both the speaker and his listener.
They set the point apart, so that it is not confused with other points.
They make the point seem more important.
They help in retention if you use a small number of points.
They tell the listener the speaker knows what he is talking about.

This last is most important, for no listener wants to take the advice of a speaker who doesn't seem to know what he wants.

■ *Try this experiment.* In one speech workshop the instructor has a student say this line aloud: "This plan has three advantages: It saves time. It saves labor. It saves money."

Then he tells him to say this line aloud: "This plan has three advantages. First, it saves time. Second, it saves labor. Third, it saves money."

Then he has him say the latter again, this time pausing after each number: "First (pause), it saves time. Second (pause), it saves labor. Third (pause), it saves money."

Try doing what these men in the session do. Note how by numbering you tend to put more force into explaining the point. Note how the pause helps the audience understand that you are offering them something new.

■ *Cautions on numbers.* If you tell a group you plan to talk about ten points, it will think "We'll be here all morning." If you have a long

> Most men think indistinctly, and therefore cannot speak with exactness . . .
> —*Samuel Johnson*

string of points, don't mention how many. One speech instructor advises against the use of numbers because it is possible to forget what your seventh or eighth point was.

In speaking your numbers use "one, two, three—" or "first, second, third—" instead of the more complicated terms such as "primarily, secondarily." Keep your numbers as easy to understand as possible.

How would you handle these points?

For most speeches you have to dig out your own points, but just to give you some practice in following the advice given in the pages ahead, let's assume your boss has read an article on safety that listed these causes of accidents:

1. inadequate knowledge
2. wrong attitudes
3. habits
4. insufficient skill
5. environment hazards
6. carelessness
7. failure to assume personal responsibility

He hands you the article and asks you to read it and to make a speech on the subject to office workers at his next monthly meeting. "Use these causes or any others, and your own ideas, of course. The speech will help prevent some of the accidents we are having," he suggests.

You read the article. You feel the list will do. You think of some office incidents and examples you can use to help illustrate some of the points. Since you have read the pages ahead, you start to plan your speech with these questions:

1. Is this an acceptable list? Or should you add other points?

2. Considering your office workers, how many points can you drop? Which can be combined with other points listed? What do you lose if you cut to four points?

3. How can you cover the points with evidence and examples that will be of interest to the group?

4. How would you arrange the points so that you held interest all through the speech?

5. How would you use numbers to help the listeners retain the points?

Planning a speech on safety may give you more trouble than similar planning on a subject with which you are expert. Do this type of planning on any speech you plan to make, and your effort will be much more professional.

Put the list of points you want to make through these five questions, and you will improve any speech.

test your skills

START WITH A LIST OF POINTS

1. You are going to make a speech on the need to reduce noise pollution. What is the first thing you must do?

2. What devices can you use to make your speech effective?

3. Following is a list of points you might want to cover. Read it and answer the questions that follow.

    a. Damage to health
    b. Loss of efficiency
    c. Cost in dollars
    d. Time lost from job
    e. Social dislocation
    f. Nostalgia for old (more quiet) days
    g. Need for corrective legislation
    h. Who will pay for research?
    i. Patents on inventions that can cut noise
    j. Prominent individuals seeking reform
    k. Portrait of a "silent city"
    l. The noiseless jackhammer
    m. Move the highways out of the cities
    n. Protests
    o. Research being done
    p. The curse of amplification
    q. Number of people suffering from noise-induced ailments
    r. Noise and politics

The questions:

A. What are the most important points covered in the above list?

B. In which order would you present those points to create the most interest?

C. Which of the points in the list could be grouped under the various main headings?

Answers to this quiz appear on page 706.

HOW TO INTRODUCE A SPEAKER

THE SPEECH of introduction serves the same purpose as a social introduction. It creates a bond of interest between the speaker and the audience and establishes a friendly atmosphere. It ought to lead us to information about the speaker that demonstrates his or her fitness for discussing this particular topic. In other words, an introduction ought to "sell" both the topic and the speaker to the audience. And it should do these things in the briefest amount of time possible.

Even though the introductory talk is short, it demands careful preparation. First, you must gather your facts. These will center on three items: the subject of the speaker's talk, his qualifications to speak on that subject, and his name. Often a fourth item will become apparent—why the subject chosen by the speaker is of special interest to the audience.

Give the title of the speaker's talk correctly and point out its relevance to the audience's interests. Try to get this information directly from the speaker. If you have to rely on a third party, a program chairman for instance, try to get the information in writing and check with the speaker just before the meeting.

Most of your preparation will involve getting facts about the speaker's qualifications. If your speaker is nationally or regionally well known, you may be able to find an accurate listing in *Who's Who* or a comparable work. On the local level you can appeal to the public relations or personnel office of the concern where the speaker works, or in some cases verify your facts by calling a close friend or a member of the family. The main idea is to get your biographical facts correct. People close to your speaker will be glad to furnish you with material.

Above all, be certain of the speaker's name and begin at once to familiarize yourself with its pronunciation.

For most introductions, the T-I-S formula serves as a handy guide in organizing the facts you have collected:

1. T stands for Topic. Start your introduction by giving the exact title of the speaker's talk.

2. I stands for Importance. In this step you show the connec-

tion between the topic and the particular interests of the group.

3. S stands for Speaker. Here you list the speaker's outstanding qualifications, particularly those that relate to his topic. Finally, you give his name, distinctly and clearly.

No clichés, such as, "It gives me great pleasure," and "It is a great privilege to introduce to you." The best way to present a speaker is to give his name or to say, "I present," and then tell the audience his name.

Some chairmen are guilty of talking too long and making the audience restive. Others indulge in flights of oratorical fancy in order to impress the speaker and the audience. Still others make the sad error of dragging in "canned jokes," sometimes not in the best taste, or of using humor that patronizes or deprecates the speaker's profession. All of these faults should be avoided by the man who wishes to make an effective introduction.

In making your introduction, manner is quite as important as matter. Try to be friendly; instead of saying how happy you are, be genuinely pleasant making your talk.

If you give the introduction with a sense of building to a climax at the end when you announce the speaker's name, the sense of anticipation will be increased and the audience will applaud the speaker more enthusiastically. This display of the audience's good feeling will in turn help to stimulate the speaker to do his best.

When you do pronounce the speaker's name at the end of the introduction, remember the words, "pause," "part," and "punch." A little *pause* just before the name is given will increase anticipation. *Part* reminds you to separate the first and last names clearly as you say them. *Punch* means the name should be given with vigor.

When you do enunciate the speaker's name, don't turn toward him. Instead, look out over the audience until the last syllable has been uttered, and then turn to the speaker. I have seen countless chairmen give fine introductory speeches that were ruined at the end because they turned toward the speaker, pronouncing his name so that only he could hear it and leaving the audience in total ignorance of his identity.   —*Dale Carnegie*

48

How to sell
your idea

**Making someone change his mind is one of the most difficult
tasks in the world, yet the public speaker must often try to
do just that. Learn to observe these simple principles of
leadership and patience and you'll find you can persuade a
hostile audience, not alienate it.**

Come out slugging! This is the typical tactic of the untrained,
wild-swinging amateur. The canny pro knows the risks of this. He spars
cautiously and respectfully. Then he goes to work systematically to
carry out his campaign according to plan.

When you make a talk or have a conversation on a controversial subject, you must choose your approach carefully. With the wrong approach, there is risk that you will run into a hostile listener reaction.
This will floor your talk before you really get started. With the right
approach, you may be able to be genuinely persuasive. This is the most
difficult and most rewarding of the communicating arts.

Let's look carefully at this matter of being *genuinely persuasive*.

If you know that a subject is controversial, you can expect that in any
audience there will be three groups of people. There will be some who
already agree with you, some who are undecided, and some who disagree. Those who agree have already been persuaded. Those who are
undecided can probably be swayed by any reasonably clear and convincing presentation of the facts. The real challenge is posed by those
who disagree. You want to induce them to change their minds.

Now inducing a person to change his mind is a very delicate operation indeed. We are proud of the ideas we hold. Some ideas have been

formed as a result of years of study and experience. Other ideas have deep-seated emotional roots. The lessons you learned at your mother's knee are planted deep and securely in your very personality. Most of us have deeply rooted ideas about religion, politics, child-raising, democracy, and even labor unions. Old loyalties make it very difficult to be coolly objective in our thinking on dozens of subjects. In another person, these tendencies look like prejudices. But if it is *my* idea, it seems completely rational and completely satisfying. Each of us looks upon cherished ideas with the same uncritical regard as an indulgent parent feels for a child. Others might see a spoiled "brat," but the parent looks through different spectacles.

If you make a blunt frontal attack on a man's cherished idea, he will react in the same way he would if you criticized his child. He will resent it. He will put up his guard against everything you say. He will surely not abandon the idea but will hug it to his breast more tightly than before.

This is a universal and completely predictable emotional reaction when you "come out slugging" at a man's idea.

For instance—Mark Antony

Shakespeare recognized this and gave us a classical example of the effective way to handle a controversial situation. You recall the famous funeral oration by Mark Antony. Brutus and others had just murdered Julius Caesar. Brutus had sold the crowd on the idea that this was necessary to save Rome. The crowd had cheered the deed and looked on Brutus and his fellow conspirators as heroes.

Mark Antony's objective was to persuade the crowd to change their minds and turn against Brutus. If Mark Antony could accomplish it, he hoped to become Caesar's successor.

He did not "come out slugging." His opener was, "I come to bury Caesar, not to praise him." He spoke respectfully of Brutus. "Brutus is an honorable man," said he. He acknowledged the plausibility of the idea that Brutus had killed Caesar for the good of Rome. Then he gently pulled and nudged his audience through a series of ideas. Each step carried them a little further from Brutus's idea and a little closer to his own.

When he was sure that he had them with him, he attacked with vigor first Brutus's idea and then Brutus. The crowd turned into a lynching mob looking for Brutus and his fellow assassins. If Mark Antony had "come out slugging" at the idea which Brutus had sold to the crowd, the lynching party would have gone after Antony instead.

In less dramatic form, that is what will happen to you if you start a controversial talk by plunging abruptly into an attack on the opposite point of view. Those who hold to the opposing view will be alienated before you begin. They will become defensive of their cherished ideas and will resist your efforts to change them. They will simply close their minds and shut out your ideas as effectively as if they wore ear muffs.

So the first tip for you is: "Don't come out slugging." Start out by acknowledging that there is another point of view, and demonstrate that you understand it. Acknowledge respectfully that such a point of view is plausible and that it may be held by a man who is neither a knave nor a fool.

Don't be a bulldozer

The next guide to genuine persuasiveness is, "Don't be a bulldozer." Don't try to bludgeon your listeners into submission with facts, figures, and what debaters like to refer to as "conclusive proofs."

Remember, your listener will accept your idea only if he first *wants* to accept it. It is literally true that we think what we "feel like" thinking. Ideas that are accompanied by favorable emotional responses are readily accepted. Ideas that come wrapped in a hostile attitude can be very easily rationalized into impotence.

If you were ever on a debating team, it's likely you were taught to tear into opposing ideas with vigor. The game was to rip and tear the opponents' ideas to shreds. Sarcasm was sharpened to knife-edge keenness, to slash the opposing ideas.

It was great fun. In fact, it was probably very pleasing to those who already agreed with you. That's where the applause came from that made you so proud.

But the applause was misleading because such debater's tactics don't persuade those who are in disagreement with you. Sometimes one may appear to win an argument because the other person simply "clams up" rather than offering *open* resistance by arguing. The resistance simply goes underground and becomes resentment. No ideas are changed by this process.

There is a saying that, "A man convinced against his will is of the same opinion still." If you bulldoze a person into apparent submission to your idea, you haven't achieved persuasion at all—just exhaustion. Don't be a bulldozer!

Emerson told a story that illustrates this principle. A husky boy was trying to get a large calf into the barn. He pushed with all his might. He whipped the calf repeatedly, swore vigorously, and tried to force the animal into the barn.

A milkmaid saw his plight. Remembering the calf's eating habits, she gently put her finger into his mouth and led him docilely into the barn. You see, she approached the matter from the calf's viewpoint and contrived to make her idea very *attractive to the calf*. Once that rapport had been established, she could have led him anywhere.

The moral for a speaker is this: Try to make your idea attractive to your listener. Try to make him want to agree rather than want to disagree. Having started with a respectful acknowledgment of his idea, proceed to build up your idea gradually.

How do you build up your idea? You do it by making the idea appealing to the listener—as the finger was to the calf. He must be helped to see that the idea has valuable benefits for *him*.

You establish rapport with him when you demonstrate that you are open-minded, that you understand his point of view, that you are sincerely interested in his welfare, and that you have something of value to offer to him. Only then will he be willing to be led toward a changed idea. Not until you reach this point may you safely start to urge the action or conviction that you are seeking to induce.

Avoid head-on clashes

The mature persuader learns not to be overeager. Like Mark Antony, he moves patiently and carefully toward his objective. He avoids head-on collisions of opposing ideas. He tries not to step on intellectual or emotional corns.

Now let's try out this approach in a brief talk. Suppose you are to give a talk in favor of building a new high school. You expect acceptance from parents who have children in school. The principal opposition is expected from taxpayers who don't have children in school. Some may be childless. Some have grown children. Some send their children to private or parochial schools.

One approach is to "choose up sides" and think of those who don't

SELL YOUR IDEA WITH STORIES

EVERY GOOD SPEAKER should have a basketful of point-proving stories that can be pulled out and used to make his audience open up and buy his idea with gusto.

Since your mere presence on the dais has put you on the line as wanting to be a *good* speaker, one your audiences will clamor to listen to again, you have a duty to learn to use stories and particularly humorous ones.

Here are some realistic facts about telling a good story:

We know humor can't be defined accurately. Granted, but neither can many other things we live very close to—like love or hate. Our styles of humor may differ from one another but the fact still remains that humor is part of every one of us.

Anybody, yes, anybody can tell a good story. If you can't do it as well as some other people you know, you can do it well enough to make storytelling a vital part of your speech arsenal. If someone else tells stories better, it's probably because he's had more practice. You can get practice, too.

When everything else has failed to win the agreement of the audience, the good story will! Many times it seems to be the *only* technique that will allow a listener to drop his prejudices and agree with you, the speaker.

Use these guideposts:

Tell stories you *know* and are completely sure of.

Avoid telling stories that depend on a "punch line" unless you are sure the audience will understand easily.

Whatever story you tell, it *must* tie in with your speech. If not, drop it like a hot potato!

Make your stories short.

Beware of the old, old, old stories *everyone* has heard before. Nothing is more deadly.

Never, never lead into a story with, "That reminds me of a story . . ."

Avoid off-color stories. You may be on dangerous ground.

Don't wait for, or show you expect, any response to your story. Just go right on with your speech.

favor a new school as opponents—even as enemies. This is what happens so distressingly often in human differences of opinion. Down this path lie misunderstanding, suspicion, hostility, and conflict. In its extreme, it leads to deep breaches like the conflict between North and South on the integration problem.

If you follow the approach of "choosing up sides," you can precipitate a bitter fight. Friend may quarrel with friend, religious groups may hurl accusations and counteraccusations at each other. You might hold the votes that you already have, but you would not be likely to win any new ones.

This approach is clearly a dead end. Let's see how we might apply the persuasive approach. We begin by recognizing that there is another point of view. Then we open our minds sufficiently to try honestly to understand it. The starting point is the area of agreement between the two points of view. All the voters will be weighing and comparing consciously or unconsciously two sets of values. On one side of the scale are the values to the community from the improved educational opportunities. On the other side of the scale, we place the taxes which we must pay.

All of us are in agreement about one side of the scale. Rising taxes have been painful for everyone. We are as close as brothers when we are worrying about high taxes.

We are in considerable agreement about the other side of the scale, too. All of us want the young people of our community to have good educations. To some of us this seems so urgent and so important that it tips the scale even though there is a heavy tax weight on the other side. To others, it isn't quite heavy enough to hold its own and the heavy tax load tips the scale.

Our challenge is to build up the weight of improved education to the point where it will outweigh heavy taxes in more people's minds. Let's plan a brief talk to accomplish this.

NOW FOR THE TALK

Fellow taxpayers and fellow citizens: You and I have a critical decision to make. It is critical to each of us, because it affects the taxes we shall pay for several years to come. It is critical to each of us, also, because it may have an important influence in determining whether Blankville will continue to be a fine place to live, to work, and to raise children.

All of us share a deep concern about our heavy tax burden. It hits all of us where it hurts—in our pocketbooks.

We know too that if taxes get too high, they discourage new people and new industry from moving in. This can hurt a community. All of us are against anything which will hurt our town.

On the other hand, we share enthusiasm for projects which we can feel will help make our community a better place to live. Our problem is to decide whether building a new high school will do more to improve our town than the increase in taxes will do to harm it.

Let us try to weigh the problem on a scale. On the one side, we put the increase in the tax rate. This is easy to weigh. It will be $2.00 per $1,000 assessed valuation. You can calculate what this will add to your tax bill.

On the other side, let's put the value to the community of offering completely modern educational opportunities to our young people. This will be more difficult to weigh because each of us views it from a slightly different vantage point.

Some of us have children who will go to that new school—or to the old one. Perhaps we are too close to be objective. We see the crowded classrooms, the inadequate laboratories, the overcrowded gymnasium, and the fire hazards. It would be good if all of us as citizens could tour the school and see the conditions for ourselves.

A citizens' committee has made an objective survey. Their report shows that our high school is clearly inferior to those in each of the neighboring school districts. It doesn't measure up to minimum standards recommended by a state educational rating agency.

This situation would be discouraging news to a prospective buyer of one of our homes. It would be a real deterrent to a new industry considering our town for a plant that might bring in many new jobs and much new business for local merchants. To us homeowners, this might make a difference of several thousand dollars in the resale value of our homes. To some, this could mean the difference between having a good job or not having one. To our town it might mean the difference between growth or stagnation.

We have most of what it takes to resume our traditional place as the outstanding school district in the area. We have a capable and dedicated faculty who are carrying on despite discouraging conditions. We have provided well for our grade school and junior high students. We have done our best for all the students—except those in the high school.

Our public school system rests on a solid base of enlightened self-interest. All the people help to educate all the children. When you were in school, all the citizens of the community "chipped in" to help pay for your education. You and your parents paid only a small part of the cost. The other citizens did this because they knew that some day you would repay the debt by helping to pay to educate other people's children.

All of us share in the blessings of living in a community with excellent educational opportunities. Let's give Blankville's children the best we can. Let's vote for the new high school!

534

Note that we have tried to aim the talk at those who disagree. We acknowledged the legitimacy of their point of view and found as much meeting ground as possible. Finally, we held out benefits to them and attempted to lead them gradually toward a favorable attitude.

Person-to-person persuasion

The principles of persuasion are the same for person-to-person conversation as for making a talk to an audience. The only difference is that it is easier to be persuasive in a conversation. That is because there is an opportunity to give a full hearing to your companion's point of view. You can understand it fully and appreciate its appealing points. You have an easier opportunity to find the maximum area of agreement with the other person's point of view. If you are really open-minded, you may want to change some facets of your own ideas. From this point, you can start to build up the values to him of your idea. If you pause occasionally and let him get a word in, you can accurately judge both his intellectual and emotional responses. If you find you have stepped on an emotional corn, you will do well to change the subject and make a fresh start some other time when the receptivity is better.

CURB YOUR REBUTTAL INSTINCT

One of the worst enemies of personal persuasiveness is the rebuttal instinct. In a discussion there is a very great temptation only to pretend to listen to the other point of view when you are in fact preparing the sparkling rebuttal speech which you will give as soon as you can break into the conversation. Your companion senses that this is taking place and he unconsciously lapses into a rebuttal preparation when it becomes his turn to listen. Thus a discussion degenerates into a subliminal battle of wits. Points may be proved, objections may be disposed of (or at least swept under the rug temporarily), but there is no true persuasion in a subliminal battle of wits. The rebuttal instinct is an insidious killer of sales. It may sometimes even kill a friendship.

The disease is so insidious that few recognize that they have it. It is so objectionable that even your best friend won't tell you.

BE PATIENT

Often, persuasion does not come at the first attempt—or the second or third. Sometimes an idea has to be mulled over, examined critically,

535

and slept on before it finds a favorable reception. To push too impatiently for acceptance might spoil its chances altogether. How many times have you heard someone say, "If you push me for an answer right now, it will have to be No. If you let me sleep on it, perhaps I can agree."

If you are perceptive enough to distinguish among the symptoms of submission, acquiescence, or agreement, you may guide the conversation to a genuinely persuasive conclusion.

Lest all these techniques sound tricky or clever, you can be assured that they are not. We are talking about intellectual honesty and a genuine concern for the welfare of others. You can be really persuasive only if you deeply and genuinely believe in your idea. Further, you can't really make an idea attractive to another unless you honestly believe that it is good for him. You can't be really persuasive unless you are wise enough to recognize that there are two sides to a question and that a reasonable person might prefer the other side. You can't be persuasive unless you too are really open to persuasion.

Persuasion must be sincere. But, to persuade, you must remember that you communicate both thoughts and emotions. If you invoke hostile emotions your ideas will fall on closed ears. If you invoke sympathetic emotions, you have a chance to be genuinely persuasive.

So, if you want to improve your ability to persuade, practice these tips until they become natural to you:

■ Don't come out slugging.

■ Don't be a bulldozer.

■ Don't push—lead.

■ In person-to-person contact, curb your rebuttal instinct.

test your skills

HOW TO SELL YOUR IDEA

This chapter discusses and illustrates four "key admonitions" to induce others to change their minds: (1) Don't come out slugging at a controversial idea. (2) Don't be a verbal bulldozer. (3) Don't push—lead. (4) Curb your rebuttal instinct. *Read the speech on pages 533–534 and tell how the speaker applies these four admonitions.*

Answers to this quiz appear on page 706–707.

49

Use visuals to prove your point

No matter how eloquent a speaker you become, there are still cases where a picture or diagram makes the point faster and better. Charts, diagrams, slide projectors, chalk boards, and other visual devices can hold audience attention and give your presentation more punch.

In 1869, a Spanish nobleman named Don Marcelino de Sautuola was out hunting and came upon a large crack in a rock that led downward into a huge echoing cave. As the Spanish lord's eyes became accustomed to the dim light, he suddenly realized he was surrounded by terrifying figures of threatening men and beasts. As the nobleman's eyes searched the darkness, he began to realize the true value of his find. The pictures he was staring at were drawn in the dim ages when man was just beginning to emerge from the dark recesses of the caves and to look out blinking over the rolling hills of the earth. These pictures had been drawn by early men twenty thousand years in the past. Twenty millenniums ago fur-clad men stood in the flickering light of oil lamps to draw pictures; pictures that would show other watchers what they wanted to say. The picture was being used to present an idea vividly.

It's a long step from the prehistoric cave dwellers to today's speaker, but the rule that the best way to get across a point is with a picture still remains unchanged.

And no better way will ever be found! The picture communicates an idea more quickly, clearly, and vividly than any other means of communication. The picture on the cave wall, the visual presentation in the speech—both stick the idea deep in the listener's mind. And that, after all, is right on target.

Let's take a closer look at this "picture presentation" of ideas; this technique called visual aids. How do they work on the viewer? What purpose do they fulfill in the straightforward selling of an idea? These are two questions that can be answered easily. There is no deep secret in supporting your speech with visuals; no mystery about what the visual can do for you and your ideas.

Here's a definition which you can use as a check every time you want to use a visual support in your speech.

A visual aid in a speech is a pictorial presentation of an idea or situation used by the speaker because it looks more like the idea than words or numbers can. For instance, a picture or diagram showing how to butcher a side of beef looks more like the actual operation than words that say, "Now take the beef and cut off a brisket, etc." Or, a pictograph or line graph showing the growth of troop concentrations in a specific area will certainly show that growth more clearly and vividly than any series of numbers could.

The reason for a visual aid is simply to present an idea in a form that the audience will understand most quickly; in a form that is as close to the real thing as possible; in a form that asks the listener to do as little translating as possible. Put into a formula it could read like this:

The Speaker's Ideas + Visual Aids = Quick Registration of Idea

In using visuals, just as in golf, gardening, cooking, or cartography, you need a knowledge of the basic rules. In golf the question is, "What club?" In gardening, "How deep do I plant?" In cooking, "When do I add the condiment?" In cartography, "What type of map shall I make?"

Beginning rules for each activity answer these questions. There are likewise basic guides to help the speaker in the use of visual aids.

Lights

The speaker must never be in the dark. Not even when slides and films are being shown? *Never!* The visual presentation supports what the speaker is attempting to develop or prove. He must always be the most important object in the room. The visual must always work for him. It is impossible for him to assume any importance if the audience can't see him.

If the type of visual presentation demands complete darkness, arrange to have a small light on yourself. If you don't, you can be sure your authority will be weakened—a serious mistake.

Size

The following statement should be dropped forever from *all* speeches:

> I have here a chart of the plant (*pause*) . . . you probably can't see it . . . but I thought it might help you understand the problem.

How could a chart no one can see help anyone understand the problem? A visual your audience can't see is a waste of time.

How can you tell that everyone will be able to see a visual? Easy! Go to the back of the hall before the speech and look. If you can see everything on the visual, it fulfills the requirements.

How to stand

The right-handed speaker usually stands to the left of the visual and directs the attention of the audience to his material. If you use a pointer, you may stand on either side. Don't, however, stand in front of the diagram or picture you want your audience to see. Think about this before you set up your material; place your diagram where it will be most visible and where you work easily. Always remember the importance of integrating the visual to support what you have to say. If you appear awkward, or the visual is cumbersome, its effectiveness will be greatly reduced.

Many speakers fail to use their good visuals fully. Always pull the eye of the viewer down to your chart or visual; point out specifically with your pointer what you want him to note carefully. Don't simply wave in the general direction of the visual and expect the viewer to pinpoint the thought.

How to speak

Remember, your audience is the listener, not that inanimate object, the visual. Yet, in nine of ten speeches you listen to, the speaker will spend most of his time addressing the visual aid! Speak to the audience. When you turn to the visual, do so to draw the audience's attention to a particular point that the diagram amplifies or makes more clear. The visual is a help; never let it take you from your listeners.

How to use color

Percy Bysshe Shelley, one of the great poets of the English language, referred to life as being "like a dome of many-colored glass." He was vividly describing the multicolored, varied nature of our everyday existence, and the effect that color has upon all of us. Look at a picture, an ad in a magazine, a photograph taken by a friend on a vacation, a new car: all are more exciting by their use of color. Color plays an important role every day in motivating us to accept, and sometimes to reject, ideas. The important fact is that it forces us to respond. The speaker is losing out if he does not take advantage of this vital force.

How to draw

Ever looked at a Japanese print? It's delicate and fine-lined, suggests softness and fragility. These are not the qualities the speaker wants to get across to his fact-hungry and critical audience. He wants to impress his listeners with the strength of his thinking. Strong diagrams and charts can help put this feeling across.

Make the pictures and lines of your visuals definite, broad, and clear. Avoid thinness and delicacy; it can easily be confused with artiness, willingness to compromise, and unwillingness to hold to a position. Simply stated visuals can help convince your listeners that you have carefully thought out your material and that they will be safe to take what you say as fact.

How to show an object

Nothing is more real or can demonstrate a particular object in your speech better than the object itself. For instance you might be showing the advantages of a new cigarette lighter, or the new design of a compact, more efficient package.

Nothing can tell your story as well as the lighter or the package. Show it.

But show it right! Here are some rules that can help your demonstration of an object:

■ Be sure your audience can see everything you point out on the object you hold. If they can't, you're going to have to enlarge that part by drawing a picture.

■ Point to the part of the object you want the audience to concentrate on. Don't just wave it in front of them. Using a physical object to support your speech is an excellent way to make your audience follow you; they can't get ahead of you.

■ Don't hold the object in front of you. If you do it will probably blend into your suit or dress. You want it to stand out for easy viewing by the audience. Hold it naturally, about shoulder level, approximately five inches from your body. Practice learning to handle objects without appearing awkward. It isn't difficult.

■ Most important! Be sure you know how to operate the device you're using. Nothing is more embarrassing to a speaker than demonstrating an object and finding out in front of his audience that he doesn't really know how it works.

■ Decide at what point you will demonstrate the object. Then don't pick it up until that time! Watching a speaker play with an object he doesn't explain frustrates an audience.

■ If you decide to carry the object in your pocket, be sure you can find it when the time comes. Your author has seen literally dozens of speakers pull the famous (or infamous) act of the bridegroom who can't find the ring. In this situation, the audience has no mercy. And the speaker deserves none.

How to use line and bar graphs

Everyone understands something he sees more quickly than something he hears. Psychologists point out that the eye is a much more effective instrument for gathering and storing information than the ear.

The reason is simple enough. Think for a minute how spoken words work; you have to add each word to the one that went before to come up with the whole meaning. On the other hand, visuals present all the information at once. The eye can grasp the whole immediately.

This is one reason that charts have become so important to business and industrial organizations. Numbers are a basic tool in business; the message they carry very often is the force that swings the balance, proves the point being made, in the end determines company action.

However, numbers when presented in bulk tend to work against themselves and lull, instead of stimulating, the thinking of the audience. This is where the value of the graph comes in.

Graphs can present in a single viewing the complete growth or decline picture of the production trend you are describing. Or they can expose, in one presentation, the shipments of a product for the last year and compare them to sales quotas.

Here are several forms of graphs; note that each type has a particular strength, each is particularly well suited to do a special job.

THE LINE GRAPH

The line graph can be used very effectively to picture rise or fall, growth or decline, over a specified period. Perhaps you wish to show the growth of population in the U.S. since the year 1790. The line graph could do this instantly.

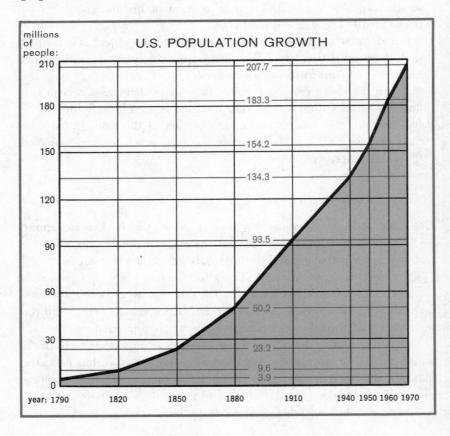

When you use a line graph, keep the following suggestions in mind:
■ Always put a heading over the graph which spells out clearly what it is supposed to tell the audience.
■ Be sure to label both legs of your graph, and be sure the labels are visible to your viewers.
■ Label both legs of your graph horizontally; remember that your audience cannot pick up your graph and turn it around (as they would a page) for easy viewing.
■ Draw your lines definitely so the last man in the last row can see easily. Nothing could be more useless than a visual that is not visible.
■ If there are important points in your graph, mark them with arrows to pinpoint the attention of your viewers. Make it easy for them to learn; they're sure to appreciate it.
■ Use color; it is one of the best ways to attract and hold attention.

THE BAR GRAPH

The bar graph is particularly well suited to present immediate comparisons of like ideas, events, or trends. For instance, if you wanted to show the size of the merchant fleets of the world, comparing the years 1939 and 1959, it would look like this on the bar graph:

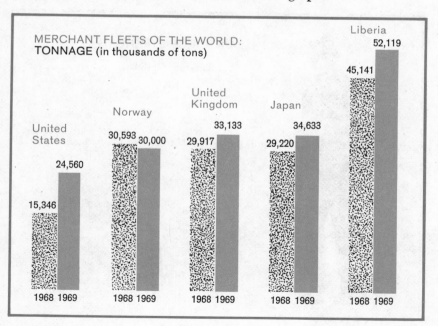

The bar graph may be used vertically or horizontally, whichever way best presents the information you are visualizing. Add these guides to the suggestions offered for use of the line graph:

■ Place your designation within the bar when possible. It will help translate the meaning of each bar quickly.

■ Set off the growth of one bar over another by using color to spotlight the difference. This follows the basic rule of visuals; the quicker the audience understands, the better your chance of their believing what you have to say.

How to use a pictograph

The pictograph is entering like a breath of fresh air into more and more visual presentations. By its use, thousands of grateful listeners are able instantly to receive and understand facts that would be dull as dust if presented in the usual form of statistical tables. An audience that is relaxed and happy is easy to talk to and easier to convince.

The pictograph serves the goal stated by a famous knight, scholar, teacher, and soldier of the sixteenth century—Sir Philip Sidney. Out-

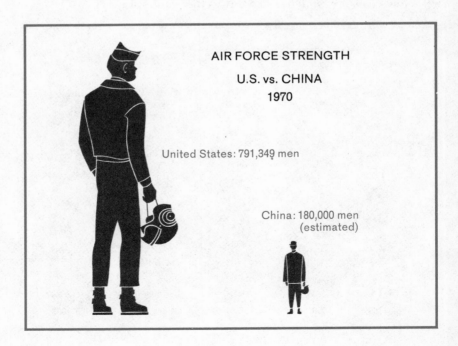

AIR FORCE STRENGTH
U.S. vs. CHINA
1970

United States: 791,349 men

China: 180,000 men
(estimated)

lining the best way to teach or persuade someone, he said: "He cometh unto you with a tale which holdeth children from play, and old men from the chimney corner."

In other words, he was saying, "Make what you have to say easy to understand and pleasant to learn, and people will remember it." The pictograph does this unusually well.

The pictograph is a symbolic presentation of the object or objects being described. You have probably seen the visual of a coin divided into parts to show how government spending is allocated to different departments. Or the use of silhouette soldiers to show the armed forces of a country. Or a factory to show an industry. The pictograph is the most effective of visuals because it visually translates the idea for the viewer.

The pictograph gives an immediate visual comparison of the idea being presented. No translation of numbers, tables, graphs is needed; the audience can see and understand almost as soon as the visual is revealed. Take advantage of the pictograph and let it work for you.

Here are some suggestions that will help you in designing a pictograph that will carry across your point:

■ Make your picture as simple as possible. Detailed drawings work against the simple and direct presentation of the idea.

■ Make the picture symbols bear the major responsibility of making the idea clear. Any labels or numbers are only extra support. Set as a standard the guide that the picture could stand alone if necessary.

■ The pictograph is frequently used to show comparisons. Heighten these comparisons by using color.

Take full advantage of the pictograph whenever you have the chance. It stimulates as it informs; it interests as it teaches; it entertains as it supports your ideas. It is frequently the difference between the speech everyone talks about and the speech no one remembers.

Try the pictograph on your next audience—and then ask them for *their* opinion!

How to use a flannel board

Here is an excellent way to present a finished-looking demonstration that is easy to prepare, easy to use, with a device that never fails to interest and stimulate an audience. The flannel board has proved its communication value every time it's been used, and the novelty of the board will enhance your speaking even more. Chances are that your listeners have never seen a flannel board used and as a visual aid technique it's bound to excite them.

Here is what the flannel board is and what it can do.

Flannel boards are pieces of plywood, fiberboard, masonite, etc., varying in size from 2' x 4' to 3' x 6' to larger, covered with a black flannel tightly drawn over the surface. On this black background you affix your charts, diagrams, and other prepared visuals.

You lay out your visuals on illustration paper, drawing the pictographs, diagrams, charts, statistics, etc., on whatever color background you prefer. When your visuals are finished, you paste pieces of sandpaper on the back (use the heaviest gauge sandpaper you can find, and paste in the corners).

As you give your speech, all you need do to exhibit your information is to press these visuals onto the flannel board. The roughness of the sandpaper will make them hold to the flannel. They'll stay there until you pick them off.

The flannel board allows you to develop and build an idea in front of your audience by laying it out as you talk. Listeners will never fail to be intrigued by this device that seems to defy gravity.

For those speakers who like their visuals in a more finished form, visual supply houses have colored and white paper designed specifically for flannel-board use with the holding surface already sprayed on the back. Whether you buy it or make it—try it. It will really pay off in successful speaking.

How to use charts and the blackboard

The chart and the blackboard offer probably the most convenient and flexible means of visualizing ideas and supporting your speech. Thousands of teachers depend on the blackboard to help them in their teaching. Charts are part of almost every well-developed business speech. Both visual techniques have their advantages and limitations.

CHARTS

Large white charts, drawn either on heavy illustration paper or on a common white pad, can be very helpful in making your idea clear to the audience. If your diagram is complicated you will probably want to prepare it completely before the speech. However, if the diagram is simple, it's often a good idea to develop it as you proceed. This technique is an excellent way of keeping the audience with you—keeping them from coming to the point before you make it.

Lay your diagrams out in an orderly fashion. Your audience has a long established habit of reading from left to right, top to bottom. It is foolhardy to try to break it now. Lay your material out in this familiar pattern and you will help your listener and viewer follow your material easily and rapidly. As with all other visual devices, use color and variety to stimulate interest. The one big weakness in charts is that everyone has seen them used many, many times before—and frequently used poorly. Nevertheless, well-drawn, simple, and original charts can work very hard for you in supporting your speech.

BLACKBOARD

The blackboard is too often regarded as a visual device for use only in the classroom. The very reason it has such wide use in teaching is because it is one of the best ways of outlining and dramatizing a thought. You can see that few mediums have the flexibility of the blackboard: the speaker can erase and present a new idea on the same surface time after time.

As with the chart, the blackboard speaker should take advantage of color to stimulate interest and to get clearer definition of his idea.

Plan how you are going to use the blackboard and be sure you write firmly enough for all your audience to see. If you are in doubt, test your writing before the speech begins!

It's easy to develop a terrible jumble in laying out your material on the blackboard. Again, trade on the pattern viewers have of reading left to right and top to bottom.

One last thought: don't work against the background of a cluttered blackboard. It's very distracting to your viewers. When you have finished with a diagram on the board, erase it and give the audience nothing to look at but you! That's the way it should be.

How to use visual projectors

Many scholars of language and communication have underlined the sharp difference between words and pictures; that words build one upon the next, that pictures present the whole idea at one time. This is a communication principle that good speakers have traded on for many years: using the picture to tell an immediate and vivid story.

Former Sheriff Ralph S. Marshall, Allen County, Ohio, made no campaign speeches. Instead, he took his wife to public gatherings, stood her ten paces away, and shot cigarettes from her mouth with a revolver. Usually he was elected.

—*Albert Benjamin in the American Magazine*

Today, many new machines have been developed to make the presentation of visual ideas easier and even more dramatic than was possible a few years ago. These machines can be divided roughly into three types: motion picture projectors; slide and strip projectors; and overhead projectors. Let's examine the strengths and weaknesses of each.

MOTION PICTURES

Here is an excellent way to present ideas in a very finished form. This type of presentation is made strong by the highly flexible flow of ideas; by the ability of the camera to move freely and easily from scene to scene; by the ability to provide a running audio track with the picture. Since we have all been brought up in the age of the "movies" and associate the movies with fun, they have a built-in appeal for all audiences.

Motion pictures can add vitality to your speech, but they have their limitations which you must learn to recognize:

■ Motion pictures demand a completely darkened room and a darkened room carries with it loss of attention and not infrequently sleep. When the lights go out, the speaker loses his identity and with it goes his control. If you use movies, try doing the commentary yourself and thereby hold your listeners' attention.

■ Be sure the machine you use is in good working order. The visual device that won't operate, the projector that "worked just this afternoon" annoy audiences mightily; they don't expect Cinemascope, but they do expect something that works.

■ Use the film to support your speech; don't let the picture become the speech. A good method is to open your presentation orally and then use the movie to support the points you want to emphasize. Then close by summarizing the purpose of the presentation and telling your listeners exactly what action you want from them. In other words, make the film a tool—*you* be the speaker, not the machine.

■ Remember, your audience has probably seen its fill of "home movies." Be sure the film is worth showing. Think of the poor viewer.

■ Check carefully to determine where you can place your projector. More than one unfortunate speaker has planned to show films as the main support of his presentation only to find that the projector obscured a full 50 percent of his audience! Another great idea with the impact of a wet muffin.

■ One last suggestion: Check the current. Is it AC or DC?

SLIDE AND STRIP PROJECTORS

More and more people have taken to collecting pictures of their trips, etc., as a record of their pleasant family life. As a result, dozens of excellent slide projectors are on the market today. Speakers have been quick to find that these projectors are just the device to hammer home an idea in an entertaining way and with lasting effect. The strip projector, which is now also being used widely, is simply a series of slides fastened together in a strip form on film.

Don't overlook the slide and strip film projector when you plan your next speech. And when you use it, keep these ideas in mind:

■ As with the film projector, the slide projector must be used in a dark room; don't let it take over. Remember *you* are the speaker, not the machine.

■ New slide and strip projectors have a long cord attachment which allows the speaker to change his own slide frames. Use it! It eliminates that tired old instruction to the much maligned machine operator, "May we have the next slide, please."

■ Several new slide projectors are available with sound attachments that play a record in coordination with the slides or film strips. We advise against them. If you replace the speaker with a mechanical device, you might just as well stay at home and let the audience listen to a recording.

OVERHEAD PROJECTORS

Here is an excellent device (used unfortunately too little) which will add a professional touch to any speaker's presentation. Some of you may have seen these projectors used in bowling alleys; they are the machines that project the bowling score onto overhead screens.

Here's how the business speaker can use the overhead projector. Visuals are prepared on transparent sheets of acetate varying in size from

3″ x 3″ to 8″ x 8″. The acetate is placed on a polished glass surface of the projector through which a strong light shines. The light projects through the acetate, picking up the illustration the speaker has made; it passes up through an optical lens and is thrown forward onto a screen. The overhead projector is a natural for the speaker. Here are some of the reasons:

■ The overhead projector can be used in a fully lighted room.

■ This type of projector is easily portable; one make of overhead projector weighs only about 17 pounds.

■ The speaker can easily prepare his own transparencies, thus avoiding the considerable cost of professional slide preparation.

■ In the lighted room, the speaker can face his audience, place the transparencies on the projector, and have them thrown over his head on a screen. This means that the speaker always faces his audience and is in close personal control of the visual device. Very important!

■ Overlays of different color transparencies can be used to show growth or change or comparison in your speech. The overhead projector gives the speaker flexibility in visual presentations not to be found in other devices.

Visual projectors can make any speech better. Look up your nearest visual aid distributor and ask him to show you what is available for you as a speaker.

Other visual aid equipment

Here are some additional visual aid materials you should be familiar with and consider for use in the next important presentation you are called upon to give. If you use them well, you'll have a big jump on the problem of giving a good speech—a speech that will show your ability and intelligence; a speech that will communicate clearly and convince people it is logical to do what you suggest.

Crayons. Get several in a variety of colors for use on charts, diagrams, graphs, etc. Look for a heavy crayon that will make a broad, distinct line on your paper.

Chalk. If you use a blackboard (you should try it), don't forget color. Try definite colors (red, yellow, green, blue) as well as white, since these colors will be most visible and will add interest and clarity to the ideas you present.

Plastic tapes. Several manufacturers now produce plastic tapes (packaged like mending tapes) of various widths and colors, which are a natural for laying out bar and line graphs. Just label your base and then strip off the color tape you need, and the visual is done!

Ink markers. Many business persons do not have the services of a professional artist to call on when they need a visual. Most have to do the work themselves. Very often, these people are self-conscious about their drawing ability and their ability to letter a diagram. There are now on the market several ink markers which make letters and lines easier to draw and more professional looking. With these markers, everyone can produce a thoroughly acceptable visual presentation.

Color transparencies. Sheets of transparent paper in a multitude of shades are available in most art stores for use as overlays in the visual presentation of an idea. Draw the basic visual and then use these overlays to develop or expand the basic idea. This is an excellent way to show the development of a plant, growth in sales, change in package design, etc. Try this device in your next speech; chances are your audience has never seen it used.

There is one request all audiences make which visuals constantly fulfill. The request is "Show me!"

test your skills

USE VISUALS TO PROVE YOUR POINT

1. What is the basic reason for using a visual aid?
2. Tell how each of the following relates to the use of visual aids:
   a. lights
   b. size of visual aid
   c. where to stand
   d. how to speak
   e. use of color
   f. how to draw
3. Study the illustration on page 544, "Air Force Strength," and tell how and why it is effective.
4. Explain how to make and use a flannel board.
5. Name some other types of visual aids and mention some materials that can be used in them.

Answers to this quiz appear on page 707–708.

50

Preparing yourself
to speak

Once the speech itself has been organized and written, the time has come to get ready for the big moment. Here Dorothy Sarnoff describes all the things you need to prepare and check: delivery, cue cards, lights, microphone, lectern, and the slightly apprehensive speaker—you!

After you have made several drafts of your speech and edited it according to the check list given on page 518, you are ready to try aloud not just single sentences or paragraphs, but the speech as a whole. Ask relatives or friends to lend you their ears. They can help you analyze the structure and delivery of your speech.

But your best friend and severest critic is your tape recorder. Deliver your talk into it. Listen objectively to the playback, pretending that the speaker is someone you do not know. Make notes and edit again, adding or deleting as necessary. Repeat, re-edit, over and over until you are satisfied. Listen for faulty structure, errors of logic, poor usage, irrelevant examples and quotations. Are some of your words stoppers, either because they may be unfamiliar to your audience or because you find them difficult to pronounce? Do you conclude three or four times instead of once?

When you are satisfied with the organization of your talk, sit down and write it out once more, preferably typing it in triple space.

You are now ready for cue cards.

Television actors use teleprompters or reminder cards as fail-safes in case they forget their lines. These latter are called idiot cards—and most professionals would rather use idiot cards than appear to be idiots.

Cue cards will give you the confidence that comes from knowing you will not falter even if some synapse in your mind short-circuits while you are speaking. They will enable you to speak more freely, almost conversationally. They will also free you to look at your audience. This is important, because that interchange of looks is the first step toward rapport. If you have to read your speech, your eyes are preoccupied with your text. With cue cards to back you up, you can look at the audience almost all the time.

If you want to sound spontaneous to your audience, buy a 6″ × 9″ looseleaf notebook with some file cards to match, and a punch. Punch the cards the long way for insertion in the book, so that they can be flipped up, like a wall calendar.

Your talk by now is on paper. Go over it. Strike out such small words as "the," "and," "but," "for," "by," "with," "at," and "in." Also drop self-evident verbs, and abbreviate other words—but be sure that when the time comes you will recognize instantly what the abbreviations mean.

Next, transcribe this shortcut version of your talk onto your cards. Look at the sample on the next page. Notice that it is *printed* with a felt tip pen. Each letter is about a half inch high, so that an entire sentence can be scooped up in a single peripheral glance. Print is easier to read than even the clearest handwriting. So resist the temptation to write script. It may be faster, but it also is harder to read. Don't use a typewriter either, unless it has jumbo type.

In using cue cards, remember to: (a) number each card; (b) number each sentence and start each at left margin; (c) leave plenty of white space between sentences.

Read the first sentence of the unabridged paragraph in the following sample three times aloud. Then turn the page and go to cue-card abbreviation No. 1. You will find that the cues enable you to recreate the whole text of the sentence without hesitation. Try it.

FULL TEXT:

No one can say that morale is high in America today. The President, in his State of the Union Message in January, spoke of "a certain restlessness" in the land. This is the understatement of the century. The "restlessness" looks dangerously like nothing less than a widespread loss of faith in America, in our political institutions, and in our whole middle-class, technological civilization.

Editorial writers say that everywhere we look, something is wrong. But they usually point to the war in Vietnam and the Negro poverty problem in our cities as the causes of most of our troubles.

553

The cue-card abbreviation:

1. NONE CN SAY MORALE HIGH AMER. T'DAY.
2. PRES. JONSON...ST. OF UNION MESG., JAN...CERTAIN RSTLESNESS IN LAND
3. UNDERSTATMNT...CENTURY
4. RESTLESNESS...DANGROUSLY...NOTHING LESS WIDE-SPRD LOSS FAITH AMER.
   IN PLITICAL INSTUTIONS
   IN WHL MIDDLE CLASS...TECNOLGICAL CIVILZA.
5. ED. WRTRS EVRYWHR...LOOK SOMTHNG WRONG.
6. BUT...USLLY POINT WR VIET...NEGRO POVRTY PROBLM...CITIES...CAUSES...MST TRUBLES.

Rehearse with cue cards as many times as is required to use them naturally. For me the magic number is generally eight. Your magic number may be two, or twenty, or anything in between. In any event, practice ALOUD as though in an actual speech situation—on your feet, not at your desk—and don't be satisfied until the speech seems almost to come by itself.

Don't memorize—familiarize!

"He who speaks as though he were reciting," says Quintilian, "forfeits the whole charm of what he has written."

The purpose of your rehearsals is not to memorize what you are going to say, but to become thoroughly familiar with the key expressions and the flow of ideas. If you memorize, your eyes are lackluster, focusing inward, trying to remember words. If you read your speeches, you are communicating with the text instead of the audience; they see the top of your head instead of your eyes. (Nothing will make a bald-headed man switch from a full text to cue cards faster than to see himself on a television playback in which his polished pate instead of his animated face holds center stage.)

When young Abraham Lincoln was on a speaking tour, his roommate reported that the effectiveness of the future President's presentations was invariably in direct ratio to the amount of time he had spent re-

HOW TO HANDLE DISTRACTIONS

ONE IMPORTANT ASPECT of your preparation for a speech is knowing what to do if an unexpected disturbance should arise. Here are four points that will help you keep control of the situation despite distractions in the hall.

1. *Recognition of counterattractions.* Sometimes there are disturbing noises or movements which compete for attention within the room. Someone is uncomfortable and gets up to raise or lower a window or to adjust the air conditioning. Someone else arrives late, bangs open a door, and moves down front to an available seat. If you can ignore the counterattraction and still hold the audience, do so. If the disturbance seriously interferes with communication, pause and wait until the disruption has stopped and the audience is again attentive.

2. *Recognition of outside disturbances.* Sometimes there are outside interruptions, such as fire sirens, clanking machinery, low-flying aircraft, or animated conversations in an adjoining room or corridor. You should ignore them unless they interfere with your communication. You can just pause and wait out the passing siren or overhead plane. Otherwise, deal with the disturbance if it causes the audience to be seriously distracted or ask a responsible person in the audience to help you.

3. *Handling hecklers.* If someone heckles you verbally, you should respond good-naturedly, maintain your dignity and composure, and keep your temper under control no matter what the provocation. If you can think on your feet and reply to the badgering with suitable repartee, the audience will usually respond favorably and apply pressure on the heckler. If you do not have the popular side of the controversy, the audience pressure may turn against you. In some cases it is wise not to try to continue in the face of obvious hostility and inattention.

4. *Handling emergencies.* Occasionally someone in the audience may faint or undergo a severe attack such as heart failure. In such cases common sense suggests that you stop your speech and summon competent medical aid. If circumstances permit you to resume, it probably is wise to condense your materials and conclude early.

hearsing them—aloud, and on his feet. Simply looking over what you plan to say does not substitute for saying it, any more than looking over a swimming pool substitutes for a swim.

I cannot say too often: Rehearse as if you were on the platform with an audience before you. On your feet. Aloud.

Now you are on the last lap of familiarization. Use that tape recorder again. Do you sound attractive? Vital? Self-confident? Warm? Knowledgeable? Informed? Vibrant? Sincere? Relaxed? Amusing? Clever? Check your ending. Do you strengthen it by pausing for effect? Is it strongly delivered?

Or do you sound dull? Tired? Cold? Uncertain? Monotonous? Affected? Tense? Confused? Perhaps even a little bit stupid? Do you conclude weakly and more than once?

Practice and check, practice and check, until you feel that you are the kind of speaker you would like to hear if you were in the audience.

D- (for *do it*) day

You have arrived at D-day. Last-minute preparations are in order.

First, the matter of dress. Remember—wear nothing that will distract your listeners from what you are saying. (One of the worst enemies a woman speaker can have is dangling, dancing earrings or a hat that hides half her face so people wonder what she looks like from the nose up.)

If you have time, go through one final tape recorder session. If there is not enough time for that before you have to leave for your talk, at least use the recorder for a last-minute check on the beginning and end of your speech.

On the spot

Be prepared to spend from a half hour to an hour checking the physical arrangements of the meeting place before the audience arrives. If possible in small meetings, and particularly in business meetings, ask to have the chairs arranged amphitheater style, in arcs rather than straight across. The more the audience can see of each others' reactions, the better it is for the speaker.

Get as close to your audience as physical conditions permit. I have at times had the lectern and microphone moved from the stage to the floor, or even sat on the edge of a platform stage dangling my legs, or moved my chair and sat among the group if it was small enough. A yawning chasm between speaker and audience is a psychological as well as a physical barrier.

LET THERE BE LIGHT

At a recent meeting in a New York hotel ballroom, the guest of honor sat on a dais beneath an overhanging balcony. Spotlights fastened to the balcony rim illuminated the tablecloth, the silver, the crystal, and the speakers' hands. Yet every face was left in shadow. Nobody had checked to see if the lights would illuminate the speakers' faces.

In Texas, before a concert, I found there was no spotlight in the hall. "We keep our eyes closed," said the chairwoman haughtily; "singers are to be listened to, not looked at." My accompanist was Josef Blatt, later head of the Opera Department of the University of Michigan. Joe was the most talented conductor and accompanist I ever had, and also the most conscientious and considerate. He refused to accept the chairwoman's verdict. Instead, on his own, he searched the city, and arrived finally at the concert hall with two borrowed spotlights which had illuminated the display sign in front of a funeral home, and attached them to the balcony rail. After the concert, the chairwoman agreed that the spotlights had added to the evening. "I had no idea," she said, "how much it adds to the enjoyment of a concert to be able to watch the expression on the singer's face. I hate to think of what we have been missing all these years!"

THE LECTERN

Make sure the lectern is the right height for you. Carlos Romulo, Foreign Minister of the Philippines, is an outstanding speaker but unusually short—just a little over five feet tall. To be seen, he always asks to have a box to stand on behind the lectern.

Incidentally, Mr. Romulo says that as a young man his lack of height caused him agonizing feelings of inferiority until one day, in Paris, he visited Madame Tussaud's wax museum.

When he found that he was fully a half-inch taller than the life-size figure of Napoleon Bonaparte, he started to gain confidence. He knew the worst was over when he found himself on a platform in Houston, surrounded by tall Texans. One of them asked him how it felt to be a man of his stature "among us Texas giants." "Well," replied Romulo thoughtfully, "I guess you might say that it's rather like being a dime among nickels."

Back to the lectern: It is important to check the light. Often it lights up not only your notes but also your Adam's apple or double chins. If you would rather have attention focused on your face than your Adam's apple, clip or Scotch-tape a sheet of paper or a napkin over the light to soften and diffuse it.

MICROPHONE—FRIEND OR FOE?

Check the position of your microphone. Generally it should be not more than eight inches from your mouth. If it is in the wrong position, you may have to lean forward or stretch up to it in an awkward manner. If the microphone is wrong for you, don't hesitate to adjust it until you are comfortable.

The closer you are to the mike, the more intimate the sound. The more forcefully you project, the farther away from it you should be. I prefer the most conversational sound possible, and keep the microphone about six inches away, at chin height. Now and then I come closer for emotional effect.

You may have to ask for a gooseneck extension to bring the microphone closer.

If the microphone squeals or screeches, you may be touching it. Some mikes, like some dogs and babies, don't like to be touched by strangers. Take your hand off, and the squealing will stop.

Sometimes the sound "p" comes from the mike with a loud pop. If so, talk into it not straight on but at an angle.

THANKS, FRED!

If there is a sound engineer—Fred, for instance—make a point of meeting him and learning his name. It can forestall crises and help you make the mike your friend. Ask him to test the mike with you and to adjust it

---

When King Charles II was asked why he read his speeches before Parliament rather than delivering them from notes, he answered, "I have asked them so often and for so much money, that I am ashamed to look them in the face."

so the tone is warm and the volume does not blast. If you are a woman, you may want him to turn the tone control knob so there's less treble and more bass. Some added bass flatters a woman's voice; an overdose of treble results in a pinched, metallic sound. Get the right sound mix for you.

Without knowing Fred's name, in a minor crisis you could be a voice crying in the wilderness. If, despite arrangements, you cannot be heard by the audience, simply call, "Fred, can you please turn up the volume? I don't think they can hear me." You are apt to get prompt action. Fred, who has probably forgotten completely to turn up the sound, and is happily munching on a hamburger as he reads the racing form, will leap to his feet, feeling the hundreds of disapproving eyes fixed on his booth, and in a moment the volume will be restored.

Fred can help in another way. If the room is too close and hot, so that you see people fanning themselves, ask him to turn up the cooling system. Nothing defeats a speaker more than a room that is too hot.

Post time

Just before speaking and while you are waiting to go on, remember:

Don't drink anything alcoholic—or, if you must, limit your intake to one drink. Pilots would be allowed to drink before flights if alcohol did not lessen their ability to have complete control of themselves and the plane. Competence cannot be preserved in alcohol. It will not make you a better speaker; it will only make you think you are better.

Be moderate in your eating. There is more than meets the palate to the old saw that a full belly makes a sluggish mind.

Study the audience while others are speaking. Do they respond quickly? Slowly? Negatively? Do they laugh easily? Is their reaction different from what you had expected? If so, you may wish to amend some statement you had intended to make; modify an argument; add a joke, or omit one. (Unless you are fully confident of your mastery of the situation, though, do not make a last-minute change in the basic structure of your speech.)

Listen to the other speakers. This is a courteous gesture, and the audience will like you better for it. Moreover, you may hear something you want to acknowledge or that bears on what you are about to say.

Confirm that your notes are in order. I have seen inexperienced speakers lose their place and go into a panic. Your notebook of numbered cue

> Half the world is composed of people who have something to say and can't, and the other half who have nothing to say and keep on saying it. —*Robert Frost*

cards insures you against ever becoming confused in this way. Dog-ear the cards for quick flipping.

Set a small key-chain timer, attached to the ring of your notebook, for five minutes less than the length of your talk plus the estimated time of the chairman's introduction of you.

BYE, BYE, BUTTERFLIES

However thoroughly you have prepared yourself, even if you are an old speaking hand the chances are that adrenalin is now pouring into your blood stream. Don't worry about a slight case of nerves; it only shows that you are a race horse rather than a truck horse. Below are prescriptions to combat butterflies. Memorize the steps and follow them while you are waiting to go on:

1. *Sit in Executive Posture.* Press against the chair with your lower back, directing your tension into your vital center. Keep your upper abdominal muscles taut. This leaves the butterflies no place to flutter around in.

2. *Permit only positive thinking.* Avoid succumbing to the negative by repeating to yourself any one of these positive catch statements:

I am:

Poised, prepared, persuasive, positive, powerful.
Composed, confident, convincing, commanding, compelling.
Effective, energetic, enthusiastic, enjoyable.
Imaginative, informative, instructive, inspirational, impressive.
Zestful, zippadeedoo, zing and zowie!

Or make up your own positive energizers. The words don't matter, as long as you saturate yourself with positive, upbeat feelings. Refuse to be negative or apprehensive.

3. *Keep running your opening remarks through your mind.* Have them literally on the tip of your tongue. You should know them well enough so that you can deliver your first four or five sentences smack into the eyes of your listeners without looking at your cards at all.

(This should also be true of your concluding remarks. Say the last two or three sentences right into their eyes—no looking down, here.)

Every speaker has his own butterfly net. Winston Churchill overcame his early fear of audiences by imagining that each of them was sitting there naked. Franklin D. Roosevelt is said to have pretended they all had holes in their socks.

I hope you won't have to go that far. Your audience is not a jury that has already found you guilty and is about to decide on your sentence. They want to like you. All you have to do is make it easy for them.

REMEMBER:

Use cue cards. Don't memorize—familiarize.

Rehearse aloud, on your feet, at least six times, editing after each playback. Make your tape recorder your editor.

Check the physical arrangements on the spot—the lectern—the microphone—the sound engineer.

Reinforce your confidence while waiting to speak. Banish those butterflies once and for all.

test your skills

PREPARING YOURSELF TO SPEAK

1. Read the brief speech that follows and make cue board abbreviations as directed on page 553:

America is the most prosperous nation in the history of the world. This affluence, however, has not brought happiness. Rather, Americans are beset by many problems: racial tensions and disorders; poverty amid plenty; a faltering economy; decaying cities; pollution of air, water, and soil; a drug problem. We have gone from one war into another; our people are divided politically, physically, and spiritually. There is a breach between the races, religions, and generations. We have the most advanced communications systems ever devised and our people are unable to communicate with one another—and often not even with themselves. We are the victims of a range of psychological ailments—from alienation of the self to severe mental disease. What terrible price have we paid for our affluence—our creature comforts? . . .

2. Why is it better to familiarize yourself with a speech rather than to memorize it?

Answers to this quiz appear on page 708.

EIGHT RULES FOR PRESENTING
AND ACCEPTING AWARDS

"It has been proved that the deepest yearning of the human heart is for recognition—for honor!"

When Margery Wilson, the author, wrote this she expressed a universal feeling. We all want to get along well in life. We want to be appreciated. Someone else's commendation, if it is only a word—let alone a gift presented at a formal affair—lifts the spirit magically.

Althea Gibson, the tennis star, managed to get this "yearning of the human heart" most aptly into the title of her autobiography. She called it *I Wanted to Be Somebody*.

When we make a speech of presentation, we reassure the recipient that he really is somebody. He has succeeded in a certain effort. He is deserving of honor. We have come together to pay him this honor. What we have to say should be brief, but we should give it careful thought. It may not mean much to those who are used to receiving honors, but to others less fortunate it may be something to remember brightly the rest of a lifetime.

We therefore should give serious consideration to our choice of words in presenting the honor. Here is a time-tested formula:

1. Tell why the award is made. Perhaps it is for long service, or for winning a contest, or for a single notable achievement. Explain this simply.

2. Tell something of the group's interest in the life and activities of the person to be honored.

3. Tell how much the award is deserved and how cordially the group feels toward the recipient.

4. Congratulate the recipient and convey everyone's good wishes for the future.

Nothing is so essential to this little talk as sincerity. If you have been chosen to make a speech of presentation, you, as well as the recipient, have been honored. Your associates know that you can be trusted with the task—one that demands a heart as well as a head.

But this must not tempt you to make the mistake of exaggerating.

At a time such as this, it is easy to exaggerate someone's virtues far beyond their real measure. If the award is deserved, we must say so, but we should not overpraise. Exaggerated praise makes the recipient uncomfortable and it doesn't convince an audience that knows better.

We also should avoid exaggerating the importance of the gift itself. Instead of stressing its intrinsic value, emphasize the friendly sentiments of those who are giving it.

The acceptance speech should be even shorter than the speech of presentation. It certainly shouldn't be anything memorized; yet being ready to make it will be an advantage. If you know you are to be given a present, with a speech of presentation, you don't want to be at a loss for words of acknowledgment that will be a credit to you and a pleasure to the givers.

Just to mumble "Thank you" and "greatest day in my life" and "most wonderful thing that ever happened to me" is not very good. A danger of exaggeration lurks here, as in the speech of presentation. "Greatest day" and "most wonderful thing" take in too much territory. You can express heartfelt gratitude better in more moderate terms. Here is a suggested format:

1. Give a warmly sincere "thank you" to the group.

2. Give credit to others who have helped you: your associates, employes, friends, or family.

3. Tell what the gift or award means to you. If it is wrapped, open it and display it. Tell the audience how useful or decorative it is and how you intend to use it.

4. End with another sincere expression of your gratitude for the gift or award you have received.

I urge you to follow these suggestions carefully when making either of these talks and you will have the satisfaction that comes from saying the right thing at the right time. — *Dale Carnegie*

51

What makes a good speaker?

You've learned a lot about preparing your speech—how to choose and organize a topic that will interest your audience, how to persuade reluctant listeners. You know how to prepare yourself, too. But now that you're on the podium, here are tips that will help make you a good speaker.

Public speaking is enlarged conversation. There is little difference between talking to one person, to ten persons, or to a hundred. You must talk louder; but the talking that goes on around your dinner table does not differ in essence from the talking that goes on at a meeting. The only real difference is that at a meeting the speaker is allowed to talk for a longer time without interruption.

Therefore, think of your speech as a conversation with the audience. Talk *with* the persons you see in front of you. Talk *to* them. But never, never talk *at* them.

It is helpful, too, in preparing and practicing your speech, to think of it as a *discussion* with people you know. Imagine that they have asked you an important question and you are doing your best to answer. As you do so, they put other questions to you, and you try to answer these. You explain, tell stories to illustrate what you mean, and cite statistics. Or someone objects, and you offer counterarguments, and produce facts to back them up. Finally, you sum up everything you've said with a "There, that's it. That's what I've been saying."

If you think of and prepare your address in these ways, it will be *good talking*.

Public speaking is purposeful communication. You talk to an audience for a purpose. You want them to feel, to think, to do something.

Therefore, during your speech, concentrate on this objective. Keep your eye on the ball.

Don't let yourself be distracted by latecomers or noises. Don't let your talking become mechanical. If you let your attention wander, your manner will become absentminded and you will not communicate.

Think what you are saying while you are saying it. Think it *hard*.

Then the audience will know that you mean what you say and will listen to you.

Profile of a good speaker

■ A good speaker is lively, interested, enthusiastic, vital. He feels alive; he sees his audience as living people. He is interested in his topic and considers it vital to such people. So he speaks of it with enthusiasm. That's the best way to interest an audience.

■ A good speaker is earnest. He doesn't talk for talk's sake, to show off his clothes, or his smile, or his diction, or his voice. He doesn't turn on the charm when he stands up only to switch it off as he sits down.

■ A good speaker has a sense of responsibility to his listeners. He realizes that if he talks for five minutes to a hundred listeners he is taking five hundred minutes out of people's lives. He tries to say something that will be worth that precious time.

■ A good speaker has a sense of responsibility to others on the program. If he has been allotted five minutes, he does not take ten. He takes care not to squeeze others off the program, or force them to hurry. They, too, may have something worthwhile to say.

■ A good speaker has a sense of responsibility to his subject. He doesn't bite off more than he can chew. He doesn't spread it thin.

■ A good speaker has a sense of leadership: he stands up tall; he talks eye to eye; he speaks responsibly and with authority, as a leader should. He is positive, friendly, straightforward.

■ A good speaker keeps his head. He doesn't let his enthusiasm carry him too far. He doesn't become a zealot.

He doesn't let his confidence become overconfidence. He doesn't let himself get intoxicated with the sense of power that comes with being in the public eye.

■ A good speaker tries to be balanced, sane.

■ A good speaker keeps his sense of humor.

WRITE BETTER, SPEAK BETTER

WRITE BETTER, SPEAK BETTER

To the beginning speaker: Be yourself. Say what *you* think, not what some columnist or newscaster thinks.

Study other speakers, but don't ape them.

Recognize and admire the fine qualities of experienced speakers. But don't feel that these are necessarily the qualities you must have. You must develop your own potentialities, work out your own style, discover what will make *you* an effective speaker.

Therefore, another word to the beginning speaker: know yourself. Do not indulge in wishful thinking about your speaking ability. Be realistic about the extent of your capabilities.

Learn to accept criticism and to profit by it.

After each performance, analyze it. Ask trusted friends about it. Try to form some objective estimate of its worth.

Discover your weaknesses; don't cover them up. Do something to correct them.

Discover your strengths. Emphasize them, develop them.

Beginners' faults

Here are several of the more common beginners' faults. If you have some, try to eliminate them.

The "er" or "and-er" habit. All of us will say an *er* if we are tired, or can't collect our thoughts, or if we've been reading or doing mechanical tasks too long. But *er*'s sprinkled throughout a speech make it tedious.

TO CORRECT: With a sweep-hand watch in front of you describe the room you are in as if to a radio audience. Try to talk for forty-five seconds without an *er*. Have someone check you, if you don't hear the *er*'s yourself. If you slip, start over for another forty-five-second try. Describe what you see out of a window. Talk of some news event or on any topic that lends itself to a short extemporaneous speech.

The apologetic opening, the apologetic tone. Only the best speakers can afford to apologize, and they do it only when a busy schedule hasn't left them enough time to prepare.

The audience will dismiss your apologetic opening as a routine; or, if you are too convincing, will start looking for faults.

If you haven't had enough time to prepare, if you don't know much about the subject, get out of the assignment as best you can. Let someone better equipped do the talking.

566

Being a copycat. Don't take your speech from, or copy the style of, the Sunday magazine section of your newspaper or the Reader's Digest. Their articles are intended for a reading audience. Their style will sound artificial coming from your lips.

Build your own talks. If a magazine article interests you, read other articles on the same subject, take notes, add your own ideas and observations. Then prepare your speech in your own words.

Fidgeting, jiggling, playing with things. Beginners sometimes drain off their extra energy by nervous playing with coins, buttons, keys, pencils, pens, notes. In doing so, they distract the audience's attention.

Don't carry small objects with you to the platform. Concentrate on your message and use up your extra energy in *vigorous* talking.

Lack of audience contact. Beginners may tend to talk only to themselves or to the front row. Public speaking is enlarged conversation, it is communication to others.

TO CORRECT: Talk to the person in the last row first; then talk to the persons closer to you.

Jargon. Professional persons tend to use a jargon which is intelligible only to other professionals. For example:

Familial societality is already a settled question biologically, structured in our inherited bodies and physiology . . . [from *Social Casework*, quoted as a horrible example by Jacques Barzun in the December 1953 *Atlantic*].

Beginners sometimes seem to feel that they will make an impression if they talk over the heads of the audience in such jargon. They will do much better if they use plain, everyday language and say (interpreting the above): "Family life is born and bred in us."

Meaningless words and phrases. Be specific. Name names. Say exactly what you mean.

AVOID: "something or other," "and so forth," "exact same thing," "all that sort of thing," "this here thing," "that there place."
ALSO AVOID: "Before I begin I should like to state . . . ," "I could talk on this for hours," "I haven't time to discuss this fully, but . . . ," "I'll have to leave this for another time," "I hope I'm not boring you with this, but . . ."

Those phrases are useless and irritating. Prepare your talk well so that you won't be tempted to fall back on them.

test your skills

WHAT MAKES A GOOD SPEAKER

Using the points made in this chapter, explain the difference between the two speeches that follow:

1. Before I begin I'd like to point out that this is a controversial subject—whether the use of private automobiles should be limited or banned. It is now known that the automobile is costly and wasteful of natural resources. The government recognizes the need for mass transit facilities and is spending money to develop them. But some feel the government isn't doing enough. There's no getting around the fact that roads are clogged, there is a lot of pollution, and matters are getting worse. Therefore, people who are against the automobile say that something must be done and soon.

2. One of the most controversial subjects in America today is whether to ban or limit the use of private automobiles. A recent study revealed that the auto industry uses up one-fifth of the nation's steel, 60 percent of its rubber, one-third of its glass, and large quantities of other diminishing resources. The government recognizes the need for mass transit and recently appropriated $340 million to form a federal railroad operating agency, the National Railroad Passenger Corporation, known as Amtrack. Many critics argue that this is an inadequate response to the vast need for more public transportation. They point out that the nation's highways are choked by the present 105 million motor vehicles (almost half the world's total), and these vehicles pollute the atmosphere with monoxide fumes and other emissions, creating a serious health threat. They also point out that the situation promises to worsen before legislation that requires "clean engines" becomes effective in 1975. These critics demand immediate action if we are to avoid greater health threats and social dislocation due to the proliferation of cars and highways and the multitude of problems they create.

Answers to this quiz appear on page 708.

When columnist Merryle Stanley Rukeyser got up to speak at a luncheon of the Pittsburgh Advertising Club, he asked President Carl Dozer, "How long shall I speak?"

Carl told him cheerfully, "Take as long as you like—we all leave at one-thirty."   —*Charles F. Danver in Pittsburgh Post-Gazette*

52

The secret of
good delivery

**In this classic exploration of the elements that contribute to
good delivery, Dale Carnegie strips the subject of its mystery and lays down four commonsense principles that will
free you of artificial restraints and let you be your natural
and effective best on the podium.**

Would you believe it? There are four ways, and only four
ways, in which we have contact with the world. We are evaluated and
classified by these four contacts: what we do, how we look, what we
say, and how we say it. This chapter will deal with the last of these—
how we say it.

When I first started to teach public-speaking classes, I spent a great
deal of time on the use of vocal exercises to develop resonance, increase
the range of voice, and enhance inflectional agility. It wasn't long, however, before I began to see the utter futility of teaching adults how to
project their tones into the upper sinuses, how to "breathe diaphrag-
matically," and how to form "liquid" vowels.

This kind of training is all very fine for those who can devote years
to improving themselves in the art of vocal delivery. I realized that my
students would have to settle for the vocal equipment they were born
with. I found that if I expended the time and energy I formerly devoted
to helping class members with the vocal mechanics of delivery and
worked on the far more important objectives of freeing them from their
inhibitions and general reluctance to let themselves go, I would achieve
quick and lasting results that were truly amazing. I thank God I had
the sense to do this.

In my course there are several sessions that have as their purpose the freeing of tightly bound and tense adults. I got down on my knees, literally, to implore my class members to come out of their shells and find out for themselves that the world would treat them with cordiality and warmth when they would do so. It took some doing, I admit, but it was worth it. As Marshal Foch, who led the Allied forces to victory in World War I, said of the art of war, "It is simple enough in its conception, but unfortunately complicated in its execution."

The biggest stumbling block, of course, is stiffness, not only physical but mental as well, a kind of hardening of one's attitudes that comes with growing up.

Crash through your shell of self-consciousness

It is not easy to be natural before an audience. Actors know that. When you were a child, say, four years old, you probably could have mounted a platform and talked naturally to an audience. But when you are twenty-and-four, or forty-and-four, what happens when you mount a platform and start to speak? Do you retain that unconscious naturalness that you possessed at four? You may, but it is dollars to doughnuts that you will become stiff and stilted and mechanical, and draw back into your shell like a snapping turtle.

The problem of teaching or of training adults in delivery is not one of superimposing additional characteristics; it is largely one of removing impediments, of getting people to speak with the same naturalness that they would inevitably display if someone were to come up to them and calmly knock them down.

Hundreds of times I have stopped speakers in the midst of their talks and implored them to "talk like a human being." Hundreds of nights I have come home mentally fatigued and nervously exhausted from trying to drill members of my classes to talk naturally. No, believe me, it is not so easy as it sounds.

In one of the sessions of my course I ask the class to act out portions of dialogue, some of which is in dialect. I ask them to throw themselves into these dramatic episodes with abandon. When they do, they discover to their amazement that, though they may have acted like fools, they didn't feel bad when they were doing it. The class too is amazed at the dramatic ability some of the class members display. My point is that once you let your hair down before a group you are not likely to hold yourself back when it comes to the normal, everyday expression of your opinions, whether to individuals or before groups. You have freed yourself from your self-consciousness.

The sudden freedom you feel is like a bird taking wing after being imprisoned in a cage. You see why it is that people flock to the theater and the movies—because there they see their fellow human beings act with little or no inhibition; there they see people wearing their emotions prominently displayed on their sleeves.

Don't try to imitate others—be yourself

We all admire speakers who can put showmanship into their speaking, who are not afraid to express themselves, not afraid to use the unique, individual, imaginative way of saying what they have to say to the audience.

Shortly after the close of the First World War, I met two brothers in London, Sir Ross and Sir Keith Smith. They had just made the first airplane flight from London to Australia to win a $50,000 prize offered by the Australian government. They had created a sensation throughout the British Empire and had been knighted by the King.

Captain Hurley, a well-known scenic photographer, had flown with them over a part of their trip, taking motion pictures; so I helped them prepare an illustrated travel talk of their flight and trained them in the delivery of it. They gave it twice daily for four months in Philharmonic Hall, London, one brother speaking in the afternoon, the other giving the talk at night.

They had had identically the same experience, they had sat side by side as they flew halfway around the world, and they delivered the same talk, almost word for word. Yet somehow it didn't sound like the same talk at all.

There is something besides the mere words in a talk that counts. It is the flavor with which they are delivered. It is not so much just what you say as how you say it.

Brulloff, the great Russian painter, once corrected a pupil's study. The pupil looked in amazement at the altered drawing, exclaiming: "Why, you have touched it only a tiny bit, but it is quite another thing." Brulloff replied, "Art begins where the tiny bit begins." That is as true of speaking as it is of painting and of Rubinstein's playing.

The same thing holds true when one is touching words. There is an

571

WHEN YOU'RE ON RADIO OR TV

TALKING on the radio or on television presents special problems. Your audience cannot see you in person, and yet you want them to think of you as a pleasant, warm, and cordial person. You cannot see your audience, can get no immediate response from them. You have in front of you only a mechanical instrument, the microphone—and, on television of course, the formidable camera.

If you let your gaze and thoughts concentrate on the equipment, you may find it difficult to get the feeling of direct communication with live listeners. Therefore, as you talk, think of your listeners. Forget the surrounding studio equipment. This will help to keep you from sounding flat and expressionless.

Though you may have many listeners, more than could crowd into any hall, they are listening to you as individuals. Therefore think of your speech as a conversation with just one or two other persons. Don't think of it as a formal address.

Sit at the table, lean your elbows on it, and talk as if these listeners were sitting at the other end of the table.

Talk *to,* talk *with* these persons, not at them. Keep the tone of active, spirited conversation. Let one sentence be a reply to a question. Let the next be an idea that has just popped into your head. Pause as if to find the right word. Think "because" or "not at all" or "in short" before appropriate sentences. Avoid appearing as if you've rehearsed your lines. Give your audience the illusion that what you are saying you are saying for the first time.

Begin with a strong, attention-getting sentence, for your listener can turn you off if you don't interest him. Restate points at intervals, for he may have tuned in late.

However, let the one or two imaginary persons you are talking to be representatives of the group most likely to be listening at that hour of the day, that day of the week. Ask yourself: Who is most likely to be listening *now?* A busy housewife, a relaxing office-worker, or someone idling through the Sunday newspaper?

The studio announcer will tell you the best distance to keep the microphone from your head or mouth, whether eight inches or a foot or two. Whatever the distance, keep it. Don't weave from side to side, or back and forth. When you are going to use louder volume at some point, move back a bit. When you are going to talk quietly in some section, move slightly closer to the "mike."

Aim your voice not directly at the center of the "mike," but slightly to one side. Breathe quietly. Try not to explode *b, d, g, p, t, k,* too much. Talk at a rate somewhat faster than you would before a "live" audience, between 140 and 180 words per minute, preferably at 150 words per minute. Practice this rate before you reach the studio.

Avoid emphasizing words by saying them more loudly. Instead, emphasize by pitch changes, pauses, and phrasing.

Though you are reading your talk, know the material well enough so that you can keep your eyes off the page at least a third of the time. Do not hold the script between your mouth and the microphone, and move the pages *quietly* to one side as you finish with them.

Prepare enough material to fill your time allotment, allowing 150 words or from fourteen to sixteen lines of typscript a minute. Prepare a little extra so you won't run short. Mark off on the script units of three, four, or five minutes, whichever is more suitable for the total length of the speech. Bracket material which can be cut in case you see that you are going to run overtime. Be prepared to cut heavily on the next-to-last page, so that you can give full time to the concluding section.

On television, face the camera that is being used at the moment (indicated by a light or otherwise). Focus on an imaginary person there and talk to him. As in the case of radio, you will be better received if you think of talking to individuals rather than to a mass audience. Don't let your gaze become unfocused, for then you will seem to be talking *past* or *through* the audience.

Make any gestures purposeful. Avoid elaborate gestures, and quick, sudden movements.

Your rate should be the normal speaking one of about 125 words per minute. You need not worry about talking to the microphone for this will be overhead, or hung about your neck, or concealed.

old saying in the English Parliament that everything depends upon the manner in which one speaks and not upon the matter. Quintilian said it long ago, when England was one of the outlying colonies of Rome.

"All Fords are exactly alike," their maker used to say, but no two men are just alike. Every new life is a new thing under the sun; there has never been anything just like it before, and never will be again. A young man ought to get that idea about himself; he should look for the single spark of individuality that makes him different from other folks, and develop that for all he is worth. Society and schools may try to iron it out of him; their tendency is to put us all in the same mold, but I say, don't let that spark be lost; it's your only real claim to importance.

All that is doubly true of effective speaking. There is no other human being in the world like you. Hundreds of millions of people have two eyes and a nose and a mouth, but none of them looks precisely like you; and none of them has exactly your traits and methods and cast of mind. Few of them will talk and express themselves just as you do when you are speaking naturally. In other words, you have an individuality. As a speaker, it is your most precious possession. Cling to it. Cherish it. Develop it. It is the spark that will put force and sincerity into your speaking. It is your only real claim to importance. I beg you, do not attempt to force yourself into a mold and thereby lose your distinctiveness.

Converse with your audience

Let me give you an illustration that is typical of the fashion in which thousands of persons talk. I happened on one occasion to be stopping in Mürren, a summer resort in the Swiss Alps. I was living at a hotel operated by a London company; and they usually sent out from England a couple of lecturers each week to talk to the guests. One of them was a well-known English novelist. Her topic was "The Future of the Novel." She admitted that she had not selected the subject herself; and the long and short of it was that she had nothing she cared to say about it to make it worthwhile expressing. She had hurriedly made some rambling notes; and she stood before the audience, ignoring her hearers, not even looking at them, staring sometimes over their heads, sometimes at her notes, sometimes at the floor. She unreeled words into the void with a faraway look in her eyes and a faraway ring in her voice.

That isn't delivering a talk at all. It is a soliloquy. It has no *sense of communication*. And that is the first essential of good talking: a *sense of communication.* The audience must feel that there is a message being delivered straight from the mind and heart of the speaker to their minds and their hearts. The kind of talk I have just described might as well have been spoken out in the sandy, waterless wastes of the Gobi desert. In fact, it sounded as if it were being delivered in some such spot rather than to a group of living human beings.

An enormous amount of nonsense and twaddle has been written about delivery. It has been shrouded in rules and rites and made mysterious. Old-fashioned "elocution" has often made it ridiculous. The business-man, going to the library or book shop, has found volumes on "oratory" that were utterly useless. In spite of progress in other directions, in al-most every state in the Union today, schoolboys are still being forced to recite the ornate "oratory of 'orators' "—a thing that is as useless as a squirrel-headed tire pump, as out of date as a quill pen.

An entirely new school of speaking has sprung up in recent decades. In keeping with the spirit of the times, it is as modern and as practical as the automobile, direct as a telegram, businesslike as a telling adver-tisement. The verbal fireworks that were once the vogue would no longer be tolerated by an audience today.

A modern audience, regardless of whether it is fifteen people at a business conference or a thousand people under a tent, wants the speaker to talk just as directly as he would in a chat, and in the same general manner he would employ in speaking to one of them in conver-sation, in the same *manner,* but with greater force or energy. In order to appear natural, he has to use much more energy in talking to forty people than he does in talking to one, just as a statue on top of a building has to be of heroic size in order to make it appear of lifelike proportions to an observer on the ground.

At the close of one of Mark Twain's lectures in a Nevada mining camp, an old prospector approached him and inquired, "Be them your natural tones of eloquence?"

That is what the audience wants: "your natural tones of eloquence," enlarged a bit.

The only way to acquire the knack of this enlarged naturalness is by practice. And, as you practice, if you find yourself talking in a stilted manner, pause and say sharply to yourself mentally, "Here! What is wrong? Wake up! Be human." Then mentally pick out a person in the audience, someone in the back or the least attentive person you can find, and talk to this person. Forget there is anyone else present at all.

Converse with this person. Imagine that he has asked you a question and that you are answering it, and that you are the *only* one who can answer it. If he were to stand up and talk to you, and you were to talk back to him, that process would immediately and inevitably make your speaking more conversational, more natural, more direct. So, imagine that is precisely what is taking place.

You may go so far as actually to ask questions and answer them. For example, in the midst of your talk, you may say, "And you ask what proof have I for this assertion? I have adequate proof and here it is. . . ." Then proceed to answer the question. That sort of thing can be done very naturally. It will break up the monotony of one's delivery; it will make it direct and pleasant and conversational.

Speak to the Chamber of Commerce just as you would to John Henry Smith. What is a meeting of the Chamber of Commerce, after all, but a collection of John Henry Smiths? Isn't it only right and reasonable that the same methods that are successful with those men individually be successful with them collectively?

Earlier in this chapter was described the delivery of a certain novelist. In the same ballroom in which she had spoken, we had the pleasure, a few nights later, of hearing Sir Oliver Lodge. His subject was "Atoms and Worlds." He had devoted to this subject more than half a century of thought and study and experiment and investigation. He had something that was essentially a part of his heart and mind and life, something that he wanted very much to say. He forgot that he was trying to make a "speech." That was the least of his worries. He was concerned only with telling the audience about atoms, telling us accurately, lucidly, and feelingly. He was earnestly trying to get us to see what he saw and to feel what he felt.

And what was the result? He delivered a remarkable talk. It had both charm and power. It made a deep impression. He was a speaker of unusual ability. Yet I am sure he didn't regard himself in that light. I am

> When he speaks,
> The air, a chartered libertine, is still,
> And the mute wonder lurketh in men's ears,
> To steal his sweet and honey'd sentences. —*Shakespeare, Henry V*

sure that few people who heard him ever thought of him as a "public speaker" at all.

If you speak in public so that people hearing you will suspect that you have had training in public speaking, you will not be a credit to your instructor, especially an instructor in one of my courses. He desires you to speak with such intensified naturalness that your audience will never dream that you have been "formally" trained. A good window does not call attention to itself. It merely lets in the light. A good speaker is like that. He is so disarmingly natural that his hearers never notice his manner of speaking: they are conscious only of his matter.

Put your heart into your speaking

Sincerity and enthusiasm and high earnestness will help you, too. When a man is under the influence of his feelings, his real self comes to the surface. The bars are down. The heat of his emotions has burned all barriers away. He acts and talks spontaneously. He is natural.

So, in the end, even this matter of delivery comes back to the thing that has already been emphasized repeatedly in these pages—namely, *put your heart into your talks.*

"I shall never forget," said Dean Brown in his Lectures on Preaching before the Yale Divinity School, "the description given by a friend of mine of a church service which he once attended in the city of London. The preacher was George MacDonald; he read for the Scripture lesson that morning the eleventh chapter of Hebrews. When the time came for the sermon, he said, 'You have all heard about these men of faith. I shall not try to tell you what faith is. There are theological professors who could do that much better than I could do it. I am here to help you believe.' Then followed such a simple, heartfelt, and majestic manifestation of the man's own faith in those unseen realities which are eternal, as to beget faith in the minds and hearts of all his hearers. *His heart was in his work, and his delivery was effective because it rested upon the genuine beauty of his own inner life.*"

"His heart was in his work." That is the secret. Yet I know that advice like this is not popular. It seems vague. It sounds indefinite. The average person wants foolproof rules, something definite, something he can put his hands on, rules as precise as the directions for operating a car.

That is what he wants; that is what I would like to give him. It would be easy for him and it would be easy for me. There are such rules, and there is only one little thing wrong with them: They just don't work. They take all the naturalness and spontaneity and life and juice out of a man's speaking. I know. In my younger days I wasted a great deal of energy trying them. They won't appear in these pages for, as Josh Billings observed in one of his lighter moments, "There ain't no use in knowin' so many things that ain't so."

Practice making your voice strong and flexible

When we are really communicating our ideas to our listeners, we are making use of many elements of vocal and physical variety. We shrug, move our arms, wrinkle our brows, increase our volume, change pitch and inflection, and talk fast or slow as the occasion and the material may dictate. It is well to remember that all these are effects and not causes. The so-called variables, or modulations of tone, are under the direct influence of our mental and emotional state. That is why it is so important that we have a topic we know and a topic we are excited about and eager to share when we go before an audience.

Since most of us lose the spontaneity and naturalness of youth as we grow older, we tend to slip into a mold of physical and vocal communication. We rarely raise or lower our voices from one pitch to another. We may get into the habit of talking too slowly or too rapidly, and our diction may become ragged and careless. In this chapter you have been urged to act natural, and you may suppose that I therefore condone poor diction or monotonous delivery provided it is natural. On the contrary, I say that we should be natural in the sense that we express *our* ideas and express them with spirit. On the other hand, every good speaker will seek to improve himself in breadth of vocabulary, in the richness of imagery and diction, and in the variety and force of his expression.

It is an excellent idea to evaluate oneself in terms of volume, pitch variation, and pace. This can be done with the aid of a tape recorder. It is useful, too, to have friends help you make this evaluation. Remember, however, that these are areas for practice away from the audience. To concern yourself with technique in front of an audience will prove fatal to effectiveness. Once there, pour yourself into your talk, concentrate your whole being on making a mental and emotional impact on your audience, and nine times out of ten you will speak with more emphasis and force than you could ever get from books.

578

PART FOUR

Learn to use your voice

53

Beware of these
speech blemishes

Nothing expresses your personality as surely as your voice, and no amount of study and planning will make you a fully effective speaker if you suffer from one of these eleven major speech blemishes. Learn what they are and how you can guard against and correct them.

How can you pinpoint the speech blemishes that destroy or shatter an otherwise appealing image . . . rob you of power, authority, persuasion, allure . . . lessen your impact . . . keep you from being lovable at first listen?

If your face has a blemish, you see it in a mirror. You go to a drugstore or cosmetic counter and buy something to cure, cover, or camouflage it. If it is bad enough, you go to a plastic surgeon and have it eliminated.

Speech blemishes can detract just as much—but how do you know they are there? Before you can cure or eliminate them, you have to recognize them.

A mirror can tell you a little something about your speech picture. It can tell you, for instance, whether you are using your hands too much; contracting the sides of your mouth, and so making your speech as well as your face ugly; being aloof, stiff, and tense; forcing your voice; talking without moving your lips.

But the best reporter of speech is the tape recorder. Many small, lightweight recorders are available at prices most families can afford; if you have a mirror in your home, you should have a tape recorder too. It won't be long before you can buy an inexpensive video-corder for instant TV playback, so that you can check yourself visually and aurally at the same time. Meanwhile, do get the tape recorder. It will enable you, in privacy, to hear exactly how you sound. You can learn your defects and shortcomings, and check the results of the easily followed suggestions in this section.

In business, a tape recorder for your speech is an indispensable aid to success. You can use it to review your ideas aloud, to edit and practice speeches and presentations, to rehearse interviews, to check your speech and conversation habits in action by recording your voice when you talk on the telephone.

If you have no recorder, you can learn a little something about your voice through either of two very simple procedures:

1. Say something with your nose almost against the middle of a large, half-opened magazine. You will hear a considerably magnified sound.

2. Face a corner of a room, as close as you can sit or stand to where the walls meet. Cup your hands lightly over your ears, and speak in your usual fashion. The sound will bounce back, amplified. And you may be surprised at what you hear!

What are the speech blemishes you should guard against? How can you recognize them?

Are you a nose talker?

This blemish is particularly common and disfiguring. When you talk through your nose, you twang. Clasp your nose between thumb and forefinger, so as to close your nostrils. Then say: "She sang seventeen songs and swooned." Your fingers will pick up the vibration caused in your nose by "m," "n," and "ng." These are the only three legitimate nasal sounds in our language.

For contrast, hold your nostrils the same way and say, "Woe, oh woe, oh woe, oh woe!" The sound should come entirely from your mouth. If you buzz, even on those "o" vowels, you are a nose talker. In the theater, the actor who wants to play a complaining and disagreeable character is apt to adopt a nasal speech pattern.

You cannot be lovable at first listen if you talk through your nose. You will be whining, lifeless, and negative. Yet your voice has to come out through your nose if your mouth does not open enough when you talk. Look into your mirror, and say, "Hi, you handsome, wonderful, lovable creature!" There should be almost a half-inch strip of darkness between your teeth throughout much of that self-admiring sentence.

> Her voice was ever soft,
> Gentle, and low, an excellent thing in woman.
>
> —*Shakespeare, King Lear*

If, instead, your teeth are fitted together like two rows of corn on a cob, or if, even worse, your lips are virtually closed, like those of a ventriloquist, you almost certainly speak nasally.

Nasality mars a woman's image even more than a man's. Have you ever heard a woman whose nasal twang was alluring? Of course not! If you want to be as persuasive as advertising tycoon Mary Wells, or as seductive as Brigitte Bardot, bring your resonance not from your nose but from your chest.

The tight, clenched jaw was once considered the "society" way of talking. "Don't move a muscle; don't let animation show in your face; avoid laughter—it makes wrinkles." We ought to be all for those laugh lines. If you lack them, perhaps you don't laugh enough; and in our problem-laden world, we need all the laughter we can get.

The clenched-jaw speaker emanates tenseness and strain. This prevented one fine woman from fulfilling a long-held and altruistic dream of recording books for the blind. Blind readers could not see her, but they could *hear* the tightness in her voice.

For more antinasality hints see pages 607–611.

Are you a shrieker?

Do you screech even when you are not angry? Do you force your voice even when you are not calling the children? Women, particularly, often do, perhaps because of the million irritants which sting them each day. If you are a wife with a strident voice, your husband's teeth are set on edge every time you speak. Stridency and shrillness are even more disagreeable than nasality. There has been only one politician—the late Mayor Fiorello LaGuardia of New York—who won and kept the affection of his constituency despite a shrill, strident voice. When LaGuardia read the Sunday comics over the radio, the whole city chuckled—because they loved the Little Flower, despite his voice.

This is another blemish that shows up in your mirror. Does your neck look taut? Do the veins and cords stand out like ropes? Are the muscles around your chin tight to the eye and the touch? If they are, you probably sound as strident as a seagull.

Try talking with a ribbon tied snugly around your neck. If you strain or force your voice, you will feel the ribbon choking you as you approach the end of each sentence.

For antistridency tips, see pages 607–611.

Are you there?

Do you usually sound weary and depressed? Does your voice have wrinkles in it. Does it lack vitality, vigor, energy, enthusiasm, intensity? Are you constantly asked to repeat because people do not hear you? The reason may be that you lack proper breath support. You are failing to project.

Whispering is for telling secrets and making love. What is a whisper? It is the ghost of a sound—one from which most of the tone and resonance are missing. A breeze whispers until it has something to vibrate against. As soon as it runs into a leaf it rustles.

To recognize whisper talk, first put a finger against your Adam's apple and say "Zzzzzzz." You will feel a vibration; "Zzzzzzz" cannot be said in a true whisper. It is a voiced tone. Now say "Sssssss." Your larynx does not vibrate. "Sssssss" is the unvoiced, whispered counterpart of "Zzzzzzz."

Next, your finger still on your larynx, make some such remark in your normal voice as "I wonder whether I'll feel a vibration." If the telltale buzz is missing, you are a whisper speaker.

Do not confuse whisper speaking with soft but supported speaking. Your voice needs support even at its lowest volume. You should have at your command projection ranging from the very quiet to the very strong with infinite gradations of volume in between.

If you whisper for effect, as Marilyn Monroe did, and still manage to make yourself heard, you are not really whispering at all—you are stage whispering, an entirely different thing. The stage whisper is supported by almost as much air pressure as a declamation. In the theater, it can be heard from the nearest seat in the orchestra to the farthest row in the balcony. In his army days General James M. Gavin was known for his low voice, but no one had trouble understanding him because he too was a stage whisperer.

The unprojected speaker, by contrast, is almost inaudible. Jackie Kennedy Onassis is one of these. Sometimes it was a strain to make out what she was saying on her famous television tour of the White House.

Some people who are perfectly audible in one situation are whisper talkers in another. There is a chain store magnate who always whisper talks when he is out socially with his wife; yet he makes himself heard at board meetings. It seems likely that he is trying, perhaps subconsciously, to tell his wife that she should moderate both the volume and the quantity of her conversation. If so, she has yet to get the message— which shows that whisper talking is no way to drive home a point.

Women may think that inaudibility demonstrates their feminine delicacy. Actually, they are substituting a meretricious femininity for the real thing.

A not too distant relative of the whisper speaker is the fader. His voice comes and goes as if he were a crystal radio in a thunderstorm. A sentence may start perfectly well, on a flowing current of breath support through which the words swim as gracefully as fishes; but toward the end the current dries up, leaving the last words to expire, flapping a little, on the wet sand.

Beware the unprojected voice if your purpose is to communicate. The only person an overquiet speaker can communicate with effectively is a professional lip reader. Projection promoters appear on pages 601–603.

Are you a foghorn?

Faulty breath support may show up not in whispering or mumbling, but in strain. An unsupported voice is like a Model T Ford trying to climb a steep hill in high gear. It moves slower and slower, starts to jerk, and finally stalls altogether. Excessive speechmaking with an unsupported voice cannot but produce hoarseness. Millions of television viewers of U.S. Republican and Democratic National Conventions in 1968 heard platform officials force their voices (and sometimes their audiences) almost beyond endurance. Representative Carl Albert, permanent chairman for the Democrats, could scarcely speak at all by the time the convention ended. The Model T had barely made it up the hill. For unforced, focused, effective speech, you must know how to feed the gas and adjust the gears.

If your throat tires quickly when you talk—if you constantly clear it, if you are chronically hoarse, though you haven't a cold, don't smoke, and are told by the doctor that there is nothing organically wrong with your throat—then you are not using your breath properly to support your voice. The result is likely to be a fuzzy, foggy, grating sound that irritates the listener's throat as well as your own.

If you need projection practice see pages 602–603.

Do you have lazy lips?

Even a lip reader may not be able to make out a mumbler, because the mumbler's lips often do not move enough to be read.

A mumbler, like a whisperer, manages to keep secrets even when he is trying to reveal them. His lips are lazy, and he fails to project. He runs his words together, sometimes omitting whole syllables.

Speak into the mirror once more. If your lips barely move, you are mumbling. To quote Ogden Nash:

> I believe that people before they graduate or even matriculate,
> They should learn to speak up, to speak out, to articulate.
> It befuddles my sense acoustic
> To be mumbled at through a potato, be it from Idaho or Aroostook.
>
> This word-swallowing, these muffled mutes and slovenly slurrings
> Can lead to calamitous misunderstandings and errings . . .
> It's easy to be manly and still make your meaning plain, whether in
>   accents of Mt. Ida, Cathay or Boston, of Des Moines or of the deep-
>   est South
>   . . . Just take that towel out of your mouth.

Another prescription, more prosaic than Mr. Nash's, is this: Speak with *lively* not lazy lips. See page 611 for antimumbling secrets.

Do you color it gray?

The average voice runs a scale of twelve to twenty notes. (A professional actor's or singer's may span thirty-six.) Some unfortunates have a speaking range of only five notes. If you are one of these, your voice has all the fascination of a faucet with a worn-out washer—you drip, drip, drip. Or, like a metronome, you tick, tick, tick. As you drone, others doze. You are a Johnny or Jenny One-Note.

Businessmen sometimes need help with a complaint like this: "When I talk, people get a sort of glazed, sleepy look." Why wouldn't they, if they have to listen to that endless drip, drip, drip, tick, tick, tick? Even

586

the hundred eyes of Argos, the monster of Greek legend, could not have stayed open. No variety of pitch. No color. Drab.

To check your voice for monotony, listen to yourself as you read aloud from a newspaper. Do you vary the pitch, the pacing, the emphasis according to the sense? Is there life, color, melody in your voice? Or does every sentence sound wooden—like the one before? Do they all end on the same note?

A tape recorder provides an accurate voice picture. Read into it and listen to the playback, pretending you are listening to someone on the radio. Decide whether you really enjoy hearing him speak.

Does your speedometer need adjusting?

President Kennedy, in most respects a fine speaker, sometimes raced so fast that some listeners had a hard time keeping up with him. President Johnson, on the other hand, used to dawdle so that a new international crisis could have arisen before he finished briefing the country on the current one.

If you talk too fast, you will not be understood—and you may leave your listeners breathless. If you talk too slowly, they will stop listening. Acceptable speaking rates vary between 120 and 160 words a minute. We read aloud a little faster than we talk. The rate should never be constant, because thought and emotion should alter pacing. Pauses for effect and changes of speed provide needed variety.

Read the following quotation aloud. (It is from a speech by the late

---

I was a member of a party of American mayors that once visited France. In Paris I attended a dinner party at which I was called upon to make a speech. I spoke for fifteen minutes. There wasn't a bit of applause. I sat down, disappointed, and listened unhappily as another man delivered a fiery oration in French. He was applauded at every pause. I joined in the applause until a neighbor whispered, "I wouldn't applaud so much if I were you, Mayor; that man is interpreting your own speech."
—*Former Mayor Bryce B. Smith of Kansas City, Missouri*

Stephen S. Wise.) Time yourself by the sweep hand of your watch. Stop at the end of sixty seconds, and mark the last word you speak:

> In his lifetime Lincoln was maligned and traduced, but detraction during a man's lifetime affords no test of his life's value nor offers any forecast of history's verdict. It would almost seem as if the glory of immortality were anticipated in the life of the great by detraction and denial whilst yet they lived. When a Lincoln-like man arises, let us recognize and fitly honor him. There could be no poorer way of honoring the memory of Lincoln than to assume, as we sometimes do, that the race of Lincolns has perished from the earth, and that we shall never look on his like again. One way to ensure the passing of the Lincolns is to assume that another Lincoln can nevermore arise. Would we find Lincoln today, we must not seek him in the guise of a rail-splitter, nor as a wielder of the backwoodsman's axe, but as a mighty smiter of wrong in high places and low.
>
> Lincoln has become for us the test of human worth, and we honor men in the measure in which they approach the absolute standard of Abraham Lincoln. Other men may resemble and approach him; he remains the standard whereby all other men are measured and appraised.

If you did not reach the phrase "Lincoln can nevermore arise" in the sixty-second period, you were reading too slowly. If you got into the second paragraph, you were beginning to rat-a-tat-tat. The faster you go, too, the more surely you will chop-talk, losing smoothness and flow, sounding like the Morse Code tapped out on a telegraph key or a $33\frac{1}{3}$ r.p.m. record played back at a 78 r.p.m. speed.

If, on the other hand, you spoke at less than 110 words a minute, your best bet is to hire out as a baby sitter. You can count on putting your listeners to sleep.

Do you have a speech tic?

Do you know people who say, "You know, you know," until you bite your lips to keep from screaming? Or, "That is"? Or, "He says, I says"? There are dozens of kinds of speech tics. One writer monitored a Hubert Humphrey TV interview for a magazine article, and counted thirty-one "I b'lieve's" in forty minutes. That's a lot of b'lieving.

Meaningless grunts like "uh" and "ur" can recur as remorselessly as a tic. Bear in mind the warning of the elder Oliver Wendell Holmes:

> . . . And when you stick on conversation's burrs,
> Don't strew your pathway with those dreadful *urs!*

The persuasive warmth and frankness of Abraham Lincoln's speaking manner prompted one old codger to walk away from a campaign speech he was delivering. "I won't hear him," the exasperated listener explained, "for I don't like a man who makes me believe him in spite of myself."

If you have a tape recorder, let it run while you are talking on the telephone. The playback will reveal whether you are a padder. Once you become aware of these tics, you will notice them in yourself and others. You will realize how irritating—and unattractive—they are.

Have you a speech mustache?

One of the trademarks of Salvador Dali, the painter, is an oversized, black, waxed mustache with exaggerated points, like horns. He was once asked if he wore it to attract attention.

"Oh, no," he replied, in fragmented Dali English, "I am really quite shy; I don't *want* attention. I don't wear this mustache to attract, but to distract. People look at it instead of *me*."

Since attention is mother's milk to Dali, we may not take his disclaimer seriously; but it really does seem that speech problems are something like an unwanted, untidy mustache. They distract from what you are trying to say. Your speech should be clean shaven.

Mispronunciations are one such speech mustache. Some of these result from sloppiness or laziness: "govment" or "gumment" for "government," "gonna" for "going to," "idear" for "idea," "Sadday" for "Saturday," "hafta" for "have to."

Mispronounced consonants. Lisping and the sibilant "s." The "s" is more frequently distorted than any other consonant. At one extreme, it becomes a "th"; at the other, a piercing whistle.

The lisp is found everywhere in the world, from humble homes to haughty salons and executive suites. A giant-sized, important executive does not stay giant-sized long if he is afflicted with a baby-sized lisp.

Often the lisp is so slight that its owner isn't aware that he has it. It is easy to check. Simply say, slowly and distinctly, a phrase containing a number of "s" sounds: "Essential hospital nursing services"

> John Joseph Cahill, former premier of New South Wales, explaining the difference in English as it is spoken in Australia and the United States: "In your country, a bison is an animal. In my country, we wash our hands in it."   —*Tony Weitzel, quoted in Look*

will do very well. Where was the tip of your tongue as you spoke? If it touched your teeth or gum ridges on those "s's" you were lithping, whether or not your ear caught the "th."

The sibilant "s" often occurs because of a gap between two front teeth, either upper or lower. It is like the whistling sound of a teakettle announcing that the water has come to a boil, but it brings irritation instead of pleasure to the listener. Take that kettle off the stove!

Other mispronounced consonants. Consonants are subject to a Pandora's boxful of abuses.

The exploding "t" was made famous by Mae West: "Come up *ta* see me some *time*." When addressed by a practitioner of the exploding "t," keep your distance—you may be sprayed.

Some people substitute a "d" for "th" ("doze" for "those"). Many of us associate this sound with old-time movie gangsters.

A familiar consonant defect is the lolling "l," as in "wowwipop"—another baby sound. Some people even make an "l" of an "n," at least according to this story:

A woman asked the butcher for kidleys. After she had repeated the word several times, he exclaimed, "Oh, you mean kidneys!" To which she rejoined indignantly: "I *said* kidleys, diddle I?"

Some New Yorkers turn the soft "ng" in "Long Island" to a hard one: "Long Guy-land." Below the Mason-Dixon line, quite the other way, the final "g" may vanish altogether: "Fussin', feudin', fightin'."

The Kennedy brothers, Boston born and Harvard bred, added the unwelcome "r" to words ending in vowels ("idear," "lawr," "Indianer," "sawr") and dropped the "r" if it was really there ("paypah" for "paper"). For tips on cleaning up consonants, see page 611.

Tarnished vowels and diphthongs. Without vowels, speech would be all snap, crackle, and pop. If you try to leave them out when you speak, you will be unintelligible. You will also sound as if you were strangling.

The vowels give your speech sheen and richness. Consonants are the pizzicato piccolo; vowels, the 'cello notes. Reader, bow that 'cello!

On paper, there are only five true vowels—*a, e, i, o,* and *u.* "Y" sometimes stands in for "i." Orally, however, these turn into several times as many distinguishable sounds.

These sounds vary from region to region. In New York City, the sentences "I brought coffee to the office for the boss" is likely to come out, "Awee braw-wt caw-wffee to the aw-w-ffice for the baw-wss." In Texas, "you" becomes "yee-ew"; "word," "ward"; "red hair," "ray-ud high-ah"—an example of a vowel that has become a diphthong.

Also, one vowel may turn into a quite different one. Some southerners say what registers on ears as "Thin he lint me the pin" when they mean "Then he lent me the pen."

In a diphthong, one vowel sound leads into another, with the stress on the first and just a dash of the second added, like the dash of vermouth in a martini. A pure vowel is iced gin, with no vermouth at all. "I" is properly pronounced as a diphthong— "ah-ee." In the South, an "I" is likely to lose its dash of vermouth. "I tried to buy pie on Friday" ("Ah-ee trah-eed to bah-ee pah-ee on Frah-eeday") becomes "Ah trahd to bah pah on Frahday." "Wire" becomes "war," "down" becomes "day-oon" instead of "daoon."

Regionalisms like these are ordinarily acceptable in one's home town. To learn whether your vowels and diphthongs are distorted beyond normal acceptability and even understanding (unless some friend or relative is brave enough to tell you), compare your speech with that of some national (not local) newscaster such as David Brinkley or Walter Cronkite.

Do you upstage yourself?

Fidgeting; frowning; raising the eyebrows; nose twitching; lifting one side of the mouth; pulling the ear or chin; biting the lips; fussing with hair, beads, pencil, fingers, or tie; swinging a leg—these are only a few of the common distractors which may be upstaging what you are trying to say.

When Senator Eugene McCarthy ran for the U.S. Democratic Presidential nomination in 1968, the camera usually focused on his head and shoulders, showing an expression as tranquil as a saint's. Occasionally, however, the shot took in his whole body, and you would see his hands in constant action, worrying his ring. The viewer's attention was drawn to that gesture and distracted from his message.

A leading businessman arranges for his secretary to be in the audience whenever he gives a talk. If he gestures too much, she signals him by putting a pencil behind her ear. You may not be fortunate enough to have a signaling secretary, but if you watch yourself you can quickly tell whether attention thieves are robbing you of impact when you talk.

Eye-eye-eye!

When you clasp someone's hand in greeting, you establish a physical contact. An "eye clasp" forms just as vital a contact. You set up a connection with another human being.

Our radios and our TV sets are silent boxes until we make a connection by turning on the electrical current. With your eyes, you can turn on the switch and make a very real connection.

Not only do your eyes *send* messages; they *receive* impressions from others' eyes. "How interesting"; "I'm bored"; "I understand"; "I'm confused"; "I am ready to end this"; "I am content to listen more"; "You irritate me."

When you speak, do your eyes talk too? Or do you avoid direct eye contact because it makes you feel uncomfortable? Does your gaze take refuge on the walls or ceilings? Do you look at your feet instead of the audience? Do you see blobs instead of individuals? There is no surer way to lose an audience!

POINTS TO REMEMBER

Use a tape recorder to identify your speech problems.
If your nose buzzes whenever you talk, you sound nasal.
If your neck grows taut when you speak, you are probably strident.
Don't whisper unless you are telling a secret.
Speak with lively, not lazy, lips.
Read aloud to check your voice for monotony.
Check how many words a minute you speak.
Watch out for speech tics.
Don't upstage yourself with visual distractors.
Contact your listeners with eye clasp.
Check your pronunciation.

54

How to improve your voice

In this series of easy exercises, Dorothy Sarnoff shows you how to eradicate speech blemishes. You'll learn the importance of proper breathing and voice support, how to project your voice and control your pitch, and how to relieve tensions that create harshness and hoarseness.

Speech can soar to the loftiest heights, but its source, as my doctor father never ceased to remind me, is still the human body. If I had paid more attention to his picture studies of the muscle systems which cooperate for breathing, I might not have come within an ace of losing my voice altogether.

My early teachers kept repeating: "Dorothy, you've got to remember there is a body beneath the tone." But I did not understand well enough what they were saying.

The result was catastrophe. When preparing for my first professional engagement, I continued practicing despite a heavy cold—and without proper breath support. The cold turned into laryngitis, and before the end of my first week with the St. Louis Municipal Opera Company, I lost my voice completely. I was rushed to the Philadelphia office of a noted throat specialist, who focused his narrow light on my vocal cords while asking me to say, "Ahhh." I could not. He shook his head. "Your cords have hemorrhaged, and you have huge nodes besides, young lady," he said. "We will have to operate. You may never sing again."

I managed to persuade him (writing out the words) to let me see if absolute silence would do the job. At the end of three weeks, the cords had improved so that he canceled the operation. For another three and

and a half months I did not utter one sound, communicating by writing on a pad. At the end of that time, to the doctor's frank astonishment, my vocal cords were again in mint condition. Several weeks later I was a finalist in the Metropolitan Opera auditions, and my singing career at last was under way.

From then on, you can be sure I gave my voice the breath support and projection all voices require. And though I have sung in hundreds of smoke-filled supper clubs, I have never had laryngitis since.

Understanding breath control

I loved all my voice teachers; but I remember Giovanni Martinelli with particular gratitude. There have been few singers who could support their voices as well as he, or explain the principles of breath support so cogently. Martinelli gave me an image that may help you understand how breath control works.

Think, he would say, of a Ping-Pong ball bobbing on the crest of a fountain. Imagine that the ball is your voice, and the fountain is the breath supporting it. If the support slackens, the ball drops away.

Without breath support, he went on, you will not be heard. Your voice will sound tired and old. You will be a constant candidate for hoarseness, sore throat, and laryngitis.

Breath support must be controlled and constant. No great energy is required. If all the people on earth were to say the same sentence at the same time, the total energy created by their breaths would be too trifling to run a six-cylinder automobile across a street intersection.

When not talking, asleep or awake we breathe through the nose. When talking, we breathe through the mouth. When we are not talking, the abdomen area balloons out, unchecked. In speech, it should be kept tucked in, contracted, ready like a spring to give support.

DON'T BE A BLOWHARD

Proper breath control is not a matter of how much air you take in, but of how you support it on the way out. A sip of air is all you need to speak a long phrase or sentence—and, unlike a deep inhalation, it will not make you tense. Singers have no time during their long musical phrases to pause for a deep breath. They take repeated "catch" breaths through the mouth as they sing. These sips are quick and delicate as a sudden, silent intake of surprise.

594

A single exhalation will carry you through eight or more lines of any jingle that comes to mind. Try this one:

> Sing a song of sixpence,
>   A pocket full of rye;
> Four and twenty blackbirds
>   Baked in a pie.
>
> When the pie was opened,
>   The birds began to sing;
> Was not that a dainty dish
>   To set before the king?

Muscle support, not deep breathing, is the prerequisite, the very philosopher's stone, of a clear, projected, lovely voice.

How your voice works

These opening sections make not so much a mechanic's guide to your voice as simply a driver's manual. Even a Sunday driver should have some notion of what makes his car work. (If your automobile has ever rolled to a remorseless halt in the midst of expressway traffic, as mine once did, you know why I say this.) I had to learn at least the rudiments of speech production before I could attain the full potential of my voice. If you are truly interested in improving yours, you too should understand the principles behind *breathing, resonating,* and *articulating*—the three systems that make up speech.

So bear with me, before we begin corrective measures for specific speech blemishes, while I summarize for you:

How your outgoing breath carries and supports your voice;

How your voice box turns exhalations into sound;

How the sound is amplified in your chest, throat, and nasal passages;

How your mouth—your tongue, lips, teeth, palate, as well as your cheeks—shapes the sounds into words.

A voice is born

When you refer to someone's conversation as a lot of hot air, you probably have in mind the burden of the remarks rather than the quality of the voice. Yet it is true that voice is simply air—resonated, amplified, shifted in pitch, and finally shaped into the sounds we call words. An extraordinary number of organs and muscles are involved.

You could not utter an intelligible word without the active or passive cooperation of your diaphragm, chest muscles, lungs, windpipe, voice box, throat, nasal passages, sinuses, mouth, and jaw.

Your diaphragm sets the whole operation in motion. It is an almost horizontal muscle, a little lower behind than before, that lies under your lungs like a bedboard under a mattress, separating your chest cavity from that of your abdomen. You have hiccups because your diaphragm has gone into spasmodic contractions. You cannot see it; you cannot even feel it; but it is working away morning, noon, and night, like the operating end of a bellows.

Each time you breathe, your diaphragm lowers, and your chest muscles automatically move your ribs outward, thus distending your lungs. (Your lungs lead an easy life; all their breathing-in work is done for them by the muscles.) Air rushes in. Then your diaphragm comes up like an elevator, pushing the air in the lungs above it into the windpipe; your rib cage contracts; and out rushes the air.

This inhalation and exhalation takes place a dozen or so times a minute from the instant your doctor first spanks your red baby bottom and you let out your first big yell.

WHEN YOU EXHALE

Speech starts on an exhalation (you can't speak intelligibly while inhaling) and the exhalation is the work of your diaphragm and the great surrounding chest and upper abdominal muscles—your vital or dynamic center, or "girdle of breath support."

To produce speech, these muscles start a current of air up your windpipe from your lungs. The air passes through your voice box, along your throat, into your nasal passages and sinuses, back to your mouth, and, finally, out into the open as spoken words.

Along the way, a number of amazing events take place.

The first way-station is your larynx, which sits on the top of your windpipe the way a factory whistle is sometimes seen sitting on top of a steamstack. Your larynx is the hard bump in your throat, more noticeable in men than women, that joggles when you swallow. It is called the Adam's apple because a piece of the apple which Adam ate in the Garden of Eden is supposed to have stuck there. Just behind your Adam's apple is your voice box, which is hung with two curtainlike membranes called vocal cords. As the current glides or rushes through, the cords vibrate, causing a sympathetic vibration in the upward-

---

TIPS ON PACING YOUR SPEECH

1. Speak at the rate that suits you and the situation. Don't be as fast as a machine gun or as slow as molasses on a cold day.

2. Note the pacing of the better newscasters on television and radio; then check yourself against them on your tape recorder.

3. Speak in phrases; don't chop your talk into jerky fragments.

4. Sound your vowels fully; don't overemphasize your consonants.

---

moving air. This vibration is what registers on your ear as sound. The faster your vocal cords vibrate, the higher is the pitch of your voice.

When a boy's voice changes at about the age of fifteen, the reason is that his vocal cords have lengthened, dropping his register a full octave. A girl's vocal cords lengthen at the same age, but so slightly that the drop in her register is all but imperceptible. Mr. Jones's voice is deeper than Mrs. Jones's because his vocal cords are about a third longer—six-tenths of an inch as compared with less than four-and-a-half-tenths of an inch. The longer the cords, the slower the vibration and, therefore, the lower the tone.

The range of your voice is probably less than two octaves. A professional singer must be able to span a full two octaves, and many achieve three. There is a case on record of a singer with the incredible span of five octaves.

RESONANCE BEGINS

Before the air even leaves your windpipe, it has begun to resonate, using your chest as a sounding board. Resonance is a reverberation that follows the principal tone in a series of almost instant echoes. It can occur only in an enclosed space. The vibrations of violin strings, for instance, reverberate in the violin box, gaining richness and fullness with each bounce. The amplifiers of your hi-fi set work the same way.

After the vibrations of your voice box determine the pitch, resonance determines the quality of the tone. If your primary resonance is in your nose, you will twang. If you resonate from the chest, you will command more respectful attention.

On its way to utterance, the current of air that carries the sound of your voice passes through a whole series of amplifiers: the throat, the nose, the sinus cavities. Among them, they raise the level of audibility by as much as twenty times.

ARTICULATION

On its upward passage the current of air has become sound. It has acquired pitch from your vocal cords, and tone from your resonators. Its audibility has been multiplied manyfold. Its quality as sound has been determined. The sound may be as pure as a church bell, or as ear-shattering as an ambulance siren. It may be as dead and dry as drift-wood. But it still has not been turned into words, or even syllables. It is like a piece of cloth about to be cut into a suit. Some of the vowel sounds are there, or are at least foreshadowed, but your mouth still has to shape them and add the consonants and the punctuation.

What a lively time it has doing that! Everything in and around your mouth that can move goes into action. Whatever cannot move back-stops the rest. Your tongue, lips, teeth, cheeks, palate—even the uvula that hangs like a tiny fleshy tongue above the entrance to your throat—all go after that current of air like a pack of hounds after a rabbit. They tear it to pieces—and then put it together again. They chop, butt, slice, add, modify, enlarge, narrow, lengthen. Your tongue darts, furrows, spreads, curls, pushes, pulls. Your lips wriggle, squeeze, pout, stretch, relax.

Consider for a moment the versatility of your tongue. Say "ah," and it lies limp as a pancake. Say "a" as in cat, and it humps its back. Say "oh," and it furrows. Say "oo," and it furrows even more. All the while it is jumping up, down, and around like a madman. For a "t," its tip touches the upper gum ridge with feathery lightness; for a trilled "r," its side touches your side teeth, while its tip rustles like a flag in a breeze. For some sounds, such as "ee," your tongue widens; for others, such as "ss," it narrows and retreats. And all this is just the forepart, which you can see easily with the help of your mirror. If you want to know what happens farther back, I believe the American Telephone and Telegraph Company has a film that can show you all you want to know. Call their public relations department.

Your lips are almost as lively. Say "p" (the sound, not the letter), and they pop. Say "mmm"; they automatically press together, so that the sound comes out your nose. Say "f" or "v," and your upper teeth almost bite your lower lip.

All these mouth movements take place at a breakneck rate, as hard to follow as the movements of a one-man band who kicks the cymbals, pounds the drum, blows the harmonica, and scrapes the fiddle all at the same time. It is not surprising in either case that the resulting sound is not always heavenly music.

So there we are—first the breath, then the sound, then the resonance, then the articulation.

The following pages deal with breath support and projection. They consist primarily of a series of simple hints. You can follow them in your own home—some even in a crowded elevator, in the subway, or on the street, without attracting attention.

A better voice is just a breath away

The first step toward proper breathing is proper posture. The fact that proper posture makes you look ten years younger and twice as handsome is a side benefit. If round shoulders and a drooping midriff helped you speak better, I would be gung ho for round shoulders and a drooping midriff. It happens, though, that an upright carriage, naturally held, puts the muscles of your vital center in the best possible position to provide the steady exhalation of air that you need to support an attractive voice. So from now on you are to hold your head a little higher and your back a little straighter. That is Executive Posture. It will help your soul as well as your voice. "Grief," Shakespeare said, "is proud, and makes his owner stoop." If you refuse to stoop, you will be one up on grief.

SIMPLE RULES FOR GOOD POSTURE

So if you plan to speak before a group of people—or simply to talk to a friend—follow these old rules:

■ Keep your chest up. Keep your stomach in.

If you are standing, add one more rule:

■ Keep your weight evenly distributed on the balls of your feet.

If you are sitting:

■ Place your feet squarely on the floor. *Never* cross your legs. (Crossed legs also impede circulation.)

■ Make a double L (as seen from the side)—one L of your feet and lower legs, and another of your upper legs and torso.

■ To help the bellows of your abdomen, touch the back of your chair with your lower (but not your upper) spine, almost pushing against it. Feel that vital center tighten! No more flab!

When a sizable voice thrust is needed, some people modify the last rule. I once knew a choir leader who made all his singers sit on the forward side of a tape which marked off the eight front inches of the chair. He said that sitting on the chair edge while maintaining the "L" position helped them to cannonade the audience with their voices; if he let them sit back, they might relax so much that the cannon would turn into a popgun.

The rules of posture, like the rules for proper breathing that follow, can sometimes be broken without penalty—if you master the rules first. Having heard that Maria Jeritza sang the aria from *Tosca* lying flat on her stomach, I decided to sing the aria from *Pagliacci* lying flat on my back. It worked—but only because I had learned how to use my support muscles. In a lying posture, these muscles had to work many times as hard.

So sometimes one can get away with breaking a rule. But the moral remains: never break a rule unless you have mastered it. If you do break it, try to break it with style.

FOUR WAYS TO BUILD YOUR BREATHING POWER

As an old preacher said, "You can put your mind into a speech, and you can put your heart into it, but if you don't put your diaphragm into it you've got no speech."

How do you put your diaphragm into it?

Let me tell you about a system that has worked for me, and that I think is bound to work for you.

To locate the muscles of the vital center that we have been talking about—the ones that provide the energy, vitality, and power you will need for dynamic speech—sit in a double "L" position, the lower part of your spine touching the back of the chair, the palm of your hand pressing flat on the area about three inches above your navel and at the bottom of your rib cage. Now stand up. Sit down. Go through the same performance again. And again. And again. Each time, you will feel the muscles under your hand tighten. Doctors call the vital center the abdominis rectus and oblique supporting muscles. Singers call it the abdominal brain.

Here are four ways to understand your vital center and help it provide solid support for your speaking voice:

1. Put your palms against a wall, standing one leg in advance of the other as if you were fencing, and try to push the wall down on a slow count of four. (This is another way to pinpoint the girdle of breath support.) You will feel your midmuscles tightening and the flab fleeing.

2. Clench one hand into a fist. Pretend it is a balloon, and try to blow it up on a single slow thin thread of exhalation. Keep the other hand pressed against your upper abdominal muscles, spanning the area where the rib cage separates. Feel them harden and contract as you blow, pulling in toward your back, flattening out your middle.

3. Stand relaxed before a mirror. If your posture is poor, your abdomen will show a melon shape, and excess fat will droop over your hips. Now assume the Executive Posture, and again pretend to blow up a balloon. Once more, see how your muscles tighten and contract, as though something back around your spine were pulling them in. You look younger, more alert, more positive, more slender. If you are a man, this posture can let you wear your belt two inches tighter.

4. Pretend to push a grand piano—to pull a full bucket from a well —to haul up an anchor—to return a tennis serve backhand—to throw a knockout punch. Exhale slowly and steadily with each action, and notice once more the effect on your girdle of breath support.

DON'T SHOUT—PROJECT

Even when you are speaking most quietly, your diaphragm and the muscles around it are supporting every word. Or they should be. Proper posture, giving those muscles complete freedom of action, is therefore the No. 1 requisite for projection.

When you have to project your voice to catch the attention of someone across the room, or to hold the attention of an audience, your muscle support digs deeper and tautens. You tap the same muscles a rider uses when he grips the barrel of a horse with his legs.

Projection is not shouting. Political candidates, addressing large crowds; sports coaches; fans at outdoor games; foremen; supervisors; teachers; cocktail partiers—all these often shout wildly instead of taking advantage of the maximum carrying power developed by the vital center. At cocktail parties, guests often force their voices and scream at each other, instead of simply projecting to make themselves heard. The noise goes from loud, to *Loud,* to LOUDER, to L O U D E S T. It is a crescendo, with mounting throat tension. Voices should not be forced;

the force should be put into *supporting* them. Even in a fairly crowded, noisy room your voice should carry fifteen feet without strain—but you may have to make those backup muscles work harder.

Earlier in this chapter I mentioned Giovanni Martinelli's image of the voice in conversation as a Ping-Pong ball bobbing on a steady fountain of air. To project at greater distances, change the image from a fountain to a hose. By adjusting the nozzle you can water the bushes at your feet, the privet hedge a dozen feet away, or the Japanese cherry tree at the far end of the garden.

FOUR WAYS TO STRENGTHEN YOUR VOICE

Any of the following simple routines, carried out consistently for five minutes at a time, four or five times a day, will soon strengthen your support muscles and have you projecting easily, with no voice strain. (Remember, do these exercises standing, chest up, stomach in. *Do not* take a deep breath.)

1. *Steam kettle.* Take a short sip of breath and, as you exhale slowly, hiss, in a fine thin stream, through your teeth. H–i–s–s–s–s–s. Count to yourself, and see how long you can make the hissing last. Don't push your breath; LET it come out. You should be able to get to thirty the first time around, and to seventy later on. Feel your girdle of breath support pulling in, getting tighter, tighter, tighter.

2. *Numbers.* Take a short sip of breath, and count aloud on a long single exhalation, as fast as you can. The first time, try for forty by tens (one–two–three–four–five–six–seven–eight–nine–ten, one–two–three–four–five–six–seven–eight–nine–twenty, etc.). How far can you count—80, 100, 120? (This is the only time you will be permitted to mumble, so take advantage of it. We are not concerned here with the sound you make, but only with your breath support.) As before, you will find that each day you can go a little further. In a few days you should be comfortable at a count of a hundred, and eventually you should reach 130. You will be getting thirty miles a gallon from your breath instead of ten. Keep it up, and you will have no further worry about breath support.

3. *Professor Higgins's candle.* Remember the scene in *My Fair Lady* where Professor Higgins showed Eliza how to blow a finely rationed thread of breath at a candle so that it flickered but never went out?

Pretend your index finger is a candle. Hold it about ten inches from your face, and direct your breath gently at it in a thin stream, keeping your mouth in a whistling position. If you are uncertain whether your breath is touching your finger, use a sailor's trick; wet your finger, and the evaporation of the moisture will sensitize it to the passing air.

Once more, monitor the bottom of your rib cage with your other hand, and feel the contraction there.. This is how your vital center should feel when you speak on the telephone or to someone less than ten feet away.

Next, hold your finger at a distance of about eighteen inches, and aim the same delicate stream of air at it. You will find the muscle tension going lower and the support deepening, as it would if you were speaking to someone fifteen or more feet away.

The farther off your finger is, the deeper the support must go to project your breath. To make the candle flicker at arm's length, you use muscles in your groin, your thigh, your buttocks, behind your knees, perhaps even at the back of your calves. They are all backing up your diaphragm to provide that extra projection.

4. *Big bass drum.* Locate your dynamic center once more by coughing or laughing, with your hand at the lower edge of your rib cage. Now start to count aloud, preceding each number by a light grunt: "Uh-*one!* Uh-*two!* Uh-*three!*" Emphasize the numbers, not the grunts. Don't separate the "uh" from the "one"; connect them. With no break in your breath, dig into each number, trying to boom like a big bass drum struck by a drumstick. You will find your breath support seems to go right down to the groin.

EXTRA DIVIDENDS

When you are out for a walk, see how far you can go on a single slow exhalation. A third of a block? A half? I once recommended this to an Irish nun, who practiced it until she could walk a whole short city block on a single exhalation.

Make a practice of climbing as many steps as you can on a single exhalation. You will soon find that you no longer reach the top of the stairs exhausted and out of breath. If you are a golfer, use the same technique going up a hill. My husband and I regularly do this at our golf club when approaching the sixteenth tee, which is at the top of a sharp rise. I think we are the only members who reach the tee breathing normally.

There are side benefits to making an exhalation go on and on. It often works like magic, for instance, against nausea. A doctor told me this is because pulling in the muscles inhibits reverse peristalsis, which is one of the causes of air and sea sickness.

You will find, too, that a constant, long, slow exhalation decreases your nervousness while you wait to speak in public or to undergo a trying interview. It can do much more than that. It can hold down panic and even reduce pain. Pregnant women practice it to help them in natural childbirth.

A beautiful Swedish woman, whom I had long admired for her radiant complexion and unfailing energy, one day confided the secret of her glow to me. "I take a catch-breath," she said, "and pop into a tub of icy water. Then I count aloud at least to sixty on a single exhalation, take another catch-breath, and repeat. That is enough. I jump out, and miraculously I am not shivering but tingling and invigorated."

I have tried it—and it is a better pickup than a martini. (But this is not for you if you have even a hint of a heart problem.)

Keep your voice as alive as you are!

Your voice can tell the best or the worst of lies about you. It can say "vigorous" when you are tired. It can say "young" when you are over seventy. But watch out if it says "fatigued" when you are rested; "weak" when you are strong; "frustrated" when you are fulfilled; "old" when you are still young!

Don't let your voice give away your age—unless, that is, you are still on the diaper side of the generation gap. Franklin D. Roosevelt managed to sound young and vibrant even in his last speeches, when he was already mortally ill. Winston Churchill's voice remained the same long after his shoulders had rounded and his step become a shuffle.

Don't give someone else voice fatigue. If you recharge your own voice instead, he may very well pick up your vitality. Voices are surprisingly contagious.

You know what sagging stockings do to a woman's image. A sagging voice is worse. Here are some vocal projection secrets that will keep your voice as snug as a fashion model's panty hose. For *voice vitality and vigor*, first follow the hints for breathing on the previous pages. Next, do the following—with energy and thrust:

Say each of the verbs below twice—quietly for the lower-case version in the left-hand column, and emphatically for the capitalized version at the right. The lower-case words should be spoken as if to someone ten feet away; the capitalized ones as if to someone at a distance of about twenty-five feet. Pretend all the while that you are on a balcony projecting *down* to the other end of the room. This will help you to resist the temptation to raise your pitch. Each time you say a word, stay two beats on the vowel of the accented syllable: ru-un, pu-ush.

run	RUN!	don't	DON'T!
quiet	QUIET!	do it	DO IT!
ready	READY!	try	TRY!
look	LOOK!	come in	COME IN!
shoot	SHOOT!	climb	CLIMB!
fire	FIRE!	stand up	STAND UP!
no	NO!	bravo	BRAVO!
go	GO!	go home	GO HOME!
rush	RUSH!	leave	LEAVE!
pull	PULL!	drive on	DRIVE ON!
hit	HIT!	stay here	STAY HERE!
push	PUSH!	move on	MOVE ON!

When you are speaking emotionally—in anger, outrage, defiance, command—your support muscles work harder. Or they should. What you should *not* do is let your pitch rise. Do you have a tendency to grow shrill in emotional situations? Then practice a few sentences like the following, remembering to give extra support from your vital center to each word you wish to stress. If you have trouble being emphatic, pound the table! Speak several ways: with strong conviction—defiance—anger—boredom—hilarity—authority—command.

1. I was born an American, I shall live an American, I shall die an American!

2. As a citizen of this great country, you must count your blessings—and demand your rights!

3. A situation like this demands strong minds, courageous hearts, abiding faith, and ready hands!

4. We are fighting by ourselves alone, but we are not fighting for ourselves alone.

5. We need dreamers, thinkers, doers—we need you!

6. I am ready to act now, and for my action I am ready to answer to my conscience, my country, and my God.

HOW TO BEAT HOARSENESS

Does your work require you to talk continuously on the telephone? Must you sometimes keep your listeners' attention despite competing noises—from a boiler factory, or a discothèque? (The boiler factory is quieter.) If so, hoarseness is bound to set in unless you know how to protect your voice.

A number of common irritants contribute to hoarseness and laryngitis. One of these is strain—caused often by irritation, or by attempting to make yourself heard above noises.

Cigarette smoke, either yours or someone else's, is another irritant to your vocal cords. Emotional tension can cause you to strain your throat. So can strenuous coughing, loud laughter, and constant throat clearing. Far from really clearing your throat, hruumping actually abuses the vocal cords. If you could look down your throat while these irritants are at work on it, you would see the normally pale cords turn an angry red. You are scratching one against the other.

Avoid clearing your throat to ease irritation. (Many professional singers strike beer and milk from their diets because they create extra mucus. If you find you have a tendency toward phlegm, you too should avoid drinking beer and milk for several hours before giving a talk.) Instead of clearing your throat, chew lightly on your tongue (this will produce saliva) and swallow.

Better still, simply pant and then swallow.

Panting puppy. You have often seen a dog stretched out on the rug, his jaw loose, his tongue hanging limply as he pants. Pretend you are such a dog. First yawn, until you feel an open throat. With mouth lax and tongue limp, pant low and slowly in your throat. Inhale and exhale audibly but smoothly through the mouth. In and out, in and out. Feel the cool air moving over the tongue, down the windpipe and then back up again. Feel the air brushing and massaging the phlegm off your vocal cords. This exercise tends to dry your throat, so swallow after it. Breathe this way seven or eight times, swallow, and repeat the process ten times over. Then rest, and start again an hour later, if necessary. Each time make yourself sound like an old-fashioned steam locomotive idling in the station.

If there is really something the matter with your throat, though, you don't need a speech teacher—you need a throat specialist. If you have acute laryngitis, he will tell you to stop talking. And Dr. Max Som, a distinguished throat specialist, advises: "For laryngitis it is not enough just to stop talking. You should not whisper either." Whispering without breath support—and that is the usual kind—can only add to your voice strain.

He adds one more thing: Whatever the temptation, don't smoke.

To avoid the onset of laryngitis, speak as little as possible whenever a serious cold descends from your nose to your throat or chest. If you strain your voice at that point, you may well invite polyps or nodes.

The rule of silence is even more golden when nodes have been removed by surgery. Tragically, many men and women must live with permanently damaged vocal cords—because they failed to take seriously their doctors' orders to observe *complete* silence for a number of weeks after the operation.

To prevent laryngitis, follow the advice for breath support I have given you. You will find that hoarseness and sore throat become as rare as May flies in December.

THESE DON'TS BEAR REPEATING

■*Don't* let your dynamic center collapse, no matter how tired you are. The energy you put under your voice will put energy into you.

■*Don't* yield to the contagion of loud voices at social gatherings, discothèques, and sports arenas. Instead, use exaggerated breath support.

■*Don't* release your frustrations and anger by shouting or screaming. You will only tear your throat apart. Get and hold attention by quiet emphasis and projection, as much as was required to blow up your make-believe balloon.

■*Don't* clear your throat under the illusion that you are clearing your vocal cords. Pant the phlegm off.

Keep your voice vital—and it will keep you vital!

Banish that blemish

How many Americans talk through their noses? The census does not ask that question; but if they were to organize a third party, I suspect they could cast enough votes to throw the next Presidential election into the House of Representatives.

And if all the strident speakers in the country joined up too, their candidate would probably win the election.

To correct both nasality and stridency, and to arrive at the velvet smoothness of chest resonance, you must work toward relieving your general physical tension. Specifically, learn to relax your jaw and tongue and open your throat and mouth so that the sound can exit that way, instead of being shunted into the passageway that makes it come out the nose.

By following these suggestions, you can relax the entire head and neck and feel better all over.

1. *The plopper*

Let your head dangle forward and hang there, eyes closed, for six slow counts.

Again counting slowly to six, raise your head from its drooping position until your eyes, gradually opening, see the ceiling. You should feel the tension begin to melt away. Repeat several times.

2. *The rag doll roll*

With your head again dangling, let your jaw hang loose, as if it were about to fall off. Roll your head slowly to one side; then back and up; then to the other side; then forward again.

To know how far your jaw can relax, first put your fingertips in front of your ears, at the spot where your lower and upper jaw are hinged together. With your mouth closed, the place is a slight bump. As you drop your jaw, the bump will go away and be replaced by a cavity.

Watch yourself in the mirror. Once properly relaxed, your lower jaw will drop behind the upper one. Don't worry about that row of double chins; they will disappear when these maneuvers are over.

Place your index finger against your chin and manipulate your lower jaw until it stops fighting you and swings free. It should become eventually as loose as Charley McCarthy's. You will feel like a ventriloquist's dummy—and you will enjoy it. (Before, with jaws clenched and lips drawn, you were more like the ventriloquist.)

3. *Slower downer*

Drop your jaw and let your tongue hang limply over your lower teeth and lip. Breathe more and more sleepily, as if you were beginning to feel the effects of an anesthetic.

Silently count a slow 1–2–3–4 on each inhalation, and another on each exhalation. By now your breathing should sound the way it would a split second before you begin to snore.

Substitute a groan for the count on each exhalation. Be sure you do not pause between the outgoing and incoming breath. The flow should be constant. Don't stop until you feel a yawn coming on.

4. *The groaner*

Tuck your tongue between your lower lip and your teeth, relaxed and thick. Now groan "Aaaaah," dragging out the sound and directing it at the point where your tongue and lip meet. You will have the sensation that the "Aaaaah" is actually outside your mouth—which is exactly where it should be.

TONGUE TALK

If I ask you to let your head sag on your neck, you will have no trouble doing it. But can you relax your tongue? Go over to the mirror and check: can you let it go limp, completely without tension, resting sleepily in the nest of the floor of the mouth? Most people cannot. It will probably hump up, it will furrow, it will pull back, it will stretch sideways. Talk to it as if to an untrained puppy. Say, "Down, tongue, down! Relax! At ease!"

Now, with jaw and tongue completely relaxed, say "la, la, la, la, la, la," as if you were a drooling baby. Your tension will soon drool away.

THE THROAT

Yawning is a number one relaxer. Can you yawn at will? Here is a way to:

1. With eyes gently closed, bring your lips together lightly.

2. Drop your jaw loosely, lips still closed.

3. Let a great big lazy yawn take over, opening your mouth and the back of your throat w–i–d–e; feel the stretch, up and sideways, of the muscles opening the throat.

If, as you yawn, you look at the back of your throat in a mirror, you will see the uvula pull up and shorten like a rising curtain. That is the way it opens to make way for sound.

In all speech (except when you are saying "m," "n," or "ng") your throat should be open. To feel the difference between a closed and an open throat, say "ng–ah, ng–ah, ng–ah" several times. On the "ah" sound, the throat is completely open. On the "ng" sound, it is completely closed. Try to have the sensation of the open throat in speech.

To combine the relaxed jaw and the open throat in one maneuver:

1. Put your elbow on a table, resting your chin on the back, not the palm, of your hand.

2. Lift your head so that your chin is about two inches above your hand.

3. With the same sensation as the yawn, say: "yah, yah, yah, yah, yah"; "yaw, yaw, yaw, yaw, yaw"; "yoh, yoh, yoh, yoh, yoh." Let your jaw relax so that it hits your hand as you pronounce each syllable. At

the same time, put your other hand flat on your chest, right under your collarbone, and feel the vibrations there. There is no nasality now—no clenched jaw—no tight flat mouth.

THE MOUTH

Make a "V for Victory" frame of the index and center fingers of one hand, putting the tops of the fingers lightly at the corners of your mouth. The cleft or point of your chin should be directly above the bottom of the "V." If, as you speak, your mouth moves out to widen the top of the "V," you are undoubtedly a nasal talker.

Say "Baa baa, black sheep, have you any wool? Yes, sir, yes, sir, three bags full. One for the master, and one for the dame, and one for the little boy who lives down the lane." Watch yourself in the mirror.

As I said before, there should be about a half inch of dark between your teeth as you talk. To help you tight-lipped, clamped-jawed speakers unlock your mouths and get the sound outside of your heads, use these two maneuvers:

1. *Knuckle down*

Put the knuckle of your index or middle finger between your teeth and try to read, aloud, the Lord's Prayer, the Gettysburg Address, or any other familiar passage. The sound will be almost unintelligible. Then remove the knuckle and repeat the same words, still opening your mouth widely to let the sound pass through unimpeded.

2. *Megaphone*

Use your lips as if they were a megaphone. "W" makes a wonderful megaphone, blowing away nasality and mumbling like a sea wind blowing away a fog. Here are some sentences to practice on:

Why do wily women win wealth and wed well?
Wilma worked woefully while Wallace willfully wandered west.
Weary Willy washes and wipes wet windows while Walter whistles.
Welcome wagons wound their way westward while warped wheels wobbled weakly.
Washington was a wizard warrior; his wisdom and wishes worked wonders.
Women worried when Warsaw's wild, wet winter weather worsened and workers wearied.
One weeping willow wisp waves wanly in the wind.
Woolite warrants washing worn, wilted white woolens well.

To remove the sound from your nose when you talk, memorize one of these sentences and repeat it aloud until you can zip through it the way in your schooldays you zipped through "Peter Piper picked a peck of pickled peppers."

MUMBLERS

The above alliterative sentences also help mumblers. The "w's" bring your lips alive. Men's lips tend, with no apparent reason, to be lazier than women's. Notice on your television set how often men speak with a literal "stiff upper lip." (And how do you suppose that phrase ever came to mean not letting events get you down?) They often look as if they had just shaved off their mustaches, and their upper lips had not yet had time to become as flexible as before.

Ordinarily, lazy lips and lazy middle muscles go, if not hand in hand, at least side by side. The mumbler is likely to leave whole syllables out of his words. "Hereditary" may become "hered'ty"; "American," "Murcan"; and the like.

Your best cure for mumbling is to recite polysyllabic words slowly, with full breath support, making sure that you give each syllable its due. Don't chop! Glide from one syllable into the next. Make full use of your vital center on the accented syllable. Give the accented syllables extra physical impetus:

administration	beautiful	zodiacal
dependability	exuberance	cantankerous
jocularity	hereditary	fertilization
monosyllabic	kleptomaniac	individualistic
polysyllabic	nonrepresentational	libertarian
somnambulator	quietude	overwhelmingly
valedictorian	theoretical	regenerative
Yugoslavian	whimsicality	unappropriated

PITCH

The owner of a leather company came to me for help because, as he complained quite legitimately, he sounded like a twelve-year-old boy. When he reached a prospective client on the telephone, he could not talk business until he had proved he was the head of the company and not the office boy. In three sessions he lowered his pitch to an attractive level and left pinched, nasal resonance behind.

A high-pitched voice is a serious handicap for a businessman not only because it irritates but because it lacks authority. In a woman it sounds like chalk squeaking on a blackboard.

An airline asked me to help one of its Spanish-speaking stewardesses, a candidate in a beauty contest. Beauty of form and figure was not the only criterion in the competition; the contestants were judged also according to their speech, and this poor girl whisper-talked and whined. She also inflected upward at the end of every sentence like a cat discussing its love affairs on a back fence. A few lessons brought her pitch down four tones, and gave her the velvet chest-tone that her lovely figure deserved. She was one of the runners-up in the contest not just because of her classic Castilian beauty, but because of her voice. My tapes show that only five of the eighty-seven contestants had voices to match their looks.

Think of how a cow moos; contrast the sound with the bleat of a billy goat. The moo is low, the bleat is high. I do not ask you to sound like a cow, but for contented listeners it is better to have the pitch of a cow than a goat.

How do we lower the voice? Low pitch and low resonance usually go hand in hand.

BE A LOW PITCHER

To find out how low your potential pitch may be, put your hand flat on your chest right under the collarbone and groan or say "Aaaaah," as if for a doctor. Now, as if you were going down cellar steps one at a time, go down the steps of your available pitches till you hit bottom. Be aware of the vibrations in your chest as your voice descends.

Next, with your hand still on your chest, say "I don't think it is going to snow." Again, go down step by step, lowering the pitch each time till you feel you cannot go any lower. Try a few sentences at the lowest pitch you can maintain naturally.

> Mend your speech a little,
> Lest it may mar your fortunes.   —*Shakespeare, King Lear*

To help make this low pitch part of your regular vocal equipment:

1. *Be a floor talker*

Sitting in a chair, place your feet squarely on the floor, twelve inches apart. Set a book between your heels. Bend over from your waist toward the book, your head dangling, your arms hanging loose. Your fingers should be like limp tassels touching the floor. Relax completely. Now begin reading, using your girdle of breath support. Your speech will automatically resonate in your chest. Your pitch will be lower. Listen carefully to this sound—it is the one you want. Then straighten up, trying to retain the voice quality you had in the dangling position. You are not supposed to read for interpretation but purely for voice quality.

2. *Use "Palmer penmanship"*

In grammar school when they taught you how to write with flowing, rounded, unbroken lines, you were told to make endless connected circles like this:

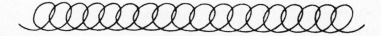

Standing chest up, stomach in, describe full rich vocal circles on

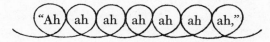

with unbroken supported sound, while you make circles with your hand for your eye to see. As each sound hits the bottom of its circle, give it renewed energy by pulling in your vital center. You should remind yourself of a broken record when the needle gets stuck in the groove. The sound rolls over and over.

Try this on "ah"—"aw"—"oh."

Remember to give each circle of sound a new push with your vital center. Dig down, down, down as though you were dredging for a new low in voice range. Scoop up your voice from the bottom of the bay— haul the bucket up from the bottom of the well.

It is also a good idea to read aloud, with your hand on your chest to remind you to use chest resonance. Never let yourself inflect up at the end of a sentence. It tends to make your overall speech sound higher and gives you the tentative sound of uncertainty instead of the positive sound of authority. Even questions can be asked effectively inflecting down. Try some:

<pre>
                        OVER TO–
    CAN YOU COME   MORROW?
                   DO IT TO–
    WILL YOU   DAY?
                GLAD
    YES I'LL BE   TO.
</pre>

Emphasizing down is much more effective than raising pitch.

<pre>
    I   I   You
      want it!   hope so!   must do it!
</pre>

There is no sound of uncertainty or hysterics this way.

To attain a voice that charms, beguiles, persuades, convinces, commands—and, above all, *communicates warmly*—you must THINK LOW constantly. (I do not mean morally; I mean physically.)

You have to keep your breath support LOW!

You have to keep your pitch LOW!

You have to keep your resonance LOW!

You have to keep emphasis and inflection DOWN!

Write on six self-adhering stickers, in big letters, and preferably in bright red ink, the words, "THINK LOW!" Place them on your telephone at the office and at home, on the mirror before which you shave or comb your hair, on your desk, in your diary. Remind yourself to "THINK LOW!"

And think low in all talking situations. If you spend much time on the telephone, turn your telephone calls into exercise sessions—hold a pencil about sixteen inches away from your lips at lap, waist, or table level, and talk down into it.

POINTS TO REMEMBER

Proper breath support is the foundation of a good voice.

The way you exhale is what counts.

Project your voice, don't shout.

Don't let your voice sound older than you are.

Use some of the "relaxers" in this chapter every day to relieve daily tensions. Use them to relax your head—jaw—throat—neck.

Make your lips lively, not lazy.

Be a low pitcher.

Be a smooth talker.

55

Your child
talks like you

**Learning to speak properly is one of the greatest steps in a
child's development—or one of his most severe hurdles. Here
are practical steps you can take to avoid speech problems
in your child and to help him develop a pleasant voice and
an articulate way of speaking.**

What makes your Johnny speak? It's a good question.
Speech doesn't just happen. It is no sudden miracle springing out of
sheer good luck, but the result of a fascinating process of development.

Johnny's speech will be influenced by his intelligence, his hearing,
his sight, his health, by how happy he is during the first five years of
life. It will also be influenced by his control of his muscles and his coordination, by how well he learns to breathe and to use his speech organs—tongue, teeth, lips, gums, larynx, and others. His speech will also
be influenced simply by his innate tempo for maturing.

You will know that he has a good working voice if with it he can
easily carry on the business of normal daily living, if he can easily be
heard and his voice is usually free of either huskiness or shrillness, if he
does not speak through his nose.

To make himself heard Johnny must have carrying power, which
means he must make good use of volume. Remember that volume in a
human voice is very similar to volume in your radio. Turn your radio's
volume up or down and you get more or less sound. So, too, should
Johnny learn to give more emphasis to important ideas than to unimportant ones. His voice should be flexible enough to express the differences he has learned to sense.

Through suitable pitch variety Johnny makes his voice interesting, lets it become a sensitive reflection of his moods and thoughts. A voice that has flexible pitch is never dull.

Johnny's speech shows a good sense of tempo. Some children naturally speak fast; others naturally speak slowly. This natural rate, provided it isn't too fast or too slow (and you'll know whether it is either of these by the reaction of other people and by your own reaction) should, of course, not be interfered with. Johnny learns to suit his timing to the occasion—speeding up or slowing down as the occasion demands. He learns to give emphasis to what he says by making use of varying pitch, by "framing" the important point. To frame it he must say the important words either faster or more slowly than he spoke what preceded these words and what will follow them. This is a technique for giving emphasis.

Good volume, pitch, and tempo go to make good tone quality. So do vibrancy and resonance. If Johnny's tone quality is good, if his voice is vibrant and resonant, he impresses people as a vital, vivid child. But these things cannot be taught Johnny. They must come naturally in imitation of the example you yourself set. How Johnny speaks is therefore not preordained. It is largely a matter of his environment.

Six ways to help your child speak better

In the beginning you are the child's world; so it is you who must fashion the child's speech.

You fashion it by what you do and by what you don't do, and by what you are.

Johnny will speak earlier and better—better all his life—if you will do certain things.

1. Stimulate him to talk from the very beginning of his life. (But only when he is in the mood for such stimulation!)

2. See that he has a motive for speaking. In his preverbal period he will ask for things by gestures, by crying, or by babbling. But as he shows that he is ready to speak and after he not merely speaks his first word or his second or third but shows signs of a growing vocabulary, let him know that his preverbal techniques for asking will no longer serve their old purpose. Give him what he wants only *after* he has asked for it—no matter how clumsy the asking may be. And don't anticipate

his wishes. If he gets what he wants without asking, he may not bother to ask.

3. Fill his world with meaning. To do this, give him many opportunities to see the connection between a thing or an experience and the word for that thing or that experience.

4. Fill his world with interest, excitement, vitality. Make his environment an alive one by talking to him from his very first days. Sounds and words are a form of play, one of the most exciting games of childhood. As soon as your child can appreciate this fact he will readily enter into the spirit of sound play to which you have introduced him.

5. As he grows a little older and is able to join you at meals, make a point of including him in family conversations.

6. You must let Johnny know that you love him. His good speech thrives on this expression of your love. Mothers start influencing the child's speech from the day he or she is born. Mother's arms, the tone of her voice, the aura of warmth that she creates—these affect the way the child breathes and eats. They also affect the way he makes sounds and learns to speak.

LOVE MAKES A DIFFERENCE

How important is this first mother-child closeness can be seen in children who have been wholly or partially denied it. Twins, for instance, each of whom gets only half of his mother's attention, are practically always late in speaking. And once they begin, they talk imperfectly for a long time.

For the opposite reason, the only child is very frequently precocious in speech development—he receives love and attention to his heart's and his speech's content. He not only enjoys more of his mother's undivided attention when he is an infant, but he is spared having this attention eclipsed by the arrival of a sister or brother.

The arrival of a sister or brother may have a marked effect upon a child's speech. When he receives the newcomer with extreme hostility and jealousy, these emotions may result in a speech defect.

But the child who spends a barren childhood in an orphanage is the best example of what a loveless childhood can do to a child's speech. The speech of children in institutions typically develops very slowly and with marked defects. Neglect and the absence of love retard a child in every phase of his development. But *nowhere* will the effects be as great and as apparent as in the child's speech.

Speech thrives when the child feels loved.

Correct your own speech habits

Your Johnny talks like you. This fact may gratify you or embarrass you, but it cannot be escaped. If it were not so, all children—from Atlanta or New York or Saskatchewan or Dubrovnik—would talk alike.

The first approach to your child's future speech, then, is via your own present speech.

Be honest with yourself—does the flatness of your voice reflect a listless attitude toward life? Is the shrillness caused by taut nerves? Does the huskiness or nasality filter out the vitality of your words? Or is your voice saccharine sweet, so that what you say is drowned in a profusion of syrupy nothings?

Shrillness, for instance, is a major vocal indiscretion of American mothers. Shrill voices grow out of taut nerves, and shrill-voiced women are likely to give their children nervous speech patterns reflecting nervous personalities.

Other women whine and, without meaning to, always seem to be complaining. One son of such a mother, four-year-old Tommy, said, "Mommy always makes me feel I did somethin' wrong." When the boy's mother was informed that her voice might be the cause of the child's feeling, she agreed to have her voice recorded. Upon hearing the record, her instant reaction was, "I don't sound like that. That's the voice of a nag—a shrew!" That was the beginning of taking the whine out of one woman's voice.

PUT LIFE IN YOUR VOICE

Still other mothers and fathers have voices so flat that they take the luster out of living and give their child's world an atmosphere of listlessness. Even though the child himself is not listless, he is likely to adopt this voice pattern and sound that way.

There are mothers and fathers with husky voices and some with nasal voices—voices that fail to bring a soothing parental quality into their child's world. And there are parents whose words tend to die somewhere in the back of their throats, who always seem to be depressed. When you actually are depressed, you're likely to say, "I'm

618

down in the mouth." Down is exactly where your speech goes when you are not up to par.

Remember that Johnny's emotions as well as his speech are affected by the speech and voices around him.

"All right," you say. "I admit it. My diction is dreadful, my voice terrible. I never thought much about these things. It is too late to start now. Certainly too late to have any effect on my child."

YOU CAN BE A GOOD MODEL

But it is not too late. To be sure, you may have a voice disorder that is caused by a deep-seated disorder in your personality. In that case, removal of the basic cause will take a long time. Meanwhile, you can approach the matter purely from a vocal point of view. You can attempt to improve your diction. You can attempt to give color to a flat voice, to tone down a shrill one. Nor from the point of view of Johnny's speech is this a waste of time, for you can destroy his chance for good speech by speaking badly. Remember, he will reproduce your vocal defects as surely as your vocal virtues.

Dr. Robert Harrington, head of the Department of Speech Therapy at Los Angeles Orthopedic Hospital, finds that 80 percent of all speech defects are wholly unrelated to any organic causes. What this means is that most speech defects are the result of imitation, pure and not so

---

An African chieftain flew to London for a visit and was met at the airport by newsmen. "Good morning, Chief," one said. "Did you have a comfortable flight?"

The chief made a series of raucous noises—honk, oink, screech, whistle, z-z-z-z—then added in perfect English, "Yes, very pleasant indeed."

"And how long do you plan to stay?" asked the reporter.

Prefacing his remarks with the same noises, the chief answered, "About three weeks, I think."

"Tell me, Chief," inquired the baffled reporter, "where did you learn to speak such flawless English?"

After the now standard honk, oink, screech, whistle and z-z-z-z, the chief said, "Short-wave radio." —*Terry Harman*

619

simple. And because these defects are the result of imitation, they can be remedied by the simple expedient of providing good models.

This power of imitation is very strong. It is so strong that, though only one-fifth of all speech defects have organic causes, the total number of people handicapped by speech defects is greater than the number of deaf, blind, crippled, and feebleminded put together.

NEVER TALK BABY TALK

Your child reproduces lisps, hesitations, stuttering, substitutions of wrong sounds for right sounds (making a word like "rate" sound like "raid," for instance), and substandard usages—in fact, the whole repertoire of distorted sounds. If a hissing *s* mars the pleasantness of your speech in the same way that a hissing radiator destroys the calm of a room, then your child is likely to hiss his *s*'s, too. And if you talk baby talk to him, he is almost certain to baby-talk back. You should never reproduce the baby's words with their inaccuracies and distortions. To do so only reinforces the baby's errors and prolongs them. Baby talk serves one purpose only—and that a bad one—it tongue-ties Johnny to your apron strings.

To coo and babble to Johnny is something else again. This is something you should do often. For your cooing and babbling to him instill in him a play attitude toward language and also make him feel that you are close to him.

It is amazing to find mothers with nasal voices, shrill voices, flat voices, mothers who can't sing a note, becoming suddenly melodious as they babble or coo to their babies.

But let's get back to *your* speech. Cooing and babbling to the baby will improve your own speech. But if you're really serious about doing something about it, you'll have to do other things as well. It's best to begin at the beginning, as my whining friend did, by having your voice recorded. Listening, you will learn many things about yourself. You may say, "That doesn't sound like me." But rest assured that what you hear is truly how you sound.

LEARN TO HEAR YOURSELF AND OTHERS

Train your ear. There are many ways of doing this—all of which are fun. Read aloud, listen to trained voices at the theater, on the radio and television, and on phonograph records. Train your ear to distinguish pleasant voices from unpleasant ones. You will gradually begin to imitate pleasant voices without even being aware that you are doing so.

In large measure the speech your child develops during his first five years is the speech he will use as an adult. It is, at least, the bedrock of that speech. Whatever superstructure is erected upon the bedrock will be the more sturdy if the bedrock itself is firm.

So subtle is this process of imitation that your child will subtly reflect the changing moods that your voice conveys. He will, of course, reflect it not only in his speech but in his whole personality.

For example, consider the mother who brought a five-year-old son to the Speech and Hearing Center at Queens College, New York. She was deeply troubled by the boy's high-pitched, shrill, and squeaky voice.

"I don't know what to do with David," she told Dr. Jon Eisenson, the clinic's director. "Other children make fun of him. I'm afraid he'll have a hard time at school."

Dr. Eisenson sprang a surprise. "Forgive me," he said, "if I talk frankly. There is really nothing wrong with David's voice that I can't correct by correcting your voice first. I recommend that you, and not the boy, should come for therapy."

The mother went to the clinic regularly and once her shrill voice was toned down, the boy's voice gradually toned down, too.

CHANGE YOUR TUNE TO CHANGE YOUR TONE

But not all parents need resort to therapy. The solution in many instances can be quite simple. When, for example, Mrs. Lewis yelled at three-year-old Arnold he yelled back at her, reproducing her angry tone exactly. Hearing her own voice echoed through her child's voice, Mrs. Lewis decided to change her tune. One day, when Arnold moved uncomfortably close to a hot plate, she restrained her instinctive, angry, "Arnold, get away. You'll burn yourself." Instead, she removed him bodily, while saying very calmly, "We don't go near a hot plate." On similar occasions later she always controlled herself, always kept her voice calm. The day came when Arnold surprised his mother by mimicking her new tone. He was about to look for a ball that had rolled under a radiator. But he stopped short suddenly. "We don't go near hot radiators," he said in the same calm tone his mother had used in connection with the hot plate. The point had struck home. And so had the tone of voice.

But Johnny may find talking like you, his parents, more difficult than will your girl baby. It is easier for infant girls than for boys to mimic

Mama's voice fairly closely. Nor are boys very successful in imitating their fathers, for they come up against the great difference between the voice quality of a grown man and that of an infant male. Because there is less difference between the infant girl and her mother, the infant girl echoing her mother is likely to have a more satisfying experience. In addition, boys characteristically have a slower rate of motor development than girls. For these reasons girls may be more precocious in their speech development than are boys.

The deeper Johnny's attachment, the more he will imitate you. When he repeats your words and the cadences in which you speak them, he affirms his rapport with you. Imitating your words, he also imitates other things about you. You become his model—a hero (heroine) if you like. And it is in this hero worship through imitation that much of Johnny's character will be formed.

He will also imitate the speech of other people he sees often, particularly people of whom he is fond.

If Johnny spends more time with children of his own age than with adults, his speech develops more slowly—all else being equal—than if he spends more time with adults, or even with older children. If he spends most of his time with children younger than himself he will make even slower progress.

It is easy to see why this is so. Because speech is so imitative the child suits his language to the occasion and tends to speak like the person with whom he is talking. This habit is so fixed that by the time he is speaking sentences, he almost invariably uses longer sentences in talking to adults, whom he apes and wants also to impress, than in talking to children, whose shorter sentences he must then imitate and whom he need not impress.

Your own vocabulary counts

The words you use and the way you use them will influence Johnny's words, too.

A child whose parents are skilled in the use of language, have large vocabularies, and talk in well-constructed sentences usually follows suit. All else being equal, he speaks his first word earlier than the child whose parents have less language skill. He begins to combine words earlier—combine them first into phrases and then into sentences. More, his sentences are longer than those of less-favored children. And he not only asks questions earlier but he asks questions that are more probing.

He has still another advantage—his larger vocabulary has more varied parts of speech. The first part of speech all children acquire is the noun. He adds other parts sooner than other children, who seem to cling to nouns and use a larger percentage of them throughout their childhood.

How important it is for Johnny to get a firm grip on vocabulary from the beginning cannot be stressed too strongly. But remember that understanding comes before words, so be patient with him in his struggle to find the right word. Watch. Wait. And above all listen carefully.

BUILD JOHNNY'S CONFIDENCE WITH WORDS

A good vocabulary will give Johnny confidence in expressing himself. This confidence will help him in playing with other children and in making sense in his dealing with adults. And when finally he takes his speech to school the command of words and the freedom he feels in using them will have a great deal to do with the kind of adjustment he makes. Words properly understood and easily used will help him to do better work in school and to be a happier child. "Give me the right word," wrote Joseph Conrad, "and I will move the world."

Give Johnny the right word and he not only will move his little world but will eventually move into the big world with greater poise, with greater peace of mind, for everybody knows that the man or woman who uses the exact word the occasion demands is in an advantageous position. Words are part of the strategy of living, part of the equipment we must give Johnny.

But suppose you are not satisfied with your own vocabulary. Suppose these remarks have aroused a few fears whether, in this respect, you are able to do what's best for Johnny. Put these fears to rest. You don't have to be a walking dictionary to give Johnny a firm grasp of words. You do, however, have to be interested in words. And you do have to use words correctly, even though your vocabulary may not be a large one.

Suit the word to the occasion

Don't teach Johnny words merely as words, words unrelated to people, objects, experiences, ideas, situations. Don't, for instance, teach him the word "monkey" in your living room. Do that at your neighborhood pet shop or at the zoo.

623

> I am not yet so lost in lexicography, as to forget that words are the daughters of earth, and that things are the sons of heaven.
>
> —*Samuel Johnson*

Make situations and take advantage of situations that will help him learn the meanings of words. If at any time you told him to keep away from the radiator because it was hot, he may have gotten it into his head that the word "hot" means anything to be avoided. One day you may find him sitting on a chair a stretcher of which has worked itself loose. When you tell him to get off the chair, he may say "hot." Touch the loose stretcher and say "loose." Repeat the word several times, each time touching the loose stretcher. Then touch the radiator lightly and, as you withdraw your fingers, say "hot." Repeat this, too, several times. The distinction between "hot" and "loose" should gradually dawn on Johnny, particularly if you touch other hot—not too hot—and loose objects, each time saying the proper word.

It is important that, from the very beginning, Johnny should learn to use the exact word to suit the occasion or situation—making allowance, of course, for Johnny's mental ability at a particular phase of his development. Don't let him learn words in a hit-or-miss sort of way. Instead, like the considerate driver, stop, look, and take time. And remember always that, at first, Johnny uses one word for many meanings. Slowly help him find the one word for what he means. Bring him to the point at which he shows no more hesitation in choosing the right word when speaking than in deciding which foot to use next when walking.

Teach your child to listen

Read aloud to Johnny all through these first five years. Even during his first year there are picture books planned for his level. By reading aloud you create a mood for Johnny. Growing accustomed to the sound of a word will later give him confidence in using it. And, as he grows older, this reading will help him to associate the word with its sound and with a context of words and ideas.

Also play phonograph records for Johnny. This is probably the most helpful listening you can give him. You can play the records over and over again and you can be very selective. The familiarity trains Johnny to recognize sounds.

Radio and television, used wisely, can also be instructive. All of these media will strengthen his interest in words—in their sound, their meaning, and their importance in his life.

Whether or not you help Johnny to learn to talk, he will learn to talk. But the learning will be haphazard. When you do teach him, his development, his level of performance, and the pleasure he takes in that performance will be immeasurably greater.

He will earlier use words in a meaningful way rather than haphazardly. He will use two- or three-word sentences at an earlier age. His grammar, the structure of his sentences, and the inflections he uses in talking will be better than those of other children.

DON'T PUSH OR SHOVE

This does not mean, however, that you should press Johnny into speaking before he is ready. Or that you should make an issue of his speech. You should teach him. But the teaching must be effortless, a sort of game, sheer fun.

It will do Johnny no good if you expect more of him than he can deliver. It is therefore important to recognize that all children are different —that some have a greater inclination to speak and a greater flair for words than others. And nobody dare single out a child and call him unintelligent merely because at one, or at two, or even at three he is not talking.

This nontalking child may be just as bright as the child who vocally seems a shining star. There may be some physical or emotional reason for his making haste slowly. Or he may be one of those who are highly intelligent but whose intelligence rigorously resists verbal expression. Such children will naturally respond with less enthusiasm to your efforts to teach them than will children who have an innate flair for speaking.

But even if yours is a word-minded child it will do him no good to be pressed into performing in a way that his present phase of development makes impossible. As a matter of sober fact it will do him no good to be pressed at any time.

The ability that Johnny has above all other abilities is the ability to grow. All other abilities depend on this one. That is why you must know what can and cannot reasonably be expected of him as he moves from the inarticulateness of birth to the relative fluency of his fifth birthday.

56

That bugaboo:
correct pronunciation

Everyone agrees that "correct" pronunciation is important when you want to make a good impression on your listeners. But just what is "correct" pronunciation, and how can you learn to recognize and use it? Here is a simple definition that can help you improve your own speech.

Power over words logically entails power over correct pronunciation—but what is *correct* pronunciation?

Is it what the actors and actresses use on the Broadway stage or the Hollywood set? Is it what the members of the Social Register use? Is it what the English professors at the great universities use? Is it what the dictionaries recommend? Is it what the political leaders of the country use? Is it what the people use in Boston? Or in the Middle West?

Correct pronunciation is none of these, exclusively; yet it is a combination, in part, of all of them.

Correct pronunciation is the pronunciation used by the great majority of educated people throughout the country. This definition, agreed upon by all language scholars, is the principle that governs the pronunciations offered in your dictionary. It is the criterion by which a skillful speaker is judged. It is the means by which our language has changed from its Teutonic character of the sixteenth century to the modern form in which we now find it. *Correct* pronunciation, in short, is no more nor less than *current* pronunciation. The *proper* way to say a word, by this token, is simply the way educated people are saying it at the moment.

Correct pronunciation has no exclusive relationship to spelling. *Fur* and *her* and *myrrh* are spelled differently but, except for the initial consonant, pronounced the same. In *psalm,* there is a *p* in the spelling but none in the pronunciation, while in *hiccough* (pronounced HIK'-əp) there is a *p* in the pronunciation but none in the spelling (though another spelling of this word is *hiccup*).

Correct pronunciation has no exclusive relationship to clearness. In *handkerchief, vegetable,* and *comfortable,* the correct pronunciations are those which run all the syllables together.

Correct pronunciation is not exclusively charming, or impressive, or clear, or cultured. It is only two things—*current and acceptable.*

The effective way to pronounce a word is the popular way. You will discover that unpopular pronunciations, no matter what authority or reasons you have for using them, are ineffective pronunciations.

There is no Supreme Court of Speech, no final arbiter to rule on the constitutionality or legality of a pronunciation. The dictionaries do not rule on how you must speak, nor do they make any pretense of doing so. They do no more than record how most educated people are currently speaking—as the multitudinous changes that are introduced into each new edition of a dictionary clearly demonstrate.

The next three chapters will point out some of the major pronunciation pitfalls and discuss the popular trends in pronunciation today; develop in you a keen ear for these trends among the people whom you know, and in the locality in which you live and work (for of course trends vary from group to group and from place to place); and teach you to use a dictionary frequently and discriminatingly when you are in doubt about how a specific word should sound.

Once your ear and mind are trained to understand and interpret pronunciation trends you will no longer be uneasy about any of the words you use. You will *know* that your pronunciation is correct because you have discovered, at first hand, through personal experience, analytical listening, and direct contact with an authoritative dictionary that the pronunciation is the one used by most educated and skillful speakers.

PRONUNCIATION SYMBOLS IN THIS BOOK

These pronunciation symbols are used in Chapters 57 through 59:

ə—the schwa, an unstressed vowel representing the "uh" sound spelled *a* in *above, e* in *sicken, i* in *clarity, o* in *melon, u* in *focus*

ăr—ar in *carriage* (KAR'-əj)

er—as in *very*

ōō—as in *moon* (MŌŌN)

ŏŏ—as in *book* (BŎŎK)

ō—as in *go* (GŌ)

57

Three pronunciation pitfalls

You should learn to recognize and avoid the three main pronunciation errors: carelessness, affectation, and pronunciation that is <u>too</u> careful. Studying the lists and examples and taking the exercises in this chapter will help you to talk more naturally and effectively.

When you speak, you want your listeners to be immediately and sharply aware of what you are trying to say. Unlike dress, speech should not be at all ornamental. It should be *functional* only. *Effective speech expresses a thought in the simplest, most economical way.* You have gained genuine power with words when you have trained yourself to speak concisely, with no superfluous sound, with no flossiness, and with no affectation.

Judged by this principle, that pronunciation is correct which is most effective. Effective pronunciation calls a minimum of attention to itself. The skillful speaker places his listeners under the spell of his ideas—he does not permit his pronunciation to break that spell. He *never* pronounces a word in a way that is alien to the habits of his listeners, for he knows that such a pronunciation breaks the spell of his thoughts by distracting the minds of his listeners from the *substance* of his words to their *form.* By making your pronunciation conform as nearly as you can to the current standard of educated speech, you avoid drawing attention to your pronunciation. You escape the danger that the form of your words is detracting from their substance.

Unfortunately, bad pronunciation habits slip easily into everyone's speech, so it's essential to be constantly on the alert for them. There are three kinds of pronunciations that weaken communication:

1. careless pronunciation
2. affected or ostentatious pronunciation
3. overmeticulous pronunciation

Once you have learned to cleanse your speech of these three vitiating influences, you have taken a long step toward gaining power with words.

Careless pronunciation

Effective pronunciation, to repeat, calls no attention to itself, either by design or by accident. Effective pronunciation meets a certain accepted standard of educated speech.

Exactly what that standard is in every instance is not too easy to say. It is a standard, you must bear in mind, that varies greatly from place to place, from time to time, and even from social group to social group.

This much can be said with assurance: effective pronunciation is completely free of grossly illiterate forms.

Substituting a *d* for *th* (*dis, dat, dese, de fadder of de family,* etc.) is discernible to the most untutored ear. Such a habit smacks so strongly of slovenliness in speech as to make the listener painfully aware that there is something unpleasant in the general character of what he is hearing. As it happens, elementary education is so nearly universal these days that few people in our country are addicted to the habit of *d-th* substitution. Those who are generally are completely oblivious of their fault and react with aggrieved astonishment when their mannerisms are pointed out to them.

If you feel that you yourself are sometimes guilty of a *d-th* substitution, consciously listening to your pronunciation for several days and working to eradicate the substitution will effect a rapid cure.

Two related habits are the dropping of the *-g* in words ending in *-ing* (*talkin', workin', hopin',* etc.) and, on the other extreme, clicking the final *-g* in these words. The ending *-ing* is one of the more difficult sounds in the English language; *-ing* and *th* are a pair of sounds never conquered by many people learning English as a foreign language.

To determine how well you pronounce *-ing,* read these words aloud:

> hoping   seeing   making   loving

If the final syllable in these words, as you say them, is identical with the word *in,* or if you detect a sharp, clear, harsh g sound at the end, you do not pronounce your *-ing* words according to preferred patterns. If you will train yourself to say words ending in *-ing* without closing your throat, you will have the sound conquered. A little practice here, as in the *d-th* problem, will produce speedy results.

There is a third facet of careless pronunciation worth discussing. A dozen and a half words, when pronounced a certain way, are usually indicative of a certain linguistic naïveté. They are thus pronounced almost solely by people with little or no experience in the language arts. Let us take a look at them:

Word	Careless Pronunciation	Preferred Pronunciation
1. accurate	AK'-ər-ət	AK'-yə-rət
2. genuine	JEN'-yōō-wine	JEN'-yōō-ən
3. attacked	ə-TAK'-təd	ə-TAKT'
4. athletic	ATH'-ə-let-ək	ath-LET'-ək
5. elm	EL'-əm	ELM (*one syllable*)
6. film	FIL'-əm	FILM (*one syllable*)
7. bronchial	BRON'-ə-kəl	BRONG'-kee-əl
8. mischievous	mis-CHEE'-vee-əs	MIS'-chə-vəs
9. grievous	GREE'-vee-əs	GREE'-vəs
10. faucet	FAS'-ət	FAW'-sət
11. intricate	in-TRIK'-ət	IN'-trə-kət
12. modern	MOD'-rən	MOD'-ərn
13. municipal	myōō-nə-SIP'-əl	myōō-NIS'-ə-pəl
14. deficit	də-FIS'-it	DEF'-ə-sit
15. accept	ə-SEPT'	ək-SEPT'
16. drowned	DROWN'-dəd	DROWND (*one syllable*)
17. February	FEB'-yōō-er'-ee	FEB'-rōō-er'-ee
18. wrestle	RAS'-əl	RES'-əl

Because careless pronunciations generally either annoy or amuse your listeners, they detract considerably from the power of your speech. Your speech must never amuse your audience, unless you consciously plan to be funny; and it must never, without qualification, annoy your au-

Bernard Shaw liked this example of the discrepancy between spelling and pronunciation in English. How do you pronounce "ghoti?" Why, "fish," of course. Pronounce the *gh* as in "enough," the *o* as in "women," and the *ti* as in "nation." Eenuf sed?

dience if you wish to gain power with words. So conspicuous are the wrong pronunciations of the eighteen words listed above that they force your listeners to focus their minds on the *form* of your speech, rather than on its *substance*. They permit your audience, if it is the average alert audience, to feel a momentary superiority over you. Nothing, as you know, so delights a listener as secretly to feel that he is superior to the person speaking; and similarly, nothing so robs your speech of power and persuasiveness as this feeling in the minds of your listeners.

Affected, ostentatious, or "elegant" pronunciation

Many people feel that a very definite and valuable kind of social prestige attaches to the pronuneiation *eyether* (either). While this form is standard in some sections of New England and in parts of the South, in the rest of the country it runs the risk of sounding stagy. Many people, it is true, have been brought up on *eyether* and say it as naturally and unaffectedly as they do their own names. Others, however, have purposely and with premeditation schooled themselves in the use of this form because they feel it lends an air of sophistication to their speech.

The conscious, deliberate use of *eyether* illustrates two negative principles of effective speech:

1. Pronunciation that indicates to the listener, in however minor or momentary a form, that the speaker feels superior is *ineffective* pronunciation. Any such attitude on the part of a speaker, whether real or imagined, is met with instant hostility. Pronunciation that causes hostility is in direct conflict with the primary purpose of speech, for an unfriendly reaction thwarts communication almost as surely as if the speaker's entire language were foreign to his audience.

2. Any pronunciation that is too conspicuous is ineffective. The listener's mind should be directed solely toward the thought of the speaker; if he can remember later that the speaker belongs to the *eyether* school, as he usually will if the speaker uses *eyether,* then some part of his attention was occupied with the form rather than the substance of what he was hearing.

Either and *neither* are entirely neutral, colorless, inconspicuous words —as they should be, since, as conjunctions or pronouns, they contain very little thought. When pronounced *eether* and *neether,* nobody will notice them. When pronounced *eyether* and *neyether,* it is certain they will be noticed and there is a chance that they will cause irritation.

631

Seven other words belong in the same category as *either* and *neither*. These, too, can be pronounced in two ways:

Word	The Inconspicuous, More Popular, Hence Effective Way	The Conspicuous, Less Popular, Hence Ineffective Way
chauffeur	SHŌ'-fər	shō-FUR'
aunt	ant (very similar to *slant*)	ahnt
vase	vayz *or* vays	vahz
again	ə-GEN'	ə-GAYN'
against	ə-GENST'	ə-GAYNST'
rather	RATH'-ər (rhymes with *gather*)	RAH'-thər
avenue	AV'-ə-noō	AV'-ən-yoō

Overmeticulous pronunciation

That a little knowledge can be a dangerous thing applies as much to pronunciation as to any other facet of human living. Thus you will often find, paradoxically, that the person who has taken a speech course or who has suddenly become interested in language or who has decided to major in English in college will begin to speak somewhat less effectively than he used to. Exactly in what respect his effectiveness has diminished may for a time elude you. But as you listen to him you are aware that his manner of expressing his ideas has intangibly lost some of its smoothness, some of its casual power; that there has developed in it that slight degree of awkwardness that forces you, from time to time, to think of his speech as a series of separate words instead of a running juxtaposition of ideas.

Speech that calls undue attention to the pronunciation of any of its component or individual parts is highly ineffective speech. While it is generally true that carefully enunciated speech is more to be desired than slovenly and garbled speech, extreme meticulousness in pronunciation is as much a fault, and for the same reason, as is extreme sloppiness. Sloppy speech is hard to understand and hence irritates the listener; overprecise speech is, in a certain sense, equally hard to understand, for while each word is clearly discernible, the complete pattern of the thought is obscured by the competitive prominence of every syllable that goes to make up that thought. The speaker who has developed the habit of crystal-clear enunciation speaks *words* instead of phrases and sentences. As you listen to the separate words, your mind must perform a kind of gymnastics to fuse these words into understandable ideas.

The person with a rudimentary knowledge of speech principles must be careful not to become self-conscious about his speech. Self-consciousness robs speech of power. One should be word conscious, yes, but not self-conscious when using words. Word-consciousness makes for confidence in speaking, but self-consciousness, in speech as in anything else, tends to undermine confidence.

Meticulousness is manifested in some pronunciations of:

1. The letter *u*
2. The vowels in unemphasized syllables
3. The letter *t* in medial or final position

THE LETTER *U*

According to some speech manuals, the correct way to pronounce *during* is *DYŌO-ring*. By the same criterion, *new* should be *NYŌO*, *tune* should be *TYŌON*, *stew* should be *STYŌO*, *lute* should be *LYŌOT*, and *assume* should be *ə-SYŌOM*.

Now let us test this principle against what we have learned about effective pronunciation.

Effective pronunciation is popular pronunciation. Except in certain parts of New England and in some areas of the South, notably Virginia, very few good speakers pronounce the letter *u* in the manner indicated.

Effective pronunciation is inconspicuous pronunciation. Except in the localities noted, this type of pronunciation is so rare that it shouts its self-consciousness in every sentence in which it occurs.

Effective pronunciation is unobnoxious pronunciation. Again excepting those sections of the country to which it is indigenous, this overemphatic sharpening and lengthening of the letter *u* is considered affected or pedantic by most skillful speakers and ordinary citizens.

If you have always sharpened your *u*'s and if your friends and business associates do the same, by all means continue to pronounce words like *Tuesday, tumor,* and *student,* as you have been accustomed to doing.

On the other hand, if you have always pronounced *tube* and *tune* as near rhymes with *boob* and *boon,* avoid schooling yourself in the meticulous pronunciation. What you are now in the habit of doing conforms to the accepted standards of present-day American pronunciation.

THE VOWELS IN UNEMPHASIZED SYLLABLES

Of, as an isolated word considered out of context, is pronounced *uv* or *ov.* So unimportant is this word, so completely lacking in emphasis in most sentences, that in reality it is almost always pronounced əʊ. For example, read these two sentences:

> He came through the front of the house.
> This is a government *of* the people, *by* the people, *for* the people.

You can appreciate how different the *of* of each sentence sounds when it is spoken.

Meticulous pronunciation erroneously gives equal prominence to all words in a sentence. Speakers addicted to this habit labor under the delusion that their clear and equal enunciation of every word in a sentence lends culture, tone, and impressiveness to their speech; quite the contrary, it makes their speech *pedantic, unpleasant,* and *almost meaningless.*

As Margaret P. McLean points out in her excellent book *Good American Speech:*

> A great many English sounds are pronounced one way when they are used alone or in a stressed position, and in different ways when combined with other words in a sentence or when used in unstressed positions. If the first, strong, pronunciation is used in place of the second, weak, it sounds very artificial and pedantic and is often called overcorrect or affected.

Speaking effectively, you will subordinate unimportant words. Note some of these:

WORD	PRONUNCIATION WHEN UNIMPORTANT
for	fər
to	tə
of	əv
him	əm
her	ər
them	thəm
from	frəm
his	iz
was	wəz

These phonetic respellings are somewhat exaggerated in order to make the point clear. But if you will read the following sentences naturally, you will be able to listen to the exact sound that the weak, unemphatic forms possess. You will discover that for many words we cannot insist on a uniform pronunciation in all positions. The sentences on the next page are quoted from *Language and Its Growth,* by Scott, Carr, and Wilkinson.

In the following list the first illustration is of the strong form and the second is of the weak form.

are	Here they are.	They are coming.
at	Shoot at him.	Stop at the next house.
be	It can't be.	He must be stupid.
could	I would stay if I could.	You could do better than this.
do	There is nothing to do.	What do you see?
for	What is he waiting for?	He is waiting for his pay.
had	The only chance he had.	He had always worked faithfully.
has	You are the only friend he has.	The boat has arrived.
he	We tried but he didn't.	John said he was ready.
his	The fault is his.	He took his departure.
my	Which is my seat?	That is my only hope.
she	Both he and she were offended.	The woman said she was tired.
should	Read as much as you should.	How should I know?
than	"Than" is a conjunction.	Braver than a lion.
was	Could you see who it was?	It was only a small boy.
you	The message was for you.	Why do you think so?

The above list is by no means complete, but it serves to make clear the fact that for many words we cannot insist on a uniform pronunciation in all positions.

T IN MEDIAL AND FINAL POSITION

Although *t* is generally articulated by means of a forcible expulsion of breath while the tongue hits the upper palate of the mouth just above the top of the teeth, a comparison of three words will show that in informal speech the sound of *t* undergoes certain changes. Say these words aloud:

tiny   *better*   *wet*

In American speech the *t*'s in these three words are not identical. Only the first word contains *t* in its pure form. In *better,* the *t* begins to approximate a *d* sound, faintly. The very tip of the tongue only is used. In *wet,* the tongue is in the same position as in *tiny* but considerably less breath is used.

Meticulous speakers make the mistake of pronouncing medial *t* (as in *better, writer, hitting,* etc.) and final *t* with the tongue in the same position and with the same amount of breath required for initial *t* (*tiny, Tom, task*). Their speech as a result sounds somewhat British in flavor.

For medial and final *t* relax your mouth, take your mind off the sound, speak naturally.

58

Recent trends in American speech

Correct pronunciation does change with the times; speech habits come in and out of fashion. The lists that follow will bring you up to date on the currently accepted pronunciation of some problem words, showing how they are commonly spoken in most parts of America today.

Just as the meaning of a word may change with the passage of time, so may the way it is commonly pronounced. What was right for one age might horrify careful speakers in another.

In his classic book *The American Language,* linguist H. L. Mencken gives the example of Benjamin Franklin. Franklin's pronunciation must have reflected the best speech of Philadelphia, then the cultural center of the North American colonies. But he favored the use of a short *a* in words like *calm* and *what.* This would have made them rhyme with *cam* and *hat*—hardly acceptable today. Franklin also defended the pronunciation of words like *get, chest* and *general* with a short *i* sound instead of an *e*—resulting in *git, chist,* and *gineral.* And Noah Webster, whose spelling book was the most widely distributed work on language in North America for over a century, vigorously advocated the pronunciation of *deaf* as *deef.* Webster was also responsible for changing the old pronunciation of *lieutenant* from *leftenant* (still used in England) to *lootenant.*

This flexibility of speech patterns is now widely recognized, and you will undoubtedly find variations from the rules set forth in the lists that follow. But they do show how these words are pronounced by most careful speakers in North America today.

"Long" A: In the following words, "long" a (ay, as in hate) is strongly favored by careful speakers over the so-called short a (as in hat).

aviator	AY'-vee-ay-tər
radiator	RAY'-dee-ay-tər
desideratum	də-sid-ə-RAY'-təm
verbatim	vər-BAY'-təm
ultimatum	ul-tə-MAY'-təm

In some words preferred usage is divided, long a somewhat more popular than short a.

data	DAY'-tə or DAT'-ə
fracas	FRAY'-kəs or FRAK'-əs
status	STAY'-təs or STAT'-əs
implacable	im-PLAK'-ə-bəl or im-PLAY'-kə-bəl
ignoramus	ig-nə-RAY'-məs or ig-nə-RAM'-əs
stratum	STRAY'-təm or STRAT'-əm
pro rata	prō RAY'-tə or prō RAT'-ə
gratis	GRAT'-əs or GRAY'-təs
apparatus	ap-ə-RAT'-əs or ap-ə-RAY'-təs

Adjectives ending in -able: Careful speech shows a preference for first-syllable accent in certain adjectives ending in -able.

am'icable	for'midable
hos'pitable	rev'ocable
lam'entable	pref'erable
ex'plicable	rep'arable
ap'plicable	rep'utable
com'parable	

In the negative form the accent is retained on the same syllable on which it fell in the positive form.

inhos'pitable	irrev'ocable
inex'plicable	irrep'arable
inap'plicable	disrep'utable
incom'parable	

Disputable is more commonly accented on the second syllable (dis-PYOO'-tə-bəl), though DIS'-pyə-tə-bəl is sometimes heard; similarly the negative is in-dis-PYOO'-ta-bəl or, rarely, in-DIS'-pyə-tə-bəl.

Words ending in -ile: In the following words, the American pattern is to pronounce the suffix -ile in such a way that it almost rhymes with hill, but with the vowel sound less protracted, i.e., -əl. The British, on the other hand, tend to rhyme the ending with *mile*. Thus, for *fertile*, we say *FUR'-təl*, Britons say *FUR'-tile*.

fertile	FUR'-təl	juvenile	JŌO-və-nəl
fragile	FRAJ'-əl	textile	TEKS'-təl
servile	SUR'-vəl	docile	DOS'-əl
versatile	VUR'-sə-təl	virile	VEER'-əl
imbecile	IM'-bə-səl	mercantile	MUR'-kən-təl
puerile	PYŌO'-ər-əl	domicile	DOM'-ə-səl
hostile	HOS'-təl	agile	AJ'-əl
sterile	STER'-əl	futile	FYŌO-təl

In *juvenile, textile,* and *mercantile,* however, rhyming the final syllable with *mile* is equally common; and MUR'-kən-teel is also occasionaly heard for *mercantile*.

In the following, *-ile* is generally pronounced as in *mile*.

infantile	bibliophile
Francophile	profile
Anglophile	exile
crocodile	reconcile
senile	turnstile

American vs. British pronunciation: In a great many words, British pronunciation differs markedly from American. Some random examples:

WORD	BRITISH PRONUNCIATION	AMERICAN PRONUNCIATION
organization	awr'-gən-eye-ZAY'-shən	awr'-gən-ə-ZAY'-shən
civilization	civ'-əl-eye-ZAY'-shən	civ'-ə-lə-ZAY'-shən
docile	DŌ'-sile	DOS'-əl
missile	MIS'-ile	MIS'-əl
fast	fahst	fast
laugh	lahf	laf
secretary	SEK'-rə-tree	SEK'-rə-ter'-ee
conservatory	kən-SURV'-ə-tree	kən-SURV'-ə-taw'-ree
laboratory	lə-BAWR'-ə-tree	LAB'-ə-rə-taw'-ree
miscellany	mə-SEL'-ə-nee	MIS'-ə-lay-nee
project (*n.*)	PRŌ'-jekt	PROJ'-ekt
progress (*n.*)	PRŌ'-gres	PROG'-res
process (*n.*)	PRŌ'-ses	PROS'-es
ate	et	ayt
schedule	SHED'-yŏol	SKED'-yŏol
medicine	MED'-sən	MED'-ə-sən
circumstance	SUR'-kəm-stənce	SUR'-kəm-stance
been	bean	bin
Celtic	KEL'-tək	SEL'-tək

PRONUNCIATION PUZZLERS

ADVERTISEMENT   As many people say ad-vər-TIZE'-mənt as əd-VUR'-tiz-mənt or əd-VUR'-tis-mənt—take your choice.

BONA FIDE   Join the common people and say BŌ'-nə fide; the Latin scholars who add the extra syllable (BŌ'-nə FY'-dee) sound pedantic.

CLIQUE   KLEEK is the pronunciation of choice, though CLIK is still widely heard.

DIVAN   When the word means a couch, the popular form is DY'-van.

FIANCÉE   Spelled with two e's, it's a woman, and pronounced fee-ahn-SAY'; with one e (fiancé) a man, and pronounced exactly the same.

POTPOURRI   This import keeps its French flavor: pō'-poo-REE'.

REMONSTRATE   rə-MON'-strayt, even though demonstrate is DEM'-ən-strayt.

RIBALD   RIB'-əld, rhyming with the imaginary word dibbled.

Words ending in -age: In many words the ending -age contains the same consonant sound represented by the letter s in pleasure. The phonetic symbol generally used to represent this sound is zh.

-AHZH PREFERABLE TO -AHDGE

barrage	ménage
camouflage	persiflage
massage	corsage
garage	espionage

Prestige (pres-TEEZH') and cortege (kawr-TEZH') have this sound.

The letter C: C is probably the most useless letter in the alphabet. Not only could we get along admirably without it, but our pronunciation and spelling would be considerably more logical and simple if it had never existed.

C is a parasite, doing nothing to earn its keep, and sponging on the letters k and s. When c has the sound of k (as in cat) we call it hard; when it has the sound of s (as in citizen), we call it soft. Generally (there are, of course, exceptions) this rule works:

C is soft before *e, i,* and *y;* otherwise it is hard. Note the following:

SOFT C (S)

acerbity	(ə-SUR'-bə-tee)	accelerator	(ək-SEL'-ə-ray-tər)
accept	(ək-SEPT')	Celtic	(SEL'-tək)
flaccid	(FLAK'-səd, but also FLA'-səd)	ceramic	(sə-RAM'-ək)
		taciturn	(TAS'-ə-turn)
succinct	(sək-SINGKT')	viscid	(VIS'-əd)
accessory	(ək-SES'-ər-ee)		

HARD C (K)

accustom	(ə-KUS'-təm)	clink	(KLINK)
catastrophe	(kə-TAS'-trə-fee)	crawl	(KRAWL)
cold	(KOLD)	viscous	(VIS'-kəs)
cut	(KUT)		

The letter *G*: *G* follows the same principle: Before *e, i,* or *y,* it is soft (*j*), as in *gem.* Otherwise, it is hard (*g*), as in *gum.* Short words of Anglo-Saxon origin are the most frequent exceptions to this rule.

SOFT G (J)

orgy	(AWR'-jee)	manger	(MAYN'-jər)
gill	(the measure is JILL)	gibe	(JIBE)
giblets	(JIB'-ləts)	gibberish	(JIB'-ər-ish)
George	(this explains the first E; without it, the word would be pronounced GAWRJ)	harbinger	(HAHR'-bən-jər)
		longevity	(lon-JEV'-ə-tee)
		turgid	(TUR'-jəd)
		orgiastic	(awr-jee-AS'-tək)
gesture	(JES'-chər)	gibbet	(JIB'-ət)
gesticulate	(jes-TIK'-yə-layt)		

HARD G (G)

go	glint
guard	grass
game	gill (of a fish)
gust	prodigal (PROD'-ə-gəl)

Words ending in *-itis*: Diseases ending in *-itis* are generally pronounced EYE'-təs, *not* EE'-təs.

appendicitis	laryngitis
arthritis	meningitis
bronchitis	neuritis
colitis	pharyngitis
gastritis	tonsillitis

59

Our wonderful, erratic language

In most languages, pronunciation follows certain predictable rules—but not in English! In our tongue, spelling just isn't a reliable guide to how a word is spoken. Here is a survey of some of the most troublesome letters and combinations that we have to deal with.

It is no wonder that English is a difficult language to pronounce. Consider some of the pitfalls that are always present in the path of the unwary speaker:

1. Spelling is no criterion.

Tough, through, though, cough, bough all end in *-ough.* In each case this combination of letters has a different pronunciation.

Consider how perplexed a foreigner learning English would be by pairs like these:

ghost—guest	plumber—hammer
palm—thumb	hymn—dim

Often the spelling of a word is not even remotely connected with its pronunciation. Consider:

victuals	(VIT′-əlz)	solder	(SOD′-ər)
colonel	(KUR′-nəl)	Sioux	(sōō)
quay	(kee)		

2. A tremendous part of the vocabulary of English comes from foreign languages. Every language on the face of the earth is represented: ancient languages, modern languages, dead languages, living languages. Hebrew, Latin, Greek, Sanskrit, Hawaiian, Japanese, Chinese, French,

and Icelandic, to mention just a few, have contributed tens of thousands of words to our present-day dictionaries. Some of these foreign words are Anglicized when they are taken over into English; some are Anglicized years later; some always retain their foreign flavor. For example:

From the French, *sachet* is still pronounced in a Gallic manner (sa-SHAY'); *valet* is sometimes Anglicized (VAL'-ət).

Sotto voce, from the Italian, has not been Anglicized (SOT'-tō vaw'-chay); *viva voce*, from the Latin, has been (VY'-və vō-see).

Weltschmerz and *wanderlust* are both from the German. The former is still Teutonic in sound (VELT'-shmairts); the latter is Anglicized (WAHN'-dər-lust).

3. Sometimes *th* is soft, as in *the* (*lithe, blithe*); sometimes hard, as in *thing* (*hearth, ether*); sometimes like *t,* as in *thyme.*

4. Sometimes *h* is silent, as in *honor;* sometimes pronounced, as in *humor.*

5. *Oo* may be heard one way, as in *book;* another as in *moon.*

6. *Ch* may be *tsh,* as in *chair; sh,* as in *machine; k,* as in *pachyderm;* or silent, as in *yacht.*

7. S may be *sh,* as in *sugar* or *sure; s,* as in *sinecure; z,* as in *reserve;* or silent, as in *island.*

8. *-Ine* may rhyme with *wine,* as in *feline;* or be sounded *-ən,* as in *genuine.*

9. G may be silent in one form of a word (*phlegm, malign, diaphragm*), pronounced in a different form (*phlegmatic, malignant, diaphragmatic*).

More perplexities of English

These nine principles do not by any means exhaust the peculiarities and idiosyncrasies of English pronunciation. They are sufficient, however, to indicate the great complexity and delightful confusion of our language. An educated Frenchman, or German, or Spaniard can pronounce perfectly any word in his language with which you may wish to confront him—and this statement holds whether he's ever seen the word before or not. Pronunciation hews obediently to definite rules in these and other languages; the exceptions, if any, are infrequent and unimportant.

But, ah, English! What a language! Confusing, perplexing, without rhyme or reason, the full scale of its intricacies can scarcely be more than hinted at. But let us see whether we can't get a little order out of the seeming chaos.

In the following words, the italicized letters are usually pronounced as indicated.

suggest	(sug-JEST')	government	(GUV'-ərn-mənt)
epitome	(ə-PIT'-ə-mee)	strength	(strenkth)
canapé	(kan-ə-PAY')	length	(lenkth)
accessory	(ək-SES'-ə-ree)	succinct	(sək-SINGKT')
ague	(AY'-gyōō)	zoological	(zō-ə-LOJ'-ə-kəl)

In the following, the italicized letters are silent.

indict	(in-DITE')	forehead	(FAHR'-əd or
malign	(mə-LINE')		FAWR'-əd)
poignant	(POY'-nyənt)	solder	(SOD'-ər)
piquant	(PEE'-kənt)	viscount	(VY'-kount)
chestnut	(CHES'-nut)	kiln	(KIL)
boatswain	(BO'-sən)	herb	(URB)
comptroller	(kən-TRŌ'-lər)	often	(OF'-ən)
gunwale	(GUN'-əl)	imbroglio	(im-BRŌL'-yō)
bagnio	(BAN'-yō)		

Words ending in *-ine* are pronounced in one of three ways: long *i* (as in *wine*), *-ən*, or long *e* (*-een*).

-ən	AS IN *wine*	-een	
aquiline	alkaline	submarine	
genuine	asinine	peregrine	
heroine	canine	nectarine	
saccharine	concubine	nicotine	
gelatine	turpentine	benzine	
	leonine	gasoline	
	saturnine	cuisine	(kwə-ZEEN')
	serpentine	guillotine	(GIL'-ə-teen)
	feline		
	bovine		

Th may be hard, as in *thing*, or soft, as in *the*. Here are the few confusing forms:

HARD (*thing*)	SOFT (*the*)
youth	lithe
cloth	blithe
bath	thence
	youths
	bathes
	swathe

A large proportion of our two- and three-syllable words ending in *-et* have come from French, in which language the pattern is pronounced *-ay*. Some of these words retain their Gallic flavor; some have been Anglicized.

ANGLICIZED (*-et*)	GALLIC (*-ay*)
bayonet	sachet
cadet	sobriquet
coronet	cabaret
tourniquet	bouquet
martinet	cabriolet
	Chevrolet
	gourmet

Words from the French usually retain the Gallic pronunciation *ahn-* for the initial letters *en-*.

ennui	(AHN′-wee)	entr'acte	(ahn-TRAKT′)
en route	(ahn ROOT′)	entree	(AHN′-tray)
ensemble	(ahn-SAHM′-bəl)		

Qu is sometimes pronounced as a simple *k*, sometimes as a *kw*.

k		*kw*
liquor		banquet
piquant	(PEE′-kənt)	quote
piqué	(pə-KAY′)	querulous
		quaint
		acquiesce
		loquacious

Ch has three possible pronunciations: *tsh* as in *chair; k* as in *chaos; sh* as in *machine.* Generally, *tsh* is used in native English words; *k* in words of Greek derivation; *sh* in words of French origin.

tsh	*k*	*sh*
chair	archangel	champagne
chase	archeology	chauvinism
arch	hierarchy	chagrin
archbishop	Archimedes	chic
champion	chaos	chicanery (shə-KAY′-nə-ree)
	chasm	
	epoch	
	archaic	
	archipelago	
	chiropodist	
	chimera (keye-MEER′-ə)	

644

Bach (the composer) retains its German pronunciation: the *a* as in *father*, the *ch* a guttural sound.

H is silent in many words. In the following, however, preferred usage usually pronounces it:

*h*omage	*h*umane	*h*otel
*h*umble	*h*umor	*h*uman
	*h*umorous	

In the following, *h* is silent:

vehement	prohibition	vehicle	herb

Pronunciation of *ng:* *Ng* is a peculiarly English sound, found in no other language (French has a similar sound, but it is much more nasal in character). It is for that reason that foreigners have so much trouble with this simple digraph; a speaker accustomed to a tongue other than English, or brought up in a home where some other language was spoken, tends to "click" his *ng*'s, thus: singger, Lonngg Gisland, goingg gaway, etc.

Now, as a matter of fact, the *ng* click is not necessarily a foreign sound. We use it in a host of words like English, finger, linger, anger, etc. What the foreigner does is use it indiscriminately and always, even in words like *singer* and *along* and *winging*.

The native American does not need rules to know when to click and when not to. And, ironically, since no rules are necessary, a perfectly fine rule, with only four exceptions, exists. Learn it if you're curious, or if you think you sometimes have difficulty with your *ng*'s:

At the end of a word, *ng* is never clicked—

lon(g)	*sin*(g)	*win*(g)	*han*(g)

but when *ng* occurs in the body of a word, drop all the letters following it. If a real word is then left, do not click.

singer; drop *-er.* *Sing,* a real word, remains. Do not click.
linger; drop *-er.* *Ling,* a nonexistent word, remains. Click (LING'-gər).
clanging; drop *-ing.* *Clang,* a real word, remains. Do not click.

And here are the exceptions. *These words are to be clicked,* though they violate the rule.

longer	younger	stronger	clangor
longest	youngest	strongest	

Pronunciation of -ate: A fairly reliable rule is that *-ate,* as a suffix in *nouns* or *adjectives,* is pronounced -ǝt; as a suffix in *verbs,* it is pronounced *-ayt.*

Verbs (*-ayt*)	Adjectives or nouns (*-ǝt*)
graduate	graduate
aggregate	aggregate
alternate	alternate
animate	animate
appropriate	appropriate
approximate	approximate
articulate	articulate
associate	associate
aspirate	aspirate

Note that the following exceptions, though nouns or adjectives, are pronounced *-ayt.*

candidate	potentate
concentrate	prostrate
irate	reprobate
magnate	sedate
ornate	inmate

Shifts in parts of speech: It is a tendency of English words to shift the accent as they add or change letters from one part of speech to another. Here are a few out of a very great many examples. The italicized syllable is accented.

*dra*ma (n.)	dra*mat*ic (adj.)
*ba*nal (adj.)	ba*nal*ity (n.)
*cred*ulous (adj.)	cre*dul*ity (n.)
*al*gebra (n.)	al*ge*braic (adj.)
*mor*al (adj.)	mo*rale* (n.)
*gar*rulous (adj.)	gar*rul*ity (n.)

Similarly, a change of part of speech may change the length of some vowels. Thus *mediocre* has a long *o; mediocrity,* a short one; *loquacious* has a long *a; loquacity,* a short one. Here are a few more examples:

tenacious	(tǝ-NAY'-shǝs)	*tenacity*	(tǝ-NAS-ǝ-tee)
maniac	(MAY'-nee-ak)	*maniacal*	(mǝ-NY'-ǝ-kǝl)
admire	(ad-MIRE')	*admirable*	(AD'-mǝ-rǝ-bǝl)
saliva	(sǝ-LIE-'vǝ)	*salivary*	(SAL'-ǝ-ver'-ee)
alkali	(AL'-kǝ-lie)	*alkalinity*	(al-kǝ-LIN'-ǝ-tee)
athlete	(ATH'-leet)	*athletic*	(ath-LET'-ǝk)
compete	(kǝm-PEET')	*competitive*	(kǝm-PET'-ǝ-tiv)

A dictionary of usage

Test your skills: answers

A dictionary
of usage

This special section contains an alphabetical list of trouble-some words, phrases, and grammatical constructions, with explanations and examples of correct usage.

Necessary rules of grammar are included to avoid repeating the rules under each word to which they apply. Thus, the correct usage of a collective noun is not repeated under AUDIENCE, COUNCIL, and other collective nouns. Instead, reference is made under each collective noun to the topic COLLECTIVE NOUNS. The grammatical rules, or topics, are listed alphabetically under an appropriate heading.

If a word causes trouble in more than one sense, the various troublesome points are numbered 1, 2, 3, etc. (See BETWEEN.) No attempt has been made to point out all uses of the words listed. Only those uses that cause confusion or trouble are included. Problems involving meaning or spelling should be looked up in the dictionary.

Words in small caps in the text also appear in their proper alphabetical place, with an explanation of their correct usage.

a, an (indefinite article) Use *an* before all words beginning with a vowel except those beginning with the sound of *y* or *w* and before words beginning with a silent *h*. In all other cases, use *a*.

> *an* attitude
> *an* era
> *an* ideology
> *an* obligation
> *an* understanding
> *an* hour
> *an* honorable discharge
> *a* humble workman
> *a* historical novel
> *a* unit
> *a* eulogy
> *a* one-sided affair

abhorrence (n.) When followed by a preposition, use *of*.

abhorrent (adj.) When followed by a preposition, use *to*.

about (prep.) 1. Never use the combination *at about*. If you are being precise, use *at*; if you are approximating, use *about*.

> He will be here about [approximately] nine o'clock and will leave at [precisely] noon.
> The program will begin *about* [not *at about*] 8:30.

2. If a sentence indicates an approxi-

mation or estimate, *about* is redundant.

> The average mystery novel is [not *is about*] 200 to 250 pages long.
> I think there were [not *about*] twenty-five or thirty people at the meeting.

above   Preferably used as an adverb or preposition rather than as an adjective or noun.

> PERMISSIBLE: The *above* outline.
> PREFERABLE: The outline given *above*.
> PREFERABLE: The foregoing (or preceding) outline.

accede   (v.)   When followed by a preposition, use *to*.

accompanied   (v.)   Use *by* when a person accompanies another. Use *with* when the reference is to some intangible thing.

> He was accompanied *by* his wife.
> The angry tones were accompanied *with* a pounding on the desk.

accountable   (adj.)   Accountable *to* a person, *for* something.

adage   (n.)   Do not modify by *old*. The word adage means an old saying or proverb.

adapt, adopt   (v.)   *To adapt* means "to make fit or suitable," "to adjust"; *to adopt* means "to take as one's own," "to accept formally."

> Many companies *adapted* their plants to the needs of an expanding economy.
> The company *adopted* the suggestions made.

addicted to, subject to   *Addicted to* means "devoted to persistently," as to a bad habit or indulgence; *sub-*ject *to* means "liable to" or "conditional upon."

> Jones is *addicted to* alcohol.
> Jones is *subject to* [liable to] colds.
> This arrangement is *subject to* [conditional upon] approval by Mr. Jones.

adept   (adj.)   When followed by a preposition, use *in* or *at*.

adequate   (adj.)   When followed by a preposition, use *for* when "enough" is meant; *to* when "commensurate" is meant.

> That amount is adequate *for* [enough for] her living expenses.
> That amount is not adequate *to* [commensurate with] the demands made on her.

adjectives   Adjectives modify nouns and pronouns. They have three degrees for comparison purposes: positive, comparative, and superlative. Adjectives of one syllable form the comparative by adding -er and superlative by adding -est.

> slow, slow*er*, slow*est*

Some adjectives with two syllables form the comparative and superlative by adding -er and -est while others use *more* and *most*.

> *more* helpful, *most* helpful, happi*er*, happi*est*

When you are in doubt as to how to compare an adjective, consult an unabridged dictionary. It will indicate those adjectives that form the comparative and superlative with -er and -est.

Comparison to indicate less or least of a quality is accomplished by using the words *less* and *least* before the adjective.

> helpful, *less* helpful, *least* helpful

Adjectives with more than two syllables always form the comparative and superlative with *more* and *most*.

industrious, *more* industrious, *most* industrious

Some adjectives are compared irregularly, such as:

good, well — *better* — *best*
bad — *worse* — *worst*

Avoid double comparisons such as *more slower, more faster,* etc. Be sure to use the comparative when you have just two to compare and the superlative for three or more. Don't say, "Jack is the best editor of the two."

adopt (v.) Not to be confused with *adapt*. See ADAPT.

adverbs Adverbs modify verbs, adjectives, and other adverbs.

1. Avoid using an adjective for an adverb. A common error is the misuse of an adjective to modify another adjective.

> He submitted a *really* [not *real*] good report to the president. (Good is an adjective and must be modified by the adverb "really," not by the adjective "real.")
> The requirements of the position are those that an *ordinarily* [not *ordinary*] intelligent man should have. (Intelligent is an adjective and must be modified by the adverb "ordinarily," not by the adjective "ordinary.")

2. Confusion sometimes arises when an adjective follows a verb. This is perfectly correct when the verb is intransitive—that is, does not have a direct object—and the modifier refers to the subject of the sentence, not the verb.

> The report sounded *strange* [not

strangely] to me in view of the circumstances. ("Strange" modifies report, not "sounded.")

When the word following the verb does *not* qualify the subject, but qualifies the action of verb, it should be an adverb. Note that the same verb can take both constructions.

> His laugh sounded *hollowly* through the room.

See also PREDICATE ADJECTIVE.

3. Some adverbs have two forms, either of which is correct.

> slow, slower, slowest
> or
> slowly, more slowly, most slowly

Most common adverbs that have two forms are listed in alphabetical position in this section.

adverse, averse (adj.) *Adverse* means "in opposition," "unfavorable"; *averse* means "having a dislike for." *Adverse* refers chiefly to opinion or intention; *averse* to feeling or inclination.

> His report was *adverse* to the interest of labor.
> He is *averse* to criticism from others.

advise, inform (v.) Use *advise* in the sense of "counsel," "warn"; use *inform* in the sense of "acquaint," "tell," "communicate knowledge to."

> I shall *advise* him not to accept the contract as it now stands.
> I shall *inform* [not *advise*] him that the contract is full of loopholes.

affect, effect **1.** The word *affect* is not used as a noun, except as a technical psychological term; *effect,* used as a noun, means "result."

> The *effect* [not *affect*] of a sarcastic business letter is to harm business.

2. The verbs *affect* and *effect* are totally different in meaning. *To affect* means "to influence," "to concern"; *effect* means "cause," "produce," "result in," "bring about."

> Passage of this bill will *affect* [influence, concern] the entire country.
> Passage of this bill can be *effected* [brought about] by cooperation of all parties.
> The change of climate may *affect* [alter, have an influence upon] his recovery.
> The change of climate may *effect* [cause, result in] his recovery.

3. *Affect* is also used in the sense of assuming or pretending.

> He *affects* [not *effects*] a blustery manner to hide his shyness.
> He *affected* [not *effected*] ignorance of the matter to avoid a fight.

ago (adj., adv.) When a qualifying clause is used after *ago,* it begins with *that,* not with *since.*

> It was over ten years *ago,* as well as I remember, *that* [not *since*] the stores were consolidated.
> *But:* It is over ten years, as well as I remember, *since* the stores were consolidated.

agree (v.) You agree *with* a person, *to* a proposal, *on* a course of action.

> I agree *with* you.
> He agreed *to* the suggestion.
> The union members can not agree *on* the kind of compensation plan they want.

Also, a thing may agree with another thing.

> The photograph *agrees* with the painting.

agreeable (adj.) Usually followed by *to,* but may be followed by *with* when it means "in conformity," or "in accordance."

> The plan is agreeable *with* [in accordance with] my understanding of what is expected of us.

ageement of verb with subject A verb should always agree with its subject in number and person. The rule is simple, but the number of the subject is not always clear. Mistakes sometimes occur when two or more subjects are joined by *and* (see COMPOUND SUBJECT); when two or more subjects are joined by *or, nor,* and the like (see ALTERNATE SUBJECTS); when a noun or a phrase intervenes between the subject and the verb (see INTERVENING NOUN) and when a verb is followed by a predicate nominative (see PREDICATE NOMINATIVE).

alike (adj.) Never preceded by *both.*

> WRONG: They are *both alike.*
> RIGHT: They are *alike.*

all **1.** When used as a noun, *all* is either singular or plural, depending upon the meaning.

> All *is* [meaning everything] forgiven.
> All *are* [meaning several people] forgiven.

2. When used with a pronoun, *all* is a noun and is followed by *of.*

> Number *all* of them.

When used with a noun, *all* is, properly, an adjective; *of* is not needed, but good writers often use it.

> Number *all* [or *all of*] the sheets.

all right This expression should always be written as two words. The forms "alright," "allright," and "allright" are incorrect.

> Are you *all right?*
> It will be *all right* to ship the goods on the tenth.

allusion, illusion, delusion An *allusion* is a reference to something; an *illusion* is a false image; a *delusion* is a false concept or belief.

> In his speech he made an *allusion* [reference] to the President's last news conference.
> The mirrors gave the *illusion* [false image] of a larger room.
> The company's accounting system creates a *delusion* [false concept] about its profits.

almost (adv.) See MOST.

already (adv.), **all ready** *Already* means "beforehand," or "by this time." *All ready* means "completely ready" or "prepared"; the *all* adds emphasis.

> I *already* [by this time] have the information for you.
> I have the information *all ready* [prepared] for you. (The "all" is not necessary, but adds emphasis.)

also-ran (n.) The plural is *also-rans.*

alternate subject 1. Two or more singular subjects joined by *or, nor, and not, but, either . . . or,* or *neither . . . nor* take singular verbs.

> *Either* the sales manager *or* the advertising manager *obtains* [not *obtain*] these data.
> *Neither* power *nor* wealth *is* [not *are*] a substitute for health.
> Not only the typing but also the spelling *was* [not *were*] poor.

2. If two or more subjects differing in number or person are joined by *or, nor, and not, but, either . . .*

or, neither . . . nor, the verb agrees with the subject nearer it. It is often wise to recast the sentence to avoid awkwardness.

> *Neither* the boy *nor* the *men were* [not *was*] able to work the problem.
> *Either* the girls *or* the *supervisor has* [not *have*] to work late.
> I understand you or *Mr. Jones was* [not *were*] to meet the train.
> He said that *he and not I* have [not *has*] been chosen.

although (conj.) See THOUGH, ALTHOUGH.

altogether, all together (adv.) *Altogether* is correct only in the sense of "entirely," "on the whole."

> The story is *altogether* [entirely] false.
> By working *all together* we can meet the deadline.

am (v.) Principal parts, *am, was,* [has, have, had] *been.* See IRREGULAR VERBS.

among (prep.) See BETWEEN, 2.

amounts Words stating amount (time, money, measurement, weight, volume, fractions) take a singular verb.

> Five days *is* the usual work week.
> Three feet *is* the correct measurement.
> Five yards *is* what I ordered.
> Three-quarters of a pound *is* enough.
> Ten dollars *is* more than I expected.

an (indefinite article) See A.

and (conj.) **1.** Frequently misused to connect two verbs when the second verb should be an infinitive.

WRONG: Come *and* visit me.
RIGHT: Come *to visit* me.
WRONG: Try *and* finish the chapter.
RIGHT: Try *to finish* the chapter.

2. Sometimes used incorrectly for *or.*

WRONG: Shipments of a fresh vegetable such as lettuce *and* broccoli. . . . (A vegetable cannot be both lettuce and broccoli.)
RIGHT: Shipments of a fresh vegetable such as lettuce *or* broccoli. . . .

anger (n.) Anger *at* that which hurts or annoys, *toward* a person.

angry (adj.) Angry *at* a thing, *with* a person.

annoyed Annoyed *with* a person, *by* that which annoys.

I am annoyed *with* her.
I am annoyed *by* her carelessness.

anxious, eager In informal usage, *anxious* is often used for *eager,* although to be *anxious* is to be worried and to be *eager* is to anticipate enthusiastically. In writing, the distinction should be kept.

I am *eager* [not *anxious*] to hear the new director's address.
He is *anxious* [worried] about the outcome of the election.

any (adj.) May modify either a singular or plural noun. For misuse of *any place,* see PLACE.

anyone, any one (pron.) **1.** Singular, followed by a singular verb and singular pronoun.

Anyone who *is* [not *are*] interested in *his* [not *their*] work *makes* [not *make*] a point of getting to work on time.

2. Of the two forms *anyone* and *any one,* the first is correct when *anybody* can be substituted in the sentence with no change in meaning. In other uses, *any one* is the correct form.

If we send *anyone,* it should be Mr. Jones.
If we send *any one* of the salesmen, it should be Mr. Jones.
Any one of the manuscripts is worthy of publication.

3. See EITHER, 2, for the distinction between the use of *either* and *any one.*

anywhere (adv.) Always written as one word.

1. Do not add an *s* to anywhere; there is no such word as *anywheres.*

2. See also PLACE.

appreciation (n.) When followed by a preposition, use *of* or *for.*

apropos (adv.) Means "with respect to" something; usually used with *of.*

Apropos of our recent talk.

apt, liable, likely (to do something) These words are frequently confused. *Apt* suggests an habitual tendency; *liable* usually means "exposed to a risk or unpleasantness"; *likely* means "probable."

Businessmen *are apt* [have a tendency] to dictate letters carelessly.
A businessman who dictates letters carelessly is *liable* to lose [exposed to the danger of losing] his customers.
He is *likely* to [probably will] vote against the bill.

argue (v.) Argue *with* a person, *for* something that is favored. When a definite viewpoint is not expressed, argue *about* something.

> I argued *with* the directors *for* an increase in salary.
> They argue *about* politics and religion too much.
> He argues *for* proportional representation.

arise (v.) Principal parts, *arise, arose,* [has, have, had] *arisen.* See IRREGULAR VERBS.

as 1. Use *as . . . as* in affirmative statements. In negative statements and in questions implying a negative answer, *so . . . as* is preferred by some authorities.

> This window display is *as* attractive *as* the last one.
> This window display is *not so* attractive *as* the last one.
> Could any ambitious young man be *so* foolish *as* to turn down the offer? (Implying a negative answer.)

2. Use *as* to express comparison when a clause containing a verb follows. See also LIKE, 1.

> Copy the report exactly *as* [not *like*] it is written.

3. An explanatory *as* clause should be placed before the main sentence. The exception to this rule is an *as* clause that states a fact necessarily known to the reader.

> WRONG: The minority abandoned its position, *as* the opposition showed no sign of yielding.
> RIGHT: *As* the opposition showed no sign of yielding, the minority abandoned its position.
> RIGHT: I need not read the fifth clause, *as* you are familiar with it.

As is overworked when used as a substitute for *for, since, because.*

4. Avoid using *as to* instead of a simple preposition such as *of, about, among, upon.*

> She has no conception *of* [not *as to*] the proper performance of her duties.
> The witness testified *about* [not *as to*] the defendant's early life.

5. For the misuse of *as* with *equally* see EQUALLY AS.

assuage (v.) The active voice is followed by *with;* the passive voice by *by.*

> *Assuage* hunger *with* food.
> Hunger is *assuaged by* food.

audience (n.) See COLLECTIVE NOUNS.

aught (n.) See NAUGHT.

averse Not to be confused with *adverse.* See ADVERSE.

aversion (n.) Aversion *to* a person, *for* acts or actions.

avocation, vocation Use *vocation* when you mean "occupation" or "line of work"; use *avocation* when you mean "hobby."

> Her *vocation* is secretarial work; her *avocation* is golf.

backward(s) Either form is correct when used as an adverb to mean in reverse order or direction. *Backward* is also an adjective that means "not progressing," "not developing normally" or "reluctant," "bashful."

> The train pulled out of the station *backwards* [or *backward*].
> The child is *backward* [not *backwards*] for his age.

bad, badly Use the adjective (*bad*)

when the subject, not the verb, is being modified. When a verb denoting action is being modified use the adverb (*badly*). See ADVERBS, 2.

> He looks *bad*. (Describes "he.")
> He was injured *badly* in the accident. (Describes how he was injured.)
> He writes *badly*. (Describes how he writes.)
> He feels *bad* about the incident. (Describes "he." See FEEL.)
> He behaves *badly* when he is disappointed. (Describes how he behaves.)

balance (n.) Frequently misused for "rest" or "remainder." *Balance* is a financial term and should be used only in reference to the difference between two amounts.

> She gave the *balance* of the money to the Red Cross.
> We expect to ship the *remainder* [not *balance*] of the order next week.
> The *rest* [not *balance*] of the audience enjoyed the program.
> The *balance* of the account. . . .
> The *remainder* of the week. . . .

band (n.) See COLLECTIVE NOUNS.

barely (adv.) This word carries a negative idea and hence should not be used with another negative.

> WRONG: She has *barely no* typing to do.
> RIGHT: She has *barely any* typing to do.

because (conj.) Frequently incorrectly used instead of *that* after *The reason . . . is. . . .*

> WRONG: Her reason for quitting her job is *because* she does *not* earn enough money.
> RIGHT: Her reason for quitting her job is *that* she does not earn enough money.

RIGHT: The reason the goods were delayed was *that* [not *because*] they were shipped to the wrong zone number.

beside(s) *Beside* means "by the side of," "close to"; *besides* means "additionally," "in addition to."

> The letter is on his desk, *beside* [close to] the file.
> *Besides* [in addition to] these two bills, there are several others.
> We have these two bills and several others *besides* [in addition].

between (prep.) **1.** Use the objective case after *between*.

> Between you and *me* [never *I*].

2. Use *between* when reference is made to only two persons or things; use *among* when reference is made to more than two.

> The friendliness *between* [not *among*] the British foreign minister and the American secretary of state promoted harmony.
> The friendliness *among* [not *between*] British, American, and Israeli delegates promoted harmony.

3. Do not use *each* or *every* after *between* or *among*. The objects of these prepositions should be plural, whereas *each* and *every* modify singular nouns.

> WRONG: Almost all the audience went into the lobby *between each* scene.
> RIGHT: Almost all the audience went into the lobby *between* scenes.
> WRONG: It is essential that harmony prevail *between every* department.
> RIGHT: It is essential that harmony prevail *among* the departments.

biannual, biennial (adj.) **1.** *Biannual* means "twice a year," through not necessarily at six-month intervals; *biennial* means "once in two years."

> The association holds *biannual* conferences. (Two conferences a year.)

Congressmen are elected *biennially*. (Every two years.)

2. Biannual is distinguished from *semiannual* in that *semiannual* means "occurring every six months."

3. *Biannually, biennially* are the adverbial forms.

bid (v. meaning to order) Principal parts, *bid, bid, bid*. See IRREGULAR VERBS.

bid (v. meaning to invite) Principal parts, *bid, bade*, [has, have, had] *bidden*. See IRREGULAR VERBS.

biennial See BIANNUAL.

biweekly, bimonthly (adj. and adv.) *Biweekly* means "once every two weeks" or "twice a week"; *bimonthly* usually means "once every two months." These expressions are confusing. It is clearer to use *once every two weeks, once every two months*. See SEMIMONTHLY, SEMIWEEKLY.

blame (v.) Blame a person *for* something, *not* something *on* a person.

WRONG: Blame the present difficulty *on* the Administration.
RIGHT: Blame the Administration *for* the present difficulty.
WRONG: The blame for the accident is *on* him.
RIGHT: The blame for the accident is his.
RIGHT: Put the blame for the accident on him. (Because the verb in this sentence is *put*, not *blame*.)

both (adj., pron.,) **1.** Pl., followed by plural verb and plural pronoun.

Both Matthew and Smith *are* [not *is*] employed in the same capacity and *make* [not *makes*] *their* [not *his*] reports directly to the president.

2. *Both* is unnecessary with the words *between, alike*, as well as *at once, equal(ly)*, and should be omitted unless the omission of the other words is preferable.

WRONG: *Both* the Democrats and the Republicans are *equally* anxious to prevent the spread of Communism. (Omit either "both" or "equally.")
WRONG: They are *both alike* in their zeal for perfection. (Omit "both.")

3. *Both . . . and* are correlative conjunctions and the constructions after them should be parallel. See EITHER . . . OR

bring (v.) Principal parts, *bring, brought, brought*. See IRREGULAR VERBS.

bring, take (v.) These words are opposites. *Bring* implies *coming* with some person or thing to another place; *take* implies *going* with some person or thing to another place.

I will *bring* the book [with me] when I come to your office this afternoon.
I will *take* the book *to* him when I go to his office this afternoon.
Please *bring* the book *with* you the next time you come to my office.
Please *take* the book *to* him the next time you go to his office.

burst (v.) Principal parts, *burst, burst, burst*. See IRREGULAR VERBS.

but (conj.) **1.** When used in the sense of *except*, some writers consider *but* as a preposition and follow it with the objective case. In formal usage, the case after *but* varies according to its use. However, when the pronoun after *but* ends the sentence, it is always in the objective case.

Everyone *but she* [not *her*] enjoyed the entertainment. (She did not enjoy it.)

No one wanted to make the change *but me*. (Pronoun ends the sentence.)

I told no one *but him* [not *he*] about the change. (I told him about it.)

2. A common error is the use of *but,* meaning "only," after a negative.

WRONG: I *cannot but* object to the title.
RIGHT: I *can but* object to the title.
WRONG: There *aren't but* ten shopping days left before Christmas.
RIGHT: There are *but* ten shopping days. . . .

When *but* means "except," it may follow a negative, of course.

Nobody but he went.
He accepted *none* of the shipment *but* the short coats.

3. See BUT THAT for the correct use of *but* with *that.*

4. *But what* is correctly used only when *except* could be substituted for *but.* The use of *but what* for *but that* is a colloquialism.

RIGHT: He said nothing *but what* [or, *except what*] any honorable person would have said.

5. See also ELSE, 1.

but that   1. A common error is the use of *but that* instead of *that* to introduce a clause after *doubt* (either the verb or the noun).

I do not doubt *that* [not *but that*] the shipment will reach you tomorrow.

There is no doubt *that* [not *but that*] the shipment will reach you tomorrow.

2. *But that* is not interchangeable with *that.* Notice the difference in meaning in the following sentences:

It is impossible *that* the signatories to the United Nations Charter will sanction the move. (They will not sanction.)

It is impossible *but that* the signatories to the United Nations Charter will sanction the move. (They are sure to sanction.)

It is not impossible *that* the signatories to the United Nations Charter will sanction the move. (They may sanction.)

3. *Unnecessary negative.* When *but that* has a negative implication, the subsequent use of *not* is incorrect.

WRONG: How do you know *but that* the apparent friendliness of our competitor may *not* be an attempt to learn more about our new project?
RIGHT: How do you know *but that* the apparent friendliness of our competitor may be an attempt . . . ?

cabinet (n.)   When used to mean a "body of advisers," *cabinet* is a COLLECTIVE NOUN.

can, could   1. *Could* is the past of *can.* Remember this when using *can* or *could* in sentences with other verbs. See SEQUENCE OF TENSES. Use *can* with verbs in the present, perfect, and future tenses; use *could* with verbs in the past, past perfect tenses.

I give
I have given } what I *can.*
I shall give

I gave
I was giving } what I *could.*
I had given

2. Use *could,* not *can,* when *would* is used in the main clause.

He *would* stop in Cincinnati on his way West if he *could* [not *can*] arrange to meet you there.

He said that he *would* recommend that the agency change its specifications so that we *could* [not *can*] get some of the business.

Even if the company *could* [not *can*] ship the order by Monday, the material *would* not reach the factory soon enough.

3. A common error is the misuse of *could* for *might* in conditional sentences. *Could* expresses ability, *might* expresses permission or possibility. See CAN, MAY.

If you have not bought the stock, you *might* [not *could*] as well forget about it.

If the certificate fails to make provision for the issuance of stock in series, it *might* [not *could*] subsequently be amended to include that provision. (The thought is that the certificate *would perhaps* be amended; there is no question that it *can* be amended.)

can, may *Can* denotes ability or power; *may* denotes permission.

Can you [will you be able to] make shipment next week?
May we [will you give us permission] make shipment next week?
I *can* [it is possible for me to] go to Alaska by plane. *May* I? [Do I have your permission?]

canvas (n.) *Canvas* is a type of heavy cloth.

canvass (v.) *Canvass* means to "scrutinize," "discuss," "solicit." Not to be confused with *canvas*.

capital, capitol (n.) *Capital* is a city that is the seat of a government. *Capitol* is the building in which Congress meets, or a building in which a state legislature meets. State capitols may be spelled either upper or lower case, but the United States Capitol is spelled with an upper case C.

Washington is the *capital* of the United States.
I hope the repairs to the *Capitol* are completed when we visit Washington.

The *capitol* at Albany is being repaired.

Capital has several other meanings; *capitol* has not.

capitalize (v.) When followed by a preposition, use *at*.

The corporation was *capitalized at* $900,000.

careless (adj.) Careless *about* appearance and dress; *in* the performance of an action; *of* others.

cause (n.) Cause *for* an action, *of* a result.

The cause *for* her change in attitude was. . . .
The cause *of* the epidemic. . . .

certainly Do not modify by *most*. I *certainly* will [not *most certainly* will].

cheap The adverb forms are *cheap, cheaper, cheapest* or *cheaply, more cheaply, most cheaply*. See ADVERBS, 3.

choose (v.) Principal parts, *choose, chose,* [has, have, had] *chosen*. See IRREGULAR VERBS.

class (n.) pl., *classes* **1.** A COLLECTIVE NOUN when used in the sense of a group of students.

2. For correct usage in the sense of "kind" or "sort" see KIND.

clean The adverb forms are *clean, cleaner, cleanest* or *cleanly, more cleanly, most cleanly*. See ADVERBS, 3.

cling (v.) Principal parts, *cling, clung,* [has, have, had] *clung*. See IRREGULAR VERBS.

close The adverb forms are *close, closer, closest* or *closely, more closely, most closely.* See ADVERBS, 3.

coincide (n.), **coincident** (adj.) When followed by a preposition, use *with.*

Collective nouns Collective nouns are singular if the writer is referring to the group as such, plural if he is referring to the individual persons or things of which the group is composed. The number of the verb and pronoun depends upon whether the collective noun is used in the singular or plural.

> The council *is* insisting on *its* right to enforce the regulation. (Meaning the council as a unit.)
> The council *are* disagreeing as to *their* authority to enforce the regulation. (Meaning that the members disagree among themselves.)

In some cases it is a matter of discretion whether the singular or plural sense shall be used, but after the choice is made, the verbs and pronouns must all agree. It is incorrect to use a singular verb in one sentence and begin the next sentence with a plural pronoun, or vice versa.

> WRONG: The Democratic party *has* elected *their* candidate as mayor for the last four terms. However, *they* have not had a majority in the City Council for several years.
> RIGHT: The Democratic party *has* elected *its* candidate as mayor for the last four terms. However, *it* has not had a majority in the City Council for several years.
> RIGHT: The Democratic party *have* elected *their* candidate as mayor for the last four terms. However, *they* have not had a majority in the city council for several years.

committee (n.) See COLLECTIVE NOUNS.

common, -er, -est (adj.) Preferable to *more common, most common.*

common, mutual (adj.) 1. *Common* refers to something that is shared alike by two or more individuals or species, as *common fear* of war, *common trait* of character. *Mutual* refers to something that is reciprocally given and received, as *mutual agreement, mutual respect.* Careful writers do not use *mutual* when *common* is the correct word.

> WRONG: *mutual* effort, *mutual* sorrow.
> RIGHT: *common* effort, *common* sorrow.

2. *Mutual* in the sense of "having the same relation to each other" is now established, although some authorities still object to it.

> *mutual* [or *common*] foes
> *mutual* [or *common*] friends

company (n.) See COLLECTIVE NOUNS.

compare to, compare with If it is desired to suggest a similarity or to state that a similarity exists, use *to.* If it is desired to indicate specific similarities or differences, use *with.*

> The speaker compared the new law *to* a plague. (The speaker merely suggested a similarity.)
> The speaker compared the British law *with* the American statute. (The speaker made a detailed comparison.)

comparison of adjectives Some adjectives form the comparative and superlative by adding *er* and *est* to the adjective; others by placing *more* or *most* before the adjective. If you are uncertain how to compare an adjective, check an unabridged dictionary. It will indicate the *-er, -est* words; use *more* and *most* for all others.

comparison of adverbs Almost all adverbs form the comparative by placing *more* before the adverb and the superlative by placing *most* before it. There are exceptions, which are listed alphabetically in this section.

complacent (adj.), **-ency** (n.); **complaisant** (adj.), **-ance** (n.) A *complacent* person is pleased with himself or with things that affect him personally. A *complaisant* person is anxious to please by compliance or indulgence.

> Don't let your *complacency* about your work keep you from knowing your shortcomings.
> If Congress were in a more *complaisant* mood, the President might be able to push the law through.

complement, compliment (n. or v.) **1.** *Complement* is that which is required to complete or make whole; *compliment* is an expression of admiration.

> This department has its full *complement* of workers. (Noun)
> A gold clip on your dress will *complement* [complete] your costume. (Verb)
> His *compliments* on my article were gratifying. (Noun)
> The president *complimented* him on the showing made by his department. (Verb)

2. The noun *complement* is followed by the preposition *of;* the verb *compliment* is followed by *on.*

complementary, complimentary (adj.) **1.** The distinction in meaning is the same as that between *complement* and *compliment.* See above.

> Practical experience is *complementary* to theoretical training.
> Two *complementary* colors mixed together make a third color.
> His review of the book was not *complimentary.*
> *Complimentary* remarks about a person's work are always appreciated.

2. The preposition *to* is used with *complementary; about* or *concerning* with *complimentary.*

compliance (n.) When followed by a preposition, use *with.*

comply (v.) When followed by a preposition, use *with.*

compounds This name applies to two or more words written together, or joined by a hyphen, or written separately but expressing a single idea. Thus, *editor-in-chief, businessman,* and *attorney general* are all compounds. The authorities often differ on whether compounds should be written separately, hyphenated, or written as one word. The following rules are a guide to writing compounds.

1. *Consistency.* Be consistent. When there is a choice, decide whether you wish to hyphenate two or more words, to write them as one word, or to write them as separate words. When you have chosen a form, follow it consistently.

2. *Meaning.* An invariable rule is to use the form that conveys the proper meaning. Although your dictionary might show two or more words joined together or hyphenated, the meaning might differ from the meaning of the same words used separately, sometimes to the point of absurdity.

> The *takeoff* was smooth.
> We will *take off* from LaGuardia Airport.
> They have a *hothouse.*
> They have a *hot house.*
> He is very *matter-of-fact.*
> As a *matter of fact,* I did go.

3. *Usage.* Do not hyphenate or join words together for the sole reason that they are frequently used together. Wait until the authorities accept them in compounded form.

4. *Adjectives.* Hyphenate two or more words used as an adjective, such as *two-story* house, *short-term* loan, *no-par* stock, *above-mentioned* law. Do not hyphenate color variations used as an adjective, such as *navy blue* dress, *light gray* paint.

5. *Fractions.* Hyphenate fractions when the numerator and the denominator are both one-word forms, such as *one-third, three-fourths, one-hundredth.*

6. *Nationalities.* Hyphenate two or more words to indicate that the person or thing shares in the qualities of both, as *Anglo-American, Sino-Japanese, Latin-American* (but not *Latin America*), *Scotch-Irish.*

7. *Coined phrases.* Hyphenate coined phrases, such as *middle-of-the-road, pay-as-you-go, drive-it-yourself, ready-to-wear.*

8. *Adverbs.* Do not use a hyphen to connect an adverb and an adjective. Do not use a hyphen to connect an adverb ending in -*ly* and a past participle in such phrases as a *happily married couple, a brilliantly lighted house.*

compound subject 1. Two or more subjects joined by *and* take a plural verb.

> Personal power, progress, *and* success *depend* [not *depends*] upon many things.
> A good quality of stationery *and* neat typing *make* [not *makes*] a good impression upon the recipient of the letter.

2. If the compound subject consists of two nouns referring to the same person or thing, the verb is singular.

> The vice president and treasurer of the company *is* out of the city [when both offices are filled by the same person].
> The vice president and the treasurer of the company *are* out of the city [when separate individuals fill the two offices].

3. When *each, every, many a,* and the like modify the complete subject, the verb is singular.

> *Each* (or *Every*) officer and member *was* [not *were*] present.
> *Many a* man and woman *has* [not *have*] voted for him.

concur (v.) Concur *in* a decision, opinion, belief; concur *with* a person.

conducive (adj.) When followed by a preposition, use *to.*

conform (v.) When followed by a preposition, use *to* or *with.*

congress (n.) See COLLECTIVE NOUNS.

connect (v.) Objects, places, or

people are connected *with* one another *by* certain means.

> France is connected *with* Italy *by* the Mont Blanc tunnel.

connection The phrase *in this connection* is never good usage; the phrase *in connection with* is generally considered trite and is overworked. There is no grammatical objection to it when it is the proper phrase to use, but a substitution is generally preferable. Try *about* as a substitute.

conscious, aware (adj.) *Conscious* emphasizes inner realization; *aware* emphasizes perception through the senses.

> He became *conscious* of the reason for his failure.
> He was *aware* of the staleness of the air in the room.

consensus (n.) An erroneous expression frequently used is *consensus of opinion. Consensus* means "agreement in matter of opinion"; therefore, the expression is clearly redundant.

consist (v.) Followed by *of* to indicate ingredients; *in,* to define or show identity.

> Margarine *consists of* [the materials] vegetable oils and coloring.
> The sinking fund method *consists in* [may be defined as] the payment of a sum. . . .
> His greatest asset *consists in* [is] his ability to understand.

contemplate (v.) *Contemplate* is a transitive verb and should be followed by a direct object, not by a prepositional phrase.

> WRONG: I am contemplating *on* making a trip.

> RIGHT: I am contemplating a trip.

contemptible, contemptuous (adj.) *Contemptible* means "despicable," "deserving of being despised." *Contemptuous* means "scornful."

> The effort to bring pressure to bear on him was *contemptible* [despicable].
> His comments on the report were *contemptuous* [scornful].

continual, continuous (adj.) *Continual* means "occurring in close succession," "frequently repeated"; *continuous* means "without stopping," "without interruption." The same distinction applies to the adverbs, *continually* and *continuously.*

> *Continual* [frequent] breakdowns in the factory delayed production.
> The machinery has been in *continuous* operation [without stopping] for sixty hours.
> He is *continually* [frequently] asking for favors.
> He drove *continuously* [without stopping] for six hours.

correct (adj.) Not comparable. If anything is correct, it cannot be *more* correct. "More nearly correct" is allowable.

correlative (adj.) When followed by a preposition, use *with.*

Correlative conjunctions are pairs of conjunctions that are used together but not next to each other. *Either . . . or, neither . . . nor, both . . . and* are correlative conjunctions. See EITHER . . . OR; NEITHER . . . NOR.

could See CAN, COULD.

council, counsel, consul 1. *Council* applies to a board or assembly and to the meeting of such a body; *counsel* applies to deliberation or advice or to the person giving such advice, as an attorney. *Counsel* may be either a verb or a noun, but *council* is never a verb. *Consul* is a government representative looking after his country's interest in a foreign country.

2. *Council* is a COLLECTIVE NOUN.

couple (n.) See COLLECTIVE NOUNS.

credible, credulous, creditable (adj.) *Credible* means "believable"; *credulous* means "easily imposed upon," "believing too easily"; *creditable* means "praiseworthy."

He is not a *credible* witness.
The readers are indeed *credulous* if they believe the editorial completely.
His summation of the case was highly *creditable*.

crowd (n.) See COLLECTIVE NOUNS.

damage, injury (n.) *Injury* is the broad, general term; *damage* is especially an injury that impairs value or involves loss. *Injury* is impairment of utility or beauty and applies generally to persons, feelings, reputation, character, and sometimes to property. *Damage* applies to property only.

The *damage* to the *house* is extensive, but it does not compare with the *injury* to the *landscape*.
He collected insurance for *injury* to his *back* and for *damage* to his *car*.
He will never live down the *injury* to his *reputation*.

data (n.) This word is plural and takes a plural verb and plural adjective pronoun. The singular form, *datum*, is now seldom used.

We have proved that *these* [not *this*] data are [not *is*] reliable.

dates from The correct expression is *dates from*, not *dates back to*.

deep The adverbial forms are *deep, deeper, deepest* or *deeply, more deeply, most deeply*. See ADVERBS, 3.

defect (n.) Defect *in* a concrete object; defect *of* an intangible quality, such as judgment or character of a person.

The failure to pick up speed is a defect *in* the machine.
The defect *of* his character is impatience.

depreciate (v.) Never followed by the words *in value*. If anything has depreciated, its value is less.

did (v.) Sometimes misused in place or *has* or *have*. *Did* represents past action; *has* or *have*, action continuing to the present moment. The misuse usually occurs with *yet* or *already*.

Did you listen to Town Meeting yesterday? (Past action).
Have you heard the results of the election yet? [not *did you hear*].
WRONG: I *did* not hear the results of the election yet.
RIGHT: I *have* not heard the results of the election yet.

differ (v.) Used in the sense of unlikeness, *differ* is followed by *from*; used in the sense of disagreeing in opinion, by *with*.

My sales campaign differs *from* [not *with*] yours.
I differ *with* [not *from*] you as to

the value of your sales campaign.

different 1. Do not use to show separate identity that has already been established.

> Three secretaries [not three *different* secretaries] asked for a Christmas vacation.

2. *Different* is followed by the preposition *from*, not the connective *than*. The use of *different than* is acceptable in only one instance; that is when *different* is followed by a clause.

> My taste in furniture is different *from* [not *than*] yours.
> Her taste in furniture is different *than* I expected it to be.

direct 1. The adverb form is *direct* or *directly*.

2. *Direct* is not comparable. If anything is direct, it cannot be *more* direct. "More nearly direct" is allowable.

disappointed (adj.) *Disappointed with* a thing or object; otherwise, *disappointed in*.

> I am disappointed *with* the car.
> I am disappointed *in* the outcome of the election.
> I am disappointed *in* him.

disinterested, uninterested (adj.) *Disinterested* means "impartial," without selfish motive or thought of personal gain." *Uninterested* means "not interested or enthusiastic."

> The teacher did not state the case in a *disinterested* [impartial] manner.
> He seems *uninterested* [lacking in interest] in his work.

displace (v.) When followed by a preposition, use *by*.

dissent (v.) When followed by a preposition, use *from*.

drive (v.) Principal parts, *drive, drove,* [has, have, had] *driven.* See IRREGULAR VERBS.

do (v.) 1. For the misuse of *did* for *has* or *have,* see DID.

2. Principal parts, *do, did,* [has, have, had] *done.* See IRREGULAR VERBS.

double negatives The use of two negatives to express a negative thought is wrong. Some double negatives, such as *don't want no, doesn't need none, wouldn't never,* are too obviously wrong for discussion. The insidious double negatives occur with words that convey a negative idea, such as *hardly, barely, scarcely, but, but that,* rather than with words that are definitely negative in form, such as *no, none, never.* See HARDLY, 1; SCARCELY; BARELY; BUT; BUT THAT, 3; NOT.

draw (v.) Principal parts, *draw, drew,* [has, have, had] *drawn.* See IRREGULAR VERBS.

drug (v.) "To stupefy with a narcotic." Principal parts, *drug, drugged, drugged.* Erroneously used as the past tense of *drag.*

due to Often misused for *owing to. Due* is an adjective and must be attached to a noun or pronoun, whereas *owing to* is now considered a preposition. *Due to* means "caused by." Test your sentence by substituting *caused by* for *due to.*

> WRONG: The labor movement is losing

prestige *due to* the methods of some of its leaders. (There is no noun for "due" to modify. The "prestige" was not caused by the "methods.")

RIGHT: The labor movement is losing prestige *owing to* the methods of some of its leaders. ("Methods" is the object of the compound preposition "owing to.")

RIGHT: The success of the firm was *due to* [caused by] the ability of its president. (The "success" was caused by the "ability.")

RIGHT: The firm succeeded *owing to* [not *due to*] the ability of its president.

each 1. When used as a subject, *each* invariably takes a singular verb and pronoun even when followed by *of them.*

Each of the reports made by the committees *was* [not *were*] a tribute to the late President.

Each of the companies filed *its* [not *their*] reports promptly.

Each *carries* [not *carry*] his [not *their*] share of the load.

2. When *each* immediately follows a plural noun or pronoun the verb is plural.

The officers *each take* [not *takes*] an oath.

3. When *each* refers to a preceding plural noun or pronoun, the number of a subsequent noun or pronoun depends upon whether *each* comes before or after the verb. Use the plural when *each* precedes the verb; the singular when *each* follows the verb.

The employees *each* are responsible for their own assignments. (Precedes the verb.)

The employees *are* responsible *each* for his own assignment. (Follows the verb.)

4. For the use of *each* after *between* or *among*, see BETWEEN, 3.

each other, one another 1. *Each other* should be used when only two things are referred to, and *one another* when more than two are referred to.

WRONG: Smith and I see *one another* often.

RIGHT: Smith and I see *each other* often.

WRONG: It will be interesting for the four of us to see *each other* again.

RIGHT: It will be interesting for the four of us to see *one another* again.

2. The possessive of *each other* is *each other's;* of *one another, one another's.*

They did not spare *each other's* [not *each others'*] feelings.

They did not spare *one another's* [not *one anothers'*] feelings.

economics (n.) Usually plural in form but singular in meaning; hence, takes singular verbs and singular pronouns. See -ICS.

Economics *is* [not *are*] of prime importance to every student of commerce. Several courses in *it* [not *them*] are required.

effect See AFFECT.

either (conj.) 1. Singular, followed by singular verb. The use of a plural verb after *either* is a common error.

Either of these sales plans *is* [not *are*] excellent.

2. Use *either* to designate one of two persons or things; *any one* to designate one of three or more.

You may choose *either* of the [two] new typewriters or *any* one of the [three] old typewriters.

either . . . or 1. The construction after correlatives should be the same; for example, if *either* is followed by a verb, *or* must be followed by a verb. The misplacement of *either*, a common error, frequently results in unbalanced construction after the correlatives.

> WRONG: You *either are required* to register by the 15th *or to drop* the course. (*Either* is followed by a verb and *or* by an infinitive phrase.)
> RIGHT: You are required *either to register* by the 15th *or to drop* the course.
> WRONG: You must *either* go today, *or* you must wait until next week.
> RIGHT: *Either* you must go today, *or* you must wait until next week.
> RIGHT: You must *either* go today *or* wait until next week.

2. When *either . . . or* connects two singular nouns that are the subjects of the sentence, the verb agrees with the second noun.

> Either the maid or the butler *is* guilty.
> Either you or he *has* eaten her porridge.
> Either the pupils or the teacher *is* going to give in.
> Either the teacher or the pupils *are* going to give in.

When the verbs sound awkward, as they often do when the first noun normally takes a plural verb and the second a singular one, reword the sentence.

> Either you or he ate her porridge.
> One of you ate her porridge.

else **1.** A common error is to combine *else* with *but*.

> WRONG: It was nothing *else but* selfishness on his part.
> RIGHT: It was nothing *but* selfishness on his part.

2. The possessive of *somebody else, everyone else, anyone else, no one else,* is *somebody else's, everyone else's,* and so on.

emigrate, immigrate (v.) *To emigrate* means "to go *from* one's own country to another for the purpose of living there." *To immigrate* means "to go *into* a country or place for the purpose of living there." *Emigrate* is followed by the preposition *from; immigrate* by *to.*

> Thousands of Jews *emigrated from* [left] Germany and *immigrated to* [moved to] Israel.

eminent, imminent (adj.) *Eminent* means "prominent," "distinguished," and is applied to persons. *Imminent* means "impending," "threatening," "close at hand," and is applied to events.

> He is an *eminent* lecturer.
> A struggle for power between the two nations is *imminent.*

See also IMMANENT, IMMINENT.

enamored (adj.) Enamored *of* a person, *with* an object.

enthuse (v.) *Colloquial.* Avoid using.

equally as Often incorrectly used for *equally . . . with, equally* by itself, or *as* by itself.

> WRONG: The Republicans are *equally as* guilty as the Democrats.
> RIGHT: The Republicans are *as* guilty as the Democrats.
> RIGHT: The Republicans are *equally* guilty *with* the Democrats.
> WRONG: The trouble in the western cities is *equally as* alarming.
> RIGHT: The trouble in the western cities is *equally* alarming.

-ever Compounds of *-ever* (*however, whichever, whoever, whatever*) are not interrogatives. A common error, particularly in speech, is to use

these compounds as interrogatives
with the thought that they add emphasis to the question.

WRONG: *However* did you find out?
RIGHT: *How* did you find out?
WRONG: *Whoever* told you that?
RIGHT: *Who* told you that?

every (adj.) Always singular. Followed by singular verb and singular pronouns.

Every large company in the industry *files its report* [not *file their reports*] with the trade association.
Everyone was [not *were*] trying to
better *his position* [not *their positions*].
Every one of the students who participated in the demonstration put
himself [not *themselves*] in the position of insubordination.
Every one but he *was* [not *were*] at
the meeting.

everybody (n.) Write as one word.
Always singular.

every one, everyone **1.** Write as one
word only when *everybody* is meant.
Thus, *every one* is always written
to refer to objects; also if *of* follows
the expression it must be written in
two words.

Everyone [*everybody*] should attend the meeting.
Every one of the department heads
attended the meeting.
All of the drawings are excellent;
every one of them deserves a prize.

2. *Everyone* and *every one* are always singular and followed by singular verbs and pronouns.

everywhere Always written as one
word. *Every place* is commonly misused for *everywhere*. See PLACE.

evidence (n.) When followed by a
preposition, use *of*.

expect (v.) Expect *of* a person;
otherwise, expect *from*.

The company expects loyalty *of* its
employees.

faced (adj.) When followed by a
preposition, use *by* or *with*.

fair The adverb forms are *fair,
fairer, fairest* or *fairly, more fairly,
most fairly*. See ADVERBS, 3.

fall (v.) Principal parts, *fall, fell,*
[has, have, had] *fallen*. See IRREGU-
LAR VERBS.

farther, further Use *farther* to refer
to distance; *further* to refer to time,
quantity, or degree.

Philadelphia is *farther* from Washington than from New York.
We went *further* into the matter.

This distinction is rapidly disappearing and *further* is more widely
used.

fatal (adj.) Not comparable. If
anything is fatal, it cannot be *more*
fatal. "More nearly fatal" is allowable.

feel (v.) Followed by a predicate
adjective and not by an adverb (see
PREDICATE ADJECTIVE), unless used
in the sense of touching physically.

He telephoned and said that he still
feels very *bad* [not *badly*]. (Predi-
cate adjective modifying "he.")
The doctor felt the bruise *tenderly*.
(Adverb describing how the doctor
touched the bruise.)
I felt *sick* when I heard the news.
(Predicate adjective modifying "I.")

few (indefinite pron.) **1.** Either
singular or plural, depending upon
the meaning.

A few *is* enough.
Many are called, but few *are* chosen.

2. See LESS for distinction between *less* and *fewer*.

final (adj.) Not comparable. If anything is final, it cannot be *more* final. "More nearly final" is allowable.

find (v.) Principal parts, *find, found, found.* See IRREGULAR VERBS.

fireworks (n.) Always used in the plural.

firstly (adv.) In formal enumerations, the use of *first, second, third,* or *firstly, secondly, thirdly, lastly* is a matter of personal preference. However, use *firstly*, not *first*, with *secondly, thirdly, lastly.*

flee (v.) Principal parts, *flee, fled, fled.* See IRREGULAR VERBS.

flock (n) See COLLECTIVE NOUNS.

flow (v.) Principal parts, *flow, flowed, flowed.*

fly (v.) Principal parts, *fly, flew,* [has, have, had] *flown.* See IRREGULAR VERBS.

forbid (v.) Principal parts, *forbid, forbade,* [has, have, had] *forbidden.* See IRREGULAR VERBS.`

forecast (v.) Principal parts, *forecast, forecast, forecast.* See IRREGULAR VERBS.

forget (v.) Principal parts, *forget, forgot, forgot* or [has, have, had]

forgotten. See IRREGULAR VERBS.

formally, formerly *Formally* means "in a formal manner"; *formerly* means "previously."

He was *formally* initiated into the club.
He was *formerly* president of this company.

former (adj.) Correct when used to designate the first of two persons or things; incorrect when used to designate the first of three or more.

RIGHT: Smith and Jones were at the convention; the *former* gave an interesting talk.
WRONG: Smith, Jones, and Brown were at the convention; the *former* gave an interesting talk.
AWKWARD: Smith, Jones and Brown were at the convention; *the first-named* gave an interesting talk.
BETTER: Smith, Jones, and Brown were at the convention; *Smith* gave an interesting talk.

forsake (v.) Principal parts, *forsake, forsook,* [has, have, had] *forsaken.* See IRREGULAR VERBS.

Fractions See AMOUNTS. For use of hyphen in writing fractions, see COMPOUNDS.

freeze (v.) Principal parts, *freeze, froze,* [has, have, *or* had] *frozen.* See IRREGULAR VERBS.

-ful The correct plural of words ending in *-ful,* such as *spoonful, handful,* is *-fuls. Spoonfuls, handfuls* [not *spoonsful, handsful*].

full (adj.) **1.** Not comparable. If anything is full, it cannot be more full. "More nearly full" is allowable.

2. The adverb form is *full* or *fully*. See ADVERBS, 3.

further Widely used instead of farther. See FARTHER.

future tense The future tense expresses action that will take place in the future. A common error is the use of the future tense, instead of the future perfect tense, to express action *completed* before a time in the future.

RIGHT: She *will finish* the book next month. (Simple future.)
WRONG: She *will finish* the book *before* the end of the month. (Completed action.)
RIGHT: She *will have* finished the book *before* next month. (Future perfect expressing completed action.)
WRONG: Next month *I shall be* his secretary ten years.
RIGHT: Next month, I *shall have been* his secretary ten years.
RIGHT: I *shall write* the letter tomorrow. [Simple future.]
RIGHT: I *shall have written* the letter by that time. (Future perfect.)

gang (n.) See COLLECTIVE NOUNS.

genial, congenial *Genial* means "cheerful" or "enlivening"; *congenial* means "compatible" or "kindred in spirit."

His secretary is always *genial*, no matter how busy she is.
The people in my department are very *congenial* and work well together.

gerunds A gerund is a verb form ending in *ing* and used as a noun.
1. Possessive nouns or possessive pronouns usually modify gerunds.

I do not approve of *your* [not *you*] reading the book.

I had not heard of the *company's* [not *company*] buying the building.

2. Because it is a verb form a gerund may take an object; as a noun, it can be either the subject or object of a sentence or the object of a prepositional phrase.

Recording test data required care.
Recording is the final step.
He thought of recording the test data.
Finish recording the data.

3. The gerund is identical in form with the active participle and is often confused with it. Notice in the following examples that the use of the gerund with a possessive gives the sentence a meaning entirely different from that given by the use of a participle.

I do not approve of the *girl's reading* the book. (Gerund)
I do not approve of the *girl reading* the book. (Participle)

4. If a verb has a noun form. use the noun form instead of the gerund.

POOR: *Accepting* the position was an ill-advised move.
BETTER: *Acceptance* of the position was an ill-advised move.

get (v.) Principal parts, *get, got,* [has, have, had] *got,* or *gotten.* See IRREGULAR VERBS.

give (v.) Principal parts, *give, gave,* [has, have, had] *given.* See IRREGULAR VERBS.

go (v.) Principal parts, *go, went,* [has, have, had] *gone.* See IRREGULAR VERBS.

good (adj.) See WELL.

goods (n. pl.) Always takes a

670

plural verb and plural pronouns.

> The goods *were* [not *was*] damaged in transit before *they* [not *it*] *were* delivered.

government (n.) In the United States, *government* is construed as singular; in Great Britain, as plural.

> Her Majesty's government *are* sending *their* representatives at once.
> The United States government *is* sending delegates also.

group (n.) See COLLECTIVE NOUNS.

grow (v.) Principal parts, *grow, grew,* [has, have, had] *grown.* See IRREGULAR VERBS.

guarantee, guaranty For the verb, always use *guarantee.* Business convention has established a specialized use of *guaranty* as a noun, which is illustrated in such expressions as *contract of guaranty, act of guaranty.* However, *guarantee* is never wrong, even in these expressions. A safe rule to follow is: when in doubt, use *guarantee.*

habitual (adj.) When followed by a preposition, use *with.*

had (v.) *Had . . . have* (or, even worse, *had . . . of*) is sometimes carelessly used in inverted sentences when only *had* is required.

> WRONG: *Had I have* been on the jury, I should have acquitted him.
> RIGHT: *Had I been* on the jury, I should have acquitted him.

An illiterate use of *had have* or *had of* occurs when the sentence has not been inverted.

> WRONG: If I *had of* been on the jury, I should have acquitted him.

> RIGHT: If I *had been* on the jury, I should have acquitted him.

hang (v. to put to death) Principal parts, *hang, hanged, hanged.* See IRREGULAR VERBS.

hang (v. to suspend) Principal parts, *hang, hung, hung.* See IRREGULAR VERBS.

hardly (adv.) **1.** This word conveys a negative idea and should not be used with a negative. The error usually occurs when the speaker or writer decides to modify a negative statement.

> WRONG: There is *no* company *hardly* which does not have an employee benefit plan.
> RIGHT: There is *hardly any* company that does not have an employee benefit plan.
> WRONG: The company *cannot hardly* take that attitude.
> RIGHT: The company *can hardly* take that attitude.

2. *Hardly* is used only in the sense of *scarcely.* The adverb of *hard,* meaning "difficult," "firm," or "solid," is the same as the adjective—*hard.* The following sentences illustrate how the use of *hardly* changes the meaning of a sentence.

> His salary as president of the company is *hard* earned.
> His salary as president of the company is *hardly* earned.

he Nominative case of third person singular pronoun. **1.** For misuse of *he* for *him,* see PRONOUNS, 1.

2. For use after forms of the verb *to be* (*am, is, are, was, were*), see PREDICATE NOMINATIVE, 2.

heavy The adverb forms are *heavy,*

heavier, heaviest or *heavily, more heavily, most heavily.* See ADVERBS, 3.

help Should not be followed by *but* when used in the sense of "avoid."

WRONG: I cannot *help but feel* that you are unwise.
RIGHT: I cannot *help feeling* that you are unwise.

her Objective case of third person singular pronoun. 1. For use as an object, see PRONOUNS, 1.

2. For misuse of *her* instead of *she* after forms of the verb *to be* (*am, is, are, was, were*), see PREDICATE NOMINATIVE, 1.

high The adverb forms are *high, higher, highest* or *highly, more highly, most highly.* See ADVERBS, 3.

him Objective case of third person singular pronoun. 1. For use as an object, see PRONOUNS, 1.

2. For misuse of *him* instead of *he* after forms of the verb *to be* (*am, is, are, was, were*), see PREDICATE NOMINATIVE, 1.

himself See REFLEXIVE PRONOUNS.

hope (n.) Sometimes incorrectly used in the plural after *no.*

We have no *hope* [not *hopes*] of receiving payment.

hope (v.) When *hope* is used in the passive voice, the indefinite pronoun *it* is always the subject. The error usually occurs when *it* is omitted from the parenthetical expression *it is hoped,* especially in a clause introduced by *what.*

WRONG: This region is now experiencing *what is hoped* will be a short cold spell.
RIGHT: This region is now experiencing what, *it is hoped,* will be a short cold spell. ("What" is the subject of "will be" and not of "is hoped.")
RIGHT: *It was hoped* by all that he would win.

hyphen For use of the hyphen in compound terms, see COMPOUNDS.

I Nominative case of first person singular pronoun. 1. For misuse of *I* for *me*, see PRONOUNS, 1.

2. For use after the forms of the verb to be (*am, is, are, was, were*), see PREDICATE NOMINATIVE, 1.

3. Avoid use of the editorial *we* instead of *I* in a letter written on behalf of a company. Use *I* when referring to the writer individually and *we* when referring to the company. *I* and *we* may be used in the same letter.

I [the writer] will look after this order and you can be sure *we* [the company] will ship it tomorrow.

-ics A few English words end in *-ic* (*music, rhetoric, logic, magic*) but the normal form is *-ics*. Words ending in *-ics* are sometimes treated as singular and sometimes as plural.

Singular when used strictly as the name of a science or study:

Politics [the science of] *is* most interesting.

Singular when used with a singular noun complement:

Politics is a *game* at which more than two can play.
Athletics is the chief *attraction* at the school.

Plural when used loosely and when denoting qualities, usually pre-

672

ceded by *his, the, such:*

> Such *politics* never *win* an election.
> The *acoustics* in the new building *are* faulty.

Plural when denoting practice or activity:

> Superb *tactics were* responsible for our victory.
> *Athletics are* necessary for every normal boy.

identical (adj.) When followed by a preposition, use *with* or *to.*

if (conj.) **1.** Often misused in place of *whether* after the verbs *ask, say, know, learn, understand, doubt.*

> WRONG: He asked *if* I could ship the goods on that date.
> RIGHT: He asked *whether* I could ship the goods on that date.

2. Avoid the use of *if and when.* Only in rare cases is *if and when* really better in a sentence than *if* or *when.*

> WRONG: *If and when* the voters in this country elect a Communist to high office, they can expect curtailment of free speech.
> RIGHT: *If* the voters in this country elect a Communist. . . .
> WRONG: He told the Union members that *if and when* the Republicans gain control of the Senate they will . . .
> RIGHT: He told the union members that *when* the Republicans gain control . . .
> RIGHT: He told the union members that *when, or if,* the Republicans gain control . . . (The writer expects the condition to be realized but has his doubts.)

ignorant (adj.) When it means "uninformed," follow by *in;* when it means "unaware," by *of.*

> He treats her as if she is ignorant *in* the subject.

> I was ignorant *of* his interest in the matter.

ill (adj.) When followed by a preposition, use *with.*

immanent, imminent (adj.) *Immanent* means "indwelling," "inherent." *Imminent* means "impending," "threatening," "close at hand."

> Honesty and fairness are *immanent* in the president's character.
> The passage of the bill is *imminent.*

immigrate (v.) See EMIGRATE.

impatient (adj.) Impatient *at* actions or characteristics; *with* persons.

imply, infer (v.) *To imply* means "to suggest," to insinuate, "to hint at." *To infer* means "to draw from," "to deduce from," or "to conclude from."

> Your letter *implies* that I have tried to evade payment of the bill.
> I *infer* from your letter that you cannot grant an extension of time.

impossible Not comparable. If anything is impossible it cannot be *more* impossible. "More nearly impossible" is allowable.

in, into, in to **1.** *In* denotes position or location; *into* denotes action, motion from without to within.

> The sport coats that were advertised yesterday are *in* the Junior Miss department.
> He was *in* the sales department but is now *in* the advertising department.
> We went *into* the room.

2. Do not use *into* for the words *in to* (adverb and preposition).

> He went *in to* [not *into*] the meeting.
> He took her *in to* [not *into*] dinner

673

inasmuch Always written as one word.

incompatible (adj.) When followed by a preposition, use *with*.

incongruous (adj.) When followed by a preposition, use *with*.

infer See IMPLY.

inferior (adj.) Should be followed by *to*, not *than*.

> Their products are always inferior from every point of view *to* [not *than*] ours.

Infinitives 1. *Tense*. Use the present infinitive, not the perfect, after past conditions, such as *should have liked, would have been possible.*

> It would have been possible *to reduce* [not *to have reduced*] the cost at that time.

2. *Split infinitives.* The infinitive sign *to* and the verb naturally go together, it is best not to split the infinitive by placing a word or words between *to* and the verb.

> WRONG: The company agrees *to substantially increase* the salaries.
> RIGHT: The company agrees *to increase* the salaries substantially.
> WRONG: *To really be understood*, it should be read carefully.
> RIGHT: *To be really understood*, it should be read carefully. ("To be" is the infinitive, not "to be understood.")

Split infinitives are preferable to ambiguity.

> RIGHT: We tried to get the states *to at least repair* the roads. (If "at least" is placed anywhere else in the sentence, the meaning is not clear.)

Split infinitives are preferable to awkwardness.

> AWKWARD: Efforts *to unite firmly* bolters from the party were a failure.
> IMPROVED: Efforts *to firmly unite* bolters from the party were a failure.

3. *Series of infinitives.* To make the parallel clear in a series of infinitives or infinitive phrases, repeat the *to* when any qualifying words intervene.

> *To punish* and [*to*] *expose* the guilty is one thing; *to help* the unfortunate is another.
> It is improper for the debtor *to take* an unearned discount and then *to refuse* to pay the difference.

inform See ADVISE.

ingenious, ingenuous (adj.) *Ingenious* means "clever," "skillful"; *ingenuous* means "frank," "innocent," "trusting."

> He concocted an *ingenious* [clever] plan to avoid the law.
> He is very *ingenuous* [trusting, easily fooled] for a man of his age and background.

injury See DAMAGE.

insofar Can be written as three separate words but one word is preferred.

interfere (v.) Interfere *with* a person, *in* something.

> I have no right to interfere *with* her *in* the matter.

intervening noun or **phrase** The intervention of a noun or nouns between the subject and the verb will sometimes cause trouble if the intervening noun is different in number from the subject. Remember that the verb agrees with the subject, not the intervening noun.

The hot days of summer *send* [not *sends*] everyone to the beach.

A parenthetical phrase coming between a subject and a verb can sometimes cause trouble. The verb agrees with the subject of the main sentence, not with the noun of the phrase.

> The community, as well as the owners of the land, *is* interested in development.

intransitive verbs See TRANSITIVE VERBS.

investigation When followed by a preposition, use *of*.

irregular verbs Almost all verbs form the past and perfect tenses by adding *ed* to the present—thus, *look, looked, looked; ship, shipped, shipped.*

However, many verbs are irregular, and there is no rule for the formation of the past and perfect tenses. Many irregular verbs are listed in their proper alphabetical position in this Dictionary of Usage. The principal parts (present, past, and past participle) are given—thus, *ring, rang, rung; say, said, said.* Form the perfect tenses by adding the auxiliaries (*has, have, had*) to the past participle. Thus, I *do,* I *did,* I *have done.*

In this section, where the past participle differs from the past tense, we have inserted the auxiliaries (*has, have, had*) to remind you that it is illiterate to use that form of the verb *without* an auxiliary. It is also illiterate to use an auxiliary with the past tense form of that verb.

> I did—[never *I have did*]
> I have done—[never *I done*]

its, it's *Its* is the possessive form of the impersonal pronoun *it. It's* is a contraction of *it* and *is* and is incorrectly used as a possessive.

> The company has expanded greatly in recent years; *its* [not *it's*] success is attributable to *its* [not *it's*] founders.
> *It's* [*it is*] too bad that the books will not be ready for delivery by September.

jury (n.) See COLLECTIVE NOUNS.

kind (n.) The explanation here applies also to *class, sort, type, size, variety, species,* and similar words.

1. The singular form is modified by *this* and *that,* not *these* and *those* and takes a singular verb.

> *This* [not *these*] kind does [not *do*] not grow readily; *that* [not *those*] kind does grow readily.

2. The expression *kind of* is followed by a singular noun unless the plural idea is particularly strong. The common error is inconsistency.

> The *kind of position* [not *positions*] that appeals to me doesn't interest her.
> The company has numerous positions open. What *kind of positions* are they?
> WRONG: The *kind of position* I prefer *are those* that offer a lot of money.
> RIGHT: The *kind of positions* I prefer *are those* that offer a lot of money.
> RIGHT: The *kind of position* I prefer *is one that* offers a lot of money.

3. It is incorrect to follow *kind of* by *a.*

> WRONG: What *kind* of *a* position do you want?
> RIGHT: What *kind of* position do you want?

4. After the plural form *kinds of,* a singular or a plural noun may be used.

> The *kinds of* writing that are the

most lucrative are novels and inspirational books.

The *kinds of books* that they publish are novels and textbooks.

knit (v.) Principal parts, *knit, knit* (or *knitted*), *knit* (or *knitted*). See IRREGULAR VERBS.

know (v.) Principal parts, *know, know,* [has, have, had] *known.* See IRREGULAR VERBS.

latter, last (adj.) **1.** The word *latter* may be used to designate the second of two persons or things previously mentioned, but should not be used where more than two have been mentioned.

RIGHT: We are now conducting a special sale of suits and overcoats; the *latter* [not *last*] are particularly good value.
WRONG: We are now conducting a special sale of hats, suits, and overcoats; the *latter* are particularly good value.
AWKWARD: We are now conducting a special sale of hats, suits, and overcoats; the *last* are particularly good value.
BETTER: We are now conducting a special sale of hats, suits, and overcoats; the *overcoats* are particularly good value.

2. Do not use the expression *the latter part of.* The correct expressions are, *toward the end of, the last part of.*

WRONG: The book will be published *the latter part of* next month.
RIGHT: The book will be published *toward the end* of next month.
RIGHT: The book will be published *the last part of* next month.

lay, lie (v.) There is an easy way to stop confusing *lay* and *lie.* Remember *lay* means "to put (or set) down," "to place," "to deposit"; *lie* means "to rest," "be in a certain position or location." *Lay* takes an object; *lie* does not. The principal parts of *lay* are: *lay, laid, laid* (present participle, laying). The principal parts of *lie* are: *lie, lay, lain* (present participle, *lying*). The common error is the use of *lay* or one of its principal parts for *lie* or one of its principal parts. Thus, the past tense of *lay* (*laid*), for example, is used incorrectly in place of the past of *lie* (*lay*). Remember that you must *lay* something down.

LAY, LAID, LAID, LAYING
You *lay* the *book* on the table, and it *lies* there.
You *laid* the *book* on the table yesterday, and it *lay* there until Mary picked it up.
I *lay* the *letters* in the same place on his desk each morning.
I *laid* the *letters* on his desk before I left the room.
The brickmason has *laid* the *stones* in an irregular pattern.
The brickmason *is laying* the *stones* in an irregular pattern.
LIE, LAY, LAIN, LYING
I *lie* [not *lay*] in the sun for an hour every day.
I *lay* [not *laid*] in the sun for an hour yesterday. (Past tense.)
The book has *lain* [not *laid*] there for a month.
The book is *lying* [not *laying*] here where you laid it.

lead (v.) Principal parts, *lead, led, led.* See IRREGULAR VERBS.

leap (v.) Principal parts, *leap, leaped* or *leapt, leaped* or *leapt.* See IRREGULAR VERBS.

leave (v.) Principal parts, *leave, left, left.* See IRREGULAR VERBS.

lend (v.) Principal parts, *lend, lent, lent.* See IRREGULAR VERBS.

less, fewer Use *less* when referring to quantity, *fewer* when referring to number.

> Her new apartment has *less* closet space and *fewer* windows.
> The staff in the New York office is *fewer* [not *less*] in number than that in the Chicago office.
> *Fewer* [not *less*] industrial accidents occurred this year than last.

let (v.) Principal parts, *let, let, let.* See IRREGULAR VERBS.

liable See APT.

lie (v. to recline) Principal parts, *lie, lay,* [has, have, had] *lain.* See IRREGULAR VERBS. See also LAY.

lie (v. to tell a falsehood) Principal parts, *lie, lied, lied.*

light (v.) Principal parts, *light, lighted* (or *lit*), *lighted* (or *lit*). See IRREGULAR VERBS.

light The adverb forms are *light, lighter, lightest* or *lightly, more lightly, most lightly.* See ADVERBS, 3.

like Use *like* as a preposition; *as* as a conjunction. *Like* takes an object; *as* or *as if* introduces a clause.

> Their product is not *like ours* in quality. (No verb follows *like*.)
> To increase sales, reduce the price *as* [not *like*] our competitors *do*.
> You are *like me* in your desire for perfection. (No verb follows *like*.)
> He treats her *as if* [not *like*] she *were* ignorant.
> I wish I could think *as* [not *like*] he does. (The verb is understood.)

likely See APT.

live (v.) Live *in* a town, *on* a street, *at* a certain address, *by* means of a livelihood.

> He lives *in* New York *on* Tenth Street.
> He lives *at* 231 West Tenth Street.
> He lives *by selling* family heirlooms.

loan, lend Many authorities object to any use of *loan* as a verb. It is best to use the word only in connection with formal banking transactions—for example, placing a loan through a banker. For general purposes, use *lend*.

> Will you *lend* [not *loan*] me ten dollars?
> He *lent* [not *loaned*] me ten dollars.
> The bank *loaned* the money at 6 percent.

lose (v.) Principal parts, *lose, lost, lost.* See IRREGULAR VERBS.

loud The adverb forms are *loud, louder, loudest* or *loudly, more loudly, most loudly.* See ADVERBS, 3.

majority (n.) 1. In a contest, *majority* means "more than half the votes cast," whereas *plurality* means "more votes than any other candidate received but less than half the votes cast."

> Smith received a *plurality* but not a *majority* of the votes. There were 21,000 votes cast, and Smith received only 10,000. Jones received 7000, so Smith's *plurality* was 3000. A majority is necessary for election.

2. *Majority* is singular or plural depending upon the sense in which it is used. It is plural when it means "most of."

> The majority [the majority as a whole] *is* against the new bill.
> A majority [the larger number as

individuals] *are* against the new bill.

many a Always takes a singular verb, even if followed by a compound subject.

Many a newspaper and magazine *has* [not *have*] published his work.

mass (n.) **1.** Do not capitalize.

2. A *mass* is offered or celebrated, not held. A *high mass* is sung, a *low mass* is said.

mathematics See -ICS.

may See CAN, MAY.

may, might (v.) **1.** When expressing possibility in a simple sentence, these words are usually interchangeable. See 2 below.

I suggest that we settle the question now; otherwise it *may* [or *might*] cause trouble several years hence.
We *may* [or *might*] decide to order a different make.

2. *Might* is the past tense of *may.* In using *may* or *might*, observe the SEQUENCE OF TENSES if *might* is not required by 3, 4, or 5. With the present, perfect, and future tenses, use *may;* with the past or past perfect, use *might.*

I give ⎫
I have given ⎬ you the information
I shall give ⎭ that you *may* understand the situation.

I gave ⎫
I was giving ⎬ you the information
I had given ⎭ that you *might* understand the situation.

As we *have seen,* it *may be wise* to allow the debtor additional credit.
I *have not heard* what happened this morning, but he *may have* persuaded her to adopt his view.
The president *said* that we *might have* a holiday.
The instructions *were* that, come

what *might,* the task should be completed by the end of September.

3. *Might* is conditional. It is used in the main clause of a conditional sentence whether the condition is expressed or implied.

Anyone *might* learn the facts from the report [if he read it].
If the product is successful, it *might be* necessary to increase the size of the plant. (The increase is conditional upon success.)
If the certificate fails to make provision for the issuance of stock in series, it *might* subsequently be amended to include that provision.

4. *Might* is used in the sense of *would perhaps* in a conditional statement.

With a little persuasion, Mr. Brown *might* [would perhaps] agree to that arrangement.
Jane *might* [would perhaps] go to the dance with Ralph if he agreed to leave when she wanted to go home.

5. *Might* is used in the subjunctive to express a supposition.

He acts *as if* the company *might* try to take advantage of his lack of legal knowledge.
He speaks *as though* he *might* sever his connections with the company.

6. *May* is used in prayer and benedictions. The subjunctive *might* denotes wish without expectation of fulfillment.

May God bless you.

7. See CAN, COULD, 3 for the misuse of *could* for *might* in conditional sentences.

me Objective case of the first person singular pronoun. **1.** For use as an object, see PRONOUNS, 1.

2. For misuse of *me* for *I* after

forms of the verb *to be* (*am, is, are, was, were*), see PREDICATE NOMINATIVE, 1.

measles (n.) Plural in form but singular in meaning. Measles *is* a disease.

metaphysics See -ICS.

might See MAY, MIGHT.

monopoly (n.) When followed by a preposition, use *of*.

mood (**mode**) The mood of a verb expresses the attitude of the speaker. See SUBJUNCTIVE MOOD.

more than one Always takes singular noun and verb, although the meaning is plural.

> More than one *defendant* is involved.

most, almost *Most* is used with an adjective to express the superlative degree. Do not use *most* for the adverb *almost*.

> He is the *most eager* of the boys.
> *Almost* all the senators voted against the bill.

Apart from the fact that *most* is not a substitute for *almost,* in many constructions it changes the meaning of the sentence when it is used incorrectly.

> I am *most ready to go.* (More ready than others.)
> I am *almost ready* to go. (Nearly ready to go.)

motive (n.) When followed by a preposition, use *for*.

mumps (n.) Plural in form but singular in meaning. Mumps *is* a disease.

mutual See COMMON, MUTUAL.

myself See REFLEXIVE PRONOUNS.

naught (n.) The name of the symbol 0 is *naught,* not *aught. Aught* means "anything," but is obsolete.

negatives 1. For comparative negative, see AS, 1.

2. See DOUBLE NEGATIVES.

neither 1. Singular, followed by singular verb. The use of a plural verb after *neither* is a common error.

> Neither of these plans *is* [not *are*] satisfactory.

2. Use neither to designate between one of two persons or things; *none* or *no* instead of *neither* to designate one of three or more.

> He decided that *neither* of the [two] plans suggested was satisfactory. (Two is unnecessary.)
> He decided that *none* of the [five] plans was satisfactory.
> *No* report submitted to date covers the subject adequately.

neither . . . nor 1. It is never correct to use *or* with *neither*.

2. The construction after correlatives should be parallel. The misplacement of *neither* frequently results in unbalanced construction after the correlatives.

> WRONG: The plan *neither meets* the approval of the president *nor of* the treasurer. ("Neither" is followed by a verb and "nor" by a prepositional phrase. "Meets the approval" is common to both the president and the treasurer.)

RIGHT: The plan meets the approval *neither of* the president *nor of* the treasurer.

RIGHT: The plan meets the approval of *neither* the president *nor* the treasurer.

3. For correct number of verb when *neither . . . nor* connects two subjects, see EITHER . . . *or*, 2.

news (n.) Plural in form but singular in meaning. The news *is* good.

nobody (n.) Always write as one word.

none (indefinite pron.) Either singular or plural, depending on the meaning.

We asked for volunteers, but *none* [not one] of them *was* willing to go.
I want *none* of them to go unless they want to.

no . . . or When *no* precedes the first word or phrase in a series and is applicable to each, connect the words or phrase with *or,* not *nor.*

No man, woman, *or* child can be happy without friends. (No man, no woman, no child).
Several of the families had *no* fuel to burn *or* money with which to buy it. (No fuel, no money.)

not *Not* is often superfluous in a subordinate clause after a negative in the main clause. In each of the following sentences, the bracketed *not* should be omitted.

WRONG: Nobody knows how much time may [*not*] be wasted in argument.
WRONG: It would not surprise me if they had [*not*] cut expenses.
WRONG: Do you think there might [*not*] be some other cause at work here?

Not is correct when its use is necessary to convey the intended meaning, but it is usually better to reconstruct the sentence.

RIGHT: Is it impossible for you to realize that the merger might *not* be consummated?
BETTER: Is it impossible for you to realize that *no* merger might be consummated?
WRONG: He does not believe that there are *not* extenuating circumstances.
RIGHT: He does not believe that there are *no* extenuating circumstances.
BETTER: He believes there may be extenuating circumstances.

nowhere Always written as one word. **1.** Do not add an *s* to *nowhere;* there is no such word as *nowheres.*

2. *No place* is commonly misused for *nowhere.*

I have gone *nowhere* [not *no place*] today.

O, oh Use *O* as a form of address (the "vocative" O); or when it is related to that which follows; use *oh* as an exclamation.

O Shepherd, speak!
O for the happy days of childhood!
Oh, I'm all right.
Oh! How did you find out?

odds (n. pl.) Always takes a plural verb. The odds *are* against him.

off Never follow *off* by *of.*

He gave me 10 percent *off* [not *off of*] the price list.

offended (adj.) Offended *at* an action, *with* a person.

omission of words Words may be omitted from a sentence if they can be supplied *clearly and exactly* from a parallel portion of the sentence. A common error, however, is the omission of a word that cannot be clearly and exactly supplied.

1. In two clauses, if one subject is singular and the other plural, it is better not to omit the verb.

> WRONG: The sky *was* clear and the stars bright.
> BETTER: The sky *was* clear and the stars *were* bright.

2. Do not omit part of a verb phrase if it is different in form from the corresponding part of the parallel verb phrase.

> WRONG: The company always *has* and always *will give* recognition where it is due.
> RIGHT: The company always *has given* and always *will give* recognition where it is due.

3. Do not omit an article, a personal or relative pronoun, or a preposition that is necessary to the grammatical completeness or to the clear understanding of a sentence.

> WRONG: He wrote to the chairman and president. (If two men are involved.)
> RIGHT: He wrote to the chairman and *the* president.
> WRONG: I have great sympathy but no confidence in that class of people.
> RIGHT: I have great sympathy *for,* but no confidence in, that class of people.
> BETTER: I have great sympathy for that class of people, but no confidence in them.

4. See INFINITIVES, 3, for omission of *to* in a series of infinitive phrases.

oneself (pron.) Formerly *one's self,* but now preferably written as one word.

only (adv., adj.) **1.** The meaning that the sentence is intended to convey determines the position of the word *only.*

> *Only* his *assistant* has authority to sign the payroll record.
> His assistant has authority *only* to *sign* the payroll record, not to prepare it.
> His assistant has authority to sign *only* the payroll *record.*
> His assistant has authority to sign the payroll *record only.*

The first sentence states that the assistant, and no one else, has the authority; the second, that the assistant has no authority beyond signing the payroll; the last two sentences state that the assistant has authority to sign the payroll record and nothing else. No hard and fast rule can be given. The writer must consider carefully the exact meaning that he wishes to convey and place the *only* accordingly. If there is danger of ambiguity or misunderstanding, the construction should be changed to eliminate the *only.* The foregoing explains the orthodox or conventional placement of *only.* It is permissible, however, to choose another position if the change does not obscure the meaning.

> ORTHODOX: In typing manuscript, use *only one side* of the sheet.
> PERMISSIBLE: In typing manuscript, use *one side* of the sheet *only.* (What is there besides the sheet to use?)

2. *Only* is sometimes erroneously used as a conjunction.

> WRONG: Your pen is the same as mine *only* that the nib is different.
> RIGHT: The *one* [or *only*] difference between your pen and mine is the different nib.

oral (adj.) *Verbal* is often misused for *oral.* See VERBAL.

over The expression *over with* is

erroneous. The *with* is superfluous.

> Our annual sale is now *over* [not *over with*].

owing to See DUE TO.

parliament (n.) See COLLECTIVE NOUNS.

Participles 1. *Dangling participles.* Participles or participal phrases, which are used as adjectives, must clearly modify the proper noun or pronoun within the sentence.

> WRONG: When *writing* this book, an attempt was made to organize the material to best advantage. (What does "writing" modify?)
> RIGHT: When *writing* this book, the *author* attempted to organize the material to best advantage.
> WRONG: The study showed that while *advancing* the cause of one group, another *group* was injured by the new law. ("Advancing" wrongly modifies "group.")
> RIGHT: The study showed that while *advancing* the cause of one group, the new *law* injures another group.
> RIGHT: The study showed that the new law *advanced* the cause of one group but injured another.

Exceptions: Certain participles may indicate a general rather than a specific action—an action in which no particular actor is implied. They do not then need a noun or pronoun to modify and are not dangling. Some participles that may be used in this manner are *allowing for, granting, considering that, speaking of, talking of, owing to.*

> *Allowing* for interruptions, the work will be completed by the end of the year.
> Generally *speaking*, our products are superior to theirs.

2. *Misplaced participles.* The mis-

placement of a participal modifier can result in a meaningless sentence.

> A classic example is, "I saw the new file *cabinet walking* up the stairs."
> RIGHT: *Walking* up the stairs, *I* saw the new file cabinet.

party (n.) See COLLECTIVE NOUNS.

past tense 1. Use the simplest past tense to express action that was completed at some time before the time a statement is made.

> The report concerns events that *occurred* many years ago.
> He *had* [not *has had*] practical ideas on every phase of the problem.

2. Avoid substitution of the past tense for the present perfect or past perfect tenses.

> WRONG: I was filing when he returned, but I *was typing* the report before that time.
> RIGHT: I was filing when he returned, but I *had been typing* the report before that time. (Past perfect.)
> WRONG: Since Mr. Scott was elected president of the club, the members *enjoyed* better socials.
> RIGHT: Since Mr. Scott was elected president of the club, the members *have enjoyed* better socials. (Present perfect.)

3. In dependent clauses, a *permanently true* fact is usually put in the present tense, even when the main verb is in the past tense. This rule does not apply to independent clauses or sentences with one verb.

> We *were taught* in school that "Hamlet" *is* Shakespeare's greatest tragedy.
> "Hamlet" *was* Shakespeare's greatest tragedy.
> San Francisco *was* the birthplace of the United Nations.

people (n.) 1. Singular in form but

plural in meaning. The plural *peoples* is used when more than one race or nation is referred to. The *peoples* of France and Italy. . . .

2. *Persons, people.* When referring to a number of individuals, use *persons*. When referring to a group, use *people*.

> Six *persons* were in the room.
> Do you know the *people* who live next door?
> The American *people* are democratic.

percent (n.) A COLLECTIVE NOUN which can be either singular or plural in meaning. If there is a doubt about its number, make the verb agree in number with the noun following *of:*

> About 20 percent of the *students* *are* ill today.
> Only 20 percent of the *work was* done yesterday.

perfect Not comparable. If anything is perfect, it cannot be *more* perfect. "More nearly perfect" is allowable.

perfect tenses The perfect tenses are formed by adding the auxiliaries *has, have, had* to the past participle. It is incorrect to use the past participle as a verb without an auxiliary.

PRESENT PERFECT TENSE:
    have (has) looked   have (has) taken
PAST PERFECT TENSE:
    had looked   had taken
FUTURE PERFECT TENSE:
    shall (will) have looked   shall (will) have taken

personal, personnel 1. *Personal* is an adjective meaning "individual"; *personnel* is a noun meaning "a body of people employed in work or service."

2. *Personnel* is a collective noun and may take either a singular or a plural verb.

place (n.) Must be used as the subject or as the object of a verb or preposition. *Place* is commonly misused with *any, every, no, some* after an intransitive verb. The adverbs *anywhere, everywhere, nowhere, somewhere* are usually better.

> WRONG: Are you going *any place* this afternoon?
> RIGHT: Are you going *anywhere* this afternoon?
> WRONG: I have looked *every place* for the letter.
> RIGHT: I have looked *everywhere* for the letter.
> RIGHT: I have *no place* to go. (Object of the transitive verb "have.")
> RIGHT: I have *nowhere* to go.
> RIGHT: He is located in *some place* in the West. (Object of preposition "in.")
> RIGHT: He is located *somewhere* in the West.

plead (v.) Principal parts, *plead, pleaded, pleaded;* preferred to *plead, pled, pled.* See IRREGULAR VERBS.

pliers (n.) Always used in the plural.

plurality See MAJORITY, 1.

possessives 1. *Compound nouns and proper names.* The possessive is formed by adding *'s* to the word nearest the object possessed.

> attorney *general's* argument
> John Brown, *Jr.'s* office
> John Brown, *II's* office
> Mr. Mason of *Consolidated's* staff
> notary *public's* seal
> aide-de-*camp's* promotion

683

Use the *of* phrase to form the plural possessives of a compound noun.

> arguments *of* the attorneys general
> seals *of* notaries public
> promotions *of* aides-de-camp

2. *Awkward or sibilant sounds.* If a word of more than one syllable ends in *s* or an *s* sound, causing a hissing or awkward sound, add only an apostrophe to form the possessive.

> *Moses'* rod   *Kansas' son*
> for *conscience'* sake
> for *goodness'* sake
> for *appearance'* sake
> for *convenience'* sake

3. Words ending in *s*. The singular possessive of words ending in *s* is formed by adding *'s*; the possessive of plurals ending in *s* is formed by adding only the apostrophe. Formerly, the accepted form for singular as well as plural nouns was the addition of an apostrophe without the *s*, but most authorities prefer the *'s* in nearly all cases.

> Mr. *Jones's* car
> the *Joneses'* car
> Misses *Smiths'* reception
> *James's* position
> *bus's* motor

The use of the apostrophe without the *s* still prevails in poetic or Biblical expressions.

> *Jesus'* life, *Achilles'* heel, *Mars'* Hill

4. *"Of" phrase.* An *of* phrase may be used to show possession. When the thing possessed is a specific number or group belonging to the possessor, the *'s* also is used, thus forming a double possessive.

> In his book he tried to imitate a novel *of* James *Street's.*
> That remark *of* the *commentator's* aroused. . . . (A specific remark.)
> Those investments *of* his *father's* are. . . . (Specific investments.)

When the thing possessed is not restricted or limited to a specific number or group, the *'s* is not used.

> In his book he tried to imitate the novels *of* James *Street.*
> The remarks *of* the *commentator* aroused. . . . (Generally speaking.)
> The investments *of* his *father* are. . . . (Generally speaking.)

5. *Appositives and explanatory words.* Whenever possible, avoid the use of appositives or explanatory words with the possessive case.

> ACCEPTABLE: His guardian, *Mr. Nelson's,* control of the money. . . .
> BETTER: Control of the money *by his guardian, Mr. Nelson,* . . .
> ACCEPTABLE: In his writings, he tries to imitate his father, *James Ludlow's,* novels.
> BETTER: In his writings, he tries to imitate the novels *of his father,* James Ludlow.

When the appositive is restrictive and therefore not set off by commas, the awkward construction does not arise.

> The defendant *Smith's* defense

When the explanatory words are parenthetical, and especially when they are enclosed in parentheses, the construction *must* be changed to avoid the possessive.

> WRONG: *Mrs. Ball's* (formerly Miss Brown) estate is. . . .
> RIGHT: The estate of *Mrs. Ball,* formerly Miss Brown, is. . . .

6. *Inanimate objects.* An inanimate object cannot actually possess anything. It is usually better to show relation by the use of the *of* phrase. However, usage has attributed possession to some inanimate objects, especially those expressing time or measure.

> one day's vacation
> *two weeks'* pay

one additional day's pay
five dollars' worth
a month's delay
three months' delay
six pounds' weight

The italicized expressions are plural. Notice that the apostrophe *follows* the *s* instead of preceding it. Many of these expressions form compound adjectives and can be hyphenated instead of written as possessives.

a one-day vacation
a three-month delay
a six-pound weight
a three-ounce bottle

practical, practicable (adj.) *Practicable* means "feasible," "capable of being put into practice"; *practical* means "useful" or "successful in actual practice." *Practical* may be used with reference to either persons or things, but *practicable* can be used only with reference to things.

Jones is a *practical* man. (A doer rather than a theorist.)
The scheme is *practical*. (It will be successful when it is carried out.)
The scheme is *practicable*. (It can be carried out.)

precedence (n.) When followed by a preposition, use *of*.

The vice president has *precedence of* the secretary of state.

precedent (n.) When followed by a preposition, use *to* or *for*.

preclude An erroneous expression is *preclude the possibility of*. Since *preclude* means to render impossible, the absurdity of the expression is obvious.

WRONG: In an effort to *preclude the possibility of* a misunderstanding. . . .

RIGHT: In an effort to *preclude* a misunderstanding. . . .

predicate adjective Some intransitive verbs are followed by adjectives. These adjectives do not modify verbs (for, in that case, they would be adverbs) but complete the meaning of the verb, or predicate. Thus they are called complements or predicate adjectives. The intransitive verb that is most commonly followed by a predicate adjective is *to be* and its forms—*am, is, was, were, have been, had been,* etc. Other verbs that are usually followed by predicate adjectives are: *feel, look, smell, sound, taste, appear.*

He *looks handsome*. ("Handsome" modifies "he" not "looks.")
The music *sounded good*. It was played well.

predicate nominative A noun or pronoun following an intransitive verb (one that does not take a direct object), thereby completing, or helping to complete, the predicate is a *predicate nominative*. As its name implies, a predicate nominative is always in the nominative case. A predicate nominative is also called a complement. All complements, however, are not predicate nominatives; adjectives may also serve as complements.
1. Forms of the verb *to be* (*is, are, was, were*) do not take an object but are followed by a predicate nominative. A common error is the use of the objective case of a pronoun (*me, us, her, him, them*) as a predicate nominative. The phrase *It wasn't me* is a colloquialism. It is technically incorrect, however, and should be avoided in writing.

685

It was *I* [not *me*] to whom you spoke.

It was *he* [not *him*] who delivered the papers.

I am *she* [not *her*].

2. A verb agrees with its subject and not with the predicate nominative. Difficulty is caused by the use of a singular subject and plural predicate nominative, or *vice versa*.

A valuable *by-product* of training conferences *is* the numerous *opportunities* afforded for management to observe the trainees' reactions. ("By-product" is the subject of "is"; "opportunities" is the predicate nominative.)

Progressive *interviews are* a useful *form* for training personnel. ("Interviews" is the subject of "are"; "form" is the predicate nominative.)

preposition at the end It is not grammatically incorrect to place a preposition at the end of a sentence; it is better to end a sentence with a preposition than to use an awkward construction. It is incorrect to place an unnecessary preposition at the end of the sentence.

WRONG: Where is the book *at?* (Preposition unnecessary).

RIGHT: Where is the book?

AWKWARD: Prepositions sometimes follow the nouns *with which* they are coupled.

BETTER: Prepositions sometimes follow the nouns they are coupled *with*.

prepositional idioms The correct usage is given under the word to be used. For example, what preposition follows *angry?* Look under ANGRY.

prescribe, proscribe *To prescribe* means "to order as a rule or course to be followed" or, in medicine, "to order as a remedy." *To proscribe* means "to denounce" or "to condemn a thing as dangerous," "to outlaw."

present tense 1. Use the present tense to indicate action that is taking place at the present time.

He told me that the company's home office *is* [not *was*] located in New York. (The office is still located in New York.

2. The present tense is used idiomatically to express future action.

Congress *adjourns* [for *will adjourn*] next week.

My vacation *starts* [for *will start*] next Friday.

3. Use the progressive form, not the simple present, to express action in progress.

WRONG: St. Vincent's Hospital, where he *is treated*, has the most modern equipment.

RIGHT: St. Vincent's Hospital, where he *is being treated*, has the most modern equipment.

WRONG: When I write in the morning, as I *write* now, I compose with more facility than in the evening.

RIGHT: When I write in the morning, as I *am writing* now, I compose with more facility than in the evening.

presently (adv.) Meaning "soon." A common error is the use of *presently* when *at present* is meant.

We expect to complete the book *presently* [soon].

At present [not *presently*] we are working on your book.

principal, principle The word *principle* is a noun only and cannot be used as an adjective. *Principle* means "a fundamental or general truth," "a rule." *Principal* is used in all other cases. As a noun, *principal* has many meanings; as an adjective, it means "chief," "main," "most important."

We have always acted on the *principle* [fundamental truth] that honesty is the best policy.

An agent may bind his *principal* to contracts entered into within the scope of his authority.

The loan, including *principal* and interest, amounted to $350.

The New England states have been our *principal* source of business during the past five years.

The *principal* of the school resigned.

proceeds (n. pl.) Used in the plural and takes a plural verb.

pronouns 1. As *objects*. When a pronoun is used as an object, it is always in the objective case. A common error is the use of the nominative case of the personal pronouns (*I, we, he, she, they*) instead of the objective case (*me, us, him, her, them*), especially when the pronoun is joined to another object. Test the sentence by omitting the first object. The omission will show the absurdity of the use of the nominative instead of the objective.

WRONG: We received a letter inviting my wife and *I* to spend the weekend in the country. (Inviting . . . I?)
RIGHT: We received a letter inviting my wife and *me* to spend. . . .
WRONG: Mr. Smith, let's you and *I* discuss the matter from every viewpoint. (Let . . . I?)
RIGHT: Mr. Smith, let's you and *me* discuss the matter from. . . .
WRONG: I know you and *he* to be my friends. (I know . . . he to be?)
RIGHT: I know you and *him* to be my friends.

2. After forms of the verb *to be* (*am, is, are, was, were*). See PREDICATE NOMINATIVE, 1.

prophecy, prophesy *Prophecy* is a noun; *prophesy* is a verb.

I hope the *prophecy* comes true.
I *prophesy* a period of prosperity in the near future.

prove (v.) Principal parts, *prove, proved, proved.* The use of *proven* for *proved* is increasing in the United States but is not considered good usage.

provided, providing 1. Many excellent writers use *providing* as a conjunction in place of *provided,* but some authorities do not sanction this.

CORRECT: I will give you the order *providing* you agree to my price.
BETTER: I will give you the order *provided* you agree to my price.

2. It is preferable not to use *that* after *provided* except where it is accepted usage in formal documents.

public (n.) See COLLECTIVE NOUNS.

quarter When referring to the time of day, the correct expression is *a quarter to* not *a quarter of.*

quick The adverb forms are *quick, quicker, quickest* or *quickly, more quickly, most quickly.* See ADVERBS, 3.

reason When a sentence begins with "The reason is" or "The reason why . . . is," the clause giving the reason should begin with *that* and not with *because.*

WRONG: Her *reason is because* she does not have the money.
RIGHT: Her *reason is that* she does not have the money.
WRONG: The *reason why* the goods were delayed was *because* they were not shipped.
RIGHT: The *reason why* the goods

were delayed was *that* they were not shipped.

reconcile (v.) When followed by a preposition, use *with* or *to*.

reflexive pronouns Formed by adding *-self* (sing.) or *-selves* (pl.) to some personal pronouns.

1. Reflexive pronouns are used to call attention to the subject and to emphasize a noun or pronoun.

> RIGHT: *He* hurt *himself* more than anyone else by his attitude.
> RIGHT: The *president himself* made a report to the employees.

2. A common error is the use of a reflexive pronoun in place of the objective case of the pronoun.

> WRONG: Best regards from George and *myself*.
> RIGHT: Best regards from George and *me*.

3. Another common error is the omission of a possessive pronoun when a word is joined to a reflexive pronoun. Test the sentence by omitting the reflexive pronoun.

> WRONG: He hurt *himself and family* by his attitude. (The absurdity of "He hurt family" is obvious.)
> RIGHT: He hurt *himself and his* family by his attitude.

regard Do not use *regards* in place of *regard* in the expressions *in regard to, with regard to.*

regardless There is no such word as *irregardless*. Misuse perhaps is caused by confusion with the word *irrespective*, which means "without respect to" and is correct.

> We should acknowledge all orders *regardless* of the amount involved.

relation (ship) (n.) when followed by a preposition, use *of, to,* or *with.*

> The relation *of* these parts is not clear.
> The relationship *of* the beneficiary *to* the insured is not close.
> Our strained relations *with* Russia are a source of worry.

remainder, rest (n.) **1.** These words are interchangeable except when *remainder* is used as a mathematical term.

2. See BALANCE for the distinction between *balance* and *rest* or *remainder*.

resentment (n.) Resentment *at* or *for* an action, *against* a *person.*

> My resentment *against* him was *at* [or *for*] his rudeness to me.

retroactive (adj.) When followed by a preposition, use *to.*

> Retroactive *to* May 15th.

rich, riches (n.) Always plural and take plural verbs.

ride (v.) Principal parts, *ride, rode, ridden.* See IRREGULAR VERBS.

right 1. The adverb form is *right* or *rightly.* See ADVERBS, 3.

2. *Right* is not comparable. If anything is right, it cannot be *more* right. "More nearly right" is allowable.

ring (v.) Principal parts, *ring, rang,* [has, have, had] *rung.* See IRREGULAR VERBS.

rise (v.) Principal parts, *rise, rose,* [has, have, had] *risen.* See IRREGULAR VERBS.

round *Round* is not comparable. If anything is round, it cannot be *more* round. "More nearly round" is allowable.

run (v.) Principal parts, *run, ran,* [has, have, had] *run.* See IRREGULAR VERBS.

same (adj.) Do not use as a pronoun. Businessmen especially are guilty of the misuse of *same.*

> WRONG: We will repair the spring and ship *same* to you.
> RIGHT: We will repair the spring and ship *it* to you.

saw (v.) Principal parts, *saw, sawed,* [has, have, had] *sawed* or *sawn.* See IRREGULAR VERBS.

say (v.) Principal parts, *say, said, said.* See IRREGULAR VERBS.

scarcely (adv.) This word carries a negative idea and should not be used with a negative.

> WRONG: There is *scarcely no* time left in which to fill the order.
> RIGHT: There is *scarcely any* time left in which to fill the order.
> WRONG: We could *not scarcely* ship the goods before August.
> RIGHT: We could *scarcely* ship the goods before August.

scissors (n.) Always used in the plural and takes a plural verb.

see (v.) Principal parts, *see, saw,* [has, have, had] *seen.* See IRREGULAR VERBS.

seek (v.) Principal parts, *seek, sought, sought.* See IRREGULAR VERBS.

seem Followed by a predicate ad-

jective and not by an adverb. See ADVERBS, 2.

semimonthly, semiweekly (adv.) Since *semi* means "half," *semiweekly* means "twice a week" and *semimonthly* means "twice a month."

sequence of tenses When two or more verbs are used in the same sentence, the time relation, or *sequence of tenses,* is important and sometimes troublesome.

1. Remember that the purpose of changing the tense in a sentence is to indicate a change in time.

> I *remember* I *owe* him a debt of gratitude. (The whole situation is in the present.)
> I *remembered* I *owed* him a debt of gratitude. (The whole situation is in the past.)
> I *remember* I *owed* him a debt of gratitude. (Implication: The debt is no longer owed.)

2. If you are writing in the past tense and wish to refer to a preceding event, you must use the past perfect tense.

> He pledged the bonds he *had bought* [not *bought*] last week.

3. After a future tense in a main clause, use the present tense in a dependent clause.

> The chairman *will open* the meeting as soon as the speaker *arrives.*

4. A fact that is permanently *true* is usually put in the present tense, even when the main verb is in the past tense.

> Even then men *knew* that tides *are caused* [not *were caused*] by the moon.
> As a child she *was taught* that honesty *is* [not *was*] the best policy.

5. The perfect participle expresses

an action that has been completed *at the time* indicated by the main verb. A common error is the use of the present participle instead of the perfect.

> He completed the report on schedule, *having worked* [not *working*] unusually long hours.
> He will complete the report on schedule, *having worked* [not *working*] unusually long hours.

set (v.)   See SIT.

shake (v.)   Principal parts, *shake, shook,* [has, have, had] *shaken.* See IRREGULAR VERBS.

shall (should); **will** (would) *Should* is the past tense of the auxiliary verb *shall; would,* of the auxiliary *will.* Few writers today observe the old distinction between *shall* and *will, should* and *would.*

sharp   The adverb forms are *sharp, sharper, sharpest* or *sharply, more sharply, most sharply.* See ADVERBS, 3.

she   Nominative case of third person singular pronoun. **1.** For misuse of *she* for *her,* see PRONOUNS, 1.

2. For use after forms of the verb *to be* (*am, is, are, was, were*), see PREDICATE NOMINATIVE, 1.

shine (v.)   Principal parts, *shine, shone,* [has, have, had] *shone.* See IRREGULAR VERBS.

short   The adverb forms are *short, shorter, shortest* or *shortly, more shortly, most shortly.* See ADVERBS, 3.

show (v.)   Principal parts, *show,* *showed,* [has, have, had] *shown.* See IRREGULAR VERBS.

shrink (v.)   Principal parts, *shrink, shrank,* [has, have, had] *shrunk.* See IRREGULAR VERBS.

since   **1.** Do not use *since* to begin a clause after *ago.* Begin the clause with *that.* This error is more apt to occur when a parenthetical expression follows *ago.*

> It is over ten years *ago,* as well as I remember, *that* [not *since*] the stores were consolidated.

2. Be certain that a phrase introduced by *since* is correctly attached to the sentence and is not a dangling participial phrase. See PARTICIPLES.

> WRONG: *Since* preparing the report, new figures are available. ("Preparing" is a dangling participle.)
> RIGHT: *Since* I prepared the report, new figures are available.
> RIGHT: *Since* the preparation of the report, new figures are available.

sing (v.)   Principal parts, *sing, sang,* [has, have, had] *sung.* See IRREGULAR VERBS.

sink (v.)   Principal parts, *sink, sank,* [has, have, had] *sunk.* See IRREGULAR VERBS.

sit, set (v.)   There is no reason to confuse these words. *To sit* means "to be seated," *to set* means "to place an object." *Sit* never takes an object, *set* always does. Principal parts, *sit: sit, sat, sat.* Principal parts, *set: set, set, set.*

> He *sits* at his desk.
> He *sat* at his desk from ten to eleven.
> He *has sat* there for two hours.
> He *is sitting* at his desk.

I *set* the thermos on his desk every morning.

I *have set* the thermos on his desk every day for a month.

I *set* the thermos on his desk yesterday, as usual.

I *am setting* the thermos on the table.

The thermos *sat* [past of *sit*] on the table for a week.

The thermos *has sat* there for a week. (Present perfect of *sit*.)

size (n.) **1.** See KIND.

2. *Size* is a noun; *sized,* an adjective. Either noun or adjective may form a compound adjective.

medium-size house or *medium-sized* house
large-size dresses or *large-sized* dresses
different-size dogs or *different-sized* dogs

3. Since *size* is a noun and not an adjective, it is incorrect to omit the *of* in these and similar expressions: that size *of* machine, that size *of* paper.

slay (v.) Principal parts, *slay, slew,* [has, have, had] *slain.* See IRREGULAR VERBS.

slide (v.) Principal parts, *slide, slid, slid* or [has, have, had] *slidden.* See IRREGULAR VERBS.

slow The adverb forms are *slow, slower, slowest* or *slowly, more slowly, most slowly.* See ADVERBS, 3.

so For the use of *so . . . as* see AS, 1.

soft The adverb forms are *soft, softer, softest* or *softly, more softly, most softly.* See ADVERBS, 3.

some For misuse of *some place* see PLACE.

somebody, someone (pron.) **1.** Always write *somebody* as one word. Write *someone* as one word when it is equivalent to *somebody;* otherwise, it is two words.

He will appoint *someone* of outstanding ability.
If *some one* person is designated to head the project. . . .

2. Singular, followed by singular verb and pronoun.

I know *someone* [or *somebody*] *was* [not *were*] here while I was away, because *he* [not *they*] left *his* [not *their*] briefcase.

some time, sometime, sometimes (adv.) **1.** *Sometime* may be used instead of *at some time,* meaning a point of time not specified. There is no distinction. The trend is to omit *at* and use *sometime.*

RIGHT: I expect to be there *at some time* in August.
PREFERRED: I expect to be there *sometime* in August.

2. Use *some time* when referring to an indefinite lapse of time. It is incorrect to use *sometime* in this sense.

It will take *some time* to prepare the report.

3. *Sometime* may be used as an adjective meaning "former."

Dr. Evatt, *sometime* Minister of Australia. . . .

4. *Sometimes,* written as one word, means "at several indefinite times"; "on some occasions."

Sometimes she works late.

somewhere 1. Always written as one word. *Some place* is commonly misused for *somewhere.* See PLACE.

2. There is no such word as *some-wheres*.

sort (n.) Pl., *sorts*. See KIND.

sow (v.) Principal parts, *sow, sowed, sowed* or [has, have, had] *sown*. See IRREGULAR VERBS.

speak (v.) Principal parts, *speak, spoke,* [has, have, had] *spoken*. See IRREGULAR VERBS.

species 1. Singular or plural. The species *is;* these species *are.*

2. For correct usage in the sense of kind or sort, see KIND.

spin (v.) Principal parts, *spin, spun, spun*. See IRREGULAR VERBS.

split infinitives See INFINITIVES, 2.

spring (v.) Principal parts, *spring, sprang,* [has, have, had] *sprung*. See IRREGULAR VERBS.

stationary, stationery *Stationary* means standing still; *stationery* means writing materials.

Some loading platforms are *stationary,* but others move.
Don't forget to order the office *stationery.*

steal (v.) Principal parts, *steal, stole,* [has, have, had] *stolen*. See IRREGULAR VERBS.

stick (v.) Principal parts, *stick, stuck, stuck*. See IRREGULAR VERBS.

sting (v.) Principal parts, *sting, stung, stung*. See IRREGULAR VERBS.

straight 1. The adverb form is *straight.*

2. *Straight* is not comparable. If anything is straight, it cannot be *more* straight. "More nearly straight" is allowable.

stride (v.) Principal parts, *stride, strode,* [has, have, had] *stridden*. See IRREGULAR VERBS.

strike (v.) Principal parts, *strike, struck, struck* or [has, have, had] *stricken*. See IRREGULAR VERBS.

string (v.) Principal parts, *string, strung, strung*. See IRREGULAR VERBS.

strive (v.) Principal parts, *strive, strove,* [has, have, had] *striven*. See IRREGULAR VERBS.

subject to See ADDICTED TO.

subjunctive mood Although the trend is away from the subjunctive mood, correct usage still requires the subjunctive in some cases.
1. Use the subjunctive mood to express a condition contrary to fact. Contrary-to-fact statements are generally introduced by *wish* or *if.*

I wish I *were* [not the indicative *was*] able to fly like a bird [but I am not].
If the company *were* [not the indicative *was*] in a sound financial position, a merger would not be necessary. (The company is not in a sound financial position.)
If I *were* [not the indicative *was*] you, I should not accept the offer.
I wish their relationship *were* [not the indicative *was*] more harmonious.

Many clauses introduced by *if* do not express impossible or contrary-to-fact conditions, but merely a condition or a doubt. In those clauses, the subjunctive is *not* generally used.

> If optimism *does* [not the subjunctive *do*] not get out of hand, there will be no sudden collapse.
> If he *is* [not *be*] in town I am sure he will call you. (Doubt implied.)
> If he *was* [not *were*] at the meeting, we did not see him [but it is possible he was there].

2. Use the past subjunctive to express a supposition or condition in clauses introduced by *as if, as though.*

> He looks as if he *were* [not *is* or *was*] ill.
> The motor sounds as though a spark plug *were* [not *is* or *was*] missing.
> It appears as if he *did* [not *does*] realize the necessity.

3. Use the subjunctive in *that* clauses when the main verb expresses demand or request.

> We asked that he *vacate* [not the indicative *vacates*] the premises.
> He gave instructions that the office *be* closed early.
> It is essential that the orders *be* shipped tomorrow.
> The requirement is that he *remain* [not the indicative *remains*] abroad for two years.
> He recommended that a Department of Welfare *be* established.

4. Use the subjunctive in formal writing to express a motion, resolution, or ruling.

> Mr. Edwards moved that the secretary *be* instructed to. . . .
> RESOLVED: That the Certificate of Incorporation *be* amended. . . .
> The Court ruled that the plaintiff *receive* [not the indicative *receives*] damages in the sum of $10,000.

such 1. Do not use *which, who, that,* or *where* with *such.* The correct combination is *such . . . as.* Frequently the better usage is to omit *such* or change it to *the, that, those,* and the like.

> WRONG: Some people give only *such* things for *which* they have no need.
> RIGHT: Some people give only *such* things *as* they do not need.
> RIGHT: Some people give only *those* things for *which* they have no need.
> WRONG: We shipped immediately *such* parts of the machinery *that* were in stock.
> RIGHT: We shipped immediately *such* parts of the machinery *as* were in stock.
> BETTER: We shipped immediately *those* parts of the machinery *that* were in stock.

2. Do not use *such as* in place of *as* to introduce a prepositional phrase.

> WRONG: Radios that you have previously purchased from us, *such as in* your last shipment, are out of stock.
> RIGHT: Radios that you have previously purchased from us, *as in* your last shipment, are out of stock.

suitable (adj.) Suitable *for* a use or purpose; *to* an occasion or requirements.

> The machine is suitable *for* that work.
> The machine is suitable *to* the requirements of your office.
> An informal invitation is suitable *to* the occasion.

superior (adj.) Should always be followed by *to*, not *than.*

> It is superior from every point of view *to* [not *than*] the other material.

surround (v.) When followed by a preposition, use *by.*

swear (v.) Principal parts, *swear, swore,* [has, have, had] *sworn.* See IRREGULAR VERBS.

swell (v.) Principal parts, *swell, swelled, swelled* or [has, have, had] *swollen.* See IRREGULAR VERBS.

swim (v.) Principal parts, *swim, swam,* [has, have, had] *swum.* See IRREGULAR VERBS.

swing (v.) Principal parts, *swing, swung, swung.* See IRREGULAR VERBS.

tactic (n.) pl., *tactics.* Most commonly used in the plural.

take (v.) 1. Principal parts, *take, took,* [has, have, had] *taken.* See IRREGULAR VERBS.

2. See BRING.

teach (v.) Principal parts, *teach, taught, taught.* See IRREGULAR VERBS.

team (n.) See COLLECTIVE NOUNS.

tense Tense indicates the time of action expressed by a verb. For correct usage in sentences that cause difficulty look under the different tenses. See SEQUENCE OF TENSES for correct usage when a sentence has more than one verb expressing action at different times.

than 1. Never use after *more and more.*

WRONG: The Supreme Court has granted *more and more* powers to the federal government *than* was originally intended. (Delete "and more" to make the sentence correct.)

2. See DIFFERENT FROM.

thanks (n. pl.) Always takes a plural verb.

that (conj.) Use only one *that* to introduce a single clause. A common error is the use of a second *that* when a phrase or clause intervenes between *that* and the clause it introduces.

I hope *that* (when you have reconsidered the matter) *that* you will cooperate. (Omit the second "that." The first "that" introduces "you will cooperate.")

that, which (rel. prons.) The grammar-book rule is to use *that* to introduce a defining or restrictive clause; use *which* to introduce a nondefining, nonrestrictive clause. Theodore Bernstein, formerly an editor of *The New York Times,* puts it this way in his book *The Careful Writer:* "If the clause could be omitted without leaving the noun it modifies incomplete, or without materially altering the sense of what is being said—or if it could reasonably be enclosed in parentheses—it would be better introduced by *which;* otherwise, by *that.*"

The museum, *which* is open every day but Monday, attracts thousands of visitors each week.
He works Tuesday through Saturday, so he can only go to museums *that* are open on Sunday or Monday.
Statutory requirements *that* fix a definite number of days for notice must be followed. (Only certain requirements are referred to.)
The proposed amendments, *which* improve the practicability of the measure, were adopted unanimously. (The clause introduced by "which" is an additional thought.)

However, the use of *which* for *that* when the meaning is perfectly clear has become acceptable usage.

them Objective case of third person plural pronoun. 1. For use as an object, see PRONOUNS, 1.

2. For misuse of *them* for *they* after forms of the verb *to be* (*am, is, are, was, were*), see PREDICATE NOMINATIVE, 1.

there Often used to introduce a clause in which the verb precedes the subject. The number of the verb is not affected by *there* but depends on the number of the subject. Contrast this construction with PREDICATE NOMINATIVE.

> There *are* not sufficient *data* available. (Plural subject.)
> There *is* a *mass* of data available. (Singular subject.)

they Nominative case of third person plural pronoun. **1.** For misuse of *they* for *them*, see PRONOUNS, 1.

2. For use after the forms of the verb *to be* (*am, is, are, was, were*) see PREDICATE NOMINATIVE, 1.

thrive (v.) Principal parts, *thrive, thrived* (or *throve*), [has, have, had] *thrived* or *thriven*. See IRREGULAR VERBS.

though, although It is perfectly correct to use *though* instead of *although*.

throw (v.) Principal parts, *throw, threw,* [has, have, had] *thrown*. See IRREGULAR VERBS.

tidings (n. pl.) Always used in the plural and takes a plural verb.

toward(s) Either is correct, but the use of *toward* is more prevalent in the United States. *Towards* is the accepted British form.

transitive and intransitive verbs The action of a transitive verb goes from a doer to a receiver, from a subject to an object. The action of an intransitive verb either does not include an object, or is limited to the subject, or the intransitive verb shows no action at all.

> He *opened* the *door*. (Transitive.)
> He *sings* beautifully. (Intransitive, action limited.)
> He *is* a good painter. (Intransitive, no action.)

tread (v.) Principal parts, *tread, trod, trod* or [has, have, had] *trodden*. See IRREGULAR VERBS.

trust (v.) Trust *in* a person, *to* a quality, trust a person *with* something.

> I trust *in* you.
> I trust *to* his discretion.
> I trust you *with* this secret.

try (v.) Often erroneously followed by *and* with a verb in place of an infinitive.

> Try *to come* [not *and come*] to New York.
> Try *to solve* [not *and solve*] the problem.

type (n.) pl., *types*. **1.** See KIND.

2. Type is a noun and should not be used as an adjective. It is incorrect to omit the *of* in these and similar expressions: type *of* machine, type *of* building, type *of* person.

uninterested See DISINTERESTED.

unique Unique is not comparable; it means "the only one of its kind." You should not say "most unique," "more unique" or "very unique."

unquestioned, unquestionable (adj.) *Unquestioned* means "that which has not been questioned"; *unquestionable,* "that which cannot be sensibly questioned."

> The statement was *unquestioned.*
> His loyalty is *unquestionable.*

us Objective case of first person plural pronoun. **1.** For use as an object, see PRONOUNS, 1. **2.** For misuse of *us* for *we,* after forms of verb *to be* (*am, is, are, was, were*), see PREDICATE NOMINATIVE, 1.

valuables (n. pl.) Always used in the plural and takes a plural verb.

variety (n.) pl., *varieties.* See KIND.

verbal (adj.) Relates to either written or spoken words. *Verbal* is used carelessly in place of *oral* with reference to spoken words.

> A contract, whether written or *oral* [not *verbal*] is binding.
> He gave *oral* [not *verbal*] instructions.
> A few *verbal* changes [changes in words] are necessary.

verbs For agreement of a verb with its subject, see COMPOUND SUBJECT; ALTERNATE SUBJECT; INTERVENING NOUN; PREDICATE NOMINATIVE. See also IRREGULAR VERBS.

very, very much **1.** These words are overworked. Although they are good modifiers, excessive use of them destroys their force. *I am pleased* is as emphatic as *I am very much pleased.*

2. Those who insist on using *very* and *very much* should observe cor-

rect usage. These terms are not interchangeable. The problem is whether to use *very* or *very much* before a passive participle.

Use *very* when the passive participle has the force of an adjective.

> A *very delighted* crowd heard the news.

Use *very much* (or *much*) when the passive participle is used in the predicate with verbal force.

> I was *very much* [or *much*] delighted at the result of the game.
> I shall be *very much* [or *much*] inconvenienced by the delay.

Exception: A passive participle that, although used as a verb, has lost its verbal force by common usage is preceded by *very.*

> I am *very* [not *very much*] tired of hearing about the matter.

voice The quality of a transitive verb that shows when the subject is acting (active voice) or being acted upon (passive voice). Voice is ordinarily not troublesome. The passive voice is less emphatic than the active.

> WEAK: The manuscript *was rejected* by the publisher.
> BETTER: The publisher *rejected* the manuscript.

wait on Do not use in place of *wait for.*

> We have been waiting *for* [not *on*] her.

wake (v.) Principal parts, *wake, waked,* [has, have, had] *waked* or *woke.* See IRREGULAR VERBS.

way Do not use *ways* in place of the singular *way.*

> WRONG: This year's sales are quite a

ways ahead of last year's.
RIGHT: This year's sales are quite a *way* ahead of last year's.
BETTER: This year's sales are *considerably* ahead of last year's.

we Nominative case of first person plural pronoun. 1. For misuse of *we* for *us*, see PRONOUNS, 1.

2. For use after forms of the verb *to be* (*am, is, are, was, were*), see PREDICATE NOMINATIVE, 1.

3. For the correct use of *we* or *I* in letters, see I, 3 in this section.

4. *We* is frequently misused for *us* in apposition to a noun in the objective case.

WRONG: It is advisable for *we* citrus growers to organize an association.
RIGHT: It is advisable for *us* citrus growers to organize an association.

wear (v.) Principals parts, *wear, wore*, [has, have, had] *worn*. See IRREGULAR VERBS.

weave (v.) Principal parts, *weave, wove*, [has, have, had] *woven*. See IRREGULAR VERBS.

well, good *Well* may be either an adjective or an adverb, but is usually an adverb except when it refers to a state of health. *Good* is always an adjective.

He *did* the job *well*. (Adverb, describing how he did the job.)
He looks *well*. (Predicate adjective, referring to state of health.)
The *situation* looks *good* to me. (Predicate adjective, describing the situation.)
The upswing in the stock market is a *good indication* that prosperity is still with us. (Adjective, modifying indication.)

what May be either singular or plural. In the singular, *what* stands for *that which* or *a thing that*. In the plural, *what* stands for *those* [persons] *who* or *those* [things] *that*.

SINGULAR: What *is* saved in price *is* likely to be lost in service and goodwill.
SINGULAR: The reports show not only what *has* been done during the period covered, but also what will be done.
PLURAL: My reasons for refusing the order *were* what I considered sufficient. ("Reasons" is the plural antecedent of "what.")

If *what* is singular in the beginning of the sentence, it remains singular. A common error is to make the second verb agree with a plural PREDICATE NOMINATIVE. In each of the following examples, *what* is definitely established as singular because it is followed by a singular verb. The second verb must also be singular, although it is followed by a plural predicate nominative, which is the complement to *what*.

What *is* needed *is* [not *are*] houses at prices that the people can afford.
What *seems* to be needed *is* [not *are*] stringent regulations.
What *causes* the delay *is* [not *are*] the three transfers.

In each of the following examples, *what* is used in the plural sense. Test the sentence by substituting *those* [things] *that* for what.

He is attempting to show by the chart what *appear* [not *appears*] to be the reasons for the decrease in sales. (Meaning "those reasons that.")
The company sold at discount only what *were* [not *was*] considered refrigerators of second quality. (Meaning "only those refrigerators that were considered.")

when 1. Do not use *when* to define

a word.

> WRONG: A sentence is *when* you have a complete thought.
> RIGHT: A sentence is a complete thought.

2. *Where* is frequently misused for *when*. *Where* should introduce an adverbial clause of place; *when,* of time.

> *When* [not *where*] a proxy is given limited power, he must act within the limitations.
> A surplus exists *when* [not *where*] there is an excess in the aggregate value of assets over liabilities and capital.
> *Where* the company is building. . . .

where **1.** Sometimes misused in place of *that.*

> I see in the paper *that* [not *where*] the corporation has declared a dividend.

2. Where should be used to introduce an adverbial clause of place, not of time. See WHEN, 2.

3. Do not use *where* to define a word.

> WRONG: Perjury is *where* a person voluntarily violates an oath.
> RIGHT: Perjury is the voluntary violation of an oath.

which For use of *that* and *which* as relative pronouns see THAT.

while When used as a conjunction, *while* means "during the time that" or "as long as." It should be used in this sense only and not as a substitute for *although, whereas,* or *but.*

> WRONG: *While* I have your order, I cannot fill it until the items are in stock.
> RIGHT: *Although* I have your order, I cannot fill it until the items are in stock.

> WRONG: *While* some of the employees cooperated, others took an antagonistic attitude.
> RIGHT: *Whereas* some of the employees cooperated, others took an antagonistic attitude. (Expressing contrast.)
> RIGHT: *While* [during the time that] the secretary took dictation, her assistant filed the papers.

who, whom (pron.) *Who* is the nominative case and is used as the subject; *whom* is the objective case and is used as the object of a verb or preposition.

> He is the client for *whom* I prepared the contract. (Object of "for.")
> Mr. Adams is the person *who* has charge of sales. (Subject of "has.")
> *Who* has charge of sales? (Subject of "has.")
> *Whom* do you wish to see? (Object of "to see.")
> Mr. Edwards is the candidate *who* I believe will win. ("Who" is the subject of "will win"; "I believe" is parenthetical.)
> Mr. Edwards is the candidate *whom* I favor. ("Whom" is the object of "favor.")

will See SHALL.

would See SHALL.

write (v.) Principal parts, *write, wrote,* [has, have, had] *written.* See IRREGULAR VERBS.

wrong The adverb forms are *wrong, wrongly.* See ADVERBS, 3. *Wrong* is not comparable. If anything is wrong it cannot be *more* wrong.

yourself pl., *yourselves.* See REFLEXIVE PRONOUNS.

Test your skills: answers

SECRETS OF GOOD LETTER WRITING

1.

Dear Sir:

On January 6 I bought a kit from your firm: Model #316-B. When I opened it I discovered that 3 parts were missing: the wing-nut bolts, the six brass screws, and the lockwedge. Without these parts I cannot complete the kit. Please send them to me as soon as possible.

Sincerely,
George Widgen

2.

Dear Sir:

This is the third time I have written to you about a kit I received with 3 missing parts. My first two letters were not answered. The missing parts are two wing-nut bolts, six brass screws, and a lockwedge.

I have already lost three weeks because of your failure to answer my letters. I would appreciate having the missing parts without further delay.

If this letter is also ignored, I shall make formal complaint to the Post Office Department.

I hope to hear from you soon so I don't have to take this step.

Sincerely,
George Widgen

3.

a. Good. The writer clearly states his problem and gives pertinent information in the first sentence.

b. Bad. The legislator can't tell what vote the writer is talking about, and his reaction to this angry personal attack will probably make him unreceptive to reasonable arguments the writer may develop further on in the letter.

c. Could be improved. The fact that this is the third complaint is important, but the writer could be much more specific. A better version might read like this: "On March 3 and again on March 27 I wrote you about rescheduling delivery of the new wrestling mats for the Lincoln High School gymnasium."

d. Ungracious. A personal letter is usually intended to give pleasure as well as information to the recipient, but this one starts with the suggestion that it's being written only because the writer has nothing better to do. Hackneyed phrases like "drop you a line" are dull and express the writer's mental laziness.

test your skills: ANSWERS

SOCIAL NOTES AND INVITATIONS

1. *Negative:*

> Mr. and Mrs. Donald Dome
> regret that they are unable to accept
> the kind invitation of
> Mr. and Mrs. Arthur Grave
> to the marriage of their daughter
> Gillian Lucy
> to
> Mr. Ian Courtney Vault
> on Saturday, the twelfth of September
> at four o'clock
> Church of the Atonement
> and afterward at
> Broken Arrow Country Club

Affirmative:

> Mr. and Mrs. George Phlippant
> accept with pleasure
> the kind invitation of
> Mr. and Mrs. Arthur Grave
> to the marriage of their daughter
> Gillian Lucy
> to
> Mr. Ian Courtney Vault
> on Saturday, the twelfth of September
> at four o'clock
> Church of the Atonement
> and afterward at
> Broken Arrow Country Club

2. a. true   b. false   c. true   d. true   e. false

3. An at-home card is a plain white card, 2¾ x 4 inches, that gives the address of the newly married couple. It is enclosed with the wedding announcement or invitation and announces when the couple will be ready to receive guests.

HOW TO WRITE FOR INFORMATION

quiz
page
88

1. concisely . . . clearly
2. a. should   b. should   c. does not require
3.
    Dear Sir:

       I am considering moving to Denver, and would appreciate receiving information about the city, including the following specific points:

       Job opportunities.
       Housing availability.
       Social life.
       Recreational facilities.
       Cultural opportunities.

       Since I must make a decision soon, I would appreciate a prompt reply. Thank you for your help.

                                    Sincerely yours,

HOW TO COMPLAIN AND GET ACTION

quiz
page
103

1. (e).
2.
    Mr. Hudgins M. Marpole Jr.
    President
    World Motor Company
    Detroit, Michigan

    Dear Mr. Marpole:

       On January 3 I received delivery of a new Howitzer III from the Hotspot Agency in Rollbeck, Iowa. The car is a sensation in this area (once a policeman stopped me just to ask how I liked it). Unfortunately, I cannot give those who ask about the car a very enthusiastic report. The engine has a whine that makes it sound like a jet. But your dealer refuses to recognize this annoying noise and claims that it is my imagination.

       I assure you that the noise is not "in my head." Indeed, my beloved car is becoming notorious hereabouts for its "sonic boom." This angers me, and I assume that you could not be pleased by the adverse publicity your product is getting.

       I think it is your obligation to send a factory representative to investigate my claim and take the steps necessary to correct the condition that is giving both of us such poor public relations.

                         With best wishes,

                         Jonathan E. Wimble

test your skills: ANSWERS

WRITING YOUR PUBLIC OFFICIALS

1. Yes. The writer tells immediately—in only eight words—how he feels.
2. Yes. He quotes the 13th Amendment to the United States Constitution.
3. He does. He says it "will make a barber cut a specific person's hair, force a woman to give a massage to a specific person." Then he gives his own interpretation to these acts: "This, I believe, is certainly a form of involuntary servitude, and hence it would be unconstitutional."
4. He does. He says there are "many other reasons for opposing the bill." Then he gives two reasons: "It doesn't define many important terms, such as 'discrimination' or 'race', and it would subject us to more federal power."
5. Yes. The representative can have no doubt of what he is being asked to do, and he has been given the writer's reasons for wanting it.

WRITING TO NEWSPAPERS, MAGAZINES, AND TV

1. c. A name is always preferable.
2. A reasonable "tone of voice" is more likely to be listened to (and possibly bring results) than an angry or hysterical outburst.
3. No. You do not know his motives; you are only guessing. You may be wrong and you are almost sure to anger him. (If you are right in accusing him of bad faith you are almost sure to infuriate him, and seeing through him isn't likely to reform his morals.)
4. b. It is better to start with what you have to say and not waste words announcing that you are *going* to say something.

APPLYING TO SCHOOLS AND COLLEGES

1. a, c, f, g, i. (b might be relevant if you were applying to a religious institution or to one where religion is a qualification for admission.)

2.

27 Lake Street
Mountainstream, Illinois
November 16, 1984

Office of the Registrar
Central College
Deanville, Ohio

Dear Sir:

I am interested in information about Central College, with the possibility of applying for admission next year.
Would you please send me a catalog and an admission form.
I expect to visit the college on June 3 or 4 and would appreciate a personal interview on either of those dates.
I would also like to arrange for a tour of the campus at that time, if it is

702

convenient. Since I hope to become a biologist, I am especially eager to see your research laboratories.

Thank you for taking care of my requests. I look forward to my visit in June.

Sincerely,
Donald Waderight

PRÉCIS, BOOK REPORTS, AND PROJECT REPORTS

quiz page **176**

1. A brief, accurate summary of something you have read.
2. a. 2   b. 1   c. 1   d. 2
3. When you finish reading a book, make a few brief notes while your reactions and impressions are fresh and strong. When you are ready to write, these notes will help to refresh your memory and sharpen your impressions. They may even provide material for sections of your report.
4. a. You should inject your own opinions into it.
   b. Right after you finish it.
   c. The questions from your basic outline that are most appropriate in evaluating that particular book.

APPLYING FOR A JOB

quiz page **205**

1. Acquaint a prospective employer with your background.
2. Name, address, telephone number, job experience (listed in chronological order, beginning with current status), education, personal data, and job objective.
3. Accompanies the résumé and "sells" you to the employer.
4. (a) Your primary assets that can help an employer (be as specific as possible in listing your achievements with other employers).   (b) Name and date of the newspaper where the ad you are answering appeared, or the name of the person who suggested that you contact the company. (c) The job you are applying for.
5. *C* is the best within conventional boundaries. It grabs the reader's interest immediately by offering a specific fact about the applicant's ability. Like most writing, it suggests the writer's personality. In this case he is a person who does not waste words but goes to the heart of a situation; here he wants to demonstrate that he is qualified for the job.

D is also an attention-getter but is more risky. It has an audacity (without offering specific information) that may charm some employers and put off others. This is the gambit of a bold and daring person, possibly just the sort of person that some companies want, especially for a sales job.

test your skills: ANSWERS

quiz
page
223

PICTURE THE PEOPLE YOU ARE WRITING TO

1. This writer is short-tempered and sharp-tongued. He must be handled gently. Admit that he is justified in his anger, but explain that it isn't easy to get the kind of deliverymen you would like and you will take every precaution not to let such a mistake happen again.

2. This sarcastic man has a perpetual sneer on his face. He enjoys people making fools of themselves. This gives him a chance to ridicule them, thus proving his own superiority. He is usually thin-skinned and any sharp reply would enrage him. But he is perverse enough to be charmed by a letter that appeals to his intellectual pretensions.

3. This reasonable letter comes from a person who is sensible and does not react violently. He expects—and should receive—a straightforward reply. The mistake is acknowledged and he is assured that an adjustment will be made.

quiz
page
232

PLAN YOUR LETTERS BEFORE YOU WRITE

A Plan Sheet for Gorgewell's reply would read something like this:

   a. Confirm the customer's claim and admit that the store is in error.

   b. Do not minimize or attempt to excuse the offense.

   c. Express own personal dismay (indirectly put self on side of the wronged customer).

   d. Tell what the store tried to do about the error, and suggest how such things happen (things the store cannot control).

   e. Try to win the customer's understanding by explaining how many credit accounts the store services.

   f. Point out that the error is part of a system that is intended to benefit the customer by keeping prices down.

   g. Attempt to win forgiveness and keep the customer's good will and patronage by an apology.

quiz
page
262

HOW TO SAY NO WITH A SMILE

1. Your attitude determines how you put your refusal.

2. Try to see the problem from the other person's point of view. Be fair.

3. B is more friendly and sympathetic because it is answered in human terms—the writer's attitude is reflected in what he says. It gives a specific reason why the request was turned down, and offers a substitute for the extension that was rejected.

704

HOW TO WRITE BUSINESS REPORTS

1. a. false   b. true   c. false   d. false   e. true
2. Investigating sources of information, taking notes, analyzing the data, making an outline, writing the report.
3. Accuracy, clearness, conciseness, restraint in language, convenience to the reader.
4. A letter of transmittal merely transmits the report from writer to reader, while the letter of presentation also emphasizes the report's importance.
5. c, d, and f.

quiz
page
288

PUNCTUATION POINTERS

1. "It's plain to see," said she, "there are too many *and*'s in that sentence."
2. The artist Marat will open a show in Richmond, Virginia, on Wednesday, April 27.
3. The suggestion, which had arrived too late, was held for the next meeting.
4. However you do it, get here by the first of the month.
5. However, I would like to see you earlier, if possible.
6. Jim Browne—he's a friend of yours, isn't he?—called today.
7. Cans made up 60 percent of the litter; bottles, 40 percent.
8. "Did the company destroy its image?" he mused.
9. Will you please send the five hundred dollar ($500) withdrawal as quickly as possible.
10. Yes, the concert will be played over Station WXYZ at 1:30.
11. Hurry! Deliver the package to the following address: 6672 Schnefel St., Kansas City, Mo.
12. The businessmen's ass'n was formed in the early 1940's. (but *1940s* is acceptable too).

quiz
page
356

HOW YOU COME ACROSS ON THE TELEPHONE

1. true   2. false   3. false   4. false   5. true   6. false   7. false   8. false
9. false   10. false   11. true   12. false   13. false   14. true   15. false

quiz
page
453

THE FIVE STEPS TO SUCCESSFUL SELLING

1. It will satisfy the customer's needs or wants.
2. *The Pre-approach* (looking for prospects and ways of attracting their interest).
   The Approach (establishing contact and making a favorable impression).

quiz
page
470

test your skills: ANSWERS

The Presentation (showing the customer how your product can serve him).

Overcoming Objections (using techniques that dissipate resistance rather than reinforce it).

The Close (getting the customer to agree to buy the product).

3. Be confident. Be clear. Be complete. Be brief.

4. You must ask the customer to buy.

quiz page **525**

START WITH A LIST OF POINTS

1. Make a plan.

2. List the points you want to cover.

Use as few points as possible.

Analyze each point for group interest.

Arrange points in order but selected to hold interest throughout the speech.

3. A. This could vary, according to the speaker's interpretation. Three major headings could be: Health effects; Cost, to the individual and society; Need for corrective action.

B. Strong point first.

Stronger point second.

Strongest point third.

(Again, the actual order will vary according to the importance the speaker gives the various headings he chooses.)

C. Using the main headings under A, we might have the following grouping:

Health effects a, q.

Cost b, c, d, e.

Need for corrective action h, i, j, n, o, r.

(The points might be combined in other combinations or used as subtopics under different headings. Note that some of the points have no place in this organization and would be discarded.)

quiz page **536**

HOW TO SELL YOUR IDEA

1. *Don't come out slugging at a controversial idea:* He approaches his subject easily by aligning himself with his "fellow taxpayers and fellow citizens," pointing out that, together, they have a critical decision to make.

2. *Don't be a verbal bulldozer:* He avoids arousing emotions through name calling, ripping into the other side's arguments, or appealing to prejudices. Instead he quietly gives facts on which both sides can agree.

706

3. *Don't push—lead:* He gives facts and then tells the advantages and disadvantages of building a new school. Many of the advantages may have been overlooked by opponents of the school—advantages that could personally benefit them. He appeals to their self-interest by showing them a way to gain greater long-term and economic profits in place of saving a few dollars on taxes.

4. *Curb your rebuttal instinct:* This is more of a problem in personal argument than in public speaking. But here the speaker recognizes and answers the objections so thoroughly that it is obvious he has really "listened" to the other side—and he has prepared a reply that may compel many to reconsider their opinion. He ends on the same conciliatory note on which he began—speaking of the community as a whole to unify his audience: "Let's give Blankville's children the best we can. Let's vote for the new high school."

USE VISUALS TO PROVE YOUR POINT

1. The basic reason for using a visual aid is to present an idea in a form that the audience will understand most quickly; in a form as close to the real thing as possible; in a form which asks the listener to do as little translating as possible.

2. a. The speaker should never be in the dark. If lights are directed only on the visual aid, the speaker ceases to be the center of attention. The aid is just that—an aid; the speaker is the "show."

   b. Make the aid big enough so it can be easily seen.

   c. Avoid blocking the aid from the audience's view.

   d. Address the audience, not the aid.

   e. Color gives a dramatic quality of "excitement" that can help motivate an audience to accept or reject an idea.

   f. Pictures and lines should be drawn so they are "definite, broad, and clear."

3. This visual incorporates the strength of a line or bar graph by "presenting all the information at once. The eye can grasp the whole immediately."

   The pictoral symbols give an immediate visual comparison of the idea presented.

   It is simple with no confusing details, focusing on one idea.

   "It stimulates as it informs; it interests as it teaches; it entertains as it supports your idea."

4. A flannel board (display board) is made of a piece of plywood, fiberboard, masonite, etc., with a piece of flannel stretched over the surface. The visual aids (on illustration paper) have a piece of rough sandpaper glued to the back; the sandpaper clings to the flannel so that the displays can be easily moved about or removed.

test your skills: ANSWERS

5. Charts, blackboards, motion pictures, slide and strip projectors, overhead projectors. Other equipment includes crayons, chalk, plastic tapes, ink markers, and color transparencies.

quiz
page
561

PREPARING YOURSELF TO SPEAK

1. Each person will have his own abbreviations; the list below is merely one possibility:

> A. AMER MOST PROSP NATION HIST WORLD
> B. NO NOT BROUGHT HAPPINESS
> C. BESET PBLMS — RACIAL . . . POVERTY-PLENTY . . . FALT
>   ECONOMY . . . DECAY CITIES . . . POLLUTION . . . DRUGS . . .
>   WAR . . . PEOPLE DIVIDED POLITLY – PHYSCLY – SPIRITLY
> D. BREACH — RACES . . . COLORS . . . GENRTNS
> E. MOST ADVCD COMM SYSTEMS . . . PEOPLE CAN'T COMM
>   ONE ANTHR . . . SELVES
> F. VICTIMS RANGE PSYCHLGCL AILMENTS — ALIENATION
>   SELF . . . SEVERE MENTAL DISEASE
> G. WHAT TRBL PRICE PD AFFLUENCE . . . CREATURE
>   COMFRT ?

2. Memorizing a speech, rather than familiarizing yourself with it, usually causes loss of animation and spontaneity. A wooden delivery is deadly to any talk, no matter how interesting the content.

quiz
page
568

WHAT MAKES A GOOD SPEAKER

The first speech violates practically every rule in the book. It is vague, wordy, dull; the speaker is obviously uninformed and not very interested himself. He takes no real point of view. He is general, fails to document his points, and gives no colorful or arresting illustrations. The words are unimaginative, and the manner of delivery is obviously wooden, probably interspersed with many *ah*'s and *er*'s. He is off on the wrong foot almost from the opening word. He tells us that before he begins he wants to warn us that this is a controversial subject; but he has already begun as soon as he opens his mouth! Compare the faults in (1) with the second speech. Note particularly in (2) the use of specific statements, the speaker's obvious knowledge, and his own position on the issue as implied by the strong statements he makes.

Index

A

a, long, pronunciation of, 637
abbreviations
  apostrophe in plurals of, 343
  in addresses, 48
  list of, 158–59
  punctuation with, 50
-able, words
  pronunciation of, 637
  spelling rules for, 372–73
academic profession, forms of address
    for, 80–81
accent
  acute, punctuation mark for, 342
  grave, punctuation mark for, 342
acceptance (reply to invitation)
  change of answer, 70–71
  combined with regret, 69
  formal, 67–68
  informal, 66, 69–70
action verbs, 335
active voice, 335
address(es)
  on business letters, 88
  on formal invitations, 59, 61
  home, form for, 40–41
  how to find, 90–91
  outside, forms for, 45–46
  recipients, form for, 41
  return, 46, 49, 61, 106–07
  on stationery, 37–39
  on wedding invitations, 48–49
address, forms of for important people,
    76–81
adjectival clause, 332–33
adjective, defined, 328
adverb, defined, 328
adverbial clause, 332–33
aequ (*us*), English words from, 315
after-dinner speeches, 495
-age words, pronunciation of, 639
alliteration, 509
  in JFK's speeches, 513
ambassador (foreign), form of address
    for, 78–79
ambassador (U.S.)
  closing of a letter to, 42
  form of address for, 78–79

writing paper for, 39
American College Testing Program
  (ACT), 137
anaphora, 508
-ance words, spelling rules for, 375
anecdotes
  in sales letters, 235
  in speech writing, 503–04, 532
  See also humor; quotations
anger in letter writing, 19
anima, words based on, 312–13, 315
announcements
  birth, 71–72
  death, 74
  engagement, 72–74
ante- (prefix), 314
anthropo (*anthropos*), words based
  on, 310–12, 316
anti- (prefix), 314
antonyms
  in dictionary entry, 297
  use of, in vocabulary-building, 304,
    308
aphorisms, 504
apology, note of, 20–21
apostrophe
  in contractions, 342, 348
  for plurals, 342–43, 350
  in possessives, 342
  punctuation mark for, 342
application forms, letters of request for
  college, 131–33
  private school, 128–31
  See also job applications
appositives, 336
  comma with, 343
archbishop (Roman Catholic), form
  of address for, 80–81
articulation, role of, in speech
  production, 597–98
-ary words, spelling rules for, 376
asking questions, procedure for,
  476–77
associate justice (Supreme Court),
  form of address for, 76–77
assonance, 508
asterisk, punctuation mark for, 342

709

-ate words, pronunciation of, 646
At Home card, 58–59
Audience Information, Office of,
    121–22
audio-visual aids, in public speaking,
    495, 510, 512
    See also visual aids
author card, 153
awards, presenting and accepting,
    562–63

B

balance (speech device), 508
balls and dances, invitations to, 61, 64
bar graphs, 541, 543–44
bene, words based on, 315–16
bereaved persons, offering condolences
    to, 434–36
Bessler Vu-Graph, 550
bi-, words based on, 310–12, 316
Biblical citations
    colon with, 348
    form of footnotes for, 159
bibliographies
    abbreviations in, 158–59
    final, 160–61
    how to prepare, 149–50
bicuspid, etymology of, 310
bigamy, etymology of, 310
biography, writing a book report on,
    169
birth announcements, 71–72
bishop (Protestant), form of address
    for, 78–79
bishop (Roman Catholic), form of
    address for, 80–81
blackboard, as visual aid, 510, 546–47
body language, 398–99
book
    bibliographical form for, 161
    footnotes for citations from, 157–58
    titles, italics for, 157
book report
    biography, 169
    definition of, 166–67
    first draft, 171–72
    history and current events, 170
    note-taking for, 167–68
    novel, 168–69
    one-paragraph review, 171–72
    outlining, 167

science book, 170–71
brace, punctuation mark for, 342
brackets
    punctuation mark for, 342
    in quoted material, 349
bread-and-butter letters, 23–24
    bride to new in-laws, 25–26
    after a house-party weekend, 24
    to a stranger, 25
    after visiting a close friend, 24–25
breath control, 594
breathing
    breath control, 594
    and posture, 599–600
    power, 600–601
    to reduce nervousness, 604
    role of, in speech production,
        595–97
    to strengthen voice, 602–03
    and voice projection, 601–02
brevity, 4–5, 10–11
    in JFK's speeches, 512
    in letters of complaint, 92–93
    in letters to the editor, 114, 116, 119
    in letters to public officials, 106–07,
        111–12
business letters
    adopting the writer's viewpoint,
        218–20
    analysis of, 213–14
    attention line, 277
    developing a personal approach,
        212–18, 222
    enclosure line, 277
    planning, 207, 209, 224
        six guidelines, 225
        plan-sheet method, 225–32
    presenting technical information,
        220–22
    purposes of, 206, 211–12
    reference number, 277
    special parts of, 277
    See also letters of refusal; plan-sheet
        method; sales letters
business meeting
    brevity, 473
    closing, 481
    leader's duties, 471–73
        clarifying points of view, 478
        easing tension, 480
        eliciting contributions, 475, 479

preparing for, 458
presenting goals, 455–56
purpose of, 454
résumés, 193
  components of, 195–97
  "consultant" entry, 202
  covering letter for, 203–05
  emphasizing scholastic record,
    198–200
  sample, 194–95
  style, of, 197–98
  when unemployed, 200–03
  when fired, 200
"Jr.," when to use, 67
judge, form of address for, 78–79

K

Kennedy (Sorensen), excerpts from,
  512–17
Kennedy, John Fitzgerald, 428, 587
  speech-writing technique
    brevity, 512–13
    closings, 516
    dependence on text, 516–17
    humor, 514–16
    use of alliterative sentences, 513
    use of quotations, 512, 514, 516
kinesics, 398
kinesthetic imagery, 507

L

labels, in dictionary entry, 296–97
Language and Its Growth (Scott, Carr
  and Wilkinson), 634
laryngitis, 593–94, 606–07
larynx, in speech production, 596
later (Lat.), words based on, 319
Latin language
  English words formed from
    anima, 312–13
    bi, 317–18
    stem words, 311–12, 315–16
    tri, 318–19
    unus, 313, 315
  importance of in vocabulary-
    building, 309–10
  plurals of words from, 370–71
leaders, punctuation marks for, 342
legal profession, forms of address
  for, 76–79
-less (suffix), 314

letters, style and appearance of
  address and date, 40–41
  closing, 42–43
  folding, 45
  handwritten/typewritten, 17, 32,
    35–36
  letterheads, 37–39
  outside addresses, forms for, 45–46
  salutation, 41–42
  selection of stationery, 36–40
  sequence of pages, 40
  signature, 43–45
  unsealed, 46
letters of application
  to college, 131–33
  to private school, 128–31
letters of complaint
  anger in, 91–92
  information to include, 93
  length of, 92–93
  samples of
    angry, 93–94
    calm, 94–95
    failure to credit returned
      merchandise, 103
    failure to record payment made,
      102–03
    firm, 96–97
    for nondelivery, 98–99
    polite, 95–96
    requesting replacement parts,
      97–98
    unjustifiable overcharges, 99, 101
  threats in, 92
letters of condolence, 28, 33–34
letters of congratulation, 26–27
  on the birth of a baby, 26–27
  on an engagement, 26
  to a son's fiancée, 26
  on special accomplishment, 27
  to a television station, 25
letters to congressmen, 10–11
letters to the editor, 11, 113–14
  getting published, 114–15
  how editors shorten, 115–16
  of a magazine, 119
  samples
    about government policy, 120
    about a municipal facility, 118,
      120
letter of explanation, 100

717

charts, 546–47
flannel board, 545–46
line graph, 541–43
pictograph, 544–45
usefulness of, 537–38
vital center, in speech production,
600, 611, 613
vivid language, devices for creating
imagery, 507
simplicity, 506–07
slang, 507
vocabulary-building
antonyms in, 304
for children, 622–24
importance of simple words, 307–08
Latin and Greek stem words,
309–10
learning by context, 293–95, 301–02
prefixes, list of, 314
suffixes, list of, 314
synonyms, 298–99, 302–04
tests
changing the form of new words,
300
definitions, 306–07
fitting new words to meanings,
295–96
matching meanings, 304–05
matching new words with
synonyms, 298–99
pick the word for the situation,
299–300
the right word for the context,
305–06
selecting the right synonym,
302–03
suggestive phrases, 305
turning the tables, 303–04
words from Latin and Greek,
311–13, 315–19
vocal cords, in speech production,
596–97
voice
breath control, 594–95
change of, 597
maintaining vitality of, 604–07
mechanism of
articulation, 598–99
breathing, 595–97
resonance, 597–98
pitch of, 611–13

range of, 597
ways to strengthen, 602–03
voice box, 595–97
vol (*volens*), words based on, 315–16
vowels, mispronunciation of, 590–91

W

wants ads, replies to, 146, 203–04
wedding announcements, 58
At Home notice, 58–59
style and wording, 59
wedding invitations
announcing postponement, 55–56
At Home card, 58–59
correct style for, 48–49
correct wording for, 49–55
enclosures, 57
folding and inserting, 49
handwritten, 55
letters of acceptance and regret for,
47
pew card, 47, 49, 57
recalling, 67
reception card, 47, 49, 56–57
replies to, 68
when to mail, 48
widows
engagement announcement of, 74
forms of address for, 46
wedding invitation of, 53
windpipe, in speech production,
596–97
woman, forms of address and signature
for
married, 37–38, 43–44
professional, 38, 44–45
unmarried, 37–38, 44
widow, 46
word repetition, 509
write-in campaigns, 105

Y

y, final, spelling rules for, 366–68
y plus *ous*, spelling rules for, 378
yawning, to relax throat, 609–10
young people
forms of address for, 46
stationery for, 38–39

Z

zip code, 37, 45–46

727

Acknowledgments

SECRETS OF GOOD LETTER WRITING, excerpt from "The ABC's of Good Letter-Writing" in *The Complete Book of Personal Letter-Writing and Modern Correspondence* by Lassor Blumenthal. Copyright © 1969 by Lassor Blumenthal. Used by permission of Doubleday & Company, Inc. HANDLING YOUR PERSONAL CORRESPONDENCE, from "Personal Letters" in *Emily Post's Etiquette*, revised by Elizabeth L. Post. Copyright © 1969 by The Emily Post Institute, Inc. Reprinted by permission of Funk & Wagnalls Company. GIVE YOUR LETTERS THE RIGHT LOOK, from "The Appearance and Style of Your Letters" in *Emily Post's Etiquette*, revised by Elizabeth L. Post. Copyright © 1969 by The Emily Post Institute, Inc. Reprinted by permission of Funk & Wagnalls Company. SOCIAL NOTES AND INVITATIONS, from "Invitations to Weddings and Receptions," "Wedding Announcements," "Acceptances and Regrets," "The New Baby," "Engagements," "Funerals" in *Emily Post's Etiquette*, revised by Elizabeth L. Post. Copyright © 1969 by The Emily Post Institute, Inc. Reprinted by permission of Funk & Wagnalls Company. HOW TO WRITE FOR INFORMATION, from "I'm Writing to Inquire . . ." in *The Modern Business Letter Writer's Manual* by Marjane Cloke and Robert Wallace. Copyright © 1969 by Marjane Cloke and Robert Wallace. Used by permission of Doubleday & Company, Inc. HOW TO COMPLAIN AND GET ACTION, excerpt from "Writing to Business Firms—And Getting Results" in *The Complete Book of Personal Letter-Writing and Modern Correspondence* by Lassor Blumenthal. Copyright © 1969 by Lassor Blumenthal. Used by permission of Doubleday & Company, Inc. WRITING YOUR PUBLIC OFFICIALS, excerpt from "Writing to Your Congressman" in *The Complete Book of Personal Letter-Writing and Modern Correspondence* by Lassor Blumenthal. Copyright © 1969 by Lassor Blumenthal. Used by permission of Doubleday & Company, Inc. WRITING TO NEWSPAPERS, MAGAZINES AND TV, excerpt from "Writing to Magazines, Newspapers, Radio and TV" in *The Complete Book of Personal Letter-Writing and Modern Correspondence* by Lassor Blumenthal. Copyright © 1969 by Lassor Blumenthal. Used by permission of Doubleday & Company, Inc. APPLYING TO SCHOOLS AND COLLEGES, excerpt from "Writing to Schools and Colleges" in *The Complete Book of Personal Letter-Writing and Modern Correspondence* by Lassor Blumenthal. Copyright © 1969 by Lassor Blumenthal. Used by permission of Doubleday & Company, Inc. HOW TO WRITE A RESEARCH PAPER, slightly adapted from "Preparation and Note-Taking" in *Modern Rhetoric* by Cleanth Brooks and Robert Penn Warren. Copyright © 1949, 1958, 1970 by Harcourt, Brace & World, Inc. Reprinted with their permission. PRECIS, BOOK REPORTS, AND PROJECT REPORTS, from "Preparing Your Final Copy," "How to Write a Precis," "How to Write a Book Report," "How to Write a Science Project Report" in *Writing the Research and Term Paper* by Travis L. Hauser and Lee Learner Gray. Copyright © 1964 by Cambridge Book Company, a division of The New York Times Media Company, Inc. Reprinted by permission of the publisher. TAKING WRITTEN EXAMINATIONS, from "Using Time Wisely," "Reading Directions and Questions Carefully," "Using Good Reasoning Techniques," "Essay Questions" in *How to Take Tests* by Jason Millman and Walter Pauk. Copyright © 1969 by McGraw-Hill, Inc. Reprinted by permission of McGraw-Hill Book Company. APPLYING FOR A JOB, excerpt from "Jobs and Careers" in *The Complete Book of Personal Letter-Writing and Modern Correspondence* by Lassor Blumenthal. Copyright © 1969 by Lassor Blumenthal. Used by permission of Doubleday & Company, Inc. PICTURE THE PEOPLE YOU ARE WRITING TO, from *Business Letters That Turn Inquiries into Sales* by Ferd Nauheim. Copyright © 1957 by Prentice-Hall, Inc. Reprinted by permission of the publisher. PLAN YOUR LETTERS BEFORE YOU WRITE, from "Plan Before You Write" in *The Modern Business Letter Writer's Manual* by Marjane Cloke and Robert Wallace. Copyright © 1969 by Marjane Cloke and Robert Wallace. Used by permission of Doubleday & Company, Inc. HOW TO WRITE SALES LETTERS, from "Sales Letters" in *The Complete Letter Writer* by N. H. and S. K. Mager. Copyright © 1957, 1968 by N. H. and S. K. Mager. Reprinted by permission of Pocket Books, a division of Simon & Schuster, Inc. HOW TO SAY NO WITH A SMILE, from "How to Say 'No' with a Smile" in *Business Letters That Turn Inquiries into Sales* by Ferd Nauheim. Copyright © 1957 by Prentice-Hall, Inc. Reprinted by permission of the publisher. HOW TO HANDLE DELICATE SITUATIONS, from "How to Handle Delicate Situations" in *Business Letters That Turn Inquiries into Sales* by Ferd Nauheim. Copyright © 1957 by Prentice-Hall, Inc. Reprinted by permission of the publisher. HOW TO WRITE BUSINESS REPORTS, from "Business Reports" in *Business Writing* by J. Harold Janis, Edward J. Kilduff and Howard R. Dressner. Copyright © 1956 by Barnes & Noble, Inc. Reprinted by permission of the publisher. SEVEN MODERN STEPS TO WORD POWER, from "Learning Words the Modern Way" in *30 Days to a More Powerful Vocabulary* by Wilfred Funk and Norman Lewis. Copyright © 1970 by Funk & Wagnalls Co. Used by permission of the publisher. LEARNING WORDS BY THE "UNFOLDING PROCESS," from "Word Building with the 'Unfolding Process'" in *30 Days to a More Powerful Vocabulary* by Wilfred Funk and Norman Lewis. Copyright © 1970 by Funk & Wagnalls Company. Used by permission of the publisher. QUICK VOCABULARY BUILDER: WORDS FROM LATIN AND GREEK, from "Words from Latin" and "Words from Classic Roots" in *30 Days to a More Powerful Vocabulary* by Wilfred Funk and Norman Lewis. Copyright © 1970 by Funk & Wagnalls Company. Used by permission of the publisher. GOOD GRAMMAR IN A NUTSHELL, from *The Reader's Digest Great Encyclopedic Dictionary*. Copyright © 1966, 1968, 1969 by The Reader's Digest Association, Inc. PUNCTUATION POINTERS, from "Punctuation" in *Complete Secretary's Handbook* by Lillian Doris and Besse May Miller. Copyright © 1951, 1960, 1970 by Prentice-Hall, Inc. Reprinted by permission of the publisher. HOW TO BECOME A GOOD SPELLER, excerpts from *Spelling Your Way to Success* by Joseph Mersand. Copyright © 1959 by Barron's Educational Series, Inc. Reprinted by permission of

728